BORN IN THE BLOOD

NATIVE LITERATURES OF THE AMERICAS

BORN IN THE BLOOD

On Native American Translation

Edited and with an introduction by Brian Swann

University of Nebraska Press | Lincoln and London

Library of Congress Cataloging-in-Publication Data

Born in the blood: on Native American translation /
edited and with an introduction by Brian Swann.
p. cm. — (Native literatures of the Americas)
Includes bibliographical references and index.
ISBN 978-0-8032-6759-6 (pbk.: alk. paper)
1. Indians of North America—Languages—
Translating. 2. Indian literature—North America—
Translations into English—History and criticism.
I. Swann, Brian.
PM218.B67 2011   497—dc22   2010037303

Set in Minion Pro and Scala Sans Pro by
Kim Essman. Designed by A. Shahan.

CONTENTS

BORN IN THE BLOOD

Introduction

Brian Swann

Translating Native American languages is a very different process from translating European languages. For one thing, the translation of European languages does not usually present real physical and spiritual dangers.[1] For another, there are the complexities of collaboration between non-Native academics and Native American culture-bearers, formerly "informants." Moreover, translators have to decide how to transform oral expression into a written form, and in addition they may have to produce their own grammars and dictionaries, as part of what Julie Brittain and Marguerite MacKenzie in this volume term "a unique constellation of factors." This constellation can also include "the interaction of language and social life," working with Native American speakers and communities in an atmosphere of "comprehensive description" whose goal is language strengthening and retention, or even "to capture as much of the language before it dies."[2] It can also involve what Carrie Dyck in her contribution calls the creation of "ethical space," where different worlds come into contact. This contact or collision necessitates dealing with translation as part of the historical process of appropriation, and with the fact that the process of collecting and translating Native American materials is replete with ironies and dilemmas. It entails facing up to the implications of Eric Cheyfitz's claim that translation, broadly conceived, was and is "the central act of European colonization and imperialism in America."[3] All of which means that in "the post-colonial era" involving "ethics, ideology, action," the translation of Native American literatures will always be more than a "linguistic" enterprise.[4] As William Clements has noted: "The transformation from oral expression to text is much more than the process that provides the focus for translation studies; it is also the anthropologist's task of 'cultural translation.'"[5]

The need for "cultural translation" is, of course, the result of the history of the Americas. From the time of discovery and conquest, the European "bore the weight of his culture" and interpreted Native American realities in his own terms, within his own cultural framework of interpenetrating "cultural-theological, literary-rhetorical, and practical-institutional contingencies."[6] In the Americas results ranged from the wholesale burning of books and codices in New Spain in order to stamp out "idolatries" (the way of Diego de Landa and Juan de Zumarraga), to a deep interest "in the beauties of Aztec literature and the mysteries of Aztec thought,"[7] an engagement fostered not only by Philip II's order that Nahuatl was to be used as the language of conversion but by the Franciscan desire for a utopian Mexican church. This is best demonstrated in the monumental work of Fray Bernardino de Sahagún.[8] In what was to become the United States and Canada, however, most early Europeans had little interest in indigenous cultures, with the possible exception of men such as John Eliot and Roger Williams and the missionaries who wrote *The Jesuit Relations*. When they heard native stories, they regarded them as childish fantasies or downright foolish meanderings, and when they heard songs they heard animal noises and shrieks of devils, "a persistent presence in early colonial representations of native American song."[9] There was little for them to pass on or to attempt to translate.[10] To most Europeans, American natives were barely human. Their ceremonies and beliefs were often regarded as satanic parodies of Christianity, their languages deficient and defective. They could, therefore, have little "literature" that needed translating. They themselves needed to be translated. Thus, the very enterprise of translation in the Americas was compromised and tainted from its origins, and despite heroic efforts in the late nineteenth and early twentieth centuries by such people as Washington Matthews, James Mooney, Francis La-Flesche, Frances Densmore, and Franz Boas, who attempted to preserve and translate as much as they could of what they regarded as dying cultures and languages, translation was used, both deliberately and unconsciously, to weaken and destroy cultures in various ways, including via mistranslation and the creation of stereotypes.[11] The process was made easier by the eventual criminalization of native languages, which separated native peoples from their linguistic and cultural heritage. Indigenous ideas and values were translated into forms accessible and useful to the dominant culture.[12] This was especially insidious and alienating, since these cultural mistranslations and distortions were fed back into the native population.[13] Such deep colonialism is far from the benign use of translation to fill what Isaac Bashevis Singer has termed "the cultural needs of a people,"[14] though it may have become part of the "invention of the other" which Hugh Kenner regards as "a central part of the Modernist enterprise."[15]

There are many problems involved in translating Native American literatures that are not present when dealing with European literatures, including the presence and involvement in native life of missionaries, especially in South and Central America, a topic that recently resulted in a heated discussion in the pages of a journal devoted to the indigenous languages of the Americas.[16] On a linguistic level, we confront the fact that while Indo-European lexical classes such as verb, noun, and adjective correspond to some Native American languages, they do not correspond to all. Many languages have no adjectival category, and some have even brought into question the universality of nouns and verbs,[17] as well as the concept of metaphor, which presents challenges for translators, since, as Jeffrey D. Anderson has pointed out, "song images cannot be examined referentially, or even solely as metaphor or all other analogical devices, which preoccupy Western poetic readings."[18] Also, through a study of the Western Apache speech genre of "wise words," Keith Basso has extended our idea of metaphoric thinking and developed a new theory of metaphor itself.[19]

Polysynthetic languages differ radically in structure from non-polysynthetic languages, requiring inventive solutions for textual ambiguities and to convey dynamics and nuances. And languages work from different visions of the world. To take two geographically diverse languages: in Mexico, Nahuatl "does not make gender or human-animal distinctions corresponding to he/she/it,"[20] which can present complications for interpretation and translation, while Cree, an Algonquian language in Canada, distinguishes animate and inanimate gender, where gender corresponds to a division of physical phenomena into those that have life and those that do not. Those that have life include humans, animals, spirits, and trees, as well as natural phenomena such as rocks and snow, and some items of personal use such as kettles and pipes.[21] (Conversely, when translating into English, other problems present themselves; for instance, the biblical injunction to "feed my sheep" will not mean much in the Arctic.)[22]

Then there is the question of "genre." What westerners regard as "myth," which carries a sense of "fabrication," a traditional native person might regard as a true account of an earlier world, a world where everything possesses some form of life.[23] The translator needs to draw on many resources to present such a universe convincingly, a world so different from the one most of us are familiar with, a world where transformation and metamorphosis are the norm, where forms are fluid and being is polysemous and ambiguous, where everything possesses some sort of life in a "participatory universe,"[24] and where "all elements of the landscape" are "*active participants* in a set of relationships with one another."[25] And how to have that world make sense in our "nonsacramental" world of "manipulable matter"?[26] The problem is how to present this mode of understanding and being without adopting an "as if" tone or a "just so" stance, without requiring a suspension of disbelief in a world where a being such as Coyote and his variants can be villain and hero, animal and human, fool and sage, god and devil all in quotation marks and often at the same time.[27]

Another obvious challenge is how to turn the "oral" to "text": how to turn a living object into an object of criticism.[28] Wendy Wickwire, who edited the stories of the Okanagan storyteller Harry Robinson, talks of her reluctance to "crystallize" his words, either on tape or in book form, since that would be to "fix" the "living stories" in time, thus "Homerizing Harry," which means that the stories "will no longer evolve as they have for hundreds of generations."[29] However, whatever the reservations, modern translators have built on the great pioneers of the early twentieth century such as Franz Boas and his students, refining their exacting dictation methods, phoneme by phoneme, word by word, and their interlinear glosses, which resulted in texts often more "ethnographic data" than "poetic narrative."[30] In the past also, various mechanical devices were often used, starting with wax cylinders, then including aluminum disks and tape recorders. Today, electronic aids are being utilized, such as the computer-created concordances John Bierhorst notes in his essay here, or what Robin Ridington in his calls "Web-based media" and "hypermedia," which includes film and video. Then, once recorded, there is the problem of what *form* to use when translating the fluidity of song or story. At first, form was not regarded as a problem. Songs were formatted as poems, stories and myths as prose fiction. This had many drawbacks, however, and today the most successful advances in form and format were created by Dell Hymes and Dennis Tedlock. Having discovered structural elements in the originals with which to order the translation, Hymes created a format for the stories that makes them look like poetry or, more particularly, like drama, following the lead of Melville Jacobs.[31] Tedlock, on the other hand, has incorporated performative elements from his taped tellings, and has noted that "when the New World texts are translated into European languages, their epistemological aspects are routinely reduced or even eliminated."[32] Translators nowadays, however, include these epistemological elements, incorporating elements in their translations that might have once have been regarded as not that important, such as audience response, the speaker's intonation, gestures, and emphasis, as well as including notes and detailed introductions that locate and help create context, a way of conveying experience, culturally embedded, with the aim of making total translation, or what Richard Preston in his essay terms "deep translation."

In addition, it should be noted that the translators of Native American literatures are often not dealing with "literature" as that term is generally understood by a Western audience. Stories often have important educational functions, and many songs are "practical"; that is, they are intended to bring something about, make something happen. Ghost Dance songs are a clear example, intended to bring back the pre-conquest world, while the great Navajo chantways, O'odham devil songs (such as those in David Kozak's contribution here), and other ceremonies may be regarded as therapeutic or healing. Also, what we might regard as myth or fiction, the Tsimshian of the Northwest regard as part of a structure of aboriginal common law,[33] while among the Western Apache stories are "a way of constructing history," a vital part of "world-building" or "place-making," showing the indivisibility of word and place.[34]

Finally, copyright and official secrets aside, we are used to the idea of having access to anything we feel like translating, that everything is grist for our mill, and past collectors/translators used various means— some fair, some foul—to gain access to what they wanted. But things have changed; cultural artifacts are no longer here for the taking. Even among native societies themselves, access to materials varies. Among the Haida, for instance, particular organizations have exclusive right to tell the stories and the myths, and among the Tlingit, Raven stories can only be told by persons of Raven and Eagle moieties, while clan legends are owned by clans and performance is restricted.[35] With increasing legislation by tribes to restrict access, even to material already in print, the situation is becoming even more complex.[36]

These challenges are virtually unique to the translation of Native American literatures, and are in addition to the usual challenges and difficulties facing other practitioners of the art of translation, a discipline that is as much a matter of translating the spaces and silences between and around words as it is of translating the words themselves, of snagging the emotional and cultural associations words trail and of breathing the atmosphere they both make and live on. The skill in translating the Native world consists of making something inaccessible into accessible enough, without making it totally accessible; to make something available without making it assimilable; to make it similar and different at the same time, while taking it seriously all the time; to keep it simultaneously intriguing and challenging; to create beauty, respect, and admiration with the desire to share and participate without the need to appropriate.

The present volume is a follow-up to *On the Translation of Native American Literatures*, which I edited and which the Smithsonian Institution Press published in 1992. Three of the contributors to that collection are represented here: John Bierhorst, William M. Clements, and Peter M. Whiteley. These two volumes work together, but the earlier one differs in that about half is devoted to Central and South America, with essays by scholars such as Miguel León-Portilla, Joel Sherzer, and Dennis Tedlock. In the present volume, however, south of the border, where the tradition of literary redaction and translation began in the Americas, is represented only by Nahuatl, a member of the great Uto-Aztecan language family that stretches down into Central America and up almost to the Canadian border, reminding us of the essential unity of Native America.

In my call for papers for a book on the translation of Native American literatures, I said that I was casting the net wide and interpreting "translation" in an inclusive way, noting that "topics could include not only linguistic and aesthetic aspects, but also, for example, the actual process itself, whether archival or in the field, as well as the personal, ethical and political dimensions of Native American translation." The result is a collection of essays on a variety of topics intended not only for the specialist but for the serious general reader.

I have arranged the book along the following lines, with, of course, inevitable overlaps and cross-communications; a few essays might do as well in one section as another. Part 1 deals with translation in a wide sense, starting with the question of whether translation should even take place (Carrie Dyck), then how "language translates culture" (Robert M. Leavitt), how Hopi time is translated (Chip Colwell-Chanthaphonh and Stewart B. Koyiyumptewa), and how Hopi place-names convey cultural and historical information (Peter M. Whiteley). There follow essays on the translation of the Bible into Naskapi and East Cree (Bill Jancewicz) and on the performative translation of a European folktale (Amber and Robin Ridington). This section concludes with William M. Clements's essay on translation and censorship and Blair Rudes's essay on the recreation of the Powhatan language. Part 2 focuses on ways and methods of direct involvement with the texts, starting with the use of audio, video, and new media (Robin, Amber, and Jillian Ridington, Patrick Moore, and Kate Hennessy), followed by Julie Brittain and Marguerite MacKenzie on translating Algonquian oral texts, David L. Kozak and David I. Lopez on the translation of O'odham devil songs, and the retranslation of a classic Haida cradle-song by Frederick H. White. Then comes "Translating Tense and Aspect in Tlingit Narratives" by Richard L. and Nora Marks Dauenhauer, an investigation into translating performance in the written text (Lynn Burley), Marcia Haag's discussion of problems involved with translating Choctaw texts, John Bierhorst's essay on the esoteric idioms of Aztec poetry, and William M. Clements on translation as context, focusing on a Powhatan song, which chimes nicely with the essay on Powhatan that ends part 1. The section concludes on a personal note with Richard J. Preston's "A Life in Translation" and M. Terry Thompson and Laurence C. Thompson's "Memories of Translation."

Almost twenty years ago, the Nahuatl scholar Willard Gingerich wrote: "It remains to be demonstrated to indifferent, skeptical or outrightly hostile audiences that there is a real native American, let alone Nahuatl, poetry at all, able to sustain serious critical scrutiny. 'Are you still working on that naugahyde poetry?' one of my best graduate professors used to ask with some regularity."[37] And more than twenty years ago, one of my own best graduate professors asked me on a campus visit why I had become interested in Native American literature. "Is it because there are no standards?" he wanted to know. Doubtless, such attitudes still exist, but they are harder to justify after a whole generation of scholars has created the rich and distinguished field of Native American studies, which incorporates, among others, the disciplines of linguistics, anthropology, folklore, history, translation studies, ethnopoetics, and literary criticism. The present volume is part of that ongoing enterprise, an attempt to make Native American literature a vital part of our curriculum and of our multifarious heritage.[38] It derives its title from a wonderful poem by Pablo Neruda, "La palabra" (The Word), which begins:

> Nació
> la palabra en la sangue,
> creció en el cuerpo oscuro, palpitando,
> y voló con los labios y la boca.[39]

> The word
> was born in the blood,
> grew in the dark body, pulsing,
> and flew with the lips and mouth.

Early in 2008, while this book was in progress, Blair Rudes died suddenly. Blair was going to make a few changes in his essay, but it appears here as he originally sent it. This volume is dedicated to his memory, and to the memory of my friends Alfonso Ortiz, William Bright, David McAllester, and Dell Hymes, who were also friends, colleagues, and teachers of many contributors to this volume.

Notes

1. Such, however, was the case when Barre Toelken worked with the Yellowman family, as described in Toelken's "Life and Death in the Navajo Coyote Tales," in *Recovering the Word: Essays on Native American Literatures*, ed. Brian Swann and Arnold Krupat (Berkeley: University of California Press, 1987), 388–401. Other researchers have encountered similar situations. Donald Bahr, for instance, found himself in difficulties when many Tohono O'odham ascribed the death of his informant, Juan Gregorio, not to natural causes but to offended animal spirits. See Bahr's *Piman Shamanism and Staying Sickness* (Tucson: University of Arizona Press, 1974).

2. J. Randolph Valentine, "Linguistics and Languages in Native American Studies," in *Studying Native American Problems and Prospects*, ed. Russell Thorn-

ton (Madison: University of Wisconsin Press, 1998), 162. Translating from "the Mesoamerican ancient world" presents another whole set of challenges and problems. See Miguel León-Portilla, "Have We Really Translated the Mesoamerican 'Ancient World'?" in *On the Translation of Native American Literatures,* ed. Brian Swann (Washington DC: Smithsonian Institution Press, 1992), 313–38.

3. Eric Cheyfitz, *The Poetics of Imperialism: Translation and Colonialism from "The Tempest" to "Tarzan"* (New York: Oxford University Press, 1991), 104. Discussions of the moral ambiguity of translation in general, are, of course, nothing new. In England the topic goes back at least to the golden age of translation, when Sir John Denham, in his preface to *The Destruction of Troy,* his version of *Aeneid* II published in 1657, talks of translation as robbery, the appropriation of another's property. But for literary translators this is not a bad thing. It is, in fact, a positive act, a "good," according to Willis Barnstone, for whom translators are "hardcore stealers" who declare their theft openly as part of the literary "tradition," "a code word for theft." *The Poetics of Translation: History, Theory, Practice* (New Haven: Yale University Press, 1993), 267.

4. Maria Tymoczko, "Translation: Ethics, Ideology, Action," *Massachusetts Review* 47, no. 3 (2006), special issue, "Translation as Resistance."

5. William M. Clements, *Native American Verbal Art* (Tucson: University of Arizona Press, 1996), 11.

6. Daniel T. Reff, introduction, *History of the Triumphs of Our Holy Faith* [1645], by Andrés Pérez de Ribas, ed. and trans. Maureen Ahern Reff and Richard K. Danforth (Tucson: University of Arizona Press, 1999), 12. Thanks to Matthew Bokovoy for this reference.

7. Munro S. Edmonson, *Sixteenth Century Mexico: The Work of Sahagún* (Albuquerque: University of New Mexico Press, 1974), 9. The Aztecs were not above book-burning themselves, as when the emperor Itzcoatl and Tlacaelel, architect of the Aztec state, ordered ancient codices and documents to be burned and new ones made to legitimize the Aztecs as descendants of the Toltec lords of Anahuac.

8. Sahagún's work in the early 1550s, in the words of J. Jorge Klor de Alva, "began to focus on topics that were clearly foreign to his basic pastoral needs." "Sahagún and the Birth of Modern Ethnology: Representing, Confessing and Inscribing the Other," in *The World of Bernardino de Sahagún: Pioneer Ethnographer of Sixteenth Century Aztec Mexico,* ed. J. Jorge Klor de Alva et al. (Albany: SUNY Press, 1988), 34. It should be noted, however, that Native languages were learned in order to penetrate the native mind for the purpose of conversion. In the prologue to his *General History of the Things of New Spain,* Sahagún noted that a doctor cannot apply medicine to the sick without understanding the cause of the sickness.

9. Olivia A. Bloechl, *Native American Song at the Frontiers of Early Modern Europe* (New York: Cambridge University Press, 2008), 61.

10. There were, however, some attempts at transcription and translation. We

have, for instance, the case of a Dutchman recording a story, and another of an Englishman attempting to appreciate a Potomac story. The former consists of a Lenni Lenape creation myth recorded by Peter Sluiter in 1679 in New Amsterdam, while in the latter William Strachey tells a story he obtained in 1612 from Captain Argall of his visit to the Potomacs when the young interpreter Henry Spelman lived with them. Argall was confused and wanted Spelman to interrupt the teller in order to have some points clarified, but Spelman refused, causing Argall to complain about haphazard native storytelling techniques. If the story "had proceeded in some order," he said, "they would have made yt hang togither the better." (For Sluiter see Ann-Marie Cantwell and DiDiana diZerega Wall, *Unearthing Gotham: The Archeology of New York City* [New Haven CT: Yale University Press, 2001], 36; for Argall see William Strachey, *The Historie of Travell into Virginia Britania*, ed. Louis B. Wright and Virginia Freund [London, 1612; Hakluyt Society, 1953], 101.) Interestingly, something like the oral storytelling technique Argall found so frustrating is still used by contemporary Native American writers such as Leslie Marmon Silko, who has said that "those accustomed to being taken from point A to point B to point C" might have difficulties with her work, since Pueblo expression resembles a spider's web, "with many little threads radiating from the center, crisscrossing one another. As with the web, the structure emerges as it is made, and you must simply listen and trust, as the Pueblo people do, that meaning will be made." "Language and Literature from a Pueblo Indian Perspective," in *Yellow Woman and a Beauty of the Spirit: Essays on Native American Life Today* (New York: Touchstone, 1997), 49. Concomitantly, in one of her stories Louise Erdrich provides an analogy between the human condition and its organic verbal expression when she writes that "in the woods, there is no right way to go, no trail to follow but the law of growth." *The Red Convertible: Selected and New Stories, 1978–2008* (New York: Harper-Collins, 2009), 123.

11. For a brief history of North American translation see Arnold Krupat, "On the Translation of Native American Song and Story: A Theorized History," in Swann, *On the Translation of Native American Literatures*, 3–33.

12. Much has been written about stereotypes via mistranslation, or the "creation" of translations, many of which have been incorporated in the national fabric, from the Walam Olum, for which consult David Oestreicher's "The Tale of a Hoax: Translating the Walam Olum," in *Algonquian Spirit: Contemporary Translations of the Algonquian Literatures of North America*, ed. Brian Swann (Lincoln: University of Nebraska Press, 2005), 3–41, to the term "Great Spirit," which Julian Rice has shown to be a missionary creation in *Before the Great Spirit: The Many Faces of Sioux Spirituality* (Albuquerque: University of Arizona Press, 1998); from the Don Juan phenomenon, for which see Richard de Mille, ed., *The Don Juan Papers: Further Castaneda Controversies* (Santa Barbara: Ross-Erickson, 1980), to Chief Seattle's speech (see Rudolf Kaiser, "Chief Seattle's Speech(es): American

Origins and European Reception," in Swann and Krupat, *Recovering the Word*, 497–536). David Murray, in his *Forked Tongues: Speech, Writing and Representation of North American Indian Texts* (Bloomington: Indiana University Press, 1991), writes that one of his main aims "is to demonstrate the complex and various ways in which the process of translation, cultural as well as linguistic, is obscured or effaced in a wide variety of texts which claim to be representing or describing Indians, and what cultural or ideological assumptions underlie such effacement" (1). A recent ludicrous example of "effacement," mistranslation used for a dubious purposes, is the late right-wing syndicated columnist Robert Novak's article "Killing the Chief" in the *New York Post*, February 22, 2007, page 33, where he laments the forced retirement of his alma mater's "mascot" "Chief Illinewek." By honoring the Chief, Novak writes, using the party line for this kind of thing, the University of Illinois was honoring Native Americans, admiring "their valor, ferociousness and indomitable spirit in the face of overwhelming odds." He claims that "Illinois" itself is Algonquian for "tribe of superior men." (In fact it means something like "he speaks in a regular way/like us/with a common tongue.") Mr. Novak might have liked to have taken heart from the fact that while Chief Illinewek is no longer with us, the descendants of the Illinois, the Kaskia and Peoria, are. They live in the northwest corner of Oklahoma consolidated with the Wea and Piankashaw.

13. The question of "authenticity" and related issues such as syncretism and hybridity haunt contemporary Native American studies. See, for instance, Elvira Pulitano's *Toward a Native American Critical Theory* (Lincoln: University of Nebraska Press, 2003) and Jace Weaver, Craig S. Womack, and Robert Warrior, eds., *American Indian Literary Nationalism* (Albuquerque: University of New Mexico Press, 2005).

14. Isaac Bashevis Singer, in "On Translating My Books," writes that "no creation in one language can fill the cultural needs of a people," in *The World of Translation: Papers Delivered at the Conference on Literary Translation Held in New York City in May 1970 under the Auspices of PEN American Center* (New York: PEN American Center, 1971), 112.

15. Hugh Kenner, *Historical Fictions* (San Francisco: North Point Press, 1990), 229. This "modernist enterprise" can have some unusual twists. For example, in "Going Native, Becoming Modern: American Indians, Walt Whitman and the Yiddish Poet," Rachel Rubenstein argues that in the early twentieth century, Yiddish "translations" of Indian songs already "translated" by the likes of Mary Austin, Harriet Monroe, Alive Corbin Henderson, and George Cronyn in their attempt to create an exemplary modern American poetry were intended to usher in Yiddish/American modernism, since "the imaginary Indian came to function in this period as a figure through which Americans could define what it means to be *modern* as well as *American*." *American Quarterly* 58, no. 2 (2006): 431–13. For

the use of Indian songs by modern poets see Michael Castro, *Interpreting the Indian: Twentieth-Century Poets and Native Americans* (Albuquerque: University of New Mexico Press, 1983).

16. See SSILA *Newsletter* 25, no. 3 (October 2005): 4–78, as well as SSILA *Bulletin* no. 248: 4–18 (ssila@lists.uoregon.edu). (SSILA is an acronym for Society for the Study of the Indigenous Languages of the Americas.) See also "Missionaries and Scholars: The Overlapping Agendas of Linguists in the Field," LSA Annual Meeting, Anaheim, 2007, organized by Lise M. Dobrin. Thanks to Julie Brittain for the last reference.

17. Marianne Mithun, "Overview of General Characteristics," in *Handbook of North American Indians*, vol. 17, *Languages*, ed. Ives Goddard (Washington DC: Smithsonian Institution, 1996), 138.

18. Anderson's essay, "Ghost Dance Songs," is in Swann, *Algonquian Spirit*, 448–71. In the same volume, Richard J. Preston in the introduction to his "Louse and Wide Lake" (215–20) makes important points about metaphor, while John Bierhorst in the present volume questions metaphor in a Nahuatl context. In *Aztecs: An Interpretation* (Cambridge: Cambridge University Press 1991), Inga Clendinnen discusses Aztec ritual relationships we tend to regard as metaphorical but which "might not be metaphor at all, simply demonstrations of the range of consubstantiation" (251–52).

19. Basso's essay, "'Wise Words' of the Western Apache: Metaphor and Semantic Theory," is in *Meaning and Anthropology*, ed. Basso and Henry A. Selby (Albuquerque: University of New Mexico Press, 1976), 93–121.

20. Willard Gingerich, "Ten Types of Ambiguity in Nahuatl Poetry, or William Empson among the Aztecs," in Swann, *On the Translation of Native American Literatures*, 362. In Nahuatl, a polysynthetic language of compound words, highly inflected, with prefixes, suffixes, and infixes, a small structural ambiguity can result in opposite interpretations, as seen in an important story from a 1558 manuscript where the hero deflowers and/or devours the mythic female or is himself assaulted and killed, as demonstrated by Pat Carr and Willard Gingerich, "The Vagina Dentata Motif in Nahuatl and Pueblo Mythic Narratives: A Comparative Study," in *Smoothing the Ground: Essays on Native American Oral Literature*, ed. Brian Swann (Berkeley: University of California Press, 1983), 200.

21. H. C. Wolfart, "Sketch of Cree, an Algonquian Language," *Handbook of North American Indians*, vol. 17, *Languages*, 398. For an elaboration on this topic focusing on Cree's sister language Ojibwa, see A. Irving Hallowell, "Ojibwa Ontology, Behavior and World View," in *Culture and History: Essays in Honor of Paul Radin*, ed. Stanley Diamond (New York: Columbia University Press, 1960).

22. The classic study here is Laura Bohannon's essay "Shakespeare in the Bush," in which the young anthropologist attempts to tell the story of "Hamlet" to a group of Tiv elders in West Africa. The essay is in *Conformity and Conflict: Readings in Cultural Anthropology*, ed. James P. Spradley and David W. McCurdy (Boston: Little Brown and Co., 1971).

23. Frederick Turner, *Beyond Geography: The Western Spirit against the Wilderness* (New York: Viking Press, 1980), 175.

24. J. A. Wheeler, "Is Physics Legislated by Cosmology?" in *The Encyclopedia of Ignorance*, ed. Ronald Duncan and Miranda Weston Smith (New York: Pocket Books, 1977), 30.

25. Susan M. Preston, "A Pair of Hero Stories," in Swann, *Algonquian Spirit*, 231.

26. Turner, *Beyond Geography*, 175.

27. The trickster is like Shelley's west wind, both destroyer and preserver. Along these lines, Arnold Krupat argues that the trickster's "double nature," "*both* subversive *and* normative," creative and destructive, is not a problem or paradox to be resolved by "irony" or other means; the trickster's nature constitutes "creative flexibility" in action. *All That Remains: Varieties of Indigenous Expression* (Lincoln: University of Nebraska Press, 2009), 1–26.

28. On the issues involved in the transfer of an oral culture to a written one see Walter J. Ong, *Orality and Literature* (London: Methuen, 1982) and *The Presence of the Word* (New Haven: Yale University Press, 1967; Minneapolis: University of Minneapolis Press, 1981). In the latter he suggests that the written word "devitalizes the universe, weakens the sense of presence in man's life-world and renders this world "profane," "an agglomeration of things" (162). See also Eric A. Havelock, *The Muse Learns to Write: Reflections on Orality and Literacy from Antiquity to the Present* (New Haven: Yale University Press, 1983), and Jack Goody, *The Domestication of the Savage Mind* (Cambridge: Cambridge University Press, 1977).

29. Harry Robinson, *Write It on Your Heart: The Epic World of an Okanagan Storyteller*, ed. Wendy Wickwire (Vancouver: Talon/Theytus Books, 1989), 190. Arnold Krupat discusses Robinson's work and the topic of stories "turned into subjects/objects of a Western criticism of Native American literature" in chapter 5 of his *Ethnohistory: Ethnography, History, Language* (Berkeley: University of California Press, 1992).

30. Paul Zolbrod, "The Flight of Dzilyi neeyani," in *Voices from Four Directions: Contemporary Translations of the Native Literatures of North America*, ed. Brian Swann (Lincoln: University of Nebraska Press, 2003), 304. Zolbrod is referring to the work of Washington Matthews.

31. For Melville Jacobs see *The Content and Style of an Oral Literature: Clackamas Chinook Myths and Tales* (Chicago: University of Chicago Press, 1959); for Dell Hymes see *"In Vain I Tried To Tell You": Essays in Native American Ethnopoetics* (Philadelphia: University of Pennsylvania Press, 1981); and for Dennis Tedlock see *The Spoken Word and the Work of Interpretation* (Philadelphia: University of Pennsylvania Press, 1983).

32. Dennis Tedlock, "Dialogues between Worlds: Mesoamerica after and before the European Invasion," in *Theorizing the Americanist Tradition*, ed. Lisa Philips Valentine and Regna Darnell (Toronto: University of Toronto Press, 1999), 163.

33. Brian Thom, "The Anthropology of Northwest Coast Oral Tradition," *Arctic Anthropology* 40, no. 1 (2002): 1–28.

34. Keith Basso, *Wisdom Sits in Places: Landscape and Language among the Western Apache* (Albuquerque: University of New Mexico Press, 1996), 6.

35. Nora Marks Dauenhauer and Richard Dauenhauer, "Raven Stories," in Swann, *Voices from Four Directions*, 27.

36. For an example of the "politicization" of publication, M. Terry Thompson and Steven M. Egesdal note that some Salishan groups today feel that all myths must belong to the tribe and hence refuse permission for publication "in any form, by any person, including their own tribal members." This, the editors say, "accounts for the absence of some well-known Salishanists among the authors" in their volume. *Salish Myths and Legends: One People's Stories* (Lincoln: University of Nebraska Press, 2008), xx–xxi.

37. Willard Gingerich, "Ten Types of Ambiguity in Nahuatl Poetry," in Swann, *On the Translation of Native American Literatures*, 359.

38. This richness and vitality is still, however, far from obvious to all. While most literary anthologies today often include a Native component, some still ignore ethnopoetics or simply take the easy path and reprint old translations. One would have thought, for instance, that the grandly and inclusively named Library of America would have found room in its prestigious pages for the first Americans. But in volume 1 of *American Poetry: The Twentieth Century* (New York, 2000), "from Henry Adams to Dorothy Parker," all we find are a couple of pages from Frances Densmore's 1910 "Chippewa Music" and Mary Austin's brief "The Grass on the Mountain" ("from the Paiute"), with no notes providing provenance or context, presenting the songs the old-fashioned way as self-explanatory self-standing "poems." (In volume 2, from e. e. cummings to May Swenson, there is only Lynn Riggs's poem "Santo Domingo Corn Dance"). When I proposed a volume to help the Library of America live up to its name, my proposal was declined.

39. Pablo Neruda, "La palabra," in *Plenos poderes* (Buenos Aires: Losada, 1962), 24.

PART ONE

1

Should Translation Work Take Place?

Ethical Questions Concerning the
Translation of First Nations Languages

Carrie Dyck

1. Introduction

For many First Nations communities, translation represents a "sea change":
while all languages are passed on through word of mouth, only a subset of
languages have writing systems, and even fewer are regularly translated.
Many First Nations languages (and many other languages) are primarily
oral; writing and translation are recent additions. Writing, literacy, and
translation work potentially leads to great changes in a language community, and their introduction raises a host of ethical questions.

This chapter outlines the potential benefits and disadvantages of translating Cayuga, an Iroquoian language. It also describes the context of
translation: the people who speak Cayuga, and the community, Six Nations of the Grand River, where Cayuga is spoken. I outline the community context in section 3, and then discuss translation and knowledge
transfer in sections 4 and 5. I also describe related issues, which include
turning the oral tradition into a written one (section 6) and the problem
of controlling access to translations (section 7). Finally, I have included
many asides about the English words used in this chapter to describe language and knowledge, for the following reasons.

This chapter describes an *ethical space* that has come into being at Six
Nations because of translation (see Ermine 2005 for an introduction to
this concept). The potential for an ethical space is created whenever First
Nations and Western cultures come into contact. Instead of just acting and
reacting, participants within an ethical space purposefully examine their

underlying motives and the effects of their interactions. (My desire for this type of overt acknowledgment is the reason for section 2.) The goal of an ethical space is to create a principled research methodology. I will present some thoughts about the latter in the conclusion (section 8).

2. "We've Been Studied to Death"

Acknowledging the ethical context, I am uncomfortable with writing this chapter because it is yet another outsider's description of the Iroquois. ("We've been studied to death," is one Cayuga speaker's apt commentary about such descriptions.)

For a cross-section of the vast anthropological literature, the reader could consult Morgan (1901a, 1901b), Speck (1945), or Shimony (1994). Annotated bibliographies of the literature on the Iroquois include Murdock and O'Leary (1975) and Weinman (1969). Fenton (1951) also reviews the literature on the Iroquois up to about 1950. This information was sourced from Martin (2008).

This chapter contains statistics and facts about the Iroquois as well as anonymous paraphrases of what Cayuga speakers have said to me. However, these are meant to provide context or to bring alive otherwise abstract concepts. I report on the Iroquois because without their language and thoughts (or more accurately, my interpretation of them), this chapter would be rather tepid and uninteresting. The purpose of writing about the Iroquois, then, is to enliven this chapter in order to provide some insight into the ethical issues that arise from translation work.

3. The Community Context

Six Nations of the Grand River is situated in southern Ontario, Canada, near the city of Brantford (see map 1-1). Six Nations has approximately 22,350 members, of whom about 50 percent live on reserve (Six Nations Elected Council 2007:44). About 300 people at Six Nations speak an Iroquoian language, either Cayuga, Mohawk, or Onondaga. (The last Seneca speaker at Six Nations died in the 1990s, but there are Seneca speakers at the Tonawanda, Cattaraugus, and Allegheny reservations in western New York [Mithun 1999].)

The Northern Iroquoian languages include Cayuga, Seneca, Onondaga, Mohawk, Oneida, and Tuscarora. (Cherokee is also an Iroquoian language, but it belongs to a more remotely related, southern branch of

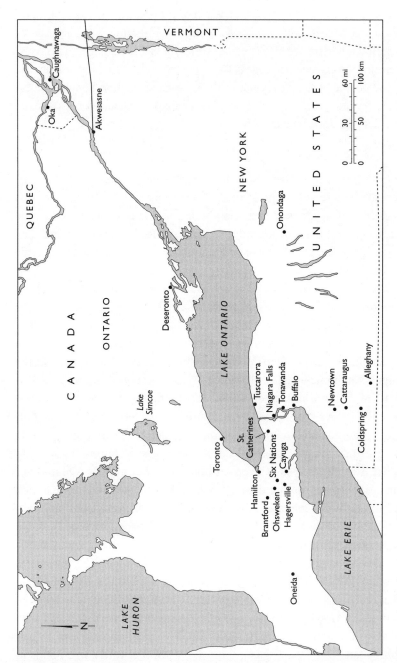

Map 1-1. Iroquoian communities

the language family.) The underlying unity of the Northern Iroquoian languages is recognized by speakers, who use phrases like "speaking Indian" or Cayuga words like *Ǫgwehǫwéhnęha:ˀ* 'the Indian way or language' to describe it.[1] There are also specific words for each language: the Cayuga word for the Cayuga language is *Gayogǫho:nǫhnéha:ˀ* 'the way or language of the people of the pipe.' Finally, the Cayuga word for a female translator is *deyewęnádenyeˀs*, which literally means 'she changes words'; a male translator is *dehawęnádenyeˀs*.

3.1. Language Status

The Iroquoian languages spoken at Six Nations can be classified as endangered: there were approximately seventy-five fluent Cayuga speakers as of 2009. Cayuga is spoken mainly in Longhouse contexts and in the immersion school setting. However, in response to fears about the state of the language, people make deliberate efforts to speak Cayuga outside these contexts.

The shift away from speaking Cayuga at home took place within living memory: for example, in one family, where the siblings are now all over fifty years of age, the older siblings grew up speaking an Iroquoian language at home, but the younger ones did not have the same exposure to the language. According to the children, the parents deliberately spoke the language at home with the older siblings because they lived in the United States at the time and were worried about language retention. However, once they moved to Six Nations the parents were less worried about language retention and did not speak the language in the home as vigilantly as in the past. To give another example, in a younger family, one woman in her early fifties spoke Cayuga at home with her mother well into her thirties, until her mother died; after that, she "didn't have anyone to talk to." In contrast, several families headed by language activists and with younger children between the ages of ten and twenty-five still make a point of speaking the language at home.

3.2. The Longhouse Religion

Many Cayuga speakers are followers of the Iroquoian Longhouse religion, founded in 1799 by the Seneca prophet Handsome Lake (Sganyadáiyo:). (The word *Ontario* appears to be a related word borrowed from an Iroquoian language into English; the *-rio* part of the word corresponds to Cayuga *-iyo:* 'beautiful' or 'great.')

Cayuga speakers express the opinion that the English words *religion* and *ceremonies* are inaccurate and that the Longhouse "religion" is more encompassing than the term *religion* implies. The word *ceremonies* is also considered somewhat objectionable; Cayuga speakers consider the word *doings* to be more appropriate, perhaps because the doings are not seen as being much different from the realm of everyday life. However, the Longhouse way is a traditional way of life, with special events and ceremonies centered around the agricultural calendar, and whose main purpose is to acknowledge and give thanks to the Creator.

At Six Nations, the oral tradition associated with the Longhouse religion is transmitted through Cayuga, Onondaga, and (more recently) English. The oral tradition is extensive; for example, the Code of Handsome Lake takes about four days to recite. This body of teachings describes how people should live simply and traditionally (some examples are provided later), and it is preached at special times of the year to promote cleansing and renewal.

3.3. Types of Oral Tradition

In addition to the Code of Handsome Lake, there are three other kinds of speeches in the oral tradition (Foster 1974:7–8): hierarchically structured speech events such as the Thanksgiving Address; political oratory, including the Great Law; and speeches associated with herbalism and private curing ceremonies. The latter will not be further discussed due to their sensitive nature (see section 7 for a few additional comments). The Thanksgiving Address is discussed in section 5.2. A few more details about the Great Law are provided below.

The Great Law (Gayanęhsra²gó:wah) tells the story of the founding of the League or Confederacy of the Iroquois, prior to the 1500s. It lays out the laws and rituals associated with the League. One example of the Great Law is the Condolence Ceremony, during which the passing of an hereditary chief is mourned and a successor is installed.

The Confederacy of the Iroquois consists of the Three Brothers (the Onondaga, Mohawk, and Seneca) and the Four Brothers (Cayuga, Oneida, and the adopted Tuscarora and Delaware; the Delaware are Algonquian). It is also called the Five Nations (for the original member nations, the Onondaga, Mohawk, Seneca, Cayuga, and Oneida), the Six Nations (add Tuscarora), and the Haudenosaunee (Hodinǫhsó:nih, the People of the Longhouse; literally, 'they (males) make the house').

The Confederate Council consists of fifty hereditary chiefs. Although it was replaced by an elected council in 1924, both councils continue to operate today, and their relative authority is a topic of long-standing dispute. (The lack of a clearly recognized central authority has an impact on access to translations, as discussed in section 7.)

Although the Great Law is a monumental body of knowledge, no Iroquoian-language version existed in print until 1992; only translations existed. (For a state-of-the-art English synopsis of the Great Law, see Fenton 1998; for a fuller description of the 1992 Iroquoian version, see section 6.1.) The 1992 monograph, consisting of Onondaga with English translation, is 755 pages long, which hints at the extent of this particular type of oral literature.

Although the type of knowledge embodied in the vast Iroquoian oral tradition can be labeled as *culture*, some speakers believe that a term like *civilization* is more accurate because it implies a more systematic, higher-status, and longer-lasting body of knowledge. When talking in English about language or knowledge, Cayuga speakers are on a constant search for more accurate or non-pejorative English labels. The Cayuga phrase that expresses a concept similar to civilization is *tsęh niyǫgwaihóˀdę:* 'our ways or beliefs').

In summary, the great and ancient Iroquoian heritage is embodied in a few languages that now have very few speakers. This creates an urgent context for language-preservation efforts, including translation.

3.4. Fear of Language Loss and Language-Preservation Efforts

Among Longhouse followers (Hadinǫhsesgehó:nǫˀ or Gaenǫhsesgehó:nǫˀ People of the Longhouse) there is a sense of obligation to pass on the Creator's gift of language: one speaker described to me a compelling dream in which she was held to account for passing along the traditional ways (including language) as a condition of being allowed to enter into the Sky World after death. While it is not my place to describe further details of the dream, I describe some aspects of its context below before returning to the topic of language preservation.

The Sky World (the realm above the sky) is in contrast with the middle realm (below or in the sky) and the earth (which rests on the Turtle's back). It is said that the earth was formed when Sky Woman fell through the hole in the sky dome that was created when the Great Tree of Light was uprooted. At that time there was no land, and so to help support her,

Muskrat dove to the bottom of the sea and brought up a lump of earth, which he placed on the Turtle's back. The earth then expanded to its present size. (For a synopsis of this body of knowledge see Herrick 1995:5–6.)

Regarding language preservation, the Six Nations community has responded to fears about the state of the language in many ways. Within the education system, Cayuga and Mohawk immersion programs for grades 1–12 were established in the 1980s and continue today. (Starting these programs was difficult: the first classes were offered by a Mohawk and a Cayuga woman who gave up their regular, better-paying jobs, cleaned out the Legion Hall in Ohsweken—the main town at Six Nations—so that it could be used as a classroom, and started preparing curriculum material to teach.)

Today, Cayuga and Mohawk adult immersion programs and adult night courses are offered at nearby postsecondary institutions and cultural centers. (Such is their dedication to preserving the language that students who enroll in the adult immersion programs typically give up better-paying jobs in return for a living stipend which is inadequate for a single person, let alone a family.)

Finally, an ongoing Cayuga and Mohawk curriculum development program, the Kawenní:io/Gawęní:yo: Language Preservation Project, is associated with the Kawenní:io/Gawęní:yo: immersion high school. This project has a coordinator and is informed by a Mohawk and a Cayuga speaker. (These are the same two women who started the original immersion school; both still work tirelessly, despite being past retirement age and in poor health.)

Although the educational programs just described aim to teach everyday language, other programs, such as the Haudenosaunee Resource Centre (HRC), aspire to preserve the oral tradition described in section 3.3. This project follows in the footsteps of the late Jacob Thomas and the late Reginald Henry (both noted ritualists and language activists, who in the 1980s each founded learning centers aimed at preserving the oral tradition). The HRC is situated in an old school building at Six Nations. All the project members except for the coordinator are men of various ages: younger learners in their twenties or thirties undertake to learn ritual speeches and are guided by older fluent speakers in their fifties. Everyone, in turn, takes direction from a handful of elders approximately in their seventies, who are called upon to explain "high language" (special ceremonial terms whose meaning is figurative and often opaque). The project mirrors in design the traditional means of training new ritualists in the oral tradition, except that the training is not done in private. (This training is described at the end of section 3.4.)

Finally, the HRC has a very popular outreach component. Members of the project make presentations (in English) to school and community groups about topics such as the Green Corn ceremony, which is a set of rituals to thank the Creator for another successful growing season and harvest (Shimony 1994:166). Project members report that the level of detail and the type of information in the presentations depended on the type of audience. This is an example of a kind of control over access to information, a topic to be further discussed in section 7. It is also an example of the strong demand for knowledge of Iroquoian civilization in translation.

The Woodland Cultural Centre (WCC; http://www.woodland-centre .on.ca/index.php) in Brantford, Ontario, under the direction of Amos Key Jr., has engaged in many language-preservation projects. Key has worked with noted ritualists and speakers to make recordings of conversational language and ceremonial speeches. As a result of the latter initiative, the WCC has archived fifteen reel-to-reel recordings of conversations, as well as Mohawk, Cayuga, and Onondaga versions of the Great Law. (Interestingly, the recordings of the Great Law were made by a single ritualist, the late Huron Miller. It was common in the past for speakers to be familiar with several Iroquoian languages, often as a result of having had parents who spoke different languages in the home.)

The WCC has fostered a tradition of engaging in research projects with both Iroquoian language speakers and academics. Some of the Iroquoian-led projects were described above, and some are described below. To give an example of the academic research, two projects funded by the Ontario Ministry of Education resulted in a Cayuga dictionary (Froman et al. 2003) and an Onondaga dictionary (Woodbury 2003). Other dictionaries funded by the Ontario Ministry of Education, but not in conjunction with the WCC, include a dictionary of Tuscarora (Rudes 1999) and of Oneida (Michelson and Doxtator 2002).

While a handful of linguists work on Cayuga, it is Longhouse followers who are in large part responsible for the preservation efforts just described. What is interesting is that they may have undertaken these initiatives in spite of Handsome Lake's prohibitions against the use of technologies such as writing and recording. As Shimony observed, "There is a conscious effort to perpetuate the Longhouse way of life precisely by several members who are most knowledgeable, and the fact that they utilize some previously disfavored means [such as writing and recording] in no way indicates any diminution of their religious convictions. To them, the means justify the ends" (1994:xx).

Writing, recording, translating, reading anthropological literature about the Iroquois, taking language courses, and obtaining postsecondary degrees are all examples of activities that I have been told run counter to the teachings of Handsome Lake, but which speakers have adopted in order to meet higher goals.

There is, however, an alternative interpretation of speakers' use of nontraditional means of preserving the language. To illustrate, one speaker asked me, "[Are] not writing systems just mnemonic devices/systems anyway?" The Iroquois traditionally used wampum belts (and other objects) as prompts for remembering significant treaties and past events. It could be, then, that some speakers see writing systems as a continuation of this tradition. Indeed, speakers learning speeches appear to use written transcripts as prompts for remembering a model speech upon which they can base their own oral compositions. (See section 5.2 for more on the process of oral composition.) If such is the case, then the use of writing, translating, and so forth can be seen as the continuation of a traditional practice that does not run counter the spirit of Handsome Lake's teachings. Similar logic could underlie the adoption of other "nontraditional" means of preserving the language.

Returning to the main topic, language-preservation efforts also take place despite an undercurrent of alarm that language loss, the loss of the traditional ways, and environmental degradation are inevitable and foretold. Michael Foster summarizes a similar viewpoint: "The story is told that there will come a time when there is only one Iroquois left who will know the ceremonies. On the last day before the calamity this lone Indian will enter the longhouse for the last time and recite the entire set of speeches and songs, and recite them perfectly. Then he will leave the longhouse and die, and that will be the end of everything" (1974:129 n. 9).

According to Foster, the traditional method of preserving the Longhouse oral tradition could account for this type of attitude: typically, the death of a ritualist triggers a crisis, which is resolved when a young man, who has discreetly undergone a private training process, steps in to perform the former ritualist's duties. In Foster's view, "The notion of 'crisis' in the taking up of ritual roles tends to engender a pessimistic view. But despite the enormous loss to the Longhouse community in the death of many key ritualists in recent years, the remarkable process of succession—of young men stepping forward at the right moment—goes on. I have seen it happen at Six Nations over the last three years, even though unhappily most of the speakers who contributed to this study have died during the same period" (1974:252).

This process of succession was also the basic model for the Haudenosaunee Resource Centre. Young men working for the project used more traditional means of learning the speeches, such as talking with knowledgeable older male speakers. However, they also analyzed unfamiliar vocabulary on a blackboard, and transcribed and translated recordings of speeches.

In summary, although translation and other preservation efforts are controversial means of preserving the Longhouse way of life, speakers still use many different tools in their desire to maintain the oral tradition. (See section 6 for further discussion of why translation is controversial.) The remainder of this chapter describes the consequences and impact of translation on the language and the community of speakers, beginning with a discussion of language and knowledge.

4. Translation and Knowledge Transfer

Translation can be viewed as a means of transferring knowledge from one group of speakers to another. The question is, how effective is translation for knowledge transfer? In order to discuss the topic, it is necessary to say a few words about the relationship between language and knowledge.

In one extreme view, the Sapir-Whorf hypothesis (Sapir 1983; Whorf 1956), language strictly determines how we perceive and think about the world: metaphorically speaking, translation as a process is as doomed as trying to change silver into gold. In reality, however, the categories of our native languages merely predispose us to think about or perceive the world in certain ways. A classic example comes from infant sound discrimination experiments: early on, infants distinguish sounds like [t] and [d] from one another, regardless of whether such sounds are found in the surrounding adult language. (For example, Gikuyu, a language spoken in Kenya, has a [t] sound but no [d] sound.) However, if the distinction between [t] and [d] is not present in the adult language, then infants lose the ability to perceive the difference between such sounds by about the age of one year (Werker and Tees 1984). Nevertheless, adults are able to relearn the distinction when they learn a second language (such as English) in which the difference between [t] and [d] is important. ("Ten" is different from "den.")

This example shows that language colors perception but is not a perceptual straitjacket: infants and adults can unlearn and relearn the ability to perceive the difference between [t] and [d]. Given that language only colors perception, then, translation is possible; however, contextualization is needed in order to promote the ability to learn novel cultural concepts or unlearn old ones. (Contextualization is further discussed below.)

Cayuga speakers recognize that language is separate from knowledge and point out that there is more to being a Longhouse follower than speaking the language: the belief systems, attitudes, and way of life are also passed down through upbringing. While, ideally, belief systems and teachings should be transmitted through the language, some people are said to have the "attitude and essence of traditional belief" even though they cannot speak the language.

This observation raises a controversial question: Can Iroquoian culture be transmitted without the medium of an Iroquoian language? To address this question, it is necessary to distinguish between concepts that are lexical (concepts conveyed through words) and those that are grammaticalized (or obligatorily expressed through grammatical categories).

Concepts conveyed through words consist of denotations (dictionary meanings) and connotations. Connotations are emotional associations (personal or societal) that are suggested by, or form part of, the meaning of a word. For example, January is the first month of the year (its denotation); in contrast, January can have negative connotations like "bad weather" and "seasonal affective disorder," or positive connotations like "New Year's." Both denotations and connotations can be translated with relative precision, although, for significant concepts, it might take a book-length work to convey the actual meaning.

To show that denotations can be translated, I could state that the Cayuga word *desda?n* means both 'stand up!' and 'stop!'; for illustration, I could add that *desda?n* is even the punch line of a joke that the late Reginald Henry told me: "A husband is driving with his wife in a truck; the wife asks the husband to *stop* so that she can investigate a yard sale. In response, the husband leans forward over the wheel, *stands up*, and drives on past." The humor of this joke can be conveyed even to people who do not know Cayuga, although it takes some explaining. Similarly, lexical meanings in one language can be described to speakers of another language, with some contextualization.

In contrast, grammaticalized concepts are more fundamental, and arguably do not translate as well. For example, Cayuga verbs obligatorily mark the difference between "we two" (or "the two of us") and "we all": when I once asked for the Cayuga equivalent of "we are fat" (a sentence in English, but a verb in Cayuga), two Cayuga women humorously supplied the word ǫgyáhsę: 'we two are fat' rather than the word ǫgwáhsę: 'we all are fat.' In Cayuga, one is forced to choose which "we" to use, allowing for the possibility of a pun. While this particular example translates well enough, the *preoccupation* with choosing between the prefixes ǫgy- 'we two' and ǫgw- 'we all' is arguably lost in translation, as are most other grammatical preoccupations.

It is even more difficult to translate the meaning conveyed by grammatical categories such as tense and aspect. (Tense distinctions convey the time in which an action takes place, while aspect distinctions describe the manner in which an action takes place.) English is preoccupied with verb tense distinctions (such as present-tense "they work" versus past-tense "they worked"). Cayuga is preoccupied with verb aspect distinctions. English also makes a few aspectual distinctions, such as "they work (all the time or habitually)" versus "they are working (an observation about a current state of affairs)." In contrast, the Cayuga verb system is all about aspect: for example, the verb ǫgí:daʔ can be translated either as 'I slept' or 'I am sleeping' (the latter could be said by someone who was trying to nap and wanted to be left alone). However, what the English translations do not convey, without further explanation, is that the word ǫgí:daʔ means something more like 'my sleeping is a fact': in Cayuga, it is more important to express whether the action is factual than to indicate the time of its occurrence. (There are ways to convey a time line in Cayuga, however.) In English, the best way to convey factuality in verbs is to use a past-tense form ('I slept'), which express an activity that actually happened; alternatively, English speakers could use a present progressive form ('I am sleeping') to make an observation about something that is actually happening as one speaks. This example shows that the English way of translating Cayuga factual verb forms is inadequate: the preoccupations of the source language cannot be conveyed in the English translation, or more precisely, Cayuga aspectual distinctions have, for the most part, no direct equivalent in English.

Returning to the main question of this section, some aspects of the Iroquoian way can be transmitted without the medium of an Iroquoian language. However, something is lost when we translate concepts without an in-depth knowledge of and empathy for the ways of First Peoples (context); it is also extremely difficult to translate the way in which First Peoples express themselves (their linguistic preoccupations or habits, their eloquence or skill, etc.). (See section 5.2 for further discussion of Dell Hymes's viewpoints on eloquence and skill.)

5. Translation in Cayuga

So far I have talked about the community context within which translation work takes place, and about the knowledge expressed in the Cayuga language. In this section I turn to describing translation proper.

5.1. Previous Translation Work

Until recently, little of the oral tradition described in section 3.3 had been written down, and little information about Cayuga existed in print. Notable transcripts and translations include Foster (1974) (described below) and Mithun and Woodbury (1980); the latter contains two short stories (one about rabbit hunting, for example) narrated by the late Reginald Henry. (Reg Henry was a gifted ritualist and linguist who spoke fluent Cayuga, Onondaga, and English and was well versed in other Iroquoian languages. His efforts to preserve the Cayuga language and Longhouse traditions are almost unparalleled. See section 6.1 for an example of his many contributions.)

Linguistic knowledge of the language is available in the Cayuga dictionary (Froman et al. 2003), a monograph about Iroquoian accent (Michelson 1988), a Cayuga teaching grammar (Mithun and Henry 1982), an unpublished description of Cayuga verb conjugations (Sasse and Keye 1998), and various journal articles and theses.

In English, knowledge of the Iroquois Longhouse tradition can be found in Foster (1974), Shimony (1994), and many other anthropological sources (some were overviewed in section 2).

The Haudenosaunee Resource Centre has produced unpublished transcripts and translations of Longhouse speeches. Similarly, linguist Michael Foster is working on transcripts and translations of the Condolence Ceremony. (The Condolence Ceremony, part of the Great Law, is a set of rituals for mourning the death of a hereditary chief and for installing a successor.) The Cayuga: Our Oral Legacy (COOL) project has also produced unpublished transcripts and translations of conversational recordings (see http://www.mun.ca/cayuga/cayuga_language.php for some examples).

Finally, dedicated community language activists have produced transcripts and translations of, for example, the large complex of speeches associated with funerals, as well as the Code of Handsome Lake. Interestingly, the Woodland Cultural Centre (which sponsored the latter project) has decided for the moment not to release the transcript and translation of the Code of Handsome Lake for fear that it will get into the wrong (outsiders') hands.

5.2. An Example of Translation: The Thanksgiving Address

One of the first and best examples of a published Cayuga transcript and translation is Foster's (1974) translation of the Thanksgiving Address. (For a shorter and more recent English translation, see Foster 1994.) The Thanksgiving Address is a speech in which the performer and audience thank the spirit forces on the earth, in the sky, and beyond the sky (this division of spirit forces was described in the second paragraph of section 3.4). Foster describes three levels of translation: a morpheme-by-morpheme level of translation showing word composition (1.b; in the interests of publishing the monograph in a timely fashion, Foster omitted this level of translation from his monograph, except in the example reproduced below); a lexical level (1.c), showing English translations of whole words; and a free translation (1.d) "in which lines are translated into idiomatic English" (1974:255–56).

1. Example from Foster (1974:255) (example numbering and orthography have been modified)

a. *hędá:*	*o:nę́h,*	*to*	*niyó:wé²,*	*nigahá:wí²*
b. and	now	that	how-it-far-perfective	how-it-carry-perfective
c. and	now	that	is how far	it is carried
d. And now the time has come.				

(One unusual feature of example 1 is that the morphemes or meaningful word-parts which are shown and translated in 1.b, are not indicated in 1.a.

Typically, for example, the fourth word in 1.a would be shown as *ni-* 'how' *-yó:-* 'it' *-wé-* 'far' *-ʔ* 'perfective'; Foster's representation is more readable.)

The morpheme-by-morpheme level of translation preserves some of the original meaning of the language because, as speakers often observe, Cayuga words "mean more than English words do." I will second-guess two interpretations of this observation, one having to do with overall word complexity (polysynthesis), and one having to do with how words are related to one another meaningfully (derivational relationships).

In general, Cayuga words are more complex in structure and in meaning than English ones. (This is a partial definition of polysynthesis.) First, most words that name objects (i.e., nouns) are actually verb forms, and verbs, in turn, convey much the same meaning as an entire English sentence. For example, the Cayuga word *gahnyaʔsesgó:wah* 'giraffe,' which functions as a noun, is a verb with the sentence-like meaning 'it has a really long neck': *ga -it, -hnyaʔs-* 'neck' *-es-* 'is long' *-gó:wah* 'great big.' Even actual nouns (as opposed to verbs functioning as nouns) can be complex in structure, with a corresponding increase in the level of meaning conveyed: for example, the Cayuga word for Caughnawaga or Kahnawake, Quebec, is Gahnáwaʔgeh, literally, 'on the rapids.' (The English words Caughnawaga and Kahnawake were borrowed from the Mohawk counterparts of the Cayuga word.)

Cayuga words are also more "meaningful" because they are related to one another derivationally, or by virtue of sharing meaningful parts, in a way that is transparent to the speakers. Example 2 illustrates how some of the words introduced previously are meaningfully related. (The meaningfully related parts are capitalized in example 2.) A basic assumption is that when two or more words share a part that is spelled (nearly) the same, they share the same meaning. For example, comparing the words in 2.c, which share *-iyo:* 'to be beautiful, good,' and the words in 2.d, containing *-wen-*, the reader can observe that the name of the Gawę:ní:yo: school means something like 'beautiful word(s).' Similarly, both of the words in 2.f share a part, *-es*, which means 'long.'

2. Example of meaningful relationships between words
   a. *-NEHA:ʔ*
      OgwehǫwéhNEHA:ʔ the Indian WAY OR LANGUAGE
      Gayogoho:nǫhNÉHA:ʔ the WAY OR LANGUAGE of the people of the pipe

b. *-HO:NǪ-*

Gayogo̲HO:NǪHnéha:ˀ the way or language of the PEOPLE
OF THE pipe

Hadinǫhsesge̲HÓ:NǪˀ or *Gaenǫhsesge̲HÓ:NǪˀ* PEOPLE OF THE
Longhouse

c. *-IYO:*

SganyadáIYO: HANDSOME Lake

Gaihwĺ:YO: Code of Handsome Lake (literally: BEAUTIFUL
words or matters)

d. *-WĘN-*

OWĘ́:Naˀ WORD, voice, speech

GaWĘ:Nĺ:yo: (name of a school)

e. *-NǪHS-*

HodiNǪHSǫ́:nih People of the LongHOUSE

HadiNǪHSesge̲hó:nǫˀ or *GaeNǪHSesge̲hó:nǫˀ* People of the
LongHOUSE

gaNǪ́HSaˀ HOUSE

f. *-ES-*

Hadinǫhs̲ESge̲hó:nǫˀ or *Gaenǫhs̲ESge̲hó:nǫˀ* People of the
LONGhouse

ga̲hnyaˀs̲ESgó:wah giraffe (literally: it has a very LONG neck)

For the most part, the relationships between Cayuga words can be viewed
as more "meaningful" than the relationships between English words because the former are more transparent and accessible to the speaker. In
contrast, for example, English speakers must look up words like *receive*,
deceive, and *conceive* in order to discover that they all share a part, *-ceive*,
which comes from the Latin *capio* 'to take'; the derivational relationships
are often not immediately obvious or accessible to English speakers.

Returning to example 1, the lexical level of translation (1.c) makes the
morpheme-by-morpheme translations somewhat more accessible to the
English speaker: 'is how far' is easier to understand than 'how-it-far-
perfective.' However, the lexical level of translation also unavoidably obscures some of the meaning conveyed in Cayuga. For example, the first
group of words in 3.a is translated as 'now' in 3.b; however, the individual words literally mean something like *ó:nęh* 'now' *giˀ* 'really' *gyę́:ˀ* 'just'
nę́:gyęh 'this one.' Meanwhile, although the phrase in 3.a is characteristic

of how an eloquent Cayuga speaker would say things, translating each individual word would not have the same effect in English writing: 'now really just this one' does not sound eloquent in English.

3. Translation of particle groups (Foster 1974:353) (example numbering and orthography have been modified)
   a. *o:nę́h, gi gyę́:ˀ, nę:gyę́h,*   *ˀǫgwaya̱ˀdayeí:ˀ*
   b. Now   we are gathered

Foster also feels that the level of free translation (1.c; defined as a translation into idiomatic English) has inadequacies:

> The free translation has proved to have special problems of its own, and I am far from happy with it. In a sense, the entire study has as its purpose the explication of the Cayuga texts. But there are many fine points of meaning that are only very inadequately rendered in English, and one approaches the whole task with some trepidation as a non-native speaker of the language. Moreover, there is the question of style. The translation should attempt to capture something of the character of oral performance beyond the literal meaning of the words. This is no easy matter, but an attempt has been made to reflect the qualities of formal oratory, particularly repetition and parallelism—those features that most define the rhythmical periodicity of the speeches. (Foster 1974:255–56)

In common with both Dell Hymes and Dennis Tedlock (see Swann 1992), Foster chooses to represent the translated text in line format or measured verse (rather than in paragraph form, for instance). (The properties of the line are discussed below.) Foster otherwise adopts Hymes's approach, describing the dynamics of the performance in the monograph, but without reflecting them explicitly in the text; that is, in contrast with the Tedlock approach, the translation is not meant to be "performable."

Like Hymes, Foster determines line breaks according to linguistic criteria, including formal markers and intonational markers (Foster 1974:188–97). Formal markers include words (technically, syntactic particles) like *negwato(h)* or *né:gwato(h)* 'and, also, moreover' and *da(h)* or *dá:(h)* 'and'; the latter word is often prefixed by a meaningless syllable *hę:*, which does not occur in conversational speech; an example is shown in 1.a. (The parentheses around the h's in the above examples signify that the "h" sound is sometimes deleted in speech.)

Intonational markers include pause, pitch (for example, musically high-toned or low-toned vowels), and stress (a stressed vowel is louder, and can be longer than an unstressed vowel). Foster notes that the intonational features used in the Thanksgiving Address are unique to the address and that different intonation and discourse features characterize, for example, the preaching style used in the Code of Handsome Lake (Foster 1974:197 n. 8). The overall characteristic of the intonation used in the Thanksgiving Address is of an almost "monotonous regularity" of features imposed on the lines: there is less intonational variation than in conversational speech, and the main distinction in the Thanksgiving Address is a two-way contrast between final and non-final tone units (or intonational groups). Non-final tone units are characterized by a pitch rise and stress on the final vowel of the line: for example, a word such as *?ǫgwaya?da-yeí:?* in 3.a displays non-final intonation. (The acute accent in this case signals the highest-pitched and loudest vowel in this tone group.) In final tone units, there is a pitch rise and stress on a non-final vowel (typically, the second- or third-to-last vowel) and a pitch fall and stress on the final vowel in the unit: for example, a word such as *nigahá:wí?* in 1.a displays final intonation: the second-last vowel is high-pitched and loud; the last vowel is low-pitched and loud. (In this case, the two acute accents signify special pitches, one higher and one lower than the average pitch of one's voice.)

Although Foster had included a two-level translation and a 283-page explanation of the Thanksgiving Address, he still felt that many subtleties had not been conveyed in the monograph. For example, much of his monograph is about major differences between written texts and oral speeches. Foster shares Hymes's conviction that to convey the genuine depth of Native American verbal art, one should describe three dimensions: the language and sociolinguistic context (the medium for the message), the text or performance itself (the message), and the performer. Hymes, in turn, emphasizes that the depth or artistry of the performance only shows through when the performer is given his or her due (Hymes 1981:9–10).

Foster dedicates much of his monograph to describing the life histories and individual stylistic differences of the performers whose recordings formed the basis for his work. He also describes speech-making as a creative process of "oral composition" (described in the next paragraph).

Similarly, Cayuga speakers view ritualists as being endowed with a special gift of eloquence from the Creator. "Speakers are proud of their ability to perform without the aid of a written text as the 'church people' do" (Foster 1974:33).

Through examining the variation and commonalities in how speeches are produced by individual ritualists, Foster discovers that the speeches have an underlying well-defined logic and order. (Speakers, of course, already know this.) For example, all ritualists first invoke thanks for the spirit forces on the earth, in the sky, and beyond the sky (the same division described in section 3.4). As a result, Longhouse followers can view both a five-minute version and a half-hour version of the Thanksgiving Address as being "the same" (Foster 1974:3–4, 43–89).

A main goal of Foster's (1974) monograph was to record several performances of the Thanksgiving Address and provide a translation. In doing so, Foster took great pains to sensitize the reader to the distinction between fluid, living, oral composition and the more "frozen" written form that he was producing. This point is significant, because turning an oral tradition into a written one represents a "sea change," with many implications and consequences to the community. This topic is discussed next.

6. Turning the Oral Tradition into a Written One

At Six Nations, translation is typically one step in the process of writing down the oral tradition. Creating a written form, in turn, has the potential to turn the oral tradition into an object or cultural artifact—a significant change: for example, while the oral tradition is lived as part of daily life, a written tradition is more removed or objectified.

However, speakers recognize that changing the oral tradition into a written one does not necessarily result in the death of the oral tradition: as one speaker put it, "The oral tradition dies out because people don't learn it, not because it is written down."

Potential advantages and disadvantages of writing down the oral tradition are described in the following sections. I equate writing with translation, since the end result (a written product) is similar.

6.1. Advantages of Turning the Oral Tradition into a Written One

Turning the oral tradition into a written one has practical advantages. For example, adult learners can gain access to a more permanent form of language for learning and memorization purposes. Some speakers consider written translation to be an essential bootstrapping tool for learning the language. For example, one learner described translation as useful for interpreting novel utterances, or words that one has not previously heard. (See the discussion of example 2 for an illustration of how this approach can be used.) Another speaker pointed out that translation would be the only way to make the language accessible if all the fluent speakers were to pass away.

In addition, outsiders can learn to value the culture and ideals represented in the writing. To paraphrase Marcia Haag (personal communication), "ironically enough" the translation takes on a life of its own, becoming part of the literature of the hegemonic language. The translation becomes different in nature from the oral tradition; it is a "work" that exists alongside other world literatures as an object of study.

Not only outsiders but also community members can learn to value their culture and ideals through a translation. For example, Amos Key Jr. related his experience of using translation to motivate young men to learn speeches for the Midwinter Ceremony, a seven-day event that takes place in January, and the most important Longhouse event of the year. Key and his brother played Cayuga recordings of speeches and stopped periodically to provide a verbal English summary of the content of the speeches. The young men grew very appreciative of the message and requested more information sessions. As this example shows, the speakers were able to communicate the values of the message to community members through a translation. (But see section 4 for discussion of why values, etc., cannot be divorced from the language.)

Translating and writing down the oral tradition can aid in language preservation in other interesting and unexpected ways. For example, the monograph *Concerning the League* "recounts the story of the founding of the League of the Iroquois . . . and it describes the laws and rituals connected with its operation and continuance" (Gibson 1992:xi). The original version was dictated in Onondaga by Chief John A. Gibson to the anthropologist Alexander A. Goldenweiser in 1912 (Gibson 1992:xi). Because the original transcription was difficult to read and understand, linguist Hanni Woodbury re-elicited the text, using "a process of reconstituting an imperfectly transcribed text by retranscribing each word of the text as it is repronounced from the imperfectly transcribed manuscript by a native speaker" (Gibson 1992:xiii n. 6) The original Onondaga transcript was repronounced by the late Reginald Henry.

Because the original transcript still existed, it was possible to reconstitute this valuable resource provided by Gibson and Goldenweiser. Interestingly, while there are many English versions (as well as a sizable anthropological industry) based on translations of this body of knowledge, *Concerning the League* is the only complete version published in an Iroquoian language. This version is *by* the Iroquois, rather than being *about* them.

6.2. Disadvantages of Turning the Oral Tradition into a Written One

Translating the oral tradition into a written one has potential disadvantages. For example, learners (and outsiders) can gain a false or surface impression of the nature of speeches (see section 5.2 for further examples): to use a categorization like Hymes's, they might pay attention to the translation without knowing the depth of meaning in the original language; they might think of the text as fixed, because it is written down; they might ignore the social and cultural concerns which gave rise to the performance; and they might fail to appreciate the artistry of the performer. Such concerns arise when an oral tradition becomes accessible in print, because it is possible to pick and choose what one reads. In response to such concerns, speakers object to perceived reinterpretations of their values and lifeways by "new agers" or people who promote versions of a pan–Native American spiritualism that does not do justice to the original sources.

In contrast, when the oral tradition is not written down, there are many safeguards to ensure the full appreciation of its depth. For example, one must at least be accepted into a community, live there for an extended period, and learn the language in order to gain any real appreciation.

Returning to potential disadvantages, linguists use written texts as objects of study, describing the language in a way that speakers may find unsettling, inaccurate, or somehow missing the essence of the language. For example, many linguists focus on the formal structure of a text more than on the meaning: a phonologist (a linguist who studies sound patterns) might describe the rules of pitch placement or measure the length of pauses; meanwhile, speakers might find such descriptions to be self-evident, beside the point, or somehow jarring. Similarly, speakers have often commented that terminology (or jargon) like "the perfective" (see 1.b) seems deliberately obscure and unhelpful for language learners. (First-year university students taking linguistics courses express a similar sentiment.)

While there are both advantages and disadvantages to having written translations, perhaps the most potentially harmful issue is the perceived lack of control caused by writing and translating First Nations oral traditions. This topic is discussed in the following section.

7. Issues of Access and Control Raised by Writing and Translating

At Six Nations there is no central authority responsible for deciding who has access to recordings, texts, and translations. The lack of a central authority is partly due to divisions like the one described in section 3.3 between traditionalists who support the Confederate Council, and those who support the Elected Band Council. In addition, the need for access restrictions was not as urgent in the past: the current loss of speakers makes language and knowledge a valuable commodity indeed.

Instead of a central authority, access and control typically grow out of individual relationships. For example, Amos Key Jr. made agreements with the people he recorded about what would happen to their recordings. Access, in this case, was controlled by someone who in turn was constrained by kinship, friendship, and community ties. Key also has a certain level of trust with the community, because he belongs to it, because he is a recognized language activist, and because he has a track record of not violating anyone's trust.

In contrast, individual linguists gain access to Cayuga language and knowledge through developing (paid) working and friendship relationships with speakers. While their degree of access can depend on many factors, perhaps the most important are the degree of perceived trustworthiness of the linguist and the speaker's sense that no opportunity to preserve the language should be wasted. To give an example of the latter, the late Reginald Henry asked to work with linguist(s) in 1998, and ended up with the author of this chapter. He explained that he was "getting on in age" and had a lot of linguistic knowledge of the language to pass on.

Linguists are not typically constrained by kinship or community ties, but they do have obligations to their host institutions and granting agencies. Such obligations create pressure to produce scholarly publications containing "data" (typically, written linguistic material). This factor can lead to loss of control if, for example, material is published, potentially violating obligations to the community, because of overriding obligations to be academically productive. It is easy to gather stories about researchers who took data or took control of data in a perceived unethical way. Remarkably (and pragmatically), many members of the Six Nations community still practice an attitude of forgiveness and tolerance toward researchers.

While formal mechanisms for access and control are in their infancy at Six Nations, the community concern is immediate; for example, speakers making anonymous comments on a questionnaire said such things as "We need to keep what we have; it is ours; it's what keeps us who we are" and "I believe we have to be careful who gets hold of [language materials]; because this is what makes us Longhouse people." Such comments might help the reader understand that translation is powerful, and possibly dangerous; the stakes are high.

Counterbalancing the above viewpoint, however, Jahner reports on a situation where Lakota elders were persuaded to allow their knowledge to be written down because "the fear of being forgotten proved great enough to justify the risks of breaking taboos against telling privileged information to outsiders" (1994:153).

Although there is no central authority controlling access to written and translated work, language activists have nuanced opinions about access and control. For example, one speaker argued that, on one hand, having non-Cayuga people learn everyday language would make a positive political statement about the importance of the language; on the other hand, however, some kinds of language materials should be accessible only to a select group: for example, some restricted ceremonies (such as individual curing rites) are seen as dangerous to a person's health if not handled carefully.

In summary, to paraphrase Bill Jancewicz (personal communication), translation (and writing) may be ethically defensible for certain genres, with the consent of the speakers of the source language. Nevertheless, in my experience, obtaining the consent of the speakers can still be problematic, particularly in a large community like Six Nations where there are diverse opinions and no central authority over language matters.

8. Translation: A Simple Matter?

This chapter illustrates that translation is not just a simple matter of *DEye-WENÁDENYEʔS* 'changing words.' The urgency and potential for harm are greater when the translated language has few speakers or when the language and knowledge are recognized as valuable resources. In addition, solutions to the moral questions raised by translation are not straightforward. For example, deciding if a translation should be made public depends on the nature of the translated ideas. Finally, such decisions also depend on the participants, who are not always *sga^ʔnígǫha:t* 'of one mind'—a central concept in Iroquoian thinking).

The process of translation raises fears and generates controversies, giving rise to changes that can only be addressed by creating an ethical space (that is, a deliberate, honest dialogue) on a case-by-case basis. Paradoxically, while there isn't much time, time is needed in order for such negotiations to take place.

Notes

I would like to thank several Cayuga speakers who anonymously provided thoughtful comments on earlier drafts of this paper. I would especially like to thank Amos Key Jr., Language Director of the Woodland Cultural Centre, for his input. Wonderfully useful comments and suggestions were also made by several contributors to this volume, notably Marcia Haag, Bill Jancewicz, Robert Leavitt, and Robin Ridington. All errors and omissions are my own. Research for this chapter was funded by grant no. 856-2004-1082 from the Social Sciences and Humanities Research Council of Canada.

1. The vowels < ę > and < ǫ > sound like the nasalized vowels in French *frein* ("brake") and *on* ("someone"). The glottal stop < ʔ > is a consonant sound, which can also be heard in place of the [t] in the Cockney pronunciation of words like "bottle." For the most part, the remaining consonants sound similar to their English counterparts. The acute accent denotes higher pitch or tone: for example, the vowel < á > has higher pitch than the vowel < a >. The colon denotes a long vowel: for example, < a: > is twice as long as < a >. Finally, underlined vowels are pronounced as whispered when an < h > follows, and as creaky-voiced when a glottal stop <ʔ> follows.

References

Ermine, Willie. 2005. Ethical Space: Transforming Relations. http://www .traditions.gc.ca/docs/docs_disc_ermine_e.cfm (accessed July 28, 2008).

Fenton, William N. 1951. Iroquoian Studies at Mid-century. *American Philosophical Society, Proceedings* 95:296–310.

———. 1998. *The Great Law and the Longhouse: A Political History of the Iroquois Confederacy*. Norman: University of Oklahoma Press.

Foster, Michael. 1974. *From the Earth to Beyond the Sky: An Ethnographic Approach to Four Longhouse Iroquois Speech Events*. The Mercury Series, Ethnology Division, Paper 20. Ottawa: National Museum of Man.

———. 1994. The Iroquoian Thanksgiving Address [Cayuga]. In *Coming to Light:*

Contemporary Translations of the Native Literatures of North America, ed. Brian Swann, 476–88. New York: Random House.

Froman, Frances, Lottie Keye, Alfred Keye, and Carrie Dyck. 2003. *English-Cayuga/Cayuga-English Dictionary*. Toronto: University of Toronto Press.

Gibson, John A. 1992. *Concerning the League: The Iroquois League Tradition as Dictated in Onondaga by John Arthur Gibson. Memoir 9, Algonquian and Iroquoian Linguistics*. Ed. and trans. Hanni Woodbury. Winnipeg, Manitoba: Algonquian and Iroquoian Linguistics.

Herrick, James W. 1995. *Iroquois Medical Botany*. Ed. and with a foreword by Dean R. Snow. Syracuse NY: Syracuse University Press.

Hymes, Dell. 1981. *"In Vain I Tried to Tell You": Essays in Native American Ethnopoetics*. Philadelphia: University of Pennsylvania Press.

Jahner, Elaine A. 1994. Transitional Narratives and Cultural Continuity. In *American Indian Persistence and Resurgence*, ed. Karl Kroeber, 149–80. Durham: Duke University Press.

Martin, Marlene M. 2008. Society—IROQUOIS. http://lucy.ukc.ac.uk/ethnoatlas/ hmar/cult_dir/culture.7849 (accessed July 28, 2008).

Michelson, Karin. 1988. *A Comparative Study of Lake-Iroquoian Accent. Studies in Natural Language and Linguistic Theory*. Dordrecht: Kluwer Academic Publishers.

Michelson, Karin, and Mercy Doxtator. 2002. *Oneida-English/English-Oneida Dictionary*. Toronto: University of Toronto Press.

Mithun, Marianne. 1999. *The Languages of Native North America*. New York: Cambridge University Press.

Mithun, Marianne, and Reginald Henry. 1982. *Watewayę́stanih: A Cayuga Teaching Grammar*. Brantford, Ontario: Woodland Cultural Educational Centre.

Mithun, Marianne, and Hanni Woodbury, ed. 1980. Northern Iroquoian Texts. *International Journal of American Linguistics—Native American Text Series Monograph 4*. Chicago: University of Chicago Press.

Morgan, Lewis Henry. 1901a. *League of the Ho-de-no-sau-nee or Iroquois. Vol. 1. A new edition, with additional matter*. Ed. and annotated by Herbert M. Lloyd. New York: Dodd, Mead.

———. 1901b. *League of the Ho-de-no-sau-nee or Iroquois. Vol. 2. A new edition, with additional matter*. Ed. and annotated by Herbert M. Lloyd. New York: Dodd, Mead.

Murdock, George Peter, and Timothy J. O'Leary. 1975. *Ethnographic Bibliography of North America*. Vol. 4. 4th ed. New Haven: Human Relations Area Files Press.

Rudes, Blair A. 1999. *Tuscarora-English/English-Tuscarora Dictionary*. Toronto: University of Toronto Press.

Sapir, Edward. 1983. *Selected Writings of Edward Sapir in Language, Culture, and Personality*. Ed. David G. Mandelbaum. Berkeley: University of California Press.

Sasse, Hans-Juergen, and Alfred Keye. 1998. Far More Than One Thousand Verbs of Gayogohó:nǫ? (Cayuga): A Handbook of Cayuga Morphology. MS. Uni-versität zu Köln, Köln, Germany, and Woodland Cultural Centre, Brantford, Ontario.

Shimony, Annemarie Anrod. 1994. *Conservatism among the Iroquois at the Six Nations Reserve*. Syracuse NY: Syracuse University Press.

Six Nations Elected Council. 2007. Six Nations Elected Council Public Report 2005–06. Six Nations Council Communications Department, Six Nations, Ontario. http://www.sixnations.ca/2007PublicReport.htm (accessed July 28, 2008).

Speck, Frank Gouldsmith. 1945. *The Iroquois: A Study in Cultural Evolution*. Bloomfield Hills MI: Cranbrook Institute of Science.

Swann, Brian, ed. 1992. *On the Translation of Native American Literatures*. Washington DC: Smithsonian Institution Press.

Weinman, Paul L. 1969. *A Bibliography of the Iroquoian Literature, Partially Annotated. Bulletin number 411, New York State Museum and Science Service*. Albany: University of the State of New York.

Werker, J. F., and R. C. Tees. 1984. Cross-language Speech Development: Evidence for Perceptual Reorganization during the First Year of Life. *Infant Behavior and Development* 7:49–63.

Whorf, Benjamin Lee. 1956. *Language, Thought, and Reality: Selected Writings of Benjamin Lee Whorf*. Ed. John Carroll. Cambridge: MIT Press.

Woodbury, Hanni. 2003. *Onondaga-English/English-Onondaga Dictionary*. Toronto: University of Toronto Press.

2

Reading a Dictionary

How Passamaquoddy Language Translates
Concepts of Physical and Social Space

Robert M. Leavitt

When I sat down to proofread the thousands of entries in *A Passama-quoddy-Maliseet Dictionary*[1] (Francis and Leavitt 2008), I expected to endure a long, tedious chore, compensated only by seeing the broad scope of the words David A. Francis and I, working with dozens of Passamaquoddy and Maliseet contributors, had compiled. But an unexpected pleasure awaited. In the words themselves and the example sentences, the Passamaquoddy world of the past hundred years came welling up from the pages. I could sense what speakers mean when they say that the language is "a unique mindset, in which I feel completely at home."[2] At a deep level, a people's cultural history and sense of collective identity are embedded in their native tongue.

The thriving, energetic culture that the Passamaquoddy language reflects is changing now as the population of fluent speakers declines. Yet in reading a dictionary, speakers' values and attitudes, sense of social and family relationships, spatial and aesthetic perceptions, and spirituality and humor take shape. How can this happen? The dictionary presents no coherent narrative, no story or history or explanation. Instead it contains a disjointed collection of one-off ideas arranged in alphabetical order.

The discussion that follows is about some of the ways in which Passamaquoddy culture is mediated by the language. The focus is on how the language itself, even in apparently isolated examples, *translates* the essence of the Passamaquoddy mind-set. The English glosses here are formulated to be literal rather than literary, in order that the content and configuration of the Passamaquoddy words may be appreciated. Readers will imagine their own, more idiomatic translations that capture the essence of the intended meanings.

A Sense of Culture

The sense of culture that comes from the dictionary would seem to have two sources: the topical content of the entry words and sentences, and the ways in which both words and sentences are constructed. Certainly the bits of oral tradition, the references to local places, and the details of community life in the dictionary present aspects of Passamaquoddy culture. But it is also speakers' elegant, eloquent formulations of words and ideas that convey a uniquely Passamaquoddy way of thinking about the world. Native speakers themselves, listening to recordings or reading transcriptions, have observed this correlation. It would be presumptuous to say that the correlation can be explained, but perhaps some light can be shed on its sources.

The Passamaquoddy mind-set is characterized in part by life experiences in the Maine–New Brunswick region that contribute the content of the words and example sentences in the dictionary. Economic pursuits include the trading, hunting, trapping, and fishing carried on since ancient times; guiding, basket making, and gardening, which developed during the colonial period; and the expanding professional, commercial, and industrial employment of today. Leisure-time activities such as storytelling and music, card playing, and baseball, respectively, also span these periods of Passamaquoddy history; spirituality and relationships with other societies have evolved continuously since the earliest times. Other themes that recur in the dictionary are marriage and family, church, and military experience. Many sentences recall ingenious acts of one-upmanship and effective strategies of social control. Until quite recently all of these activities and traditions flourished; many continue evolving among nonspeakers.

The dictionary entries[3] for *tolehp* and *wiwonikuwok* exemplify some of the attitudes with which Passamaquoddy speakers view their experiences, in this case card playing.

tolehp [d'-LAP]. *noun animate.* playing card. *Itom, naka nipayiw, eci tama tolamotuhtihtit tolehp, itom nit-oc kessahat. On-oc mecimiw nokalokittiyalan tolehp nipayiw, naka nokalokittiyatomon-na.* He said that at night, wherever they were playing cards, he said he'd go in there. And so he used to be scared to death of cards at night, he was scared like hell of [doing] it, too. (The word *tolehp* is borrowed from the French *trèfle* 'club [card suit].')

wiwonikuwok [wee-w'-NEE-goo-w'g]. *verb ai.* they grow around (something). *Mam-ote nit wiwonikuwok-otehc tuwihputik etolamotul-tihtit.* Finally they would take root there around the table playing cards (because they played for such a long time, or so frequently).

In the first of these entries we learn not only that card playing dates to the colonial period—the earliest European settlers and missionaries in the region were French—but also that the force of the Church's prohibition against card playing survived well into the twentieth century. The second word, *wiwonikuwok*, normally refers to trees, berries, and similar plants. The players' metaphorical fate evinces the kind of indirect reproach that typifies gentle teasing, still a favorite community strategy for teaching correct behavior.

The Passamaquoddy mind-set is further characterized by ways of structuring words and narratives that suggest a more participatory, interactive relationship with the speaker's surroundings than do their English equivalents. This is evident in language expressing concepts as fundamental as space, the environment, and social relationship.

A Sense of Space and Environment

Speakers of Passamaquoddy conceptualize physical space, at whatever scale, in reference to their personal point of view at the moment, that is, in relative terms, not using indicators such as fixed landmarks or latitude and longitude, whose values are independent of human presence. A spatial referent, for example, may be expressed as extending toward or away from the speaker (*ckuwawtihiw* 'on the road toward here') or indicate whether or not an object or event can be seen by the speaker (*sakhahte* 'it extends into view,' *akuwahte* 'it is situated out of sight,' *motewse* 's/he is heard walking but is not seen'). The following two entries show a locative noun and the verb from which it is derived.

elomaskutek [el-mah-SKOO-deg]. *noun locative (verb ii participle).* where a field extends away; away over the field. *Elomaskutek Kci-peskiyak tolikonul suwitokolasol.* Sweetgrass is growing where the field extends away at Marsh Pond.

olomaskute ['l-mah-SKOO-deh]. *verb ii.* there is a field extending away, there is a long field; a field extends farther (with the passage of time). *Ahaciw olomaskute tuciw kisihtasik awt.* The field has gotten bigger since the road was built.

In this way of thinking, space is active; perception of the directionality of movement, extension, and orientation gives the surrounding space its structure. In English, a "field" is usually thought of as a delimited area of open land located in a particular place: it is a thing, a noun. In Passamaquoddy the notion of field is conveyed by a verb root (*-askute-*). The verb tells how land "fields," how an open area lies and extends; "field" is experienced as a dynamic phenomenon rather than as a static object. Literal translations of *elomaskutek* 'where it fields away' and *weckuwaskutek* 'where it fields toward here' suggest the distinctiveness of this way of perceiving. The use of *elomaskutek* 'away over the field' in the sentence above identifies the speaker's vantage point; while the sentence using *olomaskute* shows a parallel, temporal meaning: 'a field extends with time.' Because all aspects of the physical environment are so constructed, it is unnatural to speak of one's surroundings as separate from the human being experiencing them; people are integral to the world in which they live. This idea also comes through in the following entry.

piskalokahte [bee-skahl-GAH-teh]. *verb ii.* it is a dark hole, it is dark interior space. *Eci-piskalokahtek emehkew.* It's very dark in the cellar.

Here the literal translation of the sentence is 'it is very dark and hollow down below.' The noun 'cellar,' *lahkap* (from French, *la cave*), is not used by the fluent speaker. In fact, when she was recorded, this speaker was responding to a literal translation from English using the verb 'be dark (night or unlit space)' and a locative form of *lahkap: eci-piskiyak lahkapok.* 'I wouldn't say it that way,' she countered. As a fluent speaker, she focuses on space as dynamic, like a field, instead of seeing a cellar as a thing. The particle *emehkew* 'below' locates the space relative to the speaker, who is seated at the kitchen table.

Other verbs further illustrate the Passamaquoddy speaker's personal sense of space. *Cicokawse* 's/he walks toward land' and *milawuhse* 's/he walks out into the water' refer to the sun and describe the changing location of sunrise as the days lengthen and shorten, respectively. The initial roots of these verbs (*cicoka-* 'ashore' and *milaw-* 'offshore') are two of a large number of spatial determiners used by speakers to indicate their immediate relationship with the environment, in this case as they stand on the south-facing seacoast of Maine or New Brunswick. Many similar initial roots, including those presented in the preceding paragraphs, have meanings that depend upon the speaker's or subject's location. Other examples are *wesuwe-* 'going back,' *ap-* 'back from having gone elsewhere,' and *nute-* (*nutiy-*) 'going or coming out.' Such initial roots, in combination with the vast number of medial and final roots, allow accomplished native speakers to convey an extraordinary range of distinctions.

In addition, to specify the distance at which an object, being, or place is located, Passamaquoddy has three locative particles. These are *yut* 'here, near me the speaker'; *nit* 'there, near you the listener'; and *yet* 'yonder, away from you and me but within sight.' The meaning of each word varies within a range according to the context. *Nit* also refers to a place whose exact location is unimportant, or which cannot be seen by either the speaker or the listener, or which is imaginary or is spoken of in the past or future, as in a story or plan.

yut [yood]. *particle.* here. *Yut-te wikuhpon kikuwoss, ksokayawtihiw.* Your mother used to live here, right across the road.

nit [need]. *particle.* there (near person spoken to, or location unspecified). *Nit ktopin.* Sit there. *Mecimi-te nit ntoliyan natonuhmon tekcokek.* I always went there to buy ice cream.

yet [yed]. *particle.* over there (away from speaker and person spoken to), yonder. *Ipa, yet lap!* Hey, look over there!

Narratives preserve the subtleties of the relative terms by which space is constructed. In a story from oral tradition that he wrote down in Passamaquoddy, Lewis Mitchell, telling how Marten discovers that Moose has fresh bear-meat, sketches the space in which the characters move about.[4] Moose's grandmother is returning Marten's cooking pot, hoping he will not notice that she and Moose have used it to cook the bear-meat. But Marten has ways of knowing everything (table 2-1).

Mitchell's skillful use of initial roots expressing direction, location, and orientation (shown in italics in table 2-1) creates a carefully balanced picture. These roots, which appear in numerous dictionary entries, establish for the listener a sense of space that is objective yet at the same time

Table 2-1. Passamaquoddy and literal English translation of "Marten and Moose"

Passamaquoddy	Literal translation
Tehpu li-*pis*omelku witapihil wikok; tehpu eli-*tuw*apit nomihtun elaqek muwinewey.	He just steps thus *into* his friend's house; just looking *in* thus, he [Marten] sees the bear-meat piled up.
Nit *peci*yamiht Mus uhkomossol, 'ta*paci*phal skuwossuwol.	Then Moose's grandmother comes *to* him, bringing *back* his pot.
Nit-te eli-*ksa*hat wikuwamok 'ci-*nuti*yaqhessu welaqotek wiyuhs.	As soon as she goes *into* the house, the smell of well-cooked meat wells up *from out of* it [the pot].
Eli-*ksiy*apit, psonte welaqotek wiyuhs.	When she looks *in*, it is filled with well-cooked meat.

entirely personal and relative—a sense of space identified with intimate spoken connections between people and the physical world around them. For example, the various forms of 'in' and 'into' indicated by *pis-* 'in through a boundary, penetrating,' *tuw-* 'into and through,' and *kse-* (*ksiy-*, *ksa-*) 'going or coming in, entering' carry distinctions critical to the effective description of action and intention in their spatial contexts. Mitchell places the emphasis on Marten's crossing Moose's threshold surreptitiously by choosing *pisomelku* 'steps in,' using *pis-* rather than *kse-*, which would refer neutrally to going in; for Marten is penetrating his cousin's secrecy (compare *eli-ksahat wikuwamok*, in the third sentence). When Grandmother looks into the pot, she enters it with her gaze (*ksiyapit*)—a 180-degree complement to the aroma coming forth from it (*nutiyaqhessu*)—and she is deeply embarrassed to have been caught in a lie.

A Sense of Social Connection

Like physical space, personal space and power are shared by all people, whatever their particular roles. Personal identity is also dynamic, determined by and depending upon shifting relations both with the natural world, as indicated in the preceding paragraphs, and with family and community. The participatory mind-set is especially evident in Passamaquoddy oral tradition, which tells in large part how the people came to be who they are today, and how they came to have their present relationship with the natural world.

wocawson [w'-JOW-s'n]. *verb ii.* the wind blows, it is windy. *Neqt neke ehtahsi-kiskahkil wocawson, wisololamson.* Once long ago the wind blew every day, it was very windy. *'Toliwiyawal Wocawson, nuci-putuwet.* They call him Wind, the one who blows. *Kil nit kisihtuwon mecokiskahk, wecawsok, eliwehsek.* You are the one who has made the bad weather, the wind, the gusts. (Lewis Mitchell)[5]

Creation stories, for example, tell how Koluskap,[6] the "culture hero" of the Wabanaki peoples, made the world habitable for human beings and taught them their place in it. In one of these stories, cited in the entry above, Koluskap must tame the wind, in the person of Wocawson, a giant white bird, who is making life difficult for the people with an unremitting gale. Koluskap journeys to the north to see Wocawson, addresses him as Grandfather, and entreats him to flap his wings less violently. But Wocawson refuses, and Koluskap must exert his power. He confines the bird so that he cannot move his wings at all. When this proves equally disastrous—no wind is as bad for the natural world as is too much—Koluskap goes back and frees one of the bird's wings, restoring balance. The wind's name, Wocawson, is not a noun, but a verb meaning 'it is windy.' Likewise, the other elements—such as rain, snow, sunshine, cold, heat—are also expressed as verbs, continuing actions or processes rather than independent things or forces, allowing speakers the possibility of interacting with them and affecting them, just as Koluskap did.

When Passamaquoddy speakers say, as they often do, that the language makes them feel "connected with the environment," or "closer to the land," they are not romanticizing or idealizing but instead recognizing relationships like those between Koluskap and Wocawson, Marten and Grandmother, or simply the spatial connection between a speaker and the field or cellar she is contemplating.

Translating a Passamaquoddy narrative literally into English is a straightforward task, but without appreciation for the mind-set of the original, the narrative's intent may not make the crossing from one language to the other. This is why Passamaquoddy stories retold in English often sound like fables or fairy tales, or wistful explanations of natural phenomena: how the turtle got his shell, why the loon has a lonesome call. The key to fuller understanding lies in the words and narrative structures of the originals as much as it does in the content and plot of the stories themselves.

Table 2-2. Passamaquoddy and literal English translation of "The Stars' Wives"

Passamaquoddy	Literal translation
Pesq 'tiyan kotokil: "Tokec-op-olu yukt possesomuk skitapewihtitsopon, tan wot-op-olu kil nisuwiyeq? Nil tehpu-op pawatom *mehqahtuwehpusossit*."	One says to the other, "If these stars were men, which one would be your husband? I would want to have only *the little red twinkling one*."
"Nil-op-olu tehpu nisuwinen-op *wisawahtuwet*, ipocol nil nmuhsacin kci-possesom."	"The only one I'd marry would be *the shining yellow one*, because I like a big star."
Tehpu nikt 'toli-pahpituwok. Nit wespasahkiwik tuhkiyahtit li-mskasuwok apc kiskatomukk . . .	They are just joking with each other. Then in the morning when they wake up they find themselves married again . . .
Wot pawatokoss *seskahtuwelicil*, eli-apskapit, wot tahk nisuwihticil, wolapewiw skitap; 'tiyukun: "Menakac, kwekihtuwin-oc nmihqonuwuhusut."	The one who wanted *the fiercely shining one*, when she opens her eyes, here is her husband, a handsome man. He says to her, "Quiet, you will ruin my war paint."
Not-olu kotok itokoss, "Nulinuwa *mehqahtuwessit*," tuhkiyat, macessit, nutuwal wenil metiyewestulicil: "Menakac, ksukahtehkomuwin nsisqi-npisun." Nihtol nit *apsahtuwelicil* possesomul, nihtol pawatokosoponil, komac puskolinaqsu ktaqhomuhsis; apsalokiqahsu naka *macikcehpute* 'siskul.	The other one, who had said, "I like *the flickering red one*," when she wakes up, when she begins to move, she hears someone speaking: "Quiet, you will knock over my eye medicine." It's that *little shining* star, that one she wanted, a very feeble-looking little old man; he has tiny little eyes and they *wobble shiftily*.
Nit-te eli-pawatomuhtits nit-te-na eli-peciyamkuhtit.	Exactly the ones they wanted to have are also the ones who have come to them.

In another passage from Passamaquoddy oral tradition,[7] Lewis Mitchell describes two star-husbands, using apt verb roots to specify how they shine and twinkle. Mitchell shapes his words both linguistically and psychologically to achieve an effect at once startling, sympathetic, ironic, and droll. When the star-husbands first appear, they are only astronomical: a red dwarf and a yellow giant. Two disillusioned sisters, fleeing from their unhappy marriage to Marten, are star-gazing in a clearing, dreaming of better prospects (table 2-2).

Seeing the stars as persons, one woman chooses *mehqahtuwehpusos-*

sit 'the little red twinkling one,' while the other prefers *wisawahtuwet* 'the yellow shining one,' who, unlike his brother, is neither shaky (*-hpus-*) nor diminutive (*-oss-*). Indeed, when this bright prodigy appears on earth he is bigger than life: *seskahtuwet* 'the fiercely shining one.' The other star, true to character, is only *apsahtuwet* 'small and shining' and *mehqahtuwessit* 'flickering red' (*-ess-* 'move suddenly'). His tiny, shifty eyes reflect the shakiness of his star. As the husbands' warnings and the last sentence of the passage imply, the marriages are ill-starred.

pqahtuwehpusu [pkwaht-wa-POO-zoo]. *verb ai.* (star) s/he is red and twinkles. *Nil tehpu-op pawatom mehqahtuwehpusossit.* I would want to have only the little red twinkling one. (LM)

pqahtuwessu [pkwaht-WES-soo]. *verb ai & ii.* (star, light) s/he, it flashes or glitters red. *Nulinuwa mehqahtuwessit possesom.* I like the flickering red star. (LM)

In applying his descriptors equally to stars and men, the storyteller does not distinguish socially between the two: both have personality traits and both are part of the sisters'—and listeners'—community. The language of Passamaquoddy oral tradition takes for granted personal interactions between the women and the stars, as it does those between Koluskap and Wocawson. The irony of the women's marriages serves as a warning to be careful what you wish for, or perhaps as a reminder to know a prospective partner well.

Social obligations are exemplified in a contemporary speaker's account of her childhood responsibilities in the community. As youngsters, she and her friends did chores for the elders in exchange for sweets or a few coins or, most desirably, just the opportunity to hear the elders converse with one another and tell stories. Of course, being children, they didn't always do the best job they could (table 2-3).[8]

The stern but indirect way in which her mother sends her back to redo the floors comes through in the storyteller's humorous tone, conveyed in part by her choice of *'kascokihpulal,* derived from *'kahsihpulal.*

'kahsihpulal [kah-see-POO-lahl]. *verb ta.* s/he wipes h/ dry briskly, dries h/ off briskly. *Pol Mali 'totoli-kahsihpulal 'temisol weci skat yalaptahsihq lamikuwam.* Mary had to wipe her dog off so he wouldn't track in the house.

Table 2-3. Passamaquoddy and literal English translation of "Children's Story"

Passamaquoddy	Literal translation
Ntiyalapekin nit pemsokhasik; eci-wisahki cel ma nkascokihpulaw not *soap*.	I crawled around there on the floor; I was in a hurry, and I didn't wipe up that soap well enough.
Weci-maceliqahay kisapenkuwit. On nmosimkun. Iya.	Then I left there so darn mad because of what she paid me. And she told on me. Yes.
Itom nikuwoss—itom, "Yali-kolcoqetul 'qatol, iya, Rose wikuwak."	My mother said—she said, "Rose's feet are getting sticky in her house."

'**kascokihpulal** [kahs-ch'-ghee-POO-lahl]. *verb ta.* s/he rubs h/ off (soft substance); s/he wipes h/ off quickly and inadequately. *Kehsikascokihpulat nicanol, cestehp sakhapit wikuwak.* She had wiped her child's face hurriedly so many times that he looked as if he were "peeking out of his house" (refers to clean face surrounded by dirty neck and ears).

In saying *ma nkascokihpulaw* 'I didn't wipe it up adequately,' which contains the root *-cok-* 'soft, formless, disorganized,' the storyteller faults herself humorously for her slapdash approach to the task. In *weci-maceliqahay* 'the reason I went away so darn mad' she inserts the root *-liqe-*, a mild expletive, into 'why I left' (*weci-macahay*). Finally, the mother's reprimand focuses on Rose's feet rather than the floor, highlighting cultural expectations of responsibility to people, as opposed to property or material goods.

The connectedness of people is reflected not just in word selection but also in the grammar of human relationships. All kinship terms, for example, are "dependent" nouns, meaning that they occur only as grammatically possessed forms—*nikuwoss* 'my mother,' *muhsumsol* 'his or her grandfather.' In speakers' minds these and similar relationships (including 'friend,' 'sweetheart,' 'godchild') are only personal. To speak of them in the abstract requires an indirect expression, such as *wemihtaqsit* 'one who has a father,' the word used to translate 'the Son' in reciting the Sign of the Cross.

An intimate connection with the world is so important in Passamaquoddy-Maliseet thought that two grammatical features of the language, "absentative" and "dubitative" forms, are called into use when a speaker is *not* fully connected to his or her environment. The absentative indicates that the speaker is talking about a person or object that no longer exists or whose whereabouts are unknown, as in *muhsumsokol* 'his or her late grandfather' or *sukoliskol* 'candies' that have been eaten up or have mysteriously disappeared. Such forms show that the speaker is separated in time as well as space from his or her subject.

When speakers cannot use personal knowledge to explain an observation or occurrence, they may use a "dubitative" verb form. In *possaq-al kmoskeyiness* 'I guess you must have been sorry,' the dubitative ending *-ess* shows that the speaker is making a supposition; the particle *possaq-al* 'must be,' another indicator of doubt, introduces the inference. In the dubitative form *tan ktalhi-peciyaness?* 'how did you get here?' the initial root *alhi* indicates bewilderment about how something happened. The dubitative also expresses the surprise that results from lack of firsthand knowledge: *nit nit eliwisuwiks?* 'is *that* what it's called?'

Even when speakers use English, their connections with others remain personal. During a conference I once attended with a colleague, a speaker of Passamaquoddy, we spent an evening at a pub with some of the other participants, who began after a while to sing. Soon their songs turned bawdy, becoming more and more obscene as they went on. Finally my friend hissed through her teeth, "That's it! I've had enough of this kind of talk. We're leaving." When we were outside, I turned to her, amazed: "But you talk that way all the time!" "Yes," she said, "but that's about people I know."[9]

A Sense of Translation

My colleague's comment sums up the connectedness that the Passamaquoddy mind-set takes for granted. The social environment, like the physical, is constructed according to the speaker's immediate perception and the relative roles of the participants. Within the community, one *knows* everyone, and knows everyone's family and developmental history. Moreover, whatever one's age, one can participate in everyone else's family and development—walking into any house without knocking, disciplining other people's children, assuming others will stay for a meal, and sitting down freely at the table wherever one goes. When my colleague expressed her disgust at the anonymous obscene songs, she reaffirmed the intimate nature of her connections to others.

In the same way, the spatial environment is constructed according to the speaker's location and distance and orientation—where one is, how close or far away, and which way one is facing. Without using absolute, arbitrary, or artificial parameters, the speaker conceptualizes and describes space both objectively and unambiguously. The language *translates*—in its etymological sense of "carries across"—this sense of place, perspective, and movement.

In Passamaquoddy the very nature of the world relies upon speakers' perceptions. Scientific, spiritual, kinesthetic, and emotional knowledge all spring from participation. Perhaps it is the loss of this culture as translated or mediated by language that young people are mourning when they say "I don't speak my language." It is not difficult to imagine how profoundly the shift to English—even apart from other social, spiritual, political, and economic changes—has affected the Passamaquoddy world.

Appendix A. Nimaqsuwehs naka Mus: Marten and Moose (Lewis Mitchell)

Passamaquoddy

Wisoki-kehsikotok, 'kani eleyiks, sehtayiw monihkuk sopayiw sipuhsisok, wikihtit Nimaqsuwehs naka Mus. Cocepinuwok, naka uhkomossuwal, nihtol-ona nutoluhkehticil.

Wot Mus wawapihiw kotunkesku; wotolu Nimaqsuwehs maleyu, peciw-ote yukt ekihkatkik piyeskomonol nihkalutuwawal eli-wolitahasuwiqewilit kisuhsol. Nit olisapiye tan elewotasik kisamilkasik wiyuhs nit-tehc mecimiw Nimaqsuwehs etoliskuweyit.

Nit li-tpiye neqt pemkiskahk Mus nehpahan muwiniyil; nokkayacqimal neqt-ote elonahsit. Katama utomitahatomuwon 'tahsoman yuhuht skat ehsomokcihi katama-te-na skat welasuweltomulcihi.

'Tiyusin, naka-te-na 'tiyan uhkomossol: "Leyu-tehc kat-tehc 'tolinomihtuwon Nimaqsuwehs, kat-tehc-ona 'possehtuwon, katama-tehc-ona 'samilluwessiwon; musa wen lakonutoc eli-wolelomoqiyiq."

Literal translation

A great many years ago, according to the old tradition, behind an island, along the shore of a little stream, there dwelt Marten and Moose. They lived in separate houses, and their grandmother is the one who looked after them.

Clever Moose is a hunter but this Marten is a lazy-bones, so that even when they do plant corn they depend on the sun to smile upon it. And where someone is storing preserved meat, that's where Marten hangs around.

It happens one day that Moose kills a bear. He drags the whole thing home in one [toboggan] load. He doesn't worry himself about feeding those who don't feed him—and certainly not ingrates.

He says to himself—and indeed, he says it to his grandmother—"The truth is, Marten won't be seeing this, or smelling it; he won't even touch his tongue to it. Nobody tell him what good luck we've had."

Passamaquoddy

"Aha," li-asitewtom kosqehsuhs. "Nqoss, wisoki nuli-nsotomon. Kwapahkuhsisomon wekessu. Nwihqehlahc wapahkuhsisomol, kisi-tuwahqosiyiq, nil-otehc nkospahla naka nkahsahqahan wecihc skat wewinaqotunuhk kcq kisi-tuwaqotek; nit-tehc-ona eli-wesuwephuk."

Yut tokec kisi-leyu. Kenuk-olu not maleyit cilomotok mawiyamkil tahalu ketunolat weyossis. Uli-kcicihtun apsi-kinuwehlosuwakon tan ehtek kehceyawik pemiptasik. Naka wen mahqalsit wapahkuhsisol wen 'kotuwakomitehtun micuwakon.

Mecimi-te-na ptewolonuwiw. Tehpu li-pisomelku witapihil wikok; tehpu eli-tuwapit nomihtun elaqek muwinewey. Nit peciyamiht Mus uhkomossol, 'tapaciphal skuwossuwol.

Nit-te eli-ksahat wikuwamok 'ci-nutiyaqhessu welaqotek wiyuhs. Eli-ksiyapit, psonte welaqotek wiyuhs. Nimaqsuwehs nuhki-wolasuweltom. Elihponolut 'toqesin, 'somokiphuwan wikuwamok.

Literal translation

"Oh yes." So the old woman answers. "My son, I take your meaning quite clearly. Our cooking-pot is broken. I'll get his pot for us to cook in; I'll wash it myself and wipe it dry so it will be impossible to tell anything's been cooked in it. And then I'll take it back."

It now happened this way. But that lazy Marten senses a feast as if he were hunting for prey. He knows quite well from a tiny sign where the big load of meat is that has been brought in. And if one borrows a cooking-pot, one is going to be boiling food.

He is always the person with extraordinary powers. He just steps thus into his friend's house; just looking in thus, Marten sees the bear-meat piled up. Then Moose's grandmother comes to him, bringing back his pot.

As soon as she goes into the house, the smell of well-cooked bear-meat wells up from out of it. When she looks in, it is filled with well-cooked meat. Marten thanks her politely. Caught at her trick, she is embarrassed, and she runs from the house with her back arched [i.e., her feet leaving her behind].

Appendix B. Koluskap naka Wocawson: Koluskap and It-Is-Windy (Lewis Mitchell)

Passamaquoddy

Skicinuwok ulamsotomoniyal kci-sipsol. 'Toliwiyawal Wocawson, nuci-putuwet. Tolawsu pihcetu lahtoqehsonuk; nit epit tehsahqiw kci-ponapskuk, mehtaluktek. Tan etuci macilqenuwit, nit-tehc petson.

Literal translation

The Indians believe in a great bird. They call him Wocawson, the one who blows. He lives far away in the north; there he sits on top of a big rock where the clouds end. Whenever he moves his wings, the wind comes up.

continued

Passamaquoddy

Neket Koluskap mec yali-wiciyemat skitapiyi, puskiw-ona nekom mace-suku 'tulok, sipsuhke.

Neqt neke ehtahsikiskahkil wocawson; wisokolamson. Ahaciw pomolamson, kospon-ote neke peciwehse naka petamoqessu. Kotama Koluskap kisi-yali-sukiw. 'Titomon, "Wocawson, wot kci-sips etolawsit lahtoqehsonuk, not nit elluhket."

'Qiluwahan. Komac pihcetu oliye, on yaka moskuwan. 'Totoli-mskuwal epilit kci-ponapskuk, wapeyu kci-sips.

'Tiyan, "Muhsumi, kotama kotomakitahamawiyik qenossok? Kil nit kisihtuwon mecokiskahk, wecawsok, eliwehsek. Kusami-macehlak kunoskiyik."

Neketok kci-sips oli-ikotohom. "Yut ntihinehpon wisoki-nihkaniw. Pihce kiskul, mesq wen etolewestuhk, nil-ote amsqahs nutaqsiyanpon. Nil-ote-na amsqahs macehlukpon nunoskiyik. Mecimi-tehc-ona nmacehlak tan eli-wolitahatom."

Nit etuci Koluskap wonakessit. Etutsonit, petkil-ote aluhkihkuk. 'Toli-wihqehlal yuhtol kci-sipsol tahalu-tehp motehehsim. 'Kolonomuwan toqiw wonoski, naka 'poneqahkan eli-psikapskiyak nisonul kci-ponapskul. Nit-te na etoli-nokolat.

Nit neke 'cimaciw, skicinuwok yaliyawolotuwok, 'kekiw-otehc. Mecimi-woluwipon, kakehsukoniw, kakehs pemoluhkemkil naka kisuhsok, kospon-ote neke 'samaqan tukcokiyak. Etuci-paqtek, Koluskap kotama 'kisi-'tahapiyatomuwon 'tul.

Literal translation

At that time when Koluskap still went around among men, he too would often paddle out in his canoe, hunting birds.

Once at that time, the wind blew every day; it blew strongly. More and more the wind blew, until at last it gusted and a storm came up. Koluskap could not travel around by canoe. He said, "Wocawson, this big bird who lives in the north, he is the one doing this."

He searches for him. He goes very far before he finds him. He finds him sitting on a big rock, a huge white bird.

He says to him, "Grandfather, do you not have pity for your grandchildren? You are the one who has made the bad weather, the wind, the gusts. You move your wings too much."

In spite of this, the big bird goes on yawning. "I was here at the very beginning. In far-off days, before anyone spoke, I was the first to be heard. I was the first to move my wings. And I will always continue to move them just as I please!"

At that point, Koluskap gets up. He is so powerful, he grows to the height of the clouds. He picks up this huge bird as if he were a duck. He holds both of his wings and throws him down into a crack between two rocks. There he leaves him.

From that time on, the people traveled around all day long. It was always calm—for many days, many weeks and months—until at last the water became foamy. It was so thick that Koluskap could not paddle his canoe.

Passamaquoddy

On nit-te mihqitahaman kci-sipsol, on macahan naci-nomiyan apc. Eli-te nokolatpon, nit-te apc eli-mskuwat, Wocawson ipocol askomawasu. 'Teweponan, 'punan apc ponapskuk, naka 'tapqehtuwan peskuwol wonoskiyil. Neke 'cimaciw kotama tutolamsonihkew tahalu pihce.

Literal translation

And then he remembered the great bird, and he set out to go see him again. He found him just as he had left him, for Wocawson lives forever. He lifted him up, put him on the rock again, and opened one of his wings. From that time on, it was not quite as windy as it had been long ago.

Appendix C. Possesomuk Nisuwihticihi: The Stars' Wives (Lewis Mitchell)

Passamaquoddy

Spikuhse sakhuhset nipawset; kiwacinaqot. Nimaqsuwehs nisuwiyek lossinuk qihiw mosihkuk weci-panapotasik kcihkuk; ahlossinuhtit, 'tosakiyaniya possesomu naka 'taskuwasiniya, tahalu-tehp wasisok eluhkehtit.

Pesq 'tiyan kotokil: "Tokec-op-olu yukt possesomuk skitapewihtitsopon, tan wot-op-olu kil nisuwiyeq? Nil tehpu-op mehqahtuwehpusossit."

"Nil-op-olu tehpu nisuwinen-op wisawahtuwet, ipocol nil nmuhsacin kci-possesom."

Tehpu nikt 'toli-pahpituwok. Nit wespasahkiwik tuhkiyahtit li-mskasuwok apc kiskatomukk tahalu olonuwihtasik, tehpu kolusuwakon.

Wot pawatokoss seskahtuwelicil, eli-apskapit, wot tahk nisuwihticil, wolapewiw skitap; 'tiyukun: "Menakac, kwekihtuwin-oc nmihqonuwuhusut."

Literal translation

The moon moves higher when it comes out; the place appears so lonely. Marten's wives lie down near some oaks, where there is an opening in the woods; they keep on lying there, watching the stars and waiting, as children might do.

One says to the other, "If these stars were men, which one would be your husband? I would want to have only the little red twinkling one."

"The only one I'd marry would be the shining yellow one, because I like a big star."

They are just joking with each other. Then in the morning when they wake up they find themselves married again according to custom, with just a word.

The one who wanted the fiercely shin-ing one, when she opens her eyes, here is her husband, a handsome man. He says to her, "Quiet, you will ruin my war paint."

continued

Passamaquoddy

Not-olu kotok itokoss: "Nulinuwa mehqahtuwessit," tuhkiyat, macessit, nutuwal wenil metiyewestulicil: "Menakac, ksukahtehkomuwin nsisqinpisun." Nihtol nit apsahtuwelicil possesomul, nihtol pawatokosoponil, komac puskolinaqsu ktaqhomuhsis; apsalokiqahsu naka macikcehpute 'siskul.

Nit-te eli-pawatomuhtits nit-te na eli-peciyamkuhtit.

Kenuk-olu wisaweyik kosona mehqeyik, piley kosona 'kaney, wahkehsukonokkiwik toqi-te komac 'siwi-ihiniya possesomuhkik eliphuts naka komac koti-wesuwessuwok skitkomiq. Naka nit li-peciyewiw:

Aqamok li-wiwisahkomuk 'kisi-wesuwessiniya. Possesomuwi-nisuwa-mahticihi katama ihiwiyik; 'kekiw kotunkiyik. 'Tiyukuwa: "Waht nit sekotiyapskek kci-ponapsq, musa sesomiw tukonehtuhkeq." Tokkiw ewecitu ciksotomuk.

Wot-olu ewasisuwit, etuci-te macehkawotilit possesomuwi-nisuwamahticihi, nit 'qiltahsin sekotiyapskek, 'panehtun. Wisoki-koti-nomihtun elomalokahk lamiw.

Nit eli-tukonehtaq, assokinaqot eli-nomihtaq: eli-pomaluktek nit emehkew, skitkomiq weceyawihtit wikihtit. Aqamotuk nemihtuhtit weceyawihtits ewasisuwihtit, kuspemok, kcihkuk, naka sipuwol. Kci-ehpit elapit, eluwe-te soqskessuwol moshunuwal elitahasihtit.

Literal translation

The other one, who said, "I like the flickering red one," when she wakes up, when she begins to move, she hears someone speaking: "Quiet, you will knock over my eye medicine." It's that little shining star, that one she wanted, a very feeble-looking little old man; he has tiny little eyes and they wobble shiftily.

Exactly the ones they wanted to have are also the ones who have come to them.

But yellow or red, new or old, within a few days the two women are both weary of being among the stars, where they have been taken, and they want very much to go back to earth. And this is how it comes about:

They are more and more impatient to go back. The star-husbands aren't around; they hunt all day. They have told them [the women], "That big, flat rock over there? Don't ever lift it up." Until now they have always obeyed.

This youngest one, however, as soon as their star-husbands walk away, dashes resolutely over to the rock and opens it up. She really wants to see the hole underneath.

When she has lifted it, it is a surprising sight she sees: the cloud-cover stretches out there below, the earth they came from, where they lived. She can even see where they used to live when they were young, at the lake, in the woods, and [she can see] the streams. When the older one looks, their hearts almost break with longing.

Passamaquoddy	Literal translation
Yukt possesomuk etuci-mocitahasoskihtit skitapihik, nit elitahamut; nomihtuniya oloqiw motewolonuwakonok nisuwihtituwa 'kisi-tuwapotomoniya elomalokahk aluhkok; 'kocicihtuniya ikonewatomuhtit. Yuhuht wolitahatomuwakon milaniya wesuwehkawotiniya skitkomikuk.	Those stars are by nature evil-minded men, as one might think of them. They see with their extraordinary powers that their wives have looked down through the hole in the cloud; they know it when they [the women] deny it. They [nevertheless] give them the pleasure of going back to earth.

Notes

1. Known as Passamaquoddy-Maliseet (or Maliseet-Passamaquoddy), this language is generally called Passamaquoddy in Maine, United States, and Maliseet in New Brunswick, Canada. The name is simplified to Passamaquoddy here.

2. Passamaquoddy native speaker Margaret Apt, community research coordinator for the dictionary project, quoted in Francis and Leavitt 2008:6.

3. Entries from the dictionary (Francis and Leavitt 2008) have been abridged and modified for this chapter, and approximate pronunciations have been added. Abbreviations used in the entries include *s/he* "he or she," *h/* "him or her, his or her" (*s/he* and *h/* represent any animate noun), *ai* "animate intransitive," *ii* "inanimate intransitive," *ta* "transitive animate." *Animate* and *inanimate* are the terms used for the two grammatical genders of Passamaquoddy.

4. Retranscribed (using current spelling) from Prince 1921. The "bear-meat" segment is found in appendix A of this chapter; see also Leavitt and Francis 1994, where a translation of Mitchell's entire text may be found. Passamaquoddy animal names are used here in place of Mitchell's original Mi'kmaq terms.

5. The story of Wocawson, from which the sentences in this entry are taken, is found in Prince 1921, and also in appendix B.

6. Koluskap, pronounced g'-LOO-skahb, is often spelled Glooscap, Gluskap, etc. in English.

7. Retranscribed from Prince 1921. This passage is another excerpt from the long narrative translated in Leavitt and Francis 1994; the "star-wives" segment is also found in appendix C.

8. Northeast Historic Film 2008 (adapted slightly here).

9. Anonymous Passamaquoddy speaker, b. mid-1940s, speaking in the late 1970s.

References

Francis, David A., and Robert M. Leavitt. 2008. *A Passamaquoddy-Maliseet Dictionary: Peskotomuhkati Wolastoqewi Latuwewakon*. Orono: University of Maine Press.

Leavitt, Robert M., and David A. Francis. 1994. The Indian Devil, Mischief-Maker. In *Coming to Light: Contemporary Translations of the Native Literatures of North America*, ed. Brian Swann, 503–18. New York: Random House.

Northeast Historic Film. 2008. *Natuwisine: Let's Go Pick Berries*. Bucksport, Maine (Passamaquoddy-language DVD produced by the Language Keepers project, under National Science Foundation grant number 0553791, Ben Levine and Robert M. Leavitt, co-investigators).

Prince, John Dyneley. 1921. *Passamaquoddy Texts*. Publications of the American Ethnological Society, vol. 10. New York: G. E. Stechert & Co. (This volume contains stories first transcribed in Passamaquoddy by Lewis Mitchell in the 1880s and later retranscribed and edited by Prince, with Mitchell's assistance.)

3

Translating Time

A Dialogue on Hopi Experiences of the Past

Chip Colwell-Chanthaphonh and Stewart B. Koyiyumptewa

Introduction

This chapter takes as its focus the question of how Hopi feelings, experiences, and knowledge of the past are, or can be, translated. Our motivation for this chapter grew out of our work together and conversations about the first author's own (non-Pueblo) experiences at ancient sites compared to how the second author perceives the role of the past in his own life and more broadly in Hopi society. From our exchanges we have to come to believe that addressing the ways in which these two disparate affinities for the material past—and ultimately closing the gap between non-Pueblo and Pueblo experiences—depend upon a thoughtful and respectful dialogue. That is, we suggest that through the methods of collaborative research we can have a richer, more complex understanding of past lives, the role of the past in the present, and even how the past may inform the shape of things to come. Because dialogue provides equitable and fruitful avenues of research and engagement, we thought it appropriate to present here a dialogue between ourselves about Hopi history, concepts of time, and the challenges and opportunities of translating the Pueblo past through the lens of anthropology and archaeology. Three more philosophically driven interludes help frame the narrative.

Time often appears self-evident, but it is neither straightforwardly a natural given nor a universal precept. Rather, time is a culturally shaped, perceived, and lived phenomenon. The disparity between how the Pueblo past is presented to the general public and how Pueblo people themselves understand their own community's past is important to acknowledge and untangle. To ignore this disparity is problematic, because we ought to care about how people who lived in these ancient villages perceived their own world—and the best, if not the only, way of doing this is by fully engaging with the living descendants of the people who once occupied these places. Disregarding Native values and viewpoints presents these places as scientific playgrounds for the national imagination instead of places of Pueblo heritage that give a deep sense of identity and belonging to Pueblo peoples. Also, it distances Pueblo people from their own history. This is of concern not just for the touristic gaze or abstract battles over heritage, but also when it comes to laws—such as the National Historic Preservation Act (1966), the National Environmental Policy Act (1969), and the Native American Graves Protection and Repatriation Act (1990)— different understandings of the material past by different stakeholders can ultimately mean the preservation or destruction of sacred objects, burial grounds, and traditional cultural properties.

Translation means cross-cultural understanding (Rubel and Rosman 2003:1). As such, translation is most fully articulated in anthropology as a formal discipline: translation is what anthropologists do. But of course intercultural exchanges have taken place for millennia, as indeed, even anthropology itself rests upon the shoulders of centuries of colonial travelers (Whiteley 2008). Over much of the twentieth century, anthropologists assumed that translation was a rather straightforward proposition, one that involved first observing others on their own terms and then writing about the others in one's own terms. However, in the 1980s anthropologists began looking at the hidden complexities of translating cultural ideas, ideals, practices, and processes into texts, driving a stake into the heart of anthropological authority (Clifford and Marcus 1986). Anthropology remains committed to the ideals of cross-cultural translation (this is deemed a worthwhile project), but anthropologists are now keenly aware of the limitations of translation—how translations can warp reality when anthropologists weave a story (Clifford 1997). Archaeologists too have come to acknowledge and grapple with how writing the past incompletely translates lived experiences, cultural meanings, and multifaceted histories (Bender, Hamilton, and Tilley 2007; Hodder 1989; Joyce 2002).

Time, as a subject of anthropological translation, has largely been the domain of archaeologists. This is not to say that all anthropologists have not used time as a mechanism to frame their subjects, as Johannes Fabian (1983) has illustrated in his classic *Time and the Other*, but rather that archaeological authority is deeply and uniquely embedded in arguments of time. (Cultural anthropologists admit that an ethnographic text represents merely an "ethnographic present," whereas archaeologists fight tooth and nail over whether Site X is older than Site Z.) Research such as ours, which seeks to combine Native American interpretations of the past with archaeological interpretations, is thus somewhat subversive because it gently challenges what lies at the center of archaeological authority. Our work involves the ethnographic study of the Hopi past: an examination of the meaning of ancient sites and places of history (see Colwell-Chanthaphonh and Ferguson 2006; Colwell-Chanthaphonh and Koyiyumptewa 2007; Ferguson, Koyiyumptewa, and Colwell-Chanthaphonh 2005). In this way, our work seeks to translate not just Hopi experiences of time, but also those of history and place. How we can translate these cultural ideas and experiences is the focus of our dialogue and discussion.

A Dialogue, Part I

CCC: Let's begin by discussing how archaeologists tend to write and think about time in the Pueblo past. For many years now, archaeologists in the American Southwest have worked to frame time in specific categories, or periods, which are tied to specific dates, for example, the Archaic Period, the Basketmaker periods, Pueblo I, Pueblo II, Pueblo III, and so on and so forth. When you see these archaeological chronologies, what do you think? In what ways is this way of tracing time useful?

SBK: As a child and a teenager growing up, I always wondered how our ancestors were living in the past. As I went into college, these terms were used often in different classes and I would imagine to myself these terms and how they fit into our teachings of the past. Paleoindians—I considered them to be the *motisinom*, the people that were here first, before the migrations from the south started. So these people were already here and Hopi refer to them in different clans, for instance the Badger clan, *motisinom*. The different clans, like the Katsina clan, I think they were here, but they weren't known as that yet. But it gives me a type of picture: the Badger clan members were the Paleoindians, they roamed, hunted, and gathered but they didn't really build any structures. With Basketmaker, I picture them experimenting with different fibers, not knowing what the outcome of their products will be. As they moved, they start experimenting with different structures, like building with rocks and adobe. I also think that during these times the population was steadily growing and the migrations were starting to happen, through the Basketmaker, Pueblo I, Pueblo II periods. With the *motisinom*, I picture them as isolated groups of people until the migration started and I see groups of people starting to show up and coming with different knowledge, skills, and incorporating that into the area.

The terms are a scientific way of classifying archaeology, but for me, from my view, I also use that to picture for myself which stage they were in; this must have been what was happening, planning and settling down. So I use those terms to picture the different stages our ancestors were at during different times.

CCC: So in your mind you combine these archaeological pictures that the chronologies create with the traditional stories about the migrations?

SBK: Yeah, I do picture that. All I can do is imagine to myself, because nobody was around when they arrived. All I can do is relate to the stories that our ancestors tell. And, the studies archaeologists have done too. So it's kind of a combination of both to picture in my mind what our ancestors were going through during ancient times.

CCC: On the flip side of that, do you think that there are some negative aspects that come along with the differences between archaeological chronologies and Hopi concepts of migrations and time?

SBK: It would be harmful if someone were to go after Hopi teachings and Hopi oral history and "disprove" it with scientific evidence. They could say, "No, your teachings are wrong because this is what I found through science." The outside world values science more than they do oral history or traditional knowledge; it's just always been that way. So, it could hurt in that sense.

CCC: So if those two ways of seeing the past—archaeological science and traditional knowledge—are set up as competing viewpoints instead of complementary viewpoints, then we might cause trouble?

SBK: Yes. I think with different studies, Hopi knowledge and scientific knowledge can complement each other. But if someone were to come up with a new idea and say, "You're wrong," then that would be harmful.

CCC: I can see that point: it is also about the attitude of the scientists, when scientists think that they alone have the answers and tell others that only they are right. It's about humility.

SBK: For instance, the Hopi talk about this blue star appearing in the sky, and according to Hopi oral history this was a time when they were to end the migration. I don't know when it actually happened, maybe around AD 1000. Anyway, this blue star appeared in the sky and it was a signal for the Hopi clans to start going to our present-day homeland. We had a person out here (an astronomer) talking about this event at one of the Cultural Resource Advisory Task Team meetings for our cultural advisers and they did prove that this star—a supernova I think it was—did really happen around the same time that Hopi was saying it happened. So, like that, science and Hopi knowledge complement each other.

CCC: And what if the opposite were the case? Say, if in the Hopi traditions, it was said that a blue star appeared, and you brought in astronomers and they said there was never a blue star that appeared in the sky. How can those kinds of conflicts be resolved?

SBK: In that case, people would think that the burden would be on Hopi because our language isn't written. The only physical evidence we may have are the petroglyphs. At this meeting, the elders were saying some petroglyphs signify that blue star. And if the scientists say, "You Hopi are wrong, there was never a supernova, it never happened." This would be damaging to our teachings because we don't have the evidence or technology like that of the scientists. We rely on what has been passed down from our ancestors.

CCC: In that sense, it seems to me that we're on an unfair playing field. Scientists, because of how they think about the past and how they think about time, and by the nature of how they approach the past, they can always point to some piece of concrete evidence if they say something. Whereas the Hopi are at a disadvantage in a society that purports to value concrete evidence because so much of their knowledge about the past is oral and passed through songs, traditions, stories. It's uneven from the very beginning, and in that sense it's always going to be harder for Hopis to try to "prove" something in the past.

SBK: Yeah.

CCC: Another question I had relates to the theme of the book that our chapter will go into, which, as you know, is "translation." After thinking about our work that "translates" the Hopi material past—and translating not just for Hopis, but for people who go to Mesa Verde or other Pueblo places, or even Paleoindian mammoth hunters for that matter—really translating time involves working together. It involves dialogue and collaboration, and that's one thing that struck me about doing this interview format, a conversation between us, because it seems to me that if we want to really understand the past more fully and if we want to create a level playing field where archaeological science and Hopi knowledge aren't in direct conflict, then the way to make this really happen is through speaking to each other as equals.

SBK: I like working with you and Dr. T. J. Ferguson. You're always asking different questions, but in turn, I'm always picking your brain about different things because you and Dr. Ferguson have been out there and you've studied different people and have worked with outside institutions. The collaboration between the tribe and different groups is really beneficial. People like you have been out there, they know the resources. And the projects that we've worked on, you've talked directly to the present-day tribes and you've also done the research on a lot of past work, and you kind of make your own conclusions, and sometimes they can be even stronger than other people's work. So I think it is to the benefit of the tribe; the tribe can learn about new portions of science and help put it in a way that makes sense to everybody. I think it's a good thing, the work that you and Dr. Ferguson and Dr. Peter Whiteley and everybody who is working directly with the tribe do. It makes the product stronger.

Interlude: The Science of Poetics

When Hopi traditionalists speak about the *motisinom* and *hisatsinom* to non-Hopis grounded in the Western tradition of positivism, this kind of language may sound definitively unscientific. When Hopi traditionalists speak of ancestors revealing themselves through natural phenomena, such as a rush of wind or a surge of water in a river, this sounds poetic to non-Hopis. In the English language, outside of poetry, it is difficult to fully grasp the significance of these statements. But when you hear Hopis speak of these matters, the gravity and sincerity of their expressions is difficult to doubt. Hence, from an anthropological perspective, taking these statements seriously and wanting to understand them, involves developing a science of Hopi poetics.

However, Hopi elders and traditionalists emphasize that their knowledge of ancient events and their ancestors relates not to poetics per se but rather to history. Perhaps, as Roger Keesing (1985) has written, we too often overemphasize the poetics of language when translating metaphors. For the Hopi people, metaphors suffuse their conceptualization of the world (Sekaquaptewa and Washburn 2004, 2006). While metaphors no doubt suffuse traditional knowledge of the past, Hopis still insist that their traditions relate real history. Many Hopis dislike the phrase "origin myth" for this reason, believing that the word "myth" suggests a fictional, untrue tale. When Hopis speak about the *motisinom* or the ancestral spirits in the here and now, they are not speaking metaphorically; they are speaking about actual people and corporal experiences.

While it is undoubtedly difficult to translate these things methodically and accurately, we resist the notion that the Hopi past is untranslatable. The idea that science and religion are mutually untranslatable was perhaps most compellingly argued by Stephen J. Gould (1999), who suggested that these two realms of knowledge constitute "nonoverlapping magisteria," that is, areas of teaching and expertise that are complementary but completely separate. But, this argument is flawed, we suggest, because it creates a false dichotomy by imagining that religious knowledge contains no scientific knowledge, and equally, that scientists are not religious in their beliefs or actions (Cajete 1999; Hedges 2008). The chimera of divisibility is particularly problematic for archaeologists who may seek precisely the historical information that is embedded in traditional religious knowledge. In short, science and religion possess elements of the other: they are not nonoverlapping magisteria, but rather they are intersecting magisteria.

To begin exploring this area of intersection, to see if it is a hair's breadth or a mile wide, requires bridging scientific and religious understandings of the world. That is, to translate Hopi notions of the material past into a language that non-Hopis can understand requires working together, collaboration (see Colwell-Chanthaphonh and Ferguson 2008). Non-Pueblo people simply don't have the conceptual, cultural, or experiential tools to fully untangle the meanings of the Pueblo material past without Pueblo contribution. In turn, until more Pueblo people gain degrees and experience in archaeological science, non-Pueblo scholars can play a central role in helping to translate Pueblo ideas of the past for the general public, government officials, and others. We do not suggest that collaboration is itself a solution to bridging these magisteria, but rather that collaboration is the mechanism by which we can seek to meet this unresolved challenge.

A Dialogue, Part II

CCC: Talking about knowledge embedded in *oral* traditions, let's turn to language. Are there Hopi words for "history" and "past"? Are there any insights in the Hopi language that could help non-Hopis understand how you think about time?

SBK: We could start from today, *pu'* or *pu'haqam*, this year. Then there is yesterday, *taavok*. Then there is *yas*, which refers to a year ago. Then *hisat*, which refers to some time ago, when, or an indefinite time. Then, *hisatti*, which refers to a long time ago, I would think in terms of days. You may also say *hisat'haqam*, which may refer to the time of the *hisatsinom* (ancient ancestors) and the migration era. I know there are probably other words that I am forgetting.

CCC: So there are these divisions of time that reference more or less an immediate past, something that just happened, that happened a while ago, or a very long time ago.

SBK: Yeah.

CCC: Before Hopis had access to the Gregorian calendar, before Hopis thought about "months" and "years," do you have any ideas on how people would have thought about those units of time?

SBK: I was just thinking: units of time can also refer to people that are living or have passed and their contributions to the village. For example we could say, "He will hold a butterfly dance this year." *Pu' pam politikivet tunatyatani.* We are able to determine when this dance will be held simply by knowing the month or season the butterfly dances are held and where it fit into the ceremonial calendar. Then we can say, "Remember sometime ago he held a butterfly dance." *Ura hisat pam politikivet tunatyata.* This example, in my opinion, would be another way of tracking units of time.

Another example would be, "Remember So-and-So, we're still using his songs in the kiva." If we can name the person that made the song, but that person has already passed on, it's still in the memory of the generation. However, as we continue to grow and forget the songs, I think that's getting farther into the past. Generations grow older and they take responsibility for different ceremonies, and new songs are made and then nobody uses the old songs. And eventually they just get forgotten. That's a good indication of different times: when they can remember who made the songs and when they used it, when they performed these songs. It's the same way with storytelling or just family history. The younger generation, they may not know who their grandfathers' grandfathers were, maybe because they don't talk about them.

CCC: Are there different levels of time? I mean, you have the more distant time periods that you're talking about, which are intergenerational time periods, and then there are also time frames within a single year. And it seems like with the Hopi ceremonial calendar, the patterns of the ceremonies—that's also a very clear way of tracing the amount of time that passes in a year. But do Hopis use the progression of ceremonies as an explicit way of tracking time, or is the progression of ceremonies, as well as plantings and such, not really related to keeping track of time per se?

SBK: It's related to time. Different ceremonies are performed during different times of the month. For example, the responsibilities for the Home Dance are passed on from kiva to kiva every year. Like this year, the kiva of which I am a member is doing the praying for the Home Dance ceremony. And then when this is done, it will jump over to the next kiva and this responsibility will not come back to our kiva until another six years. So that's another way of tracking time. So that number six—because there are six kivas in our village—is significant in Hotvela. In the village of Walpi they have five kivas, so each kiva is responsible for the Home Dance ceremony every fifth year; same with Songòopavi, which also has five kivas. So each kiva is responsible every fifth year. That helps them keep track of time. But with Hopi, just the general ceremonial calendar, they could trace different times of ceremonies through the moon and through the seasons.

CCC: And that was going on long before contact with Europeans. It seems to me that it's easy to say that *pahaanam* [Anglos] think about time in one way and Hopis think in another way. And it's true that archaeologists tend to be rigid. They create these categories of time and trace events exactly to the year. In turn, it's easy to romanticize how Native Americans think about time as more fluid or through internal experiences. But the very specific ceremonial patterns as a way of tracing time are also very specific and closely monitored. So in that sense, there's maybe not so much a dichotomy between *paha-anam* and Hopis, but rather that it depends on the context and how each group thinks about the past and when.

SBK: Archaeologists and anthropologists have to take into consideration that the ceremonial calendar was not completed until the migrations were completed. Archaeologists like Dr. Chuck Adams say this is where the Katsina cult was created, yes, and his evidence comes from pottery sherds [see Adams 1991]. We need to use these types of studies to help us look at the broader picture. My question would be: How can the faction be of use and importance when they were still migrating and coming into fruition?

When different clan groups arrived at the mesas, they would have to prove their worth as a group of people. The village chief would say, "Yes, your ceremonies will benefit all the people, so we're going to give you this part of the calendar year, and every year as we go through our ceremonies, when it comes to this part of the season or moon, this is when you'll hold your ceremony." So, there were just pieces of the calendar that were out there, the ceremonies, until they had actually completed the migrations.

CCC: Do you think in some sense that Hopi concepts of time became more complex through the generations as more and more clans joined the mesas, as the religious calendar kept adding more kivas and clans and societies?

SBK: Yeah, different groups of clans came with different ceremonies, but for other clans to join or obtain these different knowledges they would have to go through a ceremony to join different ceremonies not performed by their clan. The Katsina clan is responsible for the Katsina ceremony, and that's gained through a rite of passage. But it's the clans that brought different ceremonies: they're the ones that hold the positions as leaders. For instance, the Badger clan, we brought the Powamuya ceremony and it's the Badger clan that holds the Powamuya leadership, the ceremonial head person. Other clans that hold different ceremonies can join the Powaymuy society through initiation, but they can never hold that leadership position.

CCC: One question I have for you is whether, from a traditional Hopi viewpoint, is the past ever really past? Previously you and I have talked about ceremonies and farming and all these different activities of Hopi life: Are those all ways of connecting Hopis today to Hopis of yesterday? How does the past continue on to the present in people's lives?

SBK: This question relates to the paper that Loma'omvaya and Ferguson wrote about *navoti* [see Loma'omvaya and Ferguson 2003]. The paper is geared more toward the ceremonial knowledge of *navoti*, but *navoti* can be anything. It can be gaining knowledge from your uncle and grandfather about different farming techniques. It can be knowledge about the different soils and where different types of plants are grown. It can be knowledge on how to take care of your plants so you'll have a bountiful harvest. It's just this knowledge that has been passed on since the migrations. They will say this is the white corn, you plant it this deep in this type of soil and it takes this long for it to grow. This knowledge is passed down from generation to generation, how to properly care for these things. *Navoti* can also be for women, about cooking and traditional food gathering, the mother will go out with the daughter to find edible plants; they'll tell their daughters when to pick it, how you cook it and serve it. That's *navoti*. There's different ways *navoti* can be incorporated besides ceremonial knowledge. So there are different ways of tracing the past, the knowledge from the ancestors.

CCC: How does *navoti* contrast with *wiimi*?

SBK: *Wiimi*, to me, is the ceremonial knowledge: this is how you perform the ceremony, these are the songs that are sung. There's a rite of passage for the different prayers that are secretive. It's what you call esoteric, not available to the general public. So I consider *navoti* general information that is passed down, and *wiimi* is the ceremonial knowledge that is passed down through the generations.

CCC: Is one form of this knowledge *more* connected to the deep past than the other? I'm wondering if *navoti* could be something that only relates to two generations ago, whereas *wiimi* is necessarily many, many generations old.

SBK: I think it's all equal because without the *navoti*, planting different plants and when, Hopi wouldn't have been able to survive without that.

CCC: That makes sense.

SBK: *Wiimi* goes way back to the migrations, I guess, it has a longer connection to the past, but *navoti*, you could say, is constantly changing because the techniques are changing too.

CCC: How do Hopis traditionally gain knowledge of *navoti* and *wiimi*?
SBK: Just being around your uncles and grandparents. Hard work.

It takes a different person to farm out here, and you want to really learn, try, and ask questions. It takes trial and error too. A lot of *navoti* comes from your elders, our uncles, people that know these things.

Interlude: Time of the World and Soul

David Lowenthal (1989) has observed that when Anglos reflect on the past, they contradictorily see history as ahistorical, perpetually filtering the past through the lens of nostalgia. In our own experience, many Anglos use an immediate past to contemplate their identity: they may often think about a loved deceased grandfather, one's regrets and missteps; less often, though still often enough, do they think about their great-great-grandfather fighting in the Civil War, the long journeys of migration across the Atlantic from Ireland or Italy; and rarely, if ever, do they ponder the Ordinance of Louis the Pius or the Magna Carta.

In contrast, a Hopi elder who approaches a shrine or who picks up pottery sherds at an ancient village will immediately know the presence of his ancestors. The summer rainstorm, the appearance of a snake, the sudden burst of wind—these *are* the ancestors revealing themselves, and immediately the emergence from the previous world, the ancient migrations, the countless generations that have passed, are manifestly present in the here and now.

Time in anthropology is a big theme, hugely complex, consisting of a seemingly endless literature, akin to Borges's *Book of Sand*, "as one opens this book, pages keep growing from it—it has no beginning or end" (Munn 1992:93). While this literature is rich in theory and laden with ethnographic examples from Africa to Australia, there is no need to review it at length here. We don't want to get lost in the wilderness of philosophy to make our point: non-Pueblo archaeologists need to work in partnership with Pueblo community members to have a sensitive, nuanced, and accurate understanding of the Pueblo world, past and present.

However, it is worth drawing attention to the fact that many scholars have long worked in dichotomies, in stereotypes, arguing that some people think in lines and others in circles (Munn 1992:102). Critiquing Immanuel Kant and his adherents for a priori assumptions about time's existence and linear nature, Paul Ricoeur (1988) has argued that there is the conception of "time of the world," which is an objective measure of time's passing, marked by sequential natural events such as the solar cycle. In contrast, "time of the soul" is a subjective experience, internal to the human subject.

The implications of these different conceptions can be profound. Archaeologist Julian Thomas (1996:33), who has written on the importance of Ricoeur's ideas for archaeology, has noted, "If we emphasize the objective and worldly nature of time, we tend to promote a view of reality as a given, a set of physical conditions to which human consciousnesses must bend itself." Thomas (1996:35) points out that this is the frame in which many archaeologists and historians work; the most famous of these is perhaps Fernand Braudel, who sought to think about historical events and processes as somehow unfolding outside of human experience. Archaeologists who focus only on carbon dates, evolutionary stages, and ceramic chronologies study the past with this same assumption. The time of the soul instead emphasizes the individual connection to the world, "an inner experience which gives form to an outer reality," but this too is problematic, for then the "subject becomes a primordial being, with certain fundamental characteristics, including the giving of temporality to the world" (Thomas 1996:33). Benjamin Whorf was perhaps working in this mode when he famously, and erroneously, argued that the Hopi language has no time-referencing forms—that the Hopi language can only express a non-spatial timeless time (cf. Malotki 1983; Munn 1992:98).

Ricoeur (1988:104–26) writes that time of the world and time of the soul are equally incomplete ways of conceptualizing how time suffuses the human experience. He instead "stresses the collective and cultural character of the process of drawing on the past in order to achieve a sense of selfhood" (Thomas 1996:51). Human beings, in short, not only understand themselves but *create* themselves through stories. It is through narratives—negotiated private and public memories—that humans and human groups shape their identities. Thus, Ricoeur (1988:274) argues, time, culture, identity, and memory are intimately interconnected.

And so archaeologists do not think in certain ways because they must; chronometric dating is not the only way to think about changes in Pueblo history. Equally, Hopi elders may feel the immediate presence of the past when standing on ancient sites, but they can also appreciate and conceptualize carbon 14 and archaeomagnetic dating. These are ways each community has thought about time and the past because that is their traditions to do so. These are the stories they tell themselves. To change them for the positive, following from Ricoeur, we must only begin to renegotiate our private and collective narratives. The aim of our work thus seeks novel ways to mediate—*translate*—between these worlds.

A Dialogue, Part III

CCC: Are young Hopis today—the next generation, that is—learning this knowledge, *navoti* and *wiimi*?

SBK: I think a few, but there's also a lot of influence from the outside. They don't have the patience to learn, to really ask. They want things without really having to work for it. There are a few of the younger generation that are learning it, yet there's another part that doesn't want to have to deal with it. I think many of the younger generation think the Hopi lifestyle is a burden. They always say their uncles and their grandfathers try to teach them, take that responsibility in trying to teach them, but they're not interested in it. *Pam pi pay hisat*. That was long ago, they say. It's today now. It's a way of shutting things down, their uncles and their grandfathers. *Pam pi pay hisat*. That was long ago.

CCC: In terms of teaching younger Hopis about the past: if archaeology is used as a complementary way of understanding Hopi history, can it be beneficial? Or, do you think it maybe detracts from more traditional ways of understanding history?

SBK: It could be both. If they're really interested in the past, they would have to look at the archaeological record, the archaeology that's still standing there, and do as I did: picture how our people came to be here. The thing that always gets to me is the hardships that they had to face, the amount of labor that they had to put in to build these sites. Something like Mesa Verde is almost unbelievable, the type of work that went into that, the architecture. I always wonder: how did our ancestors live? How were they able to do that? And, this winter was the coldest winter ever recorded in Flagstaff, Arizona, where I live, and I wonder: how did they survive a winter like this? How were they able to keep warm? I'm always amazed at how we came to be here, today, at present-day Hopi, with all the struggles, the hardships. That amazes me. That would help someone appreciate really who they are as a person and where they come from. But someone who isn't interested in the past, day by day, it isn't going to matter to them.

They have that history, but they don't really know what our people went through, their struggles.

CCC: When I've gone to places like Mesa Verde and Chaco Canyon, sometimes the way they present the Pueblo past on tours or in exhibits, they emphasize some of what you're talking about: they talk about how hard it was, the difficulties of living a life in which you have to grow your own food and build your own home. But it seems to me too that for a non-Pueblo audience, those stories almost become exotic, mysterious. Most Americans today are so disconnected from really how it is they survive and they don't have genuine understandings of the rituals and ceremonies and cosmological ideas that go into these places. Whereas what I hear you saying, and what I've heard other Hopis say in our work together, is that this wonderment is not about an exotic past, but rather a deep respect for where your own ancestors have been and how the Hopi people have survived for so long.

SBK: The tourists will never understand how the ancient people lived unless they get a taste of it. The Hopi are in the modern era too, but we still have a taste of what it takes to survive. We have to work our fields every day—not all by hand anymore, some by tractor, yet it's still hard work. We have to gather our own wood, chop wood. It's a tiny taste of what it takes to survive. But people, like tourists, they don't do that. They've always had running water. Whereas, at Hopi, in my village, still into the 1980s, they still had to haul water. Either from the spring or from just one general faucet in the village. I remember having to go with my bucket and fill one of those big containers with water just so that we could have water for everyday purposes and cleaning. Today, people are out of touch with that. They have these reality shows on TV that teach us to do that, survive!

CCC: Do you think that as Hopi life on the mesas becomes more and more modern that there is a bigger and bigger risk that the people will lose this connection to their ancestors?

SBK: Yeah. The language has a lot to do with it too, because if they're not learning the language, how can you perform the songs in the ceremonies? It is a danger. The key is the language. This is already happening to some extent during the ceremonies. The person that is in charge has to give a speech on the eve of the event; a lot of these speeches are now given in English. The prayers are in English. I like one cartoon that I came upon: there was a dance, a Long Hair dance, and there was a Hopi woman that went up there and asked, "Can you dance during Easter?" And this Katsina has a question mark on top of its head, thinking, "What are you talking about?!" It's a really good cartoon because it's where we are headed, all of our ceremonies, especially the Katsina dances that fall under other people's calendar and religion, like Easter, Mother's Day, Father's Day, and so on. That's where we're headed. I take that back, we are already there. A lot of the ceremonies are done on the weekend now because the people are working. It's the convenient time to hold a ceremony. They arrange it. That's how we're doing our ceremonies now.

CCC: Talking about these things is making me think about the relationship between the past, present, and future. In your opinion, what do the past and present have to say about the future?

SBK: What we're doing today, we're still holding onto the traditions and ceremonies we have. We look to the past and are able to hold onto these up to this time. But as we get into the future, it's sad to see what direction we're headed in. We continue with our teachings, so they'll at least go on for another generation. But it's kind of hard to talk about that. We've done what we're supposed to do to this point, just based on the traditional knowledge. But I think there is an end in sight, not too far down the road.

CCC: What kind of "end" do you mean?

SBK: I mean an end to the ceremonies.

CCC: You can see that day out there.

SBK: Yeah, maybe not in my lifetime, but it is there. The only thing we'll probably be doing is powwows! But up until now that relationship between the past and present has been maintained: we've done what we're supposed to do. And there is Hopi prophecies that say, yes, it will come to an end. But we don't know when. I think it's down the road because of how we're living these days.

CCC: The work that you and your colleagues do at the Hopi Cultural Preservation Office, is that in part to try to ensure that there is a future for Hopi culture? Where does "preservation"—in terms of preserving language, eagle habitat and nests, or ancestral shrines—fit into the future? How does your preservation work fit into the future of the Hopi people?

SBK: Our hope is that if we record the ancient sites and what plants were used, like we did on the Navajo Transmission Project [Albert and Colwell-Chanthaphonh 2007] and Marvin Lalo's program to try to get the kids to learn how to write Hopi since today's kids learn by writing, and if those programs are successful in teaching people how to speak Hopi, then this end that we're talking about is still yet in the future, not in the next couple of years. The preservation is like this: yes, we're recording the eagle nests and the locations of it in hope— *hope* is the key word—that our younger generation will continue to practice the religion.

But this isn't always easy. For example, we're trying to preserve songs, yet we get criticism from our own community, saying that we're recording esoteric information through songs. I remember when I first started working at the Hopi Cultural Preservation Office they had submitted a grant proposal for a songs project. The tribal council shut it down because they thought we were going after esoteric information. We weren't! Really, it was social dance songs and bedtime songs that mothers sing to their children, just songs that are for everybody. The council didn't support it because they thought we were going after sacred songs. So there are different people throughout the villages that say, "Yeah, those guys are doing a good job." And then there are others that criticize. We can only do the best that we can.

Interlude: The Language of Time and the Time of Language

The language of time is an important avenue through which Hopis conceive of the past, the scales at which Hopis understand the passing of time and the ways in which past ancestors can be recognized. In this way, the terms *motisinom* and *hisatsinom* encapsulate vastly different kinds of meaning than the archaeological terms "Ancestral Puebloan" or "Anasazi." The *motisinom* and *hisatsinom* are labels of affinity, while also references for time periods in Hopi history. These terms mark kinship as well as the passage of time; they are the linguistic links that allow Hopis to place themselves in space and time. It is little wonder that Hopis often object to these scientific terms, arguing that they serve to conceptually, socially, and politically distance the Hopi people from their own ancestors (Michel 2006).

As we recognize the power of language to elucidate the past, a challenge emerges regarding the proper place of the Hopi language in our collaborative research, in our own dialogues. Only a handful of non-Hopi researchers speak the Hopi language; however, many Hopis express their approval on this point, saying that the Hopi language is meant only for the Hopi people. When working with groups of Hopi traditionalists, we have found that it is preferable for outside researchers to not be able to speak the language. First, this allows the group to converse in private in Hopi about sensitive issues. Second, the language barrier becomes a filtering device for the Hopi research participants, who know that when they speak in English their words are being recorded, while their Hopi thoughts and words are only for the Hopis in attendance. At the same time, because we recognize the importance of language for illuminating the past, we try to emphasize where appropriate the Hopi names for places, people, and events, while attempting to provide understanding about the broader social context in which these terms are used. Admittedly, it is a tricky game of balance.

If the researcher does not speak the Hopi language, then he or she is missing out on an opportunity to directly engage with the Hopi experience. As a result, before the researcher even attempts to translate Hopi understandings, an initial translation must occur; that is, Hopi thought must be put into English for the researcher's benefit. Even more, we propose that there are times when language itself is inadequate to relate Hopi understandings of the past. Translating emotional states is not easy (Rubel and Rosman 2003:13), and there are no clear means by which we can translate spiritual experiences into a text. Words can point to feelings; they can describe lived experiences; but the text is itself neither feelings nor experiences. The text in this sense is the filter crafted by the writer that sits between the reader and the experience.

The threat of language loss is increasing on the Hopi mesas. Although the Hopis are maintaining their language more than other tribes in the United States (Whiteley 2003), the danger is very real, and many Hopis despair at the thought of the death of the Hopi language. The loss of the Hopi language has dire implications for how Hopis connect with their own past, as prayers, songs, and oral histories and traditions are all communicated through the Hopi language. The clan migration stories, for instance, which document Hopi movements across the American Southwest over generations, and are of importance to archaeologists (Bernardini 2005), are told to English speakers only in gloss form; they are repeated in the kivas over an extended period of days. What becomes of a culture when its language dies? Many Hopis seemingly are close to Whorfians, emphasizing that the Hopi language vitally encodes Hopi worldviews.

Hence, the threat of the loss of Hopi language means the possible loss of Hopi culture, the loss of Hopi history.

Yet, we know that culture and language are never wholly fixed; rather, they are fluid, always shifting. The time of language is a continuous string of moments, linked by words learned from the past and creatively used in the present. Because these tools for conceptualizing the past—culture, language—are not static, we may say that the past itself is adjustable and adaptable. The past is an active process of remembering. Time, in other words, needs to be translated. As Richard Bradley (2003:223) has written, archaeologists typically want to create linear narratives, but those whom they typically study often did not live their lives (make their things, build their monuments, tell their stories) in a linear fashion. For most people, "time was a flexible medium." In this way, as Bradley (2003:226) wrote, archaeologists must better appreciate how "the remaking of the past in the past was both a creative act and an interpretation."

Conclusion

If anthropological translation means approximating "as closely as possible the original words and ideas of the culture being studied" (Rubel and Rosman 2003:4), then to translate the Hopi past we must study experiences of the Hopi present. To accurately translate this past perhaps means not just a literal (and linear) retelling of events in the Hopi past, but rather in some measure grappling with how Hopis themselves recall their history (see Swann 2004). Borrowing from Walter Benjamin (2007:79), we argue that "the task of the translator consists in finding that intended effect upon the language into which he is translating which produces in it the echo of the original." In short, archaeologists studying the Hopi past should seek not merely to reproduce the Hopi past in their own language (that is, scientific jargon) but also should try to reproduce the effect of Hopi understandings of history. In translation, fidelity to the original means its continued life in another form (Rubel and Rosman 2003:7).

Translating the past, in Benjamin's terms, matters because researchers must seek to engage not only with the poetry of Hopi history but also with the history embedded in Hopi narratives. Throughout this chapter we have argued that a middle ground between scientific inquiry and religious knowledge, between time of the world and the time of soul, can and must be sought to provide an accurate, respectful, and holistic understanding of the Hopi past. Furthermore, how archaeologists interpret Pueblo history has political implications. Whether ancient village sites and shrines are deemed traditional cultural properties under the National Historic Preservation Act, and whether the Hopi Tribe is deemed cultural affiliated with the Hohokam under the Native American Graves Protection and Repatriation Act, have real and immediate impacts on the Hopi people's ability to care for their own heritage. Here, with these issues, anthropology as a mechanism of translation makes most sense to tribes (Ferguson 2003).

The Pueblo material past has long been understood exclusively from the perspective of non-Native archaeologists. Only in recent years have Native American perspectives been brought to bear on archaeological sites and artifacts. Rubel and Rosman (2003:11) have suggested that "translation has become a battleground between the hegemonic forces—the target of culture and language, and the formerly subjugated non-Western world. The nature of translation must be shifted to emphasize the resistance of the latter to the domination of the former." Indeed, from this stance we can see how the translations of the Pueblo past constitute a kind of battlefield, a clash between forces of colonialism and resistance. However, with an approach of collaboration built from the foundations of mutual respect, we say it is possible to move beyond metaphors of war. Instead of clashing translations, we see Hopi interpretations and scientific interpretations as multiple readings of the same past. As with different translations of the same original text, we do not necessarily have to say that one is entirely superior to the other. Rather, they are equal but different. These translations can be read on their own terms. In this way, we hope to transform the battleground into common ground.

Note on Orthography and Pronunciation

The Hopi words were written and translated by Stewart B. Koyiyumptewa. Below is the orthography and pronunciation of the Hopi alphabet as outlined in *The Hopi Dictionary* (Hill et al. 1998).

'	glottal stop
a	somewhat as in want
aa	as in father, drawn out
e	as in met
ee	as in red, drawn out
h	as in how, but pronounced more conspicuously

i	vowel in beat
ii	vowel in bead, drawn out
k	as in ski
kw	qu in squash
k.w	k followed by w
ky	k in skew
k.y	k followed by y
l	somewhat as in leaf
m	as in may
n	as in now
ng	as in song
ngw	ng and w pronounced simultaneously
ng.w	ng followed by w
ngy	ng and y pronounced simultaneously
o	as in obey
oo	like the o in home, drawn out and with no w-sound at the end
ö	somewhat like the u in purple
öö	u in purple, drawn out
p	as in spot
q	a k-sound made at the back of the soft palate
qw	a far back k-sound pronounced with simultaneous lip-rounding
q.w	q followed by w
r	before a vowel: voiced spico-alveolar fricative; at the end of a syllable: a voiceless apico-alveolar fricative
s	as in see
t	as in stop
ts	as in cats
t.s	t followed by s
u	somewhat like the oo in good
uu	somewhat like the oo in good, but drawn out
v	before a vowel: somewhat as in very; at the end of a syllable: an f made with the action of both lips
w	as in want
y	as in young
'y	a glottal stop followed by a brief echo of an i-sound

Suggested Reading and References

Adams, E. Charles. 1991. *The Origin and Development of the Pueblo Katsina Cult.* Tucson: University of Arizona Press.

Albert, Steve, and Chip Colwell-Chanthaphonh. 2007. *Hopi Cultural and Natural Resources Report for the Navajo Transmission Project.* Manuscript on File, Hopi Cultural Preservation Office.

Bender, Barbara, Sue Hamilton, and Christopher Tilley. 2007. *Stone Worlds: Narrative and Reflexivity in Landscape Archaeology*. Walnut Creek CA: Left Coast Press.

Benjamin, Walter. 2007. The Task of the Translator: An Introduction to the Translation of Baudelaire's Tableaux Parisiens. In *The Translation Studies Reader*, ed. Lawrence Venuti, 75–83. 2nd ed. London: Routledge.

Bernardini, Wesley. 2005. Reconsidering Spatial and Temporal Aspects of Prehistoric Cultural Identity: A Case Study from the American Southwest. *American Antiquity* 70 (1): 31–54.

Bradley, Richard. 2003. The Translation of Time. In *Archaeologies of Memory*, ed. Ruth M. Van Dyke and Susan E. Alcock, 221–27. Oxford: Blackwell.

Cajete, Gregory. 1999. *Native Science: Natural Laws of Interdependence*. Santa Fe: Clear Light Books.

Clifford, James. 1997. *Routes: Travel and Translation in the Late Twentieth Century*. Cambridge: Harvard University Press.

Clifford, James, and George E. Marcus, eds. 1986. *Writing Culture: The Poetics and Politics of Ethnography*. Berkeley: University of California Press.

Colwell-Chanthaphonh, Chip, and T. J. Ferguson. 2006. Memory Pieces and Footprints: Multivocality and the Meanings of Ancient Times and Ancestral Places among the Zuni and Hopi. *American Anthropologist* 108 (1): 148–62.

Colwell-Chanthaphonh, Chip, and T. J. Ferguson, eds. 2008. *Collaboration in Archaeological Practice: Engaging Descendant Communities*. Lanham MD: AltaMira Press.

Colwell-Chanthaphonh, Chip, and Stewart B. Koyiyumptewa. 2007. *Investigation of Hopi Traditional Cultural Properties and Cultural Landscape for the Desert Rock Energy Project*. Manuscript on File, Hopi Cultural Preservation Office.

Fabian, Johannes. 1983. *Time and the Other: How Anthropology Makes Its Object*. New York: Columbia University Press.

Ferguson, T. J. 2003. Anthropological Archaeology Conducted by Tribes: Traditional Cultural Properties and Cultural Affiliation. In *Archaeology Is Anthropology*, ed. Susan D. Gillespie and Deborah L. Nichols, 137–44. Archaeological Papers of the American Anthropological Association No. 13. Washington DC: American Anthropological Association.

Ferguson, T. J., Stewart B. Koyiyumptewa, and Chip Colwell-Chanthaphonh. 2005. *Hopi Traditional Cultural Properties Along the US 160 Highway Corridor*. Manuscript on File, Hopi Cultural Preservation Office, Kykotsmovi.

Gould, Stephen Jay. 1999. *Rocks of Ages: Science and Religion in the Fullness of Life*. New York: Ballantine.

Hedges, Chris. 2008. *I Don't Believe in Atheists*. New York: Free Press.

Hill, Kenneth C., Emory Sekaquaptewa, Mary E. Black, Ekkehart Malotki, and Michael Lomatuway'ma, eds. 1998. *Hopi Dictionary/Hopìikwa Lavàytutuveni:*

A Hopi-English Dictionary of the Third Mesa Dialect. Tucson: University of Arizona Press.

Hodder, Ian. 1989. Writing Archaeology: Site Reports in Context. *Antiquity* 63:268–74.

Joyce, Rosemary A. 2002. *The Languages of Archaeology: Dialogue, Narrative, and Writing*. Oxford: Blackwell.

Keesing, Roger M. 1985. Conventional Metaphors and Anthropological Metaphysics: The Problematic of Cultural Translation. *Journal of Anthropological Research* 41 (2): 201–17.

Lomaʾomvaya, Micah, and T. J. Ferguson. 2003. Hisatqatsit Aw Maamatslalwa-Comprehending our Past Lifeways: Thoughts about a Hopi Archaeology. In *Indigenous People and Archaeology: Proceedings of the 32nd Annual Chacmool Conference*, ed. Trevor Peck, Evelyn Siegfried, and Gerald A. Oetelaar, 43–51. Calgary: Archaeological Association of the University of Calgary.

Lowenthal, David. 1989. The Timeless Past: Some Anglo-American Historical Preconceptions. *Journal of American History* 75 (4): 1263–80.

Malotki, Ekkehart. 1983. *Hopi Time: A Linguistic Analysis of the Temporal Concepts in the Hopi Language*. Amsterdam: Mouton.

Michel, Mark. 2006. Banned Books. In *Archaeological Ethics*, ed. Karen D. Vitelli and Chip Colwell-Chanthaphonh, 176–77. Lanham MD: AltaMira Press.

Munn, Nancy D. 1992. The Cultural Anthropology of Time: A Critical Essay. *Annual Review of Anthropology* 21:93–123.

Ricoeur, Paul. 1988. *Time and Narrative* 3. Chicago: University of Chicago Press.

Rubel, Paula G., and Abraham Rosman. 2003. Introduction: Translation and Anthropology. In *Translating Cultures: Perspectives on Translation and Anthropology*, ed. Paula G. Rubel and Abraham Rosman, 1–22. Oxford: Berg.

Sekaquaptewa, Emory, and Dorothy K. Washburn. 2004. They Go Along Singing: Reconstructing the Hopi Past from Ritual Metaphors in Song and Image. *American Antiquity* 69 (3): 487–513.

———. 2006. Metaphors of Meaning: In Mural Paintings, Pottery, and Ritual Song. *Plateau* 3 (1): 27–47.

Swann, Brian, ed. 2004. *Voices from Four Directions: Contemporary Translations of the Native Literatures of North America*. Lincoln: University of Nebraska Press.

Thomas, Julian. 1996. *Time, Culture, and Identity*. London: Routledge.

Whiteley, Peter. 2003. Do "Language Rights" Serve Indigenous Interests? Some Hopi and Other Queries. *American Anthropologist* 105 (4): 712–22.

———. 2008. Ethnography. In *A Companion to the Anthropology of American Indians*, ed. Thomas Biolsi, 435–71. Malden MA: Blackwell.

4

Hopi Place Value
Translating a Landscape

Peter M. Whiteley

Place-names are arguably among the most highly charged and richly evocative of all linguistic symbols. Because of their inseparable connection to specific localities, place-names may be used to summon forth an enormous range of mental and emotional associations—associations of time and space, of history and events, of persons and social activities, of oneself and stages in one's life. And in their capacity to evoke, in their compact power to muster and consolidate so much of what a landscape may be taken to represent in both personal and cultural terms, place-names acquire a functional value that easily matches their utility as instruments of reference.—KEITH BASSO, *Wisdom Sits in Places*

Introduction

In Hopi discourse, important ideas and processes involving cultural and historical order are localized and commemorated in the landscape and are indexed by place-names. Events happened at particular places: in Hopi oral history, knowing *where* something happened is an important part of knowing *that* it happened. As texts, some named places are interconnected, while others are more independent (on related Pueblo geographic sensibilities, see, e.g., Harrington 1916; Ortiz 1969, 1972; Silko 1999). Some texts are sociological, others historical, some mythological, others political, economic, religious, or ecological (cf. Thornton 2008 on Tlingit place-names). Like Hopi personal names, Hopi place-names individuate (see Whiteley 1992, 2008, in press): there are relatively few duplicates, and those that there are often index iconic symbols, such as a shrine at the edge of a village named after a particular mountain.

At Paqaptsokvi: Coyote and Red-tailed Hawk

In 1995, I was asked to assist the BBC in making a film that would include a focus on the Hopi water crisis. Peabody coal mine's pumping of aquifer water, as well as increased domestic uses, had begun to threaten the life of the Hopi springs. Springs are especially resonant places in Hopi thought, are almost all individually named, and form the principal focus in some major ceremonies, like those of the Flute societies, which have springs dedicated to their use. The drying up of powerful Flute springs like Tawapa, 'sun spring,' at First Mesa, Masìipa, 'gray spring,' below Songòopavi, Leenangwva, 'flute spring,' below Orayvi, and even Toriiva, 'twist spring'—the formerly abundant spring, seen in many old photographs, used by the Flute societies of Musangnuvi—is a dramatic instantiation of Hopi loss of powerful places and the array of cultural, including linguistic information that they anchor. I asked Herschel Talashoma of Paaqavi village on Third Mesa if there was somewhere that he would be willing to talk about in this connection. He thought about it for a while, and came up with the importance of one spring that has been drying up: Paqaptsokvi (literally, 'reeds bush place'), north of Paaqavi on Third Mesa.

Except in the sense that all springs have sacred value, Paqaptsokvi is not a ceremonial spring. But Herschel's evocation of its importance says a great deal about Hopi place values in general. Herschel is blind, and Paqaptsokvi is not easy to get to. For the last quarter mile I was his hapless (by no means fearless) guide, as, followed by a film crew, we stumbled down a steep, sandy slope below the top of a mesa edge to reach the spring, with its clump of reeds and willows on a ledge above a side canyon to the Oraibi Valley. He proceeded to tell the story of this place in relation to the importance of springs in general to Hopis, and how they do not want their water used for the slurry. As often is the case with great storytellers, he made a connection with a traditional tale, with its own embedded song, and showed how this place and its name could evoke a whole array of remembered and precious knowledge.[1] This is what he told:[2]

Kwakwháy. Piw taalawva.
Thank you. Another day has dawned.

Nu' Herschel Talashoyiwma. Nu' honanwungwa. Paaqavit angqw nu'.
My name is Herschel Talashoma. I am a member of the Badger clan.
I am from the village of Paaqavi.

Nu' yep umumi hiisavat yu'a'àykuni.
I am going to talk to you briefly here.

I' yepeq paahu: Paqaptsokvi.
Right at this place there is a spring [named] Paqaptsokvi [reed
bush place].

I' sùukya yang paavahut angqw amumum.
This is one of several springs in this vicinity.

Pay pi yang aqwhaqami paahu tsoykitota.
You see, all along through here the water is flowing out through
springs like that.

Pay pu' pi'um nanap maamatsiwya: Paaqavi; Höwiipa; Ho'atvela;
Laputsqavö.
And also each spring actually has its own individual name: Paaqavi
['reeds (spring)']; Höwiipa ['mourning dove spring']; Ho'atvela
['juniper slope (spring)']; Laputsqavö ['juniper bark pond']

Pay nu' hikikw tungwaata.
I have named just a few of them.

I'í yang paavahu tsoykitota.
These springs are flowing around here.

Pay i'í sòosokmuy hìituy amungem yang yanyungwa.
So all of these places around here are for the benefit of every living
thing.

Muumuy'ingwt pew hikwmanta. Maamàakyam.
Farmers come here to drink. Hunters.

Pu' ima piw tuutuvosipt.
And the game animals.

Pu' pay ima aapiy soosoy hìitu tsiròot, masa'yyùngqam. Pas sòosoy hìitu taayungqam yang pew it aw hiihikwya.
And all the other [living things]: birds, the other winged creatures [flying insects]. In fact every living being [that needs water] comes here to drink.

Pu' pay peetuy piw i' makvìikya'am. Pay yang pam makvìikya piw pumuy amungem.
And for some others [including humans, owls, hawks, crows, etc.] this is their hunting area. This is the hunting ground for them also.

Noqw oovi soosoyam ita' it aqw mongvasya.
So, all of us [humans, animals, and other life-forms] are benefiting from [the water at] this [place].

Pu' ima peetuy hìituy pokmuyyùngqamuy piw peqw puma hiihikwnaya—kawaymuy, moomorotuy, kanelmuy.
And some others who have livestock—horses, donkeys, and sheep—they also water them here.

Pu' yep atkya'a tukwìwya pep piw palakwayo sutsep tìiqatsngwu.
Also down below here there is an outcrop of rocks [little butte] where the red-tailed hawk always makes its nest [sits on her eggs].

Pu' akwningya hoop ooveq pu' mongwu piw sutsep qatu.
And above there to the north, and a little to the northeast, a great horned owl is always present.

Pumuy yang i'í himu'am.
This place along here is theirs.

Noqw oovi it paahu pas himu.
And so this spring is really important/precious.

* * *

Noqw, ura tuuwutsit ep panta Palakwayo niqw Iisaw.
Remember the story of Red-tailed Hawk and Coyote.

Pay pi sonqa pep naap hisat kya pam hiniwti, Palakwayo.
Now perhaps this is where that story actually happened, with Red-
tailed Hawk.

* * *

Su'its talavay, pi ooveq tsokilkyangw tawlawngwu.
Early in the morning, [Red-tailed hawk] perches on top of that outcrop and sings.

Pu' Iisaw put navotqw put aw kwangwa'ytuswa.
And when Coyote heard that, she [Coyote is here identified as fe-
male] was envious.

Pu' put aw hapi Iisaw kwangwa'ytuswangwu nìiqe pu' pam hisat put
aw tuuvingta:
She envied her so much [HT explains: Coyote envied everything
she had observed Red-tailed Hawk do—sitting high up on the nest,
singing, flying down off the nest and almost hitting the ground before swooping up, etc.] that one day she [could not help herself and]
asked her:

"Pay yaw sonqa tutuwnani, pay yaw sonqa aw unangwtapni."
"Will you help me and show me how to do all you can do?"

Pu' antsa pam put tatawkwusna, taawi'yva.
So she [Red-tailed Hawk] agreed, and [specifically] to teach her how
to pick up the [Red-tailed Hawk's] song.

Pu' pam put supki aqw wupna. Oomiq wupna nakwhanaqe.
So she helped her climb up into [that spot]. [Red-tailed Hawk] con-
sented to help her [Coyote] climb way up to the highest point [where
Red-tailed Hawk perches to sing].

Pàasat pu' puma tawlawu. Yan tawlawu.
And then they sang. This is how they sang:

Pu' kur huvam umùutimuy kuyvaman ayaalaawu'uu
Please tell your [pl.] children to keep going to pray toward the
rising sun

Ura sonwayningwuu
Remember how beautiful it usually is

ayám hapi Palatkwape'e
Over there at Palatkwapi

Palaakwayo timuy hoohoyintangwu, ura'i'
There, remember, the Red-tailed Hawk raises her young ones

Ura wungwye' tuutunglayiningwu
Remember, when they grow up to adulthood, they are really admired
for their beauty [/become highly desirable]

Ha'oo, taalti, taalti
Oh yes, it has become daylight, it has become daylight

Ha'oo, taalti, taalti
Oh yes, it has become daylight, it has become daylight

Kwaay!
[The hawk's cry]

* * *

Yan tawlat töqpit, pu' pam pangqw atkyamiq puuyaltingwu.
That's the way she [Red-tailed Hawk] cries her song. Then she takes
off from there and flies downward.

Tutskwamiq qatongokpu' pay pi ahoyningwu.
She barely touches the ground, then she flies back up again [to the
nest].

Put Iisaw kwangwa'ytuswo.
It was all that which Coyote envied.

Pu' pam put antsa aw hisat akw wupnaqe.
So one day she [Red-tailed Hawk] indeed helped [Coyote] climb
up there.

Hopi Place Value   89

Pu' puma tawlawq pu' puma angqw naama.
After they sang, then they both [took off] from there together.

Palakwayo puuyaltiqw pu' Iisaw angqw tso'o.
Red-tailed Hawk flew off, but Coyote [only] jumped off.

Noqw Iisaw piw qamasaytaqe pam pi pay pangqw pas qa atsat tso'.
Since the Coyote does not have wings, all she could do was jump.

Posqe pay pam súmoki.
She fell all the way down [hit the ground], and died instantly.

Supos yama angqö. Tuwat ang lengi'at púhikiwta. Nú'an pono piw.
Her tongue was lying out along the ground. Her eyeballs popped out.
And her stomach [was split open] too.

Yan pam pay qatsiy pep kuyva.
This is how [Coyote's] life ended there.

* * *

I' hapi yanyùngqa tùutuwutsi.
This is the kind of story [that applies to this place].

Yan it Paqaptsokvit anyungqat ang hapi pam yukiwyungwa.
These are the kinds of stories made from places like Paqaptsokvi
[HT explains: "the places themselves give rise to the stories."]

Niqw oovi put itam hopisinom tùutuwutsiyangwu.
On account of [places like] this, we Hopis tell stories.

Noqw oovi i' yang paavahu, kuuyi pas itamumi himu.
And so these springs and the water around here are very precious/
sacred to us.

Pas kur hin itam qapaahu'yyungwa.
We just *have to* have water.

Niqw oovi pu' yangqw ura itaatutskway angqw haqami owakot
kuuyit aqw oo'oyaya.

And now remember, they are shipping coal [by use of] water from our land to some destination.

Noqw itam put qa naanawakna.
We really do not want that.

Itam qa, itàakuyi haqami hintsaknani qa ooviyo.
Because we do not want to lose our water.

Ispi kuuyi pas himu'.
Because water is very, very precious.

Kuuyi súlawtiqw sòosoy hìitu taayungqam, soosoy himu taayungqa, súlawtini.
When water is gone, everything that is alive will be gone.

Pu' itam piw sinom kuuyi súlawtiqw itam sòosoyam nawus sonqa tupqölmiyan.
When the water is gone all of us people will have to go to the graveyard.

Yantaq oovi i' yang paavahu tsoykitotaqe itamumi pas himu.
That is the reason why these springs that are flowing around here are very precious to us.

Thus this place and its name embody an array of salient cultural in-formation that motivates the Hopi literary imagination and other forms of symbolic thought and practice. A fuller understanding of Hopi narra-tives requires that translation incorporate sensibilities of the landscape, and how these articulate with Hopi conceptions and representations of it. In keeping with many other Native American place-naming conven-tions, conceptualizations of the landscape and its value are distinctive in some significant ways.

Hopi Country

The Hopi landscape is a living theater. The same might of course be said for many human habitats—rural or urban, narrow or broad, arid or lush—but Hopitutskwa has its particular redolence. At times and in some places

sacred, at others mundane, it resonates with the inherited words and actions of an endless sequence of generations. That social quality is graphi-
cally displayed in a ceremony: the oldest priests, often in their eighties,
head a line of performers, which descends to the youngest at the other
end. Imagining when the eldest were the youngest, at the end rather than
the beginning, with their own lifetime's elders ahead of them, is to see the
continuity of Hopi culture stretching back to chartless points in the ancestral past. Every ceremony originated at some distant point or village
and was originally brought into the villages by its in-migrating owners.
A rooted, abiding sense of place articulates Hopi culture, with its interdependence of elaborate symbolic forms with pragmatic attention to the
reproduction of life in a harsh, infrequently watered landscape. In the
present, in quotidian practices, in ritual dramas that recapitulate ancestral arrivals of particular clans into a village, and in a vast canon of songs
and stories, words and gestures, Hopis reiterate and replay their love for
and accumulated comfort with that landscape, which though often difficult, was their appointed destiny, the place that would sustain them.
Hopi origin narratives emphasize the deliberate choice their ancestors
made in seeking out this particular landscape. This is their center, here
at Tùuwanasavi, 'earth center place,' where they emerged from the world
below, and to which, following clan migrations, they returned when their
destinies were complete, following the instructions received upon emergence from the deity of this earth, and the true owner of this particular
landscape, Maasaw.

This is unusual for a North American landscape: with its relentless pur-
suit of the new, the dominant society celebrates differentiation from the
past and values restless movement: its historical consciousness is mostly
rather slight, pivoting on capsule transformative events little more than
two centuries old. Many Native Americans, on the other hand, who have
palpably deeper ties to the land, were displaced, deracinated, or acculturated within recent memory. The Hopis continue to dwell, in a mostly
sedentary fashion, where they have since prehistoric times: many of their
practices have direct archaeological antecedents stretching back more
than two thousand years. Hopi historical consciousness, while perhaps
"cold" in Lévi-Strauss's sense, ever absorbing unfolding events into pre-
existing paradigms of significance, ironically achieves that status by its
very depth and continuity, in contrast to the shallow yet supposedly "hot"
and more authentically historical consciousness of the dominant society.

From several of the mesa-top villages (especially Wàlpi on First Mesa, Songòopavi, Musangnuvi, and Supawlavi on Second, and Orayvi on Third), one-hundred-mile vistas extend in a broad quadrant south and southwest, to the snowcapped San Francisco Peaks and the Mogollon Rim. Within a short distance of the villages, further expanses open up in other directions: northward up the peninsular-like mesas stands Big Mountain on Black Mesa; farther northwest lies Navajo Mountain (not, it should quickly be said, its Hopi name) on the banks of the Colorado River near Lee's Ferry; west toward the village of Mùnqapi, toothed ridgelines of the Grand Canyon's rims appear on the horizon marking the far edge of the observable world. Sitting by tethered eagles on a rooftop at Musangnuvi on a clear day, one's distant gaze is uninterrupted for almost all 360 degrees around the circle.

From the Hopi mesas to the horizon the country intervening is mostly treeless, except for scattering armies of junipers and piñons on the mesa-tops at the higher elevations. Where there is more water, as along the Keam's Canyon Wash, at Wepo Springs on First Mesa, on the Moenkopi Wash near Mùnqapi village, or at Pasture Canyon north of Tuba City, the verdant abundance of life contrasts sharply with the yellow-red sandstones, yellow-white sands, and yellow-gray clays that mark the broader environs. Here rather strings of emerald-leaved cottonwoods, lush patches of cattails and reeds, and sporadic willows produce a vibrant green-black ribbon—like the embroidered margin along the otherwise plain expanse of a woven Hopi *pitkuna*, 'ceremonial kilt.' And at harvest time, unwrapping from their husks ears of Hopi corn—that other gift of water in the sere high desert—the indigos, burgundies, blacks, whites, purples, yellows, and "Indian corn" multicolors emerge as jewels from a box, astonishing in their brightness.

To the south of the Hopi mesas, the broad valley spaces carved through by the major Hopi Washes—Jeddito, Polacca, Wepo, Oraibi, and Dinnebito—are intersected by a moonscape of massive, precipitous volcanic plugs (the Hopi Buttes), where golden eagles, red-tailed hawks and other raptors make their home.[3] Pronghorn antelopes and deer pass among them, and in the past, mountain sheep also;[4] coyotes, rattlesnakes, badgers, and most of the other species appearing in Hopi clan names, totems, and stories still do. On most days of summer, fall, and winter, when there is no wind—which blows without cease in the springtime—these vistas sparkle with life in the bright high plateau sunlight. D. H. Lawrence did not much enjoy his trip to the Snake Dance in 1922. Adjectives announcing his distaste are littered almost ritually through the account. The Hopi Reservation, he began,

> consists of a square tract of grayish, unappetizing desert, out of which rise three tall, arid mesas, broken off in ragged, pallid rock. On the top of the mesas perch the ragged, broken, grayish pueblos, identical with the mesas on which they stand. . . .
> It is a parched, grey country of snakes and eagles. . . .
> [The Hopi] has the hardest task, the stubbornest destiny. Some inward fate drove him to the top of these parched mesas, all rocks and eagles, sand and snakes, and wind and sun and alkali. (Lawrence 1924:685–91)

A plodding drumbeat of "grey, old, heavy, parched, pallid, arid" saturates his narrative. This view (from my fellow English Midlands native)—which I first read some years after beginning to work at Hopi—I could never fathom: "light, bright, deft, and vibrant" seem—not always, but mostly—much more apposite tropes for the Hopi landscape and its ceremonies. It was as if pounding, blunting terms, framed in a primitivist tableau, might tame and stultify a landscape and culture Lawrence found unsettling. The August sun at midday can indeed appear to blast out all color, and others reared in wooded landscapes often find the stark high-desert Southwest too much for their vision to bear. But to see the shimmer of pale azure lift off cool golden sand in the dawn light, as bright red and yellow wildflowers open multi-hued petals with *siitala*, 'flower light,' against the dark ground of a greasewood patch—or bright white and dark thunderheads marching across a turquoise sky scattering *yoyleki*, 'rain patches moving in lines across the landscape,' and stirring the bent-over corn leaves to gather their crystal raindrops and dance in the breeze—is to bear witness to a landscape saturated with vibrant life and both subtle and sharp color. These are the high-desert Colorado Plateau colors that perhaps no non-Hopi painter (with the possible exception of Louis Akin) has captured so well as that master from Songòopavi's Bluebird clan, Fred Kabotie.

Hopitutskwa

The present Hopi Reservation comprises a small fraction of Hopitutskwa, Hopi aboriginal land (see maps 4-1 and 4-2). As a defined area marked by shrines, the perimeters of Hopitutskwa have been most clearly described by traditional leaders at the mother village, Songòopavi. In 1930 to the president and members of Congress, and again in 1951 in a petition to the Indian Claims Commission, the Kikmongwi and the Wimmomng-wit (religious society leaders) described the area of Hopitutskwa. Beginning with Tokòonavi (possibly archaic for 'dark mountain,' Navajo Mountain in English), the course follows Pisisvayu (possibly 'river of echoing sounds [between canyon walls],' the Colorado River) to its junction with Sakwavayu ('blue river,' the lower Little Colorado), to the site of Sipà-apuni,[5] the emergence place, thence to Kòoninhahàwpi ('Havasupai descent trail'—the shrine Potavetaqa, 'the one with the basketry-mark petroglyph,' or migration-spiral symbol, is nearby), thence up Cataract Creek to Tusaqtsomo ('grass hill,' or Bill Williams Mountain), south to Hoonàwpa ('bear springs'), southeast to the Mogollon Rim at Yot.se'hahàwpi ('Apache descent trail,' the head of Chevelon Creek), northeast to Tsimòntukwi ('jimson-weed butte,' Woodruff Butte), northeast up the Puerco River to Namituyqa ('two points facing each other,' near Lupton), northwest to Nayavuwaltsa ('adobe gaps,' Lolomai Point), north to Kawestima (a Keresan-derived name for northern mountain, referring in Hopi to the Tsegi Canyon area), and north back to Tokòonavi.

Within Hopitutskwa there are multiple types of sites, used on a daily or periodic basis. Some are for farming, others for gathering, hunting, or grazing. There are myriad named ruins within this area; each belongs to one or a group of matrilineal clans—like Bear, Spider, Badger, Sun, Eagle, or Bow—which trace their migrations through past occupancy of such sites. There are numerous spring shrines (cf. Fewkes 1906; Stephen 1936:1076–77), other types of shrines, and clan eagle-gathering territories. Boundary shrines are guarded by ancestral spirits; religious leaders periodically make *homviikya* pilgrimages (a course of shrine visitations) to these sites to renew them and draw in their power to the centers of contemporary settlement. Hopitutskwa is not only a geographic space, it is this level of a tripartite sacred cosmography. Mountains, like Nuvatukyaʼovi ('snow butte on top place,' the San Francisco Peaks), and Aalosaqa ('the Two-Horn deity,' Humphrey's Peak in the San Francisco Peaks), and other high or moist places, like Kiisiwu ('shadow springs' near Pinon), are especially sacred. Four comprise comparable exterior directional shrines to the Rio Grande Tewa pattern (see Ortiz 1969): Tokòonavi in the northwest and Nuvatukyaʼovi in the southwest are two of these: the

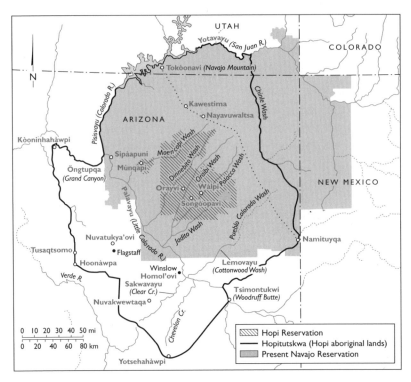

Map 4-1. Hopi lands

others lie at Kiisiwu on northeastern Black Mesa, and Weenima, the same site as "Zuni heaven" near the confluence of the Zuni and Little Colorado rivers in the southeast. These sites are particularly referenced in certain types of religious songs. It is from such areas that Hopi religious practitioners seek especially to draw moisture, and renew the life-forms toward the center of Hopitutskwa. Hopi responsibility to Hopitutskwa was vouchsafed when they arrived via Sípàapuni, the emergence place. Within this often sacred landscape, places are spoken of repeatedly in traditional narratives, sung of and to in songs, visited in pilgrimages, and renewed throughout the seasonal calendar of the Hopi ritual year.

Translating Native North American Place-names

Formal study of Native American place-names in relation to cognition and geographic environment goes back to Boas's earliest work in Baffinland (F. Boas 1885, 1888:643–48, 662–66).[6] Concerned especially with the intersection of psychology with geography, Boas recorded more than

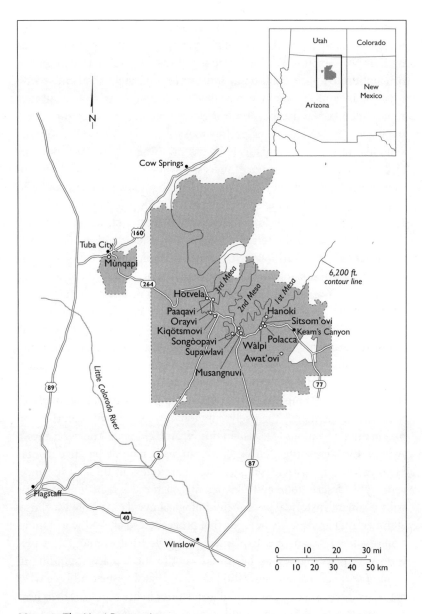

Map 4-2. The Hopi Reservation

nine hundred Inuit place-names (N. Boas 2004:59–60) and argued that these were more truly reflective of geographic forms than names imposed by European explorers, simultaneously disclosing a different cognitive orientation to space. Baffinland Inuit were intimately acquainted with topography and habitually externalized cognitive maps that accurately represented the landscape—both in snow drawings for each other preparatory to travel, and in paper drawings for Boas (F. Boas 1885). Yet despite his subsequent sophisticated work on Kwakwaka'wakw toponymy (F. Boas 1934), and the works of successors, like Sapir (1912) and perhaps most notably Waterman (1920) on Yurok geography, linguistic and ethnographic studies uniting spatial cognition with place-forms and ideas remained largely undeveloped until very recently (cf. Levinson 1996). The late renaissance of interest in indigenous systems within and beyond the Americas (e.g., Kari 1989; Hirsch and O'Hanlon 1995; Basso and Feld 1996; Johnson 2000; Solomon 2000; Samuels 2001; Cowell and Moss 2003; Rudes 2005; Yong 2007; Thornton 2008) owes in no small part to the work of Keith Basso on Western Apache (e.g., Basso 1996). Basso's magisterial synthesis of philosophical implication with ethnographic detail, linguistic forms and utterances, and sociolinguistic contexts has convincingly demonstrated the semantic depth and imaginative power of Native place-naming, and the interpretive inadequacy of only denotative translation. Basso (1996) emphasizes the textual and narrative qualities of place-names: that the names themselves metonymize extensive cognitive and pragmatic associations (see also in this regard Feld 1996; Thornton 2008). Apache and some other Native American place-naming practices (notably those of other Athapaskan speakers) are often, in the first instance, geographic descriptions, and allow mental-pictorial associations of places with resonant historical and/or mythological events. As Lola Machuse, summarizing an Apache dialogue that proceeded solely by the instantiation of a few place-names, explained: "We gave [that woman] clear pictures with place-names. So her mind went to those places, standing in front of them as our ancestors did long ago. That way she could see what happened there long ago. She could hear stories in her mind, perhaps hear our ancestors speaking. She could recall the knowledge of our ancestors" (quoted in Basso 1996:82–83).

Hopi Landforms and Characteristics

A comprehensive picture of Hopi geographic terms is beyond the scope of this chapter. But to get a flavor of how Hopi phenomenology selects among landscape forms, let me mention some typical terms that recur frequently in place-names. *Tutskwa* ('a large land space') is combined with another morpheme to form Hopitutskwa (Hopiland) and Wùukotutskwa ('a large plain'): there are several of the latter as place-names. *Tuukwi* ('butte') is combined with a modifier to form Yatkuntukwi ('Saddle Butte'), or Isvavtukwi ('coyote springs butte,' Pyramid Butte on USGS maps) south of the Hopi Mesas. *Tuyqa*, the promontory or point of a mesa that sticks out into a valley, occurs frequently: Songòotuyqa, 'sand grass point,' Antuyqa, 'ant point,' and Masatuyqa, 'wing/bird point,' fringe the Oraibi Valley. *Tuwi* represents what is called 'a cliff' in English, as in Hukyatwi, 'windy cliff' on the edge of Moenkopi Plateau, or Ponotuwi, 'stomach-shaped cliff,' on Second Mesa north of Musangnuvi. *Tupqa* ('deep canyon') combines with the morpheme for salt to form Öngtupqa ('salt canyon' in the Grand Canyon) or Lenaytupqa ('flute canyon,' Tsegi Canyon), both destinations of ritual pilgrimage. Etymologically, all these forms share an initial morpheme, *tu-* or *tuu-*, whose underlying meaning appears to refer to land, landforms, or landscape. In *tuuwa* it refers to earth and is frequently translated 'sand': Tuwangyam, the 'Sand clan,' has some particular ritual responsibilities with certain types of sand; Tuuwanasavi, earth center place, represents the central gathering point to which all the Hopi clans, after their migrations, were destined to return—it is also a specific place-name for a point a few miles south of Orayvi.

Pa- (modified in postposition to *-va*), from *paahu*, 'natural water/ spring,' appears in several geographical morphemes referring to water features. *Paayu* (*-vayu* as a suffix), 'river,' is modified to designate specific rivers: Sakwavayu, 'Blue/green River,' a section of the Little Colorado River, and also the name for Clear Creek; or Yotavayu, 'Ute River,' the San Juan River. *Paahu* (combinatory suffix form is *-pa* or *-va*), referring particularly to a spring, is very common in place-names, an index of the biological and social importance of such features: for example, Tawapa, 'sun spring,' Isva, 'coyote spring,' or Kookyangwva, 'spider spring,' all of which appear in several places as spring names. *Patupha*, a lake or other large water surface (including the ocean), appears in Wuukopatupha, 'big lake,' and Paapatupha, 'several lakes,' near the confluence of the Polacca and Oraibi Washes.

Waala (gap or notch in a mesa, combinatory *-wala* or *-wla*, pl. *-waltsa*) combines with other morphemes to form Kutsiwla ('lizard gap,' between the villages of Orayvi and Paaqavi) and Wàlpi ('gap place,' the village on First Mesa), or Nayavuwaltsa ('clay gaps,' on the north rim of Black Mesa).

Pöso refers to a corner or box canyon in a mesa wall (Spanish 'rincon'); for example, Wisokvösö, 'buzzard rincon,' between Orayvi and Hotvela, or Pöpsöva, 'rincons spring,' near Keam's Canyon. *Pööva* is a wash or arroyo; for example, Pongsikvöva, 'circle canyon wash,' the Keam's Canyon Wash. *Tsomo* ('hill, mound') appears in place-names like Kiqötsmovi ('ruins hill place') or Sitsom'ovi ('flower mound above place'), villages on Third and First Mesa, respectively. *Hahàwpi*, 'descent place,' is suffixed to particular trails, like Yotse.hahàwpi, 'Apache descent trail,' on the Mogollon Rim leading down to Cibecue, where the Western Apache dwell. *Tataypi*, a lookout place on a high point (often a low mesa or ridge), combines to form specific toponyms: Kawaytataypi, 'place to look out for horses,' northeast of Mùnqapi village, where Hopis would go in the past to spy out their wandering horseherds; or Tasavtataypi, 'place to look out for Navajos,' southeast of Second Mesa. *Tsöqavö* refers to an artificially modified (dammed) catchment or drainage area by a spring, or a precipitation run-off area; Hopis build charcos and small dams to produce these ponds, used especially for watering livestock: Laputsqavö, 'juniper bark pond' northwest of Paaqavi is one of these. Cultivated features and other sites with particular value for exploitation of certain resources are also marked features: *paasa*, a field or garden, *-viikya*, an area for a specific activity, *tipkya*, literally a birthing or infant-rearing area, or *kiihu*, a house or dwelling area. Kwaawungwvasa, 'eagle clan field,' Makvìikya, 'hunting ground,' Kwaatipkya, 'an eagle-nesting area,' and Pavawkyayki, 'cliff-swallows nesting area' (usually under a cliff overhang), may all be thought of as intermediate between actual place-names and descriptions of typical activities that occur in particular locales: they may also serve as place-names, but not in such individuating ways as *tuutungwni*, 'names' proper.

Specific place-names carry a range of cultural information, of different types, including:

1. Visual perspective or vantage point on the landform itself: Nuvakwewtaqa, 'the one with the snow belt,' a low mesa near the Mogollon Rim near Chavez Pass—during the wintertime a line of snow gathers on a slope of this feature; Löhavutsotsmo, 'testicle[-shaped] hills,' the globular volcanic hills west of Leupp; Sustavangtukwi, 'southwesternmost butte,' one of the Hopi Buttes known in English as Montezuma's Chair.[7]

2. Presence of a particular natural resource: Paaqavi ('reeds,' the name of some springs that give one village its name), Pikya'ingwtsomo ('stone-axe [material-gathering] hill,' Wildcat Peak, northeast of Mùnqapi), Hunaptuyqa ('cliff-rose point,' Preston Mesa, north of Tuba City), Pangwuvi ('mountain sheep place,' No-Trail Mesa in the Dinnebito Valley),

3. Customary practices: Yoyvwutrukwanpi ('scalp-tanning place,' northwest of Orayvi), Kòoninhahàwpi ('Havasupai descent trail,' head of a south-rim Grand Canyon trail followed by Hopi visitors to Havasupai), Leenangwva ('flute-ceremony spring,' southwest of Orayvi), Navtakinva ('grooming spring,' a spring reserved for visitors from other villages to spruce themselves up before entering a village for a dance, east of Songòopavi).

4. Historical event(s) or period: Kaktsintuyqa ('many Katsinas point,' Monument Point, a mesa west of the lower Oraibi Wash), a place where Hopis took clandestine Katsina performances during the seventeenth-century Spanish Inquisition period; Tsa'aktuyqa ('crying point,' northeast of Orayvi, a reference to a Hopi battle with Navajos); Tavuptsomo ('Tavupu's hill,' west of Ganado, commemorating the place where Tavupu, a Wàlpi man, and others in a Hopi delegation were killed by Navajos in the mid-nineteenth century),

5. Deities or other ritual figures: Sa'lako ('Shalako spring,' a ceremonial spring near Tuba City); Pöqangwwawarpi ('the War Twins racetrack,' northwest of Orayvi); Kòokyangwso'wùuti ('Spider Grandmother,' northwest of Orayvi); Taawakookopölö ('Sun hump-backed flute player,' named for a petroglyph that marks a Katsina clan ruin northeast of Mùnqapi). In some cases, referents are to ritual practices at the site, in others, to aspects of socio-religious significance.

6. Sites of historical and/or legendary clan migrations: Kiisiwu ('shadow springs,' on northeast Black Mesa, for the Badger and Butterfly clans); Tokòonavi (above), notably for the Snake and Horn-Flute clans), Palatkwapi ('Red-walled place,' whose exact site is unknown but probably in the Salt River Valley, for numerous clans from the south); Homol'ovi ('round indentations on top place,' near Winslow, for the Sun, Water, and other clans); Sakwavayki ('blue river house,' Clear Creek ruin, Sun clan); Kwastapa, ('dripping penis spring,' north of First Mesa, for the Flute clan).

Connotative references vary by Mesa-group of villages, sometimes by clan, religious sodality, or other social constituency. Connotative layering is also significantly more profound for some places and their names than others (a universal feature of toponymy). Again reflecting Harrington on Tewa place-names, some Hopi names cannot be translated: Orayvi, the oldest continuously inhabited village in North America, only parses to 'place of the Oray rock,' and while this refers to a particular formation at the western edge of the village, no further meaning for Oray has been known to Hopis for a long time. Similarly, Musangnuvi has been variously parsed as 'place of the black man' or 'place where the pillars stand,' but these fail to translate the word itself, which likely refers to Musan, the village's legendary founder who is still represented in Katsina form.

Hopi Place-names as Descriptions

The resonances of Hopi place-names echo many of Basso's depictions of Apache toponymic usage. But Hopi, in keeping with other Pueblos, offers some distinctive differences to Apache toponymy, associated with differences in society, history, economy, and worldview. Apache name-forms are almost epigrammatic topographic descriptions: for example, "Gray Willows Curve Around A Bend," "Water Flows Down On A Succession Of Flat Rocks," or "Trail Extends Across A Red Ridge With Alder Trees" (Basso 1996:23, 46, 79). At first blush, descriptive types among Hopi place-names appear similar to Apache perspectives on the landscape; for example, Nuvatukya'ovi (above), 'snow piled on top place'; Tsinngava, 'water-droplets splashing spring,' on an escarpment of Moenkopi Plateau; Sunalatukwi, 'lone butte' (one of the Hopi Buttes), a volcanic plug sticking up from the plain; or Tu'oynaqvitata 'mosaic earrings [made from a grid of small squares of turquoise stuck onto a wood base, the overall effect linguistically metaphorized to a tight stack of corn kernels] patched to the ground,' for a particular sandstone outcrop whose surface is fractured like a game board. But while resonant, in contrast to Apache names, Hopi descriptions within names appear truncated, oblique, boiled down: they are less finely observed descriptive reports of physical form than matter-of-fact identifications of an obvious single characteristic. I venture this partly reflects qualitative differences between Hopi and Apache interactions with the landscape. Western Apache entrance into modern east-central and southern Arizona probably occurred within the last three hundred years (e.g., Gunnerson 1979; Opler 1983; Perry 1991). Western Apache adaptation includes some agriculture, but historically it was principally a foraging and raiding economy. Apaches were nomadic and traversed a broad area of the Southwest and northern Mexico, especially after their adoption of horses, by raiding Spanish settlements in the seventeenth and eighteenth centuries. The precision of geographic description that characterizes Apache place-names may owe in part to social imperatives deriving from these historical and cultural features. As Harrington (1916) remarks of a contrast between Tewa and Omaha toponymy: "Conversation with Mr. Francis La Flesche, student of the Omaha and other Siouan tribes, suggests interesting comparisons between the place-names of a sedentary pueblo tribe, as the Tewa, and those of a typical Plains tribe, the Omaha. It appears that the Omaha have fewer place-names than the Tewa, but more widely scattered and more lucidly descriptive" (Harrington 1916:97–98). Tewa names, on the other hand, include some with obscure, though identifiably Tewa, etymology: "A newly settled country has its St. Botolph's Towns, a country in which a language has long held sway its Bostons. The occurrence of a considerable sprinkling of obscure names argues for the long habitation of Tewa-speaking Indians" (Harrington 1916:95).

Like Rio Grande Tewas, Hopis or their direct ancestors have been present in their specific landscape of northern Arizona continuously for at least a millennium and a half, and probably a lot longer. Hopi adaptation, while far more dependent on foraging—especially collecting wild plants and minerals, and hunting or trapping game—than is typically acknowledged in the anthropological literature, is principally agricultural. Hopi settlement is thus predominantly sedentary. Hopis continue an age-old practice of frequent distant travel within and beyond Hopitutskwa (map 4-1; see also Whiteley 1989)—to collect resources (for food, medicines, rituals, and manufactures) and to visit multiple clan and religious-society shrines.

In his seminal work on Pueblo worldview, Alfonso Ortiz (1972:137) keyed Pueblo cosmological orientation to four general principles: boundaries, levels, centers, and centripetality.

[The pueblos] all set careful boundaries to their world and order everything within it. These boundaries are not the same but, more important, the principles of setting boundaries are since all use phenomena in the four cardinal directions, either mountains or bodies of water, usually both, to set them. In pre-Newtonian fashion, all believe that the universe consists of three cosmic levels with some applying the principle of classification by fours to postulate multiple underworld levels, either four or a multiple of four. . . . [T]he pueblos attempt to reproduce this mode of classifying space on a progressively smaller scale. . . .

All the Pueblos also have a well-elaborated conception and symbolization of the middle or center of the cosmos, represented by a sipapu, an earth navel, or the entire village. . . . [T]he center is the point of intersection of the six directions, with a seventh being the center itself. . . .

. . . [D]ominant spatial orientation as well as that of motion, is centripetal or inward. That is to say, all things are defined and represented by reference to a center. The contrast has often been noted between the Pueblos and the Navajo, who have a dominant centrifugal orientation. Thus a Pueblo priest, when setting out a dry painting, will first carefully set out the boundaries, and then work his way *inward* toward the center. The Navajo singer, on the other hand, will work *outward* from the middle. (Ortiz 1972:142–43)

Ortiz's (1969:18–20) more specific representation of Tewa cosmic space emphasized concentric tetrads. Moving from the perimeter inward, aligned to the cardinal directions, the tetrads are configured by four sacred mountains, four flat-topped hills, four principal shrines on the village outskirts, and four dance plazas within the village. A critical element of Ortiz's analysis is that the four principles are not merely topological schemas but are grounded in specific named places in the landscape (1969:19). In this regard, Ortiz confirmed Harrington's painstaking examination of Tewa ethnogeography. The Tewa, Harrington found, had myriad placenames scattered over the landscape, in concentrations radiating out from particular villages. Tewa toponymic knowledge was particular, with most individuals only familiar with names within a limited radius of their communities. But for all, the place-names anchored social thought, daily life, and religious concerns in a landscape they made intelligible—both discursively and practically.

Ortiz's emphasis on boundaries, centers, and centripetal orientation is palpable in both quotidian and sacred Hopi usages of the landscape. Hopis travel by foot, horse, or nowadays mostly by pickup to distant locations for important resources to bring back into the village centers. This includes the gathering of *nepni*, 'greens,' *hekwpa*, 'spruce branches,' *palatuwa*, 'red sand,' *ööga*, 'salt,' and *kwaatu*, (fledgling) 'golden eagles.' It is also embodied in hunting practices: Hopi men travel to specific *maqviikya*, 'hunting grounds,' for *tsööviw*, 'pronghorn antelope,' or *sowi'yngwa*, 'deer,' among other game. And Hopi priests visit distant *paavahu*, (sacred) 'springs,' to collect *kuuyi*, 'water,' for ceremonial purposes back in the village kivas or plazas. All of these resources are thus returned from distant peripheries to the community settlements at the center of the Hopi world. Similarly, religious prayers and songs seek to draw in, as if magnetically, rain- and snow-clouds from the sacred high points of the cardinal directions around the perimeter of Hopitutskwa to Hopi fields, springs, and villages. Metaphorical models of the universe and the landscape in ritual altars, village shrines, or kiva architecture echo Ortiz's sense that the Pueblos classify space "on a progressively smaller scale." As well as naming the most prominent mountains, Nuvatukya'ovi is the name for a kiva at Songòopavi and the name of a shrine at other villages. Just as Hopi personal names encapsulate actions and events of the living world and memorialize them in the intersubjective space through which Hopi personal identities are constructed (Whiteley 1992), when there are correspondences of the type mentioned, place-names serve to replicate the universe in miniature—and in ritual contexts, make it manageable, more subject to manipulation by intentional human actions, especially of a symbolic nature.

Hopi place-names and the places they designate and memorialize pervade Hopi consciousness of the landscape and the Hopi literary imagination. Organized cosmologically into borders and centers, specific places may carry multiple levels of significance. Through the inherited corpus of oral traditions, Hopis continually reiterate and reenact their covenant with Maasaw, who entrusted them to care for and renew this landscape when they first emerged from below. The reticulate interconnections of named places in Hopitutskwa carry memorate history and lived practice within them. Drawing the powers of life into the center from the periphery, and renewing the pulse of the landscape through the ritual calendar, Hopis visit, speak of, dramatize, and sing of their named localities. If all the world is a stage, Hopitutkswa is the living theater of Hopi action and the Hopi imagination: the very foundation of Hopi culture. To appreciate Paqaptsokvi springs from a Hopi viewpoint requires an engagement with the Hopi literary imagination. Understanding the place's significance requires attending to its inhabitation by, among others, Red-tailed Hawks and their behavior, quotidian and mythological, including singing the envious Coyote to her doom. Translating places is not merely a question of plotting names on a symbolic map; it means ascertaining the anchor points of Hopi thought and representation of being-in-the-world.

Notes

1. Herschel's narrative, alas, ended up on the cutting-room floor somewhere in darkest Manchester, England. The only part that remained in the film *The Hopi Way* (BBC 1996) was the song of Red-tailed Hawk, as sound track during the credits.

2. Transcription by Whiteley; initial translation by Talashoma, final translation (based on Talashoma's) by Whiteley.

3. Ives's description of his 1858 journey to Hopi is good here too: approaching the buttes from the south, he reported, "While advancing the Blue Peaks [Hopi Buttes] rose up in front, like ships approached at sea-some in cones and symmetrical castellated shapes, and others in irregular masses" (Ives 1861:115).

4. Hopis indicate that mountain sheep have recently begun to make a comeback in the upper reaches of the Hopi Washes on northern Black Mesa.

5. The etymology is obscure, but if originally Hopi—the same word as Sipapu, Shipap, etc., is used by the Rio Grande Pueblos too—it may refer, as earth navels for the Tewa, to an earthly crotch (*siip* in Hopi) or navel (*sipna*).

6. Thornton's (1997) useful summary marks Schoolcraft's (1845) work as a starting point. Boas, however, may be credited with transforming toponymic inquiry into a phenomenological analysis of the interaction between environment and cognition.

7. Boas's antipathy to replacing indigenous place-names with the often banal, decontextualized, or otherwise inappropriate terms of the colonizing society is resonant here.

References

Basso, Keith H. 1996. *Wisdom Sits in Places: Landscape and Language among the Western Apache*. Albuquerque: University of New Mexico Press.

Basso, Keith H., and Steven Feld, eds. 1996. *Senses of Place*. Santa Fe: School of American Research Press.

Boas, Franz. 1885. Baffin-Land. Geographische Ergebnisse einer in den Jahren 1883 und 1884 ausgeführten Forschungsreise. *Petermanns Mitteilungen aus Justus Perthes' Geographischer Anstalt* 31 Band, 80.

———. 1888. The Central Eskimo. *Annual Report of the Bureau of American Ethnology* 6:409–669.

———. 1934. Geographical Names of the Kwakiutl Indians. *Columbia University Contributions to Anthropology* 20.

Boas, Norman. 2004. *Franz Boas: A Biography*. Mystic CT: Seaport Autographs Press.

Cowell, Andrew, and Alonzo Moss. 2003. Arapaho Place Names in Colorado: Form and Function, Language and Culture. *Anthropological Linguistics* 45 (4): 349–89.

Feld, Steven. 1996. Waterfalls of Song: An Acoustemology of Place Resounding in Bosavi, Papua New Guinea. In *Senses of Place*, ed. K. H. Basso and S. Feld, 91–136. Santa Fe: School of American Research Press.

Fewkes, J. W. 1906. Hopi Shrines Near the East Mesa, Arizona. *American Anthropologist* 8:346–375.

Gunnerson, James. 1979. Southern Athapaskan Archaeology. In *Handbook of North American Indians*, vol. 9, *The Southwest*, ed. Alfonso Ortiz, 162–69. Washington DC: Smithsonian Institution.

Harrington, John. 1916. The Ethnogeography of the Tewa Indians. *Annual Report of the Bureau of American Ethnology* 29. Washington DC.

Hirsch, Eric, and Michael O'Hanlon. 1995. *The Anthropology of Landscape: Perspectives on Space and Place*. Oxford: Clarendon Press.

Ives, Lieutenant Joseph C. 1861. *Report upon the Colorado River of the West, Explored in 1857 and 1858*. Washington DC: Government Printing Office.

Johnson, Leslie Main. 2000. "A Place That's Good": Gitksan Landscape Perception and Ethnoecology. *Human Ecology* 28 (2): 301–25.

Kari, James. 1989. Some Principles of Alaskan Athapaskan Toponymic Knowledge. In *General and Amerindian Ethnolinguistics: In Remembrance of Stanley Newman*, ed. M. R. Key and H. M. Hoenigswald, 129–49. New York: Mouton de Gruyter.

Lawrence. D. H. 1924. The Hopi Snake Dance. *Theatre Arts Monthly* 8 (12): 836–60.

Levinson, Stephen C. 1996. Language and Space. *Annual Review of Anthropology* 25:353–82.

Opler, Morris. 1983. The Apachean Culture Pattern and its Origins. In *Handbook of North American Indians*, vol. 10, *The Southwest*, ed. Alfonso Ortiz, 368–92. Washington DC: Smithsonian Institution.

Ortiz, Alfonso. 1969. *The Tewa World: Space, Time, Being, and Becoming in a Pueblo Society*. Chicago: University of Chicago Press.

———. 1972. Ritual Drama and the Pueblo World View. In *New Perspectives on the Pueblos*, ed. A. Ortiz, 135–61. Albuquerque: University of New Mexico Press.

Perry, Richard. 1991. *Western Apache Heritage: People of the Mountain Corridor*. Austin: University of Texas Press.

Rudes, Blair. 2005. Place Names of Cofitachequi. *Anthropological Linguistics* 46 (4): 359–426.

Samuels, David. 2001. Indeterminacy and History in Britton Goode's Western Apache Placenames: Ambiguous Identity on the San Carlos Apache reservation. *American Ethnologist* 28 (2): 277–302.

Sapir, Edward. 1912. Language and Environment. *American Anthropologist* 14 (2): 226–242.

Schoolcraft, Henry Rowe. 1845. Comments, Philological and Historical, on the Aboriginal Names and Geographical Terminology of the State of New York. *Proceedings of the New York Historical Society,* for the year 1844, pp. 77–115.

Silko, Leslie Marmon. 1999. Landscape, History, and the Pueblo Imagination. In *At Home on the Earth: Becoming Native to our Place*, ed. D. L. Barnhill, 30–44. Berkeley: University of California Press.

Solomon, Thomas. 2000. Dueling Landscapes: Singing Places and Identities in Highland Bolivia. *Ethnomusicology* 44 (2): 257–80.

Stephen, Alexander M. 1936. *Hopi Journal.* Ed. Elsie Clews Parsons. Columbia University Press, New York.

Thornton, Thomas F. 1997. Anthropological Studies of Native American Place Naming. *American Indian Quarterly* 21 (2): 209–28.

———. 2008. *Place and Being among the Tlingit*. Seattle: University of Washington Press.

Waterman, T. T. 1920. Yurok Geography. *University of California Publications in American Archaeology and Ethnology* 16 (5): 177–314.

Whiteley, Peter M. 1989. *Hopitutskwa: An Historical and Cultural Interpretation of the Hopi Traditional Land Claim.* Expert Witness Report for the Hopi Tribe in Masayesva vs. Zah vs. James ("1934 Reservation case"). U.S. District Court, Phoenix AZ.

———. 1992. *Hopitutungwni*: "Hopi Names" as Literature. In *On the Translation of Native American Literatures*, ed. Brian Swann, 208–27. Washington DC: Smithsonian Institution Press.

———. 2008. The Orayvi Split: A Hopi Transformation. *Anthropological Papers of the American Museum of Natural History* 87.

———. 2009. Losing the Names: Native Languages, Identity, and the State. In *Language and Poverty*, ed. Wayne Harbert, Sally McConnell-Ginet, Amanda Miller, and John Whitman, 161–79. Clevedon, UK: Multilingual Matters.

Yong, Kee Howe. 2007. The Politics and Aesthetics of Place-names in Sarawak. *Anthropological Quarterly* 80 (1): 65–91.

5

Related-Language Translation
Naskapi and East Cree

Bill Jancewicz

Introduction
Translation for Minority Languages

While some theorists have suggested that translation is impossible (Payne 1971), to a large degree Western civilization and culture has depended upon translated documents originally written in one language into some other, usually more common, language. A large portion of our current understanding of philosophy, history, mythology, and religion comes to us through translated documents. What could we know of Aristotle, Plato, Moses, or Muhammad without contemporary translations of their writings into our mother tongue? From the philosophy of Immanuel Kant to the literature of Victor Hugo, the breadth of human knowledge is inextricably linked to the translation of documents from one language to another. Despite the claim that the deeper one analyses the linguistic science of translation on a theoretical level, the more impossible translation appears, translation remains a fundamental component of our understanding of the world. It follows then that translation must indeed be possible. It has been suggested that one reason for this is that translation is neither simply a science nor even an art but rather a craft; that is, it is a skill or a technique (Azizinezhad 2006) that can be developed, practiced, and taught.

There are two different translation issues actually at stake here. One is the translation of Native-language documents into majority languages, providing wider access to the knowledge, culture, and traditions of indigenous groups. The other is the translation of documents from outside the indigenous culture into the Native language. During the research for this chapter and over the course of the Naskapi language project, this writer has had opportunity to elicit responses from native Naskapi speakers on both issues. With regard to the translation of traditional Naskapi material such as legends or oral histories into the majority languages, one Naskapi speaker responded this way: "I never thought about it before. But for me I think it's good that we translate of [sic] our language and it's not stealing. Ex; some of our great-grand-children in the future may not speak the Naskapi language and might want to know the stories their grandfathers and grandmothers told. They will have it in their hands in English." And regarding those who would assert that translation of material from outside his own culture and traditions into the Naskapi language might be unethical, he writes: "I would say they are wrong, I'll take the Bible for example, it is OK that we translated it into our language so that our people (especially those who don't speak English) will learn more and more and read about God and Jesus. We learn from it and it teaches us how we should live our lives, the way God wants us to, etc. . . . The Bible makes us strong. That's one example."[1]

This writer acknowledges that for some in the academic community, the idea of translating religious materials into First Nations languages is problematic, questioning whether it is ethical for *any* translation take place for these languages at all. Over the years SIL International has come under criticism at least in part because of the religious motivation of its members.[2] Some of these criticisms surfaced in 2006 and 2007 regarding the SIL management of the ISO 639-3 standard, in connection with the language codes used in the Ethnologue, an encyclopedic reference work cataloging all of the world's known living languages. Although the International Organization for Standardization (ISO) invited SIL International to participate in the development of these standards and has authorized SIL International to be the registration authority for the administration of the standard,[3] in 2007 the Society for the Study of the Indigenous Languages of the Americas (SSILA) proposed a resolution advocating the creation of an alternative to SIL management of the ISO 639-3 standard because of some "colleagues who are reluctant to be associated with SIL for religious, social or political reasons" (Golla 2006).

While the Linguistic Society of America (LSA) devoted a portion of its January 2007 meetings to the question of missions and linguistics (symposium "Missionaries and Scholars: The Overlapping Agendas of Linguists in the Field"),[4] this merely underlines the fact that such controversies exist, and that some steps are being taken to clarify the various positions of each side in dialogue, which is commendable. Fostering a spirit of understanding and cooperation can undoubtedly benefit the speakers of these languages whom workers on both sides of this issue are striving to serve.

Indeed, the LSA is not the first to recognize the potentially complementary relationship between anthropologists and missionaries. In *The Slippery Earth*, Louise Burkhart describes a glimpse into the traditional Nahua worldview and culture that comes to light through a dialogue between the Nahuas and the Mendicant friars who came to minister to them:

> In order to apply an anthropological perspective to the missionaries' dialogue with the sixteenth-century Nahuas, the traditional enmity between the anthropologist and the missionary must be set aside. This is not, after all, so outrageous a proposition. Both anthropologists and missionaries engage in intercultural dialogue, in contexts where the contacted cultures tend to be in a materially and politically weak position relative to the culture represented by their visitors. Malinowski saw anthropologists and missionaries as "inverted twins," the missionary's role being to translate the European's point of view for the native, while the anthropologist's is to translate the native point of view for Europeans. The missionaries to the Nahuas were sent to do the former but also did quite a bit of the latter, for themselves as well as for a broader European audience. Distance in time enriches their records by providing a historical perspective usually lacking in modern field studies. (Burkhart 1989:9)

Although translating the Bible into minority languages is indeed one of the stated goals of the work of SIL International, it is not the only one. SIL International's Web site explains:

> Studying these languages results in practical help for local people and contributes to the broader knowledge of linguistics, anthropology, and ethnomusicology. SIL publishes its research and widely distributes it to libraries, universities, governments, and international agencies.

As a leader in the research of the world's endangered languages through language survey, SIL facilitates language development to prevent the extinction of language and culture.

SIL works in partnership with local speakers to adapt or translate literature for publication on subjects such as nutrition, farming, health (including HIV/AIDS), and some or all of the Bible. SIL's involvement and the scripture translation goals for each language are decided in close interaction with churches and communities, and often with other partnership groups or organizations.[5]

SIL International's work in developing and documenting languages has been shown to have a positive effect on the preservation of those languages as well as assisting language communities to meet their own literacy and developmental goals. Of course, such quotations of statements supporting SIL International as are found on their own Web site are all very well, but what about testimony from those in the academic community who are not connected with SIL? Geoffrey K. Pullum is perhaps the only person who is a life member of the Linguistic Society of America, the International Phonetic Association, and the American Philosophical Association. Dr. Pullum wrote in a *Linguist List* posting in early 2008 an obituary for SIL linguist Desmond Derbyshire:

Regardless of one's position on missionary work, one has to view the Hixkaryana as lucky that their first extended interaction with the modern world was this gentle missionary couple, Des and Grace. As is well known, many Amerindian groups in South America have been far less fortunate. Des loved the Hixkaryana people; he respected their intelligence, kindness, generosity, and practical skills; he delighted in their language; and he cared about their welfare. They have done well in the fifty years that Des knew them, and their society is far more robust than it was when Des and Grace arrived. From a demoralized population in danger of extinction in 1959, with only about a hundred members, few children, and high infant mortality, they grew to a population of about 350 in all by the time I met Des, and today there are about 600, with access to modern medicine, frequent intermarriage with the Waiwai tribe, and high literacy rates, and a school with Hixkaryana teachers, and a government-assisted Brazil nut business. (Pullum 2008)

William Foley is a linguist and professor at the University of Sydney who specializes in Papuan and Austronesian languages. He is best known for his 1986 book *The Papuan Languages of New Guinea*, where he writes:

> The most important event in the history of New Guinea research was the establishment in the mid-1950s of the Summer Institute of Linguistics, Papua New Guinea branch. . . . The overwhelming majority of descriptive linguistic studies of Papuan languages have been provided by SIL workers. Most of the references in the back of this book are by authors working within SIL. Without their exemplary efforts, our knowledge of Papuan languages would be much poorer indeed, and this book would certainly not have been possible. (Foley 1986:13)

These are just a few statements supporting the idea that workers with SIL International have made significant contributions to the study, development, and preservation of minority languages around the world. But with regard to the specific ethical question of the translation of documents from other traditions and cultures into the languages of indigenous peoples, this author feels that it would doing these language groups a disservice to deny them access to the rich tapestry and vast areas of human knowledge currently recorded only in the majority languages.

Translation of the Bible for Minority Languages

Criticism has been leveled at SIL International not because of its linguistics or language development work per se but rather because it operates as a faith-based organization whose staff "shares a Christian commitment to service, academic excellence, and professional engagement," according to their Web site.

While it may not be surprising that Bible translation work is censured by some, it can also be admitted that the Bible is a very influential, unique, and beneficial document. It follows that those who take issue with Christianity, missionary work, or proselytizing would object to Bible translation for minority languages. However, it has been shown that the stated long-term goals and desires of the speakers of these languages provide the impetus for Bible translation. In the early history of Bible translation into English, it was those who held economic and political power that fiercely resisted the translation of these words into the common language, not the speakers themselves. It is not the purpose of this chapter to debate further the ethics neither of Bible translation nor of the place of religion in the lives of First Nations people. Suffice it to say that this assistance is provided to the First Nations communities, as in minority language groups worldwide, at their express and informed invitation. Indeed, in most cases the translation work itself is carried out by the speakers of these languages.

In keeping with SIL International's principles, this writer's relationship with the Naskapi community was initiated at the request of Naskapi language speakers themselves. All of the major decisions regarding the involvement of SIL in the language development work and the translation process were made by Naskapi speakers. Indeed, the New Testament translation this chapter describes was carried on completely under the control and auspices of the Naskapi Development Corporation, an entity wholly owned and mandated by the Naskapi community.[6]

Naskapi Language Project Background

The Naskapi community of Kawawachikamach is populated by the formerly nomadic caribou hunters living in what is now northern Quebec and Labrador in the region south of Ungava Bay (see map 5-1). Although they have been settled in their own village since the early 1980s, they have only recently transitioned into a more sedentary lifestyle; prior to the mid-1950s they were still living on the land in temporary dwellings. In contrast, the East Cree language groups have generally had a longer period of settlement in communities.

The Western Naskapi language is a part of the Cree-Montagnais-Naskapi dialect continuum, a chain of closely related languages or dialects stretching from the Rocky Mountains in Alberta to the Atlantic shore in Labrador.[7] These languages or dialects share many linguistic features.

Naskapi Historical Background

Prior to Schefferville

For centuries the ancestors of the Naskapi were nomadic hunters, living off the land and following the caribou herds across the barren lands of what became northern Quebec and Labrador. Their earliest recorded contact with Europeans was in the 1830s when the Hudson's Bay Company first established trading posts in their territory (Cooke 1976). Initially, however, rather than trading with the newcomers, the Naskapi preferred to continue living off the land and following the caribou on which they depended for survival.

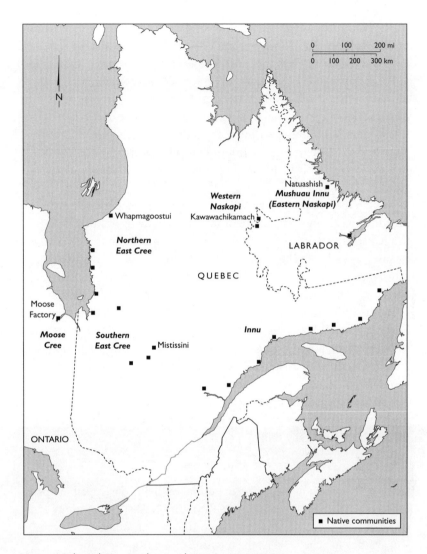

Map 5-1. Selected Cree-Naskapi and Innu communities

The Naskapis were presented with the extraordinary situation that here were strangers who had come uninvited and unwanted into their land. These strangers could not hunt, and needed the Indians' help in getting meat for the traders' own survival. Moreover, the traders expected the Indians to trade the furs of inedible animals at times when, owing to the difficulties of supply, the traders did not, in fact have enough goods to trade with them. (Cooke 1976:19)

The Hudson's Bay Company established the trading post at Fort Chimo on the Koksoak River in 1830. The Naskapi people eventually centered their trading activities at that post. The company closed the trading post at Fort Chimo in 1842 to open Fort Nascopie in Labrador. The Naskapi moved so they could do their trading there. "The Naskapis had by this date, as McLean [post manager] had forecast, become dependent on 'artificial wants' and were ever more dependent on guns and ammunition. They had therefore no choice but to follow his decision and to 'proceed to Fort Nascopie to which Post they are to be attached in future'" (Cooke 1976).

In 1870 the company closed Fort Nascopie and reopened Fort Chimo near the coast. The company relocated their trade operations from post to post solely according to their commercial motivations. The Naskapi themselves had little choice but to relocate. In each of these major migrations, they would travel by foot or canoe more than 250 across the mostly barren tundra. Even in the best times, food was difficult to come by.

In 1915 the company decided to open Fort McKenzie, halfway between Fort Chimo and Fort Nascopie. But in 1948, Fort McKenzie was closed, so the Naskapi moved back to Fort Chimo. None of these migrations had anything to do with caribou, which once was the Naskapi's primary reason to move.

The final major move was in 1956, when it was recommended to the Naskapi leaders to move to the Schefferville region after the opening of the Iron Ore Company mine.

At Schefferville

In the early 1950s a massive iron ore mine was being developed in northern Quebec. In the summer of 1956 the entire Naskapi community journeyed nearly 250 miles overland from the area around Fort Chimo on Ungava Bay to Schefferville, the townsite of the iron ore mine.

After initially living in their tents, then later at a settlement near John Lake (1956–72), and then on a government-built reservation called Matimekosh (1972–83), the Naskapi finally moved to a community of their own. After signing the Northeastern Quebec Agreement (NEQA) in 1976,[8] the Naskapi gained the resources and training required to build this community themselves, fourteen kilometers beyond Schefferville, called Kawawachikamach, in 1983. By 2010, Kawawachikamach had a population of more than nine hundred, and the community more than doubled in size and population since settling there.

Naskapi Language and the Bible

During the period of attachment to the various Hudson's Bay Company trading posts, Church of England clergy were often stationed at the trading posts. These ministers served the post workers, the Inuit, Cree, and the Naskapi. Generally, the Naskapi accepted their message and were faithful to the teachings of the church.

Early Cree Scripture Translation

Beginning in the late 1800s, Bishop John Horden and others began to translate the Bible into the some of the languages spoken around James Bay. Other Church of England ministers brought these Cree scripture portions with them when they visited the Naskapi at the trading posts. The Naskapi quickly learned to read and write using the Cree syllabic script, and adopted a local version of it as their own writing system.

Both Cree and Naskapi are written in slightly different variations of Canadian Aboriginal Syllabics, a non-roman writing system developed by James Evans in 1840 for the Cree- and Ojibwe-speaking people in what is now Ontario and Manitoba. The use of this writing system spread quickly across Canada during the latter half of the nineteenth century, with a large number of Bible translations and pieces of religious literature being published using this script (Evans 1985). While the Naskapi writing system (see figure 5-1) is similar to the writing system used for Cree, there are a few important differences. However, it was not until the early 1990s that any literature had ever been published in the Naskapi script or language. Consequently, the local Naskapi church never had its own scriptures or prayer book in Naskapi. Instead, during most of the twentieth century, Naskapi readers used materials that had been produced for the Cree groups by making orthographic and phonological adjustments and often translating from Cree into Naskapi "on the fly" during church services. Even though certain individuals became quite proficient at this process, these Cree materials remained out of reach for the majority of Naskapi speakers.[9]

Naskapi Bible Translation

In the late 1960s, linguists associated with SIL International surveyed the Native languages in eastern Canada and determined that Naskapi along with several other indigenous languages in Quebec presented significant

ᓇᔅᑲᐱ ᐃᔪᐤ ᐃᔨᑐᐅᓐ ᐊᐃᓯ ᒥᓯᓇᐃᒐᓄᐅᒡ

Naskapi Syllabic Chart

i / *ii* ᐃ	*u* / *uu* ᐅ	*a* / *aa* ᐊ			
wi / *wii* ·ᐃ		*wa* / *waa* :ᐊ	*w* ᐤ		
pi / *pii* ᐱ	*pu* / *puu* ᐳ	*pa* / *paa* ᐸ	*p* ᑉ	*pwaa* :ᐸ	
ti / *tii* ᑎ	*tu* / *tuu* ᑐ	*ta* / *taa* ᑕ	*t* ᑦ	*twaa* :ᑕ	
ki / *kii* ᑭ	*ku* / *kuu* ᑯ	*ka* / *kaa* ᑲ	*k* ᒃ	*kwaa* :ᑲ	*kw* ᒄ
chi / *chii* ᒋ	*chu* / *chuu* ᒍ	*cha* / *chaa* ᒐ	*ch* ᒡ	*chwaa* :ᒐ	
mi / *mii* ᒥ	*mu* / *muu* ᒧ	*ma* / *maa* ᒪ	*m* ᒻ	*mwaa* :ᒪ	
ni / *nii* ᓂ	*nu* / *nuu* ᓄ	*na* / *naa* ᓇ	*n* ᓐ	*nwaa* :ᓇ	
si / *sii* ᓯ	*su* / *suu* ᓱ	*sa* / *saa* ᓴ	*s* ᔅ	*swaa* :ᓴ	
yi / *yii* ᔨ	*yu* / *yuu* ᔪ	*ya* / *yaa* ᔭ	*y* ᔾ	*ywaa* :ᔭ	

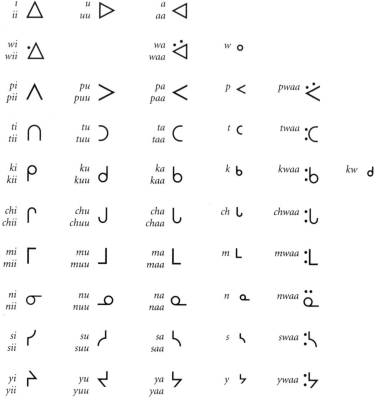

Other Symbols

The symbols ᔅ plus :ᐸ :ᑕ :ᑲ or :ᒐ are often written as contractions, thus: ᔅ:ᐸ ᔅ:ᑕ ᔅ:ᑲ and ᔅ:ᒐ.
Final *y* ᔾ may also be written ᐟ as in: ᐱᒥᐟ *pimiy* 'oil'. X is the symbol for Christ.
Although the following sounds do not exist in Naskapi, the characters are often used to spell proper names:

li / *lii* ᓕ	*lu* / *luu* ᓗ	*la* / *laa* ᓚ	*l* ᓪ
ri / *rii* ᕆ	*ru* / *ruu* ᕈ	*ra* / *raa* ᕋ	*r* ᕐ

Fig. 5-1. Naskapi syllabic chart

need for language development work, which would include Bible translation. By the mid-1970s, at the invitation of the Naskapi leadership and the Naskapi church, SIL assigned a language team to the Naskapi project full-time. Lana Martens and Carol Chase learned the language and began some translation work, but medical issues prevented them from continuing beyond that.

In 1987, Bill and Norma Jean Jancewicz were invited to take over the Naskapi language project from the previous SIL team. They moved to the Naskapi community in 1988 with their children in order to learn the Naskapi language and support the language development work. When they arrived, it was with the intention of SIL leadership that there would be a two-pronged approach to the project. Primarily, the team was tasked with initiating a related-language adaptation (CARLA)[10] translation approach, using source material from the East Cree (James Bay Cree) translation project already under way at Mistissini, Quebec. Secondarily, the team would proceed as in a traditional SIL translation project; that is, they would follow the usual stages of language and culture learning, linguistic analysis, and "direct" translation.

However, the books already being used in the Naskapi church (and indeed all around James Bay) at this time were the Moose Cree texts translated by Bishop Horden, whose New Testament was first published in 1876. Accompanying this translation there is an Anglican *Book of Common Prayer* in Moose Cree (which includes the Psalms) and a collection of *Proper Lessons from the Old Testament* in Moose Cree. Also in use but containing much less biblical material are works by Rev. William G. Walton (c. 1923) translated into the dialect of Cree spoken at Whapmagoostui (Great Whale River). All these materials were in wide circulation and use in Native communities all across northern Quebec well into the 1980s and 1990s.

Even though Moose Cree is a member of the dialect continuum to which Naskapi belongs, it is at least three languages distant from Naskapi. Northern East Cree (also referred to as the Northern dialect of James Bay Cree) is much closer to Naskapi, in fact the nearest neighbor; however, there was little biblical material available for adaptation from Northern East Cree during the early stages of the Naskapi project, and thus it was not a candidate as a source text.

Moose Cree, on the other hand, had the entire New Testament, selections of the Old Testament, and other religious materials that had been translated by Horden and his Moose Cree colleagues. All of these documents were already in regular use within the local Naskapi church when SIL began its work, and they were being read by Naskapi lay readers who were proficient, in varying degrees, at deriving a considerable level of understanding in Naskapi from these Moose Cree documents.

Two Translation Approaches

Given the existing language and church situation, it was a complicated starting point to begin to provide texts that were easily understandable in Naskapi. As already noted, two different approaches were proposed, direct translation and related-language adaptation. The first approach, direct translation, requires a trained, bilingual Naskapi mother-tongue translator to prepare a Naskapi translation using an annotated English text as a source. The second approach, related-language adaptation, starts with a completed translation in a related language which is used as a source text. Computer procedures are used to produce a draft translation in the target language, which is then reviewed and revised by speakers of the target language.

Direct Translation

Direct translation generally proceeds through the following steps. After determining the plain meaning of the source document (a process referred to as exegesis), sometimes the SIL team prepares an annotated English version (called a "front" translation), which is written taking into account the second-language ability and the vocabulary of the mother-tongue translator. This is generally used as the primary source text from which the Naskapi mother-tongue translator works to prepare his or her Naskapi translation.

The mother-tongue translator will also read the portion to be translated in other English translations, along with commentaries and historical background for that particular passage. He or she will also study the meaning of difficult words or expressions.

The Naskapi mother-tongue translators are trained to determine the meaning of each phrase of the source document, taking into consideration the intention of the original authors, the historical background of the original audience, implied information, figures of speech, and the original discourse genre. They then render that meaning as closely as possible into the target language (their mother tongue), taking into con-

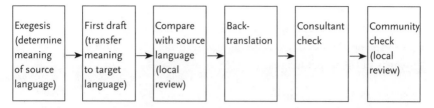

Exegesis (determine meaning of source language)	First draft (transfer meaning to target language)	Compare with source language (local review)	Back-translation	Consultant check	Community check (local review)

Fig. 5-2. Typical direct translation procedures

sideration how people in their own language community and culture will understand the message of the translation. When necessary, information that is implicit in the source document may be made explicit, or figures of speech are explained or altered so that the meaning is clear, natural, and accurate. When available, SIL's *Translators' Notes* series is used to assist the translator as well.[11]

This Naskapi "first draft" translation is then read over by the translator, comparing it to standard majority-language versions of the text for accuracy. It is also checked for clarity with (or by) two or three other Naskapi speakers to ensure that it sounds like natural Naskapi. This draft is revised during this process. After this step is accomplished, draft two is then "back-translated": that is, translated *back* into English, phrase by phrase, which provides a basis for the translation to be "consultant-checked" (see figure 5-2).

Trained translation consultants are provided with this back-translation in advance of an on-site visit. The consultant compares the back-translation of the target text with the source document to check for errors, omissions, or other inconsistencies. Finally, the translation consultant normally meets with a speaker of the target language, and over the course of one or more interviews will ask content and comprehension questions: such an interview is sometimes done with a bilingual speaker of the target language (the interview being carried on in the majority language) or sometimes through an interpreter.

A trained translation consultant is able to evaluate a translation, make suggestions for improvements, and essentially verify that the translation is accurate and clear. Naturalness is another desired quality of a translation, and this can normally be ensured by a separate "community-check" step in which the text is reviewed with other speakers of the target language to elicit their opinion or suggestions for the naturalness of the translation.

These steps make little or no use of any existing native-language translation: in a direct translation, the bilingual mother-tongue translator shoulders the entire task of transferring the meaning of the source text into the words of the target language.

Related-Language Adaptation

The second approach, which I have referred to as related-language adaptation, involves starting with passages that were already translated into Cree as a source text and then adjusting or adapting this text much as the Naskapi readers would do orally during church services. The steps used in checking a related-language adaptation are the same as those in direct translation. Related-language adaptation processes only replace the "first-draft" step: the translation is generally still subjected to all the usual checking and reviewing steps already described.

Related-Language Adaptation Using Conventional CARLA

In the early 1990s, the North America Branch of SIL was assisting in several translation projects involving languages within the Cree-Montagnais-Naskapi dialect continuum, including Western (Plains) Cree, James Bay Cree (also called East Cree, Southern dialect), Atikamekw, Montagnais (now called Innu), and Naskapi. In addition, a new language team was preparing to work with Whapmagoostui (East Cree, Northern dialect). Under the supervision of the academic affairs department of the North America Branch, steps were taken at this time to begin a detailed grammatical analysis of these languages with a view toward developing an integrated Computer-Aided Related-Language Adaptation (CARLA) approach to meet the translation needs of some of these languages. This conventional CARLA approach is well documented within SIL (Buseman 1993a, 1993b). The CARLA adaptation process is only practical when the source document is from a dialect that is closely related linguistically to the target document (for a technical description of the entire CARLA procedure, see the appendix).

Even though there was an initially strong effort by the linguistic coordinator and enthusiastic participation of several SIL language teams, including the Naskapi team, various factors worked against setting up a conventional multi-language CARLA project for Cree-Montagnais-Naskapi. Among the problems was the time-consuming task of detailed interlinear analysis of natural texts in order to collect all the information for the various dictionaries of word-parts and grammatical rules, which are required by the CARLA adaptation process. This proved to proceed at a slower pace than expected. Eventually, for personnel and administrative reasons, the SIL entity temporarily placed three of the language projects on hold, and the three remaining projects (East Cree, Plains Cree, and Naskapi) redirected their focus toward direct translation strategies.

Naskapi Language Incremental Adaptation
From Moose Cree as Source

In spite of the circumstances that sidelined a conventional CARLA approach for the Cree-Montagnais-Naskapi dialects, the local need for Naskapi scriptures remained great and immediate. In 1994 the Naskapi translation team continued with the direct translation strategy, deciding first to translate a series of excerpts from the Gospels (the *Walking With Jesus* series). Then in 1996, the local translation committee made the decision to translate the Old Testament book of Genesis. The reasons for this choice included the fact that only very small portions of this book were available in the related Cree translations used at that time in the community: Genesis was, for the Naskapi community, mostly new material, and thus had to be translated directly.

Related-Language Adaptation Using "Incremental CARLA"

At about this time the leaders in the Naskapi church felt that having the lectionary readings available for weekly distribution in leaflet form would assist the congregation in understanding the scriptures, as well as providing them with reading material that could be followed along during the services and taken to their homes afterward.[12] The SIL team assisted in the production of these leaflets, which contained the Moose Cree scriptures "respelled" in the Naskapi orthography. This respelling basically follows a few simple rules.

Early on, the SIL team recognized that a number of consistent changes took place when a Naskapi lay reader was verbally adapting from Moose Cree into Naskapi as the scriptures were read aloud at church services. Many phonological (sound) changes were predictable and regular: these changes comprised some of the features that distinguish the dialect boundaries between the source and target languages (MacKenzie:1980). For example, every single *e* vowel in Moose Cree becomes *aa* (long a) in Naskapi. Every Moose Cree *k* before front vowels (such as *i*) is palatalized;

that is, every *ki* becomes *chi* in Naskapi. The letter *l* (Proto-Algonquian [*l]) in Moose Cree is pronounced as *y* in cognate words in Naskapi.[13]

By making these simple and regular changes, a Moose Cree text could be modified before being read by a Naskapi speaker, thus easing the understanding of many of the cognate words. However, there remained a number of phonological transformations, as well as lexical and grammatical changes, that had to be implemented before the text could be considered to be in good Naskapi. For these reasons, a thorough manual review and editing stage was carried out as part of the procedure, to ensure reasonable accuracy of these readings and to incrementally improve the process. That is, each new consistent change discovered during the review was added to a master list of changes that were performed when converting a text to Naskapi. Thus, the procedure produced increasingly better results as more texts were reviewed (for a full description of the procedures used for Incremental CARLA, see the appendix).

Of course, at the end of each cycle of this procedure, a usable draft of the church readings are produced: Naskapi speakers then have a scripture translation to read in church starting from the first week. Incremental adaptation is a language adaptation procedure that is mother-tongue translator centered, rather than computer centered, providing useful output from the start.

Another benefit of the incremental adaptation procedure is that it inherently accomplishes one of the review steps described in figure 5-2. Conventional CARLA produces only a first draft, while incremental adaptation produces a reviewed first draft.

The main benefit of this approach is that adaptation can be done fairly accurately for many cycles without having to depend upon a complete grammatical analysis, because each corrected check print through the cycle depends solely on "manual" adaptation by the Naskapi speaker/ reviewer for accuracy, and because of this manual review stage the computer-aided adaptation stage (search and replace) could be allowed to run "blindly" until it was convenient to do the analysis. Each translated passage is ultimately produced by the Naskapi reviewer, not solely by a computer program.

Difficulties and Cautions

Two of the greatest difficulties with this (and any) adaptation strategy lie with the quality of the source text. The Moose Cree scriptures used for this exercise were translated by Bishop Horden more than a century ago. Very little was known about his source text, his exegesis, or his translation principles, although at this point some pretty good guesses can be made. The other difficulty is the relatively wide dialect span between Naskapi and Moose Cree. There are substantial grammatical, syntactical, and discourse-level differences between the two languages. It has become apparent that even when the procedure works well, there is an "Old Moose Cree" sound to the Naskapi version. Usually the source document's Moose Cree word order remains intact after the transfer to Naskapi, and this can skew the naturalness of the Naskapi. To be sure, some consistent phrase-level word-order differences have been noted, and in these cases the conversion tables can even be tweaked to account for these. Still, the quality of such a Naskapi version is limited, and can seldom be made "better" than the Moose Cree source text without extensive retranslation.

However, in defense of the procedure, it should be remembered that the Moose Cree scriptures, as found in the Moose Cree volumes noted above, had been accepted as the "Bible" for the Naskapi church in the first place for many years, even with all their inherent difficulties in accessibility and understanding. Just running the global changes alone (changing every "e" to "aa," for example) provided a vast improvement for the typical Naskapi reader, and the full cycle of adaptation made the Moose Cree scriptures that much more accessible and understandable to the Naskapi. It further provided a reference document for work that was already under way on the Naskapi translation in the conventional (direct translation) manner.

From East Cree as Source

During the late 1990s, the Naskapi project continued with direct translation (for Genesis, Exodus, and Luke) along with incremental related-language adaptation for the Sunday lectionary readings using Moose Cree as the source. Whenever possible, the Naskapi direct translation (such as material from Genesis) was used when the lectionary readings called for it, but for the most part the lectionary remained largely an adaptation from Moose Cree.

During this same period, the East Cree (James Bay Cree) translation team was completing a translation of the entire New Testament in the dialect spoken at Mistissini Quebec, and they were nearing publication. This dialect of Cree is much closer to Naskapi than Moose Cree, besides being a contemporary translation (unlike the Moose Cree scriptures, which consisted of texts over a century old). The Naskapi project secured permission from both the East Cree translation team and the publishers (copyright holders) to attempt an incremental language adaptation approach to produce a Naskapi version using East Cree (James Bay Cree) Southern dialect as the source, based on the steps described above for Moose Cree. In the summer of 2001, a pilot project of incremental language adaptation for the book of Philippians was tried by this method.

As the procedure was repeated for each chapter, all the changes collected from previous chapters became the basis for the changes applied to the original text for the current chapter. As with Moose Cree, a comprehensive account of all the changes made was maintained in a master database; that is, a complete list of every Cree word that had been changed to an equivalent Naskapi word.

During a routine SIL consultant visit in the fall of 2001, the book of Philippians was checked for clarity, naturalness, and accuracy according to the same criteria as the direct translation projects. This check confirmed that for the East Cree to Naskapi pairing, the incremental adaptation procedure was providing good results, and the consultant greenlighted this procedure for the entire New Testament.

Naskapi New Testament

After completing Philippians, the Naskapi translation team moved on to complete the books of Acts and Matthew simultaneously (employing two Naskapi reviewers), as well as keeping up with the weekly Sunday readings. For the lectionary cycle beginning with Advent of 2001 (Year A), the translation team decided to produce all the New Testament readings for Sundays using East Cree as the source text (rather than Moose Cree, as had been the practice before this). The congregation responded very positively to these new translations based on East Cree.

After a facilitator review in the fall of 2002, the team decided to enlist the services of another Naskapi reviewer and run the incremental adaptation procedure on larger sections of the New Testament, roughly processing two hundred verses at a time. At this increased rate it was possible to complete the procedure on the entire New Testament, bringing it to a very readable level in just under a year. Thus by June 2003 the first draft of the Naskapi New Testament was complete and ready for community review and consultant checking.

The incremental adaptation procedure for the Naskapi New Testament was breaking new ground. The source text—the East Cree (James Bay Cree) New Testament—had already been checked by a consultant and by the community according to SIL standards just a few years earlier. This new Naskapi version was being produced from a translation that was already "checked." Should the checking procedures for Naskapi be modified?

The SIL entity academic affairs department discussed the issues regarding an appropriate approach to consultant checking such material. Through discussions with a translation consultant who was familiar with Naskapi, the translation coordinator and the director of academic affairs decided to proceed as follows.

First, one book of the Bible would be adapted. After making a back-translation for the translation consultant, this entire passage would be subjected to a thorough line-by-line consultant check in the conventional way including a visit and interview with the consultant. This was initially done to ensure that the proposed incremental adaptation process was viable and did not have any obvious flaws. After this, provided the quality of the translation proved adequate, the remaining books of the New Testament would be adapted into Naskapi.

Once the entire Naskapi New Testament was drafted, the academic affairs department prepared a list of ten different discourse genres that are found in the New Testament. (A discourse genre is a style or form of language used for a particular purpose. Examples of such genres include narrative, hortatory, poetic, dialogue, and procedural.) A passage from each of these genres was selected, the total quantity representing roughly 10 percent of the entire New Testament.

Each of these selected passages was prepared for a consultant check in the conventional way: a back-translation was done, and questions were prepared by the translation consultant. In January 2004 there was another on-site consultant check, during which a series of interviews for evaluating the target text were conducted.

It was understood that should the consultant have any concerns about the accuracy or clarity of the translation during this 10 percent check, additional translation review and revision would be required. On the other hand, if the translation consultant was satisfied that the text was clear and accurate as is, it would be concluded that the 10 percent check served as an adequate representation of the remainder of the translation.

And indeed that was the case with the Naskapi New Testament: the translation consultant approved the 10 percent check of the various genres without qualification, and therefore the remainder was considered "passed" by representation, and by virtue of the fact that the East Cree (James Bay Cree) source text had been already thoroughly consultant checked.

Still, it was felt that a thorough and complete (100 percent) community review was still desirable. Therefore, over the course of several public reading sessions in the community, the entire New Testament was read through in the presence of several Naskapi speakers, who provided valuable comments and suggestions to help make the translation sound like more natural Naskapi.

Other translation teams also recommended that a final (and oral) read-through of the entire New Testament be completed by a competent and trained reviewer. During this read-through some specific grammatical issues (such as participant reference and obviation) were particularly focused upon. This kind of reviewing was found indispensable for turning up some important changes to the text that made it much more natural in Naskapi and for weeding out certain Cree-like features that had been overlooked in the other reviews.

Conclusions

The conventional suite of CARLA programs (see the appendix for a detailed account) had always held promise for language adaptation to produce Naskapi scriptures from related languages, and it is felt that such an approach might have been successful if the project had the time and technical resources to devote to it. But project circumstances prevented teams from investing the required time and resources, and ultimately the Naskapi project worked on translation independently of the potential source text projects. By beginning with direct translation, the Naskapi mother-tongue translators thus gained experience and training in basic translation principles and then applied these skills to the related-language adaptation task.

By maintaining a high level of direct involvement by mother-tongue translators in the adaptation procedure, the quality of the Naskapi-language texts that were produced by the incremental adaptation approach described in this chapter was such that they could be used immediately by the local church and community.

The SIL team's primary task was to coordinate the language adaptation task, collect and analyze the changes made by the Naskapi translators, and implement the computer search-and-replace routines. By doing this on a repeated, cyclical basis, an adaptation procedure that was initially simple to set up was improved in efficiency incrementally as more and more texts were processed through it.

When the thoroughly checked East Cree (James Bay Cree) text became available as a source text for language adaptation, the Naskapi translation project production appreciably accelerated over the direct translation approach, more than doubling the usual rate of translation output. While the procedures described here may not be appropriate for all language projects, it is felt that if the appropriate components of a high-quality source text, relatively close linguistic proximity of the source and target languages, and the availability of trained mother-tongue translators are present, the incremental adaptation approach may prove to be a workable strategy for other translation projects.

Appendix

Conventional CARLA

To accomplish a translation using a conventional CARLA approach, several components must be in place. One of these components is a series of dictionary databases, including (at least) an extensive dictionary of the morphemes (meaningful parts of words, such as prefixes and suffixes) in the source language along with a dictionary of the morphemes in the target language. Another necessary component is a thorough grammatical analysis (patterns describing the way a language is structured) of the source and target languages (see figure 5-3).

These morpheme dictionaries and grammatical analyses are written into series of computer-readable rules and then applied in sequence to analyze (that is, to morphologically parse, or separate the words into their meaningful parts) the input text using a computer program called AMPLE (A Morphological Parser for Linguistic Exploration), and then synthesize (replace source morphemes with equivalent target morphemes) and transfer (recombine those morphemes according to the structure of the target language) the analyzed text using another computer program called STAMP (Synthesis/Transfer-AMPLE Text), which generates the first draft target text. These procedures held promise that at least a first draft of the target language translation could be produced by using a translation in a source language, and they have proven successful in some SIL projects.

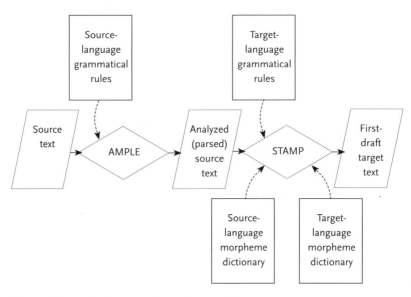

Fig. 5-3. Conventional CARLA adaptation procedure

When the appropriate dictionaries and grammatical rules are in place, the conventional CARLA adaptation process can produce a rough draft in the target language from a clear, accurate, and natural translation in the source language.

The preparation for this eventual promise for Naskapi and the other related languages in Canada proved to be a formidable task. A number of CARLA workshops were held in order to begin to gather the very large body of necessary data (dictionaries of morphemes and grammatical rules for both languages) required by this approach. One method used to gather this data was to have the various team members perform detailed interlinear analyses of natural texts (breaking down of the words of texts into their component meaningful parts, and identifying each one) in each of the languages they were working on. These analyses had to be co-ordinated across language projects in order that common metalanguage terms and analytical orthography be used by all of the researchers.

Incremental CARLA

The linguistic and technical procedures that were followed for the incremental adaptation of the Cree scriptures into Naskapi are fairly simple, but esoteric. Still, it was felt that a thorough description of these procedures might be useful to persons who might consider this approach for producing texts in related languages. The procedure initially developed for the older Moose Cree source text was later applied to the contemporary James Bay Cree source text, and is described in detail here.

Moose Cree to Naskapi Incremental Adaptation

The following steps were followed:

1. The Moose Cree text was selected from the available sources, according to the lectionary references provided by the prayer book.
2. The text was keyboarded, and changed to Naskapi phonology and spelling (following the rules outlined above, all *e* are changed to *aa*, for example).
3. A printout of the modified text was brought to a Naskapi lay reader, who carefully read the passage and made numerous corrections, usually by hand.
4. These corrections were keyboarded into the original text, and another printout was made, from which the leaflets were copied for use in the Sunday services. Each correction was carefully cataloged for future reference.
5. During the oral reading at the church service, any additional corrections were further noted.

As this five-step cycle was repeated each week, the corrections collected from previous weeks became the basis for the changes applied to the original text for the current week. From the outset (other than the very basic phonemic changes noted above), all the manual corrections were tabulated in a list: every Cree word that had been changed in any way to an equivalent Naskapi word was carefully compiled and maintained.

Computer Assistance

Computers can be very good at helping with certain repetitive tasks. As soon as the team developed solutions for efficiently handling the syllabic orthography, computers could be used for all kinds of word-processing tasks in the Naskapi language. For the steps outlined in the previous section, a series of computer programs were utilized to assist in making the changes.

The Consistent Changes program (available from SIL) provides a simple, reliable, and programmable utility that can make consistent changes throughout a text.[14] For example, a list of desired changes may be written as follows:

"e" > "aa"
"ki" > "chi"
"l" > "y"

This means:

Each time the letter "e" is encountered, change it to "aa";
each time "ki" is encountered, change it to "chi";
and each time "l" is encountered, change it to "y."

Such a list, when applied to a Moose Cree text as input, will make all the basic phonological changes to move the text closer to Naskapi. The Consistent Changes program also provides the ability to make complex and conditional replacements, and such tables are easy to update.

As noted above, during the correction/revision steps of adapting the Moose Cree texts for Naskapi, a list of words that the Naskapi reviewer changed was maintained. The Field Linguist's Shoebox program (now superseded by the Field Linguist's Toolbox program, also available from SIL)[15] uses a simple database program for maintaining such a list. At first the database only needed two fields: Moose Cree word and Naskapi word. Later, as the team gained a better understanding of both languages, other fields were added. The following is an excerpt from the Moose Cree–Naskapi database, showing the entries for three Moose Cree words: *itweyak* 'we say,' *kaakichihiwewiniliw* 'consolation,' and *kaakika* 'always, forever.'

```
\mc itweyak
\fm ischiiswaayaahk
\ps vai
\gl we[incl]_say
\chg lexical
\dt 30/Jan/2002

\mc kaakichihiwewiniliw
\fm kaachichihiwaauniyuw
\ps ni
\gl consolation[o]
\chg ki>chi
\chg we>waa
\chg win>un
\chg iliw>iyuw
\dt 08/Jun/1999

\mc kaakika
\fm kaachich
\ps vii
\gl always,_forever
\chg kika>chich
\dt 30/Jan/2002
```

Each record in the database begins with the \mc marker. The top line (after \mc) is the Moose Cree word. The next line (after \fm) is the Naskapi equivalent word form. The \ps field is "part of speech," and the \gl field is "gloss," or definition.

Periodically (every cycle), words are added to this database, and the size of this database increases with each new correction. The database is used to create another consistent changes table, with the form shown in the following Moose Cree–Naskapi lexical change table excerpt.

"itweyak"	> "ischiiswaayaahk"
"kaakichihiwewiniliw"	> "kaachichihiwaauniyuw"
"kaakika"	> "kaachich"

Such a change table, when used on Moose Cree input files, ensures that at least all the changes already recorded in the database will never have to be "corrected" again by the Naskapi reviewers. That is, once a Naskapi reviewer has changed the Moose Cree word *kaakika* to the Naskapi word *kaachich*, the correction is then made by the computer for every other occurrence of that word in later cycles.

Figure 5-4 diagrams the procedures just described for Moose Cree, which were also followed during the translation of the Naskapi New Testament based on the East Cree (James Bay Cree) New Testament.

Incremental Grammatical Analysis

As noted, besides the Moose Cree (\mc) and Naskapi (\fm) entries, there are fields in the database for part of speech, gloss (definition), and a summary of the changes noted. Analyzing the database entries can reveal other "global" (across-the-board) changes like the sound changes. For example, when observing the Moose Cree abstract noun *kaakichihiwewiniliw* 'consolation,' it was eventually discovered that the ending *-iliw* (which marks the noun as a subsequent or non-topical referent in a discourse) was a consistent change: that is, final *-iliw* in Moose Cree is always rendered *-iyuw* in Naskapi. It was further observed that abstract nouns are derived from their corresponding verbs, and *-win* is the derivational affix for such abstract nouns in Moose Cree. In Naskapi, such abstract nouns are spelled with the derivational affix *-un*.

It can be seen that as more texts are processed by this procedure, the growing Moose Cree–Naskapi database not only provides a word-by-word inventory of readers' corrections but also informs the analysis of the languages and allows more complex and effective changes throughout the text, anticipating changes according to verified corrections. For example, once it was determined from the database of corrections that the final *-iliw* should always change to *-iyuw* for Naskapi, this change was performed globally; that is, all words ending in *-iliw*, whether they had been encountered in a correction cycle or not, were changed to *-iyuw*.

The main benefit of this approach is that adaptation can be done fairly accurately for many cycles without having to depend upon any kind of prior grammatical analysis, because each corrected check print through the cycle depends solely on "manual" adaptation by the Naskapi speaker/reviewer for accuracy—and because of this manual adaptation the computer-assisted adaptation step (search and replace) could be allowed to run "blindly" until it was convenient to do the analysis. That is, each passage is ultimately produced by the Naskapi reviewer, not solely by a computer program.

Orthography Change

Because Cree and Naskapi are written in a syllabic script, a procedure for converting from the syllabic script to roman and back again also had to be developed. All the automated phonemic (sound), morphological (prefixes, suffixes, and roots), and word changes were designed to work on texts in standardized roman spelling.

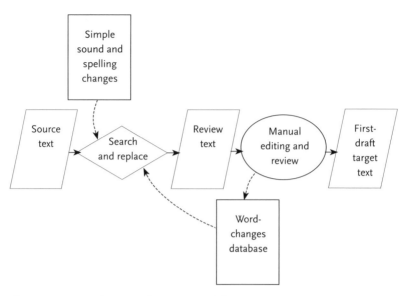

Fig. 5-4. Incremental CARLA adaptation procedure

So the input texts are all converted from syllabics or transcribed into roman spelling first, then the adaptation is done, and finally the roman output is converted to Naskapi syllabics.

Eventually, a series of batch files were created that automated most of the processing necessary to produce a Naskapi "check-print" from a Moose Cree text. However, the basic steps never deviated from those listed above. As time went on, as the wordlist database increased in size and global changes tables grew more refined, the number of corrections that the Naskapi readers had to make to the check-prints became fewer and fewer, until eventually there were only two or three corrections necessary for each page of text. Still, it was the Naskapi translators who were relied upon to produce the Naskapi translation from the Moose Cree, and not the computer. The computer just made their job easier.

In all fairness, it should be pointed out that the conventional CARLA suite of programs allows for a similar "simple" approach designed to be used by a mother-tongue translator, by using a variation of the CARLA programs referred to as CARLA Lite, which is based upon a similar word- or phrase-replacement approach. However, the team felt that even CARLA Lite involved a more complicated procedure than was warranted by the Naskapi situation, and the Naskapi community was encouraged by the fact that a readable Naskapi text was being produced through each cycle described above. CARLA Lite or Adapt-It (Waters and Martin 2006) may well have been applied to provide similar results.

Other Software Tools

Some other very useful software tools have been applied to the project: Paratext, the Bible translation software produced by the United Bible Societies, is used for all the direct editing of the various stages of the adaptation and for producing the back-translation. The Moose Cree and James Bay Cree New Testaments in their entirety are kept available for reference in Paratext. In addition, all the existing Old Testament Moose Cree passages from the *Proper Lessons from the Old Testament* were keyboarded and made accessible in Paratext.

By means of this program, the Naskapi translators are able to quickly refer to these reference materials along with the various English translations and translation helps available in Translators' Workplace, another software tool provided by SIL. To begin a cycle for adaptation and translation, the translator simply selects the source text from Paratext and runs it through the six-step cycle described above.

With the two incremental language adaptation projects (one from Moose Cree and the other from James Bay Cree) plus direct translation projects into Naskapi, there are now at least three different kinds of resulting Naskapi translated texts: one adapted from Moose Cree, one adapted from James Bay Cree, and one translated directly from English. Each of these also has its own separate back-translation. The Paratext program provided an efficient solution for maintaining, organizing, and accessing all these various translation texts.

The lexical database program Toolbox was also useful to maintain the databases of changes that were generated during the review process.

To obtain check prints, the texts were be exported from Paratext directly into Microsoft Word and formatted using various stylesheets according to the desired layout.

Notes

1. Silas Nabinicaboo, Naskapi speaker from Kawawachikamach, personal communication, January 2008.

2. SIL International, originally known as the Summer Institute of Linguistics, came by that name because when the organization was first established, the linguistics courses were conducted primarily in the summer. Courses are now held year-round and worldwide, but the name SIL was retained for continuity's sake.

3. http://www.sil.org/iso639-3.

4. http://www.lsadc.org/info/pdf_files/2007_MeetingHandbook.pdf.

5. http://www.sil.org/sil.

6. Grateful acknowledgment is made to the Naskapi Development Corporation for their support and encouragement, as well as to their Naskapi language and translation department.

7. The Ethnologue lists two dialects of Naskapi: Eastern and Western. The Eastern dialect is spoken in the community of Natuashish in Labrador. The speakers of this dialect are referred to as Innu, and their language as Innu-aimun, not Naskapi. The Western dialect is the one with which this article is concerned.

8. The NEQA provided, among other things, Naskapi local authority over their own land and affairs and access to funds for community development, including support for the maintenance of Naskapi language and culture. The translation work described in this chapter takes place under the auspices of the Naskapi Development Corporation.

9. In the 1980s, the classes at the Naskapi school that taught the reading and writing of the syllabic alphabet were called "Cree Class." It was not until the 1990s that a curriculum began to be developed (in Naskapi) for the teaching of reading and writing the Naskapi language for Naskapi-speaking students.

10. CARLA refers to Computer-Aided Related-Language Adaptation. It was formerly called CADA, Computer-Aided Dialect Adaptation. It is a process that uses collected linguistic data for two or more related languages and assists the translation process by generating a tentative draft of the translation in the target language adapted from texts in the source language.

11. *Translators' Notes* is a series of translation helps SIL developed primarily for mother-tongue translators who speak English as a second language, especially those who are translating the Bible into their first language. It aims to provide careful discussion of exegetical and translation issues in nontechnical English.

12. The lectionary is a collection of scripture readings appointed for Christian worship on a given day or occasion. At the Naskapi church the Anglican lectionary is used, with commonly an Old Testament lesson, a Psalm, an Epistle, and a Gospel reading each Sunday.

13. The analysis of Algonquian languages proposes a "parent" language from which the various Algonquian languages and dialects are descended. Linguists refer to this parent language as Proto-Algonquian. Certain consonant sounds of Proto-Algonquian vary according to the dialect considered. For example, the Naskapi word *yuutin* 'it is windy' is spelled and pronounced *lutin* in Moose Cree, *nuutin* in Innu, and *ruutin* in Atikamekw.

14. http://www.sil.org/computing/catalog/show_software.asp?id=4.

15. The Field Linguist's Toolbox is a data management and analysis tool for field linguists. It is especially useful for maintaining lexical data and for parsing and interlinearizing text, but it can be used to manage virtually any kind of data. http://www.sil.org/computing/toolbox.

References

Azizinezhad, Massoud. 2006. Is Translation Teachable? *Translation Journal* 10 (2): April. http://accurapid.com/journal/36edu.htm (accessed July 20, 2010).

Burkhart, Louise. 1989. *The Slippery Earth: Nahua-Christian Moral Dialogue in Sixteenth-Century Mexico*. Tucson: University of Arizona Press.

Buseman, Alan. 1993a. CARLA *Computer Aided Related Language Adaptation— User's Guide*. Waxhaw NC: JAARS Inc.

———. 1993b. CARLA *Computer Aided Related Language Adaptation—Tutorial (Second edition)*. Waxhaw NC: JAARS Inc.

Cooke, Alan. 1976. A History of the Naskapis of Schefferville (preliminary draft). Montreal: Naskapi Band Council of Schefferville. Unpublished manuscript.

Evans, Karen. 1985. *Masinahikan: Native Language Imprints in the Archives and Libraries of the Anglican Church of Canada*. Toronto: Anglican Book Centre.

Foley, William A. 1986. *The Papuan Languages of New Guinea*. Cambridge: Cambridge University Press.

Golla, Victor. 2006. SSILA Statement on ISO 639-3 Language Codes. *Society for the Study of the Indigenous Languages of the Americas SSILA Bulletin*. Number 249 (December 6, 2006).

MacKenzie, Marguerite. 1980. Towards a Dialectology of Cree-Montagnais-Naskapi. Doctoral thesis, University of Toronto.

Payne, Robert. 1971. On the Impossibility of Translation. In *The World of Translation*, 361–64. New York: American Center of PEN.

Pullum, Geoffrey K. 2008. Obituary: Desmond Derbyshire (1924–2007). *Linguist List* 19 (1): January 3. http://linguistlist.org/issues/19/19-1.html (accessed July 20, 2010).

Waters, Bruce, and Bill Martin. 2006. *Adapt-It: Reference Documentation Version 2.4*. Computer Program. SIL International.

6

Performative Translation and Oral Curation

Ti-Jean/Chezan in Beaverland

Amber Ridington and Robin Ridington

The Setting

In 1999, as Amber Ridington was preparing to enter the MA program in folk studies at Western Kentucky University, her father, anthropologist Robin Ridington, recorded a French folktale told by Sammy Acko, a talented Dane-ẕaa storyteller (for the full text of this story see appendix A). The Dane-ẕaa, also known as the Beaver Indians (or Dunne-za in earlier publications), are subarctic hunting-and-gathering people who live in the Peace River region of northeastern British Columbia, Canada, close to the town of Fort St. John, where Amber was born. For almost fifty years, since Robin began his fieldwork in the area, the Ridington family has referred to the area where the Dane-ẕaa live as Beaverland.

Until 1942, when U.S. Army engineers pushed the Alaska Highway through their territory, the Dane-ẕaa were nomadic hunters. They had participated in the fur trade since 1794, when the Northwest Company established the first upper Peace River trading post, Rocky Mountain Fort. In 1822 the Northwest Company merged with the Hudson's Bay Company, and Dane-ẕaa continued their interactions with this fur-trading monopoly. During the late eighteenth and nineteenth centuries, the Peace River was a major transportation route connecting eastern Canada with Arctic drainage fur and game resources. The Dane-ẕaa have, therefore, been in contact with a variety of cultural influences for several centuries. Because of this long history of fur-trade contacts, most Dane-ẕaa men spoke Cree, the traders' lingua franca, as well as some French, the language of the voyageurs.

Even after taking an adhesion to Treaty no. 8 in 1900, the Dane-ẕaa continued to travel seasonally to hunt, trap, gather, and socialize with their kin groups. Today, farms and oil and gas development dominate in the region, the Hudson's Bay Fort is long gone from the area, and the city of Fort St. John is a thriving urban center. Yet the Dane-ẕaa continue to tell traditional stories. In talking about the "narrative technology" of the Dane-ẕaa, Robin has written: "Literature is more than a pastime in First Nations tradition. It is where stories become experience and experience gives rise to stories" (Ridington 2001a:222). Similarly, Dell Hymes describes narratives in Native American culture as being produced by "thoughtful motivated minds, seeking narrative adequate to their experience, surviving and renewing" (2000:11).

Dane-ẕaa experience includes cultural exchange with Europeans, so it is not surprising that they have added stories learned from their new neighbors to their narrative repertoire. Robin first met the Dane-ẕaa in 1959, and was introduced to much of their oral literature through participation, observation, and documentation when stories were being told. Perhaps because he identified himself as someone interested in documenting traditional Dane-ẕaa culture, he was not exposed to and did not record any European folktales in the Dane-ẕaa repertoire until 1999.

Dane-zaa Oral Tradition

While the Dane-ẕaa participated in the rich mix of cultural and linguistic influences of the fur-trade era, their knowledge remained entirely within an oral tradition until the 1950s, when the Department of Indian Affairs established the first Indian day schools in their communities. Dane-ẕaa children were not allowed to speak their own language at the day school. However, they were fortunate: unlike their close linguistic relatives the Sekani and children from many other First Nations across Canada, they were not taken from their families and placed in church-run residential schools where they were forbidden to speak their language at all times.

In addition to cultural exchange with the other First Nations groups in the area, particularly the Cree and the Sekani, the Dane-ẕaa have come to share cultural traditions brought by the traders with whom they came into contact. As Robin has pointed out elsewhere (Ridington 1990:64–83), the tradition of Dane-ẕaa dreamers was strongly influenced by images and metaphors from Christianity, as well as by the changed relation to the natural environment that the fur trade brought about. The men who ran the forts (the factors) were generally Scots from the Hebrides and Orkneys, but many fur traders and other employees in forts across Canada were francophones. Some were Iroquois from eastern Canada, while others were Métis, the products of intermarriage between European men and First Nations women.

Over the course of the nineteenth century, people of French-Cree ancestry established themselves as permanent residents of the Peace River country. Some of those who were in regular contact with the Dane-ẕaa came to speak a working version of Beaver. As stated previously, many Dane-ẕaa learned to communicate in Cree and perhaps a little French. It was through the interactions of these bilingual or trilingual communities that the Dane-ẕaa were introduced to the folktales of France and other European countries. It was not unusual for Dane-ẕaa trappers to spend time on the trapline with their French-Cree neighbors. This is where the adventures of Ti-Jean (Petit Jean) in Beaverland began.

On July 28, 1999, Robin was driving through traditional Doig River territory recording stories and place-names from the elders who are his contemporaries. Accompanying him on this trip were Billy and Tommy Attachie and Sammy Acko. Sammy was born in 1952, but his older brother, Jack, who told him stories about a sort of European trickster named Chezan, was born in 1916. Their father, Ray Aku, whose stories Robin recorded in Beaver in the 1960s, was born in 1879. Like the rest of his contemporaries, Sammy grew up immersed in Dane-ẕaa oral tradition. He continues the storytelling tradition and is recognized in his community as a master storyteller who can tell many different kinds of stories from memory without hesitation, always taking care to explain how he came to know each story.

Ever since Robin began working with Dane-ẕaa elders in the 1960s, they have appreciated the value of having their culture documented, and Robin has been comfortable with his role as cultural documentarian. The stories he recorded in both Beaver and English generally told about places associated with dreamers or other important people from the past. Some stories and names described events in recent experience: the place where band members were born in the 1950s; a place named for the Cree trapper Mygoosh (who was listed in the 1899 Northwest Mounted Police census); and Broomfield Creek, where our late colleague and mentor, Howard Broomfield, camped with a small group of Dane-ẕaa, including Tommy

Attachie and Sam Acko, in 1974. Perhaps Robin's presence as a documentarian of "traditional" culture kept the focus on distinctively Dane-ẕaa stories.

"As we approached Doig on our way home," Robin told Amber, "Sammy unexpectedly launched into a story from a genre that is very much alive in the Dane-ẕaa community, but to which I had never been exposed" (personal communication). Billy Attachie volunteered that this was just one of many similar stories, and that Sammy wasn't the only person who could tell them. Indeed, he said, "Tommy got lots, oh, he start, you gotta go to Grand Prairie" (a town in Alberta that is several hours drive from the Doig River Reserve). Sammy started to tell the story in English with an introduction explaining that the story, while part of the Dane-ẕaa repertoire, must be of European origin. Robin was already recording the conversations on the drive and captured this story on a mini-disc recorder. He transcribed it verbatim, but has set it out in line-for-line ethnopoetic form to reflect the quality of the oral performance. Sammy began:

> There's one story, Dane-ẕaa, Dane-ẕaa
> They have one story about Chezan.
> Anybody tell you about that story?
> This story, it's amazes me.
> It sound like a . . .
> Long time ago there's little towns, things like that.
> That's the way this story sound like,
> And I don't know where Dane-ẕaa people pick that story from.
> Maybe from Monias [Cree word for white man] elder, or . . .
> I didn't know where it come from.
> But anyway, this story,
> It's about magic tablecloth,
> and then a magic fiddle,
> magic wine,
> and magic scissors.
> Those four things.
> It's about four things. (Acko 1999)

When Robin got back from the field in 1999, he told Mark Mealing, a folklorist at Selkirk College, about the European tale that he had found in oral circulation. Dr. Mealing provided a few Aarne-Thompson tale type references,[1] but none of the material he provided identified the protagonist as Ti-Jean. About a year later it suddenly dawned on Robin while he was corresponding about the story with his former student Blanca Schorcht that Chezan must be Ti-Jean, a popular character from French folklore. In 2000, Robin asked Sammy if he would tell some more Chezan stories, and Sammy volunteered another one (Acko 2000).

The stories are two of many that Sammy calls Chezan stories. They are about a young man named Chezan and his brothers. Chezan is a trickster character who is constantly outwitting people and using special powers to his advantage. Chezan as trickster resonates well with the well-established Native American tradition of trickster stories. Among the Dane-ẕaa, the culture hero Tsááyaa (also spelled Saya) has a trickster side to his character and is known for his ability to use special powers to outwit the giant animals that once hunted people. In thinking about the Chezan story as Sammy told it compared to the Aarne-Thompson tale type references Mark Mealing had provided, Robin noted in an e-mail to Amber:

> None of these sources contain the texts themselves, only motif abstracts. This kind of folkloristics is great for cross-references but has absolutely no literary or performative value. I am interested in performative translation. As long as a story stays within the oral tradition, it can cross language barriers and retain its integrity as a narrative. In this case, I think you could argue that the story actually retains its original meaning quite well, even though it is told by First Nations hunting people . . . Rather than transpose the story into their own cultural setting (The Odyssey becomes *Oh Brother, Where Art Thou?*), the storytellers have kept the narrative in a form that preserves its original setting. There is a lot of underlying similarity to Danne-Zaa narrative in the character of Chezan and his brothers. He is like Saya or Wyoni in being a trickster figure. Maybe that's why Ti-Jean has done so well in Quebec and the Caribbean. He fits into the form of characters like Anansi. Another point about performative translation is that maintaining orality keeps the story alive, while writing it down generally stultifies it. That point, of course, depends on finding some written versions. It would be quite interesting if similar Ti-Jean stories transcribed from actualities turned up. (Ridington 2001b)

Performative Translation

Dennis Tedlock (1991) distinguishes between oral performances of traditional texts that are rote recitations and those that are re-creations in which the narrator is also the text's interpreter. Sammy's Chezan story is clearly a re-creation, but it is just as clearly a translation. In comparing Sammy's story with motif indexes describing its European antecedents, it appears that Sammy privileged translation over transformation. He did not significantly change European references into Dane-zaa equivalents. Rather, his interpretation was faithful to the integrity of the story as oral literature. What is remarkable about his story, compared to the written versions that are found in the Western folklore literature, is how alive it continues to be in oral tradition.

The test of a performative translation is that it must work as performance. It must be able to touch a listener. Sammy heard the story in Beaver from his older brother, Jack. Sammy suggests that Jack heard it from a Cree speaker like Mygoosh, for whom a place in Doig River territory is named. Unlike a translation in which a written text in one language is carefully and with scholarly attention transformed into a text in another written language, a performative translation is integral to the act of performance. Sammy learned the story in Beaver but told it to Robin in English. He drew upon his knowledge of both Beaver and English, as well as his understanding of the story as a piece of oral literature. His translation was simultaneous with his telling of the story.

The late Harry Robinson was a master of performative translation in Native American oral literature. Anthropologist Wendy Wickwire recorded Harry telling a wealth of stories from his Okanagan heritage, as well as some historical narratives and the odd European tale such as Puss in Boots. Robinson used his own voice to carry the narrative line and cited the voices of characters in the story as directly quoted dialogue. The result is vivid and compelling. "I can go for twenty-one hours or more when I get started," Harry told Wendy, "because this is my job. I'm a storyteller" (Robinson 1992:7). Okanagan scholar and writer Jeanette Armstrong suggests that "Okanagan Rez English has a structural quality syntactically and [is] semantically closer [than standard English] to the way the Okanagan language is arranged" (1998:193). Armstrong writes that Okanagan reality (like that of other First Nations) "is very much like a story: it is easily changeable and transformative with each speaker. Reality in that way becomes very potent with animation and life. It is experienced as an always malleable reality within which you are like an attendant at a vast symphony surrounding you, a symphony in which, at times, you are the conductor" (191). She goes on to say that in Okanagan storytelling "the ability to move the audience back and forth between the present reality and the story reality relies heavily on the fluidity of time sense that the language offers" (194). The Dane-ẕaa "Rez English" in which Sammy told the Chezan story is similar to that which Armstrong describes for Okanagan.

We found the Chezan stories in the Dane-ẕaa repertoire interesting for a number of reasons and have pondered the following questions: Why would one group curate another group's traditional lore? How do we find meaning in a Native American group telling stories from a distant and foreign culture? What changes have been made to the stories? What meaning do these stories have for the Dane-ẕaa? In the remainder of this chapter we will address these questions and place the Dane-ẕaa Chezan stories within the canon of the original French Ti-Jean stories. We will examine them to see how their basic structure (plots, story lines, and motifs) have fared through performative translation across different language communities, point out regional variations in the stories, and discuss these in relation to work by other scholars studying European tales in Native American circulation.

Classification of Tale Types and Motifs in Folklore Literature

From the early days of ethnography in North America, scholars have been collecting stories of European origin found within Native American cultures and have been fascinated by them. These ethnographers include James Teit (1916), Alanson Skinner (1916, 1927), Truman Michelson (1916), Stith Thompson (1919, 1929), Franz Boas (1940), Melville Jacobs (1945), and Frank G. Speck and Horace P. Beck (1950), among others.

Stith Thompson was an influential figure in early American folklore who helped to bridge the disciplinary gulf between anthropology and literature. Thompson, who had studied the Finnish method of comparative philology known as the historic-geographic method in the early 1900s, was the first scholar to apply the methods of comparative analysis to European tales found among the North American Indians. As part of his 1914 Harvard dissertation (expanded in 1919 as *European Tales among N. American Indians*), Thompson created an index and survey of the geographic distribution of European tales found among the North American Indians at that time and cross-referenced them to European versions. He concluded that the majority of the European tales known and told by Native Americans came from French immigrants in Canada and Louisiana (1919:456).

Following this initial work to trace dissemination of tales from an origin, Thompson went on to the task of translating and expanding Finnish scholar Antti Aarne's work to classify the types of the European folktale. In 1928 he published *The Types of the Folktale: A Classification and Bibliography*, now commonly referred to as the Aarne-Thompson folktale index. This, along with Thompson's later *Motif-Index of Folk-Literature* (1932), became the standard reference works for the comparative study and archiving of European folktales for many decades. Over the years, numerous regional motif and tale type indexes from around the world have been published. Hans-Jörg Uther's three-volume work, *The Types of International Folktales: A Classification and Bibliography, Based on the System of Antti Aarne and Stith Thompson* (2004), is an adapted and expanded reference tool that has only recently replaced Thompson's volumes as the standard reference work. While Thompson's comparative approach to the study of folktales was adopted by many, the historic-geographic approach was flawed in many ways. It was based on the idea of monogenesis and even distribution of tales from a single origin. Also, it arose during a time when scientific approaches were in favor which took the examples out of context and reduced them to plot summaries; in the process, the tales lost their meanings. In addition, the methodology was very labor intensive and the task of collecting and classifying became an end in itself, leaving no time to look at the folktales' functional use and significance in living tradition. Alan Dundes has summarized the flawed historic-geographic approach in relation to mixed Native American and European folktale traditions: "Listing the European tales among the North American Indians does not in itself explain how the borrowed tale functions in its new environment. The concern of folklorists with identification has resulted in sterile study of folklore for folklore's sake and it is precisely this emphasis on text and neglect of context which estranged so many literary critics and cultural anthropologists" (1965:136).

Dundes does not, however, recommend abandoning the identification of variants and sources. He suggests that the comparative study of European folktale types and motifs can be a valuable tool for studying the historical development of particular variants over time and space. Writing during a critical time in folklore studies when context and performance were emerging as new paradigms for the study of folklore, Dundes concludes that the objective and empirical process of identification of variants can help inform the more subjective and speculative interpretation of the meanings of folklore (1965:136). Much later, in 1997, when performance and contextual orientations were well established in folkloristics, the *Journal of Folklore Research* (34.3) published a special issue devoted to type and motif indexes in which authors offer critiques, describe actual uses, and suggest future developments for comparative study using the indexes. Carl Lindahl is one of these authors who finds "Some Uses of Numbers" from the Aarne-Thompson indexes. Lindahl summarizes his perspective as follows: "Nearly all the folklorists who continue to use the type and motif indexes do so because there is currently available no better means of taking the broadest measure of the context of tale telling, of surveying and accessing the narrative backgrounds from which individual traditions and narratives emerge" (1997:271).

For this chapter, Amber scoured the early volumes of the *Journal of American Folklore* to find Ti-Jean stories.[2] She noted that many Ti-Jean stories were recorded from Quebec and published as Contes Populaires Canadien by Marius Barbeau (1916, 1917); Evelyn Bolduc (1919); Gustave Lanctot (1916, 1923, 1926, 1931); Adelard Lambert, Marius Barbeau, and Pierre Daviault (1940); and Marcel Rioux (1950), among others. However, as these sources are in French, we leave it to scholars more competent in that language to discuss them, as well as the numerous more contemporary collections of Ti-Jean stories published in French.[3] What our initial survey does tell us is that there was a thriving French folktale tradition in both French Canadian and Native American communities in the early twentieth century.

Amber also identified Aarne-Thompson tale types and motifs in the Chezan stories told by Sammy Acko. The tale types and motifs for the 1999 story, along with the text of that story, are included in appendices 1 and 2; because of space consideration in this volume, the text and the tale types and motifs for Sammy's 2000 Chezan story can be found on the Internet at http://sites.google.com/site/plumeofcockatoopress/chezan-story -by-sam-acko/chezan-story-2000. Although of no performative value, the plot summaries and motifs have been helpful in identifying and comparing the Dane-ẕaa Chezan stories to other Ti-Jean stories found in Native American and European tradition.

One of the fruits of this publication search was the identification of two "Ticon (Petit-Jean)" stories in Alanson Skinner's 1916 article "European Tales from the Plains Ojibwa" in the *Journal of American Folklore*. These "Ticon" stories happen to be versions of the two Chezan stories that Sammy told in 1999 and 2000. The stories have some differences in detail and action, but the basic plots are the same. In 1916, the stories could not have been recorded as audio actualities. It appears that they have been revised either during transcription in the field or in preparation for publication, as the English grammar of the stories has been standardized in the Skinner versions. Skinner provides no contextual information, so we cannot know whether the narrator told them in English or if these versions are translations. They most certainly originally arrived in Ojibwa tradition through the process of performative translation.

More recently, Jarold Ramsey (1987) has revisited many of the historic texts that show Native American assimilation of European folklore collected and written in the early 1900s by ethnographers. He notes that the Ti-Jean stories are by far the most popular and widespread of the European traditions assimilated by Native American communities and that within the Ti-Jean cycle the most common story is "Ti-Jean and the Seven-Headed Dragon" (207). Ramsey's analysis of a number of versions of this tale, he writes, are meant to shed light on the "intercultural literary process which, if properly documented and understood, could tell us much about the imaginative circumstances of Indian acculturation and about the internal rules and dynamics of traditional oral literatures" (206). Ramsey's article provides a strong historical base from which to study and compare examples of Ti-Jean stories found in active Native American oral tradition.

Thus far we have located only two examples of European stories in Native American tradition that were recorded in live performance. One is a French Ti-Jean story collected by Dundes (1965) from Prairie Band Potawatomi tradition in Kansas, and the other is a Russian version of the Frog Princess story collected by Nora Marks Dauenhauer and Richard Dauenhauer (1998) from a Tlingit community in southeast Alaska. We will discuss these and compare them to the Dane-ẕaa Chezan/Ti-Jean stories later in the chapter.

Oral Curation

A recurring theme in the literature about European folktales in Native American tradition is a fascination with the stability of tale types despite their transmission between distant languages and cultures (Thompson

1919, 1929; Hymes 1981:276; Ramsey 1987:206). Amber suggests that we can benefit by thinking of this stability within oral form in relation to the concept of curation. In museum studies, *curation* refers to the selection, organization, and care of items in a collection; the emphasis is frequently on preservation. In archaeology, a curated artifact is one that is prized, cared for, and often adapted (e.g., large stone knife could be retooled into an arrowhead). Drawing on the references to both stable and dynamic cultural patterns[4] contained in these definitions of curation, Amber has applied the term *oral curation* to the process of oral transmission which simultaneously maintains the plot structure and setting of a story and provides an opportunity for it to be tailored according to each performance context. Amber's intent in using the term *oral curation* is to reconceive curation so that it implies a dynamic and ongoing process rather than one that is fixed, and to point out that tradition bearers, rather than just outside professionals, are, and can be, curators of their own culture. Reconceiving curation in this way is meant to relieve it from its association with elite institutions and a history of decontextualization. As we will demonstrate, the Dane-ẕaa have adapted the Ti-Jean/Chezan narratives through ongoing performance, but have also maintained the stories' structural form through the processes of performative translation and oral curation.

Regional Variation and Indigenization

C. W. von Sydow and Albert Lord were influential scholars who contributed to the idea of emergent folklore and refocused study on living traditions instead of texts. Von Sydow's work (1932) to explain the processes of regional variation through folktale transmission[5] and Lord's (1960) identification of oral formulaic memory devices that help maintain the structure of oral histories during performance are both applicable to the Dane-ẕaa Chezan stories and to Dane-ẕaa and Native American literature in general. Also relevant to our study of oral curation and performative translation is Linda Degh's work on the art of storytelling. Degh writes: "The special gift of any storyteller consists in his being able to shape a tale. . . . The possibilities for the reshaping of the well-known forms are legion. They can occur in the tale structure (the possibilities for combination of motifs are infinite) or in the individual shaping, in the way the narrator actualizes the tale . . . and they depend on whether his manner of narrating aims at breadth, length, detail, precision, or density of content" (1969:171–72).

Drawing from these contextual approaches to studying variation within oral literature, we can see the adaptive process by which Sammy Acko, a talented Dane-ẕaa storyteller, as well as his Native storytelling predecessors, have orally curated Ti-Jean/Chezan folktales and have made them relevant for each new audience. In the preamble to Sammy's narration of the second Chezan story (Acko 2000), it becomes clear that there are both active and passive tradition bearers in the Dane-ẕaa narrative community. Again, the four people present at the narrative event are Sammy Acko, Billy Attachie, Tommy Attachie, and Robin Ridington. The story begins as follows:

> **Robin:** Do you know any other stories about that, like that Chezan?
> **Sammy:** Chezan, yeah,
> **Tommy:** Yeah, lots of story about that.
> **Sammy:** That same Chezan, he's just like outlaw those years. . . .

While Sammy is telling the story, Tommy continues to make comments and offer details from time to time. This indicates that Tommy also knows the story and is able to tell Chezan stories himself, which may well have had an effect on Sammy, the narrator for this particular storytelling context.

The type of commentary presented above is an example of metanarration, a narrative device that indexes or comments on the narrative itself or on the components or conduct of the storytelling event (Bauman 1986:98). In both of the Chezan stories, the narrated event is preceded by a metanarrative statement from Sammy in which he assesses his audience's familiarity with the story he is about to tell and comments on its origin. What is made clear by the following excerpt is that the stories are now part of the Dane-ẕaa repertoire and are considered their own.

> There's one story, Dane-ẕaa, Dane-ẕaa
> They have one story about Chezan
> Anybody tell you about that story? (Acko 1999)

There are numerous regional variations evident in Sammy's versions of the stories that indicate how they have been tailored to the Dane-ẕaa context. In the story he told in 1999, Chezan is referred to as "crazy," which in the Dane-ẕaa language can be said as "muh-tsi-nachue," meaning "his head nothing." The Dane-ẕaa use of the word "crazy" corresponds to Thompson's use of the term "numbskull" or "fool," which almost always refers to a lowly hero who outsmarts someone with power. "Crazy" may also imply uncontrolled shamanic power, as in the story of the first Dane-ẕaa dreamer, Makénúúnatane, whose initial crazy behavior was later revealed to be a sign of his power to transform. The intonations Sammy used to say the word "crazy" have a metonymic element that conjures up other stories and experiences for the Dane-ẕaa audience. Ti-Jean/Chezan is a lowly hero who ends up outwitting everyone else, a familiar scenario in the Dane-ẕaa culture hero myths. Chezan is a person with power; in Dane-ẕaa terms, a person who "little bit know something" (Ridington 1990). The hybrid character of Ti-Jean/Chezan, who is seemingly an empty-headed, sometimes crazy numbskull delights Dane-ẕaa audiences, as Chezan shows that he actually does have brains and power—hence the story's appeal and survival in Dane-ẕaa oral tradition.

Sammy told the stories in English, his second language, rather than in his native Beaver. "Indian English" is evident in Sammy's speech patterns. Although his speech is often not grammatically normative, Sammy speaks with poetic authority and uses his "Indian English" effectively to convey the action and plot of the story as well as its poetic vitality. Some characteristics of Beaver language are evident in the following passage from Sammy's performance of the first Chezan story (Acko 1999):

> but her sister told him [the princess],
> "It's OK. It's not going to kill you.
> After he sleeps there
> I will wash the place really good anyway."
> So she said,
> "OK,"
> and he sleep there by that door

Dane-ẕaa pronouns are not gender specific. In the dialogue between the two princesses, Sammy says: "but her sister told him." "Him" refers to one of the princesses. This is a good example of how Dane-ẕaa often retain elements of Dane-ẕaa grammar in their English speech.

Intonation is another feature of Dane-ẕaa English evident in this performance that conveys meaning to a Dane-ẕaa-literate audience. The intonation Sammy used in the first four lines of the excerpt above we recognize as a command or imperative. It is not so much what is being said as the intonation that makes it a command. We have heard this same tone used by parents or older siblings as they direct youngsters. Thus, a Dane-ẕaa-literate audience can get more emotional meaning from the tonal connotations conveyed during the performance of the story. Without this insider knowledge, the plot sequence of the story is still understood, but the cultural connotations conveyed by intonation help the audience find both localized and personal meaning.

Another example of localization we found in the second Chezan story includes the concept of banishment involving disappearing into "the bush." The bush is a place and concept with specific meanings for the Dane-ẕaa. It implies being away from camps, towns, and settlements. There is both power and danger in the concept of the bush. The bush is where children go for vision quests, and it is also the home of the bushman, a feral forest creature who tries to capture children and women. In the same story, localization is also evident in Sammy's use of Canadian political positions such as premiers and mayors to identify the town administrators and rulers.

And all those big shot people. Those head people.
Must be like premiers or something like that
Those town, maybe those mayors and those kind of people.
(Acko 2000)

In this way we can see how the stories are adapted with every telling to reach the understanding of each particular audience.

Many students of northern Athapaskan culture have noted that the use of "I guess" and "maybe" are typical of northern Athapaskan English. These metanarrative devices found in the Chezan stories appear to be telltale signs of indigenization. For example:

I guess those years there's no car or nothing.
They gotta travel by foot . . .

I guess there's some kind of secret in that king's daughter . . .

I guess he went between people somewhere fast
and he went to bathroom in his toque or some kind of hat.
He carry that. So I guess they caught him . . . (Acko 1999)

Rather than reflecting uncertainty, these phrases indicate that the events portrayed are hearsay and not part of the speaker's direct experience. In a similar vein, a speaker will refer to another person's supernatural power by saying something like "Maybe he little bit know something." Sammy's distinction between events that are experienced directly and those that are reported by others reflects what Scollon and Scollon (1979) identify as the individualistic "bush consciousness" of northern Native oral tradition. They describe this consciousness as a feature of what they call the "linguistic convergence" of Chipewyan, Cree, English, and French in Fort Chipewyan, Alberta. The Chezan stories reflect a similar convergence, but they also demonstrate the structural, thematic, and artistic integrity of a shared oral literature. Although Sammy has made the tales understandable to his audience, he has also maintained the basic nature of the stories as he practiced performative translation from Beaver to English. The corresponding European tale types and motifs indexed in Aarne and Thompson (1928) and Thompson (1932–1936) are easily recognized in Sammy's Chezan stories.

In addition to recurrent plots familiar to both Native American and European tradition (lowly hero outwits the powerful), the Chezan stories use dialogue, which is a fundamental feature of First Nations oral discourse (Ridington 2006:148–70). Dialogue is often repeated several times during a story with minor changes. For example, when characters experience a series of similar situations, they say nearly the same thing every time.

"Are you going to cook all night?" . . .
"Are you going to sew all night—sewing?" . . .
"Are you going to drink with us all night?" . . . (Acko 1999)

This example reflects a common pattern in Native American oral discourse. It is also very similar to the memory devices reported by Lord for the process of oral composition in Yugoslavia, and reflects patterns of dialogue found in both European and Native American narrative traditions.

In European folktales, events and numbers tend to occur in groups of three, while in Native American stories the number four is more common. In his work on "Ti-Jean and the Seven-Headed Dragon" stories found in Native repertoire, Jarold Ramsey writes: "Ti-Jean's immediate appeal and accessibility in Native terms meant that he and his stories were open to adaptive changes, including alterations of details, additions, and deletions. When Ti-Jean enters Indian narrative tradition, he becomes, as we will see, subject to Native spirit power instead of European magic, he does things according to Native cult numerology (four or five times rather than the European three times), his powers and indeed his very motives are Indianized, and so on" (1987:208). This type of adaptive change, from European magic to Native spirit power, can be seen in Sammy Acko's first Chezan story. In it, there are four magic objects—magic scissors, magic bottle, magic tablecloth, and magic fiddle—while in the French versions there are only three magic objects.

In the same article on the merits of identifying variants and sources as well as interpretation in folklore research mentioned earlier, Alan Dundes has presented and analyzed a recorded performance of a P'teejah (Petit Jean) story told in 1963 by a Prairie Band Potawatomi elder, William Mzechtenoman, in Kansas. It is unclear whether this is a performative translation or if the storyteller learned the story in English himself. In his analysis, Dundes applied a Eurocentric approach in identifying the tale as "a French version of Aarne-Thompson tale type 569 and certainly not an aboriginal tale type" (1965:140). He identified a connection to tales in European tradition, but fails to look to the canon of Native American motifs and characters, many identified and presented for comparison by Stith Thompson in his 1929 volume *Tales of the North American Indians*. Specifically, Dundes failed to place the story in the categories of Native American trickster tales and hero tales.

However, Dundes did identify ways that the Potawatomi made the story their own and made it relevant to their present-day culture. We can see indigenized elements in both the Potawatomi and the Dane-ẕaa stories which follow the Native American cultural numerology mentioned earlier. For example, in the first Chezan story Robin recorded (Acko 1999), the symbolic magic (the magic tablecloth's gifts) was changed from the European ritual number of three to the more typically Native American ritual number of four. In a similar pattern of indigenization, the magic hat in the Potawatomi tale produces four soldiers rather than the three in the French version of the tale. Dundes also suggests that the tale reflects a resistance to Potawatomi colonial domination, as the lowly Indian hero, P'teejah, is able to outthink the white man (1965:141). Dundes saw the P'teejah character as an Indian boy, but he did not take into consideration that this character could have special Native spirit powers to perform the magic tasks—as do many Native American culture heroes.

Dundes argues that the Native American telling of a European folktale will more closely resemble the original according to how acculturated the teller is. He cites the Potawatomi transformation of P'teejah into an "Indian hero" as evidence that the tale has been significantly indigenized. However, it appears that Dundes asked leading questions that may have encouraged the teller to give that interpretation.

> D. The boy was, you say, an Indian Boy?
> M. Yeah.
> D. So the Indian boy was fooling the white man.
> M. Yeah, [laughing] he put it on him. (Dundes 1965:140)

Sammy Acko's Chezan stories are generally closer to their European origins, but looking at how they are contextualized for a Dane-ẕaa audience, they have been more subtly indigenized to fit into the genre of trickster and culture hero stories.

Nora Marks Dauenhauer and Richard Dauenhauer have also analyzed contemporary Native American material with European origins from the perspective of live performance, as well as historic-geographic tradition, and point out the dynamics of cross-cultural interaction inherent in the processes of both story borrowing and story documentation (1998:58). In 1974 they recorded a version of the Frog Princess, told in the Tlingit language, which came to the community through contact with Russians during the maritime fur-trade era. Nora is Tlingit and was familiar with the story from her own childhood; she translated it into English. In looking at the cultural context of the story and its situation within the Tlingit community, the Dauenhauers have concluded that this story was specific to one family and that the majority of Tlingit do not know the story.

The Dauenhauers suggest that the Frog Princess story may not have been widely adopted in Tlingit tradition for two reasons, both of which reflect traditional Tlingit social structure and attitudes toward storytelling. The first is that the narrative may have been perceived as a clan story, and that others refrained from telling it out of respect for clan ownership (1998:77). They also suggest that this European tale is not often told because of Tlingit reluctance to tell fictitious stories, as their own myths and legends are considered to be true (76). Both of these explanations seem to reflect the hierarchical Tlingit social structure. The maintenance of Tlingit social structure seems to have limited the adoption of European tales, such as the Frog Princess example, because Tlingit have had difficulty placing them in their own worldview. The less rigid Dane-ẕaa, by contrast, appear to have no trouble placing the character of Ti-Jean within their own narrative tradition.

Like the Tlingit Frog Princess and the Potawatomi P'teejah story, the Dane-ẕaa Chezan stories that Sammy Acko told are in contemporary oral circulation and were recorded in live performance situations. Unlike the early ethnographic examples mentioned previously in this chapter that were collected as plot summaries and texts filtered through the tempering lens of the translator and ethnographer, the recording of the stories in live performance allows the narratives to be analyzed as part of living oral traditions and in terms of polyphonic contexts.

Conclusion

Exactly how Ti-Jean made his way into the Dane-ẕaa story repertoire and the details of who first told these stories to the Dane-ẕaa is not known, and probably never will be. The Ti-Jean stories are of European origin and probably come from French-Cree living around or traveling through Fort St. John in the fur-trade era. Early in this chapter we put forward a series of questions: Why would one group curate another group's traditional lore? What changes have been made to the stories? What meaning do these stories have for the Dane-ẕaa? How do we find meaning in a Native American group incorporating stories from a distant and foreign culture into their own narrative tradition?

Dane-ẕaa culture is in transition now. In many respects, newer generations of Dane-ẕaa appear to be passive tradition bearers rather than active carriers of their traditions. They can understand the Dane-ẕaa language but do not speak it. They have been told some of the stories, but are not telling them themselves. It will be interesting to see what course Dane-ẕaa culture takes and whether younger generations will continue to display their oral narrative competence in similar ways. The Chezan stories have been maintained and curated orally in Dane-ẕaa culture, primarily because the trickster elements have resonance with trickster characters from their own tradition, because they reflect the Dane-ẕaa fur-trade experience which included cultural interaction with Europeans, and because the stories themselves have become part of Dane-ẕaa oral heritage. The Chezan stories illustrate how Dane-ẕaa culture is influenced by others, yet also expresses itself. In concluding the results of his 1919 study, Stith

Thompson writes: "The study shows that the comparative stability which has characterized the tales in their migration from people to people in the old world has been retained by them as they pass over to a people . . . of an entirely alien tradition . . . the tales might become as much at home on American soil as Hindu tales now seem native to France, Germany, or Norway" (1919:456–57). The pattern of structural stability that Thompson found for European tales in Native American contexts is explained by the processes of performative translation and oral curation that we have discussed here. And indeed, some ninety years later, we have found that the Ti-Jean tales are at home in Dane-zaa narrative tradition.

The Dane-zaa today still have two living generations of tradition bearers who continue the oral nature of their literacy. Their performative translation and oral curation of the Chezan stories is continuing to evolve. Sammy's recounting of the Chezan stories to Robin in 1999 and 2000 may well have been the first time they were told in English. In the future, we would like to ascertain who else in the Dane-zaa community knows and tells these stories. Do people from all the communities know them, or is it just this group of men from Doig? Do women tell them? Do children know them? What language are they told in? Until these questions are investigated, we hope the cycle of stories will continue through oral curation. We trust that Chezan will continue his adventures in Beaverland and that the Dane-zaa will continue to tell his stories in the way that Tommy Attachie has described each singing of a traditional song: "When You Sing It Now, Just Like New."

Earlier, we quoted Robin's statement that literature "is where stories become experience and experience gives rise to stories" (2001a:222). Sammy's Chezan stories describe a world that the Dane-zaa never knew from direct experience. Hence Sammy's use of "maybe" and "I guess" in his English rendition of the stories. The world these stories describe, however, is not really any more removed from direct experience than the world in which giant animals hunted people and Saya, the culture hero, overcame them and sent them beneath the earth. Chezan, like Saya, is a trickster-transformer who uses his wits to overcome more powerful adversaries.

The stories themselves are vivid experiences in a world without the distractions of television and rapid travel from one place to another. During long nights on the trapline or in small log cabins in the bush far from the nearest road, stories were a prime form of entertainment. The elders of this era, like Sammy's older brother, Jack, and their father, Aku, created windows into a world of imagination. Here kings and princesses and magic gifts of the white man's material culture became real in the voices of the storytellers. Here storytelling became an experience in its own right. Because the stories and the worlds they created were vivid and interesting, they retained their narrative integrity from one telling to another. As the stories remained alive from one telling to another and even one language to another, they were adroitly translated and carefully curated. They retained their integrity because if they lost it, they would lose their life as oral literature.

Storytellers can only find audiences for good stories performed in a lively and knowledgeable way. Ti-Jean in Beaverland had the benefit of being curated by great storytellers like Jack Acko and his brother Sammy. It had the added benefit of being recorded as an audio actuality, rather than being entombed as a list of traits and motifs. Through performative translation and oral curation, the story has retained its integrity as a window into First Nations oral literature and experience.

Appendix A: First Chezan Story Told by Sammy Acko and Recorded by Robin Ridington (Acko 1999)

Not to be reproduced without permission of narrator and transcriber.
There's one story, Dane-ẕaa, Dane-ẕaa,
they have one story about Chezan.
Anybody tell you about that story?
This story, it's amazes me.
It sound like a . . .
long time ago there's little towns, things like that.
That's the way this story sound like, and I don't know where
Dane-ẕaa people pick that story from.
Maybe from Monias [white man] elder, or . . .
I didn't know where it come from.
But anyway, this story,
it's about magic tablecloth,
and then a magic fiddle, magic wine, and magic scissors.
Those four things. It's about four things.
Jack [Sammy's elder brother] used to tell us a story about that.
He was saying . . . There's two people, two brothers.
One, his brother's name is Chezan.
Chezan and his brother.

They travel on foot.
I guess those years there's no car or nothing.
So they gotta travel by foot.
Then from one place, they got to one little town.
From there they're heading straight towards that bigger town
where the king live.
They're headin' that way,
so this town they stop.
And then they told his brother first,
>"Are you willing to cook all night?"

His brother said,
>"No, I'm tired. I'll just going to go asleep."

But his brother Chezan is kind of crazy guys. They told him,
>"Are you going to cook all night?"

He said,
>"I will cook all night."

So from there he cook all night with the people.
The next day before they move,
they give him a tablecloth. They told him,
>"Anywhere you get hungry, anywhere, you carry this,
>you just spread it out
>and then there'll be a whole bunch of food on it.
>It will happen."

They told him.
They gave him that tablecloth.
So they move to another town.
They were walking.
Somewhere in the middle they were hungry.
He told his older brother,
>"Let's eat."

His brother said,
>"There's nothing. What we gonna eat?"

So
>"Wait,"

he told him.
He took that tablecloth out and he spread it
and then, there's all kinds of food in there.
So they eat, and then his brother told him,
>"Brother, this is something good one you have.
>Don't sell it.
>Don't give it away."
>"I'll do what I want with it,"

he told his brother.

So they went to next town.
And then that town, again they stopped to spend the night.
They told his brother again,
        "Are you going to sew all night . . . sewing?"
His brother said,
        "I'm tired. I'll just go to sleep."
Again, he sewed all night.
So next morning before they move,
they give him a pair of scissors and a cloth.
So they went to another town and he told his brother,
        "Do you want new clothes?"
        "Where you get those new clothes?"
he told him,
so he took his scissors out and that magic cloth.
It bring him all the nice beautiful clothes like these.
Sports jacket and all good clothes people have.
He dress his brother up.
So his brother again told him,
        "This is good thing you have.
        Don't sell it."
But he said,
        "That's mine.
        I can do whatever I want with it."
So they move on to another town.
Again they stop in this town,
and then they told his brother first, older brother,
        "Are you going to drink with us all night?"
He said,
        "I'm tired.
        I just want to go to sleep.
        I don't want to drink."
But his brother, Chezan, said,
        "I'll drink with you all night."
Drinking whatever liquor they have.
So he drink with them all night
and next day, they give him a bottle.
A bottle.
They told him,
        "This one, you finish it,
        it will be full again.
        Forever it's like that."
So he gives his brother a drink on his way too.
And then, the last one was,

there's scissors, bottle and tablecloth,
[Billy volunteers, "fiddle."]
Yeah, the last one was fiddle.
Then next town they stop
they told his brother again,
        "You going to play fiddle all night?"
He said,
        "No, I'm not crazy.
        I'll just go to sleep."
So again he play fiddle all night for them,
and the next day they give him a fiddle.
That's another magic fiddle.
So from there,
the next one they're coming into is city, just like a city.
Big town, and there's a king in there
and then he's got beautiful princess.
And they're headin' into this town.
I guess maybe they're having some kind of celebration or something.
So they're coming into this beautiful fine town.
And when they got into town,
I guess there's some kind of secret in that king's daughter . . .
Inside somewhere.
Every time new people come there
and then the king will them,
        "What's secret in my daughter?"
They mention anything; grass, leaves, ground, rocks, sky, everything.
Nobody mention the right one.
So every time they get the wrong one,
they put 'em in jail.
So they were all in jail.
Bunch of people, are skinny people in jail.
'Cause the day somebody got it right,
they will all go free.
So I guess his brother's scared to go there.
So he never went there,
but him, somehow, before they catch him
he told his brother,
        "Oh, boy, brother I want to go to bathroom."
But there's no bathroom.
So oh, boy, his brother give him heck.
        "There's nowhere in the bathroom around here.
        How you going to ever go to bathroom?
        This is fine town.

They just going to put you in jail.
The hat you got.
Why don't you poop in there?
Poop in there and then somehow carry it
and somewhere you can,
if you find a garbage,
you can throw it away."
He said,
"Okay,"
and then I guess he went between people somewhere fast
and he went to bathroom in his toque or some kind of hat.
He carry that.
So I guess they caught him.
He's hang onto that.
So the king told him,
"What secret is in my daughter?"
And then he open his poop in that hat.
"This one,"
he told him.
So the king got mad.
He said,
"Even these people who don't say that to my daughter
are in the bad place, in jail.
Put him in the worse place."
So they throw him in jail.
And then he got all those magic, everything with him.
When he went in jail he just opened those tablecloth
and all those jail people just got fatten up
and they were drinking and partying every night.
Somehow those two princess, those sisters, they found out.
So one of the princess told her sister,
"I like that magic he got.
There's some way we'll make him give it to us.
Why don't we ask him if we can buy it?"
So I guess they told him,
"If we can buy it from you—one."
He said,
"No. If I sleep,
I sleep inside the princess, inside the door,
by the door on the floor.
If I sleep in there I'll give 'em this,
this tablecloth or scissors."
So he said,

"No, he's too dirty.
  He can't sleep in my doorway.
  He's too dirty,"
but her sister told him,
    "It's OK. It's not going to kill you.
    After he sleeps there
    I will wash the place really good anyway."
So she said,
    "OK,"
and he sleep there by that door.
So he give 'em that scissors, I think.
And next one is that tablecloth.
Tablecloth.
And then he sleep in the middle of that floor,
closer to her bed.
In the middle, he sleep there.
And the next one, the next one was that fiddle.
The fiddle.
He sleep right close to that princess bed.
The last one is that wine bottle or whatever bottle it is.
And then he sleep right under the princess bed.
Underneath.
He give that drink to the princess,
and he end up sleeping with that princess.
And then that princess told him,
    "You going to have court again.
    And if my dad told you what secret is inside me, tell him,
    'Big star up in the air, that's inside me.'
    Tell him that and don't tell him that you're with me."
So I guess he's back in jail
and then when they took all the jail people,
they all went to court
and then I guess it's his turn.
They put him in front of king
and then king told him,
    "What secret is in my daughter?"
He told him,
    "Big star up in the air."
So he, the king have to keep his word.
He marry the princess.
So this kind of story amazes me. I don't know where it come from.

Appendix B: Folktale Types and Motifs Found in the First Chezan Story Told by
Sammy Acko and Recorded by Robin Ridington (Acko 1999)

Tale Type References (Aarne and Thompson 1961)

577	*The King's Tasks.* The three brothers; through kindness one brother receives magic objects which are used to gain princess.
592 I	*The Magic Object and Powers.* Mentions magic fiddle
851 A	*Turandot.* Princess sets riddles for her suitors to be answered on pain of death.
853 IV	*The Princess Caught,* (a) The hero is imprisoned and escapes by means of his magic tablecloth, purse, and fiddle. (b) By his magic fiddle he captures the princess and will release her only if she says no to all his questions. (c) By this means he gets her into bed and marries her.

Motif Index References (Thompson 1932–1936)

D 810	*Magic object a gift*
D 817	*Magic object received from grateful person*
D 1470.2	*Provisions received from magic object*
D 1472.1.8	*Magic table-cloth supplies food and drink*
D 1472.1.17	*Magic bottle supplies drink*
D 1395	*Magic object frees person from prison*
H 335	*Tasks assigned suitors*
H 508.2	*Bride offered to man who can find answer to question*
L 13	*Compassionate youngest son—rewarded*
L 161	*Lowly hero marries princess*
T 68	*Princess offered as prize*
T 121	*Unequal marriage*

Notes

1. The Aarne-Thompson classification system for comparing plot summaries
of European and Near Eastern folktales was first published in 1910, in Finnish, by
Antti Aarne. Stith Thompson translated the work, enlarged it in scope and detail,
and published it in 1928 under both their names as *The Types of the Folktale: A
Classification and Bibliography*. Although numerous regional motif and type indexes from around the world have been developed and published over the years,
the Aarne-Thompson bibliography continued to be a standard reference work
for comparative study of European folktales until 2004, when Hans-Jörg Uther
revised and expanded it in his three-volume work, *The Types of International
Folktales: A Classification and Bibliography, Based on the System of Antti Aarne*

and Stith Thompson. Uther maintains the Aarne-Thompson tale type numbers but revises many of the tale titles and descriptions and updates the bibliography with more recent references to documented variants (primarily from European sources).

2. Amber first wrote this paper in 2002 for a narrative folklore class at Western Kentucky University. For this volume it was greatly revised and expanded by both Robin and Amber. We are thankful to Dr. Martin Lovelace, who reviewed a draft of the paper and provided valuable comments.

3. We welcome collaboration with bilingual French-English colleagues in the future so that we can together bridge this language barrier and make use of all the relevant sources. Following are some additional sources that we are aware of but that we have not been able to use as we have not been successful in locating translations from French:

Paul Delarue and Marie-Louise Teneze, *Le conte populaire francais* (1957). This French folktale index includes a survey of North American Collections primarily from eastern provinces and states.

Evelyne Voldeng, *Les meimoires de Ti-Jean: Espace intercontinental du heiros des contes franco-ontariens* (1994). This book is about Ti-Jean stories in oral circulation in Ontario and about their origins in both the literature and oral history of France.

In 1946, Joseph M. Carriere summarized the state of French folklore studies in North America for an English audience in *Southern Folklore Quarterly* 10 (4): 219–26. In this article Carriere notes research in francophone communities in Quebec, New Brunswick, Louisiana, Missouri, and Michigan's Upper Peninsula, but he does not mention any stories found circulating in Native American groups. His footnotes, with detailed references to French-American sources, may be of interest to others studying French folklore in North America.

4. Toelken (1996:39) suggests the twin laws of dynamism and conservatism to explain variation and stability in folklore process.

5. Regional variation through oral transmission is also known in folklore as "oicotypification," and a regional variant is described as an "oicotype." Von Sydow developed this term in 1927 to explain the process of cultural adaptation of stories as they are passed along from tale teller to tale teller through time and space. The term was borrowed from botany, where it refers to a local or regional form of a plant. Von Sydow used the term in his extension of the comparative method to refocus study on living traditions instead of texts (von Sydow 1932).

References

Acko, Sammy. 1999. The story of Chezan told to and recorded by Robin Ridington while driving in a truck east of Doig River Reserve, British Columbia. 7/28/99. Ridington's Recording Log DZ99-17. Available online at http://sites

.google.com/site/plumeofcockatoopress/chezan-story-by-sam-acko/chezan
-story-1999.

———.2000. Second Chezan story told to and recorded by Robin Ridinton while
driving in a truck east of Doig River Reserve, British Columbia. 12/12/00. Ridington's Recording Log DZ00–18 Tracks 8–9. Available online at http://sites
.google.com/site/plumeofcockatoopress/chezan-story-by-sam-acko/chezan
-story-2000.

Aarne, Antti, and Stith Thompson. 1928 [rev. 1961]. *The Types of the Folktale: A
Classification and Bibliography*. Folklore Fellows Communications No. 184.

Armstrong, Jeannette C. 1998. Land *Speaking*. In *Speaking for the Generations:
Native Writers on Writing*, ed. Simon J. Ortiz, 175–94. Tucson: University of
Arizona Press.

Barbeau, Marius. 1916. Contes Populaires Canadiens. *Journal of American Folklore* 29 (111): 1–154.

———.1917. Contes Populaires Canadiens. Seconde Serie. *Journal of American
Folklore* 30 (115): 1–159.

Bauman, Richard. 1986. *Story, Performance, and Event: Contextual Studies of Oral
Narrative*. Cambridge: Cambridge University Press.

Boas, Franz. 1940. Romance Folk-Lore among American Indians. In *Race Language and Culture*, 517–24. Chicago: University of Chicago Press.

Bolduc, Evelyn. 1919. Contes Populaires Canadiens. Troisieme Serie. *Journal of
American Folklore* 32 (123): 90–167.

Dauenhauer, Nora Marks, and Richard Dauenhauer. 1998. Tracking "Yuwaan
Gageets": A Russian Fairy Tale in Tlingit Oral Tradition. *Oral Tradition* 13
(1): 58–91.

Degh, Linda. 1969. *Folktales and Society: Story-Telling in a Hungarian Peasant
Community*. Bloomington: Indian University Press.

Delarue, Paul, and Marie-Louise Teneze. 1957. *Le Conte Populaire Francais:
Catalogue Raisonne Des Versions De France et de pays de langue francaise
d'outre-mer: Canada, Louisiane, Ilots francais des Etats-Unis, Antilles Fran-
caises, Haiti, Ile Maurice, La Reunion*. Tome Deuxieme. Paris: G. P. Maison-
neuve et Larose.

Dundes, Alan. 1965. The Study of Folklore in Literature and Culture: Identification and Interpretation. *Journal of American Folklore* 78 (308): 136–42.

Hymes, Dell. 1981. *"In Vain I Tried to Tell You": Essays in Native American Ethnopoetics*. Philadelphia: University of Pennsylvania Press.

———.2000. Survivors and Renewers. *Folklore Forum* 31 (1): 3–15.

Jacobs, Melville. 1945. *Kalapuya Texts*. Seattle: University of Washington Press.

Lambert, Adelard, Marius Barbeau, and Pierre Daviault. 1940. Contes Populaires
Canadiens. Septieme Serie. *Journal of American Folklore* 53 (208/209): 91–190.

Lanctot, Gustave. 1916. Fables, Contes et Formules. *Journal of American Folklore*
29 (111): 141–51.

——.1923. Contes Populaires Canadiens. Quatrieme Serie. *Journal of American Folklore* 36 (141): 205–72.

——.1926. Contes Populaires Canadiens. Cinquieme Serie. *Journal of American Folklore* 39 (154): 371–449.

——.1931. Contes Populaires Canadiens. Sixieme Serie. *Journal of American Folklore* 44 (173): 225–94.

Lindahl, Carl. 1997. Some Uses of Numbers. *Journal of Folklore Research* 34 (3): 263–73.

Lord, Albert. 1960. *The Singer of Tales.* Cambridge: Harvard University Press.

Michelson, Truman. 1916. Piegan Tales of European Origin. *Journal of American Folklore* 29:409.

Ramsey, Jarold. 1987. Ti-Jean and the Seven-Headed Dragon: Instances of Native American Assimilation of European Folklore. In *The Native in Literature*, ed. Thomas King, Cheryl Calver, and Helen Hoy, 206–24. Oakville, Ontario: ECW Press.

Ridington, Robin. 1990. *Little Bit Know Something: Stories in a Language of Anthropology.* Iowa City: University of Iowa Press.

——.2001a. Re-creation in Canadian First Nations Literatures: "When You Sing It Now, Just Like New." *Anthropologica* 43 (2): 221–30.

——.2001b. E-mail to Amber Ridington, March 2001.

——.2006. Voice, Representation, and Dialogue: The Poetics of Native American Spiritual Traditions. In *When You Sing It Now, Just Like New: First Nations Poetics, Voices, and Representations,* by Robin Ridington and Jillian Ridington, 148–70. Lincoln: University of Nebraska Press.

Ridington, Robin, and Jillian Ridington. 2006. *When You Sing It Now, Just Like New: First Nations Poetics, Voices, and Representations.* Lincoln: University of Nebraska Press.

Rioux, Marcel. 1950. Contes Populaires Canadiens. Huitieme Serie. *Journal of American Folklore* 63 (248): 199–230.

Robinson, Harry. 1989. *Write It on Your Heart: The Epic World of an Okanagan Storyteller.* Ed. Wendy Wickwire. Vancouver: Talonbooks.

Scollon, Ronald, and Suzanne B. K. Scollon. 1979. *Linguistic Convergence: An Ethnography of Speaking at Fort Chipewyan, Alberta.* London: Academic Press.

Skinner, Alanson. 1916. European Tales from the Plains Ojibwa. *Journal of American Folklore* 29:336–40.

——.1927. The Mascoutens or Prairie Potawatomi Indians, Part III—Mythology and Folklore. *Bulletin of the Public Museum of the City of Milwaukee* 6 (3): 400–402.

Speck, Frank G., and Horace P. Beck. 1950. Old World Tales among the Mohawks. *Journal of American Folklore* 63 (249): 285–308.

Tedlock, Dennis. 1991. The Speaker of Tales Has More Than One String to Play

On. In *Anthropological Poetics*, ed. Ivan Brady, 309–40. Savage MD: Rowman and Littlefield.

Teit, James. 1916. European Tales from the Upper Thompson Indians. *Journal of American Folklore* 29:301–29.

Thompson, Stith. 1919. European Tales among N. American Indians: A Study in the Migration of Folk-Tales. *Colorado College Publication: Language Series* 2 (34): 319–471.

———.1929. *Tales of the North American Indians.* Bloomington: Indiana University Press.

———.1932–1936. *Motif-Index of Folk-Literature: A Classification of Narrative Elements in Folk-Tales, Ballads, Myths, Fables, Mediaeval Romances, Exempla, Fabliaux, Jest-Books, and Local Legends.* 6 vols. Folklore Fellows Communications Nos. 106–9, 116–17. Helsinki: Suomalainen Tiedeakatemia, Academia Scientiarum Fennica.

Toelken, Barre. 1996 [1979 first publication]. *The Dynamics of Folklore: Revised and Expanded Edition.* Logan: Utah State University Press.

Uther, Hans-Jörg. 2004. *The Types of International Folktales: A Classification and Bibliography, Based on the System of Antti Aarne and Stith Thompson.* 3 vols. Helsinki: Folklore Fellows Communications nos. 284, 285, 286.

Voldeng, Evelyne. 1994. *Les meìmoires de Ti-Jean : espace intercontinental du heìros des contes franco-ontariens.* Vanier, Ontario: Eìditions L'Interligne.

von Sydow, C. W. 1932 [reprinted 1999]. Geography and Folk-Tale Oicotypes. In *International Folkloristics: Classic Contributions by the Founders of Folklore*, ed. Alan Dundes, 137–51. New York: Rowman and Littlefield.

7

Translation and Censorship of Native American Oral Literature

William M. Clements

One decision confronting translators of orally performed American Indian verbal art concerns what to do with material that is regarded as questionable by one of the several persons who may figure into the process that begins with oral performance and ends with the publication of a written representation of that performance. The performer, the ethnographer who documents the performance, the translator, an editor, or a publisher may decide that a feature of a story or song should be withheld or transformed, usually to protect someone or something from moral or spiritual contamination. Under ideal conditions, the performer should not feel compelled to place any restraints on what he or she verbalizes, nor should anyone who contributes to the translation of the verbalization from oral performance and from an indigenous language into textualized English. But translation in the real world often involves censorship. While the very word *censorship* undoubtedly raises a red flag for most people, translators must face the reality that what their readers experience in print is often not what they would have experienced had they encountered the material in its usual performance situations because of decisions by someone to delete, expurgate, or simply ignore aspects of that material that he or she believes should not be available in their original form or content to a reading audience. The purpose here is not to condemn or support censorship per se but simply to acknowledge that it occurs and to describe some of the ways that those involved in the translation process have handled it and some of the factors that have occasioned it in the particular case of Native American oral literature.

The folklorist Richard M. Dorson, for example, used to tell a story about censorship to his beginning graduate students in folklore study. It seems that as a young folklore collector, recently returned from fieldwork in Michigan's Upper Peninsula, Dorson had submitted several stories he had recorded from Ojibwe raconteurs to one of the folklore journals specializing in regional materials. At least one of these was a trickster narrative in which the impish Winabijou's "balls" figured. The journal's editor refused to publish the story unless Dorson would agree to change the referenced body part to "ears." Some twenty-five years after he had withdrawn the material from the journal's consideration, he chuckled over the benighted editor's attempting to "castrate" the story.

When we think of censoring Native American literature, what probably first occurs to many of us is the sort of situation related by Dorson: a prudish Euro-American—collector, editor, or publisher—who cannot deal with the forthright expressions of "Noble Savages" whose perceptions of body parts and functions have not been corrupted by exposure to the repressive institutions of Western civilization. Henry Rowe Schoolcraft, who notoriously suppressed material he considered indecent from the translated texts that he and his in-laws produced from Ojibwe oral traditions, may epitomize this practice. Schoolcraft became the federal government's agent to the Ojibwes at Sault Ste. Marie in 1822. Influenced by his mentor Lewis Cass's belief that such information had the practical value of helping to implement government Indian policy, Schoolcraft used his position as a basis for learning as much as possible about his charges' way of life. This included recording and translating their stories and songs. An entry in his journal from early in his tenure (July 28, 1822) reveals his methodology: "My method is to interrogate all persons visiting the office, white and red, who promise to be useful subjects of information during the day, and to test my inquiries in the evening by reference to the Johnstons, who, being educated, and speaking at once both the English and the Ojibwa correctly, offer a higher and more reliable standard than usual" (1851:107). The Johnstons to whom Schoolcraft refers were a family who were to become his mixed-blood in-laws. In 1823 he married Jane Johnston, daughter of Irish fur trader John Johnston and granddaughter of Waubojeeg, a famous Ojibwe leader. Some of the censorship that eventually characterized Schoolcraft's representations of Ojibwe verbal art may have come from the Johnstons, who undoubtedly recognized their future kinsman's religiosity, which produced what his biographer has called his "somewhat priggish village-bourgeois outlook" (Bremer 1982:46). Nevertheless, Schoolcraft himself must bear most of the responsibility. When he published a sampling of the stories he had heard in *Algic Researches* in 1839, he stressed the fidelity of the texts to what he had actually heard. "The value of these traditionary tales," he opined in the introduction to his book, "appeared to depend, very much, upon their being left, as nearly as possible, in their original forms of thought and expression." Moreover, he claimed to have paid "great attention" to "repeating the conversations and speeches, and imitating the very tone and gesture of the actors" even at "the risk of tautology" (1839:1:43). However, he confided to his journal in an entry for January 26, 1838, "I have weeded out many vulgarisms" (1851:525). When he republished the stories in 1856 in an attempt to capitalize on the popularity of Longfellow's *The Song of Hiawatha*, which drew upon the Ojibwe narratives in *Algic Researches* for an epic account of an Iroquois culture hero, Schoolcraft noted that his textualization protocols had sometimes included "expunging passages, where it was necessary" (1856:ix).

Schoolcraft, of course, was constrained by what was publishable in the mid-nineteenth century, when "Anglo-American translators consciously took on the role of censors" (Crisafulli 1997:250) and when—despite the claims of the romantic movement—the language used in literature was expected to be formal rather than demotic.[1] He indeed was interested in ensuring that his book was marketable, so he attempted to present the stories of the Ojibwe in ways that would enhance their appeal to readers who brought a literary aesthetic shaped by romantic visions of the "Noble Savage." Though Schoolcraft himself probably did not share the notion that Indians were uncorrupted children of nature, his intended readers did. To put "vulgarisms" into the mouths of figures who, for many, represented the primitivistic ideal was unthinkable. Schoolcraft's influence—or, perhaps, similar views that were independently derived—has continued to characterize the efforts of many literary-minded translators of Native American verbal art.

Meanwhile, those ethnographically oriented fieldworkers and translators for the Bureau of American Ethnology and other late-nineteenth-century institutions who published translated oral literature developed other ways of dealing with any questionable material they encountered. More reluctant than literary translators to change what their consultants had said and less apt to subscribe to the image of uncorrupted primitivism, they were nevertheless faced with the challenge of what to do with material that violated conventional standards of decency. One course of action was simply to omit such material from their publications and sometimes not even to record it at all. Franz Boas, for example, chided Henry Tate, a Tsimshian speaker who was recording stories for the anthropologist, for his expurgation of some of those stories. In a letter dated March 28, 1907, Boas wrote:

> You write in your letter that you have omitted some of the stories which to you and to me seem very improper, but if we want to preserve for future times a truthful picture of what the people were before they advanced to their present condition, we ought not to leave out anything that shows their way of thinking, even though it should be quite distasteful to us. . . . I hope, therefore, that you may be willing to overcome your reluctance to write nasty things, since they belong to the tales that were told by your old people. For our purpose it is all-essential that whatever we write should be true, and that we should not conceal anything. (Stocking 1974:124)

When Boas published the stories collected by Tate in *Tsimshian Mythology*, he noted, "Mr. Tate felt it incumbent upon himself to omit some of those traits of the myths of his people that seem inappropriate to us" (1916:31).

Yet when it came time to publish stories that contained "nasty things" (presumably sexual and scatological material), even the most dispassionately scientific translators faced a dilemma. Outlets for publication, even academic ones, were reluctant to risk the censure of printing what they and the mainstream public considered obscene. One recourse for the translator was simply not to translate, but to leave questionable passages in the Native languages. For Boas and many other linguistically oriented anthropologists, the translation was not important anyway. They were concerned with collecting and transcribing Native-language texts, especially in languages that were in danger of disappearing. Consequently, there was no problem in printing offensive material in the Native language, ignoring it in the interlinear translations that often accompanied the texts created by ethnologists, and retaining the Native language or using euphemisms for the indecent portions of the narrative in the free translations. Frank Russell used a similar approach when he simply omitted a couple of stanzas of a Pima "Roadrunner Song" from his free translation, though he had included them using the terms "vulva" and "penis" in his interlinear translation (1904–5:313). Stressing straightforward documentation of the original-language text at the expense of full cultural understanding could also blind ethnographers to subtleties and might produce translations that misrepresented the intent of the original performer. For example, when Boas recorded a myth from a Kwagul storyteller in October 1894, he missed the sexual dimension of the language, much of which depended upon punning that he did not understand. The result was an English version of the story that inadvertently censored what the performer intended. Fortunately, Judith Berman, a modern student of Kwakw'ala, has retranslated the myth, producing an English version that captures the sexual intent of the original, whose meaning depended upon more than simply making a record of the sounds produced by the performer (1992).

For those anthropologists who emphasized the importance of translated texts more significantly, an option was to translate narratives or portions of narratives that they perceived as violating standards of mainstream decency into Latin, the language of scholars. For example, in *Myths and Tales of the Southeastern Indians*, which includes only English versions of stories from three ethnic groups, John R. Swanton presents a story he recorded from Watt Sam, "one of the few remaining speakers of the ancient Natchez tongue," near Braggs, Oklahoma. Sam's repertoire, Swanton lamented, had become so influenced by material from Cherokee and Creek storytellers that the ethnologist could not say whether any of the material presented as Natchez myths and tales originally came from that linguistic community (1929:1). Sam's stories seem to have contained more than the usual amount of "indecent" material, for Swanton found that he had to resort to Latin on several occasions. A story he calls "Corn-Woman's Son" relates how a boy becomes disgusted with Corn-Woman when he thinks that she is producing the hominy for their meals by defecating into a basket. She suggests that he return to his relatives, but only after he had hunted and killed several kinds of birds, killed her, and reduced the house where they were living to ashes. Corn-Woman revives the birds that the boy has killed, positions them on various parts of his body (for example, shoulders and head), and gives him a flute to play. The birds sing in accompaniment to his fluting. At this point Swanton switches to Latin:

"Quum profisceris," ei dicebat illa, "alicubi in via mulieribus pravis obviam venies quae te ut cum eis concumbas sollicitabunt. Cum eis vero ne concumbas quia in verendis suis dentes habent qui tuum penem abscindent. Facias tibi penem lapideum et quum mulieri quartae obvenies eum ea concumbas." (1929:231)[2]

Presumably, having a classical education and the ability to read Latin immunized the reader from the corrupting effects of this passage. It certainly was less likely to arouse the interest of censors who might take offense at its appearance in English, especially in a government publication.

Of course, even some of the translators working under the auspices of the incipient science of ethnology might opt to treat the indecent by denial. Jeremiah Curtin and J. N. B. Hewitt, for instance, writing for a more general audience than some of their contemporary ethnologists, claimed that their consultants were, for the most part, uncorrupted innocents when it came to obscenity and vulgarity. They drew "special attention" to the "freedom of these Seneca narratives from coarseness of thought and expression, although in some respectable quarters obscenity seems to be regarded as a dominant characteristic of American Indian myths and legendary lore." They had to admit, though, that generic differences might be a principal factor in Native American narrators' use of the sexual and scatological: "[A] distinction must be made between myths and legends on the one hand and tales and stories which are related primarily for the indecent coarseness of their thought and diction on the other." While the former might include only an occasional reference to "indelicate matters," they admitted that American Indians did tell "ribald tales in which the evident motive is merely to pander to the depraved taste by detailing the coarse, the vulgar, and the filthy in life" (1910–11:50). Undoubtedly, Curtin and Hewitt were imposing their own ideas about what constituted "coarseness of thought," and field researchers such as Melville Jacobs, working with Clackamas storyteller Victoria Howard, have noted real differences in attitudes, especially toward scatological themes. Jacobs believed that the Clackamas reaction to the behavior of one of the characters in a story narrated by Howard would differ significantly from that of Euro-Americans. They "probably suffered little disgust when they heard about defecation as an expression of aggression to which the loser resorted. . . . Clackamas were less rejecting of overt anality than are most persons of European heritage" (1959:44).

Unless they are preparing texts for children, most contemporary translators, I think, agree with H. Christoph Wolfart's assertion that Native

American "literary texts demand respect" and that it is "appropriate to place the literary quality of the translation above strict adherence to the social norm" (1986:385). Problems remain, though, about how to handle material that has conventionally been regarded as indecent in the European literary tradition. English, for example, offers at least three approaches to verbalizing such material: the use of technical language, often with pseudo-medical connotations; euphemistic circumlocutions; and so-called four-letter words, which still have the power to shock many readers. In most cases, none of these approaches suits an American Indian text that comes from a culture which does not attach taboos to articulating the concepts. Moreover, many—perhaps most—Native American languages do not have a vocabulary of sexual insult, the context in which many of the tabooed terms in English are used. In fact, insult may be directed at one's place in the community, as it is among the Crows as reported by Robert Lowie, who noted three common curses used by the Crows: "1) You are a ghost; 2) You have no one to talk to; 3) No one at all owns you" (1959:105). Each focus on the isolation of the cursed insultee from the rest of society. Sexual insult does not appear at all.

Boas seems to have varied his approach to translating the potentially indecent, perhaps based on his perception of the appropriate register for the genre. For example, he opts for the formal pseudo-medical "excrement" when translating the name of a character (Y!n-dzax) in a Raven story collected by Henry Tate (1916:122). Elsewhere in Tate's material, Boas seems to rely on euphemistic circumlocution: "Then the young man came again and staid with the girl, and she loved him more and more" (1916:162). A footnote gives this passage in the original Tsimshian—a practice Boas uses only occasionally (and probably in other cases where he has rendered the text into euphemistic English) throughout the lengthy presentation of Tsimshian myths. Ekkehart Malotki suggests that for some of the Hopi stories that he has translated—"simple and honest narrative[s]"—the last option, "four-letter words," is most appropriate (1983:218). This approach may indeed be the most suitable, especially as the terms lose some of their tabooed status in English, but for other specific cases one of the other options, either technical terminology or euphemisms, may seem the best alternative. The translator, particularly when dealing with sexual matters, must have a good sense of the various registers in the language from which he or she is translating in order to choose what may best represent the tone of the original, even though any of the options in English may not fully capture that tone. For example, Dell Hymes's translation of the Kalapuya story he has entitled "Coyote, Master of Death, True to Life" (in Swann 1994:293–306) suggests the potential for varying registers even in the same work of verbal art. When speaking of Coyote's being reduced to coprophagy when entrapped in a tree trunk, the narrator uses the term "feces." Later in the story when Coyote addresses a body part, the narrator uses "anus." But when Coyote licentiously speaks to himself about his intentions for Mountain Woodpecker, the benefactor who releases him from the tree trunk and whom he intends to take sexual advantage of, he uses the colloquial "fuck." The formality of the narrator's speech appropriately contrasts with the earthiness of Coyote's.

Perhaps, then, Native American verbal art has transcended the prudery of Euro-American censors, at least among serious adult readers, but the issue of censorship encompasses much more than the misrepresentation of what storytellers and other oral performers say by translators, editors, and publishers. For example, performers themselves censor what they present given their sense of the performance situation, especially the response by the audience. It is certainly likely, for instance, that Schoolcraft's consultants, especially those who were family members, realized that his attitudes toward sexual and scatological themes made it advisable for them to adjust what they were telling him. Schoolcraft probably did not have to bowdlerize some of the stories that appeared in *Algic Researches*, because Jane Johnston Schoolcraft and her brothers had already done so. In his introduction to a reissue of Franc Johnson Newcomb's presentation of Navajo stories that she had heard from several Navajo storytellers, Paul Zolbrod suggests that this might be what occurred. Unlike the version of some of this material that Zolbrod had translated in *Diné Bahane'*, which contained overt sexual conflict and violence, the stories in Newcomb's collection seem "prissy and evasive" (1990:xi). Although we cannot be sure who was the actual censor, the likelihood exists that the storytellers assessed their audience, the Euro-American woman Newcomb and perhaps her children, and told what they believed would not offend their sensibilities, even if that meant major changes in the narrative. As Zolbrod notes, the flexibility of oral tradition "allows for youthful appeal in one telling and a more ponderous adult understanding in another" (1990:xi). Geoffrey Kimball also calls attention to the tendency of Koasati storytellers to censor themselves when performing for non-Indians: "Scenes pertaining to sex or excretion are deleted, or whole stories may not be told at all." He attributes the practice to "the negative reaction" that audiences from outside the culture evinced, citing Swanton's translations of "material he considered salacious" into "turgid Latin" (in Swann 1994:705). Of course, when stories recorded from performances in which the storyteller has made changes to adapt to particular audiences make their way into print, the textmaker cannot reorient them in ways to make them conform to how they would be performed in less sensitive circumstances. What we read may be bowdlerized, but if the bowdlerization emerged from the sensitivity of the storyteller, it is appropriate for the text to reflect the particular usage in the particular performance.

Some of the sensitivity on the part of performers may stem not just from their perception of the negative attitudes toward matters sexual and scatological on the part of Europeans in general, but from gender differences—a hesitancy about performing questionable material in "mixed company." For example, in September 1934 Elizabeth Derr Jacobs collected some sixty narratives from Clara Pearson, one of the few living speakers of Nehalem Tillamook, a Salish language. Among these were several dealing with the character Wild Woman, sort of a female trickster whose adventures often have sexual dimensions. In one of these Wild Woman kills Otter by clubbing him with her clitoris, a feat about which she boasts in a song which Brian Swann has reworked from Jacobs's text (E. D. Jacobs 1990:61; Swann 1996:43). Swann has speculated that Pearson would have been much less likely to have told this story to a male anthropologist than to Elizabeth Jacobs (1996:144). Gender concerns regarding audience may also transcend sexual content of verbal art when that art is associated with gender-based groups such as the warrior societies in many Plains communities and religious organizations such as Pueblo kiva societies. Barbara Babcock speculates that Elsie Clews Parsons was able to record "girl stuff" and "girl talk"—including verbal art forms such as lullabies—that a male ethnographer would have been unlikely to hear from women in the Pueblos where she worked (1991:27). Consultants may censor female-specific information such as lore regarding pregnancy and childbirth out of a sense that men simply will not appreciate its significance.

At this more profound level, Native American performers may censor what they present to outsiders in the context of ethnographic consultation because of their own religious reasons. Some of the most egregious horror stories in the history of ethnography relate the "heroic measures" to which Euro-American observers—especially of Native American religious activities—went in order to be present at those events and to make a lasting record of them for outside readers. A particularly disturbing example of a researcher's abusing the hospitality of his hosts occurs in the work of John Gregory Bourke, the soldier who—though more sensitive than most of his contemporaries to the indigenous cultures he encountered during his tours of duty during the late-nineteenth-century Indian Wars—forced himself into the "Estufas" (i.e., kivas) of several southwestern Pueblos for the sake of acquiring knowledge about "secret" rituals. At Santo Domingo, for example, Bourke and illustrator Peter Moran attempted to insinuate themselves into the kiva just after one of these rituals had concluded in order to "jot down a few memoranda of value before the preoccupied savages could discover and expel us." The researchers were unsuccessful and, according to Bourke's published version of the story, summarily rejected. He relates the adventure lightheartedly and suggests that the Santo Domingans laughed it off as readily as he did (1984:22–23). Bourke's biographer, though, does not let him off so easily. Generalizing about his field research during the summer of 1881 and focusing specifically on the Santo Domingo incident, Joseph C. Porter writes: "A summer of fieldwork among the Pueblos had already shown Bourke how skillfully they could evade his queries. When they maintained a stubborn silence he occasionally acted in an arrogant manner, barging into their kivas or ceremonial chambers and asking questions that they were reluctant to answer. What was zealous research to Bourke was often pure and simple insult to the Indians" (1986:98).

Bourke's contemporary Frank Hamilton Cushing also placed his desire for esoteric knowledge above his consultants' need to protect that knowledge from outsiders. The governor of Zuni Pueblo himself had suggested to Cushing that he should not take notes during ceremonial performances. The point was made quite forcefully one morning when Cushing encountered several community leaders who grabbed him by the arm and threatened to destroy his notebooks if he persisted in his attempts to document their rituals. Apparently relishing this "adventure" in the field, Cushing boasted of his response: "Suddenly wrenching away from them, I pulled a knife out from the bottom of my pouch, and, bracing up against the wall, brandished it, and said that whatever hand grabbed my arm again would be cut off, that whoever cut my books to pieces would only cut himself to pieces with my knife" (1979:70). No violence ensued, but Cushing was prevented from sketching in his notebooks at least for the rest of that day by the crowds of Zunis who attended him. Both Bourke and Cushing seemed to have operated under the "implicit racist assumption"—as Leslie Marmon Silko has characterized it—"that the prayers, chants, and stories weaseled out by the early white ethnographers . . . are public property" (1979:212).

The attempts to place prohibitions on Bourke's and Cushing's ethnographic activities—only minimally successful in both cases—represent censorship. The motive, though, is not to meet standards of decency but to ensure that religious practices, some of which had been strongly dismissed by non-ethnographic observers as satanic and many of which had been characterized as depraved, even obscene by some ethnographers, remained sacrosanct. Such efforts might protect the ritual protocols from contamination that could negate their efficacy, but they also protected the ethnographers and their readers from the spiritual forces that the rituals contacted and harnessed. Barre Toelken, for example, has described how his Navajo consultants withheld from him a layer of meaning in Coyote tales because it dealt with the extremely sensitive topic of witchcraft, knowledge of which would imperil both Toelken and his adopted Navajo family as well as anyone who might listen to his recordings of the material, especially at the wrong time of the year (1987:395–96). In fact, Toelken has noted, had he pursued the issue of witchcraft with his Navajo consultants, his research "stood a strong chance of being dangerous to the informants as well as to myself and my family" (1996:16). Claire R. Farrer has described a similar circumstance among the Mescalero Apaches. Having gained access to cylinder recordings of Mescalero material done in 1931, Farrer and her collaborator Bernard Second, a ceremonial singer himself, examined what was available on those cylinders. Second refused to translate several sacred songs that were still in use in 1982, when he and Farrer made their inventory. While interpretations of and commentaries on the songs might be done, translations from the archaic ritual language in which the songs are performed was not. That language, like spoken Navajo, has power. The possibility of someone who does not understand the power they generate even listening to the recordings in the original language can "potentiate unbridled chaos and . . . threaten destruction through blasphemy" (Farrer 1994:320). Likewise, Barbara Tedlock found that one of her Zuni consultants would not explain to her some features of women's ritual behavior and noted that she "shouldn't have expected her to" (1992:96–97). Tedlock along with Dennis Tedlock noted that on some occasions the Zunis with whom they had developed close relationships "abruptly told us to absent ourselves, or flatly refused to discuss a certain topic because it was 'sacred.' At such times they reminded me that, although we were adopted family, . . . we could not be included because we were, after all, also Melika, a loan word from the Spanish 'americano/American'" (1992:234).

Matters of time and place may also contribute to storytellers' reluctance to communicate certain genres of verbal art. In many communities, including the Navajo, some types of stories should be told only during the winter. Violating the taboo on seasonal storytelling, in fact, may bring profound repercussions. Often the consequence of such violation is couched in the statement that the transgressor will be beset by snakes, probably a concrete way of articulating a more abstract spiritual peril. A note published at the beginning of the last century only samples the taboos regarding the timing of performance especially of narratives. Widely noted was the summertime restriction, reported not only among the Omaha but also among Ojibwe and Winnebago performers (Chamberlain 1900:147). Presumably, a more thorough survey would have revealed much more widely spread temporal restrictions on storytelling and the performance of other verbal art.

Occasionally, some storytelling may be restricted to night, as J. Owen Dorsey reported among the Omaha (Chamberlain 1900:146). Dennis Tedlock notes that Zuni *telapnaawe* ('traditional fictions') are performed only at night between the months of October and March (1972:xvi). Among the northern Athabaskans whom she interviewed in the 1960s, Anna Birgitta Rooth found that storytelling occurred primarily in the evenings (1976:13–14). She also noted that storytelling was strictly forbidden on Sunday (1976:17–18). Rules for storytelling, she noted, had been set by the culture hero variously identified in English as the Traveler, Noah, or the Giant. In particular, this figure had specified that once a story began, it had to be completed. Consequently, storytellers might collaborate in performance to ensure that one or the other would be able to complete the narrative. Presumably, if a storyteller was unsure about his or her ability to tell an entire story, he or she might refuse altogether to attempt it (Rooth 1976:22–24) unless in the company of another performer who could take over should memory fail. Geary Hobson has echoed the belief that some potential performers may be unwilling to narrate or sing unless they are sure that they can do so correctly. Especially someone who is still mastering a verbal art tradition may resist performing until he or she is more sure of the material: "When an Indian is learning the medicine of his or her tribe, he or she is darned well not going to prance around spilling his guts about it, since . . . to tell about something to outsiders while it is in the process of being made, lessens both its value and its potential power, and cheapens the maker" (Hobson 1979:106).

Likewise, performers may expurgate their performances in order to avoid mentioning personal names. That avoidance may be particularly pronounced for the names of deceased individuals, as it was among the Twana, Salish-speakers from western Washington. Upon an individual's death, his or her adult name—lineage property conferred upon a person in adolescence and used by no one else simultaneously—disappeared from usage until someone else assumed that name. Consequently, a narrative featuring a character with a non-current lineage name would have to censor usage of that name. Moreover, the taboo might extend to prohibitions on some word that bore a phonological resemblance to the disused name. In fact, a formal community ceremony announced the intention of a deceased person's kin to drop the "name-resemblant" term from the language, thus censoring its usage in performance of verbal art (Elmendorf 1951). In several Native American societies, one of a person's names may be esoteric. It might be appropriately used in a ritual oration or prayer when the audience consists of the spiritual realm and perhaps of other initiates into a religious organization such as a Pueblo kiva society. Even if the rest of the oration or prayer could be performed outside the ritual situation for an outsider, the performer would be likely to delete personal names or make substitutions, if he or she adhered to traditional practice.

Another issue that may contribute to performers' refusal to perform certain materials or to their censoring them in some way may be that of ownership. Some stories and songs are the possession of individuals or of groups of people (e.g., kinship groups such as lineages and clans or religious sodalities). Someone who does not have ownership rights cannot legitimately perform such material. This was the case with Tlingit narratives about contact with the Russians in the late eighteenth and early nineteenth centuries. Before those narratives could be published, translators and editors had to ensure that the clan that owned them had granted permission (Dauenhauer, Dauenhauer, and Black 2008:xiii). Though this situation is not confined to any Native American community, Farrer notes the circumstances among the Mescalero Apaches: "An 'owner' of ritual, ceremonial, or religious songs at Mescalero is the one who has the right to sing them, who knows and understands the words within the songs, as well as their metaphors and allusions, and who is considered to be the guardian of the songs and their words until he . . . determines the time is proper to pass the songs, their words, and ritual actions on to another appropriate person *in the culture*" (1994:321; emphasis added). Though Farrer's primary concern is with how the Native American Graves Protection and Repatriation Act (NAGPRA) applies to nonmaterial cultural patrimony, her comments suggest a realistic reason that performers might not perform certain material: "No one sings a song owned by another without the owner's formal permission" (1994:321). If the audience has access to mechanical recording equipment, another factor figures into the reasons for censorship, particularly of verbal art used in religious situations: "Ritual language songs and lyrics are not to be recorded on tape or through notation of any kind" (Farrer 1994:322). Such proscriptions would not have dissuaded Bourke or Cushing, who tried to bully their way into sacred precincts or to document what they encountered surreptitiously—a practice (of which many early ethnographers were guilty) that has undoubtedly contributed to censorship and perhaps expurgation regulations more than a century later.

Toelken censored some of the material he collected from Hugh Yellowman over a period of some thirty years out of concern that not doing so could potentially violate Navajo proscriptions on the narration of Coyote tales during the summer. Believing in the performative quality of language, many Navajos argue that telling tabooed stories has the potential to harm anyone who may hear them. If played during the summer, tape recordings of those stories could have deleterious effects, since, according to traditional Navajo beliefs, "spoken words create the reality in which we all live" (Toelken 1998:383). When he tape-recorded Yellowman's Coyote tales, Toelken had agreed to the stipulation that he not play the tapes during the season when it was inappropriate to perform them. Fearing, though, that other researchers might not abide by the prohibition once the tapes were out of his control, Toelken returned them to the Yellowman family to dispose of as they deemed proper (1998:385). Toelken's censorship of the stories brought him criticism from other students of verbal art, who argued that he owed to scholarship an obligation to maintain them and to follow up on his research wherever it might lead. Alan Dundes, for example, complained that "not only has he [Toelken] deprived the academic world of data that may not be able to be replicated, but also . . . the Navajo themselves have lost a precious resource" (2005:403). But Toelken argued that in the case of the material he had collected from Yellowman, he was obliged to adhere to the guidelines set by those operating within the Navajo worldview rather than the protocols of scholarship as defined by outsiders (1998:388). Moreover, as Farrer has pointed out, "Perhaps some material would be lost to Westerners" if other scholars did as Toelken, but "in purely pragmatic terms, it is already lost to us, if we do not understand what it is or cannot understand the language in which the words are cast" (1994:324). One might further note that from the perspective of total ethnographic translation of orally performed verbal art, failure to appreciate taboos and to respect them represents a failure to translate. Just getting the words is not enough, and if the ideological context that forbids translation of those words does not become part of the translator's focus, the result is a misrepresentation. One should translate what is possible: in the kind of situation described by Farrer, that would involve the prohibitive perspective toward translation rather than the "text"—that is, the words themselves.

The case of the Yellowman tapes, what Farrer learned about Mescalero ritual verbal art from Bernard Second, and the objections voiced by American Indian intellectuals such as Silko connect issues of censorship with those of cultural property and colonialism that have become more and more important for ethnographers and translators during the last quarter century or so. A number of American Indians have raised these issues. In addition to Silko, one might consult the views of such figures as Vine Deloria Jr. and Elizabeth Cook-Lynn on the cultural imperialism implicit in much outsider scholarship on American Indian cultures.[3] A significant bibliography on the subject has also come from anthropologists and their critics who have applied postmodern perspectives to the processes and products of ethnography. Stephen E. Tyler has succinctly articulated the hierarchical relationship between ethnographer and "informant" that leads to cultural imperialism:

> Having perceived the limiting meaning of the second member of the compound term "ethnography" ("-graphy" fr. *graphein* "to write"), some ethnographers have tamed the savage, not with the pen, but with the tape recorder, reducing him to a "straight man," as in the script of some obscure comic routine, for even as they think to have

returned to "oral performance" or "dialogue," in order that the native have a place in the text, they exercise total control over her discourse and steal the only thing she has left—her voice. Others, in full and guiltless knowledge of their crime, celebrate in "ethnopoetry," while the rest, like Sartre, their faces half-turned from the offending pen, write on in atonement—little finger of the left hand on the "erase" button, index finger on the "play" button—in the sign of the cuckold-counterfeiting voice in the text. (Tyler 1986:128)

As long as the outsider controls the buttons on the tape recorder, he or she controls not only what will be preserved for possible communication to posterity but also how that material will be presented—censored according to the outsider's value system—to that posterity. As the subtitle of Tyler's essay ("From Document of the Occult to Occult Document") suggests, a performance that may have culturally specific restrictions placed upon it transmigrates into a document, still restricted, but now by the prescriptions and proscriptions of academic territoriality, professional jargon, and the exigencies of scholarly publication.

One of the most thoroughly argued plaints against cultural imperialism regarding American Indian materials has been developed by Laurie Hill Whitt, who primarily focuses on the marketing of Native spirituality but also raises points that might apply to the potential censorship of verbal art. Whitt notes that a fundamental principle that has informed the culturally imperialistic agenda has been the notion that Native American cultural properties are in the public domain. This idea allows collectors, translators, and editors to assume that those properties are available without constraint and, since they are not owned by anyone, convertible into their own private property. As Whitt notes, "The notion of property belonging to no one is the functional equivalent of the notion of property belonging to everyone," even someone from outside the community (1998:148). When a collector, translator, or editor publishes a story or song taken from a Native community, he or she may copyright it in his or her own name, thus making it inaccessible to those in whose culture it originated. In the case of music, the closest analogy in Whitt's argument to Native American verbal art, "copyright laws not only fail to protect the intellectual property of indigenous communities but directly facilitate cultural imperialism by consigning traditional music to the public domain, then providing for its facile 'conversion' to private property" (1998:152). Native storytellers who have caught on to this process may, therefore, withhold material from collectors, censoring out of a fear of losing control or even access to their own cultural property.

The principal issue in the censoring of Native American oral literature concerns who is doing the censoring. Nowadays, publishers, editors, and translators of materials for adult readers face few restrictions on what they can present in terms of "decency." Consequently, they usually have no reason to expurgate, bowdlerize, or euphemize. However, the performers of that oral literature may have plenty of reasons for doing so: the nature of the audience to whom they are narrating, singing, or orating; taboos concerning when material may be performed as well as by whom and for whom; issues of ownership on an individual, kinship-group, or community level; concerns about what will be done with the material by outsiders; hesitancy to allow the spiritually naive to hear and record spiritually powerful material; and fears about loss of right of use should someone else copyright what they perform. One may argue that failure to honor indigenous censorship restrictions violates both ethical and aesthetic mandates, especially if he or she recognizes the importance of translating performance holistically. Not to respect censoring done by performers misrepresents indigenous performance values, and translators who violate or circumvent restrictions fail to achieve total translation, the ethnographic process of capturing the complete act of performance as it occurs at a particular place and time.

Notes

1. Although Henry Francis Cary's translation of Dante's *Commedia* into English was hailed for its accuracy and faithfulness to the original, Cary used highly formal terminology or euphemistic constructions to deal with Dante's occasional use of colloquial "taboo words." Crisafulli (1997) argues that these departures from Dante do not undermine the "accuracy" of Cary's translation, since he was creating an epic in English to correspond to Dante's epic and since the English blank verse appropriate to English epic did not allow for informal usages. Perhaps the same argument can be made for Schoolcraft. Unfortunately, though, we only have his translation without the source material he worked with.

2. George E. Lankford, who published an edition of Swanton's southeastern translations in 1994, took a different stance from Swanton's in regard to this and other Latinized passages. In the introduction to the new edition, Lankford wrote,

"To facilitate this analysis [of Swanton's largely unexamined texts], this new edition translates back into English the nine passages Swanton offered in Latin without translation. He participated in that quaint Victorian conceit that materials of a sexual nature should be made available only to those whose education made them impervious to prurient interests—priests and academics, presumably. This volume, like the modern era, abandons that notion" (1994:xiv). Here is what Lankford has substituted for Swanton's Latin on page 231: "'When you set out,' she said to him, 'somewhere along the way you will meet wicked women who will try to tempt you to have intercourse with them. Do not lie together with them, however, because in their private parts they have teeth which will cut off your penis.'" This represents, of course, the widely reported *vagina dentata* motif.

In their textualizations and translations of Arapaho traditions, George A. Dorsey and Alfred L. Kroeber, contemporaries of Swanton, also shifted to Latin when they encountered material in Native languages that they believed readers of English could not handle. Their more recent editor, Jeffrey D. Anderson, has handled the situation somewhat differently from Lankford by leaving the Latin in place and providing the English translations as appendix 2 to the volume. See Dorsey and Kroeber (1997). Both Lankford and Anderson apparently believe that modern readers will be more daunted by Latin than by sexuality and scatology.

In *Surviving through the Days*, Herbert W. Luthin offers still another approach to redoing material that used Latin passages when originally published. J. P. Harrington had included some Latin in his translation of a Quechan myth recorded in 1908. Luthin, who finds this usage "pleasantly quaint" and "very much a product of his [Harrington's] literary time and fashion," left the Latin in place in order not to damage "the translation's patina of age" (2002:464). He collects translations of all the Latin passages in a separate section appended to the end of the myth text.

3. Smith 1999 presents a particularly well codified response to culturally imperialistic research. She deals with both the theoretical underpinnings of cultural imperialism and responses to it and methodological issues on a practical level.

References

Babcock, Barbara A. 1991. Introduction: Elsie Clews Parsons and the Pueblo Construction of Gender. In *Pueblo Mothers and Children: Essays by Elsie Clews Parsons, 1915–1924*, ed. Barbara A. Babcock, 1–27. Santa Fe: Ancient City Press.

Berman, Judith. 1992. Oolachan-Woman's Robe: Fish, Blankets, Masks, and Meaning in Boas's Kwakw'ala Texts. In *On the Translation of Native American Literatures*, ed. Brian Swann, 125–62. Washington DC: Smithsonian Institution Press.

Boas, Franz. 1916. *Tsimshian Mythology. Annual Report of the Bureau of American Ethnology* 31:29–1037.

Bourke, John Gregory. 1984. *The Snake-Dance of the Moquis of Arizona: Being a*

Narrative of a Journey from Santa Fe, New Mexico, to the Villages of the Moqui Indians of Arizona. Tucson: University of Arizona Press. (Originally published in 1884)

Bremer, Richard G. 1982. Henry Rowe Schoolcraft: Explorer in the Mississippi Valley. *Wisconsin Magazine of History* 66 (1): 40–59.

Chamberlain, Alexander F. 1900. Taboos of Tale-Telling. *Journal of American Folklore* 13:146–47.

Crisafulli, Edoardo. 1997. Taboo Language in Translation. *Perspectives: Studies in Translatology* 5:237–56.

Curtin, Jeremiah, and J. N. B. Hewitt. 1910–11. Seneca Fiction, Legends, and Myths. *Annual Report of the Bureau of American Ethnology* 32:37–813.

Cushing, Frank Hamilton. 1979. My Adventures in *Zuñi*. In *Zuñi: Selected Writings of Frank Hamilton Cushing*, ed. Jesse Green, 46–134. Lincoln: University of Nebraska Press.

Dauenhauer, Nora Marks, Richard Dauenhauer, and Lydia T. Black. 2008. *Anóoshi Lingít Aaní Ká, Russians in Tlingit America: The Battles of Sitka, 1802 and 1804.* Classics of Tlingit Oral Literature 4. Seattle: University of Washington Press.

Dorsey, George A., and Alfred L. Kroeber. 1997. *Traditions of the Arapaho.* Ed. Jeffrey D. Anderson. Lincoln: University of Nebraska Press.

Dundes, Alan. 2005. Folkloristics in the Twenty-first Century (AFS Invited Presidential Plenary Address, 2004). *Journal of American Folklore* 118:385–408.

Elmendorf, William W. 1951. Word Taboo and Lexical Change in Coast Salish. *International Journal of American Linguistics* 17:205–8.

Farrer, Claire R. 1994. Who Owns the Words? An Anthropological Perspective on Public Law 101-601. *Journal of Arts Management, Law, and Society* 23:317–26.

Hobson, Geary. 1979. The Rise of the White Shaman as a New Version of Cultural Imperialism. In *The Remembered Earth: An Anthology of Contemporary Native American Literature*, ed. Geary Hobson, 100–108. Albuquerque: University of New Mexico Press.

Jacobs, Elizabeth Derr. 1990. *Nehalem Tillamook Tales.* Ed. Melville Jacobs. Corvallis: Oregon State University Press. (Originally published in 1959)

Jacobs, Melville. 1959. *The Content and Style of an Oral Literature: Clackamas Chinook Myths and Tales.* Chicago: University of Chicago Press.

Lankford, George E. 1994. Introduction. In *Myths and Tales of the Southeastern Indians* by John R. Swanton, xii–xx. Norman: University of Oklahoma Press.

Lowie, Robert. 1959. Crow Curses. *Journal of American Folklore* 72:105.

Luthin, Herbert W. 2002. *Surviving through the Days: A California Indian Reader; Translations of Native California Songs and Stories.* Berkeley: University of California Press.

Malotki, Ekkehart. 1983. The Story of the "Tsimonmamant" or Jimson Weed Girls: A Hopi Narrative Featuring the Motif of the Vagina Dentata. In *Smooth-*

ing the Ground: Essays on Native American Oral Literature*, ed. Brian Swann, 204–20. Berkeley: University of California Press.

Porter, Joseph C. 1986. *Paper Medicine Man: John Gregory Bourke and His American West*. Norman: University of Oklahoma Press.

Rooth, Ann Birgitta. 1976. *The Importance of Storytelling: A Study Based on Field Work in Northern Alaska*. Studia Ethnologica Upsaliensia 1. Stockholm: Almqvist and Wiksell.

Russell, Frank. 1904–5. The Pima Indians. *Annual Report of the Bureau of American Ethnology* 26:3–389.

Schoolcraft, Henry Rowe. 1839. *Algic Researches: Comprising Inquiries Respecting the Mental Characteristics of the North American Indians. First Series. Indian Tales and Legends*. 2 vols. New York: Harper and Brothers.

———.1851. *Personal Memoirs of a Residence of Thirty Years with the Indian Tribes on the American Frontiers: with Brief Notices of Passing Events, Facts, and Opinions, A.D. 1812 to A.D. 1842*. Philadelphia: Lippincott, Grambo.

———.1856. *The Myth of Hiawatha, and Other Oral Legends, Mythologic and Allegoric, of the North American Indians*. Philadelphia: J. P. Lippincott.

Silko, Leslie Marmon. 1979. An Old-Time Indian Attack Conducted in Two Parts. In *The Remembered Earth: An Anthology of Contemporary Native American Literature*, ed. Geary Hobson, 211–16. Albuquerque: University of New Mexico Press.

Smith, Linda Tuhiwai. 1999. *Decolonizing Methodologies: Research and Indigenous Peoples*. London: Zed.

Stocking, George W., Jr., ed. 1974. *The Shaping of American Anthropology, 1883–1911: A Franz Boas Reader*. New York: Basic Books.

Swann, Brian, ed. 1994. *Coming to Light: Contemporary Translations of the Native Literatures of North America*. New York: Random House.

———.1996. *Wearing the Morning Star: Native American Song-Poems*. New York: Random House.

Swanton, John R. 1929. *Myths and Tales of the Southeastern Indians*. Bureau of American Ethnology Bulletin 88. Washington DC: Government Printing Office.

Tedlock, Barbara. 1992. *The Beautiful and the Dangerous: Dialogues with the Zuni Indians*. New York: Penguin.

Tedlock, Dennis. 1972. *Finding the Center: Narrative Poetry of the Zuni Indians*. New York: Dial.

Toelken, Barre. 1987. Life and Death in the Navajo Coyote Tales. In *Recovering the Word: Essays on Native American Literature*, ed. Brian Swann and Arnold Krupat, 388–401. Berkeley: University of California Press.

———.1996. From Entertainment to Realization in Navajo Fieldwork. In *The World Observed: Reflections on the Fieldwork Process*, ed. Bruce Jackson and Edward D. Ives, 1–17. Urbana: University of Illinois Press.

———. 1998. The Yellowman Tapes, 1966–1997. *Journal of American Folklore* 111:381–91.

Tyler, Stephen A. 1986. Post-Modern Ethnography: From Document of the Occult to Occult Document. In *Writing Culture: The Poetics and Politics of Ethnography*, ed. James Clifford and George E. Marcus, 122–40. Berkeley: University of California Press.

Whitt, Laurie Hill. 1998. Cultural Imperialism and the Marketing of Native America. In *Natives and Academics: Researching and Writing about American Indians*, ed. Devon A. Mihesuah, 139–71. Lincoln: University of Nebraska Press.

Wolfart, H. Christoph. 1986. Taboo and Taste in Literary Translation. In *Actes due Dix-septième congrès des Algonguinistes*, ed. William Cowan, 377–94. Ottawa: Carleton University.

Zolbrod, Paul. 1990. Foreword to *Navajo Folk Tales* by Franc Johnson Newcomb, ix–xiii. Albuquerque: University of New Mexico Press.

8

In the Words of Powhatan

Translation across Space
and Time for *The New World*

Blair A. Rudes

Introduction

Among the numerous screen and stage events staged to celebrate the four hundredth anniversary of the founding of the first permanent English colony in the Americas at Jamestown, Virginia, in 1607, perhaps the most ambitious and widely seen was the film *The New World* (New Line Cinema 2005). The film's screenwriter and director, Terrence Malick, used the legendary romance of Pocahontas and John Smith to depict the impact that the settlement of Jamestown had on both the English and the native Virginia Algonquian people. Despite the questions that surround the authenticity of the Pocahontas story, Malick wanted to provide as accurate as possible a portrayal of life at the time. To achieve that aim, he and executive producer Sarah Green identified a cadre of recognized experts in colonial English and Virginia Algonquian architecture, crafts, language, music, subsistence, wardrobe, and warfare whom they hired as consultants to the production. Achieving authenticity with respect to the languages spoken by the English colonists and the Virginia Algonquian people in the film presented Malick and Green with one of the greater production challenges.

Recognizing that the English language spoken in North America had changed substantially over the past four centuries, Malick decided not to cast actors for speaking roles as English colonists who had American or Canadian accents. As a result, the final cast of English colonists included actors from Australia, England, Ireland, and South Africa, but no

Americans or Canadians. In addition, the producers hired a British dialect coach, Catherine Chartlon, whose job it was to research the provenance in Great Britain of the original Jamestown colonists, to identify the distinctive pronunciations of English as spoken in the colonists' place of origin in the early seventeenth century, and to train the actors to use those pronunciations in delivering their lines.

The task of achieving authenticity with respect to language spoken by the native peoples of the Jamestown area proved to be even more demanding than it was for the colonists. When English explorers and colonists first arrived at the location that would become Jamestown Colony, they were welcomed by citizens of the Powhatan Confederacy—an empire named for its leader, who reigned over a region that covered most of present-day southeastern Virginia—encompassing the Chesapeake Bay area from the southern shores of the Potomac River to the border with North Carolina. The vast majority of the citizens of the confederacy spoke dialects of Virginia Algonquian, also known as the Powhatan language.

The production staff soon discovered that no one had spoken more than a word or two of the Virginia Algonquian language since sometime in the first half of the nineteenth century (see Goddard 1978:74). As a fallback position, the staff considered using a still spoken Algonquian language; however, none of the speakers capable of teaching these languages was available to work on the film. Instead, they suggested that the production staff speak with Ives Goddard, linguistic curator at the Smithsonian Institution and the foremost authority on the Algonquian languages of eastern North America, about the feasibility of reviving the Virginia Algonquian language for the film.

The very idea of reviving a moribund American Indian language for a film was novel. By the 1970s, filmmakers began moving away from using nonsense words such as "ugh" and "how" to mimic American Indian speech and having actors in American Indian roles either speak in English or in whatever American Indian language they happened to know. It was not until the Kevin Costner film *Dances with Wolves* (Tig Productions 1990) that filmmakers began to make a serious effort to have actors speak the language actually spoken by members of the tribe from which their characters came. In that film, the actors portraying individuals from the Lakhota tribe learned to speak their lines in the Lakhota language.[1] The difference between what was done for *Dances with Wolves* and what was proposed for *The New World* was that Lakhota is a living language, and native speakers were available to translate the dialogue and train the actors to speak it. As I try to illustrate here, reviving the moribund Virginia Algonquian language posed a whole set of additional problems.

Goddard's work schedule precluded his participation on the film, so he referred the production staff to David Costa and me. Costa had previously worked with several Algonquian communities on language revitalization including two Algonquian communities in eastern Connecticut, the Mohegan and the Mashantucket Pequot; I had worked with Costa on the revitalization of Mashantucket Pequot as well as on the reconstitution of the Quiripi language of western Connecticut. Family obligations prevented Costa from getting involved in the film, so I took on the task. I did not work alone, however. Throughout the project, I received valuable, unremunerated assistance from several colleagues in Algonquian linguistics, specifically David Costa, Ives Goddard, Phil LeSourd, and David Pentland.

Background Research

Immediately after I agreed to work on the film, and before the script arrived in the mail, I began collecting everything that was known about the Virginia Algonquian language—not a particularly difficult task. Nearly everything we know about the language comes from two word lists that were prepared in the seventeenth century. Sometime between 1607 and 1609, John Smith wrote down a short list of words and phrases that he had learned and found useful. The word list was first published in 1612, and again in 1624. A few years later—in 1610 or 1611—the secretary for the Jamestown Colony, William Strachey, prepared a much longer list of words and phrases in the language; this list included the words written down by Smith as well as vocabulary that Strachey obtained from other colonists and from Indians who visited the colony. The information in Smith's and Strachey's vocabularies amounts to about six hundred words, a paltry number when one realizes that a typical desktop dictionary of English such as *Webster's Collegiate* provides definitions for more than one hundred thousand words. A small number of additional words from the language were written down by later explorers and settlers.

I was not the first linguist to examine the data on Virginia Algonquian and try to make sense of it. It had long been recognized that the language was a member of the Algonquian family of languages and, as a result, was related to other languages spoken in North America from the coast of

North Carolina (Chowan, Pamlico, Roanoke) to the mid-Atlantic coast (Munsee Delaware, Nanticoke, Unami Delaware) and New England (Mahican, Massachusett, Mohegan, Natick, Passamaquoddy-Malecite, Penobscot, Quiripi, Western Abenaki), and from eastern Canada (Algonquian, Micmac, Montagnais, Ottawa) across the Great Lakes region and the upper Great Plains (Cree, Fox, Menominee, Miami-Illinois, Kickapoo, Ojibwe, Patowatomi, Shawnee) to the eastern slopes of the Rocky Mountains (Arapaho, Blackfoot, Cheyenne). The first important study of Virginia Algonquian was prepared by Father James Geary, an anthropologist on the faculty of the Catholic University in Washington DC. His work appeared as an appendix to what is generally considered to be the linguistically most accurate printing of Strachey's word list, the 1953 edition by Louis Wright and Virginia Freund. The second major linguistic study was authored by Frank Siebert, an avocational linguist, in 1975. In addition, Ives Goddard examined Virginia Algonquian vocabulary in a number of his publications, most importantly in a 1980 article. The researches of these scholars was invaluable to my own work.

To prepare for translating dialogue into Virginia Algonquian, I needed first to get a good idea of how the language might have sounded and how words and sentences were formed. Since no sound recordings of the language were ever made, I had to rely on two assumptions. The first was that the pronunciation of Virginia Algonquian would not have been too different from the pronunciation of related Algonquian languages such as Munsee Delaware and Penobscot, for which sound recordings do exist. Second, I had to assume that Smith and Strachey had been reasonably accurate in rendering Virginia Algonquian words using the spelling conventions of early-seventeenth-century English. I also had to keep in mind that the pronunciation and the spelling conventions of English in the seventeenth century differed in important ways from the pronunciation of modern English as spoken in England and the United States. To illustrate, the spellings of the word <aamowk> 'angle' suggested a pronunciation in which the first vowel was similar to the first vowel of English *amen*, [a] in the symbols used in the International Phonetic Alphabet (IPA); the fact that Strachey used two <a>s rather than one to spell the word further suggested that the vowel was noticeably longer than the vowel in the English word, that is, IPA [aː]. By spelling <ow> for the second vowel, Strachey may have indicated either the vowel in English *low* (IPA [o]) or the vowel in English *cow* (IPA [aw] in American English but IPA [əw] in seventeenth-century English and in some dialects of present-day Canadian English). When I went looking in related languages for a word that might be pronounced something like [a·mok] or [a·məwk] and meant 'angle,' I at first came up empty-handed. It was not until I realized that Strachey did not intend the geometric noun 'angle' but the verb 'angle,' a synonym for 'fish,' that I discovered appropriate terms: Narragansett <aumaũog> 'they fish,' Penobscot áme 'he fishes,' and Western Abenaki ôma 'he fishes.' Virginia Algonquian <aamowk> 'angle' is in fact structurally the same word as Narragansett <aumaũog> 'they fish' with only minor formal differences: Natick āma:ak 'they fish,' Virginia Algonquian a:mewak 'they fish.' The Virginia Algonquian word would have been pronounced [a:mewk] due to the dropping of the vowel [a] in casual speech that is characteristic of Virginia Algonquian and other Eastern Algonquian languages.

I applied these same steps to nearly all of the words in Smith's and Strachey's word lists and concluded that Virginia Algonquian possessed the following sounds: the consonants *p*, *t*, and *k*, which were pronounced like the same letters in the English words *spill*, *still*, and *skill* (IPA [p, t, k]); *c* pronounced like the *ch* in English *chill* (IPA [tʃ]); *s* and *h* as in English *sill* and *hill*; *m* and *n* as in English *mill* and *nill*; and *w* and *y* as in English *will* and *yell*. The Virginia Algonquian language also possessed a sound similar to English *r*; however, it was different enough from the sound of English *r* that Smith and Strachey sometimes wrote it in different ways. For example, Smith wrote *nemarough* 'a man' while Strachey wrote the same word as *nimatewh*. Such spelling differences led Goddard (1980:147) to conclude that the *r* in Virginia Algonquian was similar to the single *r* in a Spanish word like *pero* 'for, because,' that is, a single, rapid tap of the tongue (IPA [ɾ]) not unlike the sound heard in American English for the spelling -*tt*- in words such as *fitting* or *fitter*. The language appears to have possessed six vowels: *i* as in English *pizza*, *e* as in English *café*, *a* as in American English *father* (IPA [a]), *a:* somewhat like the *aw* in English *law* (IPA [a:]); *ə* as in English *but*, and *o* as in English *code* (Rudes 2005a, 2005b).

The material in Smith's and Strachey's word lists offered very little information about the grammar of the Virginia Algonquian language. The few bits of information they contained indicated that the patterns for forming words and sentences in the language were essentially the same as those found in other Algonquian languages (Bloomfield 1946; Goddard 1983,

1990). Therefore, I decided that I would use the grammars of such well-described languages as Munsee Delaware and Natick as guides to what could be expected in Virginia Algonquian. In these languages, the structure of words, and of verbs in particular, is far more complicated than in English. For example, whereas in English the form of a verb such as *see* stays the same after the pronouns *I*, *you*, *we*, and *they* (i.e., I see, you see, we see, they see) and adds an ending only after the pronouns *he*, *she*, and *it* (i.e., he sees, she sees, it sees), in Munsee Delaware there are different endings (suffixes) and beginnings (prefixes) for each person, that is, *ngáwi* 'I sleep,' *kkáwi* 'you (singular) sleep,' *kawíi* 'he, she, it sleeps,' *ngawíiwun* 'we (I and others) sleep,' *kkawíiwun* 'we (I and you) sleep,' *kkawíiw* 'you (plural) sleep,' *kawíiwak* 'they sleep.' Other differences between the grammar of an Algonquian language such as Virginia Algonquian and English are noted where relevant in the following discussion of translations.

Translation

Once I had the script in my hands, the task of translating Malick's dialogue into the moribund Virginia Algonquian began. It is useful for present purposes to divide the task into three stages, recognizing that there was no neat division among the stages when I was actually carrying out the work. I term the first stage the conceptual translation, the second stage the structural translation, and the third stage the linguistic translation.

Conceptual Translation

My first job was to rewrite the lines into translatable English, which entailed turning the pseudo-Jacobean conversational English dialogue that Malick had drafted into something an Algonquian speaker living in southeastern Virginia in the first years of the seventeenth century might actually have said. Malick had done a thorough job of researching the events surrounding the founding of Jamestown and had read nearly all of the primary and many of the secondary sources. As a result, there were surprisingly few glaring historical or cultural errors, but there were some. To find them, I had to carefully read each line of dialogue and look for cultural and historical malapropisms. I refer to this part of the translation process as the conceptual translation.

There were both obvious and subtle chronological errors—anachronisms—in the dialogue. An obvious error appears in the line of dialogue in (2).

(2) POWHATAN (Original): Manacle his feet!

Powhatan would not have ordered his warriors to "manacle" Smith, because the Virginia Algonquians were still a stone age culture at the time of contact; they did not smelt metals, and thus they could not forge manacles. Unless the Spanish clerics who staffed the 1570 Ajacán mission on the lower Chesapeake (Gleach 1997:91) happened to have left some manacles lying around when their mission was destroyed, there were no manacles to be had. It would have been far more likely for Powhatan to order his warriors to restrain Smith by binding his feet together (3).

(3) POWHATAN (Revised): Bind his feet!

Another example of an obvious anachronism appears in (4). The error is the word "paper."

(4) SMITH (Original): We can make paper speak.

Although the Powhatan people may have seen paper in the hands of one or another European prior to the encounter with Smith, it is almost certain that they had none of their own. They did not know how to make it, and it is highly unlikely that the Europeans gave them, any since it was a rare and treasured commodity even among the Europeans. Thus, in translating Smith's words for Powhatan, the interpreter would have substituted a term for a similar object in the world of the Virginia Algonquian. I chose to use the word "leaves" although I could equally well as substituted "birch bark" or "scraps of cloth" (5).

(5) SMITH (Revised): We can make leaves speak.

A third example of an obvious anachronism appears in (6).

(6) SMITH (Original): We come from England, a land to the east.

No single word is anachronistic in reference; rather, it is the concept of "a land to the east." There is no evidence to suggest that Powhatan or his people knew of the existence of the European continent at the time Smith arrived. Thus, a "land" to the east would at best have meant to Powhatan that Smith and company came from the Delmarva Peninsula, which of course, Powhatan would have known was not true. The previous Europeans to visit the area—the Spanish slave traders and the missionaries at Ajacán—had arrived from the Caribbean Islands and had taken captives back to the Caribbean Islands from whence some escaped to return to Virginia. Therefore, Powhatan was almost certainly aware that there were islands out to the east (or southeast) where fair-skinned people lived. The revised lines in (7) would thus have been more compatible with the Virginia Algonquian worldview at the time.

> (7) SMITH (Revised): We come from England, an island on the other side of the sea.

The anachronisms in (8) are more subtle. Their identification requires knowledge of the climate in the area in the years leading up to the Jamestown settlement. When Powhatan orders Smith restrained for the adoption ceremony, he pretends to treat him as a prisoner and orders his warriors to give him saltwater to drink and to

> (8) POWHATAN (Original): Feed him withered roots and acorn husks!

The Carolina and Virginia regions had suffered periods of severe drought for the hundred years leading up to Smith's arrival in 1607, with resulting crop failures and scarcity of edible, wild plant foods (Blanton 2004:20). Depending upon the precise conditions when Smith was speaking with Powhatan, withered roots may have been about all there was to eat and not something to be given out to a prisoner. A more likely diet for a prisoner in times of scarcity as well as times of plenty would have been such completely indigestible items as pinecones, bark, and dust (9).[2]

> (9) POWHATAN (Revised): Feed him pinecones, bark, and dust!

The second phase of the conceptual translation involved the identification and elimination of Eurocentric ways of looking at and talking about the world. In (10) Powhatan is addressing Smith.

> (10) POWHATAN (Original): I think your people come to take our land away.

In traditional Algonquian societies, neither individuals nor groups (towns, bands, tribes) can own land in the European sense. At most, they have use of a parcel of land for a particular, often seasonal period of time. The revised wording reflects that fact (11).

(11) POWHATAN (Revised): I think you come to use the land only for yourselves.

The problem with the example in (12) is that pan-Indian metaphor (ghost girl) has been mixed with Euro-Christian concepts of monotheism and the afterlife.

(12) POWHATAN (Original): So leave me now, ghost girl, and may the Father of our people give you peace hereafter.

The information available on the belief system of the coastal Algonquians of the Southeast prior to contact is very fragmentary. There are hints in the writings of Hariot and Strachey, as well as in the 1522 "Testimony of Chicora," which recounts exploits of the Spanish explorers who looked for a site for a so-called Ayllón colony in the Carolinas (Rudes 2002; Swanton 1940). The information in these sources suggests that their beliefs incorporated a pantheon of spirits or deities that included the spirits of ancestors and the spirit of the sun as the supreme deity, and that there were stages or levels to the afterlife, sort of like purgatory and heaven in the Catholic faith or the multiple heavens of the Mormon faith. The revision in (13) is my attempt to make dialogue somewhat more compatible with what is known of Carolina and Virginia Algonquian beliefs.

(13) POWHATAN (Revised): So leave now. I will ask the spirits of our ancestors to care for you.

In (14), an attempt has been made to put Powhatan's empire on a par with the British Empire by having the "royalty," in this case Powhatan's daughter, Pocahontas, and his brother, Opechancanough, address one another in ritualistic language using indirect reference.

(14) POCAHONTAS (Original): The daughter of Powhatan greets her mighty uncle. She begs him speak to her, so that she may remember the honor all of her days.

Pocahontas speaks these lines when she encounters her uncle on the ship sailing to England. It is the first time she has seen him since her father banished her to the village of Potawomick. The fact is, there is no evidence that the manner in which Powhatan's family members spoke to one another was any different from the way any other Virginia Algonquians would speak to family members. It took centuries for the ritualistic, indirect speech patterns of British royalty to evolve; the Anglo-Saxon royalty of the fifth century spoke no differently to one another than did their subjects. The Powhatan empire was only one generation old, and it is unlikely than any formal changes in speaking, other than the development of the special title for Powhatan, had had time to evolve. I therefore revised the sentence into everyday English so that I could translate it into everyday Virginia Algonquian (15).

(15) POCAHONTAS (Revised): My uncle. May I speak with you?

Structural Translation

Once historical and cultural errors in the dialogue were eliminated, another step in editing the English was required before I could begin putting the lines into Virginia Algonquian. I refer to this step, which involves both linguistic and cultural editing, as structural translation.

The cultural part of the work involved paraphrasing idiomatic English phrases into literal English. Idioms are, by definition, language- and culture-specific and can rarely if ever be translated directly into another language. Of the many examples of lines involving idioms in the original dialogue, one appears in (16).

(16) POWHATAN (Original): How can you stand up for this creature?

The offending idiom is "stand up for." When one "stands up for" someone, one does not literally rise to a vertical position for the benefit of the person. Rather, one helps the person by speaking out on the person's behalf. To keep the translation conversational, I paraphrased the idiom "stand up for" simply as "help" (17).

(17) POWHATAN (Revised): Why do you help this creature?

In example (18), the idiom "be the light of one's life" cannot be taken literally.

(18) POWHATAN (Original): You have been the light of my life.

It has nothing to do with "light" per se. It refers instead to bringing great happiness to someone, as reflected in the revised translation in (19).

(19) POWHATAN (Revised): You have given me the most joy of all my people.

The linguistic portion of structural translation was concerned with filling in missing words in the dialogue. Malick wrote the dialogue in conversational, neo-Jacobean English because the lines were meant to be spoken. In conversational English of whatever era, a speaker may omit words in casual speech that listeners can "fill in" on their own based on the situational context—the time and place in which the conversation occurs—or the linguistic context—that which has been said previously in the conversation, a phenomenon known to linguists as "gapping." Although all languages allow for such omissions in casual speech, they differ in what elements may be omitted. A feature of the Algonquian languages is that the subjects and objects of verbs are obligatorily marked by affixes on the verb. In contrast, the subject pronouns of English may optionally be omitted in conversation. In addition, an English-speaker has a choice between using a question word or question (interrogative) intonation to express a question in casual speech, whereas in an Algonquian language a question word is required. During the very first encounter with Powhatan and in response to the question "When do you leave?" from Powhatan's interpreter, Tomoccomo (Raoul Trujillo), Smith responds by first paraphrasing the question as "Leaving?" (20).

(20) SMITH (Original): Leaving? There won't be any leaving until spring.

In order to translate the response into Virginia Algonquian so that Tomoccomo could repeat the response to Powhatan, I had to rephrase the abbreviated question "Leaving?" into the fuller "When will we leave?" (21).

(21) SMITH (Revised): When will we leave? We will not leave until spring.

The last step in translating the dialogue was the replacement of the English words and phrases in the dialogue as revised during the conceptual and structural translations with Virginia Algonquian words. I refer to this phase as the linguistic translation, and illustrate the work involved with a linguistic translation of the lines of dialogue given in (22).

(22) POWHATAN (Revised): Bind his feet! Give him saltwater to drink! Feed him pinecones, bark, and dust!

About half of the Virginia Algonquian words needed to translate any given piece of dialogue for the film were attested in the extant records, although typically they were not attested in the exact grammatical form required for the translation. The other half of the words had to be created either through borrowing a word from a related Algonquian language and adjusting the pronunciation to Virginia Algonquian norms or through reverse reconstruction, that is, finding an appropriate word that had been reconstructed for Proto-Algonquian and applying the sound changes that were responsible for the development of Virginia Algonquian pronunciation.

Ignoring pronouns and prepositions, which in Virginia Algonquian will be rendered typically by prefixes and suffixes on the main, content words of the sentence, there are ten words that require translations: 'bind,' 'feet,' 'give,' 'saltwater,' 'drink,' 'feed,' 'pine,' 'cone,' 'bark,' 'and,' and 'dust.' Of these words, seven are attested by Strachey's (1953 [1612]) vocabulary although the English glosses obscure the identity of some of the words: <cuspum> 'to tye or make fast anything' (Strachey 1953 [1612]: 204), <messetts> 'feet by a general name' (Strachey 1953 [1612]: 183), <mammaha (sucqwaham)> 'give me (some water)' (Strachey 1953 [1612]: 185), <sawwone> 'salt' (Strachey 1953 [1612]: 200), <nippe> 'wette' (Strachey 1953 [1612]: 206), <cuttassamais> 'a beggar' (Strachey 1953 [1612]: 176), <punguy> 'ashes' (Strachey 1953 [1612]: 196). The more accurate translation of these words is shown by the English glosses for the reconstructed etyma:[3] Proto-Algonquian (PA) *keθpamwa 'he ties it up' (from PA *keθp—'tie up' [Goddard 1982:28]; see Munsee koxpí·lew 'he ties him up,' Natick <kishpinum, kusp-> 'he ties (it) firmly, binds close, makes fast' [Trumbull 1903:36]), PA *mesitari 'someone's feet' (Siebert 1974:342),

PEA *mənahēw 'he gives a drink to someone' (see Munsee mŭnáheew 'give a drink to s.o.' [O'Meara 1996:181], PA *ʃiːwanwi 'it is sour, salty' (Goddard 1982:39), PA *nepyi 'water' (Hewson 1993:137, #292), PA *ketahʃameθe 'I feed you' (Siebert 1974:340), and PA *penkwi 'ashes, dust' (Siebert 1974:333). Regular sound changes would have produced Virginia Algonquian kəspam 'he ties it up,' məsitar 'someone's feet,' mənahew 'he gives a drink to someone,' ʃiwan 'salt,' nəpəy 'water,' kətahʃamər 'I feed you,' and pənkwəy 'ashes, dust.'

It was necessary to make grammatical adjustments to many of the words found in the source materials to make them fit the requirements of the translation. In particular, verb forms required changes in the prefixes and suffixes that mark features of agreement such as subject, object, tense, mood, and aspect, while nouns required changes to possessive affixes. It was also necessary at times to create novel compounds out of known words, as in the case of 'tie his feet, you all!' and 'saltwater, seawater.' In Algonquian languages, some statements that involve a verb and an object are expressed by compound verbs that incorporate the object (compare English 'he is keeping the books' and 'he is bookkeeping'). Such constructions are the rule when the object of the verb is a body part. So to express the notion of 'bind his feet!', I stripped the prefix meaning 'someone's' (mə-) and the suffix indicating plurality (-ar) from the noun for 'someone's feet' and compounded the root (-sit(e)-) with the verb meaning 'tie up' (kəsp(i)-) to create a verb stem kəspisite—meaning 'tie (his) feet.' I then changed the inflection on the verb from third person singular (-am 'he . . . it') to imperative plural (-irak 'you all . . . him!'). Similarly, I created a word for 'saltwater, seawater' by following regular rules of Algonquian word formation and dropping the initial consonant of the word for 'water' before compounding the root with the word for 'salt; it is salty' (Goddard 1990:451, 464–65) (23).

(23) kəspam 'he ties it up' + (mə)sit(ar) 'someone's feet' → kəspisiterak 'tie (his) feet, you all!'

mənahew 'he gives a drink to s.o.' → mənahek 'give s.o. a drink, you all!'

ʃiwan 'salt' + (n)əpəy 'water' → ʃiwanəpəy 'saltwater'

kətahʃamər 'I feed you' → ahʃamək 'feed s.o., you all!'

Unfortunately, none of the extant sources provide the Virginia Algonquian words meaning 'pinecone,' 'and,' or 'bark,' so I borrowed those words from other Eastern Algonquian languages—specifically, Conoy and Western Abenaki—and adapted the pronunciation to that expected for cognates of these words in Virginia Algonquian (24).

(24) W. Abenaki *goa* 'white pine' (Day 1995:291) → VA *kowew*
W. Abenaki *olômpskol* 'coniferous cones' (Day 1995:82) → VA *wəra?pəskor*
W. Abenaki *walakaskw* 'rough bark' (Day 1995:25) → VA *warakask*
Conoy *còoch* 'and' (Goddard 1974) → VA *kotʃ*

The next step in the translation was to arrange these words in the proper, grammatical order for Virginia Algonquian sentences. In the case of this particular piece of dialogue, the word order was essentially the same as the word order in the English sentence (25).

(25) POWHATAN: Kəspisiterak! Mənahek siwanəpəy! Ahʃamək kowew wəra?pəskor, warakask, kotʃ pənkwəy.
'Tie his feet! Give him seawater to drink! Feed him pine cones, bark, and sand.'

The last step in translation was to apply the changes in pronunciation that characterized casual speech. These changes included the application of main word stress, which usually fell on the penultimate syllable but could fall on the antepenultimate syllable if the penult contained the vowel *a* or *ə*; syncope (omission) of certain instances of *a* and *ə*; the contraction of the diphthong *əy* to [i]; the pronunciation of *r* as the tap [ɾ] between vowels; and the pronunciation of *r* as a voiceless tap that sounded like *s* to the English ear when final in a word. These corrections resulted in the phonetic interpretation of the sentence that would be used in teaching the lines to the actors (26).

(26) POWHATAN: [kəspisi'teɾak—mə'nahek si'wanəpi—'ahʃamək 'kowew wə'ɾa?pəskoɾ wa'ɾakask kotʃ'pənkwi}
'Tie his feet! Give him seawater to drink! Feed him pine cones, bark, and sand.'

Pre-production Training for the Actors

Since none of the Indian actors cast for speaking roles in the film spoke an Algonquian language, and many had never even heard an Algonquian language spoken, I obviously could not expect them to simply read the Virginia Algonquian dialogue and pronounce it correctly the way an Algonquian would say it. All the actors had to be taught to say their lines correctly, just as if they were learning lines in any other foreign language. As a first step in coaching the actors, I prepared CD recordings of the Virginia Algonquian lines along with the English translation of the lines and the meaning of the individual Algonquian words. I also prepared a written copy of the lines. I should note at this juncture that I am not a native speaker of any Algonquian language, although I have had many opportunities to hear Algonquian languages spoken. As a result, my pronunciation on the CD recordings, which served as the model for the actors' pronunciation, cannot be considered anything but a rough approximation of how a native speaker of Virginia Algonquian would have pronounced the lines. Having said that, I should also note that there are no living native speakers of Virginia Algonquian, nor have there been any for a couple of centuries. Thus, my pronunciation was probably just as good a model for the actors as the pronunciation of anyone else alive today. Once the recordings and written scripts were ready, they were sent to the actors so that they could have a couple of weeks to practice their lines before I met with them in person on location.

When I finally met with the individual actors, I found that each one had taken his or her own approach to learning the dialogue. Certain actors had memorized the Virginia Algonquian lines exactly as I had spoken them on the CDs. They had done an excellent job, and there was little else I needed to do to help them. Other actors had chosen to learn the pronunciation and meaning of each individual word in the sentences that made up the dialogue. Because of their attention to individual words, their pronunciation of the Virginia Algonquian lines tended at first to be choppy and unnatural. I worked with these actors every day over the next several weeks, and in the end they learned to say their lines in a convincingly natural fashion. I must say I was impressed by the seriousness with which the actors approached the task of learning the language and with their skills at quickly learning to speak the lines.

Coaching on Set

I was on set whenever scenes were filmed that involved dialogue in Virginia Algonquian in case the actors needed a quick rehearsal of their lines before or during filming of a scene. More importantly, I was there in case the director decided to change dialogue. Given Malick's well-known penchant for encouraging actors to improvise, occasions did arise in which new dialogue was needed. Perhaps not surprisingly, Malick regularly forgot that neither I nor the actors were native speakers of Virginia Algonquian and expected instantaneous translations of the new dialogue. Of course, it was not possible to provide such quick turnaround, so compromises were required. In particular, I had a standing agreement with the executive producer that I would coach the actors to say something they already knew and which was approximately the same length as the new dialogue would be and that the correct dialogue would be inserted latter through voice-overs during post-production. As a concrete example, I was once called to the set during the filming of a scene involving an exchange between Powhatan (August Schellenberg) and John Smith (Collin Farrell) and was asked to teach Schellenberg how to say "What are your intentions?" I should note that at the time Malick made the request, the cameras were already trained on Schellenberg for a close-up shot of him saying the requested phrase. I had no more than two minutes to translate the phrase and teach Schellenberg to say it. I knew from translating earlier dialogue that the phrase I needed was "Kekway kətərəntamawa:kanar?" I also knew from prior experience working with Schellenberg that he knew the word *kekway* 'what' but not the word *kətərəntamawa:kanar* 'your intentions.' I also knew that he would not be able to memorize such a long word in such a short time frame, so I told him to say *kekway* followed by eight meaningless syllables from previous dialogue he had learned so his lips would move the appropriate number of times.

Post-production "Corrections"

Each of the more than one hundred scenes of the movie were filmed numerous times, and Malick spent most of a year selecting the versions that would be used in the final cut of the film as shown in movie theaters. Although the actors may have delivered their assigned lines in Virginia Algonquian with perfect pronunciation during several takes, those takes were not necessarily the ones selected. After the theater version of the film was ready, I was sent a CD of all of the Algonquian dialogue from the selected scenes and asked to review it for accuracy. I identified about twenty lines of dialogue that had serious errors and needed to be rerecorded. Arrangements were made for the relevant actors to be brought in for voice-overs of the lines. I was flown to Hollywood to meet with the director, producer, and actors at a Warner Brothers sound studio. I coached the actors in the lines once again, after which they spoke the lines while the scene from the final cut was played on a screen in the background. The sound technician in the studio then manipulated the sound track to make the new recording fit the lip movements seen on the screen. The process was repeated until there was a seamless match between the new recording and the actor's lip movements on screen.

Postscript

The revival of Virginia Algonquian for *The New World* was a major breakthrough for the representation of American Indians in historical films and set a precedent that other directors will inevitably try to follow. Apart from its value in changing the portrayal of American Indians on the screen, the producers made a major contribution to the present-day tribal peoples of Virginia—the descendants of Powhatan's Confederacy—by funding the revitalization of the language. As I hope I have demonstrated, revitalizing a moribund language is a complex, multifaceted endeavor that is both time-consuming and expensive. It requires in-depth knowledge of the linguistic structure and history of the language involved and of related languages, as well as the history and culture of the people who spoke the language. It also requires the active participation of the community of people who wish to learn to speak the language. By hiring me as the Algonquian translator and dialogue coach and my colleagues as cultural and historical advisers, the producers financed the dedicated time of individuals with the requisite academic skills for the revitalization of Virginia Algonquian. Furthermore, as a result of hiring leaders and members of the present-day Virginia tribes as extras on the film, the producers brought together in one place the people with a desire to learn the language and the people who could help them fulfill that desire.

Following the release of the film, New Line Cinema turned over to the leadership of the Virginia tribes copies of all of the Virginia Algonquian scripts, CDs, and related materials that I created to teach the language to the actors in the film. Several of the tribes have begun planning language programs that will use my work as a basis for curricular materials, and I have agreed to serve as a consultant to the tribes in their continuing efforts to revitalize the Virginia Algonquian language.

Notes

I wish to thank David J. Costa, who read an earlier version of this chapter and provided valuable suggestions for revision.

1. Although noteworthy for effort at authentic use of the Lakhota language, *Dances with Wolves* was less meticulous with the language of the other American Indian people represented in the film, the Pawnee. On December 1, 2003, in response to an inquiry on the language spoken by the actors portraying Pawnee warriors, Douglas Parks, the foremost linguistic expert on the Pawnee language, remarked that "It has been several years since I watched Dances with Wolves, but the 'Pawnees' in the movie were not speaking Pawnee—or anything like it. My impression was that the speech is nonsense. (But maybe if I listened again I might hear a Pawnee word or two.)" (Siouan@list Archive on the LinguistList, http://listserv.linguistlist.org/cgi-bin/wa?A1=ind0312&L=siouan#3). The relative lack of attention given to the accuracy of the dialogue spoken by the Pawnee warriors is reflected in the fact that two native speakers of Lakhota are listed as dialogue coaches/translators on the crew for the film, Doris Leader Charge and Albert White Hat, but no native speaker of Pawnee is listed in a comparable role (*Dances with Wolves* [1990], International Movie Data Base, http://imdb.com /title/tt0099348).

2. For providing these dietary suggestions, I am grateful to my colleague on cultural matters for the film, Buck Woodard, whose formal title on the film was animateur and who informally served as a key cultural consultant.

3. For the distinction between Proto-Algonquian reconstructions and Proto-Eastern-Algonquian reconstructions, see Goddard (1980). Briefly, Proto-Eastern-Algonquian reconstructions are supported by cognate vocabulary in two or more of the Eastern Algonquian languages (Carolina Algonquian, Conoy, Loup A, Mahican, Massachusett, Micmac, Mohegan-Pequot, Munsee Delaware, Narragansett, Nanticoke, Passamaquoddy-Maliseet, Penobscot (Eastern Abenaki), Unami Delaware, Virginia Algonquian, Wampano (Naugatuck-Quiripi), and Western Abenaki) but do not show cognates in the other Algonquian languages (Algonquian-Naskapi, Arapaho, Atsina, Blackfoot, Cheyenne, Cree, Kickapoo, Menominee, Miami-Illinois, Ojibway, Potawatomi, Shawnee). Proto-Algonquian reconstructions show cognate vocabulary in two or more Algonquian languages which must include languages from the "other" group and may include Eastern Algonquian languages.

References

Blanton, Dennis B. 2004. The Climate Factor in Late Prehistoric and Post-Contact Human Affairs. In *Indian and European Contact in Context*, ed. Dennis B. Blanton and Julia A. King, 6–21. Gainesville: University of Florida Press.

Bloomfield, Leonard. 1946. Algonquian. In *Linguistic Structures of Native America*, ed. Harry Hoijer et al., 85–129. Viking Fund Publications in Anthropology 6. New York: Viking Fund.

Day, Gordon M. 1995. *Western Abenaki Dictionary*. Vol. 1, *English-Abenaki*. Mercury Series Canadian Ethnology Service Paper 129. Hull, Quebec: Canadian Museum of Civilization.

Geary, Rev. James. 1953. Strachey's Vocabulary of Indian Words Used in Virginia, 1612. In *The Historie of Travell into Virginia Britania (1612) by William Strachey, gent.*, ed. Louis B. Wright and Virginia Freund, 208–14. London: The Hakluyt Society.

Gleach, Frederic W. 1997. *Powhatan's World and Colonial Virginia*. Lincoln: University of Nebraska Press.

Goddard, Ives. 1974. A Preliminary Report on Conoy. Handout to paper given at the Annual Meeting of the American Anthropological Association, Mexico City, November 1974, and at the Annual Meeting of the Linguistic Society of America, New York City, December 1974.

———. 1978. Eastern Algonquian. In *Handbook of North American Indians*, vol. 15, *Northeast*, ed. Bruce G. Trigger, 70–77. Washington DC: Smithsonian Institution.

———. 1980. Eastern Algonquian as a Genetic Subgroup. In *Papers of the 11th Algonquian Conference*, ed. William Cowan, 143–58. Ottawa: Carlton University Press.

———. 1982. The Historical Phonology of Munsee. *International Journal of American Linguistics* 48:16–48.

———. 1983. The Eastern Algonquian Subordinative Mode and the Importance of Morphology. *International Journal of American Linguistics* 49:351–87.

———. 1990. Primary and Secondary Stem Derivation in Algonquian. *International Journal of American Linguistics* 56:449–83.

Hariot, Thomas. 1972 [1590]. *The Briefe and True Report of the New Found Land of Virginia*. The Complete 1590 Theodor de Bry Edition, with a new introduction by Paul Hulton. New York: Dover Publications.

Hewson, John. 1993. *A Computer-Generated Dictionary of Proto-Algonquian*. Canadian Ethnology Service, Mercury Series Paper 125. Hull: Canadian Museum of Civilization.

O'Meara, John. 1996. *Delaware-English/English-Delaware Dictionary*. Toronto: University of Toronto Press.

Rudes, Blair A. 2002. The First Description of an Iroquois People: The Spaniards among the Tuscaroras before 1522. Paper presented at the Conference on Iroquois Research, Renselaerville NY, October 7.

———. 2005a. The Evidence for Dialects of Virginia Algonquian (a.k.a. Powhatan). Annual meeting for the Society for the Study of the Indigenous Languages of the Americas. January 8. San Francisco, California.

———. 2005b. On the Status of Carolina Algonquian and Virginia Algonquian as Separate Languages. Thirty-seventh Algonquian Conference. October 22. Canadian Museum of Civilization, Gatineau, Québec.

Siebert, Frank T. 1975. Resurrecting Virginia Algonquian from the Dead: The Reconstituted and Historical Phonology of Powhatan. In *Studies in Southeastern Indian Languages*, ed. James M. Crawford, 285–453. Athens: University of Georgia Press.

Swanton, John R. 1940. The First Description of an Indian Tribe in the Territory of the Present United States. In *Studies for William A. Read: A Miscellany Presented by Some of His Colleagues and Friends*, ed. Nathaniel M. Caffee and Thomas A. Kriby, 326–38. Baton Rouge: Louisiana State University.

Trumbull, James H. 1903. *Natick Dictionary*. Bureau of American Ethnology Bulletin 25. Washington DC: Smithsonian Institution.

Wright, Louis B., and Virginia Freund, eds. 1953. *The Historie of Travell into Virginia Britania (1612) by William Strachey, gent*. London: The Hakluyt Society.

PART TWO

9

Ethnopoetic Translation in Relation to Audio, Video, and New Media Representations

Robin Ridington, Jillian Ridington, Patrick Moore, Kate Hennessy, and Amber Ridington

Introduction

This chapter describes our use of video and Web-based media to present an electronic equivalent of "interlinear" translations of ethnographic texts. The initial tape recordings of elders of the Dane-ẕaa of northeastern British Columbia were made by Robin Ridington in the 1960s. Jillian Ridington and Howard Broomfield joined the work in the 1970s and 1980s, and Jillian continues to be a partner in the projects. In recent years, Robin has added video recordings to the collection. The entire audio archive has been cataloged and digitized and is available to members of the Dane-ẕaa community. More recently, the Doig River First Nation, working collaboratively with Amber Ridington, Kate Hennessy, Patrick Moore, and Robin and Jillian Ridington, began recording video as part of their Virtual Museum of Canada exhibit entitled *Dane Wajich—Dane-ẕaa Stories and Songs: Dreamers and the Land.*

Interlinear and Ethnopoetic Translations

There is a long tradition in anthropology of presenting ethnographic texts as transcriptions of the native language, accompanied by a close interlinear translation. Some of the most important work resulted from a collaboration between a native-speaking researcher and a non-Native ethnographer. Many of the Kwakiutl (Kwakwa̱ka̱'wakw) texts that Franz Boas published were collected by George Hunt. Those of Alice Fletcher and

Francis La Flesche derived from an even closer collaboration in which the Omaha native-speaker, Francis La Flesche, was also a coauthor of the published work. In his *Ethnology of the Kwakiutl*, Boas presented lines in English at the top of each page and corresponding lines in Kwak'wala at the bottom (Boas 1921). His work, however, is not known for its poetic value or for making First Nations literature accessible to a non-Native audience. In 2000, Ralph Maud suggested that Boas's collaborative work with his Tsimshian colleague Henry W. Tate to produce *Tsimshian Mythology* (1916) misrepresents the narratives as "authentic," when in fact they were edited heavily by Tate and reflect Tate's personal and multicultural perspective on Tsimshian mythology. With this new perspective, *Tsimshian Mythology* may be seen to represent an interesting syncretic creation in itself, but perhaps not the age-old tradition as transmitted among the Tsimshian people that it was purported to be.

Some premodern ethnographies also included free, often line-for-line, verse translation. They are therefore examples of what we now call anthropological poetics. Fletcher and La Flesche (1911) were particularly successful in using this method of translation when presenting highly formalized ritual song texts, such as those relating to the Sacred Pole of the Omaha tribe. These song texts were first presented with accompanying musical notation, then with a literal translation, and finally with a free translation. Their presentation of one song is as follows:

Omaha text:
Thea'ma wagthithonbi tho ho! gthitonba
Wagthitonbi, wagthitonbi, tho ho
Te'xi ehe gthithonba
Wagthitonbe, wagthitonbe te'xe ehe gthithonba

Literal translation:
Theama, here they are (the people); *wagthitonbi*—the prefix *wa* indicates that the object has power, *gthitonbi*, touching what is theirs ("touching" here means that the touching that is necessary for a preparation of the objects); *tho ho!* is an exclamation here used in the sense of a call to Wakonda, to arrest attention, to announce that something is in progress relating to serious matters; *te'xi* that which is of the most precious or sacred nature; *ehe*, I say.

Free translation:
The people cry aloud—tho ho! before thee.
Here they prepare for sacred rites—tho ho!
Their Sacred, Sacred Pole.
With reverent hands, I say, they touch the Sacred Pole before thee.
(1911:233–42)

During the 1970s, the journal *Alcheringa*, first edited by Jerome Rothenberg and Dennis Tedlock, featured a number of experimental works using poetic translations of ethnographic texts. Unlike earlier ethnopoetics, *Alcheringa* presented translations of recorded audio documents. It also innovated the practice of including thin vinyl audio records, bound within the magazine. Tedlock's 1972 collection of Zuni narrative poetry (*Finding the Center: Narrative Poetry of the Zuni Indians*) is an excellent example of *Alcheringa*'s ethnopoetic tradition applied to a substantial body of oral literature. Tedlock set out his translations of Andrew Peynetsa and Walter Sanchez in a line-for-line form, using typography to represent performance values documented on the original audio documents.

An ethnographic text produced prior to the advent of audio recording depended on the transcriber's ear and on his or her ability to take dictation quickly using a phonetic script. Ethnographers like John Swanton and John Peabody Harrington were exceptionally talented in this regard. Harrington, it should be noted, was also a pioneer in the use of audio recordings (wax cylinders and later aluminum disks) for documenting Native American texts. A written transcription and translation depends on the translator's ability to understand the poetics of the native language as well as on the ability and patience of the native "informant." By necessity, the ethnographic texts and translations found in traditional ethnographies document a particular collaboration between speaker and ethnographer. Because of the need for a translator as an intermediary, they do not document naturally occurring performative events. The Omaha ritual song presented above accurately *re-creates* the text of an actual performance (but not its actuality) in that the ritual song texts were performed by priests of the Honga clan accurately and without improvisation or interpretation.

Swanton's sensitive transcription and translation of Haida texts has been the source of poet Robert Bringhurst's remarkable poetic translations of Haida oral literature (Swanton 1905; Bringhurst 1999). Swanton worked with a bilingual translator, Henry Moody, who, as Bringhurst explains, would "listen to the poem and repeat it sentence by sentence in a loud, clear, slow voice, proving to the poet he had heard each word and giving Swanton time to write it down" (1999:32). Swanton's sessions with Moody and a number of other Haida poets document a careful and studied rendition of oral literature in which the storyteller is the primary author of the document realized through the assistance of Moody and Swanton. The storyteller is the one who makes the authorial decisions about what to commit to writing. The resulting translation is a document of the authorial process, not a document of a naturally occurring performance event.

Tedlock provides a useful distinction between what he calls recitation and performance when he contrasts two versions of the Zuni "Word of Kyaklo" as respectively canonical and interpreted. The canonical version is, while technically an oral performance, more like the reading of a written text. The other is in Tedlock's words (and italics),

spoken
rather than chanted
interpreted
rather than reproduced
told on some quiet evening at home
rather than proclaimed on a holy day in that holy chamber
known as the kiva. (1991:311–15)

He goes on to say that

Tales have no canonical versions
no Kyaklo who recites them verbatim.
They exist only
in the form of interpretations
and it takes a multiplicity of voices to tell them. (1991:338)

The canonical version could, probably, have been written down by a skilled nineteenth-century ethnographer. The interpretive version could only have been documented as an audio recording. As Tedlock points out, Andrew Peynetsa's version came about

on a chilly evening in early spring
by the hearth in his farmhouse with his family
with me there, too
and my tape recorder. (1991:315)

Prior to the advent of audio recording, a text told by a non-literate, per-haps even monolingual, informant in collaboration with a transcriber/translator was more like a written document than an oral performance. It was of necessity studied and constructed. The text did not document intonation, gesture, or in many cases even the repetition that is so im-portant to Native American narrative tradition. Bringhurst rightly credits the storytellers with whom Swanton and Moody worked as the authors of poetic texts. The advent of audio and later film and video recording made possible a new kind of documentation. Field recordings can, of course, be as formally contrived as texts that are dictated, but they can also doc-ument performative events in their natural setting. Whether performed intentionally "on air" or captured in the natural flow of events by an eth-nographic documentarian, going from the raw audio document to a trans-lation or interpretation requires aesthetic and epistemological choices.

Most texts transcribed from audio recordings have been, of necessity, removed from the recorded actuality. Even when a written translation is accompanied by a disk or CD of the original audio document (as in *Al-cheringa*), there is an inevitable disconnect between the two representa-tions. The experience of reading is separate from the experience of listen-ing. Conventional ethnography has generally privileged the written text over the audio original; it has seen the audio as merely a means to the production of a written document. Ethnographic film, by contrast, has borrowed from the practice of subtitling films in a foreign language to produce translations that are more immediate and effective in preserving the link between text and actuality.

David MacDougall suggests that the idea to use subtitles in ethno-graphic film came about in 1961 when filmmakers Tim Asch and John Marshall were collaborating on a film about the !Kung. MacDougall says: "The idea of subtitling it was so obvious that it seems to have come to Asch and Marshall simultaneously. . . . One day Asch went to see Godard's *Breathless* at the Brattle Theater, and he remembers the moment of rev-elation when he thought of subtitling the !Kung material. But when he mentioned the idea to Marshall, he found that he had thought of it too" (1995:83).

Probably the most interesting and innovative use of subtitling as a medium for ethnographic translation comes from the artistically and financially successful Igloolik Isuma Productions. The name Isuma means "to think," and they describe their mission as making it possible for young and old to "work together to keep our ancestors' knowledge alive." In addition to a series of documentaries in Inuktitut with English (and French) subtitles made between 1989 and 2006, Isuma has made two commercially and critically acclaimed feature films, also using subtitled Inuktitut. The Isuma Web site (www.isuma.ca) describes their "unique style" as "re-lived drama." In an article about Igloolik Isuma, Katerina Soukup points out that the Inuit have adopted the Inuktitut term *ikiaqqvik* 'traveling through layers' to describe the Internet. "The word," she says, "comes from the concept of describing what a shaman does when asked to find out about living or deceased relatives or where animals have disappeared to: travel across time and space to find answers" (2006:239).

Isuma's latest feature film, *The Journals of Knud Rasmussen*, travels through layers of time to portray the defeat of shamanism by an indigenous Inuit Christianity. In one extraordinary continuous monologue lasting 9 minutes and 50 seconds, Inuit actor Pakak Inukshuk, playing Avva, a shaman whose life story explorer and ethnographer Knud Rasmussen documented at Igloolik in 1922, describes the events that led Avva to become a shaman. Rasmussen was a native speaker of Inuktitut and able to understand and document Avva's narrative. Pakak Innukshuk is in a unique position to re-create that story in the original Inuktitut. The viewer is brought into the story through the use of subtitles. The film presents complex intercultural and intergenerational translation strategies to convey Avva's life as a shaman. Avva told the original story in Inuktitut, and Rasmussen wrote it down in Danish. It was first published by Rasmussen in 1929 in *The Intellectual Culture of the Iglulik Eskimos*, which was translated into English by W. Worster (Rasmussen 1976). Zacharias Kunik and Isuma Productions then adapted Rasmussen's text so as to "re-live" it as an audio and visual actuality. Like Tedlock's interpretive version of the Kyaklo story, Pakak Inukshuk re-created Avva's narrative eighty-five years later in the Inuktitut language he and Avva and Rasmussen all shared. The feature film then translated the Inuktitut as subtitles (two lines at a time) for distribution to a variety of written language communities. While the film version omits some of Rasmussen's original and adds an introductory statement, the subtitled translation complements the Inuktitut performance effectively. The film version of Avva's statement began with a statement not in the Rasmussen original:

My mother was cursed
by an evil shaman

who befriended my father
in order to lie with her.

When my mother refused, the
shaman whispered angrily in her ear,

"All your children will be born dead!"
And so it happened that all my

mother's children born before me
had lain crosswise and were stillborn.

Pakak Inukshuk's performance is gripping and faithful to Avva's narrative as Rasmussen translated and transcribed it. Through his skill as an actor, the viewer gains an insight into the moment that Avva and Rasmussen shared those many years ago.

Subtitles, Re-creation, and Translation of Dane-ẕaa Audio Documents

Dane-ẕaa songkeeper Tommy Attachie told Robin and Jillian Ridington that each time a person with knowledge sings one of the dreamers' songs, he or she creates it anew. In Tommy's words, "When you sing it now, just like new."[1] To use Tedlock's distinction again, the singer gives an interpretation a recitation. With each new performance, the singer re-authorizes the dreamer's song that he or she holds in the mind. The same interpretive style is true of Dane-ẕaa storytelling. The audio recordings we have made of Dane-ẕaa singers and storytellers document the actualities of particular interpretive performances. Younger members of the Dane-ẕaa community no longer speak the Beaver language fluently. One strategy for making both the content and performative style of Dane-zaa oral tradition available to a new generation has been to present the original audio documents with an English translation in the form of subtitles against a visual field that shows a picture of the storyteller or photographs taken at the same time as the recording.

With the advent of digital video recording and computer-based editing, subtitling to simultaneously display a written translation along with the original performance has become available to any reasonably computer-literate ethnographer. The act of translation, of course, still remains the authorial responsibility of a bilingual translator, but the primary audio (or video) document can show the translated text in its performative context. Some of the recordings we have made with the Dane-zaa have been arranged in advance; in these, the narrators are clearly performing for an unseen audience that will experience the work in a different time and place. Others document events that are ongoing and independent of the presence of a microphone or camera. Within the category of interpretive performance documents as defined by Tedlock, we have found it useful to distinguish between those done self-consciously "on air" or "on camera" and those that document ongoing events that would have taken place in much the same way had they not been documented. The new video documents that went into the *Dane Wajich-Dane-zaa Stories and Songs* Web site (discussed later) are largely of the former kind, made in part with an outside audience in mind. In contrast, many of the songs included on the Web site as audio clips, several of which were recorded by Robin Ridington in the 1960s, were recorded in a natural and community-oriented context.

In early January 1966, Robin Ridington recorded the Dane-zaa Dreamer, Charlie Yahey, in an entirely unself-conscious setting. Robin had brought some elders from another community to visit Charlie. The Dreamer spent the best part of two days singing and telling people about his dreams of Heaven. Robin made the original recording on a portable Uher reel-to-reel machine in a community that did not have electricity. From time to time he switched on a reel-to-reel tape recorder, but he did not have enough blank tapes or spare batteries to attempt anything like a complete document of the event. Along with the rest of the thousands of hours of audio recording, this recording is now available to members of the Dane-zaa community in digital form (Doig River First Nation 2003).

In the passage presented below, the Dreamer warned that many people "go the white man's way" and do not sing and dance as they should. He said that the coming winter would be hard but that by singing he hoped to make it better. The Dreamer was aware that Robin was recording some of what went on during these two days, but he was in no way performing for the tape recorder (on other occasions he did allow Robin to record interviews in which he asked the Dreamer specific questions about his knowledge). In this passage, Charlie was speaking to his contemporaries, elders from Prophet River and members of his own community. Many years later, songkeeper Tommy Attachie (a young man, as Robin was, when the original recordings were made, and now, like Robin, an elder himself) provided a close translation of Charlie's words. Below is a short passage from this translation. The transcription of the Beaver in italics is Robin's own and is not intended to be a proper linguistic rendering of the Beaver-language text. Rather, he uses it to locate Tommy's English translation at the appropriate places in the audio document. Robin created the subtitled audio on Final Cut Express software, using a still photo of Charlie Yahey as a visual backdrop. He has used the same technique to visually present other audio documents from the 1960s, as well as to subtitle recently recorded video documents. Robin gave a draft of this paper to Gerald Yahey, Charlie's oldest grandson, and obtained his approval to use the text here.

Charlie Yahey Recorded by Robin Ridington in 1966, Catalog #CY1-5.
Translation by Tommy Attachie in 1998, Catalog #CY Tommy 3b.

Kuu gruhti alin ku. 0:04
All those animals,

Kaa echi onla.
even they pray with their songs. 0:08

T'aa kehni achu keli djuu
but some people

ke su' du'chi 0:12
are not even scared [drumming]

Achu chu dane ye dzu onli klike ahka kadzi' a' tsita.
One of these evenings, nobody will be singing these songs.

Achu adawaschi. 0:19
They don't know anything.

Ah tre Monias kuh kah che kuh ga dane.
They go the white man's way. 0:22

Achu ah wuu 'de kaa la grachi
People who don't want to sing or dance, are not going to live
forever. 0:26

Yaa da de' sal'
Beyond [inside] the Sky, that's too far for them. 0:32

[sings 0:39—speaks at 0:53; continues with sung vocables]
Chaa wu'dane—daa wu'naa na—ah ah yeh ah ah yeh—ah yeh 1:04
ha wah yeh, ah yeh [to end of phrase] 1:14 [new phrase]
Chee wu'dane—daa wu'naa la—ah ah yeh—ah ah yey wuh yeh . . .
1:47
Chuu yaske' sin daata grinta—

kaiila, iinla iinla ka du'duchi, muh nah ge, siize wut'se. 1:55
This winter, it's going to be pretty hard

Dane-ẕaa onli duh
Where the Dane-ẕaa are living.

wu'tsieh kuh naa eh duh wu't'zu.
That's why I was singing, even during the winter.

Du'ut'si eh muh ga, si de yaskee wu'tsize wu't suh ga, 2:04
Chuu, naa dehnla. 2:07.
I was singing to make the cold weather stop. [song ends 3:24]

It is difficult, of course, to represent a moving audio document in the
static medium of print on a page. Charlie Yahey's song and oratory took

place at a particular time and place. It would have lived on only in the memories of those who experienced it (and understood it) at the time. Robin's experience of the event was limited by his inability to understand anything but the gist of what Charlie Yahey said. Later, Tommy Attachie's translation gave him a fuller understanding. Listening to the performance on DVD with English subtitles cued to the Beaver text now allows Robin to understand what went on better than he did at the time. More importantly, it allows members of the Dane-za community who never knew Charlie Yahey and do not speak Beaver to gain some insight into the poetics and metaphysics of this truly powerful orator. We hope to continue with the project of translating and presenting other material from the archive in this way for the benefit of future generations.

Indigenous Culture on the Web: *Dane Wajich—Dane-zaa*
Stories and Songs: Dreamers and the Land

While Robin's documentation of Charlie Yahey's oratory in 1966 was unorchestrated, the work that Amber Ridington, Kate Hennessy, Patrick Moore, and others did in collaboration with Dane-zaa youth and elders between 2005 and 2007 was intended for a wide audience. This more recent ethnographic work was undertaken specifically for a Virtual Museum of Canada exhibition that features subtitled video narratives deliberately performed for global and local audiences.[2] Like the Igloolik Isuma productions discussed above, the Doig River First Nation's recent online exhibit, *Dane Wajich—Dane-zaa Stories and Songs: Dreamers and the Land* is an example of indigenous agency and self-expression that brought elders and youth together to document their culture.

The *Dane Wajich* project grew out of a number of collaborative digital heritage projects initiated by members of the Doig River First Nation. These drew on archival materials from the Ridington-Dane-zaa Archive and included a compact disc, *Dane-zaa Dreamers' Songs: 1966–2000*; two videos, *Contact the People* and *They Dream about Everything*; and a Web site designed and built by Dane-zaa youth, *Hadaa ka naadzet: The Dane-zaa Moose Hunt* (Doig River First Nation 2000, 2001, 2004, 2006). Doig River's 2007 production, *Dane Wajich—Dane-zaa Stories and Songs: Dreamers and the Land*, represents one of the most ambitious projects to date, and was produced by the First Nation in collaboration with ethnographers (Robin Ridington, Jillian Ridington, Kate Hennessy, Amber Ridington, and Peter Biella), linguists (Patrick Moore and Julia Miller), and multimedia professionals (Unlimited Digital, Vancouver BC). The exhibit's community-directed production process facilitated the articulation of local goals for revitalizing language, recording oral traditions, and traveling to important places in their territory. It brought elders and youth together to document stories, songs, and their relationship to the land. Through community reviews during post-production, it provided the First Nation with primary control over their representation to local and global audiences.

The project also represents a contemporary expression of oral narrative grounded in hypermedia, situated at one end of a continuum that includes the work of Fletcher and LaFlesche (1911), Tedlock and Rothenberg (1970–80) and Zacharias Kunik's subtitling and translations in *The Journals of Knud Rasmussen* (2006), which we have already described. Hypermedia is defined as combining written, theoretical, descriptive, pedagogical, and applied anthropological narratives with reflexive audiovisual and photographic representations of knowledge and experience; these are most effectively communicated audio-visually (Pink 2006). Sarah Pink points to Peter Biella's *Maasai Interactive* and Jay Ruby's *Oak Park Project* as examples of a new direction in visual anthropology that embraces hypermedia's multiple possibilities for framing research, creating stronger links with writing, and resituating video as a primary element of scholarship (Pink 2006).

Similarly, John Miles Foley, known for his ethnopoetic representation of the Milman Parry, Albert Lord, and Nikola Vujnovic recordings of South Slavic oral epic poetry from the 1930s, has recently embraced what he calls "cyber-techniques" and the "cyber-edition" as a way to include video, audio, and images of oral performances along with texts and writings about the performances. Foley, in his work with the online journal *Oral Tradition*, encourages the inclusion of "eCompanions" (in essence hypermedia Web sites) for journal articles. With these multimedia tools for ethnographic representation, texts do not lose connection to their original performance and, as Foley writes, "denature what we seek to understand and represent by reducing its diverse, many-sided identity to a print-centered shadow of itself. Sound and gesture and context and back-story are but a few of the innocent victims of this ritual sacrifice" (2005:260).

The multimedia exhibit *Dane Wajich—Dane-ẕaa Stories and Songs: Dreamers and the Land* demonstrates the potential for ethnopoetic translation in hypermedia and cyber-techniques. The *Dane Wajich* project provides a degree of reflexivity and transparency not easily achieved with textual and videographic representations of oral narratives alone. The project integrates subtitled Dane-ẕaa and English video narratives, hot-linked interpretive text, photographs of the production process, recordings of songs, and contemporary images of traditional Dane-ẕaa lands. In doing so, it addresses the current concerns faced by the community as they negotiate legacies of colonialism. As we will explain, the process of producing the videotaped oral narratives produces an aesthetic and thematic focus on intertextual representation. The co-presence of interpretive exhibit text, orthographic Dane-ẕaa Ẕáágéʔ transcriptions, and English translations places the narratives in their linguistic, cultural, and political contexts. Production photos represent the collaborative process of the creation of the exhibit's narratives.

Video recordings of narratives told by Dane-ẕaa people are central to the *Dane Wajich* project. Many participants spoke in their own language, presenting their own stories and their own perspective on their culture. Over a period of three weeks in the summer of 2005, Doig River First Nation elders, ethnographers, and a team of young Dane-ẕaa video documentarians traveled to seven significant places in their territory. They recorded narratives about Dane-ẕaa dreamers, personal experiences, and changing relationships to the land and its animal, spiritual, and mineral resources. The places, speakers, and narrative themes were chosen by Doig River elders, and the young videographers recorded under the elders' direction. These primary documents, included as translated and subtitled video clips on the Web site, were recorded specifically for the project with the knowledge that both a community and an outside audience would see them.

Linguistic Anthropology and Translation

The process of translation and transcription of *Dane Wajich* recordings was long and time-intensive. In the year that followed the recording of the videos, the linguistic and ethnographic team worked collaboratively with fluent Doig River community members to translate the mostly Dane-ẕaa Ẕáágéʔ (Beaver) narratives into English, and to orthographically transcribe Dane-ẕaa Ẕáágéʔ for use in the Web exhibit and in other local Beaver literacy programs.[3] The Dane-ẕaa narratives in the *Dane Wajich* Web site were translated principally by Eddie Apsassin, who worked with linguist Pat Moore. Eddie had been present at most of the recording sessions and was familiar with the goals of the project and with the speakers. In the past he had participated in Dane-ẕaa literacy workshops that Marshall and Jean Holdstock conducted, and he has experience translating for elders at Doig River and Blueberry River. Eddie is fluent in Cree as well as in Dane-ẕaa Ẕáágéʔ, the Beaver language, and English.

The procedure used in preparing the transcripts and translation for use on the Web site was for Pat to play the sound files on a laptop computer and have Eddie repeat each phrase or sentence clearly so that it could be transcribed using the orthography developed for Dane-ẕaa Ẕáágéʔ by Marshall and Jean Holdstock. Although rough transcriptions and translations were available, Pat and Eddie based their transcriptions and translations largely on the recorded version. After each segment was transcribed, Pat wrote English terms under the Dane-ẕaa Ẕáágéʔ. Pat Moore is familiar with some of the common Dane-ẕaa terms from his work on this project and from his knowledge of the closely related languages Dene Dháh (Slavey) and Kaska, but Eddie had to translate the terms Pat was unfamiliar with. Finally, Eddie and Pat discussed how best to express what the speakers wanted to convey as they composed the smooth English translation, a compromise between colloquial Dane-ẕaa English and standard English, which Pat wrote. Eddie provided extensive commentary about the stories and about certain Dane-ẕaa expressions the narrators used that he found especially evocative or intriguing, but these comments were not included in the translation. When passages were especially obscure or difficult to translate, they were played for elders Tommy Attachie or Billy Attachie, who were able to interpret particularly challenging terms. One of the most difficult narratives to translate was Charlie Yahey's creation story, which uses abstract metaphorical references that cannot be interpreted literally, as well as multiple unmarked third-person verbs with no clear referent. Unfortunately, as we discuss later, Charlie Yahey's narrative was not ultimately included in the Web site. Pat also recorded the Dane-ẕaa Ẕáágéʔ place-names and dreamers' names with Tommy and Billy, and together they created a standardized orthography for them.

The translation of narrative texts has been a central concern of linguistic anthropology since its inception, and approaches to translation have evolved along with the subdiscipline. Alessandro Duranti (2003) has argued that linguistic anthropology in North America has employed three overlapping research paradigms. The first is associated with the work of

Franz Boas and his students and associates, and featured the recording of narrative texts and translations, often as interlinear texts as a way of documenting both the culture and language of American Indians. Pliny Goddard's Dane-ẕaa (Beaver) texts (1916) are an example of interlinear texts and translations in the Boasian mode.

Duranti characterizes the second paradigm of research in linguistic anthropology as more centrally concerned with the use of language in social life and with the study of performance. This research on the ethnography of communication was facilitated by the development and use of tape recorders, which enabled linguistic anthropologists to capture details of interactions for later analysis. Dell Hymes was one of the central figures in the development of this second paradigm during the 1960s and 1970s (Duranti 2003:327), and he is well known for his contributions to the translation and presentation of translations of American Indian narrative texts (Hymes 1981). Hymes brought attention to aspects of the structure of narrative performance that had been obscured by the ways earlier translations were presented as prose. Scholars such as Dennis Tedlock became advocates for explicitly presenting performance features recorded on tape in their translations. Robin Ridington's documentation of Dane-ẕaa (written as Dunne-za in his early work) narratives and his use of ethnopoetic translations is another example of the work of scholars of the second paradigm.

Duranti finds that the ongoing third paradigm of research in linguistic anthropology sees language as evidence of larger social processes. Linguistic anthropologists continue to be concerned with micro-linguistic data, including details of narrative performances, and they increasingly highlight the creative potential of language for the construction of identity. This third paradigm has focused on new approaches to genres, the roles of speakers and audiences in performances, the construction of gender and ethnic identities, the use of semiotic resources, and wider power relations (Duranti 2003:332).

Although successive paradigms of research have developed within linguistic anthropology, earlier research programs have remained active, so that the documentation of American Indian languages and questions of translation continue to be central concerns for many scholars. During the process of translating the video recordings of narrative performances for the Doig River First Nation's (2007) *Dane Wajich* virtual exhibit, the linguists made use of well-established techniques. These included the preparation of interlinear transcripts with fluent speakers and the identification of intonational phrases and pauses that were used as line breaks for the Dane-ẕaa text and English translations. The translation process also facilitated reflection on the part of both linguists and Dane-ẕaa translators concerning the nature of the messages Dane-ẕaa narrators sought to convey and how they used varying narrative genres to address different potential audiences.

The storytellers and singers who contributed to the *Dane Wajich* exhibit took a leading role in determining what would be recorded and selected for the site. The participants all had a depth of experience working with linguists and anthropologists to document their language and culture, but they made individual choices about how to represent their culture and address both their immediate audience of Dane-ẕaa elders, youth, and academics as well as a wider Internet audience. The diverse nature of their performances reflects differences in their purposes and the ways they anticipated the interests of their audience. Other scholars of oral performances who have examined contemporary narrative performances in novel contexts report similar variability. Julie Cruikshank (1997), for instance, has described how storytellers at the Yukon International Storytelling Festival used different genres, including potlatch-style oratory, stories, songs, and archival documents, to engage the largely non-Native audience with indigenous issues of place and rights. Like the performers at that festival, the participants in the *Dane Wajich* project made use of different genres to express their culture in a form that could be translated for a wider Internet audience.

The ways Dane-ẕaa storytellers chose to express themselves reflected their training, their roles in the project, and their perceptions of possible audiences. Tommy Attachie, Dane-ẕaa elder and songkeeper, took a leading role in determining the nature of the project as he established the twin themes of traditions of place and the history of the Dane-ẕaa dreamers. His address at one of the first planning meetings directed the participants to share the stories, songs, and traditions associated with some of the most significant places in Dane-ẕaa territory as they traveled to each location in turn. He invoked the authority of the dreamer Gaayęą, whose drum the group had examined that morning, and who had traveled between the Dane-ẕaa communities in the early 1900s, holding tea dances at each location. Tommy Attachie's address was directed toward the assembled

Dane-zaa elders; the nature of any possible Internet audience was a secondary concern. His narrative is an example of what we have identified as performances that are not staged, but rather ongoing events that are largely independent of the presence of a video camera. A small portion of his address is reproduced below. Tommy echoes the earlier addresses of Dane-zaa dreamers as he speaks about Gaayęą's drum, the purpose for going to the places where their ancestors lived, and the possibility of reviving sacred knowledge. The Dane-zaa orthography below is based on the orthography developed by Marshall and Jean Holdstock that is described on the Web site, and the time codes are keyed to the video in the *Dane Wajich* Web site (Doig River First Nation 2007).

Tommy Attachie at the *Dane Wajich* Planning Meeting, Doig River Band Administration Complex, June 29, 2005[4]

01:19   Juuhdzenéh Ahhatááʔ kuuts'adéjiih haę.
        Today, we believe in God.
01:26   Nahhadzěʔ ajuu déhgash;
        Our hearts are not black;
01:28   nahhadzěʔ dadal.
        our hearts are red.
01:31   Ii k'aastaah juu jegúúh déhgash,
        I think the black side, the one I looked at [on Gaayęą's drum],
01:36   ii sǫ̂ ajuu úújuu.
        that must be the side that's not so good.
01:40   E ii k'aasenéhtah iidekéh,
        I am going to tell you about what we saw in the past,
01:42   gukeh wowajiich jii hahk'íh nahhanaajuunuu,
        we will talk to them about how our ancestors lived,
01:48   hǫ́hch'ii ʔéh,
        how it was back then,
01:51   ii tl'ǫ gwe náęchesne jéts'ę́ʔ.
        and after that, where the dreamers were.
01:55   Kénaasjííh dah náághaghaęché ʔ de shin
        háádaʔah dé.
        We remember where they lived, where they dreamed the songs that they brought back.

01:59 Dane guu tsʼé dayah.
       People went toward them [people went to see them].
02:01 Gwe kʼéh juuʔúú,
       That way, too,
02:03 je hááké? nááṣehjííhdẹh háákaa juuhdzenéh,
       [we'll talk about] how we live still today,
02:08 ii hehsahdǫ́h nahhaazeduu.
       and how people lived long before us.
02:12 Ii taghalé?, giidúúnaanéhjiije nááchẹ yaadéshtlʼishe,
       That drum, they rewrapped the one that the dreamer
       Gaayẹą drew on,
02:16 Gaayẹą, ii hááhgáádǫ́h makʼaahtsʼanéhtah.
       Gaayẹą's, the one we looked at yesterday.
02:21 Aja hájé lǫh sǫ́ ii kʼaatsʼanehtah kʼaachʼuu.
       It was not by accident that we looked at it.
02:24 Nááwadúútsii gúlé.
       It will come back, maybe.
02:26 Ii ghǫh ǫ̀, e dane ghaa náẹché? gwe.
       For that reason, he dreamed for people.

After Tommy Attachie established the theme of the Virtual Museum project, the participants traveled to seven locations to record stories. Although their performances were thematically unified following the general outline established at the planning meeting, each storyteller conceived of his or her audience in different ways. The types of generic differences in their accounts are clearly illustrated by comparing the performance of Sam Acko (also known as Sammy Acko) at Madátsʼatlʼo?je (Snare Hill) with the performance of Billy Attachie at Nẹtlʼuk (Osborn Creek).

Sam Acko's story, which describes events that occurred at Madátsʼatlʼǫje, is an example of the Dane-ẕaa genre of tǫhchʼiitǫ́h wawajijé? 'long ago stories,' and he begins his account with "Aadzẹhdǫ́h tǫhchʼiitǫ́h" 'A long time ago,' a common frame for this type of story. As Richard Bauman (2001) has pointed out, such framing devices carry expectations as to what type of performance will follow and facilitate the recontextualization of descriptions from one performance to the next. Sam continues by contextualizing the events of the story by explaining the difficult life people had in the past as they struggled to obtain enough food by hunting during periods of intense cold. Madátsʼatlʼǫje (Snare Hill) was one of the places where people gathered in times of hardship, because they could capture moose there by driving them into snares at one end of the hill, even after the stocks of moose at other locations had been depleted. The protagonist of the story is a young Dane-ẕaa man who maintained an exemplary lifestyle but who kept to himself so that his moose-like qualities could be concealed.

Sam Acko at Madáts'atl'ǫje (Snare Hill)
"The Man Who Turned into a Moose" July 1, 2005[5]

00:00 Aadzęhdǫ́h tǫhch'iidǫ́h jii
       A long time ago
00:03 Madáts'atl'ǫje dane yéhjii.
       they called this Madáts'atl'ǫje [Snare Hill].
00:06 Dane yadáádzéʔ háá ghędaa.
       People depended on this place to live.
00:10 Dane yadáádzé dáánejiilh.
       People depended on this place to survive.

Although Sam Acko's introduction to the story provides contextualization that could be helpful for an audience that is unfamiliar with Dane-ẕaa traditions, the main part of his account is delivered in fluent Beaver language, in a style that would be most appropriate for his immediate audience of fluent Dane-ẕaa elders steeped in local traditions. His account was challenging to transcribe and translate because of his sophisticated use of the language, including technical vocabulary such as *hadaa dzisgii* 'moose mane' and complex sentences with embedded direct discourse. It was difficult to track the many characters in the story, as they are referred to primarily with unmarked third-person verbs. When the people realized that something was peculiar about the young man, they told his brother to stay with him at all times. However, in the excitement of chasing moose toward the snares, the young man was able to elude his brother and turn into a moose in order to lead the moose past the snares, preserving a small group of moose to replenish their stocks. Although the English translations in this section typically extend well beyond the more succinct Dane-ẕaa account in an attempt to convey the action being described, it is still challenging for an English-speaking audience to visualize the events, because they are unfamiliar with the reactions of hunters and conventions for describing the hunt. In their study of Southern

Tutchone storytellers, linguists Patrick Moore and Daniel Tlen (2007) have argued that this type of sophisticated performance in native language by storytellers serves to assert the prestige of indigenous language and cultural knowledge as a countermeasure to the threat of language shift and loss of cultural knowledge.

Sam Acko at Madáts'atl'ǫje (Snare Hill)
"The Man Who Turned into a Moose" (continued)

04:58 Háá jǫ ęhtsezǫh guu naadę sǫ̀,
    All of a sudden, right in front of them,
05:04 hadaa taawadéhsat jii.
    the moose all ran off.
05:07 Jii lhígé ęhchaage gutsʼę́gúh hadaa taawaadéhsat úh,
    One moose and then another separated from the rest of the
    herd and started to run away.
05:12 "Jii naade ustlę. Juude jii naade nętleh,"
    "I'm going to go around this way really fast. You go around
    that way and turn the moose around,"
    yéhjii juude sǫ̀ yaanewóʔǫh,
    he said [the younger brother to his older brother], Everything
    happened so quickly,
05:17 ę wanehjuude juude yanáeʔaak.
    the young man was able to fool his brother who was trying
    to stay close to him.
05:20 Juude yanáeʔaak hǫ́hchʼii.
    He fooled him.
05:24 Jii lhígé déhsǫ adę lhígé déhsǫ dę.
    While the young brother ran after one moose, his older
    brother ran after the other one.
05:27 Ii watsʼęh zǫh najwé.
    Then he was gone.

While Sam Acko provides additional contextualization for a wider audience, the core of his account was not simplified for a potential Internet audience. In contrast, Billy Attachie, in his account at Nętlʼuk (Osborn River), chooses to provide a general orientation for an audience that lacks familiarity with the local language and traditions. His observations were quite general and make use of short statements that could readily be translated into English. He frames his performance by providing the date, a convention he may have adopted from anthropologists who include such information to later identify the recording.

Billy Attachie at Nętl'uk (Osborn River)[6]

00:00 Juuhdzenéh, July sixth, 2005.
       Today is July sixth, 2005.
00:09 Jǫ ats'ach'ę Nętl'uk dę;
       We are here at Nętl'uk, [the end of the flat];
00:12 jǫ laa Nętl'uk wúúzhe.
       this place is called Nętl'uk.
00:15 Tǫ́hchedǫ́h, jǫ dane náájeh, jǫ dę.
       Long ago, people used to live here, right here.
00:23 Ii kwâ wǫ́lę gwe kwâ wǫtlǫ.
       There were many houses.
00:26 Haatseh júúhje
       The first ones over here
00:28 north ts'égúúh dane nááje eh,
       lived north of here,
00:31 e ii watl'ǫh yeh ts'elęgae wadzis ęhtsę?.
       and later on they lived by the creek.

Billy's full account provides an overview of the life of Dane-zaa at Osborn River and other locations in the early twentieth century. Billy Attachie has extensive experience as a translator working with anthropologists and linguists. He may have been inclined to craft his presentation based on his perceptions of the level of knowledge of a non-Dane-zaa audience. Although he spoke in Dane-zaa Záágé?, he relied on basic descriptions to deliver a clear picture for a diverse Internet audience.

The variation in the Dane-zaa speakers' presentation styles enhances the appeal of the Web site. Viewers can experience a range of genres requiring different degrees of interpretation. The storytellers have extensive experience working with academic researchers and seeing the ways indigenous cultures are represented in publications, in films, and on television. For them, self-representation through storytelling and singing has become a common experience. The variation in the approaches they take to these performances indicates the extent of their involvement in, and knowledge of, indigenous documentary projects, as well as differences in their training and social roles.

Curation and Interpretation: The Politics of Voice

Sam Acko's narrative "The Man Who Turned into a Moose," told at Madáts'atl'ǫje, was filmed along an old seismic cut, tangible evidence of the extensive oil and gas exploration and extraction activity in the area. Photographs of the process of recording this narrative are featured prominently on the Madáts'atl'ǫje page[7] and throughout the exhibition. An example of hypermedia, these photographs, along with interpretive text and links to other places and narratives, contextualize the narrative to a greater degree than text or video alone could do. In this way we can see that the project offers a textual and audio-visually reflexive reading of the actual production of the narrative and of the representation of Dane-ẕaa culture, histories, and language.

The production of the virtual exhibit was a collaborative process, and the storytellers demonstrated agency in communication to a range of audiences. Still, translating the narratives and the inclusion of the translations and transcriptions within the exhibit raise questions that anthropologists and folklorists have been grappling with since the emergence of performance studies and reflexivity articulated in *Toward New Perspectives in Folklore* (Parades and Bauman 1971) and *Writing Culture* (Clifford and Marcus 1986). To what extent do the translations impose language as "a figurative, structuring power that constitutes the subject who speaks as well as the one that is spoken to" (Poster 1990:14)? David MacDougall's description of Asch and Marshall's initial excitement at the idea of subtitling ethnographic films is tempered by his assertion that subtitling itself does not negate ethnographic obscurations of the subject's voice, as Asch and Marshall might have hoped. For MacDougall, the act of converting raw recorded speech into subtitles is a process of creating a written text. This text is negotiated by the filmmaker and translator, and the result is the writing of a definitive version of a narrative that banishes alternative readings (MacDougall 1998:174). In other words, the process of interpretation and translation is, and has always been, subjective.

To attempt to address this methodological and epistemological concern, the exhibit curators, Amber Ridington and Kate Hennessy, had to make decisions about the form that the narrative translations and transcriptions would take within the exhibit. Financially, it was not feasible to subtitle videos in English, in Dane-ẕaa Ẕáágéʔ, and in French as required by the funder. Also, throughout the production and translation process, orthographic spellings were continually adjusted. This meant that it was essential for the design team to be able to replace words as more accurate spellings emerged. The team chose to present translations adjacent to the video window rather than within the video frame. In this way, transcriptions could be replaced as necessary without re-creating every video. More importantly, the translations and transcriptions could be viewed together, reflecting both spoken Dane-ẕaa Ẕáágéʔ and the English translations that were produced together by Doig River community members and linguists.[8] Aware of local Beaver literacy initiatives, the curators thought that giving the translations a longer amount of time on-screen would make them easier to read. While this method may not resolve the issues of authority and power that MacDougall raises, it at least represents a *process* of translation that sits alongside, rather than obscures, Sam Acko's narrative performance. In addition, for those interested in studying the textual representation more closely, the transcript is available for download as a PDF file.

The selection of these narratives and their translation and transcription were only the beginning of an interpretive curatorial process that informs our understanding of ethnopoetics and ethnography, and the many layers of translation that contribute to Dane-ẕaa representations in this hypermedia context. Talal Asad (1986) writes that one of the tasks of social anthropology that emerged after the 1950s was the use of ethnography in the translation of cultures. He, like MacDougall, also discusses the power differential in this process, in which the words of the culture as object are often replaced with the voice of authority of an outsider. One of our goals for the *Dane Wajich* exhibit, as curators and interpretive text writers, was to facilitate the community's self-representation. To this end, the curators drew on the participatory process and the inclusion of the community in reviewing multiple prototypes and drafts of the exhibit in order to make sure it represented their culture as they wanted it shown to a worldwide audience.

Even though the curators wrote the interpretive text that frames the primary video and audio documents in the exhibit, they were directed by the community to write it in the first person so that the voices of the Doig River people were prioritized. To do this, Kate and Amber had to identify and figuratively translate the messages and themes from the videos and the planning and review meetings, and re-present them in a manner that would be both comprehensible and engaging to an outside audience unfamiliar with Dane-ẕaa culture or tradition. In essence, the curators used their ethnographic skills to translate the messages and themes from the primary audio and video selected for the exhibition into textual summaries which were then supplemented by graphics, such as maps and photographs. This multimedia approach allowed them to present the material in a number of formats so that, like the narratives themselves, the material would be accessible by multiple audiences and cultures.

The community chose to assert the primacy and existence of the Dane-ẕaa language by using it as frequently as possible on the Web site. They labeled places that are more commonly known by English names with their Dane-ẕaa place-names. The interactive medium of the Web site enabled the inclusion of audio clips that were activated as the mouse rolls over the word, so that it could be heard as well as read. In addition, the primary video documents were orthographically transcribed in Beaver as well as translated into English. All of these bilingual (Beaver and English) transcriptions place Beaver first, ahead of the English translation. These cyber-techniques are political statements claiming cultural authority. Because of the historical inequality between the Beaver and English languages, it was important for the Doig River people to assert the legitimacy of their oral culture through textual representation in the exhibit. As the Canadian government exercised their colonial policy of cultural assimilation, Doig River people, like most other Aboriginal groups in Canada, were forbidden to speak their own language while they were in school. Several of the stories that were told at Aláá? Satǫ/Petersen's Crossing described experiences of punishment for using their Native language in school. Many children who were punished became ashamed of their language and chose not to teach it to their children.

However, unlike the children of many other First Nations, Dane-ẕaa children were never taken from their families and placed in residential schools. They returned to their homes every afternoon and spoke the Beaver language with their families. Until the late 1970s, most children spoke and understood Beaver. Television, which became available to the Doig River First Nation only in the 1980s, and co-education with white students had a great impact on the loss of the Beaver language; the children became immersed in an English-speaking environment. Now, language revitalization is a priority for Dane-ẕaa communities, and many elders have made efforts to teach their grandchildren their language. As May Apsassin said in her video included in the exhibit: "That's what I was saying to my family. I say, 'Go to school, hang on to your language, hang on to your tradition way of living, and you be a hundred percent good person.'"[9] The *Dane Wajich* virtual exhibit has helped to build a public presence and to strengthen a positive public identity for the Doig River First Nation as indigenous Dane-ẕaa people. Both the process of creating the exhibition and the final public product copyrighted by the Doig River First Nation are forms of social action inextricably tied to multiple forms of translation.

Indigenous Heritage and the Internet: Emerging Issues in Intellectual Property

During the fieldwork and storyboarding process, the curators assembled far more information than could possibly be included in the exhibition. Selecting which stories, what places, and what type of interpretive text to include as part of the Web site was part of the multifaceted translation process that emerged in the community exhibit review. It is within this process of selecting information to share with an outside audience that a new intellectual property rights discourse developed—which ultimately meant that a great deal of material originally selected for inclusion was removed from the exhibition.

As Amber and Kate have described (2008), the exhibit raised many questions at the heart of the politics of cultural representation: How can curators and communities balance the benefits of sharing Aboriginal cultural heritage with the necessity of protecting it? Can consensus be reached over what is appropriate to show a worldwide audience versus a local audience? How is local intellectual property rights discourse constituted? The *Dane Wajich* exhibit facilitated discussion about all of these questions and focused on emerging protocols for the use and distribution of images and sound recordings from the Ridington-Dane-ẕaa digital archive, particularly with regard to the digital distribution of these valued cultural materials to new global audiences on the Internet.

Robin Ridington has published pictures of the last Dane-ẕaa dreamer, Charlie Yahey, in a number of publications that the communities know about, value, and have access to. Yet in the course of this virtual museum project, and in the context of discussions related to the reach of the

Internet, intellectual property rights and obtaining permissions from community members to use the materials became an issue. After extensive dialogue as part of the community review process, facilitated by Amber and Kate in their capacity as project co-curators, it became clear that permission would be required from both the copyright holders and the intellectual property right holders for this Web-based project. However, we found that it is not always simple to determine who the intellectual property right holders are, especially with materials from people like Charlie Yahey who are now deceased. Some saw dreamers' songs and drawings as collective cultural property, while others began to claim it as individual and family cultural property.

The Doig River community ultimately decided that relevant families—and particularly the recognized family head or elders—should help decide how and where the materials relating to their family are publicly circulated. Throughout his lifetime, Charlie Yahey was a member of the Fort St. John band. In 1978, two years after his death, the Fort St. John band split into the Blueberry River and Doig River First Nations. Charlie Yahey's immediate descendants, who are now members of the Blueberry River First Nation, decided that they did not want pictures or recordings of Charlie Yahey included in the Doig River production, in part because they wanted to save them for use in a production of their own. The Doig River people, many of whom are closely related to Charlie Yahey through blood or marriage, still talk about their memories of Charlie Yahey and about the importance of his prophecies for their people. However, because of concerns expressed by members of the Yahey family, the curators decided not to include sound recordings of Charlie Yahey that Robin had collected, along with their accompanying translations and transcriptions, in the exhibition. Because Charlie Yahey had said on tape that through Robin's recordings "The world will listen to my voice," this decision was a difficult one.

The reasons for this materials' removal reflect emerging intellectual property rights concerns faced by many First Nations as they begin to exercise control over both their oral and material cultural heritage (see, for instance, Tuhiwai Smith 1999; Brown 2003; Karp et al. 2006). The immediate concerns that arose, however, seem to have more to do with divisions between different Dane-ẕaa communities than with an agreement about restricting access to their shared heritage. Because Robin's audio documents contain what amounts to a verbal agreement between him and

Charlie Yahey that the tapes should be made available to a wide audience ("The world will listen to my voice"), it is difficult to know whether this verbal permission to reproduce tape recordings should extend to distribution on the Internet. Neither Charlie nor Robin could have known that this technology would come into existence, although Charlie as a dreamer and prophet certainly used his powers to see into the future. Many of his prophecies tell about the present industrialization of Dane-ẕaa territory, and members of his family and larger community credit him with remarkable prophetic insight.

The Yahey family is concerned that it may not be possible to guarantee that the material is protected and handled in a culturally appropriate manner on a public medium like the Internet. They feel that their right to control the public use of their cultural heritage materials must always be acknowledged through the courtesy of asking permission. Ultimately, the Doig River community did choose to share a large selection of cultural heritage materials from their community, but they also chose to remove from the exhibit culturally sensitive materials deemed by some to be too powerful for uncontrolled access on the Internet. The approved materials include archival recordings and pictures taken without a public audience in mind as well as the newly recorded video and images, which were taken anticipating a public and global audience; both can be seen throughout the exhibition. We hope that sharing some of the details of the participatory process utilized during the creation of the *Dane Wajich* exhibit will be valuable to others working with the public display of similar politically charged cultural materials from other First Nations communities.

Conclusion

This chapter has described our use of video and Web-based media to represent "interlinear" translations of ethnographic texts. It also has placed our own work within the context of the history and development of translation, transcription, and interpretation in anthropology and ethnographic film. Indigenous-directed video projects like the Igloolik Isuma productions, as well as Doig River's 2007 *Dane Wajich* exhibition, exemplify the potential of new visual media to show original performances in indigenous languages alongside their textual translations. We hope that both the performances we have described and the accompanying interlinear translations will become a valuable resource for Dane-ẕaa, and others interested in their culture, who may wish to learn Dane-ẕaa Ẕáágéʔ with the benefit of both spoken and written materials.

Our experience indicates that translation and the choices involved in textual and visual representations are part of a subjective process. Each representation carries different connotations reflecting the decisions of each agent involved in the original and translated performances. It is only by acknowledging and detailing the processes involved in translation that a reader can understand it more fully. Many early ethnographers did not describe the process of translation, and no technology existed to enable them to create audio or video documentation of the performances. We are fortunate to have modern methods that enable us to better convey the original meanings and to represent the voice of the original speakers. Most importantly, we are aided by the best tool of all—the collaboration and cooperation of the people of the Doig River First Nation. We hope our work is worthy of their trust.

Notes

Robin Ridington and Jillian Ridington are ethnographers, Patrick Moore is a linguistic anthropologist, Kate Hennessy is a visual anthropologist, and Amber Ridington is a folklorist.

1. See the book of that title, *When You Sing It Now, Just Like New*, by Robin and Jillian Ridington.

2. Co-curators Amber Ridington and Kate Hennessy coordinated the initial production process; coordinated and facilitated the tasks of all the team members and partners; wrote, edited, and curated content; worked with multimedia designers on drafts of the exhibit design; and also conducted a number of community consultations and exhibit reviews at Doig River between 2004 and 2007. They also worked with two different chiefs, and their councillors, during the course of the project, each with different perspectives and concerns about sharing and protecting their culture with the public and on the Internet.

Throughout the production and consultation process, Robin and Jillian Ridington assisted the curators by drawing on their own wealth of knowledge and experience in Dane-ẕaa communities to provide contextualizing information for the exhibit's interpretive text, and suggestions for the use of particular archival images, texts, and sound recordings from the repatriated digital archive.

3. To address one of the community's core concerns, about language documentation and revitalization, the community also formed a partnership with linguistic anthropologist Dr. Patrick Moore (University of British Columbia) and

Dr. Dagmar Jung (University of Cologne), who had recently received funding from the German Volkswagen Foundation for Beaver language documentation. Working with Dane-ẕaa language experts such as Billy Attachie, Madeline Oker, and Eddie Apsassin, Moore, Jung, and their colleague Julia Miller were able to use these funds for extensive translation and orthographic transcription of Dane-ẕaa Ẕáágé?, both for use in the virtual exhibit and for use in local language revitalization programs and oral history projects.

   4. Online at http://www.virtualmuseum.ca/Exhibitions/Danewajich/english/ stories/video.php?action=fla/tommyatcomplex.

   5. Online at http://www.virtualmuseum.ca/Exhibitions/Danewajich/english/ stories/video.php?action=fla/sasnarehill.

   6. Online at http://www.virtualmuseum.ca/Exhibitions/Danewajich/english/ stories/video.php?action=fla/billyosborne.

   7. Online at http://www.virtualmuseum.ca/Exhibitions/Danewajich/english/ places/snare_hill.php.

   8. View an example online at http://www.virtualmuseum.ca/Exhibitions/ Danewajich/english/stories/video.php?action=fla/sasnarehill.

   9. Online at http://www.virtualmuseum.ca/Exhibitions/Danewajich/english/ stories/video.php?action=fla/maymontney.

References

Asad, Talal. 1986. The Concept of Cultural Translation in British Social Anthropology. In *Writing Culture: The Poetics and Politics of Ethnography*, ed. James Clifford and George Marcus, 141–64. Berkeley: University of California Press.

Bauman, Richard. 2001. Genre. In *Key Terms in Language and Culture*, ed. Alessandro Duranti, 79–82. Oxford: Blackwell.

Boas, Franz. 1916. Tsimshian Mythology. Thirty-first Annual Report of the Bureau of American Ethnology for the Years 1909–1910:29–1037. Washington DC.

———. 1921. *Ethnology of the Kwakiutl*. Washington DC: Thirty-fifth Annual Report of the Bureau of American Ethnology, Volumes 1 and 2.

Bringhurst, Robert. 1999. *A Story as Sharp as a Knife*. Vancouver: Douglas and McIntyre.

Brown, Michael F. 2003. *Who Owns Native Culture?* Cambridge: Harvard University Press.

Clifford, James, and George Marcus, eds. *Writing Culture: The Poetics and Politics of Ethnography*. Berkeley: University of California Press.

Cruikshank, Julie. 1987. Negotiating with Narrative: Establishing Cultural Identity at the Yukon International Storytelling Festival. *American Anthropologist* 99 (1): 56–69.

Doig River First Nation. 2000. *Dane-ẕaa Dreamers' Songs: 1966–1999*. Audio CD edited by Robin Ridington, Garry Oker, and Stacy Shaak. Rose Prairie: Doig River First Nation.

———. 2001. *Contact the People*. Digital Video (DVD). Rose Prairie: Doig River First Nation.

———. 2003. *Ridington/Dane-ẕaa Digital Archive*. Rose Prairie: Doig River First Nation. www.fishability.biz/Doig.

———. 2004. *Hadaa ka naadzet: The Dane-ẕaa Moose Hunt*. www.moosehunt .doigriverfn.com.

———. 2006. *They Dream about Everything*. Digital Video (DVD). Rose Prairie: Doig River First Nation.

———. 2007. *Dane Wajich—Dane-ẕaa Stories and Songs: Dreamers and the Land*. Virtual Museum of Canada Exhibit: www.virtualmuseum.ca/Exhibitions/ Danewajich.

Duranti, Alessandro. 2003. Language as Culture in U.S. Anthropology: Three Paradigms. *Current Anthropology* 44 (3): 323–47.

Fletcher, Alice C., and Francis La Flesche. 1911. *The Omaha Tribe*. Washington DC: Twenty-seventh Annual Report of the Bureau of American Ethnology.

Foley, John Miles. 2005. From Oral Performance to Paper-Text to Cyber-Edition. *Oral Tradition* 20 (2): 233–63.

Goddard, Pliny. 1916. Beaver Texts. *Anthropological Papers of the American Museum of Natural History* 10 (2): 67–170. New York.

Hymes, Dell. 1981. *"In Vain I Tried to Tell You": Essays in Native American Ethnopoetics*. Philadelphia: University of Pennsylvania Press.

Karp, Ivan, Corine A. Krats, Lynne Szwaja, and Tomas Ybarra-Frausto. 2006. *Museum Frictions*. Durham: Duke University Press.

MacDougall, David. 1995. Subtitling Ethnographic Films: Archetypes into Individualities. *Visual Anthropology Review* 11 (1): 83–91.

———. 1998. Beyond Observational Cinema. In *Transcultural Cinema*, 125–39. Princeton: Princeton University Press.

Maud, Ralph. 2000. *Transmission Difficulties: Franz Boas and Tsimshian Mythology*. Burnaby, British Columbia: Talonbooks.

Moore, Patrick, and Daniel Tlen. 2006. Indigenous Linguistics and Land Claims: The Semiotic Projection of Athabaskan Directionals in Elijah Smith's Radio Work. *Journal of Linguistic Anthropology* 17 (2): 266–86.

Parades, Americo, and Richard Bauman, eds. 1971. *Toward New Perspectives in Folklore*. Austin: University of Texas Press.

Pink, Sarah. 2006. *The Future of Visual Anthropology*. London: Routledge.

Poster, Mark. 1990. *The Mode of Information: Poststructuralism and Social Context*. Cambridge: Polity Press.

Rasmussen, Knud. 1929. *Intellectual Culture of the Iglulik Eskimos*. Report of the Fifth Thule Expedition, 1921–24. Vol. 7, no. 1. Copenhagen: Glydendalske Boghandel.

———. 1976. *The Intellectual Culture of the Iglulik Eskimos*. Trans. W. Worster. New York: AMS Press.

Ridington, Amber, and Kate Hennessy. 2008. Building Indigenous Agency through Web-Based Exhibition: Dane Wajich—Dane-ẕaa Stories and Songs: Dreamers and the Land. In *Museums and the Web 2008: Proceedings*, ed. J. Trant and D. Bearman. Toronto: Archives & Museums Informatics. http://archimuse.com/mw2008/papers/ridington/ridington.html.

Ridington, Robin. 1978. *Swan People: A Study of the Dunne-za Prophet Dance.* National Museum of Man, Mercury Series, Ethnology Service Paper 38. Ottawa.

———. 1981. Beaver Indians. In *Handbook of North American Indians*, vol. 6, ed. June Helm, 350–60. Washington DC: Smithsonian Institution.

———. 1988. *Trail to Heaven: Knowledge and Narrative in a Northern Native Community.* Vancouver: Douglas and McIntyre.

Ridington, Robin, and Jillian Ridington. 2003. Archiving Actualities: Sharing Authority with Dane-ẕaa First Nations. *Comma: International Journal on Archives* 1:61–68.

———. 2006. *When You Sing It Now, Just Like New.* Lincoln: University of Nebraska Press.

Rothenberg, Jerome, and Dennis Tedlock. 1970–80. *Alcheringa Ethnopoetics.*

Soukup, Katarina. 2006. Report: Travelling Through Layers: Inuit Artists Appropriate New Technologies. *Canadian Journal of Communication* 31:239–46.

Swanton, John R. 1905. *Haida Texts and Myths.* Bureau of American Ethnology Bulletin 29. Washington.

Tedlock, Dennis. 1972. *Finding the Center: Narrative Poetry of the Zuni Indians.* Trans. Dennis Tedlock from Performances in the Zuni by Andrew Peynetsa and Walter Sanchez. New York: Dial Press.

———. 1991. The Speaker of Tales Has More Than One String to Play On. In *Anthropological Poetics*, ed. Ivan Brady, 309–40. Savage MD: Rowman & Littlefield.

Tuhiwai Smith, Linda. 1999. *Decolonizing Methodologies: Research and Indigenous Peoples.* Dunedin: University of Otago Press.

10

Translating Algonquian Oral Texts

Julie Brittain and Marguerite MacKenzie

Introduction

In this chapter we discuss a number of issues pertinent to the translation of Canadian Aboriginal oral literature, specifically that of the Algonquian peoples of the Quebec-Labrador peninsula (eastern Canada). Our discussion focuses on a collection of "oral texts" (the Innu-Naskapi collection) with which we have been involved as translators since 1985 (MacKenzie) and 1996 (Brittain).[1] Working collaboratively with native speakers of the Aboriginal language, we have now published English translations of several stories from this collection (e.g., MacKenzie 2004; Brittain and MacKenzie et al. 2004, 2005). The Innu-Naskapi collection was recorded on cassette tape in 1967 and 1968. It comprises more than a hundred stories, "authored" by eight different storytellers, all of whom performed in their first language, Cree-Montagnais-Naskapi (CMN).[2] Algonquian literature distinguishes two genres (Ellis 1995): traditional tales such as myths and legends (*atanukana*), and factual stories such as personal histories, hunting stories, and the like (*tipatshimuna*).[3] Both genres are represented in the Innu-Naskapi collection. We discuss the translation of this collection into Canada's two official languages, English and French.[4]

Some of the issues we deal with may be familiar to translators in general, regardless of the source language; we hope, however, to show that a unique constellation of factors comes into play in translating literature such as the Innu-Naskapi collection. We elaborate on what we take to be the key factors in this regard: (1) the source texts are oral; (2) the source language (CMN) is very different, typologically, from the goal language(s) (English, French); (3) many of the translators (ourselves included) do not have native-speaker intuitions with respect to the source language (although we do have a thorough knowledge of the grammar and vocabulary, and one of us [MacKenzie] is a functionally competent speaker); (4) relatively few reference materials (dictionaries and grammars) exist in the source language; (5) as a consequence of (2), (3), and (4), translators take a *transcribed* version of the oral text, rather the oral text itself, as their starting point, facilitating close examination of the source language with native speakers, ideally achieving a sentence-for-sentence match of source and goal languages in advance of attempting a more literary translation; (6) practically speaking, it is often difficult for the translator to obtain a transcription that is faithful to the original oral text, and a special effort must be made to obtain "a linguist's version" of transcription (one which endeavors to transfer the oral text to "paper" as completely as possible); (7) translators also tend to be involved in researching and compiling reference materials for the source language so that the projects are "recursive" in the sense that one informs the other on a regular basis—this can create the impression of "working with a moving target"; (8) finally, in transitioning from oral to written text, a certain amount of information is lost—take the case of the storyteller who announces a change of scene in his or her tale with a physical relocation in the storytelling arena. Punctuation (in this case, a paragraph break) will compensate the reader for the visual information lost in transitioning from oral to written. However, punctuation conventions (e.g., placement of commas, periods, quotations marks, paragraph breaks) remain to be agreed upon for the source language so that transcribers often work without the benefit of editorial guidelines, each applying his or her own set of criteria.

We provide an overview of our role in the transcription process, and we describe the "processing" stages to which the Innu-Naskapi collection has been subject over the past four decades.[5] We present, if you will, a "biography" of the Innu-Naskapi collection, including the role we have played in its "life." Because this story highlights how and why the art of translation—specifically of the oral literature of the Algonquian-speaking peoples, but more generally we suppose that of many indigenous peoples—has evolved, we feel it is worth telling.[6] The kinds of translations that were made in the early life of this collection are quite different from those that have been done more recently. One reason for this change is obvious: more-sophisticated technologies are now available to manipulate audio files. Perhaps less obvious is the impact of the increased level of activity in documenting "small" languages such as those belonging to the Algonquian family.[7]

The task of the translator whose source material is an oral text is, from the start, very different from that of the literary translator whose source material is a written text; translators of languages where the majority of texts are written (e.g., the large European language groups) do not face the issue of how best to *listen* to their source material. In many cases we are working from old audio files, which may be of poor quality and difficult to hear in places. This is compounded by the fact that, while writing tends to encourage the use of standardized language, the spoken word is a less constraining medium, and narrators more liberally infuse their performances with nonstandard features of speech; here we refer to regional accent, regional vocabulary items and grammatical structures. Indeed, the narrator may seek to personalize his or her piece by drawing on these regional identifiers. As translators of oral texts working in the twenty-first century, we have the advantage over our counterparts of forty, thirty, twenty, even ten years ago, in that technology has evolved to assist us in what can often be the challenging task of hearing our source material. We now have access to digitized versions of old sound files, and specialized software (e.g., SoundForge) enables us to isolate segments, enhance them, replay them, and even to "see" the sounds through visual representations of their acoustics. All of this greatly facilitates the task of transcribing sound files, a stage we consider essential to the process of translating oral texts.

Increasingly, those of us involved in oral text translation are also involved in community-based language documentation projects such as the compilation of (bilingual or trilingual) dictionaries and reference grammars.[8] These are the essential tools of the translator, and the extent to which they are available clearly has an impact on the kinds of translations we achieve. As we have noted in passing, in under-documented languages such as CMN, the work of the translator differs significantly from that of the translator of larger languages. Necessarily, the elaboration or refinement of a dictionary entry or the description and illustration of a grammatical point will have implications for translation work. Put simply, all the different parts of our work feed one another. Many of the words we come across in the oral texts are not in the dictionaries, meaning that as we work we compile a list of words to be added to the (appropriate) dictionary.[9] Many of the grammatical inflections we encounter in oral texts are poorly understood, and research is required in order to understand how to translate them; this work feeds the reference grammars.

Conversely, we find that in the course of conducting research, whether for the purpose of language documentation or for the more theoretically oriented work we are involved with as linguists in an academic context, we obtain a better understanding of the nuances of the Algonquian language. This enables us to make better translations. An important aspect of our work as academics is that some number of the graduate students working under our supervision have utilized the oral texts as source material for master's and doctoral theses. MacKenzie, for example, has been involved in a supervisory capacity in theses by Brittain (2000), Hasler (2002), Bannister (2004), and Oxford (2007), all of which are based wholly or partially on the examination of oral texts from the Innu-Naskapi collection.[10] These works have focused on a variety of aspects of the grammars of various CMN dialects, and they make a substantial contribution to documenting the language as a whole. In the final section of this chapter we show how our translation work and the other language-related projects we are involved with are closely connected. We also discuss the special challenges presented by the fact that CMN is very different typologically from both English and French. Algonquian languages are of a typology referred to as "polysynthetic." We defer detailed discussion of this issue until the need arises; for the present it will suffice to say that polysynthetic languages tend to have highly complex verbs, such that the quantity of information conveyed by an English or French sentence may be contained in one word (the verb).

The Provenance of the Innu-Naskapi Collection

The Innu-Naskapi collection is part of the cultural heritage of a people who now occupy three distinct physical locations, as residents of two communities in Labrador (Natuashish and Sheshatshiu) and one in Quebec (Kawawachikamach).[11] While separated from each other geographically, these communities cannot be considered in isolation from one another, as they retain close ties through family, history, culture, and, of course, language. Members of the Quebec community refer to themselves and their language as "Naskapi" (when they are speaking English or French), and that is the term we use here. In accordance with community wishes, we use the term "Innu" to refer to the (language and people of the) two Labrador communities. Where there is a need to distinguish between the two Innu communities, we refer to "Mushuau Innu" (Natuashish) and "Sheshatshiu Innu" (Sheshatshiu)."[12]

CMN is the most widely spoken Aboriginal language in Canada, with an estimated 98,000 people self-reporting to be fluent or at least functionally competent in it in the 2006 census (Statistics Canada), and it remains the principal language of communication for the three communities under discussion. In terms of area, the language is traditionally spoken across much of Canada, from the Rocky Mountains in the west to the Atlantic seaboard. More recently, with the movement of Aboriginal populations to cities such as Vancouver, CMN speakers are distributed from coast to coast.

The Innu-Naskapi collection comprises audio recordings made in two locations. In 1967, in Sheshatshiu, approximately one hundred stories were narrated by seven storytellers, all of whom are now deceased (Etuat Rich, Ishpashtien Rich, Tanien Pone, Sushep Ashini, Shimun Grégoire, Shanut Rich, and Shushep Rich).[13] These recordings were made by Madeleine Lefebvre and Robert Lanari.

In 1967 and again in 1968, a Naskapi elder, the late John Peastitute, narrated approximately fifty-nine stories at the community of Schefferville, northern Quebec: thirty-six stories were recorded in 1967 and a further twenty-three the following year. In 1982 the community to which John Peastitute belonged relocated to Kawawachikamach (eighteen kilometers north of Schefferville), and this remains the permanent home of the Naskapi Nation of Quebec (http://www.naskapi.ca). John Peastitute's stories were narrated before live audiences and were recorded by Serge Melançon. Both collections were recorded under the supervision of Rémi Savard of the Laboratoire d'anthropologie amérindienne. The original audio files and all of the original associated documentation (early translations, transcriptions, commentaries, etc.) for the entire collection remain at the Laboratoire d'anthropologie amérindienne in Montreal.

In the early 1990s the Naskapi were given permission to copy the original cassette recordings of Peastitute's 1967 performances.[14] They were also allowed to copy all the associated paperwork. This subset of the collection now falls under the care of the Naskapi Development Corporation (NDC), the governing body for the Quebec Naskapi. The NDC continues to oversee the conservation, distribution, transcription, and translation of Peastitute's stories.

In 1984, copies of the audio files and paperwork for the stories recorded at Sheshatshiu were placed in the Native Languages Archive at Memorial University of Newfoundland.[15] Of the original one hundred stories, twenty-nine have been transcribed into standard Innu orthography, edited and published in book form (*Sheshatshiu atanukana mak tipatshimuna* volumes 1–4, Mailhot et al. 1999 and Mailhot et al. 2004). These books, together with (Innu) sound files for selected stories, can also be accessed online.[16] Three more books are in the process of being edited. José Mailhot is presently making French translations of the stories in this collection, and Marguerite MacKenzie is working on producing English translations. These translations are still works in progress, for which reason they are not yet available in published form, or on the Web.

Background: Communities and Dialects

The issue of the different speech varieties (dialects) that are represented in the Innu-Naskapi collection is of some significance, because it has implications for our work as translators. The Mushuau Innu and the Quebec Naskapi constitute the entirety of the Naskapi-speaking population; for this reason, it is convenient to refer to the (more westerly) Quebec dialect as "Western Naskapi" and to use "Eastern Naskapi" to refer to the Labrador variety (as does, e.g., Brittain 2001). As noted, however, the Mushuau Innu of Labrador do not use the term "Naskapi" to identify themselves as a people or to refer to their language. Although in Quebec the term "Naskapi" is embraced as part of the heritage of the community, in Labrador it is regarded as an offensive colonial designation. The difference in terminology belies the fact that the people now divided into two communities, and separated by the Quebec-Labrador provincial border, until fairly recently constituted a single speech community.

The division of Naskapi into two distinct dialects has been a gradual (and still evolving) process (MacKenzie 1979). Up until the 1960s, the people now resident at Kawawachikamach and Natuashish were still pursuing a traditional lifestyle, that of nomadic hunters (principally of caribou). Ranging across a large geographical area (the entire northern half of the Quebec-Labrador peninsula), the speech variety that linguists identified as Naskapi would have shown some internal variation even prior to the adoption of a sedentary lifestyle. Families with hunting territory in the western part of the peninsula would have interacted more with speakers of Cree, while those in the more easterly and southern areas would have had more to do with speakers of dialects of Montagnais (e.g., Sheshatshiu Innu). As trapping became more important, some Naskapi took their business north to the trading post at Fort Chimo (Ungava Bay), while others went east to the trading post at Davis Inlet. As the traditional lifestyle gradually gives way to one that is more sedentary, Fort Chimo and Davis Inlet become the locations with which each group increasingly identifies. Most of the Quebec Naskapi came from Fort Chimo. Among older Naskapi in both communities there still exists a shared set of distinctly "Naskapi" vocabulary items and grammatical structures (MacKenzie 1979, 1980). Speakers of Peastitute's generation had more in common with one another than do the generations that followed; clearly, the longer the two communities have existed, the greater the disparity between the dialects has become. In Kawawachikamach, Mushuau Innu features are progressively marginalized and discarded from the speech of the younger generations. John Peastitute's speech identifies him as Mushuau Innu.

Sheshatshiu Innu is a variety of Montagnais, the subdialect of CMN spoken in numerous communities along the Lower North Shore of Quebec.[17] Some of the narrators of Sheshatshiu stories were Mushuau Innu, and some were speakers of what has come to be known as Sheshatshiu Innu. How to deal with dialectal variation is thus an ever-present issue, in particular for transcribers preparing the texts to be published for Innu and Naskapi readers, as decisions have to be made with respect to what will and will not be understood by the target audience.

Free Translation

In this section we describe the initial work that was done with the collection shortly after it was recorded. A native speaker listens to the stories and makes a "free translation" into English. By "free translation" we mean idiomatic rather than word-for-word. Matiu Rich of Sheshatshiu made the preliminary English translations of the Sheshatshiu stories, and John Peastitute's grandson, Joe, translated his grandfather's stories. Born in 1944, Matiu Rich was twenty-three at the time the recordings were made.[18] Joe Peastitute was approximately twelve years old in 1967. These initial translations are approximate and do not provide a precise translation from the original language. The translators were relatively young, and both spoke English as a second language. While they had relatively good spoken English, their vocabulary is unlikely to have been extensive, making it difficult to provide a faithful rendition of nuances encoded by the many inflectional endings of the Algonquian verb. Some forty years later, linguists are still discovering how to translate these accurately. By way of illustration we consider how "evidential" verb forms should be translated into English; these verbs are inflected with a set of suffixes that are dedicated to encoding "source of information"—how the speaker came by his or her information.[19] In CMN, information obtained through inference based on sensory information (smell, touch, sound, sight) is encoded in the verbal inflection. The examples below are taken from James, Clarke, and MacKenzie (2001).[20] In (1a) the speaker uses the evidential form of the verb, as the information he or she is passing on is inferred from indirect sensory evidence (most likely, he or she has heard snoring), while in (1b), which is not an evidential form, the statement is based on direct evidence:[21]

(1a) *Nipa:tak*
 nipa:-tak
 He/she sleep—*evidential*
 'He/she must be asleep.'

(1b) *nipa:u*
 nipa:u
 He/she sleep
 'He/she is asleep.'

Clearly, a sophisticated understanding of both languages is required to translate grammatical contrasts of this type. Undoubtedly, the essentials of plot were communicated in this initial phase of translation—the gist of the tale—but in many cases the nuances of the original spoken narrative were lost.[22] Also, as is normal in free translations, certain phrases and sentences were not translated at all.

First Publications Using Free Translations

Shortly after the initial translations had been made, author and journalist Peter Desbarats took a selection of the translations of the Innu-Naskapi collection and "polished" the language, making it more standard and more literary. Desbarats was not familiar with the language of the peoples whose stories he would subsequently publish in "translation" in his volume *What They Used to Tell About: Indian Legends from Labrador* (Desbarats 1969). The (essential, in our opinion) step of undertaking a faithful transcription of the material—of creating "a linguist's version"—was not taken at this time.[23]

Anthropologists Rémi Savard and Madeleine Lefebvre also worked with the free translations, Savard focusing on the stories that feature the trickster figure Wolverine (see, e.g., Brittain and MacKenzie et al. 2005), Lefebvre on those featuring culture hero Tshakapesh. Both Savard and Lefebvre made literary French translations of the free (English) translations and undertook structural (anthropological) analyses of the stories. This work resulted in the publication of Savard's book of Wolverine tales, *Carcajou et le sens du monde: Récits montagnais-naskapi* (Savard 1971), and Lefebvre's *Tshakapesh: Récits montagnais-naskapi* (Lefebvre 1974).

Community Decisions: Transcription and Translation

On January 31, 1980, the Quebec Naskapi voted to relocate to Kawawa-chikamach, a move that took place gradually, between 1981 and 1983, as construction proceeded. New legislation (the Cree-Naskapi of Quebec Act, June 1984) provided the Naskapi with self-government, allowing them to take charge of their own affairs, among which were fiscal decisions. As linguistic and cultural development is a high priority for the Naskapi, an intense program of linguistic work (continuing to this day) was initiated at that time. Peastitute's stories fell under the custodial guardianship of the NDC shortly after the move to the new community. The Naskapi did not begin systematically working with the Peastitute collection until 1994; prior to this, the language consultants at the NDC, working with Marguerite MacKenzie and Bill Jancewicz (community linguist from 1988 to the present), had been preoccupied with the compilation of a trilingual Naskapi-French-English lexicon (MacKenzie and Jancewicz 1994).[24]

Work began on the Sheshatshiu (Innu) stories in the mid-1980s, as funding became available. The initial translations of these recordings were examined by linguists (e.g., MacKenzie and Mailhot) and found to be at best an approximate match to the oral texts. In order to provide more accurate translations, the original audio files were transcribed into the community orthography. MacKenzie has been more intensively involved in processing the Innu stories since 2000.

With the completion of the Naskapi lexicon in 1994, the Naskapi Legends and Texts Project (NLTP) became a priority for the Naskapi. In August and September 1994, Bill Jancewicz listened to the tapes, comparing their content with the pages of descriptive documentation, which consist of several hundred typed and handwritten pages of material. Philip Einish and Thomas Sandy, native speakers of Naskapi and linguistic consultants for the NDC, also reviewed the documentation, finding copies of field notes made by Melançon at the time of recording, as well as some transcriptions (into Naskapi syllabics) that had been made in the early 1980s. For a limited number of stories they matched transcriptions to translations.

In October 1994, Phil Einish, Thomas Sandy, and Bill Jancewicz began work on a story called *Âniskuwâyikuch* ("Ants"), transcribing the text into Naskapi syllabics and roman. Jancewicz entered the text into the computer and Sandy proofread it. Subsequently, Einish produced a rough English translation. At this time, much of the work was not done on computer, but by hand. By the spring of 1995 Thomas Sandy departed from the project; approximately a dozen of the stories had been transcribed (mostly by hand) into syllabics by that time. Early in 1996, Sandy's sister, monolingual Naskapi-speaker Alma Chemaganish, joined the NLTP. She transcribed the stories into Naskapi syllabics, directly onto a computer. At that point in the project, the procedure was as follows: Alma Chemaganish listened to the audio files and typed syllabic text directly into the computer. She read the text off the computer screen to Philip Einish, who (translated and) entered the English translation directly to computer. These transcriptions did not consistently match the oral text, as the transcribers made their own editorial decisions as they worked, tailoring the written versions they were creating to the target audience (the Naskapi community). We subsequently revisited all of the oral texts to ensure that everything was transcribed, for the sake of posterity, but also to serve as a basis for our own translation work, which is destined, not for the Naskapi reading public, but for a more general audience. We have, as we show in the next section, our own editorial decisions to make in tailoring our work to our audience, and for this reason we require maximally detailed transcriptions (the linguist's version) as our starting point.

From the outset, the Naskapi stated three principal goals with respect to the Peastitute stories: (1) to make the original recordings available to their own (Naskapi-speaking) community, as CDs, via the internet, and through local community radio; (2) to make them available as reading material (printed in Naskapi syllabics); and (3), to publish English and French translations, making the work available to a wider readership.[25] Goal (1) entails working to ensure that the audio files are good, and we are only peripherally involved in this work. We are perhaps most concerned with the transitions from goal (1) to goal (2) and from goal (2) to goal (3), as a number of interesting issues are raised in making these transitions.

Transition from Oral Text to a Written Text
(Tailored toward a Naskapi Audience)

We are by no means the first to observe that oral and written texts differ profoundly (Swann 1994; Cruikshank 1999), the former being transitory and interactive, where the "author" has firsthand knowledge of who his or her audience is, the latter being permanent, non-interactive, and where the audience is not physically present. Although ideally, from our perspective, the transcriber should be the perfect human speech-to-text machine, in practice he or she is much more than this, serving to mediate between the spoken and written word on behalf of a specific target audience. The audience of an oral performance has an advantage over the reader of the same (transcribed) performance in at least the following ways: the narrator can interact with the audience before starting the performance to establish who is familiar with the story (or he or she may make a judgment based on, e.g., the age of the audience), adding or skipping details accordingly; the narrator can announce the name(s) of the main character(s) or give a plot summary before the story begins; the narrator can use different voices for different characters, aiding the listener's ability to track who is saying/doing what (Peastitute, e.g., sometimes uses his "scary voice" when Wolverine enters the narrative [Brittain and MacKenzie et al. 2005]); members of the audience can interrupt the narrator if they need clarification (again, we have evidence of this in the Peastitute recordings); the audience of a live performance can also see the narrator's gestures.[26] Clearly, these aids to understanding the story are not available to the audience of a printed text (the reader).

The reader is far more dependent on the structuring of text through punctuation (sentences, paragraphs, separate lines for dialogue, etc.). The transcriber may decide to compensate for what is lost in transitioning from oral to written media by making additions to the original; for example, to help keep track of participants, he or she might insert additional names, or plot reminders might be added to increase the clarity of the narrative. Material may also be removed by the transcriber, for example, stylistic repetition of key words, phrases or sentences, false starts or slips-of-the-tongue by the narrator.[27] Many of the so-called quotative verbs, which introduce and/or mark the termination of direct speech (he/she said, ". . . ," he/she said), are also routinely edited out.

Finally, the transcriber may make substitutions to the original; for example, an archaic vocabulary item, or one that is judged to be from a different dialect, will be replaced where possible with the equivalent word for the target speech community. We see this in cases where Peastitute uses a distinctly Mushuau Innu word. For example, in one of the Wolverine stories, Frog is a character; John Peastitute uses *anik* 'frog' throughout (Mushuau Innu), whereas in Kawawachikamach the word is *iyik*; likewise, the demonstrative *nenua* is replaced with the local word *aniyâyuw*. This is a good example of how texts are altered to accommodate a younger audience; younger speakers of Naskapi are less likely to be familiar with what is now regarded as the more easterly variety of the subdialect (Mushuau Innu).[28]

A certain number of editorial changes made in transitioning from oral to written text have to do with the fact that CMN is a polysynthetic language, one consequence of which is that verbs tend to dominate the discourse. CMN verbs encode reference to the discourse participants (who is doing what to whom), obviating the need for the number of nouns required in a language such as English or French. In CMN, once a noun has been matched to a verbal affix, it can be dropped from the discourse. Clearly, since English and French verbs only encode minimal reference to discourse participants (e.g., subject-verb agreement), in translating from CMN to English or French we need to compensate by adding nouns. Interestingly, however, we also see transcribers adding nouns for clarification; it would thus seem that merely in transitioning from oral to written text (never mind the transition from polysynthetic language to non-polysynthetic language) an information loss is perceived by native speakers of CMN. We take up the issue of specific problems associated with translating from polysynthetic language (CMN) to non-polysynthetic language (English) shortly.

Transition from Transcription to Translation (2)–(3)

The "transcription" of Peastitute's stories for a Naskapi audience results in a printed Naskapi version that has undergone certain editorial changes, making it unsuitable as a starting point for translations (which, by implication, are destined for an audience with different needs). The linguist's version that we have now obtained for each Naskapi story aims to be an objective reproduction of the original performance, with nothing added, removed, or substituted.[29] Only with all of the information intact can we begin the work of translation; during the course of this work we will implement our own editorial decisions (and these may, depending on our target audience, overlap with those made for the community print versions). We now present sample texts from the Innu-Naskapi collection to illustrate some of the editorial decisions we have just described.

Editorial Decision Making

As we have noted, CMN is polysynthetic (as are all Algonquian languages). Because this has an impact on both on the transcriber and the translator, we take a moment to detail what we mean by "polysynthetic." A polysynthetic language can be informally defined as a language that has (potentially) highly complex words. Verbs in particular can contain a large amount of information, referring not just to events or states (as we would expect, universally) but also to nominal participants (subject, direct object, indirect object), prepositional, adjectival, and adverbial elements. Pronouns equivalent to English "I," "you," "we," and "they" (etc.) do exist, but they are only used for emphasis. Potentially, the polysynthetic verb can convey as much information as an entire sentence in a (non-polysynthetic) language such as English or French.[30] We show a rather extreme, but nevertheless perfectly grammatical, example from East (Quebec) Cree:

(2) East Cree verb
    âtichinâpihîkinuwishtikwânikiwâu (Salt et al. 2004)
    âtichin-âpih-îkinuw-ishtikwân-ikiw-âu
    upside.down-open-passive-head-transitivizer-3subject/3object
    'He/she gives him/her the package of the meat from the head of a caribou that was cleaned out.'

The non-Cree speaker would be prudent to wonder on what basis we make the claim that the string of sounds represented orthographically in (2) is indeed a single word in Cree, so we take a short detour to justify our claim. While the issue of how to define a word is the subject of ongoing debate within the field of linguistics (see Hall and Kleinhenz 1999, among others), we can sidestep what is a highly technical discussion by simply stating that we know the string of sounds represented in (2) to be a word because a native speaker would be able to pick it out from the stream of speech (the oral context) as a stand-alone linguistic entity (i.e., a word).[31] Take the case of the English forms *look*, *looks*, and *looked*. Native English speakers will all agree that each form is a word because each is a stand-alone entity—a word is a complete and independent unit. By contrast, some of the components of the word are clearly not stand-alone entities: the -*s* in *looks* and the *-ed* in *looked* cannot be uttered in isolation—they are not words. Setting aside a few knotty cases we can always come up with for any language, judging what is and is not a word is something the native speaker, regardless of the language, can always do with some confidence—Cree is no different from English or any other language. Also, when committing the string of sounds in (2) to paper, the native Cree speaker would leave spaces on either side of it to show its left and right boundaries—its beginning and its end, as we have done in (2). Thus we can observe of (2) that one readily apparent issue the Cree-to-English/French translator faces is the frequent (and often radical) absence of a one-to-one word correspondence between the source and goal language. In the case of (2), clearly the word constitutes a sentence in the sense that it conveys a complete proposition; this is not always the case for a polysynthetic language. It is pertinent at this point to mention that it is not always an easy matter for CMN native speakers to determine where one sentence ends and another begins, and this poses problems for us when we translate or try to format the Aboriginal language. Although dividing the stream of speech into words seems to be an innate skill of the language user, the identification of sentence boundaries is much more a learned skill, an artifact of literacy.[32]

Another pertinent "by-product" of polysynthesis is the paucity of nominals; once the identity of the participants has been established in a piece of discourse, the referring nominals are omitted, reference to them being retained in the verbal complex via an elaborate system of "agreement morphology." In (2) there is no separate word representing the subject or object, the identities of which are obtained by context (which we do not provide). We note also in passing that in (2) even the complex indirect object (the meat from the head of a caribou that was cleaned out) is part of the verb complex.

To illustrate further, the nominals in parentheses in (3) are "optional" in the sense of not being required by syntax.

(3) (*Ishkuess*) *uapameu* (*napessa*)
     '(a/the girl) He/she.sees.him/her (a/the boy)'

Thus, when we examine texts (oral or written) from polysynthetic languages, we typically see a large number of complex verb forms and a relatively small number of nominals. Given the loss of information between the oral and written text transition to which we have already referred, this can present a challenge, all the more so if the target audience is of a younger generation whose grasp of the participant tracking system is still developing.[33] (We note in passing that children and younger people are an important target audience for the printed versions of the stories, in the push to promote literacy in the Aboriginal language.) The transcriber, you might say, feels obliged to err on the safe side and assist the reader by inserting nominals into the written text where none appear in the oral version. We provide some actual examples to illustrate how the system works.[34] The example in (4) is taken from the transcription of a Naskapi Wolverine tale. (No additions or deletions have been made to this sentence—it is an exact transcription of the oral text.)

(4) *Wiyâpimât Kwâhkwâchâw, Asiniya pâmûhtâuwiyichî piskutinâhch.*
     wiyâpim-**ât**   Kwâhkwâchâw   Asiniy-**a**   pâmûhtâuw-**iyichî**
     see-(x>y)   Wolverine(x)   rock-(y)   walk-(y)
     piskutinâhch.
     on.the.mountain
     'Wolverine sees Rock, (pause) Rock is walking along the mountain.'

The bolded verbal suffix shows that a third-person entity (x) is acting on a further third-person entity (y): *wiyâpim-**ât*** (x>y = x.sees.y). *Kwâhk-wâchâw* ('Wolverine') is interpreted as the (x) participant because it has no suffixation. The bolded suffix on *Asiniy-**a*** ('Rock') marks it as the (y) participant.[35] The suffix *-iyichî*, which appears on the verb, *pâmûhtâw-**iyichî*** ('walk'), indicates that the (y) participant, 'Rock,' is also the subject of the next verb, *pâmûhtâw-* ('walk'). Note that this tracking morphology does not simply encode "subject" and "object," as the referring expression *Asiniya* ('Rock') simultaneously provides the identity of the object of "see" and the subject of "walk."

Peastitute does not use any names in his following sentence, but it is clear (from verbal morphology) that Wolverine (x) thinks that Rock (y) looks like a person (rather than a mere inanimate rock, of course).

(5) *"Mân   âku   iyiyuw,"   itâyimâw.*
     mân   âku   iyiyuw   itâyim-âw
     that   then   person   think.about- (x>y)
     'That's a person,' Wolverine thinks to himself (about Rock).

Again, in (5) the text is a precise transcription of the oral text. In Peasti-tute's third sentence (below), the verb ending (bold) makes it clear who is doing what to whom, but for clarity now, the *transcriber* inserts Rock's name.

(6) Original: *Châchin-ât.*
                run.to(x>y)
Transcriber addition: *Châchinât Asiniya.*
                              'He runs over to *Rock*.'

The sequence of text shown in examples (4)–(6) raises another issue for the translator of a language like CMN, which (like many other languages) does not encode a grammatical distinction between masculine and femi-nine gender, into a language like English or French, which does.[36] Third persons in Algonquian languages are marked as neither masculine nor feminine. In the case where the protagonists in the stories are not hu-man (e.g., Wolverine and Rock), we rely on community members to tell us their gender; both Wolverine and Rock are male.[37]

In the Innu story about Meshapush, the Giant Hare (MacKenzie 2004), the main character's name is not used until three quarters of the way through. Clearly, the storyteller feels no need to name the main character (perhaps his audience has been begging him for weeks to tell the story of Giant Hare, in which case it is assumed background information). In (7), the translator (not the transcriber) adds the main character's name to the first sentence of text (underlined), and occasionally thereafter. Notice also in this example that in order to create a published version for the Aborig-inal reader, the stylistic repetitions present in the original performance, which readers tell us are distracting and inappropriate, are removed (text in square brackets).

(7) *Eku anite etutet [anite] [anite] naneu, uapameu namesha, mishta-mitshetinua [namesha].*

eku	anite	etute-t	anite	anite	naneu	uapam-eu
Then	there	walk-(x)	there	there	along.the.shore	see-(x>y)
namesh-a	mishta-mitsheti-nua		namesh-a.			
fish-(y)	very-see.many-(x)		fish-(y)			

'<u>Meshapush</u> was walking along the shore when he saw some fish, a great many fish.'

The translator has added the name "Meshapush," but the transcriber (for the Innu-language print version) has not, reflecting the fact that an Innu reader, being more familiar with the stories, is judged to need less information than a non-Innu reader.

Example (8) shows a case where the transcriber has removed multiple instances of the quotative verb (*iteu* 'he/she says to him/her' or, in this case *itiku* 'he/she says to her/him'). Notice that the translator makes the same decision (in effect choosing in this case to translate the edited version of the transcription).

(8) *Tau anite nussim, itiku, anapitsheu eniku, [itiku, tau anite, itiku]*

tau	anite	nussim	itiku
x.is.there	there	my.grandchild	she.says.to.him
anapitsheu	eniku	[itiku	tau
x.makes.nets	spider(x)	she.says.to.him	x.is.there
anite	itiku]		
there	she.says.to.him		

'Over there my grandchild, she said to him, there is a spider making nets.'

Quotative verbs perform an equivalent function to quotation marks in the written version. However, what to do with the plethora of 'he/she said' constructions is an issue for anyone preparing a text, whether transcriber or translator. While all instances are recorded, those superfluous to the reader are removed and additional translations such 'he/she replied' are used for variety. Over the years, procedures have been developed to deal with long stretches of dialogue by different speakers: the name of each participant is recorded in the linguist's version next to each piece of dialogue, ensuring that the attribution is well understood. Each block of direct speech begins on a new line in the text, as is the convention in (at least) European fiction, and the notes are later removed for the published version. So that a reader can follow the often convoluted stories, which have many disparate participants, Mailhot has implemented, for the Innu texts, a system of representing direct and embedded quotes by a long dash and double angle brackets, respectively.[38]

The issue of assigning sentence and paragraph breaks is also a challenge, as in these dialects of cmn there are no specific words that indicate a new paragraph or a section, as are found in Ojibwe (R. Valentine 2001).

As we learn to do this, we use many of the same criteria as are used in English (i.e., shifts in topic or scene). Similarly, the placement of commas and periods, so necessary for the comprehension of written material, remains an ongoing challenge. This brings us to the issue of how we decide what form our translations (and the Aboriginal language texts themselves) should take.

As linguists who work with oral texts in the fashion we detail here (where working with the texts is an integral part of other, more technical research goals), we see ourselves as occupying an intellectual space that is somewhere between that of the (language) technician and the artist; we must engage in detailed grammatical analysis and, at the same time, attempt to the best of our ability to reproduce the poetic artistry we perceive in the stories, artistry that is conveyed not just through the choices of word and sentence structure but also through sound (narrator pauses, repetitions, voice tone and inflection, speed of speech, etc.). Our goal is to reproduce, as accurately as we can, every aspect of the oral performance when we commit it to paper, either in translation or in the original language, as we have endeavored to do in Brittain and MacKenzie et al. (2004, 2005). In this case the format is less like prose and more like poetry. Such a detailed format is not, however, always appropriate, and in such cases we take a pragmatic approach, providing the format that best suits the needs of the target audience. We refer here to the case of formatting texts for the community, where the format is more prose-like: narrative devices such as repetition, pausing, and voice quality are not represented, and paragraph breaks are made using criteria such as change of topic or scene. Producing what we shall call "a detailed format" is costly in terms of both time and money, and that has been a consideration for the Naskapi community in determining what kind of format they want for the Peastitute collection. How long it will take to publish the stories is especially important. Furthermore, the Naskapi can listen to the original stories on CD, so in a sense, reproducing the oral performance faithfully on paper is redundant. The texts serve a rather different function for Naskapi speakers than they do for non-Naskapi speakers, whose access to the original performance is restricted merely because they cannot understand the language. For the native speaker, the text is a supplement to the original oral text (and thus, as we observed earlier, an aid to literacy); for the non-native speaker the text is all there is, and for this reason maximum detail is the ideal; in particular, it is the linguist's ideal. We concede that our rationale for choosing one format over another is more pragmatically than theoretically determined. While we are aware of the literature that exists on the topic (Hymes 2004, among many others), we feel the debate to be too distant from our realm of expertise to enter into with any confidence. Ideally, we wish to see a (detailed format) linguist's version for every oral text we work with, and in this case the material will be available for further analysis by scholars from all disciplines.

Eventually, there will be a linguist's version for the entire Innu-Naskapi collection; as noted, this remains a work in progress. These precise transcriptions are the base forms from which other versions can be constructed, tailored to a particular audience, in the manner we have illustrated. The published Naskapi and Innu versions are aimed at making reading material available to the native speaker audience; the detailed format literary translations of these versions (e.g., Brittain and MacKenzie et al. 2004, 2005) make this rich literature available to a non-Aboriginal readership. An anthropological audience will also benefit from more precise translations, as Rémi Savard's book was based on the earlier, incomplete translations.

Concluding Remarks

We hope to have shown that the methodology we adopt in approaching the translation of Algonquian oral texts is determined by several interacting factors. Because the texts are oral in nature, we seek to ensure that our translation work informs and is informed by ongoing language documentation projects as well as by more theoretically oriented research within the field of formal linguistics. We have come to appreciate that the speech communities to whom the oral texts belong, in order to make best use of resources, transcribe oral texts with a specific goal (audience) in mind— generally to provide a written version of the stories for their own community of readers—and that editorial intervention is part of this process. We, on the other hand, endeavor to take as our starting point for translation a "linguist's version" of the oral text, one that is as faithful as possible to the original performance. Being able to identify the differences that are likely to exist between the linguist's version and the community version of a transcribed text is useful for anyone who plays a role in producing written versions of oral texts, as it allows us to make the best use of the precious resources of time, money, and skilled personnel. It also enables us, as professional linguists, to articulate an appreciation of the transcription methodologies being developed within the speech communities.

Appendix A: Oral Texts and the Enhancement of Reference Materials

Our translation work can only be done in close collaboration with native speakers of CMN. Through this work we acquire a deeper understanding of the grammar of the language so that, gradually, we can add detail to existing reference grammars and contribute to those that remain works in progress.[39] We also encounter many vocabulary items that are not yet recorded in published or online lexicons, as well as an additional range of meanings for many vocabulary items that are already listed. In this section we highlight these points by discussing specific cases. Here we discuss some cases where work on the oral texts has resulted in the reclassification of verb forms. We also show how a new analysis of the function of a particular set of words has direct implications for its translation. By way of introduction to this section, we say a word about the classification of Algonquian verbs and the general rationale underlying the lexicography of Algonquian languages.

In Algonquian languages, verbs are traditionally classified into four basic classes depending on the grammatical animacy of their subject (for intransitives) and of their object (for transitives) (e.g., Bloomfield 1946).[40] Intransitive verbs are thus animate intransitive (AI) or inanimate intransitive (II), and transitive verbs are transitive animate (TA) or transitive inanimate (TI). For each of the four verbal classes there is distinctive morphology; for instance, AI suffixes are distinct from II suffixes, as we see in the bolded segments below. Dictionaries list verbs along with their class; for example, *ishinakuan* 'it appears so' (II) and *ishinakushu* 'he/she appears so' (AI). As well as considering how verbs should be listed, the lexicographer must also decide which verbs should be included in the dictionary. Without adhering to a carefully thought-out rationale, given the potential complexity of the CMN verb, the task of compiling a dictionary could become never-ending; consider, if the Algonquian verb is thought of as a mini-sentence, then the number of words in the dictionary could in theory approximate the number of sentences we can make in a language like English (in theory, an infinite number). How do we ensure that a dictionary of Innu, for example, is neither a list of arbitrarily selected complex words nor an attempt to record every possible word in the language?

The criterion that is applied is to restrict dictionary entries to forms whose meanings are not predictable and must consequently be memorized by speakers. Complex words whose meaning is no more than the sum of their parts, on the other hand, need not be listed, as they can be derived by applying combinatorial rules; inclusion of these forms would amount to recording redundant material. The elimination of redundancy is a general lexicographic principle: English dictionaries do not list the plural forms of nouns unless there is some unpredictability involved; for example, *scissors* is an entry because it has no singular form, but *boys* is not, because its plural form is predictable both in terms of its meaning and its form if we know the meaning of *boy* and that it forms a regular (-*s*) plural. When a word acquires a meaning that is not predictable on the basis of its constituent parts, it is referred to as a "lexicalized" form and it requires listing in the dictionary. The following three cases illustrate the identification of lexicalized forms that has resulted from our work on the oral texts.

The verbal suffix -*ituwach* is referred to as the "reciprocal" suffix (e.g., Wolfart 1973). It is added to a TA verb and results in a reading such as "they do X to one another." It became clear that these verbs also, in certain contexts, give a "collective action" reading, referring to groups of people performing an action together (e.g., caribou running as a group). Context serves to make clear which reading of the "reciprocal" suffix is intended, so that the issue of ambiguity does not arise. This function of the reciprocal suffix has already been recorded for Ojibwe (Nichols 1980).

The verbal suffix -*nanu* has long been considered to be restricted to AI verbs, functioning to create a type of passive (e.g., Wolfart 1973:62; Ellis 1983:474), but work with the Innu texts shows us it can also derive forms whose meanings are unpredictable. We consider first how this suffix functions in Naskapi to illustrate how it "normally" works: in Naskapi, *michinanu* 'it is eaten' is formed by adding -*nanu* to the verb *michu* 'he/she eats it.'[41] Research to date indicates that the addition of -*nanu* in Naskapi yields an entirely predictable result, a type of passive. It would thus be redundant to give *michinanu* its own entry in the lexicon (it does not appear in MacKenzie and Jancewicz 1994).[42] In Sheshatshiu Innu, MacKenzie and her collaborators have found that translating these verbs as impersonal passive versions of their base form in many cases fails to reflect their actual meaning. In this dialect at least, we find evidence in the oral texts that forms like *michinanu* in Innu may not translate as 'it is eaten' but as the semantically quite distinct 'it is edible.' It may be the case that the use of this suffix is also more complex in Naskapi (and other dialects) than we have thus far realized; the consequence of working closely with texts in one dialect is to alert us to the need to check other dialects to the same level of detail. For Innu at least, we now have the correct facts for this small area of the grammar, and verbs such as *michinanu* will be added to subsequent lexicons. They require their own entries because their properties are not predictable based on the sum of their constituent parts.

Finally, the issue of whether or not Algonquian languages have a true passive form of the verb has been subject to debate among linguists for decades (among others, Jolley 1981, 1982; Dahlstrom 1991; Wolfart 1991; Dryer 1996). The impersonal passive form we have just discussed, in spite of its name, is not a contender (for reasons which we do not detail here). There exists another verb form in Naskapi and Innu, derived from a TA verb, which is regularly translated as a passive but still fails to display the full range of properties associated with the canonical passive attested in so many of the world's languages. One restriction is that this "passive" does not allow the subject to be specified via the inclusion of a referring noun. For the form *uapamakanu* 'he/she is seen,' it would, for example, be ungrammatical to add a noun specifying the subject, so that the following sentence ('the man is seen') is ungrammatical **napeu uapamakanu*. As we have just seen for the *-nanu* forms (above), we have recently discovered that meanings of these so-called passives are not always predictable on the basis of their constituent parts. Examples have been identified in the Sheshatshiu oral texts where the meaning of the derived form is more specific than that of their base form counterparts. The examples below illustrate the case where a straightforward passive translation is appropriate (9a), and the cases where it is not (9b–d). In the latter examples, the "passives" have more restricted semantics; these are frequently translated into English with a noun ('operation' [9b], 'homicide' [9c], and 'kidnapping' [9d]).

(9) *Base form (TA verb)*   *Derived form ("passive")*
a.   *nipaieu*   *mishta-nipaiakanu*
     'he/she kills him/her'[43]   'many were killed'
b.   *matshishueu*   *matishuakanu*
     'he/she cuts him/her'   'he/she has an operation'
c.   *nipaieu*   *nipaiakanu*
     'he/she kills him/her'   'he/she is killed; homicide'
d.   *manneu*   *matshi-mannakanu*
     'he/she takes him/her away'   'he/she is in remand, he/she is
                                          kidnapped; kidnapping'

Verbs having this type of morphology abound in the oral texts. Words such as (9b), (9c), and (9d), which have the more restricted semantics (whose meanings are unpredictable), have to be added to the lexicon. Here again, translation has played a crucial role in establishing this reclassification.

We offer the case of the reclassification of particles in Innu as a final example of how working with texts has led to the enhancement of reference materials. In CMN dictionaries, words are divided into the following four syntactic categories: verb, noun, personal pronoun, and particle. The term "particle" has been a catch-all term to cover everything that is not a verb, a noun, or a personal pronoun. Scholars in the field have long recognized the need to subcategorize this diverse group. To this end, Oxford (2008a), through close examination of the Labrador Innu texts, has subdivided particles into a number of universally familiar subcategories (e.g., prepositions, conjunctions, adjectives, quantifiers, and adverbs of manner, space, time, and degree). This groundbreaking work would not have been possible without the transcription and translation of the large body of Innu oral narratives. We now provide brief discussion of "clefting constructions" to provide an example of one area in which Oxford's reclassification has affected translation work from Innu into English.

Cleft constructions exist in English: a cleft sentence is one in which a simple sentence is taken and made into a biclausal structure in order to move a piece of the sentence to the front, usually to emphasize the moved portion. Take the (single clause) sentence "John ate a red apple." If we want to emphasize the object (stressing that it was a red and not a green apple that John ate), clefting creates a biclausal structure that allows us to bring the object to the more prominent sentence-initial position: "It was a red apple that John ate." Oxford (2008b) argues that CMN grammar makes the same (universally common) strategy available, with certain words (such as *eukuan*) being dedicated to "focusing" constituents by creating cleft constructions. Prior to Oxford's work, clefting words had not been recognized as a category in CMN.[44]

Oxford notes that when speakers of Innu-aimun translate a sentence involving a clefting word into English, they often leave out the grammatical apparatus associated with clefting (a biclausal structure involving a relative clause) and offer a simple sentence instead. There is an obvious reason for this: clefts are grammatically complex and pragmatically nuanced, but the "core" meaning of a cleft sentence is no different from that of the corresponding simple sentence. Therefore, translating an Innu-aimun cleft as a simple English sentence is much easier for the translator and still communicates the same basic meaning (although the subtle shades of emphasis provided by the cleft are lost).

In some of these cases, it is likely that the Innu translator does use some technique to communicate the pragmatic information carried by the cleft, such as stressing the English noun that corresponds to the Innu noun focused in the clefting structure. However, this will not show up in print, and even orally, a linguist may not notice it unless he or she was looking for it.

The following examples illustrate cases in which the Innu-aimun sentence contains a cleft but the English translation uses a simple sentence.[45]

(10) LITP 1.3.011[46]

Miâm	âkaneshâu	eukuan	eshinâkushit
like	Englishman	it.is.that	look.like.CIN.3

'He looks like a white man.'

Here, the English translation completely ignores the cleft in the Innu original. A more accurate translation would be "Like a white man, that's how he looks."

(11) LITP 2.4.008

Eukuan	muku	tepishkânitî	eku
it.is.that	only	IC.be.night.CIN.3'	and.then

iânapîtshet.
IC.make.a.web.CIN.3

'He only makes nets at night.'

Although there is nothing wrong with this translation, it does not use a cleft, while the Innu original does. A more grammatically accurate translation would be "It's only at night that he makes nets."

(12) LITP 2.1.004

  Pîshimuss,   tshishe-pîshimu   mâk   epishiminishkueu,
  December   January   and   February
  eukuan   tshe mâtenimin.
  it.is.that   ic.fut sense.cin.2>1
  'In December, January and February, then you will feel my presence.'

Again, the English translation ignores the cleft in the Innu version. A more precise rendering would be "December, January, and February—that's when you will feel my presence." This is not to imply that the clefted version is necessarily the best translation (a question that is mainly an issue of stylistics)—it is simply a more grammatically accurate one. The classification of *eukuan* as a clefting word alerts the linguist to the possibility of a clefted English translation.

  Grammatical reclassification of the type illustrated in this section will continue as translation work proceeds in tandem with the drive to provide more language documentation materials, as well as more general linguistic research, the focus of which tends to be to inform the field of linguistic theory.

Appendix B: Guide to Naskapi and Innu Pronunciation[47]

Vowels

There are six vowel sounds in Naskapi and Innu, three long (*î, û, â*) and three short (*i, u, a*) and a seventh (*e*) used only in Innu. The following provides an approximation of their English counterparts:

Naskapi	Innu	English sound
î	î	*ee* as in "feet"
i	i	*i* as in "bit"
û	û	*oo* as in "boot"
u	u	*oo* as in "book"
â	â	*a* as in "hat"
a	a	*a* as in "about" (seldom used in Naskapi)
	e	*e* as in "ever" or "ate"

Consonants

In order to discuss consonants, we have divided them into three sets. Each set requires a slightly different explanation:

  Set one: Naskapi *m, n, s, y, w, h* and Innu *m, n, sh, ss, y, u, h*
  Set two: Naskapi *p, t, k, ch, kʷ* and Innu *p, t, k, tsh, kʷ*
  Set three: Naskapi *hp, ht, hk, hch* (Innu *p, t, k, tsh*)

Set one consonants are pronounced much like their English counterparts in the examples below. Note, however, that *s* is sometimes pronounced as English *sh*.

Naskapi	Innu	English
m	*m*	*m* as in "*m*itten"
n	*n*	*n* and in "*n*eat"
s	*sh, ss*	*s* as in seat, or *sh* as in *sh*eet
y	*i*	*y* as in "*y*ear"
w	*u*	*w* as in "*w*eed"
h	*h*	*h* as in "be*h*ind"

Set two consonants vary in their pronunciation, depending on the context in which they occur. In English, the graphemes *p*, *t*, *k*, and *ch* represent voiceless consonants (sounds made without any vibration of the vocal cords). The voiced counterparts of these sounds are, respectively, *b*, *d*, *g*, and *j*. The feature of voice distinguishes the meaning of the following pairs of English words:

Voiceless initial consonant	Voiced initial consonant
*p*it	*b*it
*t*in	*d*in
*k*ill	*g*ill
*ch*ar	*j*ar

In dialects of the Cree-Montagnais-Naskapi continuum, voice is not a feature that distinguishes one sound from another. Set two consonants are by default voiceless; they are only voiced in intervocalic position (between two vowels) and in word-initial position. Thus, the Naskapi word for "man," which is written *nâpâw*, is pronounced "*nâbâw*," and the word for "ptarmigan," which is written *piyâw*, is pronounced "*biyâw*." The Naskapi alphabet has no need to represent the voiced variants of *p*, *t*, *k*, and *ch* because voicing occurs in entirely predictable environments. Thus, the reader should pronounce *p*, *t*, *k*, and *ch/tsh* as (respectively) *b*, *d*, *g*, and *j* where they occur in intervocalic or word-initial position.

Naskapi/Innu	English	Example
p	*p* as in "*p*it"	ispimîhch/ishpimît "above"
	b as in "*b*it"	nâpâw/nâpeu "man"
t	*t* as in "*t*in"	âstim/âshtim "come here!"
	d as in "*d*in"	âtiyûhkin/âtinûkan "traditional tale"
k	*k* as in "*k*ill"	iskwâw/ishkueu "woman"
	g as in "*g*ill"	kukimâs/kûkamess "sea trout"
ch/tsh	*ch* as in "*ch*ar"	châkwân/tshekuân "thing"
	j as in "*j*ar"	kwâhkwâchâw/kuekuâtsheu "wolverine"

The final sound in set two is the sequence *kw/ku/ku*, which occurs in English words like "*quick*" and "*equal*." This sound sequence never occurs in word-final position in English. In Naskapi and Innu, the sequence *kw/ku/ku* can occur in any position in the word and follows the same pronunciation rules as the rest of the sounds in this set; it is voiced only in word-initial position and in intervocalic position.

Naskapi	Innu	English	Example
kʷ/kw	*kᵘ/ku*	*qu* as in "*quick*"	kâkʷ/kâkᵘ "porcupine"
		gw as in "*Guam*"	kwâkwâpisîs/kuâkuâpishîsh "butterfly"

Set three consonants are the "preaspirated" set. There is no equivalent sound in English. Preaspiration means that a small release of air (represented by *h*) precedes the pronunciation of the consonant. In Innu the preaspiration has largely disappeared, although Mushuau speakers sometimes pronounce *hp* as *f*, *ht* as *th*, *hch* as *sh*, and *hk* as *h*. This set occurs in the following Naskapi and Innu words (Mushuau Innu in square brackets): *akûhp/[akûf]* "coat," *mîht/[mîth]* "piece of firewood," *kûhkûs/[kuhus]* "pig," and *ministikuhch/[ministikush]* "on the island."

Notes

1. By "oral texts" we mean audio files/sound recordings of oral performances.

2. MacKenzie 1980 (http://www.innu-aimun.ca/modules.php?name=papers& p=MM) provides argumentation that the varieties of speech referred to as Cree, Montagnais, and Naskapi constitute a single language. Previously, as MacKenzie observes, this had not been the case: "The majority of scholars favour a distinct break between Cree on the one hand and Montagnais-Naskapi on the other" (1980:1). We follow MacKenzie 1980 in referring to CMN as a single language that comprises three distinct (but mutually intelligible) subdialects.

3. We present data from various CMN dialects in this chapter. Unless otherwise indicated, data are from the Sheshatshiu Innu dialect (Labrador Montagnais).

4. While there are many monolingual CMN speakers, especially among the generation of elders, it is common to be anywhere from functional to fluent in one or both of the official languages (depending on whether one lives in Quebec or Labrador).

5. By "processing" we mean such things as transcription, translation, cultural interpretation, modification of the original for audiences of variant dialects, etc.

6. It tends to be the case that indigenous languages are also those that are least well documented (in terms of there being reference grammars and dictionaries). This is certainly the case for CMN and other Algonquian languages.

7. We take a "small language" to be a language that has relatively low speaker numbers (e.g., fewer than 100,000). Small languages are not necessarily languages in crisis, as speaker numbers are only one factor in determining the viability of a language (see Crystal 2000 for further discussion of this issue). It is, however, frequently the case (for historical reasons we do not go into here) that small languages also tend to be indigenous languages, and that these in turn tend to be under-documented.

8. French and English are the two languages represented in bilingual (or trilingual) dictionaries of CMN dialects; see, for example, Drapeau 1991 (Montagnais/French), MacKenzie and Jancewicz 1994 (English/French/Naskapi), and Salt et al. 2004 (East Cree/English). Contemporary CMN reference grammars are written in English (e.g., Clarke 1982, Montagnais; Ahenakew 1987, Plains Cree; R. Valentine 2001, Ojibwe). To the best of our knowledge, French and English are the only languages into which CMN texts are currently being translated.

9. These dictionaries are frequently online even where a published version exists. Fed by ongoing linguistic projects such as translation work, the print version quickly becomes outdated; see, e.g., MacKenzie and Jancewicz 1994 and its larger (trilingual: English-Naskapi-French) Web version, http://www.collectionscanada .gc.ca/naskapi. Salt et al. 2004 also has a larger Web version: http://eastcree.org// lex/index.php.

10. Brittain 2000 was published as Brittain 2001. Hasler 2002, Bannister 2004, and Oxford 2007 can be downloaded at http://www.innu-aimun.ca/modules. php?name=papers. Oxford 2007 was published as Oxford 2008a. Henceforth we refer to published versions.

11. The community of Natuashish has recently relocated from Davis Inlet, Labrador. Davis Inlet was formerly known by its Aboriginal name, Utshimassits.

12. The term "*mushuau*" means "barrens," referring to the northern part of the Quebec-Labrador peninsula that is the traditional hunting territory of the Mushuau Innu.

13. José Mailhot has compiled biographies of each of the narrators: http://www .innu-aimun.ca/modules.php?name=stories&p=bios.

14. This consisted of eight cassette tapes, some of which were recorded on one side only, totaling fourteen cassette sides (thirty-six stories). The 1968 recordings were not copied, as they were of very poor quality.

15. The archives are located in the Aboriginal Languages Research Laboratory, in the Department of Linguistics, Memorial University of Newfoundland: http:// www.innu-aimun.ca/modules.php?name=cura&p=lab. The process of digitizing the tapes is ongoing.

16. The Web address is http://collections.mun.ca/cdm4/browse.php?CISO ROOT=%2Finnu.

17. The term "Montagnais" is not used in Labrador.

18. Matiu Rich died in a drowning accident at a tragically young age.

19. These inflections are attested in the Quebec and Labrador CMN dialects, but they have fallen from use in the more westerly Cree dialects (James, Clarke, and MacKenzie 2001; Blain and Déchaine 2006, 2007). While many languages indigenous to the Americas attest to an obligatory system of evidentials (e.g., Tariana, a North Western Amazonian language; Aikhenvald 2004), it is a linguistic feature found elsewhere in the world (e.g., Turkish, Tibetan: Aikhenvald and Dixon 2003; Speas 2004).

20. Both Labrador Innu communities use the same standard (roman) orthography. Vowel length is not marked. James, Clarke, and MacKenzie (2001) use a more detailed orthography than is the accepted community norm for Labrador Innu.

21. In Algonquian languages no distinction is made, either through verbal agreement or the use of pronouns, between "she" and "he." We reflect this fact in our English glosses and translations.

22. We have not, as part of our work, gone back and made a detailed comparison of these translations (which we have access to), but we have compared them against subsequent translations to a sufficient extent to allow us to draw some general impressions.

23. The only exception to this is that some transcription into Naskapi syllabics was done (by hand) for a few of the Peastitute stories, probably shortly after the recordings were made. The identity of the transcriber is unknown, but community members speculate it was the work of the late Elijah Einish (Bill Jancewicz, personal communication).

Naskapi people read and write their language using a syllabics system developed for the Cree and Ojibwe in the 1830s (by James Evans). Naskapi can also be written using the roman alphabet system, and that is what we use here for a non-Naskapi readership. A description of Naskapi syllabics appears in MacKenzie and Jancewicz (1994:xvi–xxii).

Innu people use a French-based roman writing system where *i* and *u* represent *y* and *w* in addition to the vowel sounds. A more detailed guide to Innu pronunciation can be found in Clarke and MacKenzie (2007) and at http://www.innu -aimun.ca/modules.php?name=lessonbook.

24. From 1988 to 2007, Jancewicz (Summer Institute of Linguistics) also worked with NDC linguists to create a Naskapi-language version of the Bible (New Testament). This project was officially completed in September 2007. Jancewicz was invited to Kawawachikamach to complete the translation project.

25. In meetings we have had with Naskapi elders on the advisory committee for NDC-funded language projects, they have expressed a desire to have the stories translated into English and French in order to disseminate their literature to a wider audience. There is a sense within the Naskapi community that other peoples can come to a better appreciation of who they are as a people through their literature. The Innu of Labrador, on the other hand, have not expressed a desire

to have a wider audience for their literature, although they have not discouraged the translation and dissemination of their stories.

26. In CMN certain demonstratives are accompanied by gesture (*maan* Northern East Cree, "there he, she, it is," accompanied by hand gesture or pointing with the lips: www.eastcree.org online lexicon). When these appear in the oral texts, we know there would have been a gesture.

27. A number of researchers have observed that repetition is a stylistic device used to highlight the theme of the narrative in Algonquian oral texts (L. P. Valentine 1995 and Spielmann 1998 for Ojibwe; Brittain and MacKenzie et al. 2004 for Naskapi).

28. Texts may also be footnoted with cultural information to assist a younger reading audience that may be less familiar with traditional aspects of Naskapi life (traditional clothing, foods, hunting knowledge, etc.).

29. The process of checking transcriptions to ensure that nothing has been edited out is still ongoing for the Innu portion of the collection.

30. Baker 1996 provides a technical account of polysynthesis.

31. This statement, while simple, is nonetheless not simplistic; it does not represent an oversimplification of the issue (which is: What is it a native speaker knows about the structure of language such that he or she can make this complex judgment call?).

32. Here we note that in many texts spaces are not made between words, especially in cases where the text is likely to be read aloud—the human brain is able to identify the word boundaries (e.g., Saenger 1997 for medieval English).

33. There is also the issue of intergenerational language change. As Crystal (2000) notes, languages that are under pressure (and CMN is arguably one of these) tend to undergo rapid change so that grammars can change rapidly within a few generations. Participant tracking is one area of the grammar where we see a change, with younger generations of speakers using a more restricted range of the participant tracking devices made available by the grammar (José Mailhot, personal communication).

34. To avoid overly complicating this discussion with technical terms, we label participant-tracking suffixes "x" and "y." Note, however, this is a simplification of the situation; we are illustrating the "Obviative system" in this section; the affixless "x" form (*Kwâhkwâchâw*) is "proximate," while the "y" form, *Asiniya*, is obviative, matching the obviative morphology of the verb (*-iyichî*).

35. We capitalize *Kwâhkwâchâw* and *Asiniya* because they are characters in the story, so the words function as names.

36. Mandarin Chinese, for example, has only one third-person singular pronoun. It is not true to say that Algonquian languages lack gender, however, as technically "gender" refers to any criterion used to make a formal division among nouns. In Algonquian, nouns fall into one of two semantically based genders: an-

imate (most sentient entities fall into this category) and inanimate (non-sentient, abstract entities).

37. Another of the characters in the stories, Frog, is female.

38. Double angle brackets are used in French, rather than the "curly quotes" used in English. Note that chevrons cannot be used as quotation marks in Naskapi syllabics, as they resemble two of the syllabic characters and their presence would cause the reader confusion. For this reason, Naskapi only uses curly quotes.

39. A grammatical sketch exists for Sheshatshiu Innu (Clarke 1982). A reference grammar for Naskapi, to which Brittain, Jancewicz, and MacKenzie are contributors, is currently a work in progress. An increasingly common practice is to locate reference grammars at a Web site, enabling researchers to contribute their results as they become available; see, for example, the East Cree reference grammar at http://eastcree.org.

40. Nouns in Algonquian languages fall into one of two formal classes: animate and inanimate. See note 36.

41. These forms are referred to as "impersonal subject passives."

42. Nor do these forms appear in Drapeau's Montagnais lexicon (Drapeau 1991) or in the East Cree lexicon (Salt et al. 2004).

43. In (9a), *mishta-* is a preverbal element that contributes the meaning of 'many'; in (9d), *matshi-* is a preverbal element meaning 'bad.'

44. The following discussion is based closely on Oxford 2008b.

45. LITP = Labrador Innu Text Project, reference to the larger collection of oral Innu texts that the Sheshatshiu collection we focus on belongs to. We leave Oxford's more detailed orthography (representing vowel length) intact.

46. The following abbreviations are used to gloss the Innu data in this appendix: fut = future tense; IC = initial change; CIN = Conjunct Indicative Neutral; 1 = 1st person; 2 = 2nd person; 3 = 3rd person; 3' = Obviative.

47. The pronunciation guide we provide here is based on the guide provided in the *Naskapi Lexicon* (MacKenzie and Jancewicz 1994).

References

Ahenakew, Freda. 1987. *Cree Language Structures: A Cree Approach*. Winnipeg: Pemmican Publications.

Aikhenvald, Alexandra Y. 2004. *Evidentiality*. Oxford: Oxford University Press.

Aikhenvald, Alexandra Y., and Robert M. W. Dixon. 2003. *Studies in Evidentiality*. Amsterdam: John Benjamins.

Baker, Mark. 1996. *The Polysynthesis Parameter*. Cambridge: MIT Press.

Bannister, Jane. 2004. Adverbial Hierarchies in Innu-aimun. Master's thesis, Memorial University of Newfoundland.

Blain, Eleanor, and Rose-Marie Déchaine. 2006. The Evidential Domain Hypothesis. In UBC *Working Papers in Linguistics: Proceedings of the Eleventh Work-*

shop in the *Structure and Constituency of Languages of the Americas (WSCLA)* 11, ed. Atsushi Fujimori and Maria Amelia Reis Silva, 12–25.

———. 2007. Evidential Types: Evidence from Cree Dialects. *International Journal of American Linguistics* 73:257–91.

Bloomfield, Leonard. 1946. Algonquian. In *Linguistic Structures of Native America*, ed. H. Hoijer et al., 85–129. New York: Viking Fund Publications in Anthropology.

Brittain, Julie. 2000. The Distribution of the Conjunct Verb Form in Western Naskapi and Related Morphosyntactic Issues. PhD diss., Memorial University of Newfoundland.

———. 2001. *The Morphosyntax of the Algonquian Conjunct Verb: A Minimalist Approach*. Outstanding Dissertations in Linguistics Series. New York: Garland (Routledge).

Brittain, Julie, and Marguerite MacKenzie, with Alma Chemaganish and Silas Nabinicaboo. 2004. Umâyichîs: A Naskapi Legend from Kawawachikamach. In *Voices from Four Directions: Contemporary Translations of the Native Literatures of North America*, ed. Brian Swann, 572–90. Lincoln: University of Nebraska Press.

Brittain, Julie, and Marguerite MacKenzie, with Alma Chemaganish, Philip Einish, and Silas Nabinicaboo. 2005. Two Québec Naskapi Stories Narrated by John Peastitute: "Wolverine and the Ducks" and "Wolverine and the Geese." In *Algonquian Spirit: Contemporary Translations of the Algonquian Literatures of North America*, ed. Brian Swann, 121–58. Lincoln: University of Nebraska Press.

Clarke, Sandra. 1982. *North-west River (Sheshâtshît) Montagnais: A Grammatical Sketch*. Mercury Series 80. Ottawa: National Museum of Man.

Clarke, Sandra, and Marguerite MacKenzie. 2007. *Labrador Innu-aimun: An Introduction to the Sheshatshiu Dialect*. St. John's: Department of Linguistics, Memorial University of Newfoundland.

Cruikshank, Julie. 1999. The Social Life of Texts: Editing on the Page and in Performance. In *Talking on the Page: Editing Aboriginal Oral Texts*, ed. Laura J. Murray and Keren Rice, 97–119. Toronto: University of Toronto Press.

Crystal, David. 2000. *Language Death*. Cambridge: Cambridge University Press.

Dahlstrom, Amy. 1991. *Plains Cree Morphosyntax*. Outstanding Dissertations in Linguistics Series. New York: Garland.

Desbarats, Peter, ed. 1969. *What They Used to Tell About: Indian Legends from Labrador*. Toronto: McClelland and Stewart.

Drapeau, Lynn. 1991. *Dictionnaire montagnais-français*. Sillery, Quebec: Presses de l'université du Québec.

Dryer, Matthew S. 1996. Passive vs. Indefinite Actor Construction in Plains Cree. In *Papers of the Twenty-Seventh Algonquian Conference*, ed. D. Pentland, 54–79. Winnipeg: University of Manitoba.

Ellis, C. Douglas. 1983. *Spoken Cree*. Edmonton: Pica Pica Press.

———. 1995. *Atalohkana Nesta Tipacimowina: Cree Legends and Narratives*. Winnipeg: University of Manitoba Press.

Hall, Tracy Alan, and Ursula Kleinhenz, eds. 1999. *Studies on the Phonological Word*. Philadelphia: John Benjamins Publishing Company.

Hasler, Laurel Anne. 2002. Obviation in Two Innu-aimun Atanukana. Master's thesis, Memorial University of Newfoundland.

Hymes, D. H. 2004. *"In Vain I Tried to Tell You": Essays in Native American Ethnopoetics*. Lincoln: University of Nebraska Press.

James, Deborah, Sandra Clarke, and Marguerite MacKenzie. 2001. The Encoding of Information Source in Algonquian: Evidentials in Cree/Montagnais/Naskapi. *International Journal of American Linguistics* 67:229–63.

Jolley, Catherine A. 1981. The Passive in Plains Cree. *Journal of the Linguistic Association of the Southwest* 4 (2): 161–84.

———. 1982. On the Plains Cree Passive: An Analysis of Syntactic and Lexical Rules. In *Ohio State Working Papers in Linguistics* 26, ed. Brian D. Joseph, 1–33. Columbus: Ohio State Working Papers in Linguistics.

Lefebvre, Madeleine. 1974 *Tshakapesh: Récits montagnais-naskapi*. Quebec: Ministère des affaires culturelles.

MacKenzie, Marguerite. 1979. Fort Chimo Cree: A Case of Dialect Syncretism? In *Papers of the Tenth Algonquian Conference*, ed. W. Cowan, 227–36. Ottawa: Carleton University.

———. 1980. Toward a Dialectology of Cree-Montagnais-Naskapi. PhD diss., University of Toronto.

———. 2004. "Giant Hare": Translation and Notes for Innu Legend "Meshapush." In *However Blow the Winds: An Anthology of Poetry and Song from Newfoundland and Labrador and Ireland*, ed. John Ennis, Randall Maggs, and Stephanie McKenzie, 569–71. Waterford: Scop Productions.

MacKenzie, Marguerite, and Bill Jancewicz. 1994. *Naskapi Lexicon—Lexique Naskapi-Naskapi Iyuw Iyimuun Misinaaikin*. Kawawachikamach: Naskapi Development Corporation.

Mailhot, José, et al., eds. 1999. *Sheshatshiu atanukana mak tipatshimuna, Myths and tales from Sheshatshit, collected by Madeleine Lefebvre and Robert Lanari in 1967, Booklets 1&2*. St. John's, Newfoundland: Innu Text Project.

——— . 2004. *Sheshatshiu atanukana mak tipatshimuna, Myths and tales from Sheshatshit, collected by Madeleine Lefebvre and Robert Lanari in 1967, Booklets 3&4*. St. John's, Newfoundland: Innu Text Project.

Nichols, John D. 1980. Ojibwe Morphology. PhD diss., University of Minnesota.

Oxford, Will. 2007. Towards a Grammar of Innu-aimun Particles. Master's thesis, Memorial University of Newfoundland.

———. 2008a. *A Grammatical Study of Innu-aimun Particles*. Algonquian and

Iroquoian Linguistics Memoir 23. Winnipeg: Algonquian and Iroquoian Linguistics.

———. 2008b. Effects of the Classification of Innu-aimun Function Words on Translation. Manuscript, Department of Linguistics: Memorial University of Newfoundland.

Saenger, Paul. 1997. *Space between Words: The Origins of Silent Reading*. Palo Alto: Stanford University Press.

Salt, Luci, Elsie Duff, Marguerite MacKenzie, and Bill Jancewicz. 2004. *Eastern James Bay Cree Dictionary, Northern Dialect: Cree-English*. Vol. 1. Chisasibi: Cree School Board.

Savard, Rémi, 1971. *Carcajou et le sens du monde: Récits montagnais-naskapi*. Collection Civilisation du Québec, série cultures amérindiennes 3. Quebec: Ministère des affaires culturelles.

Speas, Margaret. 2004. Evidentiality, Logophoricity and the Syntactic Representation of Pragmatic Features. *Lingua* 114:255–76.

Spielmann, Roger. 1998. *You're So Fat! Exploring Ojibwe Discourse*. Toronto: University of Toronto Press.

Statistics Canada. *2006 Census Results for CMN*. Accessed August 11, 2008: http://www12.statcan.ca/english/census06/analysis/aboriginal/share.cfm.

Swann, Brian, ed. 1994. *Coming to Light: Contemporary Translations of the Native Literature of North America*. New York: Vintage Books.

Valentine, Lisa Philips. 1995. *Making It Their Own: Severn Ojibwe Communicative Practices*. Toronto: University of Toronto Press.

Valentine, Randolph. 2001. *Nishnaabemwin Reference Grammar*. Toronto: University of Toronto Press.

Wolfart, Hans Christoph. 1973. Cree Preverbs and Their Syntactic Function. Master's thesis, Cornell University.

———. 1991. Passives with and without Agents. In *Linguistic Studies Presented to John L. Finlay (Algonquian and Iroquoian Linguistics*, Memoir 8), ed. H. C. Wolfart, 171–90. Winnipeg: Voices of Rupert's Land.

11

Translating the Boundary between Life and Death in O'odham Devil Songs

David L. Kozak with David I. Lopez

I do not think it a stretch to say that translating Native verbal arts occupies an unseen boundary with its comings and goings between what is actually said, what is interpreted, then invented out of those words, and the written text that is presented as a faithful rendition of what was originally stated or sung. And while translation is of course reliant upon getting the words straight, I think the heart of translation is centrally about re-expressing the rhythms and movements expressed by those words. As we are all very much aware, words have the ability to move us. And it makes no difference what language we speak, since every language possesses genres intended to emotionally move its speakers. This is, I think, a fine way to define the "art" in the verbal art found in Native American oral traditions. Ideally, the translator's task is as much about technical accuracy as it is about the art. Realistically, however, a translation is tipped to one or another side of the technical-aesthetic continuum. In this chapter I am particularly interested in identifying and translating the art of Native American oral traditions.

Tohono O'odham shamanism traverses an imagistic boundary between the empirical and sentient world, called *kawk jewed* 'hard earth,' and the afterlife and flowery world, called *si'alig weco* 'below the eastern horizon.' This tradition's healing music articulates this boundary in both diagnostic (*duajida*) and healing (*wusota*) song-poems. The songs are of a dreamt liminality encouraging the hearer to contemplate the order of society, the beauties of nature, and the seductions of the spirit world. Central to this poetics are lyrically inspired images that collapse the distance between life and death, between human and non-human, that blur the distinction between past and present, fuse self with other, and represent the boundary in song as a shifting cosmological and geographical space of interaction between those living humans who inhabit the earth and non-living spirit entities. It is a spatial-mood-poesis that shares attributes with other Uto-Aztecan languages in the Southwest and beyond. The hypothesized spatial-mood-poesis I consider in this chapter differs from yet is related to the chromaticism identified in the role of flowers and other dazzling imagery so well described by Jane Hill in her essay "The Flower World of Old Uto-Aztecan" (1992). In it she identified the pervasiveness of nouns in Uto-Aztecan verbal arts that emphasize the symbolism associated with flowers, bright colors, landscapes, and shimmering phenomena in its link to the afterlife destination. The boundary metaphor and symbolism found in song I propose here focuses on the fluidity of movement to pregnant stillness (itself a category of movement), geographical distance and the songs' hero's return to the living world. It is an emphasis on verbs of motion, whereas Hill paid close attention to descriptive nouns. It is a lyrical signature that emphasizes the life and movement side of the boundary, whereas the dazzling and flowery world emphasizes a description of the afterlife. It is a difference between action and image. In sum, the flower/chromatic symbolism refers to a well-defined and normative location in O'odham philosophy, whereas the boundary spatial-mood-poesis refers to a negotiable and shifting cognitive space.

Whereas the chromatic symbolism is ever-present in Tohono O'odham song-poetry of the afterlife location, only a small percentage of this song-poetry speaks of traversing the boundary between life and death. It is an understated poetic language of personal transformation and inner turmoil. The passage from life to death and back again is symbolized lyrically as a border crossing that is densely meaningful. Such songs are an understatement, a calm or muffled expression of the calamity of death. This border crossing is a thematic or mood marker that functions as a signature element in song much in the way that the much more common imagery of frenetic motion, dizziness, bright colors, or flowers are a mood marker found in O'odham song-poetry. I call this signature a spatial-mood-poesis that is at times metaphorized by physical geography as expressed in expansive distance and often with an accompanying cessation (if momentary) of motion. It is a contemplative stillness of the song's hero.

Song-poetry is a vibrant aspect of today's O'odham oral literature. It is a Native Southwest poetic tradition belonging to what George Herzog (1928) dubbed the "dreamt mythic song series." Herzog rightly observed that song-poetry was obtained from a dreamt source, from a spirit who sings a song (*ñe'i*) or songs to a dreaming human. Taking a cue from the O'odham theory of music translation, efforts must pay special attention to lyric content as a stylized form of storytelling. Lyrical storytelling features a journey taken around the O'odham landscape, and individual songs are "verbal images" (Bahr, Paul, and Vincent 1997:4), snapshots, acquired at moments along this journey. Each song can be likened to a direct quote of a spirit's mood, thought, or action, and songs typically narrate intriguing nature scenes. The dreamt song is ideally memorized by the human dreamer who does not alter the lyric and melodic structure. Humans, therefore, do not author or compose a song. Rather, O'odham songs originate in a land of the spirits, not the land of living human communities. Humans dutifully repeat what was learned from the spirit world. Song inspiration is divine, a sacrament for humans, and songs are a sacred liturgy.

The contents of O'odham song lyrics feature two related signature characteristics: nouns that describe the landscape, and verbs that tell of the song subject's actions. O'odham verb and noun structure lend themselves to translation into English. Yet, one significant translational difficulty relates to how song language differs from everyday spoken O'odham. Song language frequently employs a different phonemic structure for a given noun or verb. This presents challenges even for fluent native speakers. For example, the word for "flame" or "flash" is at times *sisiwoname* in song language and *siwod* in everyday speech. Or take "wander," which is *yoimeta* in song language and *oimed* in everyday speech. One may liken this phonemic shift as something akin to the English use of vocables such as "sha-doo-be-wah" in a 1950s top ten hit. This would be inaccurate, however, as O'odham music theory claims that all phonemes are meaningful units of sound that when combined contribute to the ultimate meaning of song lyrics. Thus, the main technical challenge in translating O'odham song lies in phonetic rather than grammatical features.

Songs present the first-person journeys whereby an "I" (typically a living human) travels to various locations in the desert to observe second-person spirits (non-living "yous" or "its") in action. In our book on devil sickness, David Lopez and I stated: "We have come to understand the journeys of the 'I' as the first-person experiences of narrators of events that happen to the person during these nocturnal journeys" (Kozak and Lopez 1999:115). These dream journeys describe beautiful landscapes and brightly colored chromatic phenomena and interactions with anthropomorphized spirits. Thus, there is an extensive use of first-person language, and an additional emphasis on nouns. Songs often raise two questions for an audience to consider: Who are the "I's" in each song, and what is the "I" doing? Hallmarks of the dreamt mythic song series tradition, therefore, center on the descriptive features in the narration, first- and second-person referents, on fleeting feelings and emotions, and chromatic nature imagery. It is wonderful mood music. The Tohono O'odham song-poem formula goes something like this: the "I" refers to a human and the "you" or "it" to a spirit where the "you" takes the "I" on a dream journey, with the "I" coming away with power, that is, with prophetic, transformative knowledge that may be used to diagnose and treat an O'odham-specific spirit sickness.

As has been widely noted, the movement (often frenzied) of the song's "I" or "it" is a signature feature of Tohono O'odham song-poetry. Movement is equal in consequence to the presence of descriptive nouns with flowers and other chromatic imagery serving as prototypical examples (Hill 1992). Bahr, Paul, and Vincent (1997) note this for oriole songs, although most if not all O'odham healing songs contain verbs related to the hero's movements. Verb forms, the action taken by spirits or humans, are significant features of this music, and while their positioning at the end of lines has been noted (Shaul 1981), their significance in relation to translation has received less attention. Herein lies an interesting translational question: To what extent does verb position reflect a wider cultural and aesthetic sensibility in Tohono O'odham culture? Does this grammatical structure, for instance, impose on speakers a way to view the world and the spirit world (cf. Harrison 2007:236)? They are questions I am unprepared to answer here, and they may be unanswerable. The questions suggest a Whorfian relation between the spoken word and worldview, questions that are provocative but without definitive answers.

For this chapter I reviewed several hundred published songs and noted the pervasive use of verb forms related to walking, running, crawling, falling, climbing, flying, striding, wandering, floating, shaking, staggering, thundering, entering, fleeing, zigzagging, and so on. Some of these verb forms are paired with the physical and emotional state of dizziness (*nodag*) (Kozak and Lopez 1992), a state frequently though not exclusively caused by the song's "I" or "it" drinking ceremonial wine or ingesting jimson weed (datura). In fact, the movement is frenetic, ceaseless, with an overriding sense of an inability to sit still. It is a manic-ness of spirit and youthful exuberance. With so many songs that privilege motion, the "I's" stillness in a song is quite striking. In fact, it may be rare save songs that deal specifically with death. Thus, the central translational question for this chapter is to determine the meaning and significance of stillness as expressed in some healing songs. I have come to conclude that what the stillness expresses is the song's "I's" contemplation of life and death as expressed to the song's hero in terms of geography and place.

A powerful example of the spatial-mood-poesis hypothesis is found in a set of four devil songs recorded and documented by Frank Russell sometime in 1902 (Russell 1908). Before discussing these songs, I wish to point out that "devil" in O'odham is *jiawul*, a cognate of the Spanish *diablo*. Now the O'odham conceptualization of devil is quite at variance with what is typically understood in Christian belief and imagery. The O'odham devil is a spirit cowboy, that is, a deceased O'odham male who was a cowboy during his lifetime. Devils and devil kids (a reference to their playfulness; read cowboying) are commonly said to dwell inside various mountains in the O'odham landscape. At best, devils are morally ambiguous, as are many other types of spirits. At worst, they cause illness and accidents, sickness and death, out of loneliness for their living relatives rather than out of some evil characteristic or nature. There is simply no relation between O'odham devils and the Christian Satan. For those interested in a more detailed discussion of devils and a methodological statement on the translation and interpretation of this music, please refer to *Devil Sickness and Devil Songs* (Kozak and Lopez 1999). The reworked translations from Russell are provided here:

1. Beside Broad Mountain I listen to many songs
   Beside Broad Mountain I listen to many songs
   I come running
   To listen to their voices
2. Evening draws near, it is falling
   Evening draws near, it is falling
   From inside, the devils come rushing out
   They breathed on and massaged me

3. I entered Rotten Mountain and heard the songs sound
   I entered Rotten Mountain and heard the songs sound
   And inside I listened to the songs
   And inside I saw
   There I saw the devils rocking their heads
4. Devil kids come running
   I stand among flowers
   And the distant hard land's edge stretches before me
   My breath, here I pant

The Broad Mountain referred to in song 1 is known in the region by whites as Estrella Mountain and is visible from much of the Gila River Indian Community, where the singer of these songs lived. Rotten Mountain of song 3 is probably the one south of the village of Chui Chu on the northern reaches of the Sells Reservation. Note that the songs in this set progress from movement, "I come running," and "the devils come running out," to stillness when it states, "I listen to their songs," and then to a spatial reference in "the distant hard land's edge stretches before me." Importantly the set concludes with "My breath, here I pant." Thus, the set presents an audience with pairings or dichotomies. For instance, it is of movement across the landscape from one mountain to another. It is of movement or transition from day to night, and lastly the narrative progresses from inside to outside. If my hypothesis is correct, then any song that links stillness and references to distance and spatial arrangement is a spatial-mood-poem contemplative of life and death.

The final song of this set supplies the evidence to fulfill the criteria. It is a spatial-mood-poem of an "I" who arrives at the boundary between life and death. The "I" stands among flowers (land of the dead), looking toward a "distant hard land" (land of the living). It is of movement ceased with its implied hesitation found in the final line, "My breath, here I pant." The key to understanding the significance of the boundary, the art, the spatial-mood-poesis signature, lies in answering what the hesitation and stillness refers to. The "I" is in an existential quandary over remaining with the devils and their playfulness and music in the flowery world, or of returning to the hard earth and the living. Song 4's final words, "here I pant," might at first imply breathlessness caused by running, but this is not what the referent intends. This is because it is not the song's "I" who is running about, but rather the frantic spirits which the "I" listens to and observes. The breathlessness suggests anxiety, fear, uncertainty, perhaps even a difficult choice. The boundary is breathtaking. My final translational claim is that the pairing of stillness with the physical boundary is what helps us to understand the life-and-death issue. Art resides in how "pant" is understood. Art is in the mood the pant presents to the audience.

This song set presents the spatial-mood-poesis as composed of references to landscapes of distance, of end-of-life questions, anxiety, that draws on metaphors of boundaries and distance. That boundary demarcates the fragile region between living and dying, this world and the afterlife location. It is a liminality-centered communitas-oriented poetic form. Thus, it is a mood poetic form that uses the natural environment to teach the living about the land of the dead, the place where all O'odham will eventually reside.

David Lopez, the O'odham man with whom I worked closely during my dissertation research in the early 1990s, died on February 12, 1998. He and his wife, Connie, enjoyed traveling away from home. They would often come to stay with me in my Scottsdale, Arizona, apartment. We talked, laughed, sang songs, gossiped, and told jokes over food and beer, discussing the meaning of one or another O'odham or English word. David's love of language and life changed as his diabetic condition worsened and his visits to a dialysis treatment center increased to three times per week. This put an end to their wanderings. He knew of, and was melancholy over, his impending death. During the last two years of his life his easy-to-laugh nature turned gradually into anger, resentment, and hermitism. His outlook on life and his heart grayed over thoughts of the end of his life. And as with some O'odham who know medicine songs, David came to identify with one song in particular. At the time of our collaboration I didn't pay attention to his identification with this song. For him it was a quail song, a *duajida* or medicine song that, according to David, was received in a dream of his grandfather Juan Lopez. It is a song that speaks a language of muffled apocalypse, of prophecy, of the draining or graying of life (Bahr 1991), of confronting the boundary of the land of the living and dead. The song is sung in a plaintive voice, with the word "dying" being drawn out for many beats, and with a falling tone. A translation of this dramatic tonal effect onto the printed page can be seen below. It admittedly does not do justice to the effect that David was trying to achieve, but it is the only way I could determine as to how to convey it. It surely reveals the limits to which translation can replicate the art found in the original.

During the last time that David and I spoke of and recorded songs and our discussions, he sang and spoke about of the following quail song and devil song.

Kuñ si yai mu mu	I here dying
Kuñ si yai mu mu	I here dying
Kuñ si yai mu mu	I here dying
Ali wus alt kokomai alt gagicu baña woi na mu	all the little dusty quails
Gama huda ñu whoi baña mali	westward direction me lead
Ama tato	they leave

Here I am d
        y
           i
              n
                 g
here I am d
        y
           i
              n
                 g
here I am d
        y
           i
              n
                 g
the many little grey quails
lead me to the west
where I am abandoned

David said this about the song:

About that quail song, I think it is about my late grandpa from Covered Wells who almost died. They are like those *ñeñewal a'al* [devil kid spirits] that we sing about. This song is about when my grandpa, he almost died, and it's the quails that saved him. They run toward him and carry him to the west. They say the same thing as the devil kid songs that it's not time to die. And I guess this song, well, they gave him this song. And he sang this song, and at times he used it to cure people.

And there's another one almost similar to this quail song, one that Baptisto [David's father] sang at times, and he used it to cure people too. And it's the same way like that, like we know about devil kids because that's the way it sounded. The song is about devil kids and when the sun goes down that's when the devil kids come out. They threw all that stuff [curing powers] on him [Baptisto] and made him learn the song and how to cure. What Baptisto sings in his song and that tells them what happened to my late grandpa Lopez or somebody that did die and it's not time for whoever it is to die. And those devil kids, when he is going to the shadow of death, but the devil kids meet him and took him to the west where he'll be safe, and come out, come to the, what you call . . . the human world, whatever you call that in English and this is what they said to him.

Ñeñal hu li ya ha li wa se ni woi na him mu
Devil kids they me-meet

Ñeñal hu li ya ha li wa se ni woi na him mu
Devil kids they me-meet

Wa se ni woi na him mu
Over there I-meet

Hu no niña tan wa ma toi nip e mel him e
westward toward I-carry

Hu ña wuli ya ha li wu so ni woi na kim e
In the west I-leave

I met the devil kids
I met the devil kids
in the distance we met
to the west they carried me
in the west they left me

Translation is about fidelity to the language of origin and to its meaningful poetic and aesthetic reconstitution in another language. It is, in Bahr et al.'s words, to "show the art" of Native oral traditions (Bahr, Paul and Joseph 1997). In other words, there are quantitative and qualitative aspects to attend to. Most non-Native scholars—whether they are anthropologists, folklorists, or linguists—who do the work of translation typically emphasize one or the other in their work. This suggests to me incompleteness in the translational process that might reasonably be viewed as a call for more effort and collaboration than a condemnation of the effort itself. In this chapter I focused on the latter, the qualitative aspect. It remains to be seen if the spatial-mood-poesis hypothesis will hold true for analyzing other O'odham song poetics in particular and other poetic traditions among the many other languages in the Uto-Aztecan language family in general.

To conclude, I find that the two songs sung by David Lopez above conform to the hypothesized spatial-mood-poesis formula. They reflect a movement to stillness and directional (east to west) aesthetic. The song's "I" is carried to the west, to the human community. They speak of a poetic boundary that is traversed, celebrated in this quiet and understated event in the "I's" life. Revealing the art of O'odham song poetry in the foregoing songs is nothing less than translating the personal apocalypse of coming close to death, and of the (ultimately momentary) return to life to live one more day.

References

Bahr, Donald. 1991. A Grey and Fervent Shamanism. *Journal de la Societe des Americanistes* 77:7–26.

Bahr, Donald, Lloyd Paul, and Vincent Joseph. 1997. *Ants and Orioles: Showing the Art of Pima Poetry.* Salt Lake City: University of Utah Press.

Harrison, K. David. 2007. *When Languages Die: The Extinction of the World's Languages and the Erosion of Human Knowledge.* New York: Oxford University Press.

Herzog, George. 1928. *Musical Styles in North America.* Proceedings of the Twenty-third International Congress of Americanists.

Hill, Jane H. 1992. The Flower World of Old Uto-Aztecan. *Journal of Anthropological Research* 48 (2): 117–43.

Kozak, David, and Camillus Lopez. 1992. Swallow Dizziness: The Laughter of Carnival and Kateri. *Wicazo Sa Review* 8 (2): 1–10.

Kozak, David, and David I. Lopez. 1999. *Devil Sickness and Devil Songs: Tohono O'odham Poetics*. Washington DC: Smithsonian Institution Press.

Russell, Frank. 1908. *The Pima Indians*. 26th Annual Report of the Bureau of American Ethnology. Pp. 3–389. Washington DC. Reprinted by the University of Arizona Press, Tucson.

Shaul, David. 1981. Piman Song Syntax. Proceedings. Seventh Annual Meeting of the Berkeley Linguistics Society. Pp. 275–83. Berkeley, California.

12

Revisiting Haida Cradle-Song 67

Frederick H. White

Introduction

The significant development concerning traditional Native American literature and Native American cultural research has invoked attention to the intricacies of Native languages that previously had been ignored, if even considered at all (Basso 1984; Bringhurst 1999; Hymes 1981; Kroeber 1981; Kroskrity 1986; Swann 1992; Tedlock 1972). This attention has sparked a review of the volumes amassed during the early part of the twentieth century by the premier anthropologist Franz Boas and his protégés (1911, 1922). This return—to the texts gathered by Boasians as well as other collections—is replete with stories and songs of the tribes of North America.

My interest in this chapter is to consider a Haida song that John Swanton collected during the Jesup North Pacific Expedition during the winter of 1900–1901. My purpose in looking at this song is to reexamine the original text's content and context in order to offer a modern paraphrase with regard to aspects of Haida culture possibly neglected in the original analysis. In order to provide a greater contextual understanding of the song, I find it apropos to address two factors in the process of discussing the song. The first concerns the problematic categorization of Native American literature, and the second provides background to the collection of which Cradle-Song 67 is a part. In essence, what will result is an ethnohistorical elaboration of the cradle-song within its cultural significance.

The Classificatory Question

A result that was prevalent in accumulating literature from many American Indian tribes was the subsequent classification into anglicized genres of narratives, songs, prayers, or poems. This categorization was usually a product of the earliest collected literature, and the problem that went unseen or unquestioned was the reason or explanation for the cataloging of the text into one of the aforementioned categories. Cagle clarifies: "Before the American Indian Literary Renaissance in the late 1960s, most of what was identified as American Indian poetry was actually oral stories and songs recorded in verse as poetry by missionaries, ethnographers, and anthropologists who were inclined to define Native artistic forms in relations to their own cultures" (2007:30). The translators often also provided the subsequent title for the text and the typical tribal attribution for the text rather than any individual (Day 1951:viii). Swann further notes the paucity of consideration to the translation process: "Certainly there was no explicit attention to structure, and texts were presented in plain prose, in block form, with little or no attempt to represent the verbal artistry" (1996:xxviii). Hence, while tribal affiliation retained importance, the actual person providing the song did not. In this case, the song or poem itself was the sole focus within the context of the tribal affiliation, rather than the individual attribution. The text had preeminence over the individual, though the translators recognized the need for some sort of context and allowed the tribal affiliation to suffice (Day 1951:ix).

The early classification practice regarding elements of Native American oral traditions as songs or poems has at least two implications that must be addressed before accepting the classification provided. First, the designation of the text as a poem or song may wrongly imply that the author is somehow an artist and that the song or poem is a result of a honed artistic ability. Second, the categorization may reflect the translator's preference or bias and not necessarily that of the author of the text. Historically, the author's ability to provide such a text does not necessarily mean that that person is an artist who devotes his or her life is to such endeavors. The poem, song, or prayer may merely reflect an occasion commemorated by the individual experiencing the event in question, and such occasions and commemorations of such events were certainly not limited to a chosen few.

Bierhorst offers the explanation that the singer or orator "does not consider himself the originator of his material but merely the conveyor.

Either he has heard it from an elder or he has received it from a supernatural power" (1971:4). While this sentiment is certainly accurate historically, present-day indigenous authors and poets do not necessarily have such claims for their literature, that of receiving the content of their craft from an elder or a supernatural power. Bruchac, however, evokes contemporary spirituality when he claims, "Our abilities as writers—as novelists and poets, playwrights and essayists—are a gift given to us by the Creator. It is our obligation to return that gift, to make use of it in a way that serves the people and the generations to come" (1995:xix).

Then comes the problem of categorizing the texts. Often, the evidential preference of the translator or editors imposed a need to have the texts fit nicely into a Western category for the purpose of enjoyment from the Western perspective. Thus, what seems like a simple classificatory exercise for the song has become a cultural imposition that ultimately obfuscates important indigenous features in the song. Kroeber addresses this imposition by explaining, "My experience teaching such material, however, has shown me that Americans who only know Western literature are baffled by Indian oral narratives" (1981:1). He continues with the observation that "very often it is not so much their unfamiliarity as our preconceptions that make it difficult for us to understand traditional Indian tales" (1981:2), and though the comment refers to Indian tales, the same sentiment applies to songs and poetry. Fortunately, now that we have more contextual information regarding the occasion of the text and its content, it is easier to render such texts as songs or poems with greater regard for cultural accuracy.

Background to Cradle-Song 67

With the nineteenth century quickly passing, Boas and his contemporaries feared the national loss of linguistic and cultural knowledge because of the expected disappearance of the indigenous communities. He therefore commissioned many of his graduates to capture as much information about languages and cultures of North America as possible before the inevitable demise of indigenous communities. Swanton depicted his efforts and explained: "My primary task being the investigation of the religious ideas, social organization, and language of the Haida Indians" (1905:9). The general scope of the works was to gather, assemble, and publish information about the cultures and languages of handpicked indigenous communities (Boas 1911, 1922). Commonly referred to as ethnologies, literally the study of nations, the works were often focused on cultural and linguistic descriptions, including phonemic and grammatical information, and included as much narratives and songs as possible.

With this motivation for documenting Haida, Swanton began his cultural and linguistic salvific enterprise on Haida Gwaii in the first winter of the twentieth century to record Haida narratives. Bringhurst reports that Swanton started recording the Haida language immediately upon his arrival, but that he was also learning the Haida language as he gathered the narratives and songs (1999:420). As a student of Boas, he was astutely aware of the details of language that Boas deemed it important to capture along with important cultural information. Bringhurst records a shift in priorities, as Boas originally was interested in Haida myths insofar as they would enlighten details about kinship, lineages, crests, family guardian spirits, significance of masks, intratribal and intertribal marriage roles, and artifacts, but Swanton's focus quickly focused on the Haida language itself (1999:153). Boas ultimately yielded to Swanton's focus, and his efforts at documenting the Haida language amassed an unsurpassed collection and analysis of Haida language through family narratives, history, and music.

Music is an essential part of Haida communities, and Enrico and Stuart acknowledge both the substance and the intricacies of music among the Haida. They claim that music "was so much a part of traditional Haida life that even the untrained observers managed to pass on some information about its use, and one can piece together a fair idea of the traditional importance and variety of music among these people" (1996:4). They also offer eight categories for songs: (1) house-building and mortuary potlatches; (2) lullabies; (3) mourning; (4) warfare and making peace; (5) vengeance potlatch; (6) supernatural manipulation or manifestation; (7) songs of play; and (8) miscellaneous (1996:4–5). Among the Haida, rank and status were inherent but not fully realized without appropriate potlatches—celebrations or ceremonial events to establish such honor. Potlatches were also community events which, according to Drucker, "brought to expression basic principles involved in social status and served as a major force for social integration" (1963:131).

Swanton's recording of the Haida songs during that winter eventually found publication in three categories: (1) cradle-songs, (2) mourning songs, and (3) miscellaneous songs. One of the many Haida words for "song" is *sgalaang*, but the Haida recognized many different types of songs (Boelscher 1989; Enrico 2005), some of which might fall within the category of cradle-songs, but there were also lullabies that were not necessarily limited to children in a cradle. The Haida term for this song is *git ǩagáandaaw* (Lawrence 1977:436) or *gid qagaan* (Enrico and Stuart 1996:21), which classifies this song as a lullaby.

The title of the Swanton collection that contains this lullaby is *Haida Songs* (1912). There are 106 songs in the collection, with 88 cradle-songs representing the bulk of the collection. The rest are 12 mourning songs and 6 miscellaneous songs. Three of the 88 cradle-songs are from different tribes: numbers 23 and 24 are Tsimshian, and number 55 is Tlingit, both western neighbors of the Haida along the Canadian and United States west coasts. Most of the songs, 67 of them, are from the Skidegate dialect, though the last 15 are from the Massett dialect. The lullaby song number 67 is considered and acknowledged to be a song by the Haida, and attributed as a cradle-song by Swanton. He explains: "As has been stated in a discussion of the songs, the cradle-songs are the property of various families. For this reason the songs which form the bulk of the collection here presented are arranged according to the families to which they belong. The names of the families will also be found in the publication before referred to" (1912:3). This song is one of four from the family *Qa'ial lanas*, and parenthetically, Swanton provides the information "Songs of Qa-i l'naga'-I" as the one who owns the song (1912:44).

The Haida Lullaby

Swanton recorded and translated Cradle-Song 67, and I reproduce it here almost exactly as found in the original publication of the song with the exception of /g̊/, which in the original has the dot below rather than above the phoneme. The following footnotes are found in the first line, "1. *kûgwaî'ya* is equivalent to *qa'ga*; 2. *gê'tgagî* is equivalent to *ge'tgaqa*" (Swanton 1912:47). In Swanton's orthography, /ñ/ is a voiced velar nasal (normally represented as /n/) and has the same sound in English found at the end of words such as *sing*, *thing*, or *wing*. The sound for L is "something like *tl* or *kl*; in both the tip of the tongue touches the back of the teeth, and the air is expelled at the sides" (Swanton 1912:4). And though it is not found in the general introduction, the /'/ seems to be a glottal stop. The sound found at the beginning of *tcînañ* is similar to the voiceless palatal affricate, but the tongue is much more relaxed and flat, rather than tight and taut against the palate. A final note concerns /g̊/, a voiceless uvular stop that Swanton refers to as "sonans."

Cradle-Song 67

TcînAñ	*sִı̣lִg̣â'*	*nAñ*	*kûgwaî'ya[1]*	*skoa'gagîn*	*g̣ê'tgagî[2]*	*hao.*
His grandfather	place	some one	went a long time ago	behind	was there	

Lû'g̣a gû'g̣a	*ga*	*sLdA'ldañ*	*Lûg̣agû' g̣a*	*ga*	*qîngîñgî'ñg̣a:*
On his canoe	planks	they put on their sides	on his canoe	thing	is great on the water

Wa'g̣An	*dîʼnA+ñ*	*hîʼdja+la'i*	*wA'g̣an*	*dîʼnAñ*	*kudju'g̣aasañ.*
For it	my child	is a boy (baby word)	for it	my child	is going to be a leader.

Yâ'ña,	*yâ'ña,*	*kîlsLa'-ig̣an.*	*Yâ'ña,*	*yâ'ña,*	*kîʼñgetg̣an.*
Be careful	be careful	my chief.	Be careful	be careful	my master!

Gloss

His grandfather's place someone went a long time ago behind was there.

On his canoe planks they put on their sides on his canoe thing is great on the water;

For it my child is a boy (baby word), for it my child is going to be a leader.

Be careful, be careful, my chief! Be careful, be careful, my master.

Swanton's English Translation

My child is a boy because he is going to do as his grandfather
    did when one went to his place long ago.
After he had been there, his canoe was so deeply laden
    (with gifts), that they had to put the weather-boards
on it (to increase its capacity);
For it my child is going to be a leader.
Be careful, be careful, my chief! Be careful, Be careful,
    my master!

A preliminary review of the interlinear and the free translation reveals that the word order is completely changed in the free English rendition. This must occur, because Haida is osv (object subject verb) or sov word order (see as Campbell 1990:1032 for a discussion of Haida word order), whereas English is svo. The word at end of the first line, *hoa*, is an untranslatable vocable; Enrico and Stuart regard it as a nonsense syllable that "is virtually never an archaic speech form or a foreign word, and virtually never an animal call" (1996:459). It is also important to note the repetition in the Haida version, and that the use of repetition in most oral cultures is usually for emphasis, even in literate cultures (Boas 1955). The repetition begins in line two, and interestingly, the word for "on his canoe," *Lûĝagûĝa*, is separated in its first mention into two words, *Lûĝa gû' ĝa*. There is another word repeated in this line, *ga*, which is curiously translated as "planks" the first time and "thing" the second time. The third line contains a phrasal repetition, *Waĝ̇An dînA+ ñ*, which is translated both times as "For it my son" (the addition sign indicates the lengthening of the vowel *a*). The last repetition found in line four and vocalized four times is also phrasal: *Yâ' ña*, is translated as the imperative "be careful" but could also mean "be watchful" in the sense of "be wise."

The significance of the changed order has tremendous influence upon the subsequent interpretation of the song. The first line refers to the grandfather, and in Haida the latter possession is marked with /nang/. Translated as "someone," *nang* can refer to "my," "your," "our," "her," or "his" because it does not necessarily distinguish a specific pronominal classification (Enrico 2003:869). It is usually through the context of the discourse or interaction that the pronominal referent is discerned and understood. Though Swanton translated *waĝ̇An* as "for it" both times, it is also possible to translate this simply as "just because" (Enrico 2005:1894).

Discussion

The dynamics of oral narration are all but lost among many American Indian tribes, though within many tribes efforts are being made to keep the tradition alive. Among the Haida, some have noted that the tradition known as the "high words" refers to use of the language in a formal code in which the speech has elements of formality filled with metaphor and allusions (Swanton 1905, 1912; Boelscher 1988). This elevated language usage is rarely practiced anymore due to the loss of ability resulting from a slow process of language death (Enrico 2003:7), but there are some very good efforts with all three dialects—Skidegate, Massett, and Kaigani—to revitalize the Haida language, and this dynamic usage can be recovered.

At the time of Swanton's recording, the use of high words was prominent, especially within the *git kagaandaaw* (lullaby) practice that honored the *yahgid* children, literally, those that were high-caste children. The prominence of *git kagaandaaw* suggests the importance of children in the Haida society and indicates that such attention bordered on spoiling the child (Day 1951:57). The result of such practices led to a socialization of the children to their status within the community and also socialized the child to intimate knowledge of the kinship system (Goodwin 1990; Schieffelin 1990; Scollon and Scollon 1981). With the knowledge instilled from the songs concerning the kinship system, the child acquired the intricacies of detailed relational practices that must be observed among his family. Ochs and Schieffelin make the following claims with regard to language acquisition and socialization that can be realized and confirmed among the Haida:

1. The process of acquiring language is deeply affected by the process of becoming a competent member of a society.
2. The process of becoming a competent member of society is realized to a large extent through language, by acquiring knowledge of its functions, social distribution, and interpretations in and across socially defined situations, i.e., through exchanges of language in particular situations. (1984:277)

The complexity within the Haida language revealed particular aspects of the kinship system, and learning the terms of immediate family members provided the essential information necessary to determine how to relate to the person according to his or her lineage. The Haida kinship terms clearly indicated how the person was related to the speaker and thus, what the protocol was for interaction with that person. The *git kagaandaaw* socialized the children by providing essential kinship knowledge, including the specifics of how to properly address others and refer to oneself. Ochs and Schieffelin conclude that with such socialization, even in participating in simply as audience, "the infant develops a range of skills, intuitions, and knowledge enabling him or her to communicate in culturally preferred ways" (1984:311). Such is the case of Cradle-Song 67.

The significance of the term for grandfather is perhaps most enlightening to the context of the song, because there is a Haida myth that attributes their existence to salmon. Significantly, the word for "salmon," *tcin*, is the word from which "grandfather" is derived. One story of the Haida's origin explains how the salmon began to emerge from the ocean; as they emerged they were in the form of *xáayta*, or Haida, the human people. Another important factor related to the grandfather is the reference of place. Concerning narratives of origins, location, or history, Basso refers to the magnitude of place as not just a singular location but also a place-world (1996:6). This place-world embodies two salient questions: What happened here? and What will happen here? In this cradle-song, the reference to the "place" is water, the oceans and rivers.

In Haida mythology, the Creator blesses his children from below. Blessings come up from the waters, not down from the heavens. Bringhurst elaborates on this theme: "Manna falls only rarely from the heavens; it emerges daily from the waves" (1999:65). As the grandfather goes to the place of blessing, the water, he is so overwhelmed with gifts that the canoe must be modified to contain the blessing. The reference to the place also suggests that it is the point of origin, the place from whence the Haidas emerged. The significance of the grandfather's journey to this place and his subsequent return with wealth and gifts speaks of the status of the grandfather. He is a great chief and must therefore have a great canoe.

Haidas have been well known for their skill in canoe building. The style included having high projected bow and stern, "a sharp vertical cut water or forefoot, and a rounded counter" (Drucker 1963:72). Their canoes have been up to sixty feet long and eight feet wide, made from a single red cedar. Drucker discusses the prominence of canoes on the northwest coast of Canada and United States with this important insight: "While all the northern tribes made both large and small canoes of this style, the Haida canoe makers were especially esteemed for their craftsmanship." He further explains that "the mainland group sought to buy the Haida-built craft when the tribes assembled at the olachen-fishing grounds on the Nass River every Spring" (1963:73). Thus, in the song, the craft is essentially a canoe fit for a great chief, and as such, returning from the "place," it should supernaturally be filled with gifts.

As we come to the final stanza of the song, we see repeated admonishments but with different status terms. In the Haida social system there was a ranking of status (Blackman 1981; Boelscher 1988; Kroeber 1967) that categorized the social order according to the order of nobles (chiefs), commoners, and slaves. Another subcategory of rank was the servant, not quite a commoner and not as low as a slave. Within these different ranks, the guiding principle that linked succession was both matrilineality and clan membership. For traditional Haida succession, it must be through the mother that any son achieves the status of a chief due to matrilineal rule the Haida observed (Van Den Brink 1974). It is also from the mother that every Haida inherits clan membership, Eagle or Raven. Thus, the song serves to socialize the child in at least three aspects of the culture not evident in the English gloss or in the free English translation:

    a. The child is socialized to the terminology of his own rank
    b. The child is socialized in the use of addressing the rank of others
    c. The child is being socialized to his position in society

It is not simply a song to put the child to sleep. It is a song to socialize function and status for the child as he grows.

A significant observation concerns the repetition in the song. Repetition has many functions, including emphasis, instruction, and tradition. There are four different repetitions throughout this song: the words *Lûǧa gûǧa* and the phrase *waǧAn dînA+ ñ* are sung twice; *Yâ'ña* is sung twice in the penultimate sentence and twice in the last sentence. This is noteworthy because, as Bierhorst explains, "The four directions (east, west, south, north), corresponding to the four faces of the human body (back, front, left, right), are held sacred in many cultures." He continues, "By extension, the 4 itself is also sacred and fourfold repetitions occur frequently in song and myth" (1971:4). In this song we can see all the functions of repetition occurring to emphasize history, to instruct social functions, and to maintain tradition.

These aspects of Haida culture contribute significant understanding about the song, because the child will need to know how to address others and how to refer to himself. The boy will be prepared to lead his village, and thus he must be aware of his destiny and have the essential knowledge to be and in being a leader. The words for "chief" and "master" are the words he must learn and know when to use, and since they are being used by his mother to address him in the song, he will learn how to respond to them as well.

The song is sung on various occasions. The most obvious comes from its category *git kagaandaaw*, the lullaby, which is sung to sing the child asleep for a nap or for the night. The song was also sung in order to instill soothing during such events as a potlatch, totem pole raising, or during a naming ceremony celebration. Enrico and Stuart explain further functions of the lullabies in the Haida community, "Their role in the house-building potlatch, however, was responsible for their elaborateness, their content, and their ownership lineages" (1996:21). But whatever the occasion, the song provides socialization for the child concerning his rank or destiny, how he must think of himself, and the terminologies of respect for the people of power in the village.

A Revised Modern Paraphrase

While much is to be applauded in his work, Swanton leaves opportunity to improve his efforts with a greater ethnohistorical perspective that incorporates meaningful stories and tribal accounts of history. I concur with Swann's statement that "it is too easy to make fun of the early collectors. The fact is, their contributions were enormous, and numbers of them did make an honest attempt to break through ingrained cultural habits" (1992:5). Yet Swanton was a rare scholar who invited scrutiny and was neither so unapproachable nor so uncorrectable that he would not allow revision of his work. He humbly regarded his work and its significance. In fact, Swanton wrote Boas a letter in response to his mentor's query about Haida manuscripts Boas had received from him nearly forty years earlier,

> Dear Professor Boas,
> Please feel free to make any disposition of my Haida text mate-
> rial you desire. I fear much of it is pretty crude but had hoped that
> it might be good enough for a better linguist to correct. (Bringhurst
> 1999:195)

The student/professor dynamic was still there. Even though at this time Swanton was sixty-nine and Boas was eighty-two, Swanton invited and expected scrutiny for his Haida texts and translations.

With the information provided in this chapter, I present a modern paraphrase of Swanton's translation.

Because my child is a boy,
he is going to do as his grandfather did
when he went to his place long ago.

And while there they filled
his great canoe so much with gifts
they had to increase its capacity with boards.

Be carefully wise,
be carefully wise,
my chief!

Be carefully wise,
be carefully wise,
my master!

In the first stanza, the importance of the child's heritage is immediately evident. His leadership and exploits are directly related to his mother's father, as is Haida custom. We also have a veiled reference to the place of origin, the place from whence the Creator bestows his blessing, which overflows into stanza two. Here the reference to the Creator's blessing is more explicit and so lavish that the canoe has to be altered to make room for the blessing. It is important to note that as a key figure in the Haida community, this boy's canoe will be extraordinary. While the Haida seems to reference greatness on the water, the canoe is also great because of its size and its owner. These make this canoe great. As the song ends, the singer admonishes the child to be wise and invokes important Haida terms for this boy's future status. The repetition of the admonishment is common in many cultures' use of language to discipline and also to socialize. The expectation of such admonition is, of course, obedience; and heeding the words of parents and elders is indicative of a well-reared child.

This paraphrase captures Swanton's parenthetical additions in the English gloss as well as the socialization practices for the addressee of the lullaby. By comparing the versions of the song, this paraphrase captures the focus and purpose of the song, not only to lull a child to sleep, but also to instill in the child the knowledge of place, of kinship, and destiny.

Conclusion

As translated by Swanton, Cradle-Song 67 reveals an adherence to the literal form of the song with little consideration to significant background knowledge that informs the translation of the song and its content. I have suggested an ethnohistorical review and offered a paraphrase of this song with a concern for form and content. The scope of my paraphrase results in an incorporation of the information concerning the significance of *tcin* in Haida mythology. The story of the emergence of the *xáayta* from salmon helps to keep the idea of the grandfather's journey to and return from the "place" in perspective. Just as Swanton did, the paraphrase retains the essential status of chief that the child will inherit.

This ethnohistorical perspective incorporates salient information concerning the form of the song, *git kagaandaaw*, which is not just for infants but also for toddlers who are beginning to learn the language. Seen from the perspective of language socialization, the song provides a model for socializing the boy to his rank and destiny, as well as providing important linguistic and behavioral expectations for interaction with others of the noble class. Thus, the song's conclusion repeats the sentiment that it behooves him to "be careful" of his rank and destiny, or to be thoughtful, as the word suggests, with wisdom. The song ends with the admonition to be wise and tend to life with wisdom. This lullaby contributes to the child's informal education about his environment, his history, his identity, and his role in the community both as he hears the song and in preparation for the future.

Note

I would like to acknowledge and express my gratitude for the valuable support of Pennsylvania State System of Higher Education Faculty Professional Development Council Grant, which generously funded part of the summer 2008 research and travel to Haida Gwaii for the research necessary to produce this chapter.

References

Basso, K. 1984. Stalking with Stories: Names, Places, and Moral Narratives among the Western Apache. In *Text, Play, and Story: The Construction and Reconstruction of Self and Society*, ed. E. Bruner, 19–55. Washington DC: American Ethnological Society.

———. 1996. *Wisdom Sits in Places.* Albuquerque: University of New Mexico Press.

Bierhorst, J., ed. 1971. *In the Trail of the Wind: American Indian Poems and Ritual Orations.* New York: Farrar, Strauss, and Giroux.

Blackman, M. 1981. *During My Time: Florence Edenshaw Davidson, a Haida Woman.* Seattle: University of Washington Press.

Boas, F. 1911. *Handbook of American Indian Languages.* Vol. 1. Bureau of American Ethnology, Bulletin 40. Washington DC: Government Printing Office (Smithsonian Institution, Bureau of American Ethnology).

———. 1922. *Handbook of American Indian Languages.* Vol. 2. Bureau of American Ethnology, Bulletin 40. Washington DC: Government Printing Office (Smithsonian Institution, Bureau of American Ethnology).

———. 1955. *Primitive Art.* New York: Dover.

Boelscher, M. 1988. *The Curtain Within: Haida Social and Mythical Discourse.* Vancouver: University of British Columbia Press.

Bringhurst, R. 1999. *A Story as Sharp as a Knife: The Classical Haida Mythtellers and Their World.* Vancouver: Douglas & McIntyre.

Bruchac, J., ed. 1995. *Smoke Rising: The Native North American Literary Companion.* Detroit: Visible Ink.

Cagle, A. B. 2007. American Indian Poetry. In *Encyclopedia of American Indian Literature,* ed. Jennifer McClinton-Temple and Alan Velie, 29–32. New York: Facts on File.

Campbell, G. 1990. *Compendium of the World's Languages: Abaza to Lusatian.* Vol. 1. London: Routledge.

Day, A. G. 1951. *The Sky Clears: Poetry of the American Indians.* Lincoln: University Nebraska Press.

Drucker, P. 1963. *Indians of the Northwest Coast.* Garden City NY: Natural History Press.

Enrico, J. 2003. *Haida Syntax.* Vols. 1–2. Lincoln: University of Nebraska Press.

———. 2005. *Haida Dictionary.* Juneau: Sealaska Foundation.

Enrico, J., and Stuart, W. 1996. *Northern Haida Songs.* Lincoln: University of Nebraska Press.

Goodwin, M. 1990. *He-Said-She-Said: Talk as Social Organization among Black Children.* Bloomington: Indiana University Press.

Hymes, D. 1981. Reading Clakamas Texts. In *Traditional Literatures of the American Indian: Texts and Interpretations,* ed. K. Kroeber, 117–29. Lincoln: University of Nebraska Press.

Kroeber, A. 1967. *The Indians of California.* In *The North American Indian: A Sourcebook,* ed. R. Owen, J. Deetz, and A. Fisher. New York: MacMillan, 1968.

———, ed. 1981. *Traditional Literatures of the American Indian: Texts and Interpretations.* Lincoln: University of Nebraska Press.

Kroskrity, P. 1986. Ethnolinguistics and American Indian Education: Native

American Language and Cultures as a Means of Teaching. In *American Indian Policy and Cultural Values: Conflict and Accommodation*, ed. J. Joe, 99–110. Los Angeles: American Indian Studies Center, UCLA.

Lawrence, E., ed. 1977. *Haida Dictionary*. Fairbanks: Alaska Native Language Center.

Ochs, E., and Schieffelin, B. B. 1984. Language Acquisition and Socialization: Three Developmental and Their Implications. In *Culture Theory: Essays on Mind, Self and Emotion*, ed. R. Shweder and R. Levine, 209–82. Cambridge: Cambridge University Press.

Schieffelin, B. 1990. *The Give and Take of Everyday Life: Language Socialization of Kulali Children*. Cambridge: Cambridge University Press.

Scollon, R., and S. Scollon. 1981. *Narrative, Literacy and Face in Interethnic Communication*. Vol. 7 of R. O. Freedie, ed., *Advances in Discourse Processes*. Norwood NJ: Ablex.

Swann, B., ed. 1992. *On the Translation of Native American Literatures*. Washington DC: Smithsonian Institution Press.

———, ed. 1996. *Coming to Light: Contemporary Translations of the Native Literatures of North America*. New York: Vintage.

Swanton, J. 1905. *Contributions to the Ethnology of the Haida*. Publications of the Jesup North Pacific Expedition 5(1); American Museum of Natural History Memoirs 8(1). Leiden: E. J. Brill; New York: G. E. Stechert.

———. 1911. Haida. In F. Boas, ed., *Handbook of American Indian Languages*. Bureau of American Ethnology, Bulletin 40 (1): 205–82.

———. 1912. *Haida Songs*. Publications of the American Ethnological Society, vol. 3. Leiden: Brill.

Tedlock, D. 1972. *Finding the Center: Narrative Poetry of the Zuñi Indians*. New York: Dial Press.

Van Den Brink, J. H. 1974. *The Haida Indians*. Leiden: Brill.

13

Translating Tense and Aspect in Tlingit Narratives

Richard L. Dauenhauer and Nora Marks Dauenhauer

In memory of Ron Scollon (1939–2009)

Part One: The Critical Challenge

I.

So I am in the eighth grade and I am assigned this book report and I write about Damon Runyon short stories and I begin it like this: "I am in the library last week and I see this book and I check it out."[1] My book report was severely red-penciled by my teacher, although she lightened up at the end when she saw what I was trying to do. I learned from the experiment not to mix genre and style, but to use the style appropriate to the genre and level of formality. This is a message that comes early and stays late in our schooling, including the academic writing we are trained to do, and—perish the thought—translation. I learned that one does not attempt pastiche to meet an expository writing assignment. On the other hand, we commonly use the present tense in English-language narratives, but usually only when telling funny stories. "This guy walks into a bar and says to the bartender," and so forth. The frame is set for humor. But we use the present tense for serious themes as well—the historical present: "It is early evening and President Lincoln is heading to Ford Theater," or, "President Kennedy's motorcade is slowly working its way through Dallas."

We noticed some time ago that Tlingit verb tense and aspect are not only different from English linguistic structure but are used differently in narrative structure. Briefly stated, Tlingit narrators tend to use the perfective aspect of the main verb to advance the story, and the imperfective aspect to fill in detail at that stage before moving on. Within this larger imperfective narrative space created by the perfective aspect of the main verb moving the text forward, there are more subtle patterns of repetitive forms, including perfective and imperfective habitual; progressive and decessive epimodes; a range of epiaspect durative suffixes used with both perfective and imperfective verbs; and the creation of secondary imperfectives by adding any of various durative suffixes. In Tlingit, this pattern is used for comic and tragic narratives alike. The question arises as to how to translate these imperfective forms into English without coding some undesired or unintended meta-messages.[2]

II.

The Tlingit perfective very roughly equates to the English past tense, and the Tlingit imperfective to the present, with the major distinction that where the English verb system is time based, Tlingit is aspect based. Our linguistic treatment here is admittedly oversimplified. The bottom line is that all English verbs are marked for time in ways that Tlingit verbs are not. Conversely, Tlingit verbs are marked for other things that are not always easily expressed in English, or even expressible at all. English is time based: "This article would have been being written last summer"— and we wait for the other shoe to drop—"except I got lazy." All languages have their special ways of making certain distinctions, some of which are translatable, some not. For example, "Do you eat pork?" versus "Are you eating pork?" Or "Do you speak German?" versus "Are you speaking German?" Or "I stopped to smoke" versus "I stopped smoking." We are frequently asked to translate titles of conferences and similar events into Tlingit. Typically the English phrases have snappy-sounding gerunds, such as "Supporting Our Troops." These require a paraphrase in Tlingit, a choice of forms such as "We are supporting," "Let's support," "We will support," and so on.

Where the narrative distribution of Tlingit perfective and imperfective parallel English style, there is no problem translating, but where they do not parallel English style, how do we translate into English without sending the wrong signals? How do we use the English imperfective in a serious story without making the storyteller sound illiterate; or, conversely, how do we use a perfective without making a funny story sound serious where it shouldn't? For example, even where Tlingit Raven stories are outrageously funny, non-Native audiences often feel uneasy laughing, because they erroneously think that Raven is some kind of god-figure and that laughing would be disrespectful or even sacrilegious. Although we did not entirely ignore this problem in the past, we are only now starting to take a serious look at how Tlingit narrators use these grammatical features as elements of style, and what the implications are for translation. The present chapter is a preliminary report of work in progress.

When we started this project, I thought I knew about tense and aspect, having majored in Slavic languages and what-not. One quick scan of the Wikipedia entry on "grammatical aspect" cured me, and, as the entry on grammatical tense affirms, there is considerable confusion and disagreement among specialists. Part of the confusion for Tlingit and related languages is that much of the analysis of topics such as tense and aspect in European and other languages is good as far as it goes, but with Athabaskan and Na-Dene languages, the research launches into new territory where established terms and treatments often no longer fit, requiring new terms and new explanations.

Tlingit is rich in durative suffixes that add dimensions to the verb regarding frequency, repetition, habituality, and duration of the action. While the listing of the suffixes with examples in the Story-Naish *Tlingit Verb Dictionary* (1973:356, 360–61) is instructive, the traditional terms are not entirely satisfactory in explaining their distribution. Leer takes a different approach, explaining, "Durative suffixes are suffixes that combine with the root to create the stems of the Durative epiaspectual forms" (1991:152). He notes that most of these suffixes are given distinct names by Story and Naish and that, while he lists them for reference, he does not use them. Here is Leer's list of durative suffixes[3] with the Story-Naish terms and examples (Leer 1991:152–53; Story and Naish 1973:360–61):

-k ~ g ~ kw	repetitive	da.ús'kw, he's washing (clothes)
-x̱	habitual	kadahéix̱, he's planting
-ch ~ -j	frequentative	at ya.áx̱ch, he hears something
-t ~ -d	successive	at únt, he's shooting
-x' ~ -x'w	collective	at sa.ínx', he's packing stuff (in boxes)
-t'	[unnamed]	at kasagánt', he's burning trash
-s'	serial	kadagwáls', he's knocking
-l'	[unnamed]	at kalax̱ákwl', he's grinding something.

In addition, the suffixes can be applied to other verb stems to add or express a dimension of frequency. For example, verbs of motion have no primary imperfective. But various suffixes can be added to create secondary imperfectives, for example, using the stem -goot, "to go on foot," first with progressive and perfective forms and then with secondary imperfectives (Story and Naish 1973:354–55):

yaa nagút	he is going along (progressive)
aadéi woogoot	he went there; left for there (perfective, atelic)
át uwagút	he came; arrived there (perfective, telic with post-position -t)
át woogoot	he was going around there (perfective, atelic with post-position -t)
yoo yagútkw	he goes to and fro (repetitive)
kei gútch	he goes up (usitative)
gunayéi gútx̱	he starts going (habitually) (usitative; habitual)
yaa gagútch	he goes along (stopping at intervals) (usitative)

Instead of subdividing the durative suffixes, Leer suggests the concept of the epiaspect to address features of grammar that are not mutually exclusive with aspect, but that can be applied to perfective and imperfective aspects alike. This can be presented in a chart with columns from left to right. Within each column the categories are mutually exclusive, but categories from columns to the right can be applied to items to the left.

Simplified Chart (after Leer 1991, chapter 6; some columns deleted)

1. Mode	2. Status	3. Epimode	4. Clause type	5. Epiaspect
imperfective	realis	prohibitive-	main	progressive
perfective	irrealis	optative	subordinative	durative
future		decessive	attributive	
perfective habitual				
etc.				

That is, in column 1 the mode of a verb is imperfective or perfective or future, or perfective habitual, and so forth, but can't be more than one. Moving to the right across the chart are categories that can be applied to the first column. For example, a verb can be realis or irrealis (positive or negative). Thus, within that column, positive and negative are mutually exclusive, but either can be applied to imperfective, perfective, future, and so forth. Moving across the chart, one comes to the epiaspect column. This contains two categories: progressive and durative. This means that these can be applied to perfective and imperfective verbs. As all of this applies to this chapter, we note that perfective aspect verbs are used to move the story forward, and other forms are used for action or detail within the new frame. At this stage of our research, the pattern of perfective and imperfective seems fairly clear, but we are still uncertain of the distribution pattern, if any, of the epimodes, epiaspects, and the perfective and imperfective habitual.

III.

In this chapter we won't go deeply into literary theory on translation, but we do need to touch on a few points. In one of the classic studies, *Toward a Science of Translating*, Eugene A. Nida (1964) distinguishes three stages of translation: the literal transfer, the minimal transfer, and literary transfers. For example, a literal transfer from Russian *u menya kniga* would be "at me book." As a minimal transfer into English, it would be "I have a book." This is the minimal level for normal English grammar. Literary transfers would be various final forms that differ in meaning and style, such as the variety of Bible translations that exist, or of Dostoyevsky and Tolstoy. Perhaps an equivalent of our sample sentence would be "I possess a tome," "I possess a volume," or plain old "I have a book."

In this chapter we are not concerned with the literal transfer level of translation, other than to explain that it becomes a serious consideration regarding translation of certain types of verbs, especially eventive verbs. These are verbs that in Tlingit have no imperfective, and are perfective in form, but are conventionally translated into English as present tense. For example, "I am tired" is perfective in Tlingit, because one must have already achieved the state of tiredness before being able to make the statement. (Of course, in English, this is a present perfective form not unlike Tlingit, but we will let such sleeping linguistic dogs lie.) Likewise the usual ways of saying "I know" and "I see" are not present or imperfective in Tlingit, but are perfective, the grammatical logic being that one must have acquired the knowledge prior to being able to say "I know," and one must have received the optical image prior to being able to say "I see." Thus, at this stage, we cannot be overly dogmatic in lumping all perfective verbs together, and translation can't be formulaic, but needs to be decided on the basis of the individual verb and its context. Likewise, motion verbs have no primary imperfective, but do appear in secondary imperfective forms with a variety of suffixes indicating repetitive, habitual, occasional, customary, or durative action. Also, the phrase "my name is" is literally something like "people habitually call me," with an appropriate suffix on the verb.

The point here is that we are not concerned in translation with the use of suffixes that are more or less lexicalized. For example, the verbs *to sew*, *to shoot*, *to sweep*, and *to knock* each have a durative suffix that is always used in the imperfective: *sewing* for the repetitive, circular action of pushing the needle and thread through the fabric and pulling it out; *shooting* for the idea that more than one shot is being fired; *sweeping* for the repeated back-and-forth action of the broom; *knocking* for the repeated action of the knuckles on the door. These are required by the grammar. Rather, we focus here on durative forms that are optional, and become a feature of style and intended meaning. For example, in line 33 of his "Mosquito" story (Dauenhauer and Dauenhauer 1987:74–75), Robert Zuboff says,

áx' yéi haa wooteex̱   we were living there.

Here the -x̱ durative suffix is optional. He could have said *wootee*. This is a perfective form meaning "we lived there" or "we were living there." Here the durative suffix emphasizes the extension of time, and suggests "we were living there" as a better translation than "we lived there." Likewise, *at únt* is the normal way of saying "he is shooting," with the -*t* suffix, obligatory for the imperfective. *At únx̱* would be "he habitually shoots," where the -x̱ indicates habitual action and is not obligatory.

Although we do some linguistic analysis here, our main concern is translation and not a discourse on the Tlingit verb. We will focus primarily on stylistic distribution of the perfective and imperfective aspects in Tlingit, and how these should be translated into English. The linguistic dimension is covered in Jeffry Leer's PhD dissertation, "The Schetic Categories of the Tlingit Verb" (esp. section 8.1.4.1, pp. 342–56 ff., "past narrative sequence"). In this highly technical treatment of subtypes of the verb, Leer describes how the "narrative now" window is followed by a perfective verb form and how "the perfective typically serves to indicate the shift to a new narrative-now window" (1991:345). For detailed analysis of what Leer would call a habitual narrative sequence, see Gillian L. Story's "An Analyzed Tlingit Procedural Text" (1995). We direct readers interested in more linguistic detail to Leer and Story.

IV.

As examples of this challenge in translation, we look at representative passages in two of our translations published twenty years ago, first from Robert Zuboff's "Mosquito" (Dauenhauer and Dauenhauer 1987:72–81). Zuboff opens with a narrative frame typical of Tlingit storytelling, wherein he explains who he is and his connection to the story, in this case through his Tlingit name, that derives from and alludes to events in the story. The most dramatic example of what we are describing comes in lines 12–17:

X̲at woox̲oox̲ Geetwéin.	Geetwéin called me over.
Ch'águ aayí	The one of long ago,
ch'aakw woonaa.	he died long ago.
Yées yadák'wx̲ x̲at sitee.	I am a young man.
Yées yadák'wx̲ x̲at sateeyídáx̲	From the time I am a young man
s'eenáa yaakw ax̲ jee yéi wootee.	I had a seine boat.

In our 1987 translation we translated lines 15 and 16 with the English past tense, "I was a young man" and "From the time I was a young man." But the Tlingit in both places is imperfective (or "present"). He has advanced the story with perfectives—"Geetwéin called me over" and "he died long ago"—and fills in the detail in the "narrative now" with imperfective forms. The perfective in line 17 ("I had a seine boat") now advances the story, and he describes his boats in the imperfective, as in line 22:

déix̲ ax̲ jeex' sitee wé yaakw tlénx'
I have two of these big boats.

Again, we translated this with the English past tense, "I had two of these big boats."

One more passage will suffice to describe this feature of Tlingit narrative style as used by Robert Zuboff. The story transitions from the opening narrative frame to the "story proper" with lines 29–31, "Geetwéin said to me, 'I would very much like to explain to you this name of yours.'" The narrator advances the story in two sentences (lines 32–35) with perfective verbs that we translate with English past tense:

We were living there	wooteex̱	perfective
	(wootee) + durative -x̱	
in the Interior.		
Our life there		
was so hard.	woot'éex'	perfective

He then uses a sequence of imperfective forms to fill in the detail in lines 36–49. The underlined verbs in this passage are all imperfective forms in Tlingit that we have translated with English past tense.

The salmon.	
From the ocean	
they <u>would come up</u> for us to eat.	[kei x'ákch; x'ák +durative -ch]
The salmon.	
And how <u>good they tasted</u> to us,	[haa x̱'éi yak'éi]
the salmon.	
It <u>was</u> very	[yat'éex']
hard	
to live in the Interior.	
It <u>was</u> so hard	[wáa t'éex'i sáyú]
the people	
<u>ate</u> each other.	[wooch isx̱á]
There <u>were</u> cannibals	[k̲udzitee]
at that time.	

A closer translation reflecting the imperfectives would be as follows.

We were living there
in the Interior.
Our life there
was so hard.
The salmon.
From the ocean
they come up for us to eat.
The salmon.

And how good they taste to us,
the salmon.
It's very
hard
to live in the Interior.
It's so hard
the people
eat each other.
There are cannibals
at that time.

The progressive epiaspect is also used to fill in detail. It is not marked for time in Tlingit, and we usually translate it with a time reference corresponding to the main verb. So in lines 60 and following there is a sequence of perfectives in which a brother went hunting, didn't come back, a younger brother went hunting, and didn't come back. Then, in line 71, the youngest brother is/was crying and is/was searching for his older brothers:

yaa nasgáx̱ áyá du hunx̱u hásgaa yaa k̲unashéen.

We translated this as "he was crying as he kept on searching for his older brothers," but it could also be translated "he's crying as he keeps on searching for this older brothers." There is a similar pattern a few lines later. The boy spotted the cannibal (perfective) and it is coming toward him (progressive).

The familiar perfective-imperfective pattern continues throughout the story, for example in lines 77–81, with three perfectives followed by an imperfective:

k̲usax̱a k̲wáanch áwé shaawax̱ích.
Wudzigeet, .
áa wdzigeet.
Wáa sá du toowú yak'éi wé k̲usax̱a k̲wáan.

In a literal translation:

The cannibal struck him on the head.
He fell,

he fell there.
How good the cannibal feels.

In our 1987 translation we used the past tense for the last line, "How good the cannibal felt."

V.

This pattern is not restricted to a single storyteller, but is characteristic of Tlingit narrative in general. A brief look at the opening of "Glacier Bay History" by Susie James will confirm this (Dauenhauer and Dauenhauer 1987:244–59). Her opening frame is with a long sequence of imperfective verbs describing Glacier Bay, especially the area that is now Bartlett cove, where the National Park Visitor Center is located. Her opening plays with a delicate balance of then and now, building to the pivotal moment when the inappropriate action of a young girl in puberty isolation has cosmic repercussions. Here are lines 1–13 and 20, with the Tlingit imperfectives underlined, that we translated in 1987 as English past tense.

The name of it is G̲athéeni,
that land of ours.
G̲athéeni,
the Bay Where the Glacier Was.
It was where people <u>lived</u>.
Salmon of all kinds <u>ran</u> there.
That's why the people <u>lived</u> there; they made it a village.
Many kinds of salmon are there.
Good salmon <u>ran</u> there.
It was while people <u>were</u> still living there,
the houses:
maybe as many as five houses <u>stood</u> there,
the houses.
. . . .
We <u>were</u> living there.

Line 4 is the Tlingit place-name for Glacier Bay; we probably could have translated that line as "Glacier Bay." The only perfective in the passage is in line 7, *wé aanx̲ wududliyéx̲*, "They made it a village." Otherwise, these are all imperfectives, and could be translated literally with English present tense:

line 5, people live
line 6, salmon run
line 7, people live
line 10, while people are living
line 12, are standing there
line 20, we are living there.

Line 9 has an interesting form, the decessive imperfective. Decessive is what Leer calls an epimode. It refers to action of limited duration bound on either side by other action. As an epimode, it can be applied to various modes, including imperfective, perfective, and future. The decessive has no simple equivalent in English.

This passage illustrates what Leer calls the "narrative now," but it is clearly in the historical past, describing an idyllic situation that is about to change rapidly. The dramatic tension increases in lines 22 and 24 (literal translation): "What is she thinking [imperfective] . . . at the time of her enrichment [perfective; a term for puberty seclusion]?" The narrator then describes the training of a girl who has reached puberty. The verb forms are mostly imperfective, including several imperfective decessives. One remarkable form is in line 25:

yéi anúkjeen   thus she is curtained off [literally, seated]

This is literally an imperfective + durative suffix (-ch > -j) + decessive (-een). In 1987 we translated this as "one was curtained off." There is a lot going on in the Tlingit verb, but we are no closer to translating it than we were over twenty years ago.

The tension builds with more imperfectives culminating in line 37 with a perfective durative decessive and an imperfective negative in a rhythmically and grammatically run-on sentence:

ťéex' tayeet woo.áayjeen gaat; yeedát tlél yéi át utí
the sockeyes used to run up under the ice; it's not that way anymore.

Something happened to upset the balance of nature. This is finally explained in lines 51 and 52:

She knew the glacier was there.
That's why she called the glacier like a dog.

The verb in line 51 is *awsikóo*, a classic eventive verb that is always perfective in Tlingit and that has no imperfective. It could be translated as English past or present. Line 52 is perfective, and is the defining action of the story, moving the story to its heart. The young girl unknowingly violates a taboo, the glacier advances on the village, and the people evacuate Glacier Bay.

VI.

These examples show how imperfective and perfective verbs are used in Tlingit narratives. It raises the immediate question to us of whether we need to rethink our earlier translations and all the Tlingit imperfectives we translated as English past tense. These read well in English, which is the main point of a translation. So, on the one hand, it makes sense to translate as we have into English. On the other hand, are we missing something that might be conveyed by using more literal present-tense forms? Can we use the historical present in the Glacier Bay history? Or would that make the translation more awkward, call undue attention to the lines, and be more on the level of Nida's literal transfer rather than minimal transfer? We are undecided. But we have thought about using present tense in translating Tlingit Raven stories, the comic genre in Tlingit oral literature. The same narrative pattern occurs in Raven stories, and the precedent of using present tense when telling funny stories in English might make such a translation sound more acceptable for that genre, where it would be less jarring and disruptive, and might not send an inappropriate meta-message about the skill and intention of the storyteller.

Part Two: Three Raven Stories

Raven is the trickster figure, and Raven stories are the comic genre in Tlingit oral literature. They can be told by anyone, whereas most other Tlingit stories are clan property with transmission restricted to clan members or others appropriately related or designated (see Dauenhauer and Dauenhauer 2006b for more on the place of Raven stories in Tlingit folklore). While Raven stories are typically pedagogical and etiological, they are not exclusively children's literature; rather, they are told at an adult level, and children are socialized by hearing the stories along with adults. Although Raven is sometimes popularly labeled as a "creator," we prefer to think of him as a repair man or jack-of-all-trades, who takes the created world and makes it more user-friendly. He is not altruistic, but is driven by his hunger, greed, and lust. Any benefits to the world (sun, moon, stars, fresh water, the salmon run, fire, etc.) are usually secondary or leftovers.

Raven is a negative example or model, not to be imitated. He is incapable of an open, honest relationship with others. He gets his way by tricking others. Raven either dares his victims to do something dangerous or he manipulates and tricks them into doing something foolish. Raven usually gets away unscathed, but his victims don't. In "Raven and the King Salmon" the fish is lured to his death, but the small birds, although cheated, deceived, and physically transformed, survive. In other stories in the cycle, Deer is killed and the brown bears die painful deaths. In the teaching units we are developing to accompany the stories, we suggest that parents and teachers discuss the personality of Raven with children and young people and talk about the nature of lies, deception, and dares. Raven is a smooth talker and a sweet talker. Temptation is never ugly, but always attractive and appealing. Yet a single bad judgment can lead to injury or death and can damage our lives forever. In the modern age, the lives of all of us are full of dangers, including drugs, alcohol, unsafe sex, and sexual predation and exploitation.

The final stage of proofreading and editing these stories is undertaken with support from the National Science Foundation, Award No. BCS-0756468 to Tlingit Readers, Inc. We are happy to include the translations here as a preview of our forthcoming bilingual collection of Tlingit Raven stories, to be published as volume 5 of the University of Washington Press series Classics of Tlingit Oral Literature.

I. Raven and the Great Blue Heron

Told by Willie Marks, transcribed in Tlingit and translated by Nora Marks Dauenhauer, and edited by Nora Marks Dauenhauer and Richard Dauenhauer.

It was the Great Blue Heron
to whom [Raven] egged [the Seagull] on.
Before his eyes
that Heron swallowed it.
Maybe it was a trout   5
I don't know what kind of animal it was.
He egged him on.

When he went up to that Heron
he'd turn around and go to the other [and say],
"That guy over there is talking about you,   10
that—that—bum, the one sitting over there."
Here he isn't speaking to him at all.
But still he keeps on saying that's what he said.
He knows that fish
is already dissolving inside him.   15
"When I fight
with a guy like me,
first I usually kick him upward under the edge of the ribcage."
That's how he's coaching him,
so that the fish   20
will pop out of his mouth, right?
At some point he did as he said.
He and the Heron
began fighting.
Just the way [Raven] was trying [to get him to do],   25
he kicked his belly upward.
The fish he had swallowed
popped out of his mouth.
Raven flies down, acting innocent.
"Enough! Enough! Enough!   30
You might kill each other."
Here he'd already swallowed it.
That's the way I know it.

Willie Marks (Kéet Yaanaayí; July 3, 1902–August 7, 1981), the father of
Nora Marks Dauenhauer, was of the Eagle moiety, Chookaneidí clan, and
was a child of Lukaax̱.ádi. He was well known as a fisherman and wood-
carver. He raised his large family at their homesite at Marks Trail in Juneau and on the family fishing boat, the *New Annie*. For a full biography
see Dauenhauer and Dauenhauer 1994:452–62.

The story was recorded in 1972 (probably on October 24, 1972) by Nora
Marks Dauenhauer, working with her father, Willie Marks, at his home
at Marks Trail in Juneau. It was first transcribed in January 1973 and was
translated in April 1976. Activity was renewed in 1981, with a revised
translation and a glossary project started May 1981. Because of its short

length and important social commentary, the story is ideal for experimental projects and publication where space is limited. This story is a gem of transactional analysis, illustrating the "Let's You and Him Fight" pattern, in which one person manipulates two others to destroy each other for the benefit of the manipulator.

In 1984–85 an interactive computer version was programmed with text, translation, notes, and an interactive glossary. This was completed on November 20, 1985. An English translation was featured in the *Alaska Quarterly Review, Special Issue: Alaska Native Writers, Storytellers and Orators* (Vol. 4, nos. 3 & 4, 1986, pages 89–90); the facing Tlingit text was included in the 1999 *Expanded Edition* (Vol. 17, nos. 3 & 4, 1999). A bilingual version was published in the *Naa Kaani*, the Sealaska Heritage Foundation Newsletter, in 1988.

We note here that our previously published translations of this story (Marks 1986, 1999) are ornithologically incorrect. Although *láx'* is popularly translated as both "crane" and "heron," and is so glossed in the Story-Naish Tlingit noun dictionary, *láx'* is more accurately "Great Blue Heron" (*Ardea herodias*), and "crane" is *dóol* in Tlingit (Sandhill Crane, *Grus canadensis*).

In its relatively few lines of length, this story illustrates many aspects of Tlingit oral literature and the problems that arise in translation. It is extremely laconic and highly contextualized. This is a Raven story, yet the first and only appearance of the noun "Raven" in the Tlingit text is five lines from the end! This is an example of contextualization: people familiar with the narrative tradition know from previous experience that this is a Raven story; the text itself is ambiguous. Note also that the noun "Seagull" appears in the English translation but never appears as a noun in the Tlingit text. Again, listeners know who the characters are by virtue of having heard the story before. Newcomers will not know this, and the information somehow must be provided.

A literal translation of the opening lines of the story is:

That Great Blue Heron it was
to him that he egged him on.
Beneath his eyes it was, he swallowed it.
That trout probably.
By the heron.

The relative absence of nouns and reliance on pronouns is typical of much of Tlingit oral literature. In field test classes, we learned that readers find the story unintelligible without some indication of what the nouns are. As a result, our final translation is looser, replacing some of the pronouns with nouns. For an insightful study of this problem in folklore theory and practice, see Toelken (2002).

II. Raven and the Deer

Told by Katherine Mills, transcribed in Tlingit by Nora Marks Dauenhauer, and translated by Nora Marks Dauenhauer and Richard Dauenhauer.

There's
just a little short one.

The Raven and the Deer:
they were pretty chummy people.
They walked around together.   5
But the Raven was already planning ahead, because
he wanted to get that Deer so he can have him for dinner.
And so—
I'm supposed to be talking in Tlingit!
Raven made the Deer   10
his partner.
This is when
he's beginning to think about
about how he'll kill the Deer for his dinner.
He's very hungry.   15
But the Deer is his partner.
That's why
he started going around with him then. They were going around
        everywhere.
All the while, in fact, he's searching there for a place
        to kill him.   20
At one point he saw the ravine.
It's a long way to the bottom, but not too wide.
There's
a rotten tree extending across it.

It's lying across it. Perhaps there used to be a trail
        over it long ago.   25
That tree was very rotten.
Raven sees what shape it's in.
Then he would hop across it.
"Watch me!
Partner, watch me!"   30
Then he'd keep on hopping out.
Oh,
was he hopping around there.
He does his hopping like he's partly flying.
Then he'd hop across it to the other side.   35
"Now! It's your turn, Partner.
It's your turn.
Walk on over it to the other side."
But the Deer was reluctant to walk over across
the tree.   40
He sees the shape it's in. "Nothing will happen to you, Partner.
Watch me, Partner!" Then he'd hop across it again.
After a while,
while [Raven] was hopping up and down in front of him,
Deer tried it.   45
Then he starts out across.
All of a sudden the tiny tree
broke.
Then the Deer
fell to the bottom.   50
Then he died.
This is when Raven flew down there.
But there's no way that he might get into him.
He doesn't have anything resembling a knife.
"If o-o-o-o-nly—oh, whe-e-e-re can I eat through
        my partner?"   55
he keeps on saying.
At what point was it he noticed a way around it?
Right then and there
the Deer's anus
seems just right to him.   60

This was when
he began to eat his way
through the Deer through his anus.
That's how he did it.
Then he ate him up.   65
There wasn't a piece of him left there.
Without a knife.
Just because of his desire,
he started in on the meal.
Right through the anus then.
This is all there is.

Katherine Brown Mills (Yakwx̱waan Tláa; June 5, 1915–August 16, 1993)
was of the Raven moiety and T'ak̲deintaan (Kittywake) clan, and a child
of Kaagwaantaan. She was involved in the Tlingit language movement
from the very beginning and taught Tlingit language and culture in the
Hoonah schools for many years, as well as being one of the leading in-
structors of traditional singing and dancing. In 1991 she performed at the
Festival of American Folklife on the National Mall in Washington DC. A
more detailed biography will be included in our forthcoming volume of
Tlingit Raven stories.

Many individuals and organizations helped in the development of this
text and translation. The set of stories from which it is excerpted was recorded in Anchorage in February 1989 (probably February 4) by Edna
Belarde Lamebull, director of the Indian Education Program of the Anchorage School District and niece of Katherine Mills. Also present were
Nora and Richard Dauenhauer and Dr. Patricia Partnow. We thank Edna
Lamebull for sharing the tape with us, and we thank her and other members of the immediate and extended family of Katherine Mills for their
support of this project in general, and for their patience in waiting for
the results. The complete original recording includes (side 1) 1. Raven and
the Salmon Box (in Tlingit); 2. Raven and the King Salmon (in Tlingit);
3. Raven, Brown Bears, and the Fish Tail (in English and Tlingit); (side 2),
4. Raven and the Deer (in Tlingit); 5. Raven and the Whale (in Tlingit);
6. The Old Man with the Club, or Why Raven Never Gets Full (in Tlingit).

The stories were transcribed and translated in first drafts over the next
few years, as time allowed, as a project of the Sealaska Heritage Institute
in Juneau, Alaska, with funding from the National Endowment for the

Humanities. Our primary efforts during this period were on publications of other genres of Tlingit oral literature, so proofreading and editing of Raven stories was set aside; it was resumed February 3–5, 1998, and continued through 1999 and the spring of 2001. In January 2001 a draft was completed of a glossary for the Tlingit text, and a study guide with suggested activities.

The stories were told as discrete units, with pauses and stops in between. Her delivery is evenly paced, with pauses after most sentences. Pauses between phrases of a sentence are often minimal. Also, in some places, two grammatical units are linked in the same breath unit, which we note by using a period and starting the new sentence in the same line. She often does this in passages of dialogue, with no pause between turn taking. This style increases the pace of the story by creating the sensation of rapid movement and fast-paced dialogue. Dialogue is enlivened by use of different voices for the various characters, distinct from the narrative voice. Her ending formula translates as "That's all there is," "That's as far as it goes," or "That's as big as it is."

Lines 8–10. Katherine Mills was an excellent stylist in English. Here she begins the story in English, and then remembers (lines 8 and 9) that she was asked to tell it in Tlingit, so she changes languages in line 10.

Lines 11, 30 ff., 55. Partner. One of Raven's favorite manipulative strategies is to pretend "co-membership." This word has a skillful evolution in the story: it is first factual and neutral; then Raven uses it to create trust, encourage, and betray the Deer; and at the end Raven gleefully eats his partner.

Lines 31ff. Hop. The Tlingit text is rich in the variety of verb forms for this word. The verb "hop" appears seven times in five different grammatical forms.

III. Raven Loses His Nose

Told by Austin Hammond, transcribed in Tlingit and translated by Nora Marks Dauenhauer, and edited by Nora Marks Dauenhauer and Richard Dauenhauer.

Raven
doesn't do any deep-sea diving.
Even so, this story
about it exists.

They say he heard about   5
this fat,
where people are using it as bait [for jigging halibut].
Raven really loves to eat only fat.
But even with this he's still thin.
He saw   10
where people are baiting their hooks for halibut.
This was when
he went there.
He lifted the sea
like a cloth.   15
He went under it.
After this
he's untying them
where they're tying on the bait.
Long ago, they only tied   20
the bait
on the hooks.
Well,
people couldn't feel it
when he untied them.   25
When the hooks were pulled up,
there was nothing on them.
Then as soon as they were baited—into the sea again.
Well,
after a while,   30
the same thing again.
He's untying them again.
How many times is he doing this?
Yes, they don't feel
Raven there.   35
This is when that fisherman
is thinking about it.
That's why
this
bite expert   40
was just the man.

They rowed ashore for him, so they say.
So once again,
while they were going to the beach [to get the bite expert],
[Raven] went down again.   45
Here he's just
trying to work on them lightly.
But he overdoes it. He put his mouth to it as he was
        removing the bait.
That man, the bite expert,
felt it.   50
As he's feeling it
suddenly
he told his hook to get it.
This was when that hook
caught [Raven] through the nose, they say.   55
They're pulling him up.
He's watching the bottom of the boat, just like it's this ceiling,
like here.
As he's getting closer to it, he kicked the bottom of the boat.
They pulled the line.   60
(Whoever is Raven's paternal uncle,
please forgive me.)
He kicked the bottom of it.
They pulled the line.
All of a sudden   65
it fell into their hands.
That nose of his
was stuck to it.
They didn't know what it was.
When they went ashore   70
all the people looked it over.
But that Raven, poor thing, swam ashore without his nose.
He carved
a piece of bark.
He stuck his nose in it.   75
Could anyone guess how it came into his hands?
"Visor hat" is what it's called.

He started walking again.
He started from the house at the end of town.
He's asking, 80
"Where did they jig
the Alien Nose?"
So he goes from door to door.
"It was caught next door," they say, [giving him the brush off].
That's why he'd start out again. He'd come to another one. 85
"Was it here that someone jigged up
the Alien Nose?"
"No. That was next door."
He goes to all the houses.
Finally he got here 90
right to the place where it's sitting.
He asks,
"Was it here that someone jigged up the Alien Nose?"
"Yes. It's right here,
over there." 95
This
down had been put all around it.
That was when he looked it over.
"My!
Oh!" 100
It was amazing to him, too. "My!
This is great!
Not too shabby,
the way it is."
Just as he's looking it over 105
he pulled off
the bark.
He stuck [his nose] back on in place of it.
This was when he ran outside.
That's why Raven's nose— 110
you can see the way it is—
doesn't fit too well there.
Well, this is how it was told to me.
Please excuse me,
my paternal aunts. 115

Austin Hammond (Daanawáak; October 18, 1910–July 3, 1993) lived in Haines, Alaska, and was for many years steward of the Raven House, a position shared since his death by Nora Marks Dauenhauer and two other clan members. Austin was of the Raven moiety, Lukaax̱.ádi (Sockeye Salmon) clan, and was a child of the Kaagwaantaan. For a full biography see Dauenhauer and Dauenhauer 1994:207–50.

The story was told by Austin Hammond during the Rasmuson Conference on Alaska Native Art, Portland Art Museum, May 15–16, 1989; recorded by the Sealaska Heritage Foundation and Museum staff (probably by Tim Wilson); and transcribed and translated by Nora Marks Dauenhauer in December 1999. At the end of the first day, Austin Hammond told this story to contextualize one of the art objects with the motif of Raven's nose. This story is ideal for intermediate Tlingit learners because it is rich in locational and directional words, relational nouns, and uses a small number of verbs, but repeats them in various grammatical forms. A draft glossary for the story was completed in July 2001. For a contemporary play based on another version of this story, see Nora Marks Dauenhauer's *Life Woven with Song* (2000).

Line 5. They say. This is a common phrase in Tlingit and other Native American storytelling, where the present tradition bearer asserts that he or she is reliably transmitting what the elders have passed down.

Lines 14–15. We have paraphrased here. A literal translation is: "The sea / this for example, I lifted it like a cloth." It is possible that this is Raven speaking or thinking, but it is more probable that the storyteller was pointing to some fabric close at hand. Other storytellers have also used this verb stem (to handle fabric) to describe a land-dwelling character going underwater.

Line 55. We could also translate this as "beak," but Tlingit uses the same word as "nose."

Line 57. This ceiling. The story is being told indoors.

Line 61. The storyteller, a man of the Raven moiety, is humorously apologizing in an aside to males of the opposite (Eagle) moiety.

Line 97. Down. The Alien nose as artifact is being displayed in a place of honor.

Lines 112–15. The audience responds with laughter and enthusiastic applause overlapping with the final lines of the story. The storyteller makes a humorous apology to women of the opposite (Eagle) moiety.

Part Three: Conclusion

We still don't know where we're going with this. We still don't fully understand the use of the progressive, durative, iterative, repetitive, and habitual forms and how they relate to tense and aspect, and how storytellers use them as elements of style—much less how to find something corresponding in translation. We need to explore shifts of tense and aspect as signals for boundaries of dramatic units (line, verse, stanza, scene, act) as Scollon (2009) examined for Mandeville's Chipewyan narratives. We need to reconnect with the substantial bibliography on style, text, texture, and context by Dell and Virginia Hymes, Barre Toelken, and others.

In the meantime, we continue to enjoy the stories and play with ways to make them even more enjoyable. For now, we'll see how we like these working translations. We hope that our attention to these linguistic details makes for a more colloquial or conversational style in translation. We'll lean back and enjoy the stories, and see how they look on the page and sound to the ear.

Notes

1. Richard Dauenhauer is primary researcher and author of this chapter; Nora Dauenhauer is primary transcriber and translator of the Tlingit texts; both sections were edited by both.

2. I enjoyed conversations and e-mail communication on this topic with our late friend and colleague Ron Scollon, who was preparing a collection of Chipewyan narratives by François Mandeville for publication (Scollon 2009), and who was examining the same stylistic feature in those stories. A possible future direction for our work is to link it to the act/scene analysis long advocated by Dell Hymes, which we have avoided simply because we have not had the time to pursue it. Scollon discovered that for the Chipewyan texts there is a congruence between shifts in verb aspect and the change of acts and scenes.

3. Tlingit has one of the most complex sound systems in the world, with, for example, about twenty-four sounds that do not occur in English. Here is a brief and rough pronunciation guide. (1) Underlined letters are uvular: x = German ich, x = German ach. (2) Tlingit l is voiceless. (3) The apostrophe indicates a glottalized sound. Glottal stops such as t' and k' are fairly common in Native American languages, but glottalized fricatives such as s', l', and x' are not. (4) When w follows a consonant, it indicates labialization: a sound at the back of the mouth such as k or x can be made with the lips rounded. (5) Combining all of the above features (glottalized fricatives, velar and uvular, rounded and unrounded) creates four sounds that are found in no other language on earth, as far as we know:

x', x'w, x̲' and x̲'w. (6) Tlingit is a tone language. The acute accent indicates high tone; low tone is not marked. For more on this, including a CD, see Dauenhauer and Dauenhauer 2006a.

References

Dauenhauer, Nora Marks. 2000. *Life Woven with Song*. Tucson: The University of Arizona Press.

Dauenhauer, Nora Marks, and Richard Dauenhauer. 1987. *Haa Shuká, Our Ancestors: Tlingit Oral Narratives*. Classics of Tlingit Oral Literature 1. Seattle: University of Washington Press.

———. 1994. *Haa K̲usteeyí, Our Culture: Tlingit Life Stories*. Classics of Tlingit Oral Literature 3. Seattle: University of Washington Press.

———. 2006a. *Sneaky Sounds: A Non-Threatening Introduction to Tlingit Sounds and Spelling*. Juneau: Sealaska Heritage Institute.

———. 2006b. Tlingit. In *The Greenwood Encyclopedia of World Folklore and Folklife*, ed. William M. Clements, 4:117–28. Westport CT: Greenwood Press.

———. Forthcoming. *Du Yaa Kanagoodi, Walking Along the Beach: Tlingit Raven Stories* (tentative title). Classics of Tlingit Oral Literature 5. Seattle: University of Washington Press.

Leer, Jeffry A. 1991. The Schetic Categories of the Tlingit Verb. PhD diss., University of Chicago.

Marks, Willie. 1986. Raven, Seagull and the Crane. In *Alaska Quarterly Review, Special Issue: Alaska Native Writers, Storytellers and Orators*, ed. Nora Dauenhauer, Richard Dauenhauer, and Gary Holthaus, 89–90. Anchorage: University of Alaska Anchorage.

———. 1999. Yéil K̲a Láx̲'/Raven, Seagull and Crane (with facing translation in Tlingit). In *Alaska Quarterly Review, Alaska Native Writers, Storytellers and Orators The Expanded Edition*, ed. Jeane Breinig and Patricia H. Partnow, 26–29. Anchorage: University of Alaska Anchorage.

Nida, Eugene A. 1964. *Toward a Science of Translating*. Leiden: Brill.

Scollon, Ron. 2009. *This Is What They Say: Stories by François Mandeville*. Translated from Chipewyan by Ron Scollon with a Foreword by Robert Bringhurst. Vancouver: Douglas McIntyre and University of Washington Press.

Story, Gillian L. 1995. An Analyzed Tlingit Procedural Text. In *Language and Culture in Native North America: Studies in Honor of Heinz-Jürgen Pinnow*, ed. Michael Dürr, Egon Renner, and Wolfgang Oleschinski, 312–31. Munich: Lincom.

Story, Gillian L., and Constance M. Naish, comps. 1973. *Tlingit Verb Dictionary*. Fairbanks: Alaska Native Language Center, University of Alaska.

Toelken, Barre. 2002. "Gleaning" and the Proactive Audience: An Athabascan Perspective for Modern Folklorists. In *Discourses in Search of Members, Festschrift in Honor of Prof. Ron Scollon*, ed. David Li, 451–62. Lanham MD: University Press of America.

14

Translating Performance in the Written Text
Verse Structure in Dakota and Hocák

Lynn Burley

We all know someone who can really tell a story—a person whose voice commands our attention, who encourages us to lean closer, waiting for the next detail, the next twist in the story. This person's talent may be learned or intuitive, but part of the artistry he or she displays comes from our expectations of a story, our Western culture that dictates how a story is to be told and how a story is to unfold. We learned about stories long before we started school, in our nursery tales, our fairy tales, our children's books, and while the stories got longer and more complex as we got older, the basics never really changed much. For many of us, the major change was the venue; we no longer listened to stories, but read them. Even the occasional trip to the theater or the nightly drama of television was not really the telling of a story in the same fashion, because the visuals changed the fundamental act.

We generally do not see a story as a performance when we read it, although we greatly appreciate those who can perform a story; they are always the ones in the center of a group of people at any get-together. Our Western stories are not written with a performance in mind. We expect our comfortable and reassuring patterns: the paragraphs and the chapters, laid out in the familiar book form. How, then, do we learn to read a whole new set of stories that are meant to be, first and foremost, performances, when the form they come to us in lacks any indication of the performance? Some would say we should not take the performance and turn it into the written story, particularly if we are going to turn it into the Western story and obliterate any resemblance to the original performance. Others, like myself, say that while a performance would be the best way to hear these stories, we cannot rely solely on that method. The stories might be lost forever, or never reach as large an audience as possible, or deny people the treasures of Native American stories because they do not have the opportunity to hear them.

Many of the Native American stories that we have today were originally collected in the early twentieth century by linguists who worked with many tribes, documenting their languages. During this era, texts were collected from many communities as data for linguistic and ethnographic study. These texts were written in block form with little attention to structure (Sherzer and Woodbury 1987). For instance, Paul Radin's work in "Winnebago Texts" of 1908 to 1912 is pages of paragraph-style text, despite the fact that Winnebago (since renamed Hocák) is best suited to a verse structure and does not conform easily to paragraphs. While Radin did note where some pauses occurred in several passages and did divide the passages into lines, no attempt was made during the translation or in the subsequent publication in English as *The Trickster: A Study in American Indian Mythology* (1956) to preserve any narrative structure of the original.

Other narratives suffered a similar fate. Stith Thompson's *Tales of the North American Indians* (1929), a collection from about fifty tribes, are all written in paragraph form even though all of them were originally performances. Zuni myths collected in the 1880s were often simply translated in outline form, and sometimes additional lines or whole passages not in the originals were added to the translations, presumably to make them more accessible to westerners. Other stories of the Zuni were just summaries, and these were published in a different order than the Zuni intended the stories to be heard (Tedlock 1983). The order of the stories in many Native American cultures is important, because the stories either build upon one another or are meant to be heard at only certain times of the year.

Others during this era—particularly Franz Boas, an anthropologist, and his students, but others were also involved—collected and translated myths and stories without attention to the narrative structure from such tribes as the Navajo, Hopi, Coos, Caddo, Kwakiutl, Dakota, Wishram, and others (see Bierhorst 1985; Hymes 1981; Sherzer and Woodbury 1987). For example, Stephen Riggs in *Dakota Grammar, Texts, and Ethnography*

(1893) gives a word-by-word gloss of the Dakota (Santee dialect) in eight myths, but he presents both the Dakota and the English translation in paragraph form. Even Native Americans conformed to Western structure as Mourning Dove, an Okanogan, did in *Coyote Stories*, a collection of twenty-seven stories originally published in 1933.

This method of transforming artistically performed oral narratives into paragraphs or summaries was commonly practiced by those who collected the stories; not until the 1960s did scholars began to focus on capturing the performance of the storyteller rather than just the story itself. There are several reasons to consider for this lack of attention to narrative structure. First, as Tedlock points out (1983), there were no tape recorders to aid the field worker, who was more likely to be interested in content rather than style, since the substance was the story, not the manner in which it was told. Also, without the tape recorder, the field worker was forced to repeatedly stop the storyteller in order to write out the dictation, which hampered any possibility of hearing the normal pauses and breaks (Tedlock 1972). Second, many believed that style was untranslatable anyway. Both Boas and A. L. Kroeber believed that the literary form was a property of the native language and hence could not be rendered into English. As Arnold Krupat discusses in "On the Translation of Native American Song and Story: A Theorized History," translators had to recognize that Native languages were both like and unlike European languages. "All English translations from native language performances cannot help but place themselves in relation to Western conceptions of art (literature) or of (social) science," he states, "as they inevitably privilege *either* the Sameness of Native American verbal expression in forms aspiring to what is accessibly recognizable as literary, *or* its Difference, in forms committed to scientific authenticity and accuracy" (1992:4). Most did not look for the similarity in the native language and only perceived the dissimilarity and proceeded to make the narrative appear as the audience would expect.

Given that all of these texts were oral narratives meant to be performed in front of a native-speaking audience, much of the voice, style, and artistry were lost in translation. However, attempts have now been made, led by Dennis Tedlock and Dell Hymes, to recapture these features. How can one capture dramatic features on the written page? One way is to think of how we hear a story. Translators invented ways to add in textual markings where the pauses a speaker makes occurred and a way to indicate the lengths of those pauses. Also, such voice features as loudness, tone, and pitch became part of the written word. Westerners might expect that it is not all that difficult to convey some of these elements in text. We are rather used to conventions that indicate such elements as loudness by using capital letters and pauses by putting in spaces between words or lines, but perhaps what we are not used to is the extent to which these features are applied in the translations of Native American stories.

Tedlock found ways to retain the voice in translating Zuni narratives. He felt "unhappy with the flat prose format which had always been used in presenting" field narratives (1972:xviii). So as he listened to taped oral performances, he worked out a mode of presentation that combined the poetic with the dramatic features. By breaking what had been translated as whole paragraphs into lines and strophes by the length of pauses, Tedlock has been able to recover a sense of the silences contained in the original. The pauses fall within lines as well as between lines, but sometimes there are no pauses at all between sentences.

Tedlock also considered other aspects of the Zuni narratives. Loudness ranged from nearly shouting to nearly whispering, and he also found that there was often heavy stress on the last syllable of a line to indicate the importance of an idea. Pitch was a factor, too, in lines that were chanted or by drawing out a vowel sound to indicate a long time or distance. Tone of voice could be indicated by putting in parenthesis some adjective so that a voice rendered as high or raspy could be read so. Tedlock also translated the natural parts of the narrator's story, such as spontaneous laughter or the mistakes made by backing up to say something forgotten, instead of cleaning it up as was done previously. Also, typically, Tedlock retained many repetitions that had previously been edited out, since the repetitions are a common feature of oral discourse serving poetic ends. What Tedlock has done is to allow the reader to read the tale with as much of the original performance as possible. Kenneth Roemer has shown the difference that Tedlock has made in his translations (1983). Below is the first version of the opening of the Zuni narrative "Coyote and Junco," which Roemer made using typical English phrasing and word order and eliminating repetition:

Once upon a time long ago Old Lady Junco had her home at Standing Arrows. Coyote was at Sitting Rock with his children. Old Lady Junco was separating the chaff from pigweed and tumbleweed by

tossing them in the air above her basket. Coyote was hunting for his
children when he came upon her. (1983:46)

The next version is Tedlock's (1972) as it appears in *Finding the Center:
Narrative Poetry of the Zuni Indians*. In order to compare Tedlock's version, Roemer offers a guide to reading Tedlock's text aloud. For this passage, the reader is to pause for half a second for each new line at the left-
hand margin, two seconds for a dot separating lines and no pause at all
for indented lines. A vowel followed by dashes is to be held for about two
seconds. A loud voice is used for words in capitals and a soft voice for
small type. Also, some lines are to be chanted at an interval of three half-
tones, as indicated by split lines.

SON'AHCHI.
LO————-NG A
SONTI   GO
§
AT STANDING ARROWS
OLD LADY JUNCO HAD HER HOME
and COYOTE
Coyote was there at Sitting Rock with his children.
He was with his children.
and Old Lady Junco
was winnowing.
Pigweed
and tumbleweed, she was winnowing these.
With her basket.
she winnowed these by tossing them in the air,
She was tossing them in the air
        while Coyote
Coyote
was going around hunting, going around hunting for his
        children there
when he came to where Junco was winnowing. (1972:77)

It is evident which version is preferable if style and originality are considered. Tedlock's version, of course, cannot capture entirely the performer's personality or the context of the telling, but it comes closer than the

traditional Western style. Tedlock's use of pauses to indicate silence and features such as tone and pitch, as well as including spasmodic features (not shown here) such as spontaneous laughter, render his translations closer to the originals than anyone had been able to do before.

At about the same time, Dell Hymes was also working on translating narrative as verse, but he focused his attention on recurring initial elements which he believed to be the regulatory principle within the narratives of Chinookan as well as other Native American oral narratives (1977). In such myths as Louis Simpson's "The Deserted Boy," a Wasco-Wishram text (an eastern dialect of Chinookan), Hymes has found that recurring initial particles that have been translated as *now, then, now then, now again*, and others are more than they appear to be in English. These particles mark measure with an initial particle pair defining the verses, which, when grouped into sets of three and five, compose stanzas.

However, not all narratives systematically use these initial particles. In those cases, it is possible to discern a pattern using other markers. A change of location, a lapse of time, or a change in participants of the action can indicate a unit as well as any set of three or five items or actions of a participant. Repetition of a noun or verb also suggests a new unit. These elements combined with the narrative form mark a pattern Hymes identifies as form-meaning covariation. He states that "while certain elements regularly serve to mark verses, this role is dependent upon the organization of the whole" (1977:440). So one of the particles may occur with its normal lexical meaning and would not indicate a narrative pattern. On the other hand, an element not normally occurring as an indicator of a new verse may appear as such depending on the other criteria. By using these syntactic criteria and content of the narrative together, Hymes is able to divide the narrative form into scenes, stanzas, verses, and lines.

Do all Native American oral narratives fit into one of these two patterns? William Bright (1980) has combined both approaches in his presentation of the Karok myth cycle, finding that initial particles mark verses where they occur and that length of pausing also marks lines and groups of lines. Others, Hymes reports (1992), have used a similar combination with varying results. According to Hymes (1980), there is a pattern in the narratives that goes beyond the simple use of pauses and particles; all Native American oral narratives have some kind of formal pattern. If there are particles, they will play a role in the organization, but the fundamental consideration is the "presence of a certain conception of narrative action" (9). Two basic types of this patterning have been found: in pairs or fours as in Karok and Zuni, or in threes and fives as in the Chinookan languages and their neighbors Sahaptin and Kalapuyan. For example, in Tedlock's translation of "Coyote and Junco" (1972), Hymes (1980) finds that there is a four-part introduction of the actors, a four-part exchange, and four times the song is lost and returned in two scenes. This patterning has to be deliberate; it simply could not just be chance.

Overall, the dichotomy between these two approaches is more about their focus than about how oral narratives can actually be written as verse. While one approach centers on the speaking of the narrative and attending to the performance, the other focuses on the patterning within the narrative based on numbers, but neither approach disregards the other. The two approaches are not mutually exclusive; what matters is what is to be found in the narrative.

While it is evident below that pairs of numbers are recurrent in many ways in the myths, it is not clear why a particular pair of numbers, two and four or three and five, are so important. Many cultures, not just Native American, have attached special significance to certain numbers based on natural phenomena, the body, or religion. Many Native American tribes consider four and seven to be sacred; we can see the significance of four in the four directions, the four times of day (dawn, morning, noon, sunset), the four times of night (dusk, evening, midnight, aurora), four phases of the moon, four seasons, four parts to growing things (root, stem, leaf, fruit), four stages of life (babyhood, childhood, adulthood, old age), and so forth. Seven is also seen as sacred; again for the directions including the four cardinal directions plus center, above, and below, and as the number for sacred prayers or ceremonies (e.g., reciting seven prayers in a row or holding ceremonies on the seventh day after a new moon). Various cultures view three and five as sacred; three may be based on the triangle of earth, sky, and water or fire, air, and water. The number five may also pertain to the natural world but expanded: earth, fire, water, air, and ether. Our bodies also incorporate the number five: five senses, five fingers per hand, five toes per foot.

Whichever numbers a particular culture deems sacred, they do play an important role in the myths. Originally, these stories were told not just for entertainment purposes (after all, the audience had repeatedly heard most of them throughout their lives) but for instructional value, self-awareness, and understanding of the world and one's place in it. Felix White Sr. of the Hocák remarks that as four has always been a significant number in his culture, stories always reflected this in structure as well as number of stories to be told in a sitting (Danker 1985:29). Perhaps the more elements that can be incorporated into a story that can reinforce its importance as a part of the culture, the better the audience adheres to the lessons of the stories. When used as instructional devices, the story must be a part of the lives of the people, as real to them as the earth, moon, sun, animals, and other natural elements that are in their daily lives. These stories weren't just told and forgotten until the next telling; people discussed them, thought about them, used them to guide their behaviors and interactions. Sacred numbers running throughout them only helped to make the stories more understandable and real.

Being able to render Native American myths as performances rather than as simply words on a page is a huge leap forward, but that is not all there is to these myths. Part of the performance, in addition to hearing the original voice and discovering the patterning of numbers, is the form of the story. One group of Native American languages that has mastered both of these elements is known as the Siouan languages, a group of about twenty languages with probably Crow and Dakota as the most familiar. Unfortunately, many of the Siouan languages are already extinct or nearly so.

Siouan myths are best represented in verse form, and central to remaining faithful to this form is the interpretation of narrative particles found in the originals. Narrative particles are "little" words that to westerners seem to be fillers and are interpreted variously as *then, well, like that, now, still, even, yet, and, because*, and so forth. In early translations these particles were ignored, because to English speakers the excessive number of them and the many repetitious uses are quite unlike anything found in Western stories. However, Siouan myths have a certain essential characteristic patterning to its narratives, which depends on how these narrative particles, and pauses, work together to form patterns of pairs and fours. Such patterning allows us to appreciate the artistry of these narratives, which is otherwise lost in the more typical Western translations where the verse form is replaced by paragraphs.

In both languages to be examined here, Dakota and Hocák, a half dozen or so narrative particles play a role in introducing the discourse units of each myth. Hocák, formerly known as Winnebago, is spoken by about 250 speakers in Wisconsin and Nebraska, although the tribe has recently undertaken measures to increase the number of speakers. Dakota has more speakers, up to 5,000, and is spoken in North and South Dakota, Montana, Nebraska, Oregon, and Minnesota. Both languages are part of the Mississippi Valley branch of the Siouan family. In Hocák the main narrative particles are *zheegú, háá, eesge, higú, zheejága,* and *hagorehizhá,* and each narrative particle has a specific function within the context of the myth: *zheejága* and *hagorehizhá* establish a time frame, and *zheegú, eesge, háá,* and *higú* relate narrated events to one another. In Dakota the narrative particles *uŋkaŋ, hećen, tuka, ito, hehan,* and *wanŋa* relate events to one another, while *e, iŋyuŋ kaked,* and *iho* establish time frames.

We can see how the formal patterning in Hocák, a language where the patterning occurs in twos and fours, interacts with the narrative particles to create structure in the myth titled "The Sumac." First, "The Sumac" is a story about how Wakjákaga, the Foolish One, climbs up a hill while searching for people and hears the sound of a drum beating. He decides there must be people dancing nearby. When he shouts to them, he gets no response: the people keep on dancing. He decides he will show them what good dancing really is, and he dances from noon to sundown. When he finally looks over, all the dancers have stopped, and Wakjákaga shouts to them again, but still gets no response. He climbs down the hill and over to where the people are, only to discover that the yellow and red feathers he thought they were wearing are actually the leaves of the sumac, set to "dancing" in the breeze. The drum he had heard was only the beating of his own heart from the exertion of the climb.

This is a rather short and bland story by Western standards, but when it is told as the performance it was meant to be, it really comes alive. To capture this, Kathleen Danker, who originally translated this myth as part of her dissertation, "The Winnebago Narratives of Felix White, Sr.: Style, Structure and Function," has found the number four to be significant in Hocák, along with groupings of two; there are four scenes in each of four acts, with an introduction and a conclusion. The lines within each verse are grouped in twos or fours as well, where nearly every line begins with one of the narrative particles. A careful examination of these lines reveals that the interplay of content and form is not accidental and that the narrative particles are used to mark this patterning as part of the artistry and as part of the structure. Below is a synopsis of the action in the myth. In nearly every verse, the action occurs in pairs:

I	i	Wakjákaga sees the hills and trees
		hurries towards them
	ii	comes to the hill
		climbs the hill
	iii	stops
		listens
	iv	listens again
		climbs again
II	i	steps onto hilltop
		looks over to other side
	ii	calls to dancers
		they don't pay any attention to him
	iii	hollers, "Hey!"
		says, "Hey! I've come back!"
	iv	assumes they are competing for best dancer
		decides to show them how good dancing is done
III	i	places short things from his backpack on ground
		places other backpack contents on the ground
	ii	war whoops (calls) again
		says, "YII-YI"
	iii	the dancers don't pay any attention to him
		decides to put an end to that
	iv	dances around
		does not stop all afternoon
IV	i	dances hard
		looks down to hill below where dancers are
	ii	beats his chest
		war whoops again
	iii	ignored again
		wonders what is going on
	iv	picks up backpack
		goes down hill
		arrives where dancers are
		realizes dancers are sumac leaves (Danker 1985:74–81)

Only in one instance does the action not occur in a pair, but it is described in a pair: in III.ii there is only the war whooping. First, the narrator says he must have warwhooped, then he imitates Wakjákaga doing it.

This may be because the action of calling is one of the more important actions in the story, which does occur a total of four times. The most important actions in this myth do occur in pairs and fours. In act I, Wakjákaga climbs the hill where he is able to see the dancers (scene ii), then climbs again (scene iv). He stops to listen in scene iii, and listens again in scene iv. In act II he calls to the dancers, who pay no attention to him (scene ii), then calls again, and still no one looks at him (iii). In act III, in preparing to dance, Wakjákaga places short things from his backpack on the ground, then sets more things on the ground (scene i). At the end of act III, he dances (scene iv); at the beginning of act IV, he dances hard (scene i).

There are other parallels within the myth. Overall, Wakjákaga calls to the dancers four times, and four times he does not get an answer. Also, the sound of the drum beating is imitated four times: twice in act I, once in act II, and lastly in act III. It is also notable that when Wakjákaga sees the dancers' feathers, the colors are described in a pair, red and yellow, but later, when he realizes the feathers are the leaves of the sumac, the colors are described in a foursome—red, yellow, intensely yellow, and a mixture.

The movement of the myth is also depicted in fours. In act I, Wakjákaga comes to the hill and climbs the hill. In act II, he steps onto the hill, and finally, in act IV, he goes down the hill. This patterning of the action suggests that the focus is the hill, the place where Wakjákaga comes to, dances, and leaves. This fits well because, first, the climb up the hill is what makes Wakjákaga's heart pound, and second, there must be enough distance between Wakjákaga and the sumac leaves for him to be fooled.

The narrative particles also contribute to the patterns found in the myth. Danker recognized four stanzas and an introduction and conclusion partially by recognizing one or another of the narrative particles, such as *hagore-(hi)zhá* or *zheejága*, which can occur either alone or in conjunction with another, as markers. With four exceptions, every verse also begins with a narrative particle; three of the four exceptions are the beginning of a direct quote. It may seem that this makes it easy to tell where stanzas and verses would be, but of the fifty-eight lines of "The Sumac," twenty-nine begin with a narrative particle, and another sixteen are quotes. Only eight lines are not marked. (See the appendix for an outline of "The Sumac" with the pattern of the narrative particles and the pitch following each.) Nearly every line begins with one or the other of the particles, including quotations, and is almost always followed by rising pitch.

The introduction and conclusion are marked by *háá*, and the time frame is established at the beginning with *hagorehizhá*.

Danker (1983) states that the myths typically begin with *eegi* ('and') to indicate that any one story is part of the larger cycle of stories about Wakjákaga and that the storyteller is resuming where he last finished in the cycle (28). In this case, the storyteller, Felix White Sr., may not have started "The Sumac" with the traditional *eegi* because, as Danker (1993) states, White will usually begin with this story when asked to tell a number of stories together (525), and so forego the "and," since this is considered a beginning for him.

We can find the same patterning and use of the narrative particles in the Dakota myths. As an example, we can explore the myth "Legend of the Head of Gold," as written by Walking Elk and published by Stephen Riggs (1893). All of the texts in this publication were written out by native speakers and so were not performed. There is evidence that the Dakota-speakers were probably aware that the texts were meant for a Western audience. For example, at the end of "Legend of the Heart of Gold," Walking Elk adds an explanation of the myth, telling the reader why the hero acts as he does, and also comments that his actions are like those of Sitting Bull (109). It seems highly unlikely that such a comment was part of the original myth. Still, the narrative particles appear to mark lines and could easily be used to mark verses, and the patterns of two and four are evident if not as prominent in the Hocák.

"Legend of the Heart of Gold" is about a boy whose father gives him to the Great Spirit so that he does not die of starvation. The Great Spirit takes the boy in and leaves him to watch over his home and horses while he goes on two journeys, but warns the boy to stay out of a small house on the grounds. Once the Great Spirit leaves on the second journey, one of the horses urges the boy to go into the small house and dip his head into the pool of yellow, because when the Great Spirit comes back with many men, they will eat both the horse and the boy. Believing it, the boy goes in, dips his head into the golden pool, and returns to gallop away upon the horse. The Great Spirit goes after them but the boy throws an egg back, which opens up the earth and creates an ocean. The Great Spirit tries to cross but drowns, and the boy goes safely on to a village. But here they are attacked, and the boy turns his golden head and causes almost everyone to fall off their horses, whereupon the boy leaves them. They attack again, and this time the boy destroys them all.

The patterning of twos and fours shows up many times in this myth. The boy hero is the youngest of four sons, and the action occurs in four places: the hill, the Great Spirit's house, the ocean, and the village. There is also an introduction and a conclusion. More prevalent is the pattern of twos. The Great Spirit tells the boy twice to watch over his house, and twice he warns him to stay out of the small house. Twice he leaves on a journey, and twice he returns with many men. When the Great Spirit catches up with the fleeing boy, twice he tells him to stop and twice he warns him he will die. When confronted with the ocean, the Great Spirit has to urge his horse to cross twice. And finally, once the boy is free of the Great Spirit, twice he is attacked by men.

This patterning is set off by narrative particles in every case. The four major scene breaks are introduced by *hećen iho*, which is glossed as 'so behold.' This transition occurs in one other place as well, when the boy stays behind a second time as the Great Spirit sets off on his second journey. This indicates a transition where the boy is again alone, but the scene does not change. For almost every action in the text, *uŋkaŋ*, which is variously glossed as 'then,' 'when,' or 'and,' appears at the beginning of the line. This narrative particle can be used to determine what this myth might look like in verse structure. Below is the outline of the first scene after the introduction:

hećen iho	They go westward to seek the Great Spirit
	and come on a large hill
uŋkaŋ	and as they come to it
	a man comes toward where they stand
uŋkaŋ	and the man speaks
	what do you seek?
uŋkaŋ	and the Old Man speaks
	I want the Great Spirit to take my child
uŋkaŋ	and the man says he is the Great Spirit
	and agrees to take the child home

Here, *hećen iho* sets the scene; *uŋkaŋ* begins each verse, and each verse can conceivably be broken into two lines. The final scene also works in patterns but not in exactly the same way. Again, *hećen* introduces the scene and four verses follow: three introduced by *uŋkaŋ* and the fourth by *ćaŋkeŋ*, another particle meaning "therefore." The internal "ands" are a different word, *ka*, which connects closely related events within a sentence.

hećen	the boy safely crosses the ocean
uŋkaŋ	The boy comes to a village
	and they are there
uŋkaŋ	and they are attacked from behind
	and they fight
	and the boy turns his head
	and his hair is gold all over
	and the horse becomes golden
	and those who attacked fell off their horses
	and he spared them
	and they left
uŋkaŋ	and again they attack
	and he destroyed them
ćaŋkeŋ	Therefore, the people think highly of him

Instead of pairs each time, we have one central section with eight events, all centered around the point of the story, the boy's golden head.

When the narrative particles appear repetitiously in the originals, they are usually edited out because in the traditional way westerners tell stories, repetition of words simply does not sound good. In the above example, Riggs left most of the "ands" in or changed them to "but" so that the prose form reads as a long, run-on type of sentence: "**But** from behind they came to attack, **and** fought with them; **but** the boy turned his head around, **and** his head was covered with gold, the horse also that he sat upon was golden, **and** those who came against them, he caused to be thrown off, **and** only a few remained when he left them" (1893:109, emphasis added).

This occurs in all the myths Riggs translated. A passage in "The Fallen Star" reads much the same: "The young man went, **and** came to where people lived, **and** lo! they were engaged in shooting arrows through a hoop. **And** there was a young man who was simply looking on, **and** so he stood beside him **and** looked on" (1893:91, emphasis added). So if the repetition of the particles is left out, then the translation seems to be something quite different than the original; but if the repetition is left in, then it reads rather haltingly and not as smoothly as we are accustomed to. How can we resolve this problem?

This problem can be resolved through rendering the myths in verse form, which is exactly what Kathleen Danker and many others have done.

Danker was able to do this by using the repetitions as indicators of lines along with some other criteria, such as the parallelism found in the forms; the alliteration, assonance, pauses and intonation; and the structuring function of the other narrative particles. She uses downward arrows to indicate falling pitch; upward arrows indicate rising pitch. Bold arrows indicate a drawn-out syllable. Superscript numerals indicate length of pauses in seconds, with ^{sp} indicating a pause of less than .7 seconds. Evidence of verse structure can be found in a passage in "Wašjígega Snares the Sun—Version Two" from her original translation of the Hocák narrative (Danker 1985:205, 227). Here, *zheegú* is repetitive, and coupled with the intonation and pitch patterns, it clearly indicates verse (NARR stands for "narrative particle"):

III iii 2 **zheegú↑** hatazazanak↓
      NARR flickering light
      Because it was a flickering light.

      zheegú↑ rukánákánáp↓
      NARR reflect brightly
      Because it reflected brightly

      zhee(gú)↑ gišíníšíní↓^{1.6}
      NARR to gleam
      Because it shone.

There are other instances where the narrative particle creates a discernible pattern such as at the end of "The Buzzard," another narrative translated by Danker (1985:108, 130):

IV iv 4 **zheegú↑**^{.99}
      NARR
      And then

      ruuxa(h)irešgúní↓
      chase-him-they-must
      they must have chased him

5 **zheegú↑**

NARR

And then

ná(áh)íñoj(h)íñánášge
wood-to hit him-they-also
they hit him with sticks

However, this parallelism does not always work out so well in translation. There are instances where the narrative particle begins lines in a series, but there is no English word or phrase that neatly translates into these slots as in the above examples. The following example from Danker's "The Sumac" (Danker 1985:76, 87) appears to have some kind of parallel form as the ones above, but the translation cannot reflect this very well:

I iv 4	**zheegú↑**	zhige↑sp	
	NARR	again	
	Then again		
	zheegú↑	xee	rooti↑
	NARR	hill	he-climb-it
	he climbed the hill		
	zheegú↑	máášjá↑	úšgúní↓[1.89]
	NARR	strong	he-must-do-it
	he must have done it energetically		

Although *zheegú* appears at the beginning of each phrase, there is no good way to render these instances in English. In this case, while we may ignore the repetition in the translation, the parallel use of the narrative particle clearly indicates separate lines.

It is clear that in both Hocák and Dakota, sacred numbers play an important role in structuring verse, and I believe that as much of that patterning should remain in the translations as possible. The discourse particles found in both languages are obvious markers that show an overall structure of stanzas and lines. While they may seem repetitive or intrusive to some, they are necessary in structuring the story and conveying the artistry in the telling. Translating Native American myths into verse structure rather than typical Western paragraph form better preserves the original creativity and elegance that must be part of the story as well. Being diligent in preserving the repetitions that occur because of the sacred number patterns may sound a bit odd to Western ears, but since it is an integral part of the stories, they should remain in translation. Discourse particles are important in structuring the story, but the individual artistry of the storyteller is just as important, and that is likely why the pattern sometimes does not quite fit. More often than not, however, the basic structure can be found through the particles, along with the pitch, loudness, and tone of the storyteller.

Suggested Reading

For more information on discourse particles in general, Deborah Schiffrin's *Discourse Markers* is the place to start. Her work gives the reader a grounding in how those little words we take for granted—*oh, well*, and *y'know* as well as our connectives, casuals, and time words—function to structure text in conversation. *Approaches to Discourse Particles*, edited by Kerstin Fischer, explores two theoretical views on how particles work. Of particular interest is chapter 6, "Pragmatic Markers in Translation: A Methodological Proposal," an article by Karin Aijmer, Ad Foolen, and Anne-Marie Simon-Vendenbergen on translating particles.

For more on verse structure when translating Native American languages, Joel Sherzer is definitely one to read. Sherzer and Kay Sammons published an edited volume titled *Translating Native Latin American Verbal Art*, a collection of performances with linguistic analysis and discussions of translation problems.

There are many good collections of translated Native American stories and myths that allow us to catch a glimpse of the heart and psyche of a people. Specifically for Hocák, David Lee Smith has an excellent collection detailing the creation and trickster stories as well as other myths and legends: *Folklore of the Winnebago Tribe*. Lewis Spence has a large collection of Siouan myths as well as other North American tribes titled *North American Indians: Myths and Legends*. Brian Swann's comprehensive collection, *Coming to Light: Contemporary Translation of the Native Literatures of North America*, contains stories from a wide variety of cultures and languages of North America and many of these translations follow the original verse structure. Karl Kroeber's *Native American Storytelling: A Reader of Myths and Legends* is another excellent source that samples from across languages and cultures.

Pronunciation Guide

The symbols used in this chapter follow those used in Kathleen Danker's dissertation, from which all the Hocák examples were taken. The few Dakota words used in this text also use these symbols.

Vowels

i	sounds like the vowel in b*ea*t
e	sounds like the vowel in b*ai*t
a	sounds like the vowel in b*a*t
u	sounds like the vowel b*oo*t
o	sounds like the vowel b*oa*t
á, í, ú	nasalized vowels, as though an *n* followed them

Consonants

p	sounds like the first sound in *p*ot
t	sounds like the first sound in *t*ot
k	sounds like the first sound in *c*ot
b	sounds like the first sound in *b*ought
g	sounds like the first sound in *g*ot
ć	sounds like the first sound in *ch*urch
j	sounds like the first sound in *j*udge
s	sounds like the first sound in *s*ought
š	sounds like the first sound in *sh*ot
x	the German sound in *Ich*, no English equivalent
h	sounds like the first sound in *h*ot
zh	sounds like the middle sound in vi*s*ion
m	sounds like the first sound in *m*oat
n	sounds like the first sound in *n*ote
ñ	a flap of the tongue against the roof of the mouth, pronounced as *n*
ŋ	sounds like the final sound in si*ng*
w	sounds like the first sound in *w*et
y	sounds like the first sound in *y*et

Appendix: "The Sumac"

Act	Scene	Line	Gloss
Intro	1	háá↑hagorehizhá↑ zheegú↑.93	yes
	2	eesge↑ zheegú↑	SO NARR
I i	1	HAGORE-(HI)ZHÁ↑1.5	one time
	2	—	
ii	1	HÁÁ↑	YES
	2	—	
	3	eesge	SO
	4	zheegú↑	NARR
iii	1	háá zheegú↑	yes NARR
	2	gajá↑ zheegú	AFTER NARR
	3	HEE↓2.1 (quote)	hey (interjection)
	4	zheegú↑sp	NARR
iv	1	(hi)gú-zhiga↑	STILL-AGAIN
	2	—	
	3	hii↓1.36 (quote)	hii (interjection)
	4	zheegú↑	NARR
II i	1	zheeja-ga	Finally
	2	zheegú↑	NARR
	3	zheegú↑	NARR
	4	—	
ii	1	HEE↑ (quote)	hey (interjection)
	2	gajá↑ zheegú	AFTER NARR
	3	higú↑	STILL
	4	—	
iii	1	hee↓1.36 (hi)gú-zhige(quote)	hey (interjection) STILL-again
	2	zheegú↑	NARR
iv	1	HÁÁ↑ (quote)	YES
	2	HEE↓sp zheegú (quote)	hey (interjection) NARR
	3	zheegú↑ (quote)	NARR
	4	(hi)-gú (quote)	STILL

Act	Scene	Line	Gloss
III i	1	eesge↑	SO
	2	—	
	3	—	
	4	—	
ii	1	zheejága↑ zheegú↓$^{2.1}$	finally NARR
	2	YII↑YI↓ (quote)	yii-yi (war whoop)
iii	1	—	
	2	HAA↑ zheejága↑ (quote)	ha (interjection)
iv	1	zheegú	NARR
	2	—	
	3	—	
	4	zheegú↑$^{2.62}$ zheeg(ú)	NARR
			NARR
IV i	1	zheejága↑ hagore-(hi)zhá	finally one time
		zheegú↑	NARR
	2	—	
IV ii	1	háá↑ zheejága↓sp zheejága↑	yes finally
			finally
			(quote)
	2	—	
iii	1	zheegú↑sp	NARR
	2	zheegú↑	NARR
iv	1	eesge↑ zheegú↑	SO NARR
	2	tee hagore-(hi)zhá	this one time
	3	zheegú↑sp	NARR
	4	—	
	5	HII↑sp(quote)	hey (interjection)
	6	— (quote)	
Conclusion			
	1	háá↑ zheegú	yes NARR
	2	—	
	3	—	
	4	HIIHÁ↑ eegi↓	now and

References

Aijmer, Karin, Ad Foolen, and Anne-Marie Simon-Vendenbergen. 2006. Pragmatic Markers in Translation: A Methodological Proposal. In *Approaches to Discourse Particles*, ed. Kerstin Fischer, 101–14. Studies in Pragmatics 1. Ed. Bruce Fraser. Oxford: Elsevier.

Bierhorst, John. 1985. *The Mythology of North America*. New York: William Morrow.

Bright, William. 1980. Coyote's Journey. *American Indian Culture and Research Journal* 4:21–48.

Danker, Kathleen A. 1985. "The Winnebago Narratives of Felix White, Sr.: Style, Structure and Function." PhD Diss., University of Nebraska–Lincoln.

———.1993. Because of This I Am Called the Foolish One: Felix White, Sr.'s, Interpretations of the Winnebago Trickster. In *New Voices in Native American Literary Criticism*, ed. Arnold Krupat, 505–28. Smithsonian Series of Studies in Native American Literatures. Washington DC: Smithsonian Institute Press.

Hymes, Dell. 1977. Discovering Oral Performance and Measured Verse in American Indian Narrative. *New Literary History* 8:431–57.

———.1980. Particle, Pause and Pattern in American Indian Narrative Verse. *American Indian Culture and Research Journal* 4:7–51.

———. 1981. *"In Vain I Tried to Tell You": Essays in Native American Ethnopoetics*. Philadelphia: University of Pennsylvania Press.

———.1992. Use All There Is to Use. In *On the Translation of Native American Literatures*, ed. Brian Swann, 83–124. Washington DC: Smithsonian Institution Press.

Kroeber, Karl, ed. 2004. *Native American Storytelling: A Reader of Myths and Legends*. Malden MA: Blackwell.

Krupat, Arnold. 1992. On the Translation of Native American Song and Story: A Theorized History. In *On the Translation of Native American Literatures*, ed. Brian Swann, 3–32. Washington DC: Smithsonian Institution Press.

Mourning Dove. 1990. *Coyote Stories*. Ed. Heister Dean Guie. 1933. Lincoln: University of Nebraska Press.

Radin, Paul. 1949. *The Culture of the Winnebago: As Described by Themselves*. Indiana University Publications and Linguistics, Memoir II. Baltimore: Waverly Press.

———.1956. *The Trickster: A Study in American Indian Mythology*. New York: Schocken.

———.1985. "Winnebago Tales." *Journal of American Folklore* 22:288–313.

Riggs, Stephen Return. 1893. *Dakota Grammar, Texts, and Ethnography*. Ed. James Owen Dorsey. Contributions to North American Ethnology, vol. 9. Washington DC: Department of the Interior.

Roemer, Kenneth M. 1983. Context and Continuity. In *Smoothing the Ground: Es-*

says on *Native American Oral Literature*, ed. Brian Swann, 39–54. Berkeley: University of California Press.

Sammons, Kay, and Joel Sherzer, eds. 2000. *Translating Native Latin American Verbal Art: Ethnopoetics and Ethnography of Speaking.* Washington DC: Smithsonian Institution Press.

Schiffrin, Deborah. 1987. *Discourse Markers.* Studies in Interactional Sociolinguistics 5. Ed. John Gumperz. Cambridge: Cambridge University Press.

Sherzer, Joel, and Anthony C. Woodbury. 1987. Introduction. In Native American *Discourse: Poetics and Rhetoric*, ed. Joel Sherzer and Anthony C. Woodbury, 1–16. Cambridge: Cambridge University Press.

Smith, David Lee. 1997. *Folklore of the Winnebago Tribe.* Norman: University of Oklahoma Press.

Spence, Lewis. 1984. *North American Indians: Myths and Legends.* London: Senate.

Swann, Brian, ed. 1994. *Coming to Light: Contemporary Translations of the Native Literatures of North America.* New York: Vintage.

Tedlock, Dennis. 1972. *Finding the Center: Narrative Poetry of the Zuni Indians.* New York: Dial Press.

———. 1983. On the Translation of Style in Oral Narrative. In *Smoothing the Ground: Essays on Native American Oral Literature*, ed. Brian Swann, 57–77. Berkeley: University of California Press.

Thompson, Stith. 1929. *Tales of the North American Indians.* Cambridge: Harvard University Press.

15

Toward Literature

Preservation of Artistic Effects in Choctaw Texts

Marcia Haag

The Challenges of Translation in the Verbal Arts

The Insuperable Problem of Language Structure

The central problem of translation, namely, the competition between faithfulness to meaning and preservation of form, grows more attenuated as translation moves from simple conveyance of information to artistic forms. Generally, in working with translations among European languages, the translator struggles with word choices when one language contains a particular word that denotes or connotes an idea that the other language does not. Then the translator seeks synonyms, or may resort to a phrase that more completely captures the sense intended. The translator may also have to deal with problems of grammatical structure: a language may lack a particular verbal tense or mood overtly marked in the original language's morphology, necessitating a substitution or use of calques that catches the meaning but misses the elegance of expression or the element of surprise or charm that the original depicted. One of my favorite examples is Gustavo Adolfo Bécquer's lines from *Rimas XXI* (1965): "Qué es poesía . . . Poesía eres tu." The subject of the *rima* has been "poesía," and this form continues to the last line. Literally, the last line means "poetry are you," or perhaps "poetry is you," or "you are poetry." In the first pass the English is funny, in the second it is boring, and in the third the meter is ruined. The fact that Spanish allows preposing of a predicate in the normal course of events permits the charm of the unexpected change in subject.

When languages begin to depart greatly from each other, the translator is forced to make consequential choices. If the translator chooses to remain faithful to the structure of the original language, differences, not to say mismatches, in structure, word choice, and discourse function in the target language (the language into which the work is translated) are part of what the reader grapples with. The reward is greater authenticity at the price of increased strangeness.

A pair of translations of the same work, the Yuchi story "Wolf and Fawn" by William Cahwee, taken from the volume of translations of Native literatures *Voices from Four Directions* (Swann 2004), illustrate radically different foci. The first, by Josephine Barnett Keith, Josephine Wildcat Bigler (both speakers of Yuchi), and Mary S. Linn (a linguist), attempts to show as closely as possible what the original language depicted or coded. They put information about the grammar in brackets to help the reader know what is contained in the Yuchi language while keeping the phrase and clause structure as faithful to the original as possible.

> Long time ago,
> the old people [now deceased] would get together.
> They would talk about bad things [referring to ghosts and evil].
> And sometimes one would get scared
> when they got together [for the purpose of telling stories].
> They talked together, sitting there.
> They were there talking together.
> Someone said that Wolf was there [emphatic, true].
> And he [an animal] was going there,
> Through the brush, he was going,
> Wolf,
> and Fawn, he was there. (Swann 2004:377)

It is of interest that the translation team chose not to use synonyms, add modifiers, or use tools from the English literary armamentarium to render the sense of this passage. Neither did they rely on the common interpretation of the narrative. For instance, in the second line, most readers of English would assume that "a long time ago" those "old people" who are the subject of the sentence would indeed now be deceased.

We are lucky to have William Cahwee's own translation of his story following the team's translation. It is remarkably different from the team's, and if the first translation strives to be as faithful as possible to the Yuchi language, Cahwee seems to be far less concerned about this in favor of getting to the important narrative points of the story.

> The story I told was about this Wolf and the Deer.
> And this Deer run up to this Wolf,
> I mean, this Wolf come up to this Deer and ask him,
> he said,
> "You know, I'd like to be spotted like you are," he said.
> He said,
> "Can you tell me," he said, "how you got spotted like that?"
> (Swann 2004:380)

The reader will note immediately that the two translations do not seem to be related to each other in any strict or even loose linguistic way, yet they are both right: the translation team has painstakingly rendered the Yuchi into English in the closest structural and lexical way possible, and the author is after all the author: he is entitled to say what his text means with a unique authority. The reader cannot help but notice, however, that the author has a different level of fluency in English than he has in Yuchi. Would he translate differently if he had a larger vocabulary and another set of storytelling devices?

A Word about Native American Languages

Laypeople—that is to say, non-experts in the structure of languages—tend to hold a number of well-motivated beliefs about the languages of the Americas. I will briefly discuss three of these to couch my later remarks about the structure of Choctaw in particular.

One idea is that of polysynthesis. In simplest terms, this concept refers to the tendency (but not an inevitable one) for American languages to incorporate several grammatical constituents, particularly into the verb. Hence, the word-form that includes the verb will commonly include grammatical particles that pertain to verbal properties such as tense and aspect, but also those that mark subject, object, other participants in the sentence, information about the direction of movement, and in the most extreme case, called noun incorporation, even include the word that names the direct object. An example follows here from Mohawk, an Iroquoian language (Baker 1988:103).

Wa-hi-'sereht'anvhsko.
past-he-my car-stole
He stole my car.

The reader will note the often-observed fact that one such word is a full sentence on its own. For a more detailed analysis, the reader might consult Mithun (1999).

A second idea is that American languages are verb-oriented rather than noun-oriented, making them more "dynamic" and less "static." This idea borrows from grammar school definitions of "parts of speech": verbs express actions, and nouns express things. This idea is correct as far as it goes: linguistically, verbs are canonically associated with predicates and nouns with arguments, or what the predicate pertains to. If a language is structured to include in its predicate not only the verb but an incorporated direct object, all the information about the relationships among the participants in the sentence, and all the information about the way time is organized, it will be predicate-heavy indeed. Not many linguists, though, will endorse a necessary relationship between massive predicates and "dynamism." Indeed, these same languages may just as readily "nominalize" an entire clause (more formally, make it an argument of the sentence), but the notion that American languages have gigantic nouns seems not to have captured the layperson's imagination.

So, does the structure of a language shape the way we view the world? This question deserves a careful answer, and indeed, this idea even has its own named hypothesis, the Whorfian Hypothesis, or the Sapir-Whorf Hypothesis, after Edward Sapir's brilliant student Benjamin Whorf, who was one of the first to academically ponder this question (Whorf 1956). First, it must be the case that persons who speak languages that use a multitude of special honorifics and politeness forms (e.g., Japanese and Korean) or elaborate kinship systems (languages of Australia) organize their societies in a way such that these categories are salient. Peoples who live in cities and in jungles must have relevant vocabularies to describe and organize their experiences.

But what about structure itself? Can the ways that syntax and morphology are organized have a bearing on how speakers of languages view the world? Here the problem is not how vocabulary items reflect a society, but what concepts have been grammaticalized. Linguists like to point out that "it's not what you *can* say, it's what you *must* say." It is perhaps fair to say that, while grammar probably does not hardwire the language component of the brain, it constantly directs the speaker of a language to categorize, not the universe itself, but the description of the universe, in particular ways and not in others.

Particular Points of Structural Variance in Choctaw and English

Among the many points of Choctaw grammar that can cause translation difficulties, two are sketched here. Perhaps surprisingly, the grammatical structures that are most difficult to grasp in learning Choctaw are not necessarily those that cause translation problems. To illustrate, the difficult French negation rules are cumbersome and unintuitive for the English student of French, but map readily to English concepts.

Je n'en ai pas acheté.
I didn't buy any of them.

The rules governing the annoying two-part negator *ne pas* and the placement of the indefinite pronoun *en* have to be memorized, but the concept—the meaning of the sentence—is completely consonant with its English counterpart.

In contrast, the English and Choctaw *concepts* of how definiteness and specificity are handled are not mapable to each other, even though the mechanism for the marking itself, a set of affixes, is quite simple.

English wrings as much work as possible from the articles *a* and *the* and a few other demonstratives. A native speaker knows how to use these to refer to new information, to things already in evidence, to particular things, and to general members of a set. If these will not pick out something to a fine enough degree, we also can use a range of other constructions, such as relative clauses, adverbs, and even idioms to make finer distinctions. But these are not *grammaticalized*—they are tools the speaker may use to clarify an utterance, not mandatory.

In strong contrast, Choctaw has a large, finely articulated, and morphologically efficient system to mark definiteness, contrast, specificity, and the like. A large set of affixes marks information about how specific something is, whether it has been mentioned previously, when in the discourse it was mentioned, whether it contrasts with something else in the discourse, how particularly it contrasts, whether it is part of a set, and other distinctions that are literally not possible to categorize in English.

The result in translation is that at some point, not only do English words fail, but some of the distinctions cannot even be made in a meaningful way. More precisely, we can perhaps capture the essence of the Choctaw distinctions, but only at the cost of a cumbersome sentence that would never be uttered by an English-speaker.

In this example contrasting the Choctaw New Testament with the King James version of Bible, taken from Haag and Willis (2007:124), we see that the English pronoun *he* covers for a much finer set of distinctions in the Choctaw definiteness system. The Choctaw markers and glosses are in bold.

> and when **he** was come into the house (King James Bible, Matthew 9:28)
> Mihma **yammak ash osh** aboha ont chukoa ma (Choctaw New Testament)
> And when **the one being discussed** entered the room (gloss)

In a second example, Choctaw makes a clear distinction between the two participants in the sentence, one that simply does not occur in English:

> We know that God spake unto Moses. (King James Bible, John 9:29)
> Moses **ak okano** Chihowa **yat** im-anumpuli beka toka il-ithana. (Choctaw New Testament)
> We know that Moses **the particular one in contrast to others was the one whom** Jehovah **the definite subject of this clause** used to talk to. (gloss)

It is important to note that these texts were translated from English into Choctaw by native speakers of Choctaw, and that those translators inserted the definiteness markers where none existed in English because the Choctaw texts could only be fully understood with them in place. Again, it is not what Choctaw-speakers can say, but what they must say.

Clause Structure

A second important and systemic difference between Choctaw and English is the tight structure of clauses, which permits many—a dozen or more—predicative expressions to be packed into a single sentence. This is the routine way of speaking and writing, and achieves great elegance.

Here is a single Choctaw sentence in broad (not literal) gloss taken from the story "Amofi anoti Sinti" ("My Dog and the Snake") by Henry Willis (Haag and Willis 2001:228):

> And so because I wanted to eat cake I hurried out to the henhouse went in put my hand in the highest nest something bit my hand and I was terrified and I cried screaming loudly so the dog heard me and ran and came in and jumped higher than both my head and the nest saw the snake snatched it put it in her mouth took it outside gnawed it to death turned back came and licked my hand lay down at my feet to watch protecting me.

In Choctaw, the narrative sense of this story, its development in time, and the roles of the actors are quite clear because of the definiteness markers mentioned above, and also because the clauses have special marking that shows which subject they are predicated of and whether they are modifying clauses or main predicates. In English, the prose is stark and needs to be heavily parsed, but is understandable in the barest narrative sense.

But what about the preservation of artistic effects? We cannot translate the grammatical markers that make the Choctaw story so compact, but to leave them out would give the impression that the Choctaws are a terse, laconic folk who lack anything we would term a "style." It would seem that one tack the translator could take would be to find the English sentence structure that might reflect the way an elderly man with a country upbringing would recount a story of his youth.

Returning to the Choctaw sentence above, the translator might notice that the first clause begins with a discourse device *mihma* 'and so,' and concludes with a marker with no English equivalent, but which marks it as being picked out in time. The translator might then begin: "And so, because I did indeed want some cake to eat" or "And so, because I sure did want to eat that cake my mother had promised me" (we know this from the previous sentence).

The result here is not a pure translation or a retelling of the story in English that is the second language of the author, but a careful movement to what, we dare to hope, would be the effect of the Choctaw version on the reader if he understood the language.

We are fortunate to have Mr. Willis's own translation of his story (2001:229).

Then, having a taste for cake, I rushed into the hen house and reached my hand into the highest hen's nest, and something bit my hand. I was terrified and responded with a screaming, loud cry that my dog heard and so came running and jumped higher than both my head and the hen's nest. Seeing a snake, she snatched it with her mouth, took it outside, and gnawed it to death, then turned and came back to lick my hand and lay down near my feet to watch and protect me.

The reader may note that while the author uses three English sentences to do the work of one in Choctaw, he preserves much of the sense of a pressing flow of events by the use of series of verbs, commas, and simple conjunctions.

Three Choctaw Poems and Three Translation Strategies
The Special Problems of Choctaw Poetry

What if the sound and form of a text are a major part of its essence? Unless we are willing to reduce poetry to the meanings of its words and phrases, and this is indeed an option, some care must be given to the effects of such phenomena as meter, word length, choices of vowels and consonants, numbers of syllables or other units per phrase, stress, and other purely phonological matters that profoundly influence our decision to name a text a poem.

If a language like Choctaw relies on nuanced grammatical markers such as the definiteness markers we examined earlier, markers that cannot be translated with any economy into English, what hope can we have of rendering a poem that sounds "beautiful" and conveys meaning in both languages?

Besides its different grammatical structure, Choctaw, like very many American languages, has a prosodic structure—the organization of syllables—that is unlike that of English and other European languages. Hence, what counts as poetic meter in English has no correspondence in Choctaw. Instead, Choctaw poetic effects must make reference to their own phonology.

In briefest terms, the crucial phonological feature of Choctaw word structure is that words do not contain stressed syllables in the way that English does: we cannot count metric feet by locating a stressed syllable and its dependent stressless sisters and allow a certain number of these to form a poetic phrase. Instead, Choctaw has "light" and "heavy" syllables: a light syllable is an initial consonant and a short vowel, while a heavy syllable consists of an initial consonant and long vowel, or any vowel and up to two consonants to close it. So, Choctaw words have a strong rhythm based on how heavy the syllables are: a heavy syllable literally lasts longer than a light one.

Only one of the poems shown below refers to Choctaw phonology in its structure. But the more interesting question here is: What would count as a poetic form in Choctaw? Poetry as we think of it, even loosely, is not a traditional form, and if there had been a traditional form of a recited verbal art, we no longer know what it was like.

Three poems appear here, written in Choctaw by three authors whose experience with poetry originates with English. It is irrefutable that the Choctaw poems are modeled on the authors' ideas of what a poem should be, and not on traditional forms.

The Hymn as Cultural Touchstone

The slim volume *Chahta vba isht taloa holisso* ('Choctaw Hymn Book') was written and compiled perhaps as early as 1829 by Alfred Wright. It featured translations and compositions by important bilinguals of the day, including Cyrus Byington and David Folsom. By 1858 it was in its sixth edition. The Hymn Book contains 168 hymns plus additional prayers. There is no written music, nor are there instructions about the melodies to accompany the verses; this knowledge is transmitted orally.

Structurally, each hymn is composed of lines of generally three or four words arranged into stanzas of four lines. Each hymn has between six and eight stanzas, and these are always sung to completion. The melodies are of common Protestant hymns and folk tunes. The hymns have the advantage that more than one can be sung to the same melody, thus increasing their utility in a congregation. The hymns are always referred to by number, not by title. Melodies are simple, with a small vocal range. The hymns are most often sung a cappella, with female voices singing an octave above the male in unison.

The themes of the hymns are few: redemption and God's love. Unsurprisingly, their vocabulary is small and repetitive, but the phrases contain full grammatical inflection. The Choctaw light/heavy syllable pattern lends itself well to 3/4 and 4/4 time signatures; indeed, it is naturally iambic. Most stanzas end with one of the emphatic particles -*shke* or -*oke*;

it is helpful that both these particles bear phonological stress. The lines rhyme only coincidentally. The cue that a stanza has ended is generally signaled with one of the emphatic particles.

Here is a verse from arguably the most popular Choctaw hymn, number 48, sung to the melody of "Amazing Grace." It is written in one of the dominant orthographies. The Greek letter upsilon (υ) denotes a vowel very much like schwa.

Shilombish Holitopa ma!
Pim anukfila hυt
Okhlilit kυnia hoka
Ish pi on tomashke.

A rough translation: "Holy Spirit! Since our minds are completely darkened, You will surely shine upon us."

It would be difficult to overstate the importance of Choctaw hymns in the lives of modern Choctaws, especially in Oklahoma. For many, the lyrics are their only connection with the language. We may speculate about why the hymns have replaced the traditional dance songs, such as the Jump Dance and the Steal Partners Dance, which have been sparsely preserved by some dedicated societies such as the Choctaw/Chickasaw Heritage Society (recording available privately) and the ethnographers Frances Densmore (1943) and James Howard (1990). Importantly, the dance songs do not have lyrics, only vocables, so they may have been considered only a means to keep the dance steps going, and not directly comparable to songs with lyrics that carry meaning. The near total conversion of the Choctaws to Protestant faiths may have made the hymns more directly relevant to modern Choctaw lives.

A newcomer to Choctaw culture is struck quickly by how much hymn-singing goes on as part of daily life. A gathering of Choctaws is likely to sing a few hymns together to pass the time, or as part of a family gathering. Churches commonly hold weekend-long services that feature singing in common for many hours in the evenings. One of the peak events at the important Choctaw Nation Labor Day Festival in Tuskahoma, Oklahoma, is the audience hymn-sing, reservations for which must be secured weeks in advance. Senior choirs and adolescents have posted audio files of their performances online.

While the traditional dance songs are treated as cultural artifacts, the

Choctaw hymn, called "Gospel," has begun to evolve as a musical form. Young musicians, composing in English, have begun to create new songs that feature instrumentation, soloists, vocal virtuosity, and more personal lyrics. These performing groups attend public and private gatherings and make recordings of their work, generally produced privately.

The hymn may be the first template for Choctaw verse.

Willis: "Your Life"

"Chimilhfiopak" ("Your Life") was written by Choctaw-speaker Henry Willis on the occasion of a sister's funeral. The poem was written in Choctaw and translated into English by Mr. Willis, his wife, Carole Willis, and their daughter Julianne Willis Judd. The poem marks the simple metaphor of a life as the journey of a single day, its destination the arrival into a timeless new place. While the author intended a deliberate Christian religious tone, it can be seen that this effect is mild and that there is very little imagery that could be termed strictly Christian.

I will reproduce all four stanzas of the poem, with each line of Choctaw followed by literal but broad glosses. (I have not glossed at the deepest linguistic level in my belief that linguists are likely to be the only beneficiaries of such detail.) I then give the author's own English translation.

I have used the orthography in which the poem appears, one of the common ones, with the upsilon indicating schwa and an underscore marking a nasal vowel. I have not indicated the metrical system, since the author does not appeal to it in creating the poem.

> Yakni apaknaka iluppa ish'la kʋt
> land upon this you-arrive[1] here (subject)
> chimilhfiopak ʋt
> your-breath (same subject)
> hʋshi akuchaka imma hʋshi ʋt awakaiya ako̱ chiyuhmi tok.
> where sun comes-out toward sun (subject) rise from there like (past)

Author's translation:

> You came upon this earth,
> your life,
> like the sun rising in the east.

In this first stanza, the Choctaw meanings are fairly consonant with those in English. The translators chose English words that might seem more natural or more commonly used in particular contexts. So, the translation uses simply 'came' rather than 'came here' and 'this earth' rather than 'this land' to suggest birth as an arrival from a different world. The Choctaw word for 'breath' also includes the sense of one's spirit or life-force. The poem treats 'you' and 'your life' as different ways of naming the same thing.

> Micha yakni apaknaka ish-nohọwa moyyoma ka̲,
> And land upon you-keep walking still-absolutely
> chimilhfiopak ʋt
> your-breath (subject)
> lhamko mikmʋt shohpakali achukma kʋt
> strong and-then shining good
> hʋshi ʋt ont tabokoli akọ chiyyohmi tok.
> sun (subject) go and reach sky zenith very much like (past)

Author's translation:

> And while you were walking upon this earth,
> your life,
> was strong and bright as the midday sun.

In the second stanza, several grammatical forms that mark aspect, or the expression of the development of an action over time, were not expressed directly, since these tend to be simply assumed in English. The choice was made to make a comparison 'strong and bright as the midday sun' over a more literal version 'strong and quite shining, much like the sun as it reaches the sky's zenith,' which to some tastes would have been equally charming.

> Himak a̲ Hʋshi ʋt okʋtolat mahạya ka e-chibanohọwa tok
> now sun (subject) falls into water and going along we-walk-
>   accompany-you (past)
> himak ʋla kia il-anowat a̲ya atukat ont aiʋlhit mahạya.
> now arrive here but we walking go along (nom) truly moving

Iluppa hikiat ia hokano
here standing, go, in contrast
chishno akbano hosh ish-nohowa makachi pulla.
you yourself alone are the one who you go on walking surely must

Author's translation:

Until now we have walked with you as the sun has moved west,
however, we are coming to a journey's end.
From here on
you shall ever walk alone

In the third stanza, the English translation seems to be much briefer than the Choctaw suggests it should be. The Choctaw words themselves seem to be about going and moving again and again. The Choctaw actually contains many grammaticalizations to challenge the translator. In particular, the Choctaw contains many aspect markers, definiteness markers, and nominalizations, from which the translator chooses such English expressions as 'journey's end.' Where we have simple English 'you' in the last line, the Choctaw has three emphatic markers referring to 'you,' which are simply omitted in the translation.

Yohmi kia ish-onak ma
so however you-will-arrive-there and then
lawa kʋt chi-afʋmmachi
many (subject) you-will-meet
micha na
and so
yukpa hosh chi-ayokpachi afehna achi hoke.
happy it is you-welcome very much will indeed.

Author's translation:

However, when you reach there,
many will meet you,
and
with gladness they will welcome you well.

The final stanza shows unusual correspondence between the Choctaw and English, thanks to words in both languages that mean 'meet' and 'welcome.' The English version again omits what seems to be redundant emphasis in Choctaw. Note that the Choctaw final stanza ends with the emphatic -*oke* particle.

Artistic Effects in "Your Life"

There are three salient effects in this poem. The first is that the Choctaw version is itself minimally figurative. The second is that the translators tried to be faithful to high-register but common English rather than attempting more figurative language. The third is that no attention was paid to the sound of the Choctaw poem in any deliberate way.

This poem is a very simple allegory, which is not elaborated upon. This might explain the avoidance of rich vocabulary in favor of common words and straightforward construction. While the Choctaw language includes a huge number of words with particular nuances, none of these is exploited. For instance, the language includes words for skipping, creeping, lolling, marching, and all other imaginable ways of moving, but the author sticks to the basic words for 'go' and 'move.' Similarly, he uses the basic Choctaw phrases for 'east,' 'west,' and 'noon' (these are structured differently in Choctaw than in English) rather than talk about light and shadow, moods, or other tropes that beginning poets would commonly attempt to harness. The author instead gives the clearest image he can using common words.

In translating the poem, the translators seem to value this clarity over imagery, even when the Choctaw itself offers a chance to peek at an idea with a different lens. For instance, the Choctaw word for *east* is a compound meaning 'sun comes out,' the word for *west*, 'sun falls into the water,' and the word for *noon*, 'reach the sky's zenith,' but no advantage is taken of these images. The title word *ilhfiopak*, 'wind, breath, life,' is rendered in the most abstract of its glosses, the one that would match common English usage.

In concentrating on the clarity of a single idea, the author seems to have given no thought to the phonological effect of the poem. He does not arrange the stanzas into sets of equal-numbered lines; he does not make the lines of similar lengths. Looking more closely at Choctaw phonology, he does not pay attention to groups of phrases that might carry an accent, or to numbers of heavy-light syllable groupings. He is not concerned with alliteration, with the qualities of consonants or vowels in words that are phrased together, or with rhyme.

Looking at the poem in what it might attempt rather than what it avoids, the author succeeds at re-creating important features of the Choctaw hymn. This is after all a eulogy, delivered in a church. In this view, the author would avoid fancy language in favor of solemnity. He would seek to concentrate the listener's attention on the poem's message and not on its cleverness. With respect to language, the author chooses a translation perfectly aligned with the hymnal style, exemplified in the line "you shall ever walk alone." Common English churchy expressions such as this one are chosen over more creative and more faithful translations.

If modern consumers of literature should find much to complain about in this poem, the Choctaw audience seems to find it proper and moving. If the Choctaw hymn serves as the grounding for Willis's style, it must be said that the author departs greatly from hymnal style in choosing a personal topic, creating an allegory, and using a free meter. In these ways, "Your Life" is an evolved form and perceived as a poem by Choctaw people.

McKinney: "A Leaf That Reminds Me of Thee"

William H. McKinney was an educated nineteenth-century Choctaw minister about whom we know little except that he assisted Alfred Wright in the Choctaw translation of the Psalms in the mid-nineteenth century and left behind one poem in manuscript, "A Leaf That Reminds Me of Thee" (1878, archived in the Western History Collections at the University of Oklahoma). McKinney wrote both an English and a Choctaw version of the poem.

Although McKinney does not say so, there is little doubt that the English version is the original poem and the Choctaw is a translation of it. We can see this because of its studious adherence to the European and American poetic conventions of this time: it uses a particular vocabulary ('bark' rather than 'boat'), has particular conventions in word reduction ('o'er' rather than 'over'), and has a rhyming *abababab* stanza.

The first stanza of the three appears here, divided into two portions of four lines each. The English poem appears first, followed by McKinney's Choctaw version and my own, more literal gloss, again to English. In this instance, since McKinney does not concern himself with poetic effects in Choctaw, I use one of the standard orthographies. Stress and vowel length are not determinable from this orthography. The author's own Choctaw spelling is completely idiosyncratic.

> How sweet is the hour we give
> When fancy may wander free
> To the friends who in memory live!—
> For then I remember thee!
>
> Then, winged, like the dove from the ark
> My heart o'er a stormy sea,
> Brings back to my lonely bark
> A leaf that reminds me of thee!

McKinney's Choctaw, lines 1–4:

> Hʋshi kanʋlli achukma il-ima ka̱
> Nowat a̱ya kʋt yoka keyu hosh chianukfihi̱llit
> I̱kana yʋt anta ka̱ ikhaiyanak mʋt:
> Chishno ma̱ isht ikhaiyana-li hoke!

More literal English gloss:

> We give a good hour
> walking unbound thinking about you
> When the friends living there remember
> It's you I do remember!

Choctaw, lines 5–8:

> Yohmi ka̱ isanahchi yʋt pʋchi yoshoba holba hosh
> Peni akohchat sacho̱kʋsh ʋt mahli okpulo
> Okhata i̱tʋnnʋp a̱ cholusa ha̱ falamichit ishtʋlak ma̱
> Iti hishi yʋmma isht chi'thaiyana-li hoke.

English gloss:

And so then, its wings like a dove
Brought from the boat, my heart will then bring back

From the storm, from the other side of the ocean, quietly
That leaf that reminds me of you indeed.

Translation Decisions in "A Leaf That Reminds Me of Thee"

The whole focus in examining this work should be the author's decisions
in translation from English to Choctaw, the reverse of the problem of the
Willis poem; there is little point in concerning ourselves with deliberate
artistic effects in the Choctaw version, though it is worthwhile to point
out what did happen in that version.

One of McKinney's salient problems is the lack of a separate vocabulary for use in a poetic register. McKinney may distinguish a 'bark' from
an 'ark' from a 'boat,' and from other seagoing vessels in English, but the
land-locked Choctaws have a single word that must serve, *peni*, albeit with
the possibility of modifiers, for them all. Importantly, there is no older or
alternative pronoun set that will allow one to translate 'thee': there is only
the word for 'you,' and it is used in all contexts: indeed, Choctaw culture
is notably egalitarian, as is reflected in the paucity of titles and honorifics
in general.

The Choctaw version includes the ubiquitous emphatic discourse
marker -*oke* that serves as an exclamation point, something that is completely consonant with both the spoken and written language.

But McKinney does not take advantage of other Choctaw words that
would make his translation far richer. There are a number of Choctaw
words that effectively mean 'wander,' but he has translated with the mundane 'walk along.' 'Sweet' is rendered with the all-purpose word for 'good.'

More interesting still are the changes—some slight, some significant—
in the syntax. The first line in the English version, "How sweet is the hour
we give," is rendered in a simple clause, even though Choctaw possesses
a huge set of tools (the definiteness markers mentioned earlier) that can
exquisitely emphasize the word for 'sweet.' In line 2, McKinney cannot
easily get at the English concept of 'fancy wandering free' and replaces it
with a related but different figure. In line 3, the friends have gone from
living in memory to being the ones who do the remembering.

In lines 5 through 8, the figure of the dove returning with a leaf is rewritten rather thoroughly. The 'lonely bark' is omitted completely and replaced with a longer description of the stormy sea, and includes a concept
('quietly') that does not appear in the English version.

The main illustration here is the allusion to the biblical dove returning to Noah's ark with an olive twig, a sign of literal salvation. The Choctaws were thoroughly Christianized at the time this poem was written, and would have readily understood this allusion. But lacking a Choctaw word to serve in place of the key word *ark*, there is no easy way for Mc Kinney to highlight this allusion.

In the second and third stanzas, not given here, the Choctaw translation begins to deteriorate somewhat more: the translations have only seven lines each rather than eight, and a number of the poetic figures are radically rewritten or simply left out.

So, what does this translation have to give us? First, it shows again the emphasis that authors and translators commonly place on rendering the semantic sense of a poem in the most straightforward way, at the expense of better-chosen words and certainly with little or no regard for the sound of the translation.

It is important to point out that McKinney, though seemingly eager to show off his education in the verbal arts, took time to make the poem available to his Choctaw-speaking community, as if their sharing the poem, at least in its conceptual essence (and we may debate if he succeeded), was important. It may be that he sought to introduce his community to the notion of poetry as it was written at the time—again, in imitation of an art form outside the traditional culture, and different from the hymn tradition. It is entirely possible that he could have crafted a better Choctaw poem, using even his own criteria for what a poem should be, and it is our loss that we do not have such an example.

Morgan: "On the Banks of the Walnut Creek"

The last poem is a recent work by Phillip Carroll Morgan, "A Sakti Bok Hahe" ("On the Banks of the Walnut Creek") (Morgan 2000). Dr. Morgan is a Choctaw/Chickasaw man raised speaking English, who decided to learn the Choctaw language as an adult. He is a scholar of nineteenth-century Choctaw literature and has published a number of poems. Several of them were written originally in Choctaw and then translated to English, as is this one. I repeat the author's own orthography.

Nitak lawa allanakni washoha-lih
A sakti Bok Hahe pisachukma
Nunikwelih okshinili hashtomi
Nitak lawa ilaualli samanta

Oka micha shinukat banakachi
Iyi hapi shinuk hofobi okatula
Hokola Amafo akashtala ttok
A sakti Bok Hahe

Morgan's own translation to English:

Many days as a boy I played
On the banks of beautiful Walnut Creek
Fishing and swimming in the warm sunshine
Days of good fun and peace.
The water ripples and so does the sand
Our feet sink in the packsand deep
Just like my Grandfather's roots did
On the banks of the Walnut Creek

Artistic Effects in "On the Banks of the Walnut Creek

This poem is different from both of the other examples in that it changes and manipulates the Choctaw language—a daring move, since purists might strongly object to the seeming violence to the grammar. The author has reduced the number of grammatical markers to the barest minimum and uses rich vocabulary items and word order to let the images fall out in order. He avoids the employment of much tense, aspect, mood, contrast, specificity, and complex clause structure that would call for the large and abstract set of Choctaw grammatical markers. To avoid modifying phrases and clauses, he chooses single words that carry a good deal of content. This is in strong contrast to the other authors: Willis, who uses very common words in idiomatic phrases with their attendant grammatical markers; and McKinney, who chooses the most accessible and easiest Choctaw replacements for English words and concepts.

Morgan has carefully translated his poem into English that preserves virtually all the sense of the Choctaw—granted that the Choctaw is stripped to its notional content.

Phonologically, the Choctaw poem is composed of short stanzas that each contain three accented phrases: noun phrases contain an accent on their penultimate syllable, and verbs carry a rising final pitch. The final line, "A sakti Bok Hahe," is shorter than the others, but the pattern of the established meter induces the reader to place an accent on each noun of the phrase: a sákti Bók Hahé. This gives a satisfying ending in repeating the theme of the poem in a deliberate way, each word stressed. This is the only one of the three poems in which the sound of the Choctaw language participates in the art form.

It would seem that Morgan has found a way to overcome his handicap of being not fully fluent in Choctaw. Rather than commit barbaric errors in attempting to control the sophisticated grammar, he exploits content-loaded vocabulary and natural word and phrase rhythm and chooses a simple clause structure.

Some Remarks on Poetry

It is fair to ask the question, Why should we accept any of these works as *Choctaw* poetry? We know of no poetic tradition in the culture: their artistic reference is not to other Choctaw poetry; rather, all are undoubtedly inspired by European and eventually American forms in verse—the hymn, the soaring Tennysonian style of the nineteenth century, and the sparse, personal, lyrical style of the twentieth. That each of the three featured authors has begun writing poetry anew, based on styles relevant to his own literary experience, bespeaks the isolation of Choctaw literary forms. We might wonder if new authors will write poems inspired by any of these, which would be the start of a literary tradition. It cannot be said that the small group of extant poems in Choctaw constitutes a tradition, and truthfully, the endangered status of the language jeopardizes the chances of Native authors producing work that would not be largely derivative of existing or future English-language verbal arts.

With respect to the problem of poetry translation, it is educational to observe the great difficulty that the authors have for the most part overcome in making a second text that will stand on its own. In all cases, the fine points of Choctaw grammar are given up, even though a certain depth of meaning is lost thereby.

Conclusions

What contribution to the problem of translation do these samples of Choctaw stories and poems make? These authors all chose to preserve artistic effects in their translations at the expense, sometimes the great expense, of faithfulness to the structure of the Choctaw language.

Looking again at the two Choctaw grammatical features outlined here, contrast and clause structure, no author chose to render into English any of the exquisitely articulated degrees of contrast available in Choctaw. Recall that use of the contrastive particles is obligatory. This is perhaps surprising, because transference to English of such contrast could have been accomplished with a few extra descriptive words. But, while an English translation is available, the high degree of contrast is not obligatory, and perhaps more important, it is not the way an English-speaker would normally put things. With respect to clause structure, only the English translation of "My Dog and the Snake" shows transference of the densely packed Choctaw clauses. "On the Banks of the Walnut Creek" avoids both grammatical features in Choctaw through skillful placement of phrases.

The ubiquitous emphatic discourse marker *-oke* gets more recognition. Mr. Willis translates with "they will welcome you *well*," while Mr. McKinney, interestingly, inserts *-oke* into his Choctaw translation to render the English exclamation point, when he has paid little notice to other points of grammar.

It is likely that professional translators, and certainly linguists, would be far more concerned with precision in language structure, especially when differences are significant and meaningful. Even given this limited sample, if authors themselves concentrate on overall literary effects of their work, they take a different point of view, not one grounded in the native language. We would welcome a bigger literature with a longer tradition to see if this might bring an evolving sophistication with respect to Choctaw language-specific literary effects, and how they survive in translation.

Note

1. Hyphenated words such as "you-arrive" indicate that the joined words correspond to one word in Choctaw.

References

Baker, Mark. 1988. *Incorporation: A Theory of Grammatical Function Changing.* Chicago: University of Chicago Press.

Bécquer, Gustavo Adolfo. 1965. *Rimas: Estudio y edición de Juan M. Diez Taboada.* 1871. Madrid: Ediciones Alcalá.

Densmore, Frances. 1943. *Choctaw Music.* Washington DC: Government Printing Office.

Haag, Marcia, and Henry Willis. 2001. *Choctaw Language and Culture: Chahta Anumpa.* Norman: University of Oklahoma Press.

———. 2007. *Choctaw Language and Culture: Chahta Anumpa*. Vol. 2. Norman: University of Oklahoma Press.

Howard, James. 1990. *Choctaw Music and Dance*. Norman: University of Oklahoma Press.

McKinney, William H. 1878. A Leaf That Reminds Me of Thee. MS. University of Oklahoma: McKinney Collection, Western History Collections.

Mithun, Marianne. 1999. *The Languages of Native North America*. Cambridge: Cambridge University Press.

Morgan, Phillip Carroll. 2000. A Sakti Bok Hahe. MS.

Swann, Brian, ed. 2004. *Voices from Four Directions: Contemporary Translations of the Native Literatures of North America*. Lincoln: University of Nebraska Press.

Whorf, Benjamin. 1956. *Language, Thought, and Reality: Selected Writings*. Cambridge: MIT Press.

16

Translating an Esoteric Idiom

The Case of Aztec Poetry

John Bierhorst

A typical Cherokee "sacred formula"—better, *i:gawé:sdi* 'to say, one'—
begins with the words:

> Ha! White Sparrow Hawk! You live Above. You have
>   just come to scream: "Your soul has just been
>   separated!"
> Ha! Blue Mourning Dove![1]

Similarly, out of the cryptic literature of the Yucatec Maya, the compilation known as *Ritual of the Bacabs* gathers up incantations put together
with such blind phrases as:

> Who is its mother? O glyphs in the skies, O glyphs in the
>   clouds, for you are always in skies, for you are
>   always in clouds. Throw it down![2]

Mystifying in much the same way, the collection of Aztec *conjuros* recorded by Hernando Ruiz de Alarcón in the early 1600s preserves, among
dozens of comparable examples, one that starts:

> Come quickly! Come, Red Chichimec! Here stands the
>   priest, its sign is 1 Water.[3]

370

Whatever the meaning concealed in these various yet similar phrases—from three widely separated cultures—here evidently is the language of control, expressed in imperious declaratives ("You have just come to scream"), demanding interrogatives ("Who is its mother?"), and outright imperatives ("Come!"). In short, all three repertories—Cherokee, Maya, and Aztec—may be classed as incantatory. Further, all three are bristling with enigmatic figures of speech—to an extent rare in Native American literature, even for incantations (by comparison, the equally insistent petitions of the Navajo chantway singer or the Kwakiutl prayermaker are transparent, both in the original idiom and in translation).[4] As the latter-day investigators Anna Gritts Kilpatrick and Jack Kilpatrick have said of the Cherokee texts, these "abound in terms that merely skirt their true meanings," in "ritualisms," and in "tricky wording."[5] Similarly, Ruiz de Alarcón, complained that the evidently magical *conjuros* were "nothing but a string of metaphors, not only in the verbs but also in the nouns and adjectives."[6]

Why the veiled diction? What can be its purpose? Forthrightly, the Cherokee scholar Alan Kilpatrick offers the answer: "to baffle and confuse the uninitiated."[7] Essentially the same, if subtler, is the explanation given by Ruiz de Alarcón, who observes that the very obscurity of the utterance enhances its prestige; or, as he writes, "the Devil, its inventor, influences their [i.e., the native practitioners'] veneration and esteem through the difficulty of the language." A comparable, native answer that may serve for all is contained in the *Ritual of the Bacabs* itself, indicating that the practitioner is using an idiom of authority, the so-called *suyua in thanab* 'language of Suyua' (referring to a legendary place of ancestral origin). This, the *suyua in thanab*, is the parlance of riddle-like metaphors that Maya chiefs, in theory at least, had to learn before assuming office. Thus the *Bacabs* practitioner can mention whomever he wishes to control, saying, "He falls into Suyua, my house of command!"[8]

A fourth repertory that may be considered in this select company is the vast corpus of *cantares* 'poems (accompanied by music)', recorded in the Aztec language in Mexico City or its environs during the second half of the 1500s. Two manuscripts have survived, the *Cantares Mexicanos*, collected between 1550 and 1590, and the *Romances de los Señores de la Nueva España* 'ballads of the lords of New Spain', dated 1582 (some sixty years after the Spanish Conquest of 1521). Unlike the *conjuros* 'incantations', the *cantares* remained untranslated in their own time and so were wrapped in mystery from the moment they became written texts. Judging by the largely spurious glosses contained in the manuscripts, it is clear that even the native scribes, though fluent in Nahuatl, were baffled by the material they had taken in dictation from the adept singers. The linguist undoubtedly most competent to interpret the songs and very possibly the overseer of at least one of the two compilations, the missionary-ethnographer Bernardino de Sahagún, seemingly ruled against translation, stating, "For the most part they sing of idolatrous things in a style so obscure that there is no one who really understands them, except themselves alone."[9]

The *cantares* were not to be taken up again until the 1600s, when a new generation of antiquaries begin to sift through the mass of texts. Now with a new agenda, not of missionization but of nation building, they combed through what they thought were the shards of an ancient testament, searching out bits of found poetry that could be presented as Mexico's answer to the pastoral tradition of Greece and Rome, the writings of Plato, the quasi-historical *cantares de gesta* of medieval Spain, even the songs of biblical poet-kings.

A more realistic appreciation might have been achieved if the new critics could have considered a tradition closer to home, the native Mexican *conjuros*.

Cantares Compared with Conjuros

Less rigidly technical than the incantations, with obvious entertainment value, even satiric elements, and syntax that frequently relaxes into a discursive manner, the *cantares*, nonetheless, are fundamentally ritualistic. Like the *conjuros*, the *cantares* rely heavily on the imperative mode. The codex *Cantares Mexicanos*, preserving ninety-one songs, is a virtual textbook of imperative particles—*ma, maca, macac, macamo, macaoc, macuel, macueleh, ma huel, maic, ma ihui, manel, manen, manoceh, manozo, manozocuel, maoc, maquin, matel, mazan, mazano, mazaoc, mazazo, mazazoc, mazazocuel, mazazo ihui, mazo, mazoc, mazohui, tla, tlaca, tlacuel, tlaic, tlanel, tlaoc, tlaza, tlazan, tla zanen, tlenozo* 'let it be! let it not be! let no one! let it not be indeed! let it just not be! let it be soon! let it soon be this! let it really be!' and so forth[10]—a greater vocabulary of particles expressing wishes and commands than in any other Nahuatl source, including the *conjuros* and even the voluminous sixteenth-century *Vocabulario* of the great lexicographer Alonso Molina. Declaratives are more frequent than imperatives, but the declaratives are often coercive (as in the drill sergeant's "You *will* shine your boots" or the hypnotist's "You *are* becoming sleepy"). Notice, for example, how the imperative is actually replaced by the declarative in otherwise duplicate passages: "*Let there be* green-swan flowers, roseate-swan flowers, twisting!" replaced by "Green-swan flowers, roseate-swan flowers, *are* twisting!"[11]

As with the *conjuros*, the songs make much use of the verbs 'to come,' 'to arrive,' 'to come forth,' as though the words themselves had the power to summon. Even the casual reader will note the insistent use of the verbs 'come' *huitz*, 'come' *huallauh*, 'arrive' *ahci*, 'arrive' *ehco*, 'appear' *moquetza*, 'come forth' *quizaco*, 'bring forth' *quixtia*, 'bring down' *temohuia*, and 'descend' *temo* in *Romances* songs I, II, III, V, VI, VIII, IX, X, and so forth, and throughout the *Cantares Mexicanos*, not to mention the recurring verbs 'summon' *notza* and 'call forth' *nahuatia*.

Even more so than the *conjuros*, the songs are "dramatic," in the sense that the speaker may assume more than one voice within a single song. Though the texts are monologues, it is often as if two or more speakers are present, their roles played by the same ritualist.[12]

Moreover, in true incantatory style the ritualist addresses figures of power or authority and, often, speaks for them. In the *conjuros* these figures are deities; in the songs, they are the supreme deity (or his son, Jesucristo) or, just as often, historical kings and military leaders. Thus in the *conjuros* we find the ritualist saying *niquetzalcoatl* 'I am Quetzalcoatl' and *nimictlantecutli* 'I am Mictlanteuctli [lord of the underworld]';[13] in the *Romances* (2:16 and 2v:1), *nitemilotzin* 'I am Temilotzin [a native general during the Conquest]' and *niyoyotzin* 'I am Yoyontzin [an alternate name for the fifteenth-century king of Texcoco, Nezahualcoyotl].'

In "dramatic" fashion a single song may refer to the same figure in the first person, the second person, and the third person. Thus *Romances* song II has *niyoyotzin* 'I am Yoyontzin'; *titecpiltzinn i necāhualcoyotl tecuitli yoyotzin* 'you, O prince, O Lord Nezahualcoyotl, O Yoyontzin!'; and *neçahualcoyotzin* 'it's Nezahualcoyotzin!'[14]

In the *conjuros* the ritualist calls on warrior spirits and other spirit helpers: *inic nauhcā niquintzatzilia* 'from the four directions I summon them.'[15] Subsequently, when they've done their work, 'the earth will be drunk [with the blood of their victims]' *tlalli ihuintiz*.[16] And by the same token (in *Cantares Mexicanos* song XIX, fol. 15v, lines 5–6), the ritualist summons warrior spirits, thus: *xochimecatica nauhcampa ca cenca huel xihxittomonilpitica noyollo* 'noose these hearts of mine as flower garlands from the four directions'; later, in a different context but with the same purport, 'there's earth-drunkenness' *tlalihuintihua* in *Cantares Mexicanos* song LXXXVII (fol. 77v, lines 3–4).

To facilitate his petition, the *conjuros* ritualist repeatedly speaks with the voice of *icnopiltzintli, centeotl* 'Pitiable Little Child, Corn Spirit,' that is, the child of the gods who was buried alive so that crops could grow from the earth. The myth of this corn spirit is recorded in a sixteenth-century Aztec version and is still current in Mesoamerica. In a modern Nahuatl variant from northern Veracruz State, the child corn-god continues to be called *pilsintsij*, and in one version it is said that the little boy "began to weep at being so badly treated." Among the Nahua, Huichol, Cora, and Tepecano of the Western Sierra Madre, where the analogous Corn Woman myth is preserved, it is reported that the story is told with much weeping.[17] Accordingly, in one of the Aztec *conjuros* the ritualist breaks into actual lamentation, using the vocables of the *cantares*:

> Aya ohuiya oh ayaye ohua aye ohua! I am poor! I am Pitiable Little Child, I am Corn Spirit! *ayauhuia oh, ayaye, oa, aye oa. Ninotolinia, niycnopiltzintli, niceteotl.*[18]

Identical vocables may be seen throughout the *Cantares Mexicanos*: *aya, ohuiya, oh, a, yaye, ohua, aye*, and so forth.[19] The expression *ninotolinia* 'I am poor,' moreover, is one of the staples of *cantares* phraseology. The idea, evidently, is that the pitiableness of the singer will elicit supernatural compassion. Similarly, in the *conjuros*, the translators J. Richard Andrews and Ross Hassig find "admissions of poverty as a ploy for compassion."[20]

To bring forth the agents of supernatural power, the *conjuros* ritualist—rather than merely summoning the spirits—may claim to have "made" them. The same idea, with variations, is stated and restated throughout the *cantares*, as the incoming "princes," or warriors, are said to be made, given birth, created, or brought to life.[21] Occasionally, as in *Romances* song II, they are said to be the 'flesh' *nacayotl* of the creative power or its agent; and in general they are 'marvels' *ilhuizolli* (as in *Romances* song XIV).

Differences between *Cantares* and *Conjuros*

Unlike the *conjuros*, which are based on religion exclusively, the *cantares* draw upon history and politics; and evidently for this reason they were called "profane" by European observers, who distinguished them from another native song genre, the nonpolitical *macehualiztli*, recognized as "sacred." The native name for the *cantares* genre, derived from the verb *ihtotia* 'to dance,' is *netotiliztli*—better, *nehtotiliztli*.²² In performance both *macehualiztli* and *netotiliztli*, unlike the *conjuros*, include dancing accompanied by drums and other musical instruments.

While the battles waged in the *conjuros* are between the agents of personal harm and the spirits of succor, the warfare imagined in the *netotiliztli* favors Mexico against its geopolitical rivals. With Mexico (i.e., the twin boroughs of Tenochtitlan and Tlatelolco) stand its partners in the so-called Triple Alliance: Acolhuacan (with the city of Texcoco as its seat) and Tepanecapan (seated at Azcapotzalco until the Tepanec War circa 1430, thereafter at Tlacopan). Mexico's traditional antagonists are Chalco, a confederation to the south, and, especially, Huexotzinco and Tlaxcala, a pair of confederacies on the other side of the mountains some distance to the east. These longtime enemies of the imperial power at Tenochtitlan, not incidentally, became the allies of Cortés in the siege of Mexico, 1521. In the songs, blame for the Conquest is shifted from the conquistadores to the native enemies, notably Huexotzinco-Tlaxcala, while the city of Mexico, tragically destroyed, fondly remembered, becomes an object of cult.

Cantares in Translation

A typical song from the *Cantares Mexicanos*, song XIV, begins with the enigmatic yet apparently declarative statement (referring to a brilliant bird, the "trogon"):

There's a trogon on the mat, a trogon reviving. There!

Something of the magician's art can be sensed in these words of legerdemain, announcing a phenomenon beyond the powers of earthly observation as though it were an accomplished fact; or, as noted above, it is *not* an accomplished fact, it is a wish, equivalent to the imperative "*Let* a trogon be on the mat, a trogon reviving. There!"

An even better view of this art can be glimpsed in the Nahuatl text, which includes an intensifying particle (*zan* = just! or indeed! or yes!) and a succession of affective vocables (*ohuaye, a, i* = aaah!, oh!, ah!, expressing anguish), here printed in italic:

Zan tzinitzcan im petlatl ipan *ohuaye* on tzinitzcan i[n] celiztoc *a*
   oncan *i*

Exhaustively translated, with exclamation points added to convey the emotive content:

Yes! there's a trogon on the mat, aaah! it's this one, a trogon who's reviving, ah! There! and oh!

It might be wondered if the extra material is simply euphonic, added to give a certain rhythm, without affect. Whatever the truth of such a conjecture, it must be granted that the sound of weeping or complaining is part and parcel of the genre. Having witnessed live performances, the sixteenth-century cleric and chronicler Diego de Durán could write, "All their *cantares* are composed of metaphors so obscure that scarcely anyone understands them . . . so sad that merely the sound and the dancing produce sadness . . . so sad that to hear them makes me sorrowful—and sad."[23] A rationale for the "sadness" has been offered above, in connection with the *conjuros*. In sum, the ritualist is demanding supernatural pity, and undoubtedly the technique has become an automatic feature of the *cantares* style, whether or not the vocables are stretched and trimmed to produce "a kind of meter," as vaguely asserted by the contemporary chronicler Motolinía.[24]

By suppressing this song-weeping, if it may be called that, translators help to conceal the ritualism of the *cantares*, adding to the impression that what we are reading is poetry in the Western sense. Exhaustive translation, however, would make the reading all but impossible. In any event, a close look at the metaphorical content should be sufficient to bring the reader into contact with an undeniably genuine, if ritualistic, poetry—even if the insistent whine of its vocables is muted.

Translating with a Concordance

Computer programming has given translators of difficult idioms a welcome tool. Thanks to the "searchability" of "keyboarded" texts and the "outprinting" of voluminous concordances, it becomes possible to stack up all the occurrences of a puzzling term and intuit its meaning in much the same way that children pick up basic language and thieves, untutored, learn argot. Arzápalo Marín's 1,100-page edition of the *Ritual of the Ba-*

cabs, incorporating both a word concordance and a phrase concordance for the entire manuscript, demonstrates how a recent translator was able to push our understanding of a ferociously thorny text to a higher level than had been achieved by the Mayanist Ralph Roys a generation earlier. A concordance for the *Cantares Mexicanos* has also been published, and a searchable version of the *Romances* is now available online.[25] In what follows, an attempt will be made to show how these tools can elucidate the Aztec *cantares*—which escape the confines of the (albeit excellent) dictionaries and grammars of Classical Nahuatl.

Returning to the opening phrases of song XIV, or just the single phrase *on tzinitzcan i[n] celiztoc a* 'it's this one, a trogon who's reviving, ah!,' it can be pointed out that modern Mexicanists have been puzzled by the conjunction of terms. In fact, over a period of eighty years, the phrase *on tzinitzcan i[n] celiztoc a* was translated three times by sober, well-prepared investigators, who chose to write:

1. the tzinitzcan arouses me[26]
2. *im Dienste des geliebten Herrn* 'in the service of the beloved lord'[27]
3. *en preciosa soledad* 'in precious solitude'[28]

Remember that the words are *on tzinitzcan i[n] celiztoc a* 'it's this one, a trogon who's reviving, ah!' But in each of these three cases the translator, apparently, is unable to accept that a trogon can revive like a dormant plant; and indeed the idea accords with neither mundane experience nor conventional European poetic imagery. To get rid of it, the translator, in examples 1 and 2, rewrites the text, gluing the *i* to the *celiztoc*, making *iceliztoc*, a grammatically impossible construction, hinting at some kind of action (cf. the verb *i[h]celia* 'to give or apply') (in example 2 the noun *tzinitzcan* 'trogon' is given as "precious lord" following Olmos 1972:213 "señor muy amado," an option—but it is not *netotiliztli* usage); or, in example 3, the rewriting pertains to the condition of solitude (cf. *icel* 'alone' and *itzto* 'to hold vigil'), and, in addition, makes an adjective, 'precious,' out of *tzinitzcan* 'trogon' (a bird that does, admittedly, have precious feathers—but this again is not *netotiliztli* usage). Here, in a nutshell, are the two wrongs of Aztec "poetry": mundane experience (example 2) and conventional European sentiment (examples 1 and 3). The *netotiliztli* belongs to neither.

A closer look at the troublesome verb *celiya* (combining form *celiz*) leads
to the raw data underlying the observations offered immediately above.
Here, then, is the complete extract for *celiya* 'to sprout, freshen, green,
or revive' from the Aztec song corpus, arranged alphabetically with the
manuscript folio and line numbers at right, C for *Cantares Mexicanos*, R
for *Romances de los Señores de la Nueva España* (untranslated vocables
underlined):

001   cehCELIYA noyol noconcac-<u>on</u> huehuetl comon-   C76v:23
My heart sprouts *forth. I've heard the drums. They're rumbling*

002   -ihhuixochitl in cehCELIYA ye mocuic
    tocon-<u>ya</u>-yehua ahua nomatzin   C52:1
feather blooms, sprouting *ones, songs of yours that you sing. Hail, nephew*

003   tonpilihui-<u>a</u> o cehCELIZtiuh toyollotzin toyolia
    ica teo-   C43:22
you're becoming a child. Our hearts, our souls go greening. *With holy*

004   i nahuaqueh <u>ao</u> cehCELIZtoqu-<u>i</u> a in <u>iye</u> xochitl
    oncan to-   C48:21
the Ever Near. The flower sprouts. *There! We*

005   Itzmolini xochitl, CELIYA, mimilihui, cueponi
    <u>yeehuaya</u>   C33v:19
Flowers are sprouting, reviving, *budding, blossoming*

006   itzmolini ye nocuic CELIYA notlahtollaaquillo
    <u>ohua</u> in toxochiuh   C27v:8
my songs are greening. My word-fruit sprouts. *Our flowers [are arisen]*

007   Zan ca tlauhquechol CELIYA
    pozontimani-<u>a</u> moqu-<u>i</u>-pacxochiuh   C30:29
Now the roseate swan is reviving. *Your crown flowers foam abroad,*

008   tlauhquechol CELIYA pozontimani <u>ya</u>
    mocpacxochiuh tenan   R7:11
A roseate swan is reviving. *Your crown flowers foam abroad, O mother*

009   in tocpacxochiuh tla CELIYA xochitl-<u>i</u> cueponi-<u>a</u>
    xochitl-<u>i</u> oncan   R19:7
these flower crowns of ours. Let flowers sprout, *let flowers open. There*

010   dios in xochitica CELIZtihcac <u>a-ayyahue</u> ica
    mitzonahahuiltia   R23:10
O God. They're sprouting *as flowers. With these they give you pleasure.*

011   zan tzinitzcan i CELIZtihcac <u>ooy</u> cempohualxochitl
       ontoz-   C48:25
These marigolds are sprouting as trogons. As parrot
012   ipalnemohuani ye oncan CELIZtimani-*a* in
       cuauhtli-*n* ocelotl ye oncan   C9:29
O Life Giver. There! a jaguar, an eagle, sprouts. There!
013   on tzinitzcan i CELIZtoc a oncan i zan nen
       ninentlamati-*a*   C7v:1
a trogon reviving. There! As best I can [I seek him in this grieving]
014   onoqu-*i* nepapan CELIZtoc i xihuitl ye nican-*aya*
       mochi ca   C41v:16
that exists, every green herb that is here. [Dwell in] all [the earth.]
015   ipan tochihuacoh hualcehCELIYA hualitzmolini in
       toyollo xochitl   . C14v:5
like them we come to do: our hearts come sprouting, come green; the flowers
016   OnacaxochiamatlapalCELIZtiuh ye ontzauctiuh   C58:21
They pass away reviving as reed flowers, these colored banners, as captives
017   <u>aya</u> cuicatica-*ya* oncehCELIZtihcac
       onquetzalmiyahuayohtihcac *<u>aya</u>*   C20:17
it's sprouting songs, it's covered in tassel plumes
018   -tlapepetlantoc, oncan onCELIZtoc in cozahuiz
       xochitl oncan nemih   C7v:18
lightning strikes. Golden flowers are reviving. There, they are alive
019   OncuahuicehCELIYA <u>ohuaye</u> oceloitzmolini
       in tecpillotl   C21:26
Nobles [and kings] are sprouting as eagles, greening as jaguars
020   teyolquihmatcan ontlacehCELIZtimani-*<u>ya</u>*
       onquetzalahhuachquiyauhtimani   C60:16
There's freshening in that place of heart pleasers, plume-dew raining down
021   ontzinitzcan-*i*-CELIZtihcac <u>ay-yahuen</u> ica
       mitzonahuiltiah a   C64:9
they're trogon-sprouting, and with these they give you pleasure, ah!
022   tlapalcamohpalcamilcehCELIYA moyol *i-<u>yancaya</u>*
       yectli-*<u>ya</u>* mocuic   C47v:4
your heart sprouts colors of tawny and brown, your beautiful songs,
023   o xiuhquecholcehCELIZtoc <u>ohuao aye</u>.   C46v:30
Oh, these are sprouting as turquoise swans!
024   Mexihco in xiuhquecholCELIZtiuh   C58:31
to Mexico. They're off to be revived as turquoise swans.

025   -atempan xiuhquecholCELIZtiuh macpalxochitl ic
      ontzauctiuh   C58:27
Plume-Shore! Handflowers pass away as turquoise swans reviving, *captured*

Evidently, the verb *celiya* 'to sprout, freshen, or green, especially after a period of dormancy,' hence 'to revive,' has a secure place in the diction of these songs. Moreover, the term connects with its approximate synonyms *itzmolini*, *mimilihui*, and *cueponi* (see lines 005, 006, 015, 019), which in turn have the counterparts *tlapani*, *tlatlatzca*, *tomolihui*, and *xotla* (not included in the twenty-five lines shown here), all told amounting to about one hundred occurrences signifying revival, or resurrection. Not only "flowers" but gorgeous birds, including trogons (011, 013, 021), are found to be "sprouting," or "reviving"—as well as "eagles and jaguars" (012, 019), a standard locution meaning "warriors."

As for *tzinitzcan* 'trogon' (normally designating a brilliant red-bellied bird of the genus *Trogon*), the term has forty occurrences in the corpus, including:

101   TimoTZINITZCANtzetzeloa-*ya* in centalal
      moteca-*ya*   C45V:2
You're scattered as trogons, *and they're poured out everywhere*
102   Ma TZINITZCANahhuechotihuian ahhuachotiuh
      in tzacu-*a*   C57V:23
Let's go have them be a raining mist of trogons, *off they go to fall as dew, these captives*
103   nicTZINITZCANamatlapaltzetzeloa-*n*
      cuicayehcahuilo   C38V:13
I strew them as tinted trogon *banners made to arrive as songs*
104   zan TZINITZCAN in zacuan ye tlauhquechol ic a
      tictlatlapal-   R23V:3
[you're reciting songs] in colors—as trogons, troupials, roseate swans.
105   cuica ye nican xiuhtototl quechol TZINITZCAN *iya*
      quechol attohua   R37V:3
Cotingas, swans, trogons *sing here. The swan goes first,*
106   tepilhuan zacuameh teoquecholtin TZINITZCAN
      tlatlauhquecholtin   C6V:10
princes are troupials, spirit swans, trogons, *roseate swans*

107　TZINITZCAN tlauhquechol ic nic-ya-ihmati-a
　　　nocuicatzin　　　　　　　　　　　　　　　　　C3:10
as trogons, as roseate swans I design my songs
108　TZINITZCAN tlauhquechol onpahpatlantinemi　R12v:14
Trogons, roseate swans, are flying,
109　In on TZINITZCAN tonpilihui-a　　　　　　　C43:22
O trogon, you're becoming a child!

Expanded, line 106 adds the phrase *moyehyectihtinemih-o in onmatih-o in ixtlahuatl ihtic-an* 'they live in beauty, they that know the middle of the [battle]-field.' Military allusions in lines 012, 016, 019, 025, 102, and 103 confirm the impression that war is the subject of the genre. At this point, three rules may be postulated for interpreting it:

Rule 1: Observe that interconnections and a repetitive vocabulary unify
　　　　the diction.
Rule 2: Nouns that take the same verb are interchangeable.
Rule 3: Nouns in tandem or in series are approximate synonyms.

　　　Rule 1 is qualified by several songs in the *Cantares Mexicanos* that either reinterpret the diction for literary or Christian devotional purposes (songs I–XIII) or amplify it by introducing a tangentially relevant Bible story (songs LV and LVIII). Rule 2 generally excludes verbs low in figurative value, such as the verb "to be." Rule 3 may accommodate paired nouns that are complements rather than overt synonyms, such as "eagle, jaguar" = warrior (cf. English "cloak and dagger" = intrigue).
　　　From the information shown thus far, a lexicon that includes special usages may begin to take shape:[29]

celiya, intransitive verb. 1: to sprout or freshen, of vegetation turning green after dormancy. 2: to revive, of deceased warriors. *For discussion see above.*
quechol, noun. 1: categorical name for any bird, especially in the sense that birds are divine. 2: any bird of fine plumage. 3: warrior, especially a slain warrior dwelling in the sky world or a deceased warrior newly returned to earth, *proposed English equivalent:* swan (in the sense of "swan knight"). *See section entitled "Noble Speech and the War Cult" below.*

tlauhquechol, noun. 1: roseate swan, designating a revenant warrior—see QUECHOL. 2: the roseate spoonbill, *Ajaia ajaia*.

tzinitzcan, noun. 1: (any?) bird of the genus Trogon. 2: warrior, especially a revenant warrior. *See examples above; see also section entitled "Noble Speech and the War Cult" below.*

It may be granted that for the phrase *on tzinitzcan i[n] celiztoc a* it is no longer possible to avoid the translation 'it's this one, a trogon who's reviving, ah!'

Noble Speech and the War Cult

Because the *cantares*, or *netotiliztli*, as a whole are highly repetitive and constantly synonymic, they are well suited to analysis by means of the back-and-forth comparisons that a concordance allows. The presentation, obviously, does not lie far from the mainstream of corpus linguistics, which uses computerization to derive rules from large samples of "real world" speech. Yet the procedure here applied to the *cantares*, though machine-assisted, is very much a hand method that borrows from traditional linguistic methods as well as the automata of digitization.[30]

Fortunately, we do not start from scratch. The *netotiliztli*, though largely a closed idiom, exhibits a certain amount of overlap with the more broadly used diction known as *tecpillatolli* 'noble speech' as distinguished from *macehuallatolli* 'commoners' speech.'[31] Comparable to the Yucatec "language of Suyua," the *tecpillatolli* is an acquisition of the ruling classes and hence an idiom of command, used especially in the elegant *Florentine Codex* orations that mark rites of passage (at least for those who are *pilli* 'noble' or *tecpilli* 'ruling noble') and occasions of state (in the presence of the king).[32] In this broader diction, for example, the warrior is called *cuauhtli* 'eagle' or *ocelotl* 'jaguar,' as is well known; and, in the special sense that the warrior passes to and from the other world (in a process of sacrifice and reincarnation), by the names of precious birds, *quechol* 'swan' and *zacuan* 'troupial.' Thus the midwife addresses the newborn male infant:

> your home is not here, for you are an eagle (*cuauhtli*), a jaguar (*ocelotl*); you are a swan (*quechol*), a troupial (*zacuan*); a companion (*coatl*) and bird of the Ever Present, the Ever Near. This is merely your nest, you are only hatched here, simply arrived, come forth, issued forth here on earth. Here you burgeon (*xotla*), you blossom (*cueponi*), you sprout (*itzmolini*). Here you make a nick [in the shell],

break [out of the shell]. . . . You were sent to the edge of the flood, to the edge of the blaze [i.e., to the battlefield]. Flood and blaze [i.e., war] is your duty, your fate. . . . Your actual home . . . is beyond, the home of the Sun, in the sky.[33]

The precious "birds," or companions of the supreme spirit, mentioned above, are mentioned again in a description of the afterworld where dead warriors go—and from which they return:

> . . . the home of the Sun, in the sky: those who go there are the ones who die in battle . . . or are just captured to die later, who, perhaps, are stripers [victims of sacrifice who have been painted with stripes] . . . ; all [who die in battle or are captured and sacrificed] go to the home of the Sun. It is said that . . . when the Sun appears, when it dawns, then they shout and cry out to it. . . . And after they've spent four years, then they're changed into precious birds, hummingbirds, flower birds . . . chalk butterflies, feather butterflies [i.e., potential captives chalked and feathered for sacrifice], calabash-cup butter-flies [i.e., sacrificial victims as drinking vessels of the gods], and they sip there where they dwell. And they come here to earth in order to sip [or inhale] all the different flowers: the [flowers of the] *equi-mitl*, or skull-rack tree; [and] the cornsilk flowers, the spear corn-silk flowers.[34]

Among the precious "birds" identified as warriors, but less well known in the *tecpillatolli* as a whole than the "swan," the troupial, or the hum-mingbird, is the *tzinitzcan* 'trogon,' mentioned frequently in the *cantares* and encountered in the concordance extracts printed above. What the *Florentine Codex* passages contribute is the ethnography documenting the promise of reincarnation that underpins the war cult; and also the special vocabulary that this ethnography shares with the *netotiliztli*. Notice the nouns and verbs *cuauhtli, ocelotl, quechol, zacuan, xotla, cueponi, itzmo-lini* in both groups of texts—or, to use a term increasingly heard among linguists—in both corpora.

Translating *Cantares Mexicanos* XIV

Song XIV may be considered the first piece in the *Cantares Mexicanos*, since numbers I–XIII in the same manuscript are somewhat attenuated, with one foot in oral tradition and the other in a newer literary mode.

Starting with song XIV we encounter the diction (and subject matter) of the *netotiliztli* in full force. The literal translation:

There's a trogon on the mat, a trogon reviving! There! As best I can I
   seek him in this grieving flower song.
Where is he? Where is he? We await him here beside the drum. Yes,
   there's grieving. On account of you there's sadness in this house of
   green places.
Whose child is this? Could it be the child of God Jesucristo? For
   indeed He paints him, He does the painting: He paints this song.
His flower painting, is it really coming? From the flower house
   within the sky?
Let people see, let people marvel in a house of colors. Let God Life
   Giver's creations be here.
By making us aware of his creations, God Life Giver torments us,
   causes us to crave his garden of song flowers.
Already in a springtime, in a springtime we are walking here, upon
   this field. A green-swan downpour roars upon us in Water Plain.
Lightning strikes from the four directions. Golden flowers are
   reviving. There! the Mexican princes are alive!

The Nahuatl text is given in an endnote;[35] the annotation is presented up front, as follows, including for each term a few comparable usages from the computer-generated study aids described above. The text sources (by folio and line number) are from the *Cantares Mexicanos* (C) and the *Romances* (R):

trogon (*tzinitzcan*); brilliant bird; warrior (see above).
mat (*petlatl*, mat, seat of authority [see *Florentine Codex*, bk. 6, ch. 17];
   place where songs are performed [Tezozomoc, *Crónica mexicana*
   ch. 53]). *Comparable usages:* on this mat of jewels in beauty I compose these songs of mine (C38v:10); etc. *Alternate meaning:* the sky
   world, cf. you've been to the Jewel Mat of Golden Flowers, beyond,
   O my prince (C22v:10); it's on the Painted Flower Mat that God, the
   Only Spirit, sings, eternal are those hearts of his in Heaven, in his
   home (C70v:17–18); etc. *Meaning in the present context:* place where
   songs are performed, the dance floor (as it represents either the sky
   world—or the battlefield, cf. heart flowers are created, there! on the
   field of battle princes are born [C18v:8–9]; etc.).

reviving (*celiztoc*); coming back to life (see above).

there! (*oncan*, in that place, yonder). *Comparable usages:* within the sky, only there! (c9:15–16); among the shield walls there! one lives, one fights (i.e., on the battlefield) (c8v:1); etc. *Significance in the present context:* over there on this dance floor (as it represents either the sky world or the battlefield, see "mat," above).

as best I can (*za nen ninentlamati*, just uselessly I agonize or just uselessly I do all that I can). *Comparable usages:* sing before the face of our father, God Life Giver? how but uselessly could I? I am poor (c23:15–16); etc. *Significance:* the singer expresses humility, recognizing that songs are created in heaven and merely brought to earth by the singer, cf. the myth of the origin of music.[36]

grieving (*icno-*, pitiable, inspiring compassion). *Comparable usages:* Let me somehow grieve, I, a singer . . . lifting flowers of bereavement, music of bereavement (c23:19–21); etc. Cf. call out, cry out to the Master, Our Lord . . . and then he will take pity on you, he will give you what you deserve, what you ought to have, *xicnotza, xictzatzili in tlacatl, in totecujo . . . auh vncan mjtzicnoittaz, vncan mjtzmacaz, in tlein molhvil momaceoal* (*Códice florentino*, lib. 6, cap. 18, fols. 76v–77). *Significance:* the singer's grieving, or affected sadness, is calculated to elicit divine favor; thus the supreme spirit takes pity and releases spirit warriors from the sky world.

on account of you (*moca*), the pronoun refers to the reviving warrior. *For example:* the roseate swan is reviving . . . you [the revived one] are merely borrowed (R7:11–14); etc.

house of green places (*xopancal-*, summer house, lit., green-time or green-place[s] house). *Comparable usages:* he comes singing through tears from the house of green places (c11:7); beyond in the house of green places (c12:6); etc. *Figurative meaning:* the sky world, paradise. *Alternate meaning:* paradise on earth; cf. flowers are drizzling into this house of green places (c10v:10–11); Green Places are here in this house of green places! (c15:6–7); etc. *Meaning in present context:* place where songs are performed, the dance floor or music room as it represents paradise.

child (*pil-*, child [offspring] or childe [prince]). *Comparable usages:* he's hatched in the waters, the house of jade waters, a child [or prince, *tepiltzin*] (c44v:30); a yellow jaguar [warrior] is roaring, a white eagle [warrior] . . . they're princes [*tepilhuan*] of Huexotlalpan:

the Chichimec lord Coxanatzin and my child [or my prince, *no-piltzin*], Lord Tlamayotzin! Let them all be borrowed! (c24v:9–10); etc. *Meaning in present context:* born-again warrior (see "reviving," above, and "princes," below).

he paints him (*quicuiloa*, he makes a picture of him [with the black and color used by the pictograph artist]; immortalizes him [i.e., the dead warrior], *Florentine Codex*, bk. 6, ch. 14 [p. 74: *tetlapalaquja tetlil-anja*]). *Comparable usages:* With flowers God is making paintings: they're companions [i.e., fellow warriors] (R7:3–4); God has formed you, has given you birth as a flower, he paints you as a song (c27:24–25); Life Giver, yes, it's true: you paint us: there Beyond you show us mercy (c64:23–24); oh, I'm in agony! friends, I utter so many! causing these hearts of mine to walk on earth, painting them here where we live (c9:8–10); etc. *Figurative meaning:* God causes him to be made or born anew, as the artist creates a human figure with paint.

song (*cuicatl*). *Comparable usages:* I come created as a song, come fashioned as a song (R2:13–14); as songs you've come alive (c15:17); God has formed you, has given you birth as a flower, paints you as a song (c27:24–25); flowers are shrilling [warbling (of birds) *or* shrieking (of warriors in battle)] (c69:2); as a song you've been born, O Montezuma: as a flower you've come to bloom on earth (63:7); etc. *Figurative meaning:* warrior or warrior king returned from the sky world (just as songs are brought down from the sky world; for "flowers" see below).

house of colors (*tlapapalcalli*). *Comparable usages:* yonder in the House of Pictures (*amoxcalli*) (c18:14–15); etc. *Figurative meaning:* the sky world. *Alternate meaning:* the dance floor as it represents the sky world, cf. flowers sprinkle down on this flower court, this house of butterflies . . . this house of pictures (c11v:1–7); etc. *Meaning in the present context:* the dance floor.

flowers (*xochitl*). *Comparable usages:* Cacao flowers, popcorn flowers are sprouting in Mexico, they're budding, they're blossoming: lords, eagles, jaguars [i.e., warriors] lie outspread, they form buds, they blossom (R8v:4–11); where do the flowers go, where do they go, they that are called eagles and jaguars? (c8:3); our good flowers walk abroad [or march along, i.e., of warriors] (R40v:8–9); etc. *Figurative meaning:* warriors

springtime (*xopantla*, summer, lit., green-time or green-place[s] location, *freely* springtime, greenery). *Comparable usages:* to the greenery you come (c52:29); etc. *Figurative meaning:* dance floor as it represents paradise (cf. house of green places, house of colors, above).

walking (*nenemi*, to walk, to move or march in battle [*Florentine Codex*, bk. 12, chs. 34, 36, pp. 97, 104]).

field (*ixtlahuatl*, field [of battle] or the field[s] [of heaven] [see *Florentine Codex*, bk. 6, pp. 11, 58, 74, 172]). *Primary meaning:* battlefield, cf. on the field, in battle, *ixtlahuacan yaonahuac* (c18v:8–9); etc. *Second meaning:* the dance floor as it represents the battlefield, cf. there's a singer! drums have appeared, songs are spread here in Chalco, on the field in Cocotitlan (c31v:13–14); etc. *Third meaning:* heaven, cf. you, in the midst of the field, a roseate swan, fly onward, in the Place Unknown (c22:30–31); etc. *Meaning in the present context:* the dance floor as it represents the battlefield.

swan (*quechol*); warrior (see above).

downpour (*quiahuitl*). *Comparable usages:* a cotinga mist is raining down and ah! they're your creations (c47v:26); etc. *Note:* the *xiuhtototl*, lit., green (or blue) bird or turquoise (-colored) bird, is *Cotinga amabilis*, the lovely cotinga. *See also:* you're singing in Cotinga House, the painted place . . . you're assembling them, O Life Giver, they're sprinkling down as a multitude . . . Here! in Mexico! (c20:12–18); etc. *Figurative meaning:* descent from the sky world.

Water Plain (*atlixco*, lit., on the face or surface of the water, on the bosom of the flood, upon the flood). *Primary meaning:* Atlixco, a town in the Huexotzinco region, traditional enemy of Mexico, site of battles (cf. in Huexotzinco, in Atlixco [c40:8]). *Second meaning:* in battle (the "flood") or on the battlefield (cf. upon the field, upon the flood [c24v:27]). *Third meaning:* the lake-surrounded city of Mexico (cf. in Willow Place . . . where the tunas lie [i.e., Tenochitlan, principal borough of the city of Mexico] . . . in Water Plain [c60:8–10]). *Note:* "Huexotzinco," lit., willow place, itself is a cryptic name for the city of Mexico (cf. here in Mexico which is the same as Huexotzinco [c63:27–28]). *Meaning in the present context:* battlefield either in the proverbial enemy town of Atlixco or in the beleaguered city of Mexico.

lightning strikes (*tlapepetlani*). *No other usages in C or R, but compare:* this jaguar earth is shaking and the screaming skies begin to rip . . . and they that come to stand on earth are spines [i.e. warriors] of His [the supreme spirit] from Flower-Tassel Land [i.e. the sky world] (c63:19–22); an eagle flood shall lie outspread before His face, the earth rolls over, the sky shakes (c33:23–24); the skies are roaring (R6v:2–3); etc. *Significance:* a perturbation of the universe accompanies the arrival of spirit warriors from the other world.

there (*oncan,* see above). *Comparable usages:* Among the shield walls, there! [i.e., on the battlefield] (c8v:1); etc.

Mexican (*mexica,* pertaining to the city-state of Mexico, either pre- or post-Conquest).

princes (*tepilhuan,* princes, nobles, noble warriors). *Comparable usages:* eagle-jaguar princes (c1v:14); princes, lords, eagles, jaguars, ah! he's descended (c9v:10–12); here they are, the princes! (R3v:18); etc. *Meaning in the present context:* warriors (arriving from the sky world).

We may now restate the translation, noting, to begin with, that the first four stanzas ask a question, answered by the second four stanzas:

Let a warrior be revived here! I try to seek him in a "grieving" song (eliciting supernatural compassion from the divine power within the sky).

Where is he? We await him here! There's "grieving," there's "sadness" (i.e., song-making) on account of you (the warrior), here in this "house of green places" (the dance floor as it represents paradise).

Whose child is this warrior? Isn't he the child of God—Jesucristo? For indeed God "paints" him, i.e., creates him—as a "song" (as an incoming warrior).

Is he really coming?—this "flower" (i.e., warrior), from the "flower house" (from paradise within the sky)?

Let people marvel in a "house of colors" (i.e., the dance floor), let God's creations (i.e., warriors brought by Jesus) be here.

God makes us aware of his "creations" (his revenant warriors), causing us to crave his garden of "flowers" (warriors).

Already, as if in a springtime (or in "green places"), we are walking (or marching) on the battlefield. A "green-swan" "downpour" (i.e., a rain of revenant warriors) roars upon us in Mexico.

Lightning strikes from the four directions (i.e., there is a perturbation of the universe). Golden "flowers" (warriors) are reviving; they are Mexican warriors; they live.

Finally, to paraphrase the entire eight-stanza song: On behalf of the Mexica (the native people of Mexico City) a singer calls for a delivery of Mexica warriors, to be brought from the sky world by the supreme warrior God, acting through Jesucristo as agent, or "muse"; and as the ritualist sings, the warriors—like songs produced in the sky world—come streaming down to earth.

A Chain Reaction

Once the key terms in the first song have been stacked up with their counterparts throughout the *netotiliztli*, the concordance takes over, setting up integrated translations of passages everywhere in the *Cantares Mexicanos* and *Romances* manuscripts. It can be seen that the "swans" as otherworldly heroes, the "painting" that brings them back to life, and the quasi-botanical "reviving" of these "flower"-like spirit warriors form the principal theme of the whole song-corpus. Endlessly repeated, yet with fresh variation in each song, the basic metaphor equates the warriors descending from the sky world with the music—the songs themselves—that likewise descend from above. Song, which memorializes the slain warrior—and in effect is all that remains of him on earth—then *is* the warrior. The striking figure is more than a simile, more even than a metaphor. It is an article of faith.

Modern readers who find the underlying theory hard to accept may be assured that there is nothing quite like this in Western tradition, not even in the intricate lore of the warriors' paradise Valhalla, with its slain and reviving heroes supervised by the spirit Odin, patron of war and poetry.[37] Aztec warriors themselves needed to be reminded of the theory's essential truth. In various songs in both the *Cantares Mexicanos* and the *Romances* the doubter's questions are allowed to surface and he is encouraged to 'believe' *neltoca*: 'can our hearts believe?' *cuix ontlaneltoca toyollo* (C14:4); 'let there be faith!' *ma ontlaneltoco* (C24v:25); 'their hearts have been converted to the faith' *ontlaneltocato iyollo* (C12:24); 'and now you're believed, ah! O priest!' *ye tomoneltoca ya om ohuaye teohua* (R15:3). Although there are differences, the Vedantic theory of reincarnation as it applies to the practice of war—expressed in the god Krishna's argument with the reluctant war chief Arjuna in the *Bhagavad Gita*—may be roughly compared.

Certain songs in the *Cantares Mexicanos* demonstrate that the theory can be played with, even satirized. Song LVII, for instance, is a 'cradle-song' *cozolcuicatl*, in which a seductive maiden lures a ghost warrior from the sky world, "laying" him in her cradle as though he were her newborn child (or her lover)—including in the seventh stanza a parody of a typical American Indian lullaby that reads, "Stop crying, you little babe, I'll lay you in your cradle, your father will come, he will rock you."[38] And the genre is flexible enough to permit not mere allusions to Christian lore (as in song XIV translated above) but—as already noted—lengthy quotations from Bible stories. For example, song LVIII, a "bringing-out song," retells the Creation, the Flood, the Nativity, the Resurrection, and, at last, Christ's instructions to the apostles and the crucifixion of the apostle Philip, all for the purpose of getting to Philip's death so that he may be resurrected as a ghost warrior in the Aztec manner. This as a means of paying him honor, using the technique of "telling it up from the beginning," as Navajo ritualists would say (meaning that the story of a particular hero may start with the earliest events in the underworld, followed by the Emergence and the gradual unfolding of Navajo history). In each of these two cases (the cradlesong and the bringing-out song) the point of departure for the Aztec singer is the *cantares* ritual, or ghost song ritual as it may be called, developed passage by passage, song by song—revealed through the close study of concordances—in a kind of chain reaction that spreads through the entire repertory.

Revitalization

Keeping in mind that the *Cantares Mexicanos* and *Romances* manuscripts represent not salvage ethnography but a living genre observed in public performance by various writers during the second (not the first) generation after the Conquest of 1521, we may ask whether song XIV can be understood as a call to arms, not literally of course, but as an act of covert defiance. In fact, Sahagún himself, who warned against these performances, stated unequivocally, 'they insist on returning to the old songs in their houses or in the residences of their chiefs . . . and they use other songs to persuade the people [i.e., in public] to do their bidding, whether it's war or other business that is not good, and they compose songs for this purpose, and they do not wish to give them up' *porfian de boluer à cantares antiguos en sus casas ò en sus tecpas . . . y otros cātares vsan para persuadir al pueblo à lo ellos quiere, ò de guerra, ò de otros negocios que no son buenos, y tienen cātares cōpuestos para esto, y no los quieren dexar.*[39]

War, indeed, is the pervasive theme of the *cantares*. Passages that appear to be exercises in philosophy are expressions of the war ethic and of the concept of the warrior as 'bereaved one' *icnotl*,[40] resolved in favor of militarism (not pacifism) when the *netotiliztli* are considered as a whole. Moreover, as noted above, echoes of the Spanish Conquest are heard throughout the corpus.

These elements, taken together, accord with a minimum definition of what may be called revitalization. Although it came too late to incite rebellion, the *cantares* movement, to give it a name, staged a recurring drama of resistance during the ostensibly pacific third quarter of the sixteenth century, celebrating a war ethic at odds with the newly dominant culture.[41] If it is understood that in this drama dead warriors are being brought back from the other world, it will be seen that the songs of the *Romances* and the *Cantares Mexicanos*, cryptic though they may be, exhibit a signal feature of the classic revitalization movement, that is, a movement among at least a segment of a subdued population that appeals to the supernatural when the opportunity for open rebellion has since passed.[42]

Nothing here is meant to imply that the songs *in their entirety* are new compositions. In recent years, the question of antiquity seems to have become a matter of concern for Mexicanists, anxious to protect the *cantares* from the suggestion that they are not pre-Columbian.[43] This shouldn't be necessary. A precontact motivation for the songs as we know them is easy to supply. They glorify the war cult, deal with laggards and dissenters, and assure the warrior of his immortality. Moreover, Sahagún, as quoted above, makes it clear that the singers were keeping old songs even as they composed new ones. He states the matter again in a different place: "They sing the old *cantares* that they used to perform in the time of their idolatry . . . and if they perform some *cantares* that they've composed since their conversion, treating the things of God and his saints, these are cloaked in many errors and heresies."[44] Song XIV, translated above, may serve as an illustration. Treating God, or Christ, as the agent responsible for distributing revenants is no doubt a disturbing deviation from Catholic doctrine, and it is reasonable to ask whether this is a well-meant syncretism or a token of defiance. In either case, portions of the song, perhaps most of it, may well have been repeated or adapted from a pre-Cortésian model. The point is that even an old song, with or without improvised Christian content, may take on a revitalistic function in a post-Conquest setting. Contemporary documents record that the songs were often proscribed by colonial authorities, generally without much success, or, at least, the authorities required that the songs be reviewed and examined before they could be performed. Less suspicious than the expert linguist Sahagún, Father Durán, admitting that the texts were "obscure," cheerfully claimed to have found them "admirable" after they had been "explained" to him.[45] Though undoubtedly a pre-Columbian idiom, the obscure language of command with its heavily veiled metaphors served a new purpose in the 1550s, 1560s, and 1570s—the great years of the post-Conquest *cantares* activity—as it enabled the native ritualists to elude sixteenth-century censorship.

The status of veiled lore fifty years after the conquest of Mexico may—despite obvious differences—be compared with the situation in North Carolina fifty years after Cherokee removal. In the words of the pioneering investigator of the Cherokee formulas, James Mooney, these texts "are not the disjointed fragments of a system long extinct, but are the revelation of a living faith. . . . Thus when one shaman meets another who he thinks can probably give him some valuable information, he says to him, 'Let us sit down together.' This is understood to mean, 'Let us tell *each other* our secrets.'"[46]

Notes

1. J. F. Kilpatrick and Kilpatrick 1965:129.

2. Translated from the Spanish in Arzápalo Marín 1987:316, using the concordance, 445–1100, to adjust the translation in light of parallel passages.

3. Translated from the Nahuatl in Ruiz de Alarcón 1984:87 or 1982:120.

4. For example, in Wyman 1970 and Boas 1930. A few Creek and Seminole formulas comparable to the Cherokee, Maya, and Aztec texts are given in Sturtevant 1979—suggesting that the genre here under consideration has two centers, the Creek-Cherokee area of the southeastern United States and the Aztec-Maya sphere within Mesoamerica.

5. J. F. Kilpatrick and Kilpatrick 1967:4, 53.

6. Ruiz de Alarcón 1982:60.

7. A. Kilpatrick 1999:25.

8. Arzápalo Marín 1987:18–21, 413; Roys 1965:67; Roys 1967:88–98.

9. Sahagún 1583:[iii].

10. Bierhorst 1985b:185, 323. Here and throughout this article, Nahuatl terms are written in a modernized Franciscan orthography (described in Bierhorst 1985b:9), omitting the Jesuit-style *h* to signal the glottal stop and the usual overbar (macron) on long vowels—except that in a few cases, to preserve the flavor

of the original text, the orthography is paleographic, i.e., uncorrected (and in the concordance extracts the text has been rewritten in Jesuit orthography).

11. *Cantares Mexicanos*, fol. 36, line 3, and fol. 53, line 8.

12. The "dramatic" aspect of the *conjuros* has been pointed out by Andrews and Hassig in Ruiz de Alarcón 1984:27; cf. p. 102. Dramatic monologues in the *Cantares* are discussed in Bierhorst 1985a:45–6, 509, 525.

13. Ruiz de Alarcón 1982 or 1984: tract 2, ch. 1; tract 5, ch. 1.

14. The idea that Nezahualcoyotl and other old kings were composers of songs that mention their names, first put forward by the early-sixteenth-century historians Torquemada and Alva Ixtlilxóchitl, is discussed in Bierhorst 1985a:97–105, 2001, and 2009a.

15. Transcribed and translated by in Ruiz de Alarcón 1982:106.

16. Ruiz de Alarcón 1982:105 or 1984:77.

17. The Aztec version is in Jonghe 1905:31–32; the Veracruz variant is in Sandstrom 1991:187, 245–46. For other Mesoamerican variants see Bierhorst 2002:68–74, 90–98, 220–21, 222–23.

18. Ruiz de Alarcón 1953:92 (trat. 2, cap. 14). Apparently unaware of the corn myth and misreading the name *ce[n]teotl*, Ruiz de Alarcón mistakenly explains the vocables as an outburst of joy (*algazara de alegría*) over the prospect of a successful outcome. Cf. Ruiz de Alarcón 1982:158 and 1984:113. On the name Centeotl see Ruiz de Alarcón 1984:322.

19. See the concordance to vocables in Bierhorst 1985b:729–36.

20. Ruiz de Alarcón 1984:259.

21. See the entries *chihua, tlacati, yocoya, yoli* in Bierhorst 1985b.

22. The distinction is made in Motolinía 1971b:386 (parte 2, cap. 27), and in López de Gómara 1988:147 (cap. 104); see also Bierhorst 1985a:92. Both terms, *macehualiztli* and *netotiliztli*, mean 'dance,' but of different styles. The subgenres named in the *Cantares Mexicanos* (*chichimecayotl, cococuicatl, otoncuicatl*, etc.) and described in Hernández 1945: libro 2, cap. 6, under the heading *netotiliztli* confirm the *cantares* as *netotiliztli*.

23. Translated from the Spanish in Durán 1967 (1): 195–96 (*Libro de los Ritos,* cap. 21).

24. Motolinía 1971a:69 (tratado 1, cap. 13); cf. 1971b:91 (parte 1, cap. 34).

25. Bierhorst 1985b and 2009b.

26. Brinton 1968:87.

27. Schultze Jena 1957:33.

28. Garibay 1964–68 (2): 88.

29. For more information, with sources, see Bierhorst 1985b.

30. On corpus linguistics see Biber, Conrad, and Reppen 1998; Baker 2006.

31. Molina 1970 (*Lengua Mexicana y Castellana* section): folios 50v, 93, 93v.

32. *Florentine Codex*, bk. 6.

33. Translated from the Nahuatl in *Códice florentino*, lib. 6, cap. 31, fols. 146v–

147. Cf. *Forentine Codex*, bk. 3, appendix, ch. 3, where the warriors newly returned to earth are *tlazototome* 'precious birds'; and bk. 6, ch. 3 (p. 12), where the
warriors are *tlazoti[n]* 'precious ones.'

34. Translated from the Nahuatl in *Códice florentino*, lib. 3, apéndice cap. 3,
fols. 28v–29.

35. *Cantares Mexicanos*, fol. 7v, lines 1–20: Çan tzinitzcan im petlatl ypan
ohuaye on tzinitzcan i celiztoc a oncan y ça nē ninentlamatia, in çan icnoxochi-
cuicatica ỹ noconyatemohua ya ohuaya ohuaya. / Yn canin nemiya y canon in
nemi toconchia ye nican huehuetitlan a ayiahue, ye onnentlamacho, ye moca
tlaocoyalo a y xopancalitec a ohuaya ohuaya / Ac ypiltzin? ach anca ipiltzin
yehuayan Dios jesu chͬo: can quicuiloã tlacuiloa quicuiloã cuicatl a ohuaya
ohuaya. / O ach anca nel ompa huiz canin ilhuicac yxochintlacuilol xochin-
calitec a ohuaya ohuaya. / Yn ma ontlachialoya in ma ontla'tlamahuiçolo in tla-
papalcali ma nican y ypalnemohua ytlayocol yehuan dios ohuaya et. / Techtolini-
ian techtla'tlanectia y ycuicaxochiamilpan in techontla'tlachialtian ypalnemohua
ytlayocol yehuan Dios a ohuaya et. / Ya y xopantla y xopantla tinenemi ye nican
ixtlahuatl ytec y, ça xiuhquecholquiahuitl çan topan xaxamacay yn atlixco ya
ohuaya ohuaya. / Çan ye nauhcampa y ontlapepetlantoc, oncan onceliztoc in
coçahuiz xochitl oncã nemi in Mexica in tepilhuan a ohuaya ohuaya.

36. In this myth the first, or original, musician travels to the sky world in order
to obtain songs, which he brings back to earth. See Jonghe 1905:32–33; Mendieta
1971:79–81.

37. Thompson 1955: motifs A465.1 God of poetry (Odin), A485 God of war
(Odin), A661.1 Valhalla (The hall of warriors who go to Odin, [who] die and are
resurrected daily), E155.1 Slain warriors revive nightly.

38. Compare these lullabies, from the Zuni: "Go to sleep, my little baby, while
I work; Father will bring in the sheep soon" (Hofmann 1964:3); from the Seminole: "Sleep well, your mother has gone to get a long turtle, little boy, go to sleep"
(Densmore 1956:204); and from the Aguaruna: "Little chick, chick, hey! . . . I'll
spread a little featherbed, little chick, chick, hey!" (Guallart Martínez 1974:16–17).
The sexual meaning of "lay" and the ambiguous term "father" (in battlefield parlance the captor is the captive's "father") mark the *Cantares* version as a parody.

39. Sahagún 1583:iii.

40. Bereaved because he is dissatisfied with mundane life, yearning for battle and immortality in the sky world. See *Códice florentino*, lib. 6, cap. 3, fol. 11v;
cf. *Florentine Codex*, bk. 6, p. 14: 'our bereaved eagles, our bereaved jaguars, who
have no pleasure, who are discontent, who live in torment, who live in pain on
this earth' *in tocnoquauh, in tocnocelouh, in aiavia, in avellamati, in toneoatinemj,
in chichinacatinemj in tlalticpac*. Also p. 12: 'may they in peace, in repose attain
the sun, which endures, shines' *manoço ivian, iocuxca itech onaciz in tonatiuh in
manjc in tlanexti*.

41. The emphasis placed by Stephanie Wood (2003:x and passim) on the "di-

versity in native responses to the invasion and occupation" and the probable truth in her intimation that a majority of native people were collaborators, either actively or passively, is not being questioned here.

42. Bierhorst 1985a:60–69.
43. Recently, León-Portilla 2002.
44. Sahagún 1969:bk. 10, ch. 27, p. 164.
45. Durán 1967 (1): 195–96 (*Libro de los Ritos*, cap. 21).
46. Mooney 1891:309.

References

Alva Ixtlilxóchitl, Fernando de. 1975–77. *Obras históricas*, ed. Edmundo O'Gorman. 2 vols. Mexico: Universidad Nacional Autónoma de México.

Arzápalo Marín, Ramón. 1987. *El ritual de los bacabes: Edición facsimilar con transcripción rítmica, traducción, notas, índice, glosario y cómputos estadísticas.* Mexico: Universidad Nacional Autónoma de México.

Baker, Paul. 2006. *Using Corpora in Discourse Analysis.* London: Continuum.

Biber, Douglas, Susan Conrad, and Randi Reppen. 1998. *Corpus Linguistics: Investigating Language Structure and Use.* Cambridge: Cambridge University Press.

Bierhorst, John. 1985a. *Cantares Mexicanos: Songs of the Aztecs.* Stanford: Stanford University Press. Corrected in Bierhorst 2009a or b, online at www.utdigital.org/book/index.php?page=cantaresMexicanos.php.

———. 1985b. *A Nahuatl-English Dictionary and Concordance to the Cantares Mexicanos with an Analytic Transcription and Grammatical Notes.* Stanford: Stanford University Press. Corrected in Bierhorst 2009a or b, online at www.utdigital.org/book/index.php?page=dictionary.php.

———. 2001. Cantares Mexicanos. In *The Oxford Encyclopedia of Mesoamerican Cultures*, ed. Davíd Carrasco, 1:139–41. New York: Oxford University Press.

———. 2002. *The Mythology of Mexico and Central America.* 2nd ed. New York: Oxford University Press.

———. 2009a. *Ballads of the Lords of New Spain: The Codex Romances de los Señores de la Nueva España.* Austin: University of Texas Press.

———. 2009b. *Ballads of the Lords of New Spain: The Codex Romances de los Señores de la Nueva España: Online Edition.* Austin: University of Texas Libraries and University of Texas Press, www.utdigital.org.

Boas, Franz. 1930. *The Religion of the Kwakiutl Indians, Pt. 2: Translations.* New York: Columbia University Press.

Brinton, Daniel G. 1969. *Ancient Nahuatl Poetry.* New York: AMS Press. Reprint of the 1890 ed., originally published in 1887.

Cantares Mexicanos. See Bierhorst 1985a.

Códice florentino, [Bernardino de Sahagún] . . . [1979]. 12 books in 3 vols. Mexico: Secretaría de Gobernación.

Densmore, Frances. 1956. *Seminole Music*. Bulletin 161. Washington DC: Bureau of American Ethnology.

Durán, Diego de. 1967. *Historia de las Indias de Nueva España e islas de la tierra firme*, ed. Angel M. Garibay K. Vol. 1, *Libro de los ritos y ceremonias . . . and El calendario antigua*. Vol. 2, *Historia*. 1867–80. Mexico: Porrúa.

Florentine Codex: General History of the Things of New Spain, Fray Bernardino de Sahagún, ed. Arthur J. O. Anderson and Charles E. Dibble. 1950–83. Santa Fe NM: School of American Research and University of Utah Press.

Garibay K., Angel M. 1964–68. *Poesía náhuatl*. 3 vols. Mexico: Universidad Nacional Autónoma de México.

Guallart Martínez, José María. 1974. *Antología de poesía aguaruna: traducción de textos originales aguarunas*. Series Ensayos, no. 3. Lima: Centro Amazónico de Antropología y Aplicación Práctica.

Hernández, Francisco. 1945. *Antigüedades de la Nueva España*, traducción de latín y notas por Joaquín García Pimentel. Mexico: Pedro Robredo.

Hofmann, Charles. 1964. Four-page leaflet accompanying the LP album *War Whoops and Medicine Songs: The Music of the American Indian* (FE-4381). New York: Ethnic Folkways Library.

Jonghe, Édouard de, ed. 1905. Histoyre du Mechique: Manuscrit français inédit du XVIe siècle. *Journal de la Société des Américanistes de Paris*, n.s., 2:1–41.

Kilpatrick, Alan. 1999. On Translating Magical Texts. *Wicazo Sa Review* 2 (autumn): 25–31.

Kilpatrick, Jack Frederick, and Anna Gritts Kilpatrick. 1965. *Walk in Your Soul: Love Incantations of the Oklahoma Cherokees*. Dallas: Southern Methodist University Press.

———. 1967. *Run toward the Nightland: Magic of the Oklahoma Cherokees*. Dallas: Southern Methodist University Press.

León-Portilla, Miguel. 2002. ¿Hay composiciones de origen prehispánico en el manuscrito de Cantares Mexicanos? *Estudios de Cultura Náhuatl* 33:141–46. www.ejournal.unam.mx/culturanahuatl_nahuatl/cultura_nahuatl33.html.

López de Gómara, Francisco. 1988. *Historia de la conquista de México*. 1552. Mexico: Porrúa.

Mendieta, Gerónimo de. 1971. *Historia eclesiástica indiana*. Mexico: Porrúa.

Molina, Alonso de. 1970. *Vocabulario en lengua castellana y mexicana y mexicana y castellana*. Mexico: Porrúa. Imitative facsimile of the 1880 printing of the edition of 1571.

Mooney, James. 1891. "The Sacred Formulas of the Cherokees," *Seventh Annual Report of the Bureau of [American] Ethnology . . . 1885–1886*, 301–97. Washington DC: Smithsonian Institution.

Motolinía, Fray Toribio de Benavente. 1971a. Historia de los indios de la Nueva España. In *Colección de documentos para la historia de México*, ed. Joaquín García Icazbalceta, 1:1–249. 1858. Mexico: Porrúa.

————.1971b. *Memoriales o libro de las cosas de la Nueva España y de los naturales de ella*, ed. Edmundo O'Gorman. Mexico: Universidad Nacional Autónoma de México.

Olmos, Fr. Andrés de. 1972. *Arte para aprender la lengua mexicana*, ed. Rémi Siméon. 1875. Guadalajara: Edmundo Aviña Levy.

Romances de los Señores de la Nueva España: see Bierhorst 2009a.

Roys, Ralph L. 1965. *Ritual of the Bacabs*. Norman: University of Oklahoma Press.

————.1967. *The Book of Chilam Balam of Chumayel*. 1933. Norman: University of Oklahoma Press.

Ruiz de Alarcón, Hernando. 1953. "Tratado de las supersticiones y costumbres gentílicas que oy viven entre los indios naturales desta Nueva España." In *Tratado de las idolatrías, supersticiones . . .*, ed. Francisco del Paso y Troncoso, 2:17–180. Mexico: Ediciones Fuente Cultural (Librería Navarro).

————.1982. *Aztec Sorcerers in Seventeenth Century Mexico: The Treatise on Superstitions*. Ed. Michael D. Coe and Gordon Whittaker. Albany: Institute for Mesoamerican Studies, State University of New York at Albany.

————.1984. *Treatise on the Heathen Superstitions that Today Live among the Indians . . . .* Ed. J. Richard Andrews and Ross Hassig. Norman: University of Oklahoma Press.

Sahagún, Bernardino de. 1583. *Psalmodia christiana, y sermonario de los sanctos del año, en lengua mexicana*. Mexico: Pedro Ocharte.

————.1969. *Historia general de las cosas de Nueva España*. Ed. Angel M. Garibay K. 4 vols. 1956. Mexico: Porrúa.

Sandstrom, Alan R. 1991. *Corn Is Our Blood: Culture and Ethnic Identity in a Contemporary Aztec Village*. Norman: University of Oklahoma Press.

Schultze Jena, Leonhard. 1957. *Alt-Aztekische Gesänge*. Quellenwerke zur alten Geschichte Amerikas, vol. 6. Stuttgart: Kohlhammer.

Sturtevant, William C. 1979. Southeastern Indian Formulas. In *Native North American Spirituality of the Eastern Woodlands*, ed. Elisabeth Tooker, 282–93. New York: Paulist Press.

Tezozomoc, Fernando Alvarado. 1975. *Crónica mexicana* Ed. Manuel Orozco y Berra. 1878. Mexico: Porrúa.

Thompson, Stith. 1955. *Motif-Index of Folk-Literature*. 6 vols. Bloomington: Indiana University Press.

Torquemada, Juan de. 1975. *Monarquía indiana*. 3 vols. 1723. Mexico: Porrúa.

Wood, Stephanie. 2003. *Transcending Conquest: Nahua Views of Spanish Colonial Mexico*. Norman: University of Oklahoma Press.

Wyman, Leland C. 1970. *Blessingway*. Tucson: University of Arizona Press.

17

Translating Context and Situation

William Strachey and Powhatan's "Scorneful Song"

William M. Clements

One of the earliest references to singing among North American Natives appears in a chronicle of Hernando de Soto's exploratory expedition of La Florida, during which he and his Spanish cohorts ventured as far west as the Mississippi River after passing through much of what is now the southeastern United States. Soto's party made their journey between 1539 and 1543. Inevitably, they would have encountered verbal art in the form of oratory as a component of diplomatic courtesies from the Indians they encountered, and they also experienced their singing. As reported by the chronicler Garcilaso de la Vega—known as "the Inca"—who based his account on excerpts from manuscripts prepared by participants in Soto's expedition and perhaps conversations with a few of them, the Native singers used vocal music to synchronize their oar work as they traveled by boat. The Indians, he notes of the occasion in question, pursued the Spanish, "rowing to the sound of their songs, and among many other things that they said (according to the interpretation of the Indians whom the Spaniards had with them) was to praise and aggrandize their own strength and bravery and to condemn the weakness and cowardice of the Castilians." More precisely, with regard to the latter point, "they said that now the cowards were fleeing from their arms and forces, and that the thieves feared their justice, and that it would do them no good to flee from the country, for all of them would soon die in the water." Moreover, if the Spanish "would soon be food for birds and dogs on land, in the river they would soon make them food for the fishes and marine animals, and thus their iniquities and the vexation that they were giving the whole world would be ended." The Inca noted that "at the end of every song they raised a great shout and outcry" (Clayton, Knight, and Moore 1993:508).

This chronicle did not see print until 1605, more than half a century after the musical performance it describes, but it may very well be the first (undoubtedly it is among the earliest) record of Native American singing presented as a text in a European language. Though the chronicler did not attempt to capture and translate the words of the song, he did ascertain their gist and implies their function. He also successfully preserved some of the situation and context informing the song's performance. It was not until after the publication of *La Florida* by the Inca that the first attempt to represent the words of an American Indian song from a community in what is now the United States occurred, but even then no attempt at translation was made. Moreover, this representation of the song's words had to wait more than two centuries before seeing print. Interestingly, though, the Powhatan song that William Strachey, secretary of the English colony at Jamestown, wrote out in 1611 and 1612, and which was published by the Hakluyt Society in 1849, seems to have been similar to what the Inca described: a "scornful song" in which the Indian singers disparage the prowess and manhood of their European counterparts and imply the appropriate repercussions that should befall the interlopers into their territory.

The priority of Strachey's textualization grants it particular importance in the history of European and Euro-American interest in Native American orally performed verbal art. However, appreciating it as fully as allowed by what is available in the textualization and supplementary sources involves more than simply acknowledging its primacy. Like his contemporaries, Strachey held conventional notions about American Indians as representatives of mankind in the state of nature. He also shared the challenges his fellow colonizers in Virginia faced when dealing with the language in which the song he transcribed was performed. Consequently, the ethnopoetic value of his "translation" does not emerge transparently. Nor does it lie principally in Strachey's representation of the text (what was sung) and texture (how it was sung) of the performance. Instead, the value of Strachey's documentation of the Powhatans' "scornful song" in the early seventeenth century lies in other components of performance: context (what the singer(s) and audience brought to the occasion) and situation (the specific circumstances where and when that occasion occurred). The purpose of this chapter is not to argue that text and texture are unimportant but to suggest that context and situation are also significant when we consider orally performed verbal art as an event that happens during a period of time rather than a literary artifact. Until recently, few textualizations of oral performance from anywhere in the world have adequately recorded or even acknowledged all components of performance. It seems unreasonable, then, to expect Strachey and other earlier sources for Native American verbal art to have anticipated the need to document all those components. Assessing his work with the Powhatan "scorneful song" by attempting to recover from it as well as from other sources as much as we can learn about an example of American Indian sung poetic performance that happened four centuries ago is, I believe, a worthwhile undertaking, even if we cannot reconstruct every component of it to a degree that provides complete contemporary satisfaction.

Born in London in 1572, William Strachey attended Cambridge without being graduated and read law at Grey's Inn apparently without being admitted to the bar. Instead, he fell in with the literary and intellectual circle who frequented the Mermaid Tavern during the first decade of the 1600s. He may have shared ale or sack with John Donne, Ben Jonson, perhaps even Shakespeare himself (Culliford 1965:42–46). As was "typical of the young gallant of the day," Strachey might idle away his time "in the playhouses, in the taverns, at the bearbaiting, cock-fighting, or gaming—in general sharing the pleasures of the fashionable world or of the dubious society that clustered on its fringes" (1965:57). Without means, without a profession, without any experience in trade, and without even a smattering of a religious vocation, Strachey sought to support himself in any way he could. For instance, he partnered with John Marston in a theatrical venture (the Children of the Queen's Revels) and was apparently involved in an attempt to publish a pirated French travel book, for which he wrote a prefatory poem. When his literary ambitions did not materialize, Strachey decided to seek his fortune overseas and in 1607 took a post as secretary to the newly appointed British ambassador to Turkey. He apparently had a falling out with his employer, though, and was back in England the following year. This is when he turned his prospects westward to Virginia.

Strachey sailed to Virginia as a "gentleman settler" on the *Sea Venture* in a convoy of eight ships. Also on board the *Sea Venture* was Sir Thomas Gates, who was to become deputy governor of Jamestown. Some six weeks into the trip (and about one week from landfall at the mouth of the James River), a storm separated the fleet, and the heavily damaged *Sea Venture* landed in the Bermudas. After nine months there, the party made it to Virginia aboard two ships they had constructed while on the islands. In addition to the unfortunate delay of his arrival in Virginia—which did not occur until May 1610—Strachey's experience shipwrecked on Bermuda had the fortuitous result of his writing a letter about his adventure which many literary historians view as one of the sources for Shakespeare's final play, *The Tempest*. When Strachey arrived at Jamestown, he (and Deputy Governor Gates) found the colony in disarray, fewer than a hundred of the original population surviving. They had just endured the famine of the previous winter, "the starving time," and were on the verge of abandoning Jamestown. The departure was stopped by the arrival of the new governor, Thomas West, Third Lord De La Warr, who established a firm government, which included Strachey as secretary, an important position which he held for a year. The time spent in America by Strachey seems to have marked the turning point in the fortunes of Jamestown. As Strachey's biographer notes, "Accounts covering the life of the colony from 1610 to 1612 emphasize the emergence of order, the rise of a new spirit and enthusiasm among the colonists, the pacification of the Indians, and increase in planting, until the venture became almost self-supporting" (Culliford 1965:122).

However, Culliford's summation may be too rosy, especially regarding the "pacification of the Indians." Strachey's tenure in Virginia occurred during what has recently been identified as "the first . . . of England's many colonial wars with American Indians" (Fausz 1990:3).[1] The colonists' relationship with the indigenous inhabitants of Virginia, the loose confederacy of Algonquian-speaking communities now generally referred to as Powhatans, had never been amicable. For example, on the night of April 26, 1607, the colonists' first night ashore in Virginia, a skirmish with a small party of Indians resulted in two Englishmen suffering wounds. A month later two colonists died when Indians attacked the newly erected fort at Jamestown. During the next couple of years, relations between the two groups remained tense, though that tension abated somewhat when the Powhatans formally recognized John Smith as a legitimate leader of a group who could potentially be a part of their confederacy.[2] By 1609, though, tensions had increased as the colonists failed to respond appropriately and reciprocally to the Powhatans' treatment of them as allies.

The Algonquian-speaking communities that formed the Powhatan Confederacy came to appreciate that Jamestown offered as much a threat on the east as did their traditional Siouan-speaking enemies on the west. Smith's allowing colonists to invade Powhatan communities and appropriate food supplies seems to have precipitated the hostilities now called the First Anglo-Powhatan War (Fausz 1990:20–22). During the next five years—encompassing the entirety of Strachey's time at Jamestown—armed hostilities recurred sporadically, producing more than two hundred English fatalities.

When Lord De La Warr assumed the governorship of Jamestown in June 1610, though, the tide may have already begun to turn against the Powhatans, who had been ascendant especially as the population of Jamestown languished during the "starving time" of the previous winter. The English began to take the war to their adversaries in such actions as the Battle of Paspahegh on August 10. Sixteen Indians and no colonists died in an attack led jointly with others by the governor's nephew William West on a community a few miles from Jamestown. Apparently, the only English fatalities that resulted from hostilities through the rest of 1610 were fourteen prospectors for gold, who were killed when they were lured ashore at a site about thirty-five miles upriver from De La Warr's headquarters. But in late 1610 or early the following year, the Englishmen built a fort at the fall line where they spent the winter under constant threat of Powhatan attack. During the siege of Fort La Warr, more than thirty colonists perished from hostile activity—one fatality being De La Warr's nephew William West. As George Percy, the deputy governor, described this incident, "My Lord generall [i.e., Lord De La Warr] all this Tyme Remayneinge att the Falles where nether sicknes nor skarsety was wanteinge had dyvers encownters with the Indyans some of his men being slayne amonge the Rest his Kinsman Capteyne William Weste and Capteine Bruster narrowly escaped" (Smith 2007:1107). Disheartened by his losses and suffering ill health, De La Warr left Virginia on March 28, 1611. The following day, the Powhatans attacked the garrison at Jamestown. "From forest cover the Indians taunted Puttock [the officer on duty at the fort's blockhouse] until he rashly charged them with his entire force of about twenty men," all of whom perished (Fausz 1990:37). Strachey, who was present in Jamestown when this disaster occurred, apparently did not leave Virginia until later in 1611.

For Strachey personally, the most significant result of his Jamestown experience was the production of his *Historie of Travaille*, which he conceived and began to write while still in America. His hopes for financial success and literary acclaim from this work fell through, though, when John Smith's *Map of Virginia* appeared in 1612. Strachey spent the rest of the decade revising his book (a second full copy dates from 1618) and unsuccessfully attempting to interest financial backers in it, but he died in obscurity in 1621.

Probably the reason that Strachey's *Historie* failed to attract contemporary attention and bring celebrity and material comfort to its author stems from its largely derivative nature. His biographer has dismissed it as "purely a compilation" and cites a multitude of published sources upon which Strachey drew (Culliford 1965:165–84). Most significantly for his hopes of publication, Strachey's major source of information specifically about Jamestown (i.e., Book One of the *Historie*) was Smith's *Map of Virginia*: "One third of this first book consists of extracts from John Smith's *Map*, rearranged, in a few places condensed, and in a few expanded, but in no way rewritten. Strachey borrowed about four-fifths of Smith's work and included every passage actually describing the people, the country, or its products" (Culliford 1965:178). Smith, though, had already left Jamestown by the time Strachey arrived, so some material in the *Historie* does represent Strachey's observations and experiences. Much of that deals with the people whose territory the English colonists were appropriating, the Powhatans. Despite its dismissive treatment by Culliford and its contemporary failure, the *Historie* is the best account of this society written by someone who actually observed and interacted with the Powhatans: "the most authoritative study of Virginia Indians in the early colonial era" (Hantman 1992:73). As Helen C. Rountree, an ethnohistorian who has provided the most thorough characterization of early-seventeenth-century Powhatan culture and society, notes, Strachey "was not prepared to be an ethnographer in the modern sense, but he had a wider and more detailed curiosity about Indian life than any other writer of his time." Though his tenure at Jamestown coincided with a period of unrest "which confined him primarily to the English fort and to the male Indian visitors who came there" (Rountree 1989:4), he nevertheless produced a work that remains the most complete single source on their language and literature.

The Powhatan language, now usually referred to as Virginia Algonquian, seems to have disappeared.[3] Once Powhatans were brought into

English settlements, Rountree indicates, they were expected to learn English; few if any of the English colonists reciprocated. By 1700, she estimates, "the necessity of dealing at close quarters with English people—at work, in trading, or in legal matters, meant that all Powhatans spoke some English. . . . [Moreover,] by then there were young Indian adults who spoke no Powhatan at all" (1993:173–205). English writers contemporary with Strachey recorded little of the language. Thomas Hariot, for example, whose *A Description of Virginia* (1588) predates Strachey's *Historie* by almost a quarter century, notes regarding the tongues used in that part of the world that "The languages spoken of every government is different from any other, and the further they are distant the greater is the difference" (Smith 2007:896). Even though some references to what may have been a dictionary of some Virginia language(s) compiled by Hariot have been noted, that work is apparently no longer extant (Townsend 2004:187 n. 5). John Smith included a brief Powhatan vocabulary in his *Generall Historie*, a successor to the 1612 *Map of Virginia* (Smith 2007:300–303), but this does not come near to matching the extensive word list that Strachey, who also dismissively remarked that the Powhatans "have but few words in their language" (Strachey 2005:51), appended to his manuscript. That list, entitled "A Dictionarie of the Indian Language, for the Better Enabling of Such Who Shalbe Thither Ymployed," consists of both Powhatan and English terms with their assumed equivalents. Despite his "execrable script"—which may be experienced by modern readers in John P. Harrington's facsimile reproduction of sixteen sheets from the 1618 version of the dictionary (1955:189–202)—modern linguists have given Strachey high marks for his language skills: "Among Strachey's virtues were the fact that he was generous and diversified in his linguistic sampling, and that he often rendered the same gloss two of more times in varying recordings so that it is possible to form a reasonable opinion of the probable pronunciation. In comparison with most of his contemporaries, his 'ear' for an exotic language appears to have been of a superior order, but in common with other English writers of his period he had little conception of consistency in sound representation or of uniform orthography" (Siebert 1975:292).

Perhaps Strachey's literary aspirations from his years at the Mermaid Tavern had made him more sensitive to the nuances of the spoken word than the military, political, and commercial functionaries who were also writing about the Powhatans. Perhaps the influence of Donne, Jonson,

Marston, and Shakespeare helped him to realize that this spoken language could communicate artistically. At any rate, Strachey's *Historie* has the distinction not only of producing the most complete information on Virginia Algonquian available but also of including perhaps the first attempt in English to capture Native North American poetic expression in manuscript: to translate it, if not linguistically, then ethnographically and semiotically.

Some of Strachey's contemporaries had remarked on the verbal art, especially singing, of the Virginia Indians, though usually reserving their comments for the nature of the music rather than the content of the lyrics. Smith, for instance, characterized their "hellish notes and screeches" (2007:318). George Percy, who wrote of his experiences in 1606 and 1607, noted Native singing in the context of dancing: "One of the Savages standing in the midst singing, beating one hand against another, all the rest dancing about him, shouting, howling, and stamping against the ground, with many Anticke tricks and faces, making a noise like so many Wolves or Devils" (Smith 2007:926). Writing of 1609, Henry Spelman indicated that when "they will gather themselves together they have a kind of howling, or hubbabub, so differing in sound one from the other as both parts may very easily be distinguished" (Haile 1998:494). Strachey stands out from his contemporaries not only because he devoted more attention to a particular song performance but because he was not so dismayed by the nature of Powhatan singing; for example, "When they sing they have a pleasaunt tange in their voices" (2005:54).

The song performance, which Strachey unfortunately prefaces with a description of musical instrumentation lifted almost verbatim from Smith (Strachey 2005:79; Smith 2007:290), represents a "kind of angry song against us, in their homely rymes, which concludeth with a kynd of petition unto their okeus [Their Indian name for their gods—Strachey's note], and to all the host of their idolls, to plague the Tassantasses (for so they call us) and their posterities" (Strachey 2005:79). In particular, the song Strachey transcribes is a "scorneful song" celebrating the Powhatans' killing of Captain William West "and two or three more" and capture of two other Englishmen at Fort La Warr in early 1611:

1. Matanerew shashashewaw erawango pechecoma
   Whe Tassantassa inoshashawyehockan pocosack.
   Whe whe, yah haha nehe wittowa, wittowa.

2. Matanerew shashashewaw erawango pechecoma
   Capt. Newport inoshashaw neir mhoc natian matassan
   Whe whe, etc.

3. Matanerew shashashewaw erawango pechecoma
   Thom. Newport inoshashaw neir inhoc natian moncock:
   Whe whe, etc.

4. Matanerew shashashewaw erawango pechecoma
   Pochin Simon moshashaw ningon natian monahack,
   Whe whe, etc. (2005:79–80)

Although he does not attempt to translate these words (and vocables), Strachey does provide a paraphrase. The song, he believes,

> maye signifie how they killed us for all our poccasacks, this is our guns, and for all that Captain Newport brought them copper, and could hurt Thomas Newport (a boy whose name in deede was Thomas Savadge, who Captain Newport leaving with Powhatan to learne the language, at that tyme he presented the said Powhatan with a copper crowne, and other gifts from his Majestie, said he was his sonne) for all his monachock, that is his bright sword, and how they could take Symon (for they seldome said our surname) prisoner for all his tamahanke, that is his hatchet, adding, as for a burden unto their song, what lamentation our people made when they kild him, namely, saying how they would cry whe, whe, etc., which they mockt us for, and cryed againe to us yah, ha, ha, Tewittawa, Tewittawa; for yt is true they never bemoane themselves nor cry out, gyving up so much as a groane for any death, how cruell soever and full of torment. (2005:80)

Any modern attempt to translate the song text must be speculative. Strachey wrote out what he heard, and that of course was shaped by his own language's phonology as well as by personal idiosyncrasies. Even one of his contemporaries might not have known exactly how to vocalize what Strachey intended, and that problem has become more pronounced with the passage of four centuries. As folklorist Wm. Hugh Jansen put it regarding attempts to represent dialect through manipulation of spellings in textualizations of English-language folktales, "The reader struggles to determine the sound represented by the peculiar spelling, then tries to guess the word that would match that sound" (1975:84). Moreover, Strachey's spellings of the Powhatan language are inconsistent, a result perhaps of the looser orthography of his age, of errors he made in rewriting a second version of his manuscript (the version which the Hakluyt Society published in 1849), and of difficulties that the Hakluyt Society editor may have had with Strachey's penmanship. Nevertheless, using Strachey's own published Powhatan vocabulary, that of John Smith, the dictionary for Proto-Algonquian developed by George F. Aubin (1975), and Frank T. Siebert Jr.'s (1975) lexicon of Virginia Algonquian, we can attempt to match a few of the words of the song with English equivalents or, more likely, near-equivalents. Smith's vocabulary confirms Strachey's paraphrased version of the song: the stanzas do seem to deal successively with guns (Smith: *pawcussacks*; Aubin: **pa:škesikani*), copper (Smith: *mattassin*; Siebert: *matassun*), a sword (Smith: *monacooke*), and an ax (Smith: *Tomahack*). The stanzas also seem to treat sequentially the colonists in general and then three individuals, apparently persons from whom the Powhatans had acquired arms: Captain Christopher Newport, who had charge of the Virginia Company's first expedition, which selected the site for Jamestown in 1607, and who had been at least indirectly responsible for the Powhatans' acquisition of some English armaments, including a few firearms (Fausz 1990:21); Thomas Savage, an English boy who had acquired enough of the Powhatan language to serve as an interpreter and who remained a principal player in Powhatan-English affairs for the rest of his relatively long life; and perhaps Simon Scrove, a "saylor" who apparently was taken prisoner when William West was killed.

The first word in each stanza may indeed be the ultimate insult against the English in this scornful, taunting song (sung perhaps from the forest to lure Puttock to his death on March 29, 1611). It probably represents the Virginia Algonquian equivalent of the Proto-Algonquian **mat-a:p:ew*, which combines a prefix meaning "bad" with a noun final meaning "man" (see also **na:pe:wa*, which means "man"; Siebert: *nematough*). "Matanerew" probably means "bad man" not in the sense of one who perpetrates evil but in reference to a male who does not fulfill the requirements of maleness. In other words, English masculinity is being called into question. Perhaps William West and his colleagues had indeed died badly; the Powhatans apparently wanted those at whom they were aiming this taunt to think that they had. They may have been especially thinking of the fate of George Cassen, which John Smith reported from the testimony of a Powhatan witness: "When he would punish any notorious enemy or malefactor, he causeth him to be tyed to a tree, and with Mussell shels or reeds, the executioner cutteth off his joynts one after another, ever casting what they cut of into the fire; then doth he proceed with shels and reeds to case the skinne from his head and face; then doe they rip his belly and so burne him with the tree and all" (2007:298). Probably Cassen did not face this procedure as a Powhatan would. Rountree sums up the Powhatan ethos that informed this song: "As was the case with other Woodland tribes, a 'real' man died not only stoically but also deriding his tormentors. The Powhatans probably had mocking death songs for their men to sing, like those of other tribes. Death with honor was the only possible end for a captured man, unless he could escape, and Indian men went to war carefully conditioned for such an end. The Powhatans were firmly locked into this way of thinking" (1989:84). Apparently, at least three individuals as well as the collective battle casualties from the Jamestown colony are being accused of having died badly, and the "scorneful song" became a vehicle for taunts and derision.

The Powhatans perhaps did not know whom they had killed. As Strachey notes, they had misunderstood the nature of the relationship between Christopher Newport and Thomas Savage. The apparent verb in the second line of each stanza may imply that Englishmen generically and collectively, and the individuals, Christopher Newport, Thomas "Newport," and Pochin Simon, were killed (Aubin: *ne?θa:we, "he was killed"). Their deaths allowed the Powhatans to acquire the very armaments that they were now using against other Englishmen. The vocables that conclude each stanza were probably anything but "meaningless nonsense syllables," but—as Strachey suggests—imitations of the weeping that accompanied the dishonorable deaths of the individuals named in the song and which would attend future deaths of the unmanly colonists. Perhaps this song was repeatedly used to taunt the colonists; hearing it frequently could account for Strachey's ability to reproduce it.

In fact, the three individuals whom the song mentions had not suffered death at the hands of the Powhatans in 1611 or earlier. Christopher Newport did not die until 1617, and that sad event occurred in his native England, not in Virginia. Thomas Savage, who began living among the Powhatans so that he could master their language and serve as an interpreter

soon after the English arrived in Virginia, had returned to his country-
men in 1609. He worked as go-between for the English and Powhatans
during the next several years, received a tract of land from the Accomac
weroance (a sort of "subchief" or district leader) which is still called "Savage's Neck," and died in 1635. Pochin Simon is harder to identify. He may
indeed be Simon Skrove, though the name preceding his given name is
that of a son of Powhatan, a *weroance* who oversaw the community of
Kecoughtan at the mouth of the James River. Rountree also notes the existence of a recidivist runaway named Simons who made several attempts
to cast his lot with the Powhatans several years after the composition and
performance of the "scorneful song" (2005:163). Certainly Powhatan himself would have known both Newport and Savage, but the composer(s) of
the song may not have so readily distinguished among the outsiders who
were invading their territory.

I think the view advanced here is more likely than that proposed by
Rountree: "The common people were singing the latest hit song, which
derided the Strangers for being such fools as to be killed in spite of their
supposedly superior weapons. Guns! Swords! What good did they do for
such incompetents? Just let the morons' leaders try to buy the Real People off with copper! Our Real Men can capture and kill foreigners whenever they want to!" (2005:146–47). She dates the song, though, from the
beginning of the planting season of 1610, perhaps nine or ten months before the deaths of William West and others at the siege of Fort La Warre,
which Strachey claims provided the impetus for the song's composition.

When one takes its English audience into account, the rhetorical purpose of the song is evident,[4] and for those colonists who understood its
import, it undoubtedly rankled, perhaps even to the point of precipitating
the foolhardy engagement that cost Puttock and nineteen others from the
Jamestown garrison their lives. A tradition of using songs as a prelude to
martial engagement figured into Powhatan military polity. Smith had witnessed a highly formal mock battle, staged for his benefit, during which
the warriors were "all duly keeping their orders, yet leaping and singing
after their accustomed tune, which they use onely in Warres" (2007:289).[5]
But certainly the Powhatan warriors who used the song to heap scorn on
their enemies realized that many of the colonists would not understand
what they were articulating. Strachey seems to have been unusual in his
interest in the Powhatan language. Consequently, the role of the song for
its other audience, the Powhatans themselves, must be taken into account.

Characterizations of the "other" (most likely the literal meaning of *tassantassas*, a term the Powhatans used to refer to the English) have twofold significance. They serve to characterize whoever exists outside a group's boundaries—whether marked racially, ethnically, religiously, or by caste or class. Meanwhile, through negation they define what it means to be a member of the group itself. The "other" is consummately "not us" in that he or she believes those very ideas and behaves in those very ways which we reject. If we value industry, the other comes across as lazy; if we emphasize the importance of cleanliness, the other wallows in filth; if we define some foods as unclean, the other's diet consists largely of those very foods; and if we believe that a man should confront death with dignity and fortitude, the other meets his or her demise with whimpering and sniveling. By ridiculing the other for doing exactly what we eschew, we strengthen our sense of what we do indeed value. Characterizations of the other, then, may serve as an integrative force by showing us what we must think and how we must behave if we really want to be fully accepted members of our group. As Jansen (1964) has noted, such characterizations—"the esoteric-exoteric factor in folklore"—become more pronounced when a community feels its identity threatened by outsiders.

The arrival of the English at Jamestown had introduced an emphatically different other to the Powhatan consciousness. The invaders diverged much more from what the Powhatans regarded as normative than did traditional others such as the Siouan-speaking communities west of the fall line. Moreover, these new others, though relatively few in number and decidedly inept in their attempts to adapt to life in Virginia, did bring death with them in the form of more sophisticated armaments than the Powhatans possessed. Though we can roughly guess the number of deaths among the Englishmen during the first half decade or so at Jamestown from disease, accident, malnutrition, and the hostilities that culminated in the First Anglo-Powhatan War, trying to assess how many Indians died during that period poses probably insurmountable difficulties. Most likely, though, the toll exacted from the indigenous population was high and, during the winter of 1610–11, may have seemed disproportionate to the number of Englishmen who were perishing, especially in light of the near obliteration that the English community had suffered the previous winter. Taking the war to the Powhatans had resulted in fewer English casualties, and the administration of De La Warr seems to have alleviated some of the sanitary and nutritional issues that had contributed to the high mortality rate at Jamestown from natural causes. In the spring of 1610 the Powhatans may have sensed that the English were almost defeated, but events had turned around. Perhaps, then, part of the motivation for singing the "scorneful song" the following year was to rally Powhatan spirits. It reminded them that even though the English seemed to be rebounding from their near extinction, they nevertheless did not evince the fundamental masculinity that was crucial to Powhatan warrior identity. So even if the past few months had not gone well, in the long run—especially with the departure of De La Warr on the eve of the attack when the song may have been sung—the Powhatans could count on their ascendancy. They had strength of character and fortitude that their English adversaries lacked, and they had even obtained a supply of arms that resembled the weaponry in the colonists' hands. The song also reminds Powhatan warriors of their own responsibility in the face of death: not to behave as English "bad-men" but to face the inevitable as "good-men" should. Scorn for the English was noted in other situations. For example, a commentator at the time reported that Nansemond's people filled the mouths of the English whom they killed in retaliation for a sacrilege with bread "as it seemeth in contempt and scorn" (Haile 1998:329–30).

What does an attempt to understand the context and situation of the performance of orally expressed verbal art have to do with the craft of translation, particularly when the enunciated words—the "text" itself—remain elusive? Performance involves, of course, not only what is said. A performance is an event that takes place during a particular expanse of time before a particular audience at a particular place. Capturing the performance in print and making it accessible to readers involves a process akin to what anthropologists have done in ethnography through making various actions by humans available and accessible to readers who were not on the scene when those actions occurred. Thinking of ethnography as akin to translation has long been a commonplace among anthropologists (Asad 1986), but it is also fruitful to reverse this perspective by thinking of translation as ethnography. If Strachey and his contemporaries came up short linguistically, many of them—especially someone such as Strachey who had literary aspirations—possessed observational skills and the ability to render their observations in writing. While we cannot deny that Strachey's observations were in many ways unsophisticated and colored by conventional European ideas of the nature of "savages," we do learn some things about Powhatan sung performance from his presentation that might otherwise be lost. Moreover, we can utilize other sources more or less contemporary with Strachey as well as the work of ethnohistorians such as Rountree, Fausz, and Gleach to reconstruct perhaps not too speculatively not only the general cultural context out of which the song emerged but the specifics of the situation that engendered one particular performance of it.

The ethnography of speaking has led to the recognition that a complete representation of discourse involves more than simply documentation of what was said. Several models for such an ethnographic rendering of speech behavior have been proposed (Bauman 1984; Hymes 1974), and their specific application to dealing with orally expressed verbal art through the process that Roman Jakobson (1992) called "transmutation," the intersemiotic movement from one medium of communication to another, has emerged from the rethinking of what constitutes verbal art that the ethnography of speaking engendered (e.g., Fine 1984). Drawing upon and expanding the model suggested more than forty years ago by the folklorist Alan Dundes (1964; *text*, *texture*, *context*, and *situation*), we can suggest a four-part approach to considering translation as an ethnographic act and to evaluating what we can know about the Powhatan "scorneful song" presented by Strachey. On one hand, the translator must be concerned with *text*, what the performer enunciates. The words of the performance must first go through a process of textualization, during which they move from the medium of oral performance to written or printed text. The most important criterion of textualization is that it present the words of performance verbatim without omitting materials (especially vocables in the presentation of the words of Native American songs), without adding anything to them, and without making substitutions or rearrangements. If the words must be translated interlingually as well as intersemiotically, that translation should favor source language in the manner suggested by the ethnopoetics movement. Evaluating Strachey's work in terms of its presentation of the text itself is problematic. While Strachey made a good effort to capture the sounds he heard in the song, he lacked the phonological skills to do so with complete accuracy. What he heard was filtered through the phonology of Elizabethan English and then through his inconsistent and often illegible handwriting. His piecemeal translation of only a few of the nominals in the text seems to find confirmation in what Smith had contemporaneously recorded and in the subsequent work of linguists with Virginia Algonquian and Proto-Algonquian, but he does not attempt anything beyond a few attempts to match vocabulary. And while he may have found adequate denotative matches, he undoubtedly did not understand the associations and implications that some of the Powhatan words might have for native speakers.

Texture, another component of a fully developed ethnographic translation, focuses on how the words of the performance were rendered. It includes such concerns as the tempo and pacing of what was said or sung as well as paralinguistic complements to the words themselves. Texture also involves features of the physical presence of the performer: the speaker or singer's postures, gestures, and facial expressions and the way he or she physically relates to the intended audience. The most important work in regard to textural representation of Native American orally performed verbal art has been that of Dennis Tedlock (1983), who has shown how one can work with an audio recording of a performance to produce an intersemiotic translation that suggests—often very specifically through typographic manipulation—matters of pacing, tempo, and paralinguistics especially. Tedlock has been less successful in dealing with the physical dimension of performance. Hymes (1981) has shown how some aspects of texture can be recovered even when an audio recording is not available, as long as a punctiliously documented text in the original language can be accessed. Presumably, Strachey's rendering the Powhatan song in lines emerged from the performance itself, but Strachey provides only clues about how it otherwise might have been sung. Had his material on musical instruments (which immediately precedes the song in his *Historie*) not been appropriated from John Smith, we might take that as having some bearing on the singing of the song—though one doubts that pipes and rattles would have figured into a performance that might have occurred in the emotional heat leading up to armed conflict. Although Strachey uses "they" to refer to the maker(s) and presumably the performer(s) of the song, we cannot even be certain whether this was a group or solo performance. Nor do we know if the vocables that imitated weeping and sobbing required a different vocal timbre than that used in the words of the song.

What we do have, however, is some idea of *context* and *situation*, the other two elements that ideally figure into ethnographic translation, though some of that information comes from sources that supplement

Strachey's account. *Context* refers to the set of ideas that inform the performance of verbal art: the cultural and social background as well as personal factors affecting the performer and audience. *Situation* indicates the distinctive circumstances that factored into the specific performance, including specific time, particular place, and audience composition. Most often, ethnographers of speaking have handled these matters in introductory essays to the material they present and (perhaps) through notes that respond to particular issues in the textured text. About the Powhatan "scorneful song" we know important contextual information, some of it based on the work of ethnohistorians rather than derived directly from Strachey's narrative. For instance, we know that the song emerged out of a period in the First Anglo-Powhatan War when the tide seemed to be turning, if only slightly, against the Powhatans. We also know that the song responds to the symbolically and strategically important killing of several Englishmen, including the governor's nephew, and that these deaths contributed to the abandonment of an English outpost and perhaps to the eventual departure of the governor for England. We also know that the song reflects Powhatan perspectives on how men should face death and that its intended audience consisted of comrades of individuals who, according to the song at least, had not met their deaths appropriately. We can also infer that the song's maker(s) and performer(s) realized the presence of a secondary audience of their own people who might need some encouragement, particularly given the revival of the English presence after its near annihilation during the "starving time."

Most of this context information is evident or at least implied in the historical record either directly or as reconstructed by ethnohistorians. Pronouncements about situation must be more speculative, though clues exist that provide some grounding for speculation. Among issues that we do not know are who created and performed the song, how many individuals may have been involved in producing it, and whether Strachey based his presentation upon only one hearing or, more likely, several performances. One of those performances probably occurred outside the walls of the garrison at Jamestown, particularly since Strachey seems to have spent most of his time in Virginia there and would have not been as likely to have heard the song elsewhere. A particularly appropriate situation for its performance would be as a way to lure the English away from the protection of the fort so that they would have to face their adversaries in battle. That is exactly what occurred on March 29, 1611.

In sum, I think we can, on the basis of Strachey's "text" as well as supplementary sources, recognize that Powhatans in the early seventeenth century were using song performance as rhetorical strategy to undermine the confidence of their adversaries and bolster their own self-image. Perhaps sensing that the infusion of new blood into the Jamestown colony, which may have seemed to be on its last legs when Strachey arrived and which had indeed throughout much of late 1610 made inroads into Powhatan dominance in the region, members of the Confederacy were especially concerned with asserting their superiority in what they viewed as a fundamental indicator of manliness, the ability to face death with equanimity. Taunting the colonists with specific instances of their comrades' shortcomings in this regard—and by implication foregrounding their own manliness—they served notice that those who were "bad-men" in this regard could not expect to survive effectively in what for them was a new world. In fact, they had almost disappeared as completely as the Roanoke colony on more than one occasion since 1607. But now things seemed to be improving, so the Powhatans may have sought to remind the colonists repeatedly of their weaknesses. That the song apparently was performed just after the departure of Lord De La Warr, the engineer of Jamestown's resurgence, suggests that the Indians were insinuating themselves into the consciousness of the settlers at a time when they might be able to take advantage of a momentary lapse in their morale and physical defenses.

When dealing with orally performed verbal art, all four components—*text*, *texture*, *situation*, and *context*—constitute the performance. Although I have done so above, one should not separate text from context, texture from situation. Performance is an integrated phenomenon, and while students of orally expressed Native American verbal art have tended to highlight text, perhaps to the point of not even considering the other components, that tendency represents the influence of a print-oriented literary culture. Native American literary cultures have until recently been exclusively performance-oriented rather than text-focused, though, and the failure to take that into account misrepresents them. We also do them a disservice by not trying to recover some of their tradition, even though that tradition may exist only in sources such as Strachey's *Historie* that fail in many respects to meet current expectations. The work of the translator of Native American orally performed verbal art involves much more than a faithful rendering of the original and a respectful favoring of source language in that rendering. Translation must be total in the sense that it ethnographically represents as much about the performance as possible, and it must recognize that a tradition of performance can be recovered, if only partially, from sources that did not have the advantages offered by recent developments in performance theory, the ethnography of speaking, ethnopoetics, and recording technology.

Notes

1. Frederic W. Gleach objects to Fausz's use of the term "war" to refer to the conditions existing between Powhatans and English during the first few decades of the seventeenth century as representing too Eurocentric a perspective and as suggesting a series of military engagements much more formal than what was actually occurring (Gleach 1997:43–54). Fausz's term, though, does reflect the intensification of those engagements at particular times in the course of Powhatan-English relations.

2. Varying interpretations for the famous incident involving Smith, Powhatan, and Pocahontas have been proposed. One holds that the event amounted to a ceremonial integration of the Jamestown colony into the Powhatan Confederacy (at least potentially) and acknowledgment of Smith's role as military commander of the Jamestown colonists. See, e.g., Fausz (1990:17) and Gleach (1997:116–20). Of course, many commentators believe that John Smith completely fabricated the incident. For instance, see Rountree (2005:76–82).

3. In addition to Siebert (1975:285–453), more recent work to revive Virginian Algonquian on the local level is in progress. See, e.g., these Web sites: "Vocabulary Words in Native American Languages: Powhatan," www.native-languages .org/powhatan_words.htm; "Powhatan Words Used in 'Pocahontas,'" www.geo cities.com/bigorrin/pocahontaswords.htm; and "Welcome to Our Powhatan Dictionary Courtesy of the Wicocomico Indian Nation," www.wiccomico-indian -nation.com/pages/dictionary.html.

4. See Abrahams 1968.

5. Also see Strachey 2005.

References

Abrahams, Roger D. 1968. Introductory Remarks toward a Rhetorical Theory of Folklore. *Journal of American Folklore* 81:143–58.

Asad, Talad. 1986. The Concept of Cultural Translation in British Social Anthropology. In *Writing Culture: The Poetics and Politics of Ethnography*, ed. George E. Marcus and James Clifford, 141–64. Berkeley: University of California Press.

Aubin, George F. 1975. *A Proto-Algonquian Dictionary*. Canadian Ethnology Service Paper no. 29. Ottawa: National Museums of Canada.

Bauman, Richard. 1984. *Verbal Art as Performance*. Prospect Heights IL: Waveland.

Clayton, Lawrence A., Vernon James Knight Jr., and Edward C. Moore, eds. 1993. *La Florida by the Inca*. In *The De Soto Chronicles: The Expedition of Hernando de Soto to North America in 1539–1543*, 2:25–560. Tuscaloosa: University of Alabama Press.

Culliford, S. G. 1965. *William Strachey 1572–1621*. Charlottesville: University Press of Virginia.

Dundes, Alan. 1964. Text, Texture, and Context. *Southern Folklore Quarterly* 28:251–65.

Fausz, J. Frederick. 1990. An "Abundance of Blood Shed on Both Sides": England's First Indian War, 1609–1614. *Virginian Magazine of History and Biography* 98:3–56.

Fine, Elizabeth C. 1984. *The Folklore Text from Performance to Print*. Bloomington: Indiana University Press.

Gleach, Frederic W. 1997. *Powhatan's World and Colonial Virginia: A Conflict of Cultures*. Lincoln: University of Nebraska Press.

Haile, Edward Wright, ed. 1998. *Jamestown Narratives, Eyewitness Accounts of the Virginia Colony. The First Decade: 1607–1617*. Champlain VA: RoundHouse.

Hantman, Jeffrey L. 1992. Caliban's Own Voice: American Indian Views of the Other in Colonial Virginia. *New Literary History* 23:69–81.

Harrington, John P. 1955. The Original Strachey Vocabulary of the Virginia Indian Language. *Anthropological Papers no. 46. Bureau of American Ethnology Bulletin 157*, 189–202. Washington DC: Government Printing Office.

Hymes, Dell. 1974. *Foundations in Sociolinguistics: An Ethnographic Approach*. Philadelphia: University of Pennsylvania Press.

———. 1981. *"In Vain I Tried to Tell You": Studies in Native American Ethnopoetics*. Philadelphia: University of Pennsylvania Press.

Jakobson, Roman. 1992. On Linguistic Aspects of Translation. In *Theories of Translation: An Anthology of Essays from Dryden to Derrida*, ed. Rainer Schulte and John Biguenet, 144–51. Chicago: University of Chicago Press.

Jansen, Wm. Hugh. 1964. The Esoteric-Exoteric Factor in Folklore. In *The Study of Folklore*, ed. Alan Dundes, 43–51. Englewood Cliffs NJ: Prentice-Hall.

———. 1975. A Folktale—On Paper? *Mid-South Folklore* 3:83–87.

Rountree, Helen C. 1989. *The Powhatan Indians of Virginia: Their Traditional Culture*. Norman: University of Oklahoma Press.

———. 1993. The Powhatans and the English: A Case of Multiple Conflicting Agendas. In *Powhatan Foreign Relations, 1500–1722*, ed. Helen C. Rountree, 173–205. Charlottesville: University Press of Virginia.

———. 2005. *Pocahontas, Powhatan, Opechancanough: Three Indian Lives Changed by Jamestown*. Charlottesville: University Press of Virginia.

Siebert, Frank T., Jr. 1975. Resurrecting Virginia Algonquian from the Dead: The

Reconstituted and Historical Phonology of Powhatan. In *Studies in Southeastern Indian Languages*, ed. James M. Crawford, 285–453. Athens: University of Georgia Press.

Smith, Captain John. 2007. *Writings and Other Narratives of Roanoke, Jamestown, and the First English Settlement in America*. New York: Library of America.

Strachey, William. 2005. *The Historie of Travaile into Virginia Britannia Expressing the Cosmographie and Comodities of the Country Together with the Manners and Customes of the People*. N.p.: Elibron Classics. (Originally published in 1849)

Tedlock, Dennis. 1983. *The Spoken Word and the Work of Interpretation*. Philadelphia: University of Pennsylvania Press.

Townsend, Camilla. 2004. *Pocahontas and the Powhatan Dilemma: An American Portrait*. New York: Hill and Wang.

18

A Life in Translation

Richard J. Preston

Introduction

When I was a child, I made about thirty solitary trips between my divorced parents, one in Chicago, the other in Fort Collins, Colorado, on the Union Pacific Streamliner *City of Denver*. Each trip was a thousand miles all by myself, and they were great adventures that I looked forward to eagerly. And at night, in an upper bunk, I would slide open the small window and look out through the darkness rushing by, and see in the distance a house, visible only by a lighted window or two. I used to wonder what it was like, living in those prairie farmhouses—how life looked from the inside of other people's homes.

As an adult, after several brief careers and adventures, I wound up making about thirty trips to James Bay, in northwestern Quebec and northeastern Ontario. There I and (often) my family sojourned in Cree coastal communities where it became my vocation to try to understand what it had been like living the traditional seasonal round in the bush—how life looked from the inside of other people's homes.

Near the end of my first summer at Waskaganish, I had the great good fortune to find a mentor in John Blackned, a man who was born in the bush in about 1894. When I first met him, he was sixty-nine, and was regarded in his and other Cree communities as a remarkable repository of traditional knowledge. For seven summers during the 1960s, I learned to be his scribe, recording in careful detail all that he wanted to tell me. I continued to see John during my later, more brief trips, speaking of points in the stories and getting a few additions. John aged well and continued to go to the bush into his nineties, with his two unmarried sons. Although he has no direct descendants, my recordings of his voice, telling his stories, remain available in the Cree region and in archives.

At the time of this writing, I have spent forty-five years thinking and writing about those stories, and so now you can understand my choice of the title of this chapter. It does not require forty-five years to do this, but that's just the way it has worked out. From the first story John told me, I was intensely interested and, to the extent that I was able, vicariously followed the paths of the events he related. Sometime in the third summer of my fieldwork, my understanding "broke through" when I had learned—actually become immersed in—enough narratives for them to, in some sense, substantially cross-reference their meanings and implications of meaning within my mind. I had a moment of epiphany that I still regard as a spiritual experience, when my normal, more-or-less intellectual recognition of the coherence of a story gave way to a welling up into consciousness that silently but clearly said the words "Yes, that makes sense . . . and it really does." The next forty-two years brought some additional depth of insight, several fruitful surprises, even some small epiphanies, but no great revelations.

I was not then, and am not now, fluent in Cree (or any language other than English), and this has necessarily limited my ability to see more deeply and accurately. Indeed, Crees who interpreted for me were sometimes hard put to understand the meaning and implication behind or beyond John's words, and I know of only one non-Cree whose fluency I regard as adequate to the task. Fluency is crucially important, but it is always, even at its best, a limited facility to mix and match words about experience. While I had four graduate courses in linguistics, and have taught it, I did not do any serious linguistic analysis in Cree, and have found only modest help from the many professionals who have done very good work in Cree linguistics. The gap is deep between language regarded primarily as a code to be contemplated and language in action as a vehicle for conveying experience.

My task here is to try to explain my perspective—or how I regarded, respected, and re-presented the stories for an audience that may never see the places or experience the "old ways" Cree culture that John experienced. The translation of Cree words was done by Crees who knew English, but the translation beyond the words, of the experiences that the stories were intended to preserve and convey to others, was done mostly by myself. My translations are, of course, only the best I can do. I am not seeing through my mentor's, or his grandmother's, eyes, but I try to approximate what I believe to be the storytellers' original intentions.

The translation you are about to read is my personal perspective, and was not done with a clear step-by-step method, but with only a general notion of an underlying tragedy. As I wrote, the series of steps just fell into place and took me deeper than I had expected. My intuitions were working, and it is okay that I did not consciously know how they were taking me where I was going. I believe this is the most creative piece that I have written, and that, with my own learned and embodied rules for storytelling, it has been as true to cultural form as I could make it. Just how that whole long process happened is not something I can put into word form, and that is not a problem as long as we wind up with a fair kind of integrity with Cree oral tradition.

Concepts and Background of the Problem

There are several useful types of perspectives on translation of Native American narratives. Each has a contribution to make and to refine. Each favors particular skills. Principal among them are fluency, linguistic analyses, interpretive "thick" descriptions, embedding the narrative in its cultural context, and being open to spiritual understandings.

Fluency in the language minimally enables the most nearly literal translation of words, phrases, and ideas. Fluency is not an end point reached at some age, but a lifelong process of learning how to speak the language.

Linguistic and semantic competence in the formal analysis of language reveals abstracted "structural" implications and enables definitional and comparative statements.

Interpretive or "ethno-poetical" depiction of expressive aspects of the language and thought systems of another culture enables greater breadth and depth of cultural understanding, where anthropology tries to merge with literary criticism.

Cultural contexts may refer to many kinds of setting, but in our present case the reference is to culture as an idiom of experience. The word *idiom* is usually used to refer to the figurative use of a word or phrase. But it may have a wider generality of reference, up to and including the whole symbolic system of a culture as composed of "webs of significances"—that is, meanings beyond the obvious and specific parts. Beyond the concept of cultural systems, then, is a fourth perspective, that of culture, oral tradition, and language as overlapping, aesthetic wholes, where memory and action recognize and express a gestalt that is not literal, particularistic, or time-apportioned but is remembered as a (simultaneous) whole.

The final perspective is spiritual, the lifelong maturing holism of deepening and widening apperception and understanding of our experiences, of where our choice of expressive words to convey experiences comes from, and of the extent to which our words succeed in conveying experiences. At this level of understanding and action, the stories are a source of guidance for how we are to live with each other, now, tomorrow, and for the rest of our lives.

Let's look at these different perspectives more closely:

Fluency

Our task here is learning how to speak the language, and to do so with a level of skill that allows us to speak with mature expressiveness. This is more than simple translation, and is a major achievement for most people. Fluency entails the ability to understand the full range of meanings embedded in the language and the culture. "The understanding of a simple poem, for instance, involves not merely an understanding of the single words in their average significance, but a full comprehension of the whole life of the community as it is mirrored in the words, or as it is suggested by their overtones" (Sapir 1949:162).

Linguistic or Formal Analysis

Through close analysis of speech events, the descriptive linguist's task is to explain how the language "handles" its utterances. Linguists have collected a great deal of Native oral tradition, but primarily for the record of the utterance itself, to be described with analytical precision. Linguistics is firmly scientific, and most linguistics stop at the boundaries of "hard" analysis. A grasp of phonology, morphology, syntax, and semantics points the way to more precise and full understanding of a speaker's intention. It is about the form of the language, and how it shapes and how it "carries" its content. But it only points the way to meanings and understanding. Some "applied" linguists have gone on to provide dictionaries and language-learning curricula.

This low estimation of descriptive linguistics as only a modest contributor to the translation of idioms from one language to another and from one tradition to another is a contentious claim. I am not the first, or the best able, to make it. Let's go back eighty years to Sapir.

All in all, it is clear that the interest in language has in recent years been transcending the strictly linguistic circles. This is inevitable, for an understanding of language mechanisms is necessary for the study of both historical problems and problems of human behavior. One can only hope that linguists will become increasingly aware of the significance of their subject in the general field of science and will not stand aloof behind a tradition that threatens to become scholastic when not vitalized by interests which lie beyond the formal interest in language itself.

... It is peculiarly important that linguists, who are often accused, and accused justly, of failure to look beyond the pretty patterns of their subject matter, should become aware of what their science may mean for the interpretation of human conduct in general. Whether they like it or not, they must become increasingly concerned with the anthropological, sociological, and psychological problems which invade the field of language. (1949:165–66)

Sapir, had he lived longer, might have coined the title of Dell Hymes's 1981 book, *"In Vain I Tried to Tell You,"* given the reluctance of most linguists to embrace the larger problems. American descriptive linguistics followed the narrower path and refined an orthodoxy. The narrowing of the contexts for research for the sake of descriptive precision was not limited to linguistics. During this period, from the 1920s through the 1960s, anthropology, sociology, and psychology were also comparably timid. Psychology was mired in a narrow behaviorism, sociology in Ogburnian quantification, and anthropology in ahistorical functionalism.

Interpretive or Ethnopoetical Descriptions

Interpretive description is perhaps more accurately called the depiction of webs of signification. It was not until the 1970s that Dell Hymes made the opening into the larger context of language as cultural communication—into an ethnography of communication—and subsequently, in the 1980s, helped define and advocate ethnopoetics. But this opening of the field of linguistic inquiry was essentially an extension of description with the goal of finding a way into interpretation—itself a vast field already developed in the literate disciplines, especially literary criticism. Clifford Geertz, Victor Turner, and Harold Schneider brought the interpretive turn into anthropology at about the same time that Hymes and a few colleagues were urging linguists to move toward interpretation.

The interpretive turn was a response to the limitations of formal analysis. Linguistic sophistication does not necessarily make us see as we do when we are immersed in a literature and find breadth and depth of understanding. Our task here is "thick description"—discerning how to understand what is meant from within the contexts of the oral milieu of the home culture, and then converting or re-presenting it to the written milieu of the receiving culture. The interpretive turn was intended "to enlarge the universe of human discourse," and it has done so.

This is moving toward the realm of deep translation, from the interpretation of culture as a system of symbols to the translation of culture—a translation of one aesthetic idiom of experience to another, based on an intuitive grasp of the cultural structures of meaning or the art of its expression.

Discerning an Idiom of Experience

Here our task is to see language, culture, and personality as a single, dynamic gestalt—an idiom of experience. As we saw above, nearly a century ago, Edward Sapir, anthropology's humanist pioneer and its only generally acknowledged genius, pointed linguistics in a far more broadly conceived and literate direction—a psychology of language that he envisioned in tandem with a psychology of culture. But the great majority of linguists did not follow Sapir's lead, and chose instead a narrower range of formal analysis—what George Trager much later termed micro-linguistics, in contrast to macro-linguistics. Sapir's vision of linguistics took in the aesthetic side of language, for he was also a poet, essayist, critic, and composer. And his anthropology was also broadly, optimistically humanistic, aiming for a psychology of culture that explicitly embraces the notion of the spirit of a culture, or the spirituality inherent in a culture (Sapir 1949). We now have examples of this spirituality-in-culture.

The folklorist Barre Toelken has provided a profound and exemplary treatment of one Navajo trickster story that he has considered and reconsidered over three decades. I am under the impression that the process of his own maturing has been a vehicle for the maturing of his understanding of a myth. To me, the 1981 paper is beautiful, and makes a persuasive case for the ethnopoetic approach and format. But it goes further and touches the spirituality inherent in the culture.

> Thus, the stories act like "surface structure" in language: by their articulation they touch off a Navajo's deeper accumulated sense of reality; they excite perspectives on truth by bringing a "critical mass" together which is made up of ethical opposites (one thinks of the Zen koan here); they provide culturally enjoyable correlatives to a body of thought so complicated and profound that vicarious experience in it through entertainment is one of the only access points available to most people. (1981:110)

Toelken's 1987 paper, "Life and Death in the Navajo Coyote Tales," is a challenge, and I can only hint at the significance he draws from his later experience. In a very few pages, he reiterates the two levels that he has previously opened so effectively to our view, put simply, (1) the entertainment level and (2) the moral level. Then he adds (3) the medicinal level, with several examples of how the narrative, or its evocation in a part or reference, is deeply believed to have the power to cause changes in the world—changes that are healing. Then, in a late evening's surprise, an elderly healer tells him of the fourth level, which is witchcraft—damaging, analytical, individual-centered, acquisitive, competitive, destructive, alienating, deadly—a mirror opposite of level 3. After careful thought, he decides that he must draw a line in his inquiry. For urgent moral reasons, he will leave level 4 alone, and to do this he must also leave alone level 3, witchcraft's mirror image.

I have struggled with this. I can easily recognize Cree narratives in terms of Navajo levels 1 (entertainment) and 2 (morality). Is the Cree level 3 comparable to the essentially sacred Navaho level 3? Is there a Cree level 4? I think the Crees have a rather different way of depicting the spiritual, and I will return to this at the end of the chapter.

Stories and Spirituality

The notion of culture as an idiom of experience opens the question of spirituality, where the translation of culture requires that we proceed with primary loyalty to the integrity of the idiom—realizing its existential primacy. Perhaps the title of Biedelman's collection in honor of Evans-Pritchard, *The Translation of Culture,* may be taken as an omen of things to come, but in any event, Evans-Pritchard's *Nuer Religion* is a classic example of contemplating the spirit of a culture in Nuer actions, notions, and concepts.

It is difficult for most of us to hold in consciousness the fact that the spiritual domain incorporates practical actions along with the mythos. It is also necessary.

A Reflexive Point of Reference

Here let us pause and think of our own language and its analysis. The gap between fluency, a linguistic analysis, and the cultural meaning of what is said may be relatively minor, or it may be fundamental. It may be fundamental because language is an imperfect vehicle, a code to convey subjective meanings and experiences, and so refers to memories or images in the listeners' minds. And it is fundamental because what the listener brings to the words will differ with the life experience and cultural context of each individual.

Casual conversation may be trivial, but as we move into the realm of legends and myths the plot thickens. We are challenged to use our life experience and our tacit psychologies of language and of culture to grasp what is being offered in webs of significance (Geertz), in the lived experience of others, or (on the other analytical extreme) in structural juxtapositions (Lévi-Strauss). If we have personal experiences that we can bring to bear on a comparison with the content of a narrative, we may be able to intuit what is to be discerned.

Now, however, we are seeing through a glass, darkly. Some people spend their careers in attempts to "decode" a particular genre, or even a single narrator. Some mythic traditions, such as the "Abrahamic" traditions of Judaism, Christianity, and Islam, have inspired centuries of painstaking hermeneutical study by a great many scholars, to try to discern the meanings of the texts. For example, we have William Blake characterizing the Bible as the great code of art.

Breadth and depth of cultural understanding, then, is a forest of symbols that extends far beyond the normative particularities of language structure. Of course, this is no less true for the understanding of Native American traditions. This has been the main focus of my career as an ethnographer of James Bay Cree people, and it is the main focus of this chapter.

And So, Back to the Crees

Because the text that follows tells the story of the birth and maturation of a Cree man whose understandings develop in a way radically different from others in his culture, it makes good sense to start by describing how Crees traditionally took on their own breadth and depth of cultural understanding. Normally, a child started to grow within the small and intimate domain of a family tent, and was encouraged to watch, listen, and imitate, and in this way to take the main responsibility for his or her own learning. The older persons would not often teach so much as monitor the development of the child's ability to learn next steps, and provide the opportunity for this further learning. A "walking out" ceremony, with the child taking his or her first steps outside of the tent while carrying the toy equivalents of their adult working tools, marked the venture into the domain of the world immediately outside the tent. Then, as the years passed and the individual grew in skill and understanding, the domain around the tent opened into the larger world of the adult hunter-trapper.

In many (perhaps most) cultures, people's perspectives and behavior are regarded against some standards or norms that define "right" thoughts and actions. The Crees traditionally were more open to individual differences, and this makes a big difference. For the Crees, the result of individuated learning was a sense that there was no single or "right" way to view the world and act in it; rather, each person developed his or her own characteristic perspective and ways of acting, and usually respected the somewhat different perspectives and ways of others, both human persons and non-human persons. Each had his or her insights into the world, and, necessarily, his or her own blindnesses. Different perspectives were expected and accepted; at least up to a point. But each person was responsible for the consequences of his or her actions, and going too far could lead to the consequences spiraling into a mysterious and anomalous condition. The deeper meanings of many of the atiukan-myth narratives tell us of the consequences that follow when the point of acceptability is crossed.

I hope to show how it is reasonable for you to take seriously the claim that there are deeper meanings in these narratives, moving us from winks to epistemology. To a significant extent, you, as the listener, become partly responsible for the narrative's meaning—for understanding what the winks, or the other messages beyond the words, convey.

We will return to spotting some visible winks and to the quest for Cree epistemology following the reading of an English text of a Cree atiukan-myth. The text is formatted in rough approximation of the ethnopoetic convention—the pacing of speech given by the Cree storyteller.

The Child That Was Not Born Naturally

Once there was a man who had a lazy wife, and he told her that someone was going to come near her.
"And when this person comes to you, you will take our child and put it under the boughs inside our tent."
And an atoosh (cannibal) came.
And the woman remembered what her husband said and put her child under the boughs, and gave him a bone awl to hold.
And when the atoosh got to the woman he just killed her right away and cut her down both sides of her abdomen. She was pregnant, and the atoosh threw away the baby that was inside her.
And the mice came, and took the baby away to care for it.
This atoosh had a young one with him, and the young one was looking all around inside the tent, and when he came near the child that was hidden and pulled the boughs aside, the child stuck the young atoosh with the bone awl.
He stuck the young atoosh in the nose and gave him a nose-bleed.
The young atoosh went crying around the tent.
The big atoosh heard his son crying. He didn't know that the "moose" was in the tent (he called persons that he had killed "moose").
When the man came back, the atoosh had already killed his wife.
He came up behind the big atoosh and killed him with a spear, and killed the small one with an axe.
And he thought to himself, "Maybe my wife hid the child."
Then he looked for the child. He didn't see him and thought the atoosh had eaten him.
He called him and the child moved his hands and the father found him.
The father didn't know about the young baby, he thought the atoosh had eaten the baby too.
He went to a place where he had used to hunt before, and made a new tent to stay in.
The man went out and found a female lynx, and made her his wife.

He made another tent, away from the one his son and he slept at.
And he told his son never to go on that trail, because his son didn't know about the lynx.
The man made another trail and told his son if he wanted to go out, go on that trail. His father was afraid that if the boy saw the lynx he would try to kill it for the fur.
And every morning the man went out the trail to his wife.
And the years went by and his son grew up.
The father made some toys for him, like a bow and arrow. And the boy was always losing his toys.
They didn't know about the baby that the mice had kept.
This one had grown up some, and the mice would come and steal some of the older boy's toys.
The father told his son, "You are throwing your toys away. You are not watching where you put them. You don't watch where your arrows go and then you lose them."
When his father told him this, the boy shot an arrow and watched to see where it went.
And he saw the mice come and carry it off.
When he saw that, he followed them and found the small tent where the mice were staying.
He knew it wasn't his own tent.
When he got to the tent he went in and found the young boy and saw his toys hanging up all around.
And he didn't know it was his brother.
And the mice told the boy that when the atoosh killed his mother and threw the baby away, they took the baby and looked after him.
The mice told him to go home and not to tell his father.
And in the other tent, where the lynx woman was, he had a brother there, too, but he didn't know that.
Every morning, when his father went out hunting, the boy went and got his little brother and brought him to his tent to play with him.
And the mice told the little brother to always come back in the evening. The mice weren't going to steal the baby, but when he was old enough they would give the man back his son.
The father didn't know that the boys are playing together in the tent while he is out hunting.

The mice told the older brother, "Be sure and come and get your brother and play with him when your father goes out in the morning." The mice know that the father will see the different footprints, one set larger and one set smaller. They told the older brother that if his father asks about the smaller footprints, he should tell him that he was just putting his foot down on the front part.

And the man came back from his hunting and saw the footprints in the snow, and he said to himself, "I wonder why some of them are big and some are small?"

So his father asked the boy how come his footprints are like that and the boy remembered what the mice told him and he said, "Well, I put my feet like that." And he showed him.

When the man would go out, the boy took some food to eat that the man had killed and took it to the mice, but the man didn't know that they had this son yet.

When the mice had taken care of the baby they would come and steal some food to keep the boy alive.

And the mice thought that they would give the man back his son someday and surprise him.

Then one day the mice told the older brother to take the younger brother to the tent and when the old man comes, tell him, "This is my younger brother from when the atoosh killed my mother."

And when the man came back from hunting he found his son and another young boy and the boy told him the story.

The man had a beaver that he had kept dried and he took it and folded it up and told his two sons to go and give it to the mice.

And after that, they always took food to the mice.

So the man lived with his two sons, and still he told them never to go on the trail where he goes every morning.

And soon the sons were pretty big, and the younger one said to his brother, "How come he doesn't want us to go on this trail; how come he is afraid for us to go there?"

"Let's go on the trail and see what kind of a place he has got there." So they went on the trail and found the tent and the big female and all the little lynx, too.

So they said to each other, "Let's go get our bows and arrows so we can kill them."

So they went back on the trail, and came back and killed all the young lynx and the big female too. They didn't know that they were related to them and to the big one—they would call her "aunt".

"Let's take one only and show it to our father," they said.

And the two young boys took the lynx and covered it with a cloth and when the father came in they said, "Here is what we brought for you," and pulled the cloth and showed the lynx.

And the father went right out, crying.

They said to each other, "I guess we made a mistake, the lynx was our brother and the big one was our aunt."

And the man went out to the trail and found the dead wife and all the young ones, too.

So the boys said to each other, "I guess we're in trouble . . . our father is going to kill us."

After the man had gone out to the place, the brothers went out and saw lynx coming from all directions.

And they got their bows and arrows and started shooting at them. They took their father's bow and arrows, too, and shot them.

When their father came back, they thought he was going to kill them, so they took his bow and shot at him and killed their father.

Afterwards, they said to each other, "Who is going to be our father now that we have killed him?"

The older brother said, "Well, I guess we will have to hunt, like our father was doing. I guess we can do it."

After that they left and went to another place.

And the two brothers were always together.

Then the older one told his brother, "I guess it's about time that I stay with a woman."

The younger one said, "Well, mine is not going to be like the human one my father had."

And the older brother said he wanted one like his mother (human).

The older one said, "I'm going out to look for a couple of women for us."

And the younger one said, "No, just look for yourself."

One morning, when they were just waking, the older brother found a toad close to his covers.

So the younger brother took the toad, and threw it outside and said, "You are too filthy to be inside a tent."

And one night the younger brother woke up and said to himself, "I wonder why he doesn't make a fire?"

And he looked and saw two women lying close to his older brother. So, the younger brother said, "Make a fire," and went back to lie down—then he saw these two women making a fire.

The older brother said to his younger brother, "These two women who are staying with us—one of them only I'm going to sleep with tonight."

The younger brother didn't say anything to the other woman. He said, "These two women that you found, I don't want anything to do with them."

The two women were sisters, and the oldest sister sleeps with the older brother.

So the younger sister says, "Why should we share this older boy when there are two men here. I should be sleeping with the younger brother."

So the younger sister wants to stay with the younger brother.

The younger brother says, "I'm not going to stay with you anymore, I'm going to go away."

The younger brother remembers when his father stayed with the lynx, and he says to himself, "Well, that's the way I want to be."

So the older brother says, "It's going to be pretty hard when you do that, it's going to be a lot of work."

The younger brother thinks, "When I leave my brother this evening, I'll find a woman to stay with."

When he went out he found a beaver house, and he saw this female beaver and said, "Will you stay with me?"

The boy tells this woman, "You can make a tent there where we can stay."

The beaver woman has a brother, and the brother knows that she wants to go and stay with that boy.

The boy goes out and kills all the rest of the beavers and brings them to the tent.

So he stayed with the beaver for one night, and slept with her.

Then the boy looked at the beaver woman and said, "I don't think her hair is very nice." So in the morning when he got up, he said, "Well, I'm not going to stay with you anymore, you are not too pretty." He didn't like the teeth so much.

So he left the beaver woman.

He said, "When I stop this evening I'm going to look for a wife again. He found another beaver house, and while he was sitting near this beaver house, he said to himself: "If only a female caribou would come so I could stay with her."

So he only stayed near this beaver house for a little while, and then he saw a female caribou and said to her, "Can I stay with you?"

And he had his toboggan with his tent and all and he said, "Can you pull this toboggan over there and make a tent?"

So she took it and made a place to stay.

It only took her a couple of minutes to make the tent, and he saw a fire coming out and he thought to himself, "My, she's fast."

So he killed all the beavers in that house and took them to his wife. He looked at his wife sitting there and said to himself, "She's pretty there, the way she looks."

But when she went outside, the way she stood up, he saw her rear end—all of her.

And he thought to himself, "If somebody sees her I guess they're going to laugh at her for showing all herself."

She cooked the beaver and when they went to bed he slept with her. In the morning when she went out he saw her rear end again.

So he said to the caribou, "Well I'm not going to live with you anymore if you show all of yourself every time you get up.

So he took the tent down and packed it on the toboggan and told her he was not going to stay with her anymore.

"Don't come with me."

Then he found a porcupine woman and he said he would stay with her.

So he told her to go and take the toboggan and make the place to stay.

And he saw a fire coming out—but she was kind of slow—it was late. He killed beavers again and took them to his wife.

The tent poles were all clean, and he said to himself, "She makes a tent nice."

So he told her to cook the beaver.

He looked at her and thought that her nose was big and pointed and she's too black.

After they ate and went to bed he slept with her.

The woman thought, "I guess he is going to kiss me on the nose."
The next morning he said the same thing to her, "I'm going to leave you, on account of your nose."
All of these females—beaver, caribou, and porcupine—they went home crying to their mothers.
He left and took his tent and things.
In the evening he found another beaver house and he thought to himself, "I guess I can't get married the way I am going now. This is the last time I'll look for a woman."
He said to a whiskey-jack, "Can I stay with you?"
He told the whiskey-jack to go and pull the toboggan, but she couldn't do it.
She could only go a little bit at a time and so she took a long time.
He killed the beaver and looked for the tent—and still she didn't have a fire going.
Finally he saw a fire coming out.
He took the beaver home and threw the beaver in, and she tried to pull it in.
She was too small and broke her legs trying to pull the beaver in.
She told the boy to tie her legs up so they would be straight, and that's how the rings around the legs of the whiskey-jack got there.
"Try to cook the beaver," he said to the bird. It was pretty late, about midnight, and she hadn't even cooked the beaver yet.
Finally she cooked the beaver.
After they ate they went to bed.
The next morning he told her, "If you didn't break your legs I would have stayed with you."
So he left her and took his tent and things.
He said to himself, "I guess I'm never going to get married. The first one I stayed with, I should have stayed with her."
This female beaver was saying to her mother, "He didn't like my teeth and my hair."
And her mother said, "He's going to marry you, that boy."
The boy thought to himself, "I think I'll go back to that first one I stayed with—that beaver girl."
So he stopped at the beaver house, and thought to himself and said, "If only that beaver girl would come here."

And he saw the beaver girl coming again, with her hair and teeth all fixed up.

So he said to her, "Make a place to stay."

He killed all the beaver in that house and took them to the girl.

"Cook one of the beavers," he told her, and she told him she wouldn't eat female beavers, only male beavers.

So after they ate they slept together again. In the morning he woke up and said to himself, "This is the one I am going to stay with." And he did.

So she told him, "If you stay with me it will be hard work—whenever we come to a creek you will have to put a tree across for me to walk on."

Every time they came to a creek he would do this.

Soon the young man thought, "This is too much work."

Finally they came to a little creek and he thought, "I'm not going to put a tree across—I'll see what she will do."

He went across the creek, but she didn't go across. She went into the water.

He left his toboggan to show her where to build the tent, but when he got back it was dark, and the toboggan was there but no tent.

So he was saying to himself, "I wonder where I left my wife. Maybe she is at the little creek where I didn't cut a pole for her to go across on."

So he went back on the same trail.

When he reached the creek he saw his wife in the water swimming. He called to her, "Come on to the shore."

"You didn't cut the tree for me to cross, and I like it here in the water." she said.

"Come on to shore," he said.

"No," she says, "I can't stay with you—I'm in the water now."

The woman said, "You come in the water and come to me, back in the water."

He told her that he had never done this.

So she told him to throw his mitten to her, and watch it.

She took it with her teeth and swam under the water, then she came up and threw it back to him. He looked at it and it was all dry.

She said to him, "If you will come into the water you will be dry like this."

He thinks, "If I go into the water I will be drowned."

She said, "You see how your mitten is, all dry. You will be like that too. Watch me and see how I swim."

So he tried this and floated in the water and went to his wife.

He said, "You can't do what the human does, so I guess I will change into a beaver."

So she said, "Only if you change to a beaver, that's the only way you can marry me." And afterwards, he changed into a beaver.

"The way you make the beaver houses—that's not the way it is going to be—I'll change things around," he said, "The houses do not have many doors, and that's why you get killed by trappers."

So he started making beaver houses, and he made doors where they can escape when someone is after them and breaking into the beaver house.

And he put lots of sticks on top. And that's why beavers are busy all the time, because the boy stayed with the beavers. They are building doors.

The people had never seen beaver make houses like that, and they told the boy's older brother about this.

So he said he would go see his brother. He knew that he was staying with a beaver woman.

The older brother thought, "I guess it's going to be hard to kill beavers because of his staying with them."

So he took a couple of men and went to see his brother.

They found the house and broke into it but he was not there.

He found another one and knew that his brother was in there.

And the brother knew that his older brother was after him, breaking the beaver houses in.

So he said to his wife, "Where I swim, you'll swim, too."

He had made a beaver house a long ways off and that's where they were swimming to. But the older brother conjured to find where they went.

While they were inside his brother came and put sticks all around so that there was only one door.

The younger brother heard noises on the top, so he told his wife to go.

She tried to go out by the doorway and someone hit her on the head.

The older brother started breaking through the house and talked to him from the top, "You see how hard it is when you live like the beavers. Come on out."

So he came out and went to his wife. She was lying down, dead already.

So the younger brother was going to stay with his older brother again, and the older brother was going to look after him.

So he went with his older brother.

The older brother took the dead beaver to cook it.

So he was going to eat his sister-in-law.

His brother wanted him to eat female beaver, but the younger brother told him he wouldn't eat female beavers, only male beavers.

So he stayed with his brother, and the older brother thought, "Why doesn't he eat the beaver? Why is he doing that?"

All the time the younger brother had stayed with the beaver, the older brother had had a hard time killing beavers, and he was kind of mad.

So he thought that he would tell his younger brother something to make him eat his wife. So he went out and killed some beavers, but he didn't cook them.

He cooked the female that he had killed.

So he told all the men that he stayed with to eat beaver.

So at the feast they gathered around the tent and started eating, the younger brother too.

So the younger brother said to his older brother, "The female beavers I said I wouldn't eat; you'll see what it will be like after I've taken a bite from this beaver."

So the younger brother cut a piece and took a bite and swallowed it.

He went running out and they heard a noise like thunder.

When the older brother heard the noise he ran out—they were near a river—and he saw open water (this was mid-winter).

He saw his younger brother way out in the river, swimming.

And the younger brother called to his older brother and told him, "Don't ever bother me again."

And he dove under the water and they never saw him again.

The older brother still tried to beat him, but he couldn't, he never found him again.

The younger brother swam around underwater, and hid under a stone.

Then he went out into the water, way out into the bay.
People say there's a man way out in the bay and that's the man.
The younger brother turned into a beaver.

Now that we have the English text in front of us, what do we do? With a respectful appreciation of hermeneutical theory, we ask what steps will best approximate the way a Cree storyteller would understand and communicate the story. We have seen some winks; now let's try to go into thick description, to a wider context or gestalt of persons and relations, and finally toward epistemology, or ontology, or probably better stated, to a Cree spiritual counterpart to guiding our actions and discerning our fundamental categories of knowing and being.

From winks and girlfriends, thick description takes us to a youth's radical, not fully human perspective on the world, based on his early childhood experiences while being raised by mice. Not experiencing his human mother and knowing his father only after early childhood led to a radical interpretation of whom he wanted to marry, and then to the consequences of his choice of actions. Other recorded versions of this myth favor the English title "The Beaver Wife" and focus on the winks—several girlfriends and a toad. But behind the winks lies an interpretive story of gathering misfortune, where a birth is precipitated and perhaps contaminated by a cannibal monster, and the boy's life course leads to a partly non-human perspective on the world, to parricide and marriage to a non-human, and then to his own transformation into a large, beaver-like person who becomes a widower, a cannibal of his wife, and is finally ostracized from humans and from other animals in the perpetual solitude of an anomalous, monstrous person.

There seems to be something approximating a blend of destiny, fate, and tragedy in this story of interferences in marriage relationships, and their consequences. The boundaries of relationships between humans and the other animals are fundamental, and crossing them invites the reorganization of the world in unexpected ways, a task better left to the trickster. Although the younger brother's perspective on the world is partly not human, he nevertheless recognizes the risk of allowing the toad to sleep next to them. In reply to my question later, John said that if he hadn't thrown the toad out of the tent, it would have transformed into the appearance of a woman—older people used to call the toad by the term for an older sister.

By looking for the implications of these events, we are shown something approximating a Cree ontology, balancing personal autonomy with social responsibility or respect for others, and both with environmental necessity, comparable perhaps to the Ojibwa ontology described by Hallowell, and to other subarctic cultures.

What do we need to know in order to find the deeper, idiomatically Cree implications of symbolic expression in this story? First, we need to expand the cultural context of the story. The focus should be on the characteristic actions of persons and the character, respectful, interfering, or otherwise, of the relationships between them, and the consequences of their actions. We are limited in the resources we can bring to the task, by the limits of using English language and the limits of a lack of knowledge of Cree semantics and traditional experience. But we can provide some of the wider context, and through this, some apperception (i.e., perception of inner meaning, relating new events to events already known) of what is going on in these events. In the rest of this chapter I will provide a start.

Being birthed by an unwitting but monstrous person has, through the younger brother's life, unwitting and monstrous results. So we need to know more about the effects of contact with monstrous persons. The cannibal atoosh (*wiitiko*) comes to the woman after an ominous warning by her husband, about her laziness. A lazy wife is not a casual lifestyle problem, since the sloppy and disorganized condition of the camp may provide an opening to other kinds of beings, and it is disrespectful to herself and her family as well.

Preparing to eat the woman, the atoosh cuts the woman open in an unusual way, not a typical cut down the center of the abdomen, but two parallel cuts, one to each side of the center (significantly, missing the fetus). This special treatment is also described in the Chou—a story when starvation is broken by the kill of a beaver that is "provided" by the man's mistabeo spirit. In 1964 I saw these parallel cuts done with a first kill, and the fur singed off before the skin was removed from the carcass, although I do not know whether the young man, recently graduated from residential school, knew of a reason beyond its being a traditional practice.

Being suckled and kept by mice means that we need to know more about how mice view the world, how they nurture their young, and how the young act as they grow more mature. We know only that mice try to live in enclosed spaces with shredded wood for bedding, steal their food, and conceal themselves for protection from numerous predatory species. The story describes their having a small tipi, their theft of food from the father (and perhaps from the hunter's lazy wife), and their concern to conceal themselves.

These characteristics set the stage for the younger brother being kept safe and comfortable (but away from his father and brother) through his early childhood, and his non-human morality in stealing not only food but also his older brother's toy bow and arrows. The mice have their own characteristic autonomy, and they did not alter it for the sake of the human child. In order to have his brother's company, the mice-parents persuade the older brother to join in the deception of their father. We can guess ahead in the story, how the sequence of lies told to their father would lead to bigger and bigger consequences, although we would not be likely to see their parricide as a likely outcome. We need to understand how disrespectful actions can get out of proportion, then out of control, and so lead to tragic consequences. For this story, for all its humorous winks, is existentially tragic (although we need a Cree gloss for "tragic").

The younger brother was reared to be secretive, and from a human perspective he is dangerously disrespectful. This is curiously close to the character of the trickster figure, who, although present in each of us, is not often so manifested in our actions. As the younger brother starts to mature, he makes choices according to his individual perspective (that reflects his non-human nurturance) and is not able to avoid some damaging consequences. His move into becoming a hunter is marked by impatience to follow a forbidden path, eagerness to kill animals whom he does not recognize as relatives, and then from fearfulness, deciding to kill his father. He had no sense of a human woman to form his perspective on marriage, and after trying all those girlfriends he chose the beaver. This first and then final choice among non-humans is behaviorally the most humanlike of the animals. But beavers are also very good food for humans. Here is a worldwide mythical problem. It is—must be—unthinkable that a man's wife could also be his food. It is such a fundamental confusion that life is almost unimaginable under such conditions.

Beavers eat available vegetation, but may also adapt to the human norm of eating meat. Like the beaver woman in the story, they care for their appearance, grooming and oiling their body and sometimes grooming others. The adults live with each other as families in a relation of friendly non-interference and domestic composure, stay in strong lodges through the seasonal cycle, keep their children until they are fully mature, show their young affection, and show the will and ability to work in independent coordination and to live well together. They play and talk to each other, from whimpers and moans to sounds we may associate with delight or gossip. They take easily and well to domestication with humans and easily become pets.

Of the possible choices the younger brother tries, only the beaver woman is amphibious, a water-and-land person. We all recognize water as the source of life . . . but not as a viable environment for humans after they are born. And the magic of a human somehow going to live in the water is a claim of transcendence of a radical constraint comparable to, say, flying with the geese. Like the merger of a man's food and his wife, it is crossing an impossible boundary, and once crossed in our story, in order to respect the autonomy of the beaver woman, the change works out to be irreversible.

The father's choice of marriage to a lynx and its success with many children of this union has something to do with the personal character, the hunting strategies, and the meat diet (and litter size) of a lynx. This was no arbitrary choice from whoever might be available; it was a good and informed choice. Lynx, too, have their own characteristic autonomy. They are secretive and rarely seen by hunters, yet they are tolerant of the presence of humans in their areas. This is a good fit with the secrecy of the marriage and the proximity to the camp where the sons are living. Lynx are fairly solitary, nocturnal hunters, and so the visits to his wife by the father come conveniently at the end of the Lynx-woman's hunting time and the beginning of the man's hunt. From the number of Lynx children indicated in the story we can assume that the marriage lasted for some years, before they are killed by the brothers. Females raise their young alone, as she does in the story, and the young are not sent off on their own until they are about a year old. The story tells us that other lynx came after the brothers, who shot them all. These may have been grown children of her union with the man.

But this marriage results in the death of all the human-lynx family, at the hands of the survivors of the father's first family. It seems that these anomalous marriages are mutually exclusive in an existential sense.

In a brief interlude, while the brothers are living together, a toad tries to sleep with one of the brothers. This might have resulted in the toad's transformation into a human-like creature that could deceive the human partner and lead to disaster. So it was important that it was rejected as a potential wife, the first of several yet to come, and therefore was thrown out of their tent. And it may not be trivial that the toad itself is a transform from a tadpole water person, and as an adult is similar to a beaver, in living both in and above the water.

Caribou, porcupine, and whiskey-jack women are simply not similar enough in their personal characters to be considered as potential wives, and their importance to the story is in showing the naïveté of the younger brother. Caribou are vegetarian herd animals that, from the Cree hunting song's point of view, appear to be almost erotically eager to give themselves to humans. They are migrators and have no shelter, and are a major food source. Not a good marriage prospect. Porcupines are also vegetarian, and while she nicely debarks his tipi poles, there seems little else to recommend this choice of a mate. The whiskey-jack is the most unlikely choice of all. She is neat in appearance but far too small to do women's work, and has a reputation for thieving. Each of these types of creature has a distinctive, autonomous character, and each has a characteristic insider's view of the world they live in, far from a human's perspective. Perhaps they cannot, or would not wish to conceive of how a human would fit into their world.

The other person of importance is the older brother, who survives the guilt of parricide and matures into a shaman. He uses his conjuring power to find and retrieve his wayward younger brother until, seeing his appearance so transformed, he tests him to see if he has lost his humanity, by giving him meat from his beaver wife to eat. The act of starting to eat his wife is cannibalistic, and the younger brother becomes fully transformed into an atoosh with the appearance of a very large beaver, just as the world around them is transformed by an impossible midwinter breakup to allow his escape. When it is suddenly clear that his younger brother can no longer be human, he tries to kill the monstrous being, but for all his conjuring power he cannot match the power of his brother. In the end, he has killed his father and failed in his attempt to kill his transformed brother.

This is a story about marriage. But much more importantly, it is a story about the far boundaries of who a person may marry, and behind those boundaries, about the risks of transformation. Here we are getting close to the spiritual center. The trickster chooses to dance on the edge of chaos, and some shamans are able to risk some kinds of temporary transformation. But the great majority of persons are well advised to keep a self-disciplined personal respect for stability and autonomy of their personhood and that of all the others around them, and not risk misfortune or even chaos in trying to change who they are.

When people are responsible for their self-discipline of choices and actions, the world is less likely to step in with external, punishing discipline. For example, the discipline of attending carefully to tracks enables a hunter to locate and follow his prey, and in this way reduce the chances of failing in the hunt. Respect for the prey is the conscious feeling that goes with this attention to visible clues, and into the hunting songs that invite the response of the prey. Prey means food for humans, and emphatically not their mates and mothers of their children. Food is first—primary—but a food-person is not permissible as a mate. And humans are emphatically unthinkable food for other humans—that way lies the chaos of transformation into an atoosh. Disciplined respect for others is the best way to minimize the chances that contingencies may get out of hand and be damaging, and maintaining respect is the best way to hold, even in dire hardship, to deep, I would say spiritual, hope for the life that we know is possible, even when it is not visible.

No wonder that anomalous births were regarded as dangerous, and that newborn infants with distortions of human form were left to die. Risk of transformation is always present, and especially so in the generation of a new life. Stories of full-term pregnant women who are suddenly scared by seeing nearby an unexpected animal (a beaver, bear, or seal), and then give birth to an infant with a misshapen face and with body hair, and who then choose to let the baby die, are cautionary lessons. And it would be very undesirable to allow such an infant to mature and eventually marry, for then humans would become less human.

In summary, humans' individuated personal and spiritual autonomy combines practical action, traditional knowledge, and mystical experience. Although it varies with each individual, it is not set in isolation from the rest of the world, but is embedded in experience and knowledge of the great community of persons (of many kinds) that live in the world, less a matter of spirit-oriented contemplation than it is intuitively known, and repeatedly tested against experience. The practical action is characterized by fortitude and hope. The traditional knowledge combines the social reservoir of memory culture and the techne of knowing how to use this knowledge in action. And mystical experience, normally requiring solitude, requires open receptivity to new knowledge that is more often than not unanticipated in the course of daily events. Transformation is a spiritual as well as physical and social event, and, because it is approaching chaos, is potentially damaging in the lives of all but the exceptionally powerful, and perhaps even them as well.

At the deepest level, we find ourselves facing the possibility of chaos and dangerous and perhaps monstrous events. In this we have a parallel with Barre Toelken's deepest level in the trickster myth he so profoundly depicts for us, of witchcraft and other dangerous powers. But it is a parallel, not an identity. As the Cree idiom of experience faces the possibility that the familiar form of the world may become something beyond the contingencies already characterizing the hunter's life, there is a sense of urgency to protect the stability provided by the respect relations within the great community of persons. In our story, it is a younger brother who has never known his human mother that throws the world into disarray. In life, it could be an act of witchcraft that compares with Toelken's Navajo idiom, but it could also be something else, including the mistake of simply nurturing a monstrous infant to adulthood. And so, at a fundamental level, we have an ultimately mysterious, contingent world that all persons must try to live, and live well, within. And that is the spiritual lesson that this younger brother is teaching us.

Last Reflections on Theorizing Cree Oral Literary Form

Back in the late 1960s, I asked Chris Wolfart about what Cree linguists could tell me in relation to the meanings I was trying to discover in Cree narratives, and he wished me good luck in finding anything at all. The answer finally came in a booklet that Chris sent me thirty years later, Robert Bringhurst's "Prosodies of Meaning: Literary Form in Native North America," reissued in 2008 as part of *The Tree of Meaning*. Bringhurst is doing macro-linguistics rather than micro-linguistics. Sapir is there, and a roster of other luminaries and others who, regrettably, missed their chance to be luminaries. Early on, Bringhurst indicates what may be lost in culturally skewed translation, and in the end pages, what may be gained in a good translation. In a useful way, it may be seen as a theorizing of what Barre Toelken is telling us about the Navaho Coyote story, and what I am trying to tell you about the Cree Younger Brother story.

Basically, we find in "Prosodies of Meaning" a theorizing parallel to Sapir's concept of drift in language and culture. Drift is the dynamic of what Sapir called "society as unconscious artist." As Sapir conceives the unconscious patterning of behavior in society, these processes are form-giving according to a universal cultural algebra, intuitively learned, embodied, and then taught by each individual.

In parallel with Sapir, Bringhurst sees (and knows experientially) a pan-human structure of stories and thought, and of the not-quite-told and not-quite-thought. When the stories are heard, both the idiom and the deep structure of rhyming intuitions of thought/events shine through, for those who have ears to hear. It is an unconscious recognition of natural (ecologically discerned) patterns of events/meanings that may become known consciously through intuition and thence into cognitive appraisal and emotional attachment, and then may be set into word form (Robert Frost, in a letter to Louis Untermeyer—suggests that for him, a poem starts as a lump in the throat or a tug at the heart).

Once performed in an aesthetically appropriate word form, other storytellers may replicate the performance so that the capable listener can hear it, from the winks all the way down into the intuited and finally unconscious recognition of the grammar of events and meanings. I wish you a good journey.

Suggested Reading

Bringhurst, Robert. 2008. Prosodies of Meaning: Literary Form in Native North America. In *The Tree of Meaning: Language, Mind and Ecology*, 206–56. Berkeley: Counterpoint.

Preston, Richard J. 2002. *Cree Narrative: Expressing the Personal meanings of Events*. 2nd ed. Montreal: McGill-Queens University Press.

Sapir, Edward. 1949. *Selected Writings of Edward Sapir in Language, Culture and Personality*. 1929. Berkeley: University of California Press.

Toelken, J. Barre. 1987. Life and Death in the Navajo Coyote Tales. In *Recovering the Word: Essays on Native American Literature*, ed. Bryan Swann and Arnold Krupat, 388–401. Berkeley: University of California Press.

Toelken, J. Barre, with Tacheeni Scott. 1981. Poetic Retranslation and the "Pretty Languages" of Yellowman. In *Traditional Literatures of the American Indian: Texts and Interpretations*, ed. Karl Kroeber, 65–116. Lincoln: University of Nebraska Press.

19

Memories of Translation

Looking for the Right Words

M. Terry Thompson and Laurence C. Thompson

This is not a technical essay on the sport of translation. It is some reminiscences about the experiences of a pair of linguists while studying several of the twenty-three Salishan languages of the Pacific Northwest during the active working years of our lives, between 1960 and 1995. We realize how very fortunate we were to be able to work with elders of the Lummi, Lushootseed, Thompson River Salish, Klallam, and Tillamook.

As linguists working on dying unwritten languages, where much if not all of the traditional culture survives only in the memory of elderly speakers, it is hard to translate from the native language into English. In the case of things, the speaker must describe the item and its uses, and then the translator must try to find an English word that fits the description. Often these objects show up only behind museum glass or in photos from times past. It is one thing to translate from one living language to another, and quite another from a dying one. This calls for a linguistic archaeology of sorts, re-creating the traditional world before deciding how to capture it fairly in English.

Language and culture are also inextricably intertwined. Translating from a language, not only words but the worldview behind them is necessary. Translating one European language into another poses little problem because there is so much shared culture. Though the languages may differ greatly in structure, such as between Finnish and Swedish, or Basque and Spanish, the modern cultures overlap greatly and ease the translator's task. Translating Salish into English is quite different from translating from Swedish into Finnish. It is more like trying to pound square pegs into round holes, and often the holes are black holes.

The cultures vary greatly, and the way culture is encoded in words varies greatly. To become an expert in Salish culture so as to get things right in English requires access to a community often distrustful of outsiders, especially those asking intimate questions about things existing mostly in the graying heads of the language's last speakers. There is iceberg tip after iceberg tip, and the translator must recognize the entire berg to get the idea right.

As we have analyzed the grammars and built dictionaries for several languages, we have come across some interesting, frustrating, funny, and sometimes emotional problems in the exercise of translation. All field linguists have these experiences in routine research. English-speaking linguists like us normally find difficulty working with the traditional languages of Africa, Asia, Australia, and the Americas. We have been fortunate, since all of our language experts spoke English fluently. We have great admiration for those who must translate through a third language. And there is a special place in the world of translation for those who share no common language with their consultants, when actions are the only means of communication. We admire the dedication and frustration of those who must translate their daily experiences into another language.

Larry's beginning experience as a linguistic field worker was two years in Vietnam (1950–52), resulting in a number of articles and a grammar of Vietnamese, a tone language. At that time French was the second language in Vietnam, and Larry's French was fluent, so he found it too difficult to get much information on the language in Saigon. He had to drive, in a French military convoy, up into the hill country to find speakers who would teach him Vietnamese—through French.

His first experience with the very different Salish languages was in the 1950s, when he first started teaching at the University of Washington. He began his study with Martha Abbott, who grew up on the Lummi Reservation north of Seattle. She was willing to try to teach him some of her Lummi language. In the beginning it was frustrating for both of them. The Salish languages have a number of sounds English speakers have trouble getting their tongues around, and they were unwritten; the spoken language first had to be translated into phonetics, so that took most of the time at first. The Salish languages also have a wealth of suffixes. One word in Thompson River Salish has been documented as having eleven suffixes.

Mrs. Abbott had not used her language for a long time and sometimes had trouble remembering the right word. One day she phoned Larry: "You woke me up in the middle of the night! You know that Lummi word I couldn't remember yesterday? I dreamed about my grandfather and he told me what it is." Then she proudly said the word, and Larry grabbed a pen and paper and asked her to say it again. And again.

Louise George, who spoke the Skagit dialect of Lushootseed, also north of Seattle, worked with Larry from 1956 to 1964. He was teaching linguistics at the University of Washington, including a course on the field methods of collecting spoken material from a native speaker for the phonetic and grammatical analysis of an unwritten language. That was when Terry joined the study, first as a returning graduate student, later through marriage. Mrs. George spoke English well, and was very patient with the students who were learning this difficult task. Time after time she responded to "Would you say that again, Mrs. George?" with a repetition of her translation of the English into Skagit. After a very short time she understood the importance of using exactly the same Skagit words for each repetition. Larry had a bit more difficulty teaching the students to always ask a question using the same English words each time.

One young man was trying to get one small piece of the grammar straight, and when it was his turn to elicit information, having exhausted several other activities, such as "I will go, you will go, he will go" and "X threw it to Y," he asked for the translation of a more aggressive verb: "bite." He asked how to say "The bear bit him," then "The bear bit her, the bear bit John, the bear bit me," and finally "I bit the bear." There was a pause, then Mrs. George quietly said "I don't think you'd say that." That was when the class learned theory doesn't always match reality.

Annie Zixtkwu York, of Spuzzum, in the south-central part of British Columbia, worked with us for more than twenty-five years, from 1966 until her death in 1991, translating the nɬeʔkepmx (Thompson River Salish) language into English and translating English into nɬeʔkepmxcin. We kept at this project long enough to build a grammar, a dictionary, an ethnobotany, a volume of texts, and a number of articles and monographs on that language. In the process, two instances of translation have always stuck in our memory. In both cases, the root of an obviously ancient word had been satisfactorily integrated into modern life after the older word had probably not been used for several generations in its original meaning.

To set the scene: Annie's home was at a narrow place in the Fraser River Canyon, with high cliffs on each side of the big and unnavigable river. The very nearness of two major railways and the Trans-Canada highway in such a narrow canyon made for a lot of traffic noise, with echoes. One railroad track was about fifty feet from the house, making the noise overwhelming when a train passed. One day the railroad ties were being replaced just outside Annie's house, with a number of very large, very noisy machines operating. Since there was no hope of communicating in any language, we went outside to watch the show.

The first machine was a guillotine which chopped through the ties just inside the rails.

Then came a machine with grabbers on each side to pull the end pieces of tie from under the rails and drop them into the ditches on each side.

Then came two men to toss the center sections into the ditch.

Next came a machine with prongs making a space in the gravel under the rails, and pulling a new tie in from the side.

Last came a machine with very large fingers which "fluffed up" the gravel around the ties to make it level.

When the activity passed on down the track, we went back inside and Annie began to coin names for the various machines. That was when one of the frustrations of translation resolved itself happily. We earlier had found the word *pəxʷpstes*, meaning "to make bread rise," puzzling since bread was not a traditional food. Annie included the root of that word (*pəxʷ-*) in the name of the machine that fluffed up the gravel. After some discussion with Annie, we finally decided it means "to introduce air into something." And then she remembered the word for "gas on the stomach": *pəxʷenek* (the suffix *enek* means "stomach").

Later, we found another wrinkle on that same word root. In the related language of Flathead, it is in the word for "fish bladder." Fish bladders were blown up, tied off, and used as small floats in fishing.

One of the most intriguing dictionary entries in our entire experience began when Annie attempted an English translation of *semt*, a word used in the course of one of our sessions. The meaning of that particular word in that particular sentence was not at all clear. She finally explained the meaning to us with the illustration of spilling perfume on the floor. "Every time you pass by, you get a whiff of the perfume and you remember spilling it," she said. "One day you realize you have passed by, maybe several times, without noticing, although the odor was still there." Another example is passing a place closely connected with a person who has died. Whenever you pass by there is a little tug of memory of the person, but one day you realize you were busy and passed that way several times without feeling the tug of memory. We have, so far, not found a satisfying English translation for *semt*. There are several glosses that come close, but this wordy translation is, so far, the only one we have found that really explains it.

Martha Charles John was a Klallam friend and language expert who lived near the Little Boston Reservation on the Olympic Peninsula of Washington, not far from Seattle. We studied the Klallam language with her for a number of years, in the 1960s into the early 1970s shortly before her death. When we were seeking someone who could speak Klallam, several people who couldn't speak the language told us we should talk to Martha John. We later realized they were sure she could get rid of us tactfully. Her small house in the woods was hard to find. When we finally drove down the long rutted dirt driveway into her yard she appeared, looking very stern, with her large dog standing firmly and protectively in front of her. We told her we wanted to study her language, to write it down and tape-record it for posterity. She brightened, gave us a big smile, and said, "Come right in. I've been waiting for somebody like you." She told us several times during those years that she was glad she had at last found some people who were interested in systematically preserving her language, since there were only a few elders left who could still speak Klallam fluently. Early in our work with her, we told her we wanted to put all of the information she gave us about the Klallam language, including tape recordings, into the permanent manuscript collection at the University of Washington so that young Klallams a hundred years from now would still be able to hear and learn about their language. She was excited at the prospect and decided she would concentrate on that instead of pinning her hopes on the local youngsters.

During that period, none of the younger people, all monolingual speakers of English, seemed to have enough time to spend with her to learn to speak such a complex language. She had despaired at the thought of her beautiful language disappearing. That put some pressure on us.

The beginning of our study with her happened during the Red Power movement. One day we got a long-distance call to our home in Hawaii from an unidentified person demanding that all of the material we had collected with Martha John be turned over to "us" immediately, "since that language belongs to us." Larry told the caller it must be Martha John's decision to give it to them, and gave him her phone number. She later told us, when she reported receiving a call from an unidentified person, she impatiently explained that she would be happy to share the Klallam language with him if he would come to her, as the Thompsons had done, and learn to write it down and speak it. Her comment was, "I guess they got interested in something else."

After such a tactless and disturbing experience, she decided she didn't want any other Indians to have the language material, and that it would only be preserved for "the Klallam youngsters a hundred years from now." We had planned to give copies of the written and tape-recorded material to the newly formed libraries on the Klallam reservations at Little Boston and Elwha, but we respected her wishes when she nixed that idea. Even though the community was unfailingly kind and polite to us, it did put us in the delicate position of being "the white man who has taken everything else and now is stealing our language."

In the meantime, a summer program had been arranged for the Klallam youngsters from the Elwha Reservation, near Port Angeles, Washington. The planners wanted to incorporate teaching some of the Klallam language into the summer's activities. Having become accustomed to seeing us because of our small amount of work in that area with a few elders, they asked us to spend some time helping compose some beginning lessons, translating from English into Klallam. A few of the Klallam elders who still spoke the language agreed to be teachers and, among other things, taught the children how to count, tell their Indian names ("My name is . . ."), and ask "What is this?" After six weeks the youngsters, especially the very young ones, did well with the simple lessons.

Near the end of that summer program, the community took the youngsters on a school bus to visit Martha John. It was far enough away to make a nice day trip, and caused a lot of excitement. When the bus arrived at her small house, the children noisily descended on her and greeted her in Klallam. Then they each told her, in Klallam, "My name is . . ." Since she had no electricity and used a wood stove for heating and cooking, there were many things in her house that brought "What is this?" in Klallam. When she told them, in Klallam, they repeated the words with a fairly accurate pronunciation. As could be expected, she was touched and very happy.

She told us to give them any information they wanted, so we quickly sent copies of our notes and tapes to the libraries at both reservations. In this case, simple translation by children healed some unspoken fractures between Indians and the Others—in this case, the Thompsons. One of Larry's former students, Timothy Montler, is still (2010) doing extensive work on Klallam, and has continued to receive friendly cooperation.

In earlier days, Martha John was often asked to tell stories to the Boy Scouts, and one they always enjoyed was about Chipmunk and the Witch.

Chipmunk was playing on the new thin ice one day, when Old Witch came along. Chipmunk encouraged her to come out on the ice to play. She wanted to catch him, so she pretended she really wanted to play, and begged him to come to her since she was afraid the ice wasn't strong enough to support her. She couldn't see very well, so Chipmunk tossed a few chipmunk turds onto the ice and said, "See? I threw rocks on the ice and it didn't break." Old Witch went out on the ice to catch him, the ice broke, and as she was sinking into the cold water she grabbed at him. Her long fingernails scraped his back and that's why Chipmunk has a striped back.

The Boy Scout version of the story as she told it had Chipmunk throwing pebbles instead of chipmunk turds: what she called the "cleaned-up" version of her translation into English. She laughed about it to us, but considered it only proper for the Scouts. "Their parents wouldn't like it."

Cleaning up stories for translating to outsiders was/is a common practice, showing sensitivity about many of the traditional stories being considered "dirty" by non-Indians. The translation of those portions of a story by good storytellers was sometimes very interesting, often imaginative, usually showed a depth of understanding for the reason for disapproval and, above all, a great sense of humor about the whole thing. Franz Boas, in the 1880s, used explicit Latin in the translation of those "naughty" sections of a story.

In 1967 we interviewed William Samson, a Thompson River Salish (nɬkeʔkepmx) man who lived in the Fraser River Canyon south of Lytton, British Columbia. He gave us a word for the name of a place on the mountainside above his home where the deer were most frequently found by hunters. But then, he told us, there is another name for where the deer might be, and still another name. None of these were words we had heard before. He finally relented and explained each of these were for different times of day, reflecting the line of shade and sun followed by the deer when grazing on that particular mountainside in the steep canyon. In such a rugged country of big mountains and big rivers, the movement of the sun on that mountainside was, of course, unique.

One day he was giving us the names of various birds and animals of the area, and translating them for us. Since we weren't familiar with the critters of British Columbia, we were satisfied to get the names with his English translations and then look them up later in our bird, fish, and animal books. One word was translated as "crown hawk." We couldn't find such an English name for a hawk in any of our books, and our friend Dale Kinkade, a real birder, couldn't identify that kind of hawk either. Finally, Mr. Samson said it lived in a hole in the ground, and we thought that was a very strange place for a hawk to nest. Then it dawned on us that the "g" sound in Thompson River Salish is not voiced and becomes a "k" sound. Our "crown hawk" became a perfectly normal "ground hog."

From 1969 to 1972 we were fortunate to spend some time studying the Tillamook language, a Salishan outlier on the north coast of Oregon long thought to be extinct. We worked with the last known speaker of Tillamook, Minnie Scovell, of Garibaldi, Oregon. She had married into an English-speaking family when she was quite young and didn't remember her language very well, since she hadn't spoken it often for many years. Translation from English wasn't very successful, but we found Larry could read to her, in Tillamook with English translation, from Melville Jacobs's written phonetic notes from the 1930s. She could usually repeat the words and phrases in what was obviously native pronunciation. That was good for tape-recording Tillamook to preserve the sounds of the language. Of her five sons, two middle-aged bachelors lived with her and her husband. They had been raised in English, except for occasional visits with their grandmother. They proudly said they knew some Tillamook, and with decidedly English accents laughingly produced "Bring in some wood," "Close the door," and "Sit down and shut up." According to their mother, the translation was accurate.

We never really thought of our work as translation, but since bilingual dictionaries are also expected to have one-word entries, it was often the most difficult part of the job. We remember the pleasure, frustration, and great fun of those years, a life spent in translation.

Note

Laurence C. (Larry) Thompson was always the major half of this team of linguists. Though his work was cut short by a major stroke in 1983, he has been unwavering in his support for all of his students (including Terry) in their continued expansion of his earlier work. After 1965, when we moved from the University of Washington to the University of Hawaii, we traveled to the mainland United States and Canada each summer for research. Until 1995, we spent time with several Northwest American Indian groups, often working with two or three different languages during a summer.

Our research during this entire period was supported by the National Science Foundation and the National Endowment for the Humanities. We also received support from the Guggenheim Foundation, the Jacobs Research Fund, the British Columbia Provincial Museum, and the University of Hawaii Foundation. The original idea for this piece was a demand from Dell Hymes that we write about our many interesting experiences in the field. We owe considerable thanks to Steven M. Egesdal for suggestions about the content and to Albert Schutz for helpful editing.

John Bierhorst is the author, editor, or translator of more than thirty-five books on the Native literatures of North, South, and Central America. A specialist in the language and literature of the Aztecs, he is the author of *Cantares Mexicanos: Songs of the Aztecs*, *A Nahuatl-English Dictionary*, *History and Mythology of the Aztecs: The Codex Chimalpopoca*, and *Ballads of the Lords of New Spain*.

Julie Brittain teaches linguistics at Memorial University, Newfoundland. Her research interests include theoretical models of syntax and morphology, with a focus on Algonquian languages. Other research interests include first-language acquisition (Cree), the oral literatures of native North America, and strategies to maintain and revitalize indigenous languages. She is Director of the Chisasibi Child Language Acquisition Study (CCLAS), a research project begun in 2004 that is investigating the linguistic stages through which Cree children (ages two to six) pass as they acquire the grammar of their first language.

Lynn Burley is an Associate Professor in the Department of Writing at the University of Central Arkansas. She teaches primarily linguistics courses, including semantics, world languages, and linguistics for educators. She has published previously on Siouan languages in the *Encyclopedia of Linguistics* as well as in composition in chapters in *A Delicate Balance: Teaching, Scholarship, and Service in the 21st Century College English Department* and *Miss Grundy Doesn't Teach Here Anymore: How Popular Culture Has Changed the Composition Studies Classroom*. She is now working on a book on the role of linguistics in K–12 education.

William M. Clements teaches anthropology, literature, and American Indian studies at Arkansas State University. He has published several books, articles, chapters, and reviews on American Indian literature, including *Native American Verbal Art: Texts and Contexts*. He has also published on American religious folklife, Italian Americana, and other topics in literature, folklore, history, and popular culture.

Chip Colwell-Chanthaphonh is Curator of Anthropology at the Denver Museum of Nature and Science. He received a PhD from Indiana University and a BA from the University of Arizona, and has held fellowships with the Center for Desert Archaeology and the American Academy of Arts and Sciences. He has published more than two dozen articles and book chapters and has authored and edited seven books, including *History Is in the Land: Multivocal Tribal Traditions in Arizona's San Pedro Valley* (with T. J. Ferguson), which received Honorable Mention in the 2007 Victor Turner Prize juried book competition. He also sits on the editorial board of the *American Anthropologist*.

Nora Marks Dauenhauer was born (1927) in Juneau, Alaska, and was raised in Juneau and Hoonah, as well as on the family fishing boat and in seasonal subsistence sites around Icy Straits, Glacier Bay, and Cape Spencer. Her first language is Tlingit; she began to learn English when entering school at the age of eight. She has a BA in anthropology from Alaska Methodist University and is internationally recognized for her fieldwork, transcription, translation, and explication of Tlingit oral literature. Her creative writing has been widely published and anthologized. Her Raven plays have been performed in several venues internationally, including the Kennedy Center in Washington DC. In 1980 she was named Humanist of the Year by the Alaska Humanities Forum. In 1989 she received an Alaska Governor's Award for the Arts, and in 1991 she was a winner of the Before Columbus Foundation's American Book Award. From 1983 to 1997 she was Principal Researcher in Language and Cultural Studies at Sealaska Heritage Foundation in Juneau. Her books include *The Droning Shaman*, *Life Woven with Song*, and, coedited with Richard Dauenhauer and Lydia Black, *Russians in Tlingit America: The Battles of Sitka 1802 and 1804*.

Richard L. Dauenhauer, born and raised in Syracuse, New York, has lived in Alaska since 1969. From 1981 to 1988 he served as the seventh Poet Laureate of Alaska. In 1989 he received an Alaska State Governor's Award for the Arts. In 1991 he was a winner of an American Book Award from the Before Columbus Foundation. He is widely recognized as a translator, and several hundred of his translations of poetry from German, Russian, Classical Greek, Swedish, Finnish, and other languages have appeared in a range of journals and little magazines since 1963. He holds degrees in Slavic languages, German, and comparative literature. Since moving to Alaska, much of his professional work has focused on applied folklore and linguistics in the study, materials development, and teacher training of and for Alaska Native languages and oral literature. He has taught at Alaska Methodist University and Alaska Pacific University in Anchorage, and part time at the University of Alaska Southeast in Juneau. From August 1983 to March 1997 he was Director of Language and Cultural Studies at Sealaska Heritage Foundation, Juneau. In August 2005 he accepted the position as President's Professor of Alaska Native Languages and Culture at the University of Alaska Southeast.

Carrie Dyck is an Associate Professor of linguistics at Memorial University of Newfoundland. She has been working with Cayuga speakers since 1992 on projects ranging from the digitizing of Cayuga sound files to a dictionary and grammar of Cayuga, and research on Cayuga phonology (sound patterns).

Marcia Haag is an Associate Professor of linguistics at the University of Oklahoma. She has worked since 1991 on the Choctaw language. With her longtime collaborator Henry Willis, she has written two books on Choctaw grammar directed to the general student, *Choctaw Language and Culture: Chahta Anumpa* (2 vols.). She has served as a language consultant to the Choctaw Nation of Oklahoma and has written a number of articles on Choctaw and Cherokee linguistics. She and Mr. Willis are currently working on the translation of the 1826 journal of Peter Pitchlynn, the first chief of the Choctaws in Oklahoma.

Kate Hennessy is an Assistant Professor specializing in media at Simon Fraser University's School of Interactive Arts and Technology. Her research explores the transformative role of new media in the documentation and safeguarding of cultural heritage, and the potential of new technologies to mediate culture, history, objects, and subjects in new forms. Her work with the Doig River First Nation in northeastern British Columbia engages participatory ethnographic methods while facilitating collaborative community media projects as videographer, media skills trainer, and multimedia producer.

Bill Jancewicz moved to Kawawachikamach, near Schefferville, Quebec, with his family in 1988 to continue a Bible translation project initiated by SIL International. In 1992 he began working at the Naskapi Development Corporation head office as their resident linguist, assuming the responsibility for the final editing of the *Naskapi Lexicon*, published in 1994. He served on the *Eastern James Bay Cree Dictionary* editorial staff, published in two volumes in 2004. He was the project leader for the translation of the Naskapi New Testament, published in 2007. He directs the production of reading material in Naskapi, as well as training speakers in linguistics, syllabic literacy, and vernacular media recording. He has developed computer systems for Naskapi and Cree vernacular texts and currently serves as font, keyboard, database training, and language resource person for Naskapi, Cree, and Innu communities.

Stewart B. Koyiyumptewa is a member of the Hopi Tribe and is from the village of Hotevilla, located on Third Mesa in Northeastern Arizona. He is a member of the Badger and Butterfly clans. Currently the Archivist for the Hopi Tribe's Cultural Preservation Office, he is engaged in a variety of projects, such as the Hopi oral project, ethnographic research, and collaborative work with universities, museums, libraries, and state and federal governments. Aside from his work, he dedicates his time to his wife and two children and is actively involved in the Hopi culture as a husband, father, and farmer.

David L. Kozak is a Professor of anthropology at Fort Lewis College in Durango, Colorado. He conducted research on the Sells (O'odham) Reservation in the 1990s on oral traditions culminating in several publications. He coauthored *Devil*

Sickness and Devil Songs with David I. Lopez. As a medical anthropologist he has conducted research on Type 2 diabetes in the Gila River Indian Community.

Robert M. Leavitt is Professor Emeritus of the University of New Brunswick in Fredericton, where he directed the Mi'kmaq-Maliseet Institute for fourteen years. Most recently he and Passamaquoddy elder David A. Francis coauthored *A Dictionary of Passamaquoddy-Maliseet*. Leavitt is currently working with Maine filmmaker Ben Levine in the Language Keepers project, filming speakers of Passamaquoddy-Maliseet in natural conversations and producing subtitled DVDs. He is the author of numerous other publications on Native languages, culture, and education.

David I. Lopez (1940–1998) worked as a farmer, cowboy, and school custodian. He was a ritual curer who collaborated with three generations of anthropologists, interpreting O'odham oral literature. He is the coauthor of *Rain House and Ocean, Piman Shamanism and Staying Sickness*, and *Devil Sickness and Devil Songs*.

Marguerite MacKenzie teaches linguistics at Memorial University, Newfoundland, and works with speakers of Cree, Innu (Montagnais), and Naskapi on dictionaries, grammars, texts, and language-training materials. She is coeditor of the *Naskapi Lexicon*, the *Eastern James Bay Cree Dictionary, Southern Dialect*, and the *Eastern James Bay Cree Dictionary, Northern Dialect*. Over the past thirty-five years she has participated in training programs for Aboriginal language teachers and offered courses in the structure of the local language to community members in a number of northern villages as well as assisting the Cree of Quebec to implement Cree as the language of instruction in the primary grades. She is currently directing a multi-year research project with the Innu of Labrador and Quebec to produce language reference materials, including a trilingual dictionary and a substantial audiotape archive of Innu oral narratives from Labrador in transcription and translation.

Patrick Moore is an Assistant Professor in the Department of Anthropology at the University of British Columbia. His work has focused on the languages and oral traditions of Northern Athabaskans in Alberta, British Columbia, and the Yukon, where he lived from 1976 until 2001. Since coming to UBC he has participated in collaborative digital language and culture documentation and archiving projects with the Kaska, Tagish/Tlingit, and Beaver First Nations. He is the co-author (with Angela Wheelock) of *Wolverine Myths and Visions*.

Richard J. Preston was born in 1931. He began his sojourns in the James Bay region in 1963, mentored by John Honigmann, and spent most of his academic career at McMaster University, Hamilton, Ontario. Since retiring in 1996, he has continued research as Professor Emeritus.

Amber Ridington is a doctoral candidate in the Department of Folklore at Memorial University of Newfoundland and holds an MA in Folk Studies from Western Kentucky University. For her doctoral work focusing on the narrative context of the Dane-ẕaa Dreamers' song tradition, she was awarded the Memorial University Aldrich Fellowship and a Social Sciences and Humanities Research Council of Canada doctoral scholarship. Since 2001 she has collaborated with Aboriginal and community groups in Kentucky, Alaska, and British Columbia to design, produce, and facilitate museum exhibits, interactive media projects, and documentary videos. This applied work has sparked her interest in the implications of new media for transmitting oral traditions and material culture. Find more about Amber and her work at www.amberridington.com.

Jillian Ridington is an ethnographer, writer, editor, and independent researcher and has produced many radio programs for the CBC and Vancouver's CFRO. She earned her MA in sociology at the University of British Columbia, and joined Robin Ridington and Howard Broomfield in working with the Dane-ẕaa in 1978. In addition to her work with First Nations, she has written extensively on women's and environmental issues and on issues affecting people with disabilities. She is coauthor, with Robin, of *When You Sing It Now, Just Like New.*

Robin Ridington is Professor Emeritus of anthropology at the University of British Columbia. He has a BA from Swarthmore College and a PhD in anthropology from Harvard University. He first met the Dane-ẕaa in 1959 and has been documenting their culture since 1964. His narrative ethnography, *Trail to Heaven*, describes how he learned from Charlie Yahey and other Dane-ẕaa elders. With Jillian Ridington, he coauthored *When You Sing It Now, Just Like New.* His latest book, *The Poets Don't Write Sonnets Anymore*, combines ethnographic and poetic commentary on the contemporary world we share with the Dane-ẕaa.

Blair A. Rudes was, at the time of his sudden death in 2008, an Associate Professor of English at the University of North Carolina, Charlotte, and was working on his three-volume *The Catawba Language.* His interests were wide-ranging, and his publications include the *Tuscarora-English, English-Tuscarora Dictionary* as well as essays, articles, translations, and edited volumes. He was the Mayan-dialogue coach for *The Ruins*, a film directed by Carter Smith and released by Dreamworks in 2008.

Brian Swann is the author of many books of short fiction, poetry, and poetry in translation, as well as books for children. He has edited a number of volumes on Native American literature, the most recent of which is *Algonquian Spirit: Contemporary Translations of the Algonquian Literatures of North America.* He teaches at the Cooper Union for the Advancement of Science and Art in New York City.

Laurence C. Thompson and M. Terry Thompson have been studying Northwest American Indian languages since 1957. After moving to the University of Hawaii in 1965, they traveled to the Northwest every summer until 1995 to continue the study of Thompson River Salish; they also did some work in Klallam and worked with the last known speaker of Tillamook. Their major publications include *The Thompson Language*, *Thompson River Salish Dictionary*, *Thompson Ethnobotany*, and *Salish Myths and Legends: One Peoples Stories* (ed. M. T. Thompson and Steven M. Egesdal). *nłeʔkèpmxcín: Thompson River Salish Speech* (Egesdal, M. T. Thompson, and Mandy Jimmie) is in press.

Frederick H. White, PhD, is an Associate Professor in the English Department at Slippery Rock University of Pennsylvania, where he teaches composition, literature, and linguistics. His research explores and examines historical, linguistic, and literary topics regarding Native American cultural issues, including education, identity, language revitalization, oral literature, and contact narratives, all with a keen interest in his own Haida culture. His book *Ancestral Language Acquisition among Native Americans: A Study of a Haida Language Class* addresses the question of how Native American and First Nations students learn and participate in the classroom. Most importantly, he analyzes how those styles of learning and participation affect acquiring their ancestral language. His novel *Welcome to the City of Rainbows* was co-winner of the 2006 Native Writers Circle of the Americas First Book in Prose.

Peter M. Whiteley has been Curator of North American Ethnology at the American Museum of Natural History–New York since 2001. From 1985 to 2000 he was Professor of anthropology at Sarah Lawrence College, Bronxville, New York. He holds a PhD in anthropology from the University of New Mexico, where he was a student of the late Alfonso Ortiz, and an MA from Cambridge University. His principal publications include *Deliberate Acts: Changing Hopi Culture through the Oraibi Split*; *Rethinking Hopi Ethnography*; and *The Orayvi Split: A Hopi Transformation*. Since 1980 he has conducted extensive ethnographic research with the Hopi, and briefer periods with the Hupa, Cayuga, several Rio Grande Pueblos, and Akwesasne Mohawk.

beavers, 440–41

Beck, Horace P., 144

Bécquer, Gustavo Adolfo, 348

Benjamin, Walter, 79

Berman, Judith, 172

Bible, 426; lectionary, 123, 136n12; New Testament, 119, 125, 126–28, 353; Old Testament, 119–20, 123; SIL International and, 111–12, 113–14, 117, 119; translation into Choctaw, 353; translation into Cree, 117, 119; translation into Naskapi, 110, 114, 117–29

Biedelman, T. O., 425

Biella, Peter, 222

Bierhorst, John, 4, 6, 287–88, 370–97, 455

Bigler, Josephine Wildcat, 349

Blackned, John, 419

Blake, William, 426

Boas, Franz: and censorship, 171, 172; ethnographic work of, 2, 144, 288, 327; on geographic environment, 96–97, 106nn6–7; and Haida language, 289; and interlinear translations, 211, 212, 223–24; modern linguists and, 4, 286; on Native American literary form, 328; and translation of "indecent" material, 174, 452

Bolduc, Evelyn, 146

Book of Common Prayer, 119

Book of Sand (Borges), 72

Borges, Jorge Luis, 72

Bourke, John Gregory, 177

Bradley, Richard, 79

Braudel, Fernand, 73

Bright, William, 331

Bringhurst, Robert, 213–14, 215, 444–45

Brittain, Julie, 1, 242–74, 455

Broomfield, Howard, 140, 211

Bruchac, J., 288

Bureau of American Ethnology, 170

Burkhart, Louise, 111

Burley, Lynn, 326–47, 455

"The Buzzard," 340–41

Byington, Cyrus, 356

Cagle, A. B., 287

Cahwee, William, 349–50

Canadian Aboriginal Syllabics, 117

canoes, 294

cantares, 371–72; and conjuros, 372–75; ritualism of, 376; war as theme of, 375, 381, 390–91

Cantares Mexicanos, 371, 375–76, 377, 389; as lexical resource, 378–82, 384–88; and revitalization movement, 391; Song XIV in, 383–89, 390, 391

Carcajou et le sens du monde: Récits montagnais-naskapi (Savard), 250

caribou, 442

Carriere, Joseph M., 164n3

Cary, Henry Francis, 184n1

Cass, Lewis, 169

Cassen, George, 408

Cayuga, 17–40; dictionary, 24, 29; language preservation efforts, 22–26; number of speakers, 20; oral tradition, 21–22, 23, 24–25, 29; pronunciation, 40n1; translation complexities, 27–28, 31–35

censorship: inadvertent, 172; of "indecent" material, 169–71, 173–75, 184; and intellectual ownership, 180–82, 184; key question in, 184; to maintain religious sanctity, 177–79; by performers, 175–76, 179–80, 184; and translation, 168

ceremonies, 2, 5, 68–71, 76, 92, 357

Chahta vba isht taloa holisso, 356

Charlton, Catherine, 190

Chase, Carol, 119

Chemaganish, Alma, 251

Cherokee, 18, 20, 370, 371, 392

Cheyfitz, Eric, 1

Chezan stories, 141, 142, 143, 144, 146–47; linguistic convergence in, 152; oral curation of, 148, 149, 155; regional variations in, 149–50; transcription of, 147, 157–62, 163

Chipewyan, 152, 324n2

Choctaw, 352–68; grammar, 352–55, 367–68; orthography, 358, 362–63, 365; poetry and hymns, 355–58, 362, 367; pronunciation, 355–56, 361–62; vocabulary, 361, 364, 365

Choctaw/Chickasaw Heritage Society, 357

Choctaw Nation Labor Day Festival, 357

Christianity, 2, 139, 365, 391, 426. *See also* Bible

civilization, 22, 109, 169

clans, 63, 70, 154, 295

cleft constructions, 263–65

Clements, William M., 2, 6, 168–88, 398–418, 455

Code of Handsome Lake, 21, 30, 34

colonialism, 182; resistance to, 80, 391; and translation, 1, 2, 9n3; and wars against Native Americans, 401, 402, 410–11, 416n1

Colwell-Chanthaphonh, Chip, 61–83, 455–56

Coming to Light: Contemporary Translation of the Native Literatures of North America (Swann), 342

Commedia (Dante), 184n1

community participation, 1, 24, 233–34; in translation efforts, 127, 128, 259, 260, 269

Computer-Aided Related-Language Adaptation (CARLA), 119, 128, 133–34, 136n10; conventional, 122–23, 129–30; incremental, 123–24, 130

computers: concordances created by, 4, 376–77, 382, 389; Consistent Changes program, 131; corpus linguistics, 382; cyber-techniques, 222, 234; Field Linguist's Shoebox program, 132, 136n15; incremental grammatical analysis by,

133; and translation, 120, 129, 131–32, 135, 376. *See also* Internet

conceptual translation, 194

Concerning the League (Gibson), 36–37

concordances, 4, 376–77, 382, 389

Condolence Ceremony, 29–30

Confederacy of the Iroquois, 21–22

conjuros, 370–71; and *cantares*, 372–75

connotations, 27, 102, 151, 238

Consistent Changes program, 131

Contes Populaires Canadien, 146

contextualization, 27–28, 229, 230, 315

Cook-Lynn, Elizabeth, 182

corpus linguistics, 382

cosmological views, 75, 95, 103–4, 105

Costa, David, 191

Costner, Kevin, 190

"Coyote and Junco," 329, 332

Coyote Stories (Mourning Dove), 328

Coyote tales, 87–90, 106, 178, 181

creation beliefs, 49, 67, 294, 342

Cree, 3, 117, 138, 140; oral tradition, 427–44; as polysynthetic, 254–55; and translation, 117, 420–21. *See also* East Cree; Moose Cree

Cree-Montagnais-Naskapi (CMN), 242–43, 267n2; cleft constructions, 263, 264–65; demonstratives and gestures, 252, 270n26; dialects, 248; gender in, 3, 257; grammars and dictionaries, 263, 268n8, 271n39; nominals, 255–57; as polysynthetic, 245, 253, 254–55; pronunciation, 265–67; punctuation, 252, 258, 259, 271n38; repetition in, 252, 270n27; sentences and paragraphs, 258–59; as underdocumented, 244, 267n6; verbs, 249, 261. *See also* Cree; Montagnais; Naskapi

Crisafulli, Edoardo, 184n1

Cronyn, George, 11n15

Crow people, 174

Cruikshank, Julie, 226

Crystal, David, 270n33

Culliford, S. G., 401

culture, 22, 91, 92, 151, 295, 447; attempts to suppress, 2, 139, 234; cultural imperialism and imposition, 182–84, 288; drift in, 444–45; as idiom of experience, 425; and language, 43–45, 79, 424, 446–47; preservation efforts for, 76–77; representation of, 235; revitalization of, 391; time and, 61–62; and translation, 36, 421–22

curation, 233–34; oral, 147–48, 149, 155, 156, 157

Curtin, Jeremiah, 173

Cushing, Frank Hamilton, 177–78

cyber-techniques, 222, 234

Dakota: language, 334, 343; mythology, 337–41

Dakota Grammar, Texts, and Ethnography (Riggs), 327–28

dance, 76, 94, 226, 334, 357

Dances with Wolves, 190–91, 206n1

Dane Wajich—Dane-ẕaa Stories and Songs: Dreamers and the Land, 211, 218, 221–23, 232, 238n2; and intellectual property rights, 235–37; storytellers' role in, 226–27, 228; translation in, 223–24, 232–33

Dane-ẕaa: about, 138; cultural transition of, 155; and gender, 150; intonation, 150–51; language banned in schools, 139, 234; language loss, 155, 234; language preservation efforts, 234–35; oral tradition, 139–42, 143, 155, 156, 217–18, 228–32; orthography, 223, 224, 227; translation techniques for, 217–21, 226

Danker, Kathleen, 334, 337, 339, 340

Dauenhauer, Nora Marks, 154, 301–25, 456

Dauenhauer, Richard L., 154, 301–25, 456

Daviault, Pierre, 146

Davis Inlet, 248, 268n11

death: life-death boundary, 276, 281; Powhatans' view of, 408, 411, 414

Degh, Linda, 148

De La Warr, Lord (Thomas West), 401, 402, 410–11, 415

Deloria, Vine, Jr., 182

Denham, Sir John, 9n3

denotations, 27

Densmore, Frances, 2, 357

Desbarats, Peter, 249

A Description of Virginia (Hariot), 404

"The Deserted Boy" (Simpson), 331

Devil Sickness and Devil Songs (Kozak and Lopez), 279

dictionaries and grammars, 1, 129, 261–62, 449, 453; Cayuga, 24, 29; Cree-Montagnais-Naskapi, 263, 268n8, 271n39; and field linguists, 447; Passamaquoddy, 43–52; and translation, 244–45, 268nn8–9

Dine Bahane' (Zolbrod), 175

Discourse Markers (Schiffrin), 342

Dorsey, George A., 185n2

Dorsey, J. Owen, 179

Dorson, Richard M., 169

dreamers, 139, 218–19, 227

dreams, 277, 278

drift, 444–45

Drucker, P., 289, 294

dubitative form, 52–53

Dundes, Alan, 146, 153, 154, 181–82, 412

Durán, Diego de, 376, 392

Duranti, Alessandro, 224–25

durative suffixes, 303–4, 306

Dyck, Carrie, 1, 17–42, 456

East Cree, 115, 254; Northern dialect, 119; as related-language translation source, 125–26. *See also* Cree

Egesdal, Steven M., 14n36

Einish, Philip, 250–51

Eliot, John, 2

English language, 174, 242, 259, 261, 267n4, 446; cleft constructions in, 263–64; definiteness and specificity in, 352; gapping and interrogatives in, 199; "Indian English," 150–51; nouns in, 46, 253, 254–55; seventeenth-century, 189 90, 192; structure, 292, 353; verb tenses, 28, 301, 302, 305, 308, 310

Enrico, J., 289, 292

epiaspect, 304–5, 309

epimode, 311

Erdrich, Louise, 10n10

ethnographic film, 215–16

ethnography: and anthropology, 182–83, 411; and audio recordings, 213, 214, 225, 413; and censorship, 170–72, 173, 175; collecting Native American stories, 144, 327–28; of communication, 225, 423; and cultural imperialism, 182–83; early efforts of, 238, 403; and intellectual property rights, 177–78; and language preservation, 288–89; salvage, 390; of speaking, 412, 414; and translation, 211–17, 233, 411, 412, 413

Ethnology of the Kwakiutl (Boas), 212

ethnopoetics, 213, 214, 399, 412; and interpretive depiction, 421, 423–24; and translation, 217–21. *See also* poetry

euphemism, 171, 174, 184

Eurocentrism, 153, 196–97, 416n1

European languages, 1, 303, 348; differences with Native American languages, 1, 3, 328, 352. *See also* English language; French language; Spanish language

"European Tales from the Plains Ojibwa" (Skinner), 147

Evans, James, 117

Evans-Pritchard, E. E., 426

evidential verb forms, 249, 269n19

Fabian, Johannes, 63–64

Farrer, Claire R., 178, 180–81, 182

Fausz, J. Frederick, 401, 416n1

Fenton, William N., 18

Ferguson, T. J., 66, 71

Field Linguist's Shoebox program, 132, 136n15

film portrayal, Native American, 190, 205, 206n1

Finding the Center: Narrative Poetry of the Zuni Indians (Tedlock), 213, 330–31

Fischer, Kerstin, 342

Flathead, 449

Fletcher, Alice, 211–12, 222

Florentine Codex, 382–83, 394n40

"The Flower World of Old Uto-Aztecan" (Hill), 276

fluency, 420, 421, 422

Foley, John Miles, 222

Foley, William, 113

folklore, Native American: assimilation of European tradition in, 147, 154; comparative approach to study of, 145; differences with European, 152–53; indigenization in, 151, 153–54; migration of, 156; regional variation in, 148–52, 164n5; types and motifs, 144–47

Folklore of the Winnebago Tribe (Smith), 342

Folsom, David, 356

form-meaning covariation, 331

Fort Chimo, 116, 248

Foster, Michael, 25–26, 29–30, 33–35

Francis, David A., 43

free translation, 30, 33, 248–49

French language, 138, 140, 242, 267n4, 447; folklore tradition, 146, 164n3; grammar and structure, 253, 352

Freund, Virginia, 192

Frost, Robert, 445

gapping, 199

Garcilaso de la Vega, 398

idioms, 198–99, 376, 422–23, 445; definition of, 421
Igloolik Isuma Productions, 216, 237
incremental grammatical analysis, 133
indigenization, 151, 153–54
inflection, 245, 249, 269n19, 356
Innu, *115*, 263–64, 269n25; orthography, 269n20; pronunciation, 265–67. *See also* Cree-Montagnais-Naskapi (CMN); Montagnais; Sheshatshiu Innu
Innu-Naskapi collection, 242–43, 260; free translation in, 249; provenance of, 245–47; samples from, 254–60
The Intellectual Culture of the Iglulik Eskimos (Rasmussen), 216
intellectual property rights: and censorship, 180–82, 184; and cultural imperialism, 183–84; ethnographers' ignoring of, 177–78; and Internet, 235–37; language activists' views of, 39; to stories and songs, 5–6, 14n36, 154, 180–82, 183–84
intergenerational language change, 256, 270n33
interlinear translations, 211–17, 226, 237–38
International Organization for Standardization (ISO), 110
Internet, 221–23, 231; and intellectual property rights, 235–37; as medium, 4, 234. *See also* computers
interpretive depiction, 421, 423–24
intonation, 150–51, 199, 215; markers for, 33–34, 226, 340
Inuit, 98, 216
Inukshuk, Pakak, 216, 217
Inuktitut, 216–17
"In Vain I Tried to Tell You" (Hymes), 423
Ives, Joseph C., 106n3

Jacobs, Elizabeth Derr, 176
Jacobs, Melville, 5, 144, 173
Jahner, Elaine A., 39

Jakobson, Roman, 412
James, Susie, 310–12
Jamestown, 403, 407, 409, 410–11, 414, 415; depiction in *The New World*, 189, 190; Strachey and, 400–401, 402
Jancewicz, Bill, 39, 109–37, 250, 269n24, 457
Jancewicz, Norma Jean, 119
Jansen, Wm. Hugh, 406–7
The Jesuit Relations, 2
John, Martha Charles, 450, 451, 452
Journal of American Folklore, 147
Journal of Folklore Research, 146
The Journals of Knud Rasmussen, 216–17

Kant, Immanuel, 72
Kawawachikamach, 114, 116, 245, 246, 248, 250
Keesing, Roger, 67
Keith, Josephine Barnett, 349
Kenner, Hugh, 3
Key, Amos, Jr., 24, 36
Kilpatrick, Alan, 371
Kilpatrick, Anna Gritts, 371
Kilpatrick, Jack, 371
Kimball, Geoffrey, 175–76
Kinkade, Dale, 453
kinship systems, 52, 293
Klallam, 446, 450, 451
knowledge: and action, 443–44; and translation, 26–29, 109
Korelber, Karl, 342
Koyiyumptewa, Stewart B., 61–83, 457
Kozak, David L., 275–85, 457–58
Kroeber, Alfred L., 185n2, 328
Krupat, Arnold, 13n27, 328
Kunik, Zacharias, 222
Kwakw'ala, 172, 211

La Flesche, Francis, 2, 103, 211–12, 222
Lakhota, 190–91, 206n1
Lambert, Adelard, 146

Matthews, Washington, 2
Maud, Ralph, 212
Maya, (Yucatec), 370, 371
McKinney, William H., 362–65, 366, 368
Mealing, Mark, 141–42
Mescalero Apaches, 180–81
metanarration, 149, 151
metaphor, 139, 276, 292; and Aztec song, 376, 389, 392; of boundaries and distance, 276, 281; Hopi view of, 67; new theories of, 3, 12n18
Métis, 140
Michelson, Truman, 144
micro-linguistics, 424
migrations, 64, 70, 71, 78, 101
Miller, Huron, 24
Mills, Katherine Brown, 318, 319
minimal transfer, 305, 312
missionaries, 3, 111, 112
Mistissini Quebec, 125
Mitchell, Lewis, 47–48, 50
Mohawk, 18, 23, 350–51
Mohegan, 191
Molina, Alonso, 372
Monroe, Harriet, 11n15
Montagnais, 248, 268n17. *See also* Cree-Montagnais-Naskapi (CMN); Innu
Montler, Timothy, 452
Moody, Henry, 214
Mooney, James, 2, 392
Moore, Patrick, 211–41, 223, 230, 458
Moose Cree, 119–20, 123–24, 131. *See also* Cree
Moran, Peter, 177
Morgan, Phillip Carroll, 365–67
morphemes, 30–31, 99, 129
Motif-Index of Folk Literature (Thompson), 145
motisinom, 63–64, 66, 67, 77
Mourning Dove, 328
Murray, David, 11n12
music, 183, 289–90. *See also* songs

"My Dog and the Snake" (Willis), 354, 368
myths, 14n36, 67, 333; about Native Americans, 169, 170, 173; Dakota, 337–41; Haida, 298; Hocák, 334–37, 341, 344–45; numbers in, 332; and performance, 333; and religion, 426; rendered in prose, 4–5; rendered in verse, 339–40, 341–42; Zuni, 179, 327, 329–31
Myths and Tales of the Southeastern Indians (Swanton), 172
Mzechtenoman, William, 153

Naa Kaani, 315
Nahuatl, 2, 382–83; lexicon, 372, 377–82, 384–88, 392n10; as polysynthetic language, 3, 12n20
names: geographic, 96–98, 102–3; personal, 105, 180
narrative particles, 333, 334, 336, 337, 339, 341
narratives: classification of, 287–88; construction of space in, 47; formal patterning in, 331–32, 334, 338; oral-to-written transformation of, 1, 4, 13n28, 328–29, 412; repetition as device in, 252, 270n27, 295, 329, 340; social connections depicted in, 49–53; written as prose, 225; written as verse, 141, 289, 331, 332. *See also* oral tradition; performance, oral; storytelling
Naskapi: Bible translation project, 110, 114, 117–29; community support for translation, 259, 269; and Cree, 117, 119–20, 123–24, 131; dialects, 136n7, 247–48; historical background, 114–16; lexicon, 250, 269n24; and Naskapi Legends and Texts Project, 250–51; pronunciation, 265–67; and related-language translation program, 122–35; revitalization efforts, 136; self-government of, 116, 136n8, 250; syllabic